Educational Psychology

Educational

Allyn and Bacon
BOSTON LONDON TORONTO SYDNEY TOKYO SINGAPORE

SECOND EDITION

Psychology

A Learning-Centered Approach to Classroom Practice

Rick McCown
DUQUESNE UNIVERSITY

Marcy Driscoll
FLORIDA STATE UNIVERSITY, TALLAHASSEE

Peter Geiger Roop
APPLETON AREA SCHOOL DISTRICT

Editor-in-Chief: Nancy Forsyth
Editorial Assistant: Kate Wagstaffe
Executive Marketing Manager: Kathy Hunter
Developmental Editor: Mary Ellen Lepionka
Editorial-Production Administrator: Susan Brown
Editorial-Production Service: Colophon
Composition Buyer: Linda Cox
Manufacturing Buyer: Megan Cochran
Cover Administrator: Linda Knowles
Cover Designer: Susan Paradise

A Simon & Schuster Company
Needham Heights, Massachusetts 02194

Library of Congress Cataloging-in-Publication Data
McCown, R. R.
Educational psychology/R.R. McCown, Marcy Driscoll, Peter Roop.
2nd ed.
p. cm.
Rev. ed. of: A learning-centered approach to classroom practice. ©1992.
Includes bibliographical references (p.) and index.
ISBN 0-205-17420-5 (alk. paper)
1. Educational psychology. 2. Teaching. I. Driscoll, Marcy Perkins. II. Roop, Peter. III. McCown, R. R. Educational psychology and classroom practice. IV. Title.
LB1051.M396 1995
370.15—dc20 95-18552
CIP

Printed in the United States of America

10 9 8 7 6 5 4 3 2 1 99 98 97 96 95

PHOTO CREDITS

Will Faller: pp. 1, 7, 13, 20, 26, 37, 38, 60, 65, 89, 100, 124, 134, 152, 174, 180, 187, 194, 202, 214, 218, 242, 255, 278, 295, 298, 310, 320, 326, 337, 349, 354, 359, 364, 374, 388, 395, 397, 402, 404, 408, 422, 427, 444, 462, 469, 470, 480, 492
Robert Harbison: pp. 47, 72, 110, 247, 455
Stephen Marks: pp. 477, 494
Cable News Network: pp. 24, 25, 98, 99, 172, 173, 276, 277, 352, 353, 420, 421

Contents

Part I Development

Part II Diversity

Part III Learning

Part IV Motivation and Classroom Leadership

Part V Effective Instruction

Part VI Evaluation

Preface to

Educational Psychology SECOND EDITION

Learning is the measure of teaching. We, the authors of this text, believe that the value of teaching is in the learning it fosters, and that teaching and learning form a single integrated concept. They are parts of the same sublime process.

Rick and Marcy are educational psychologists at universities in northeastern and southeastern United States, respectively. Peter is a classroom teacher in the midwestern United States. We formed our partnership to create an introductory text that reflects the very latest thinking in the field and that melds the principles of educational psychology with the maxims of classroom practice. We also wanted to create an instrument that would encourage the thinking process involved in the professional development of classroom teachers. We believe we accomplished these goals, using a learning-centered and a student-centered approach. Together, we designed our book and accompanying materials to emphasize reflection coupled with active learning. In particular, we aimed to support the process of reflective construction in which teachers as learners engage.

Authentic classroom experience is reflected throughout the text — more than in any competing text. Case studies, essays by teachers, and examples derived from actual classroom experience help connect theory to real practice.

The view of the teaching-learning process that best describes our own classroom practice is social constructivism. Indeed, one of the working assumptions of this text is that learning is active construction in social contexts. The social constructivist and learning-centered approach of this book is reflected in our pedagogy and supplements in a number of ways. For example, as you will see, the pedagogy was developed both to provide teaching models—students see the problems that real teachers face and learn how expert teachers solve those problems—and to promote critical thinking, collaborative learning, and authentic problem solving on the part of readers themselves.

Our purpose here is not to persuade you, the instructor, that our approach is best. Rather, our purpose is to inform you of our biases so that you can critically evaluate our writings and teaching suggestions and can use or adapt them to your own purposes and teaching style. We hope our contribution makes learning both more meaningful and more enjoyable for you and your students.

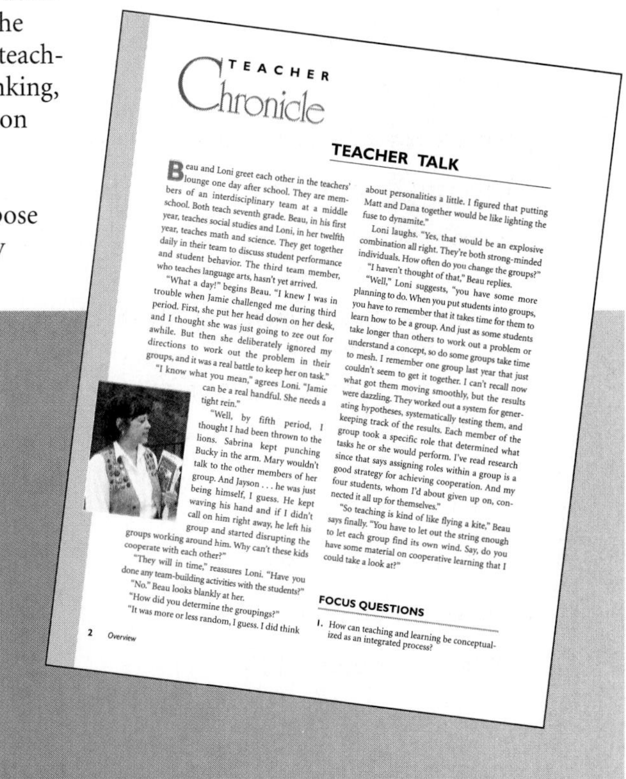

TEACHER Chronicle

TEACHER TALK

Beau and Loni greet each other in the teachers' lounge one day after school. They are members of an interdisciplinary team at a middle school. Both teach seventh grade. Beau, in his first year, teaches social studies and Loni, in her twelfth year, teaches math and science. They get together daily in their team to discuss student performance and student behavior. The third team member, who teaches language arts, hasn't yet arrived.

"What a day!" begins Beau. "I knew I was in trouble when Jamie challenged me during third period. First, she put her head down on her desk, and I thought she was just going to zee out for awhile. But then she deliberately ignored my directions to work out the problem in their groups, and it was a real battle to keep her on task."

"I know what you mean," agrees Loni. "Jamie can be a real handful. She needs a tight rein."

"Well, by fifth period, I thought I had been thrown to the lions. Sabrina kept punching Bucky in the arm. Mary wouldn't talk to the other members of her group. And Jayson . . . he was just being himself, I guess. He kept waving his hand and if I didn't call on him right away, he left his group and started disrupting the groups working around him. Why can't these kids cooperate with each other?"

"They will in time," reassures Loni. "Have you done any team-building activities with the students?"

"No." Beau looks blankly at her.

"How did you determine the groupings?"

"It was more or less random, I guess. I did think about personalities a little. I figured that putting Matt and Dana together would be like lighting the fuse to dynamite."

Loni laughs. "Yes, that would be an explosive combination all right. They're both strong-minded individuals. How often do you change the groups?"

"I haven't thought of that," Beau replies.

"Well," Loni suggests, "you have some more planning to do. When you put students into groups, you have to remember that it takes time for them to learn how to be a group. And just as some students take longer than others to work out a problem or understand a concept, so do some groups take time to mesh. I remember one group last year that just couldn't seem to get it together. I can't recall now what got them moving smoothly, but the results were dazzling. They worked out a system for generating hypotheses, systematically testing them, and keeping track of the results. Each member of the group took a specific role that determined what tasks he or she would perform. I've read research since that says assigning roles within a group is a good strategy for achieving cooperation. And my four students, whom I'd about given up on, connected it all up for themselves."

"So teaching is kind of like flying a kite," Beau says finally. "You have to let out the string enough to let each group find its own wind. Say, do you have some material on cooperative learning that I could take a look at?"

FOCUS QUESTIONS

1. How can teaching and learning be conceptualized as an integrated process?

2 Overview

INSTRUCTIONAL AIDS

We have provided a rich array of materials to help you in teaching this course. The INSTRUCTOR'S RESOURCE MANUAL, written by Rick McCown, Marcy Driscoll, Peter Roop, Marlynn Griffin, and Gwendolyn Quinn, highlights cooperative and collaborative strategies and student assignments, and incorporates a case-based approach. For each chapter interactive cases are provided in the form of handout MASTERS, and questions are provided to support case analysis as a class activity or in assessment. Our IRM also includes a chapter-at-a-glance feature, a summary, a list of key concepts, a list of chapter-relevant acetate TRANSPARENCIES — over 100 of them in all, teaching suggestions for introducing chapter content and using the pedagogical text features, cross-references to the Assessment Package, and a Media Guide.

The text has been totally updated, including extensive material on *constructivist-social constructivist viewpoints* (Chs 7, 8, & 12) and new material in the Assessment & Evaluation chapters that reflect advances in authentic performance assessment and the use of portfolios.

The MEDIA GUIDE provides text tie-ins to the CNN VIDEO created specifically for our book, and to CLASSROOM INSIGHTS II, a video of classroom footage that illustrates educational psychology principles in action. In addition, the Media Guide explains how you and your students can interact with us and other instructors and students on AMERICA ONLINE, the Internet, and other electronic resources. Rick and Marcy have instituted electronic office hours and scheduled faculty workshops, for example, along with a teacher interview series and many other events.

The ASSESSMENT PACKAGE, created by Marlynn Griffin and Gwendolyn Quinn, is far more than the usual test item file. In addition to multiple-choice and essay items with answer feedback, our assessment package provides alternative, authentic assessments for every chapter along with criteria for scoring them or creating your own scoring rubrics. These features provide opportunities for you to use performance or portfolio assessments in teaching the course — a great way to model these concepts for your students.

A STUDY GUIDE by Vicky Zygouris–Coe supports the learning of students using our text package, and a variety of other supplements are also available for sale to students, including a READER in educational psychology and an interactive CD–ROM on classroom management.

The following pages explain how the book is organized and present the pedagogical features.

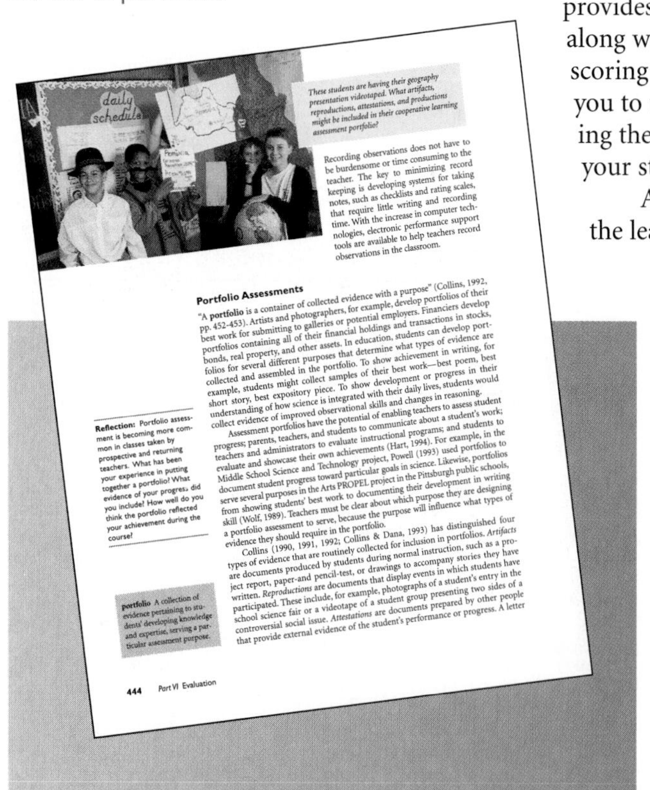

These students are having their geography presentation videotaped. What artifacts, reproductions, attestations, and productions might be included in their cooperative learning assessment portfolio?

Recording observations does not have to be burdensome or time consuming to the teacher. The key to minimizing record keeping is developing systems for taking notes, such as checklists and rating scales, that require little writing and recording time. With the increase in computer technologies, electronic performance support tools are available to help teachers record observations in the classroom.

Portfolio Assessments

"A **portfolio** is a container of collected evidence with a purpose" (Collins, 1992,
pp. 452-453). Artists and photographers, for example, develop portfolios of their
best work for submitting to galleries or potential employers. Financiers develop
portfolios containing all of their financial holdings and transactions in stocks,
bonds, real property, and other assets. In education, students can develop portfolios for several different purposes that determine what types of evidence are
collected and assembled in the portfolio. To show achievement in writing, for
example, students might collect samples of their best work—best poem, best
short story, best expository piece. To show development or progress in their
understanding of how science is integrated with their daily lives, students would
collect evidence of improved observational skills and changes in reasoning.
Assessment portfolios have the potential of enabling teachers to assess student
progress; parents, teachers, and students to communicate about a student's work;
teachers and administrators to evaluate instructional programs; and students to
evaluate and showcase their own achievements (Hart, 1994). For example, in the
Middle School Science and Technology project, Powell (1993) used portfolios to
document student progress toward particular goals in science. Likewise, portfolios
serve several purposes in the Arts PROPEL project in the Pittsburgh public schools,
from showing students' best work to documenting their development in writing
skill (Wolf, 1989). Teachers must be clear about which purpose they are designing
a portfolio assessment to serve, because the purpose will influence what types of
evidence they should require in the portfolio.
Collins (1990, 1991, 1992; Collins & Dana, 1993) has distinguished four
types of evidence that are routinely collected for inclusion in portfolios. *Artifacts*
are documents produced by students during normal instruction, such as a project report, paper-and pencil-test, or drawings to accompany stories they have
written. *Reproductions* are documents that display events in which students have
participated. These include, for example, photographs of a student's entry in the
school science fair or a videotape of a student group presenting two sides of a
controversial social issue. *Attestations* are documents prepared by other people
that provide external evidence of the student's performance or progress. A letter

Reflection: Portfolio assessment is becoming more common in classes taken by prospective and returning teachers. What has been your experience in putting together a portfolio? What evidence of your progress did you include? How well do you think the portfolio reflected your achievement during the course?

portfolio A collection of evidence pertaining to students' developing knowledge and expertise, serving a particular assessment purpose.

444 *Part VI* Evaluation

ORGANIZATION OF THE BOOK

We have tried to be very clear about our view of the teaching–learning process, including how it works, what it affects, and what factors affect it. By making our view explicit — in the form of assumptions — students will have a basis of comparison for the development of their own views. In the opening chapter students are asked to think about their view of teaching and learning and you will encounter the three basic assumptions that underlie our view. The first of these assumptions will come as no surprise to those who have read the preface to this point.

1. Teaching and learning are aspects of the same process.
2. Your view of the teaching–learning process affects your classroom practice.
3. Reflective construction (explained in Chapter 1) is necessary for the development of teaching expertise.

The remainder of the book is organized into six parts. The working assumptions associated with each part are listed below. These assumptions further explicate our view of the teaching–learning process and are the main themes of this book. Each assumption is explained fully in chapter content.

To encourage reflection on the teaching–learning process, each chapter concludes with the question: "How can your knowledge of _____ make you a more effective teacher?"

Part 1 Development (Chapters 2 & 3)
- Development is complex and multifaceted.
- Development affects learning.
- Life conditions affect development.

Part 2 Diversity (Chapters 4 & 5)
- Learners are diverse.
- Students' diversity and individuality affect their learning.
- Inclusive classrooms provide learning opportunities.

Part 3 Learning (Chapters 6, 7, & 8)
- Learning is shaped by the learner's environment.
- Learning is a function of complex mental activities.
- Learning is active construction in social contexts.

Part 4 Motivation and Classroom Leadership (Chapters 9 & 10)
- People are naturally motivated to learn.
- Needs and values affect motivation.
- Classroom management is a shared concern.

Part 5 Effective Instruction (Chapters 11 & 12)
- Teachers and students are both learners.
- Teachers coordinate the context for learning.
- Instructional technologies support teaching and learning.

Part 6 Evaluation (Chapters 13 & 14)
- Assessment serves multiple purposes.
- Assessment improves teaching and learning.
- Authentic activity provides a basis for assessment.

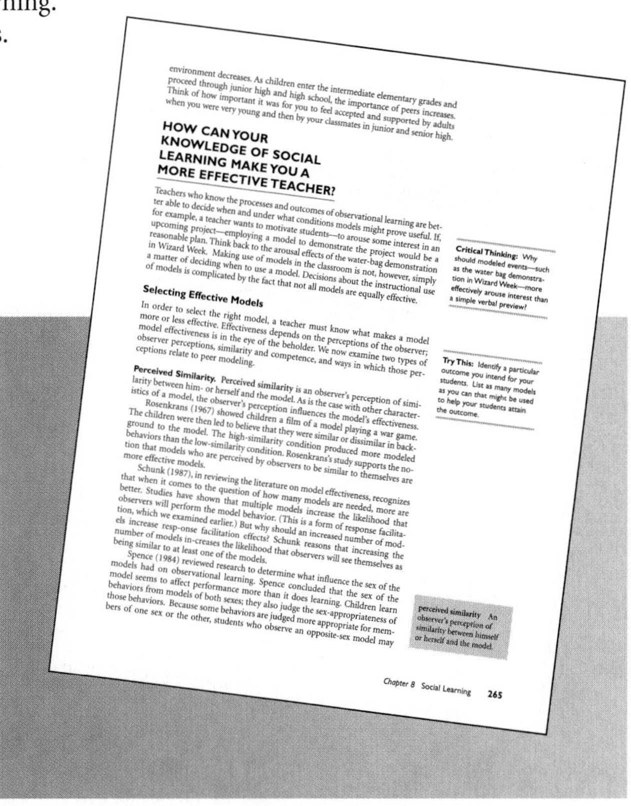

environment decreases. As children enter the intermediate elementary grades and proceed through junior high and high school, the importance of peers increases. Think of how important it was for you to feel accepted and supported by adults when you were very young and then by your classmates in junior and senior high.

HOW CAN YOUR KNOWLEDGE OF SOCIAL LEARNING MAKE YOU A MORE EFFECTIVE TEACHER?

Teachers who know the processes and outcomes of observational learning are better able to decide when and under what conditions models might prove useful. If, for example, a teacher wants to motivate students—to arouse some interest in an upcoming project—employing a model to demonstrate the project would be a reasonable plan. Think back to the arousal effects of the water-bag demonstration in Wizard Week. Making use of models in the classroom is not, however, simply a matter of deciding when to use a model. Decisions about the instructional use of models is complicated by the fact that not all models are equally effective.

Critical Thinking: Why should modeled events—such as the water bag demonstration in Wizard Week—more effectively arouse interest than a simple verbal preview?

Selecting Effective Models

In order to select the right model, a teacher must know what makes a model more or less effective. Effectiveness depends on the perceptions of the observer; model effectiveness is in the eye of the beholder. We now examine two types of observer perceptions, similarity and competence, and ways in which those perceptions relate to peer modeling.

Try This: Identify a particular outcome you intend for your students. List as many models as you can that might be used to help your students attain the outcome.

Perceived Similarity. Perceived **similarity** is an observer's perception of similarity between him- or herself and the model. As is the case with other characteristics of a model, the observer's perception influences the model's effectiveness.

Rosenkrans (1967) showed children a film of a model playing a war game. The children were then led to believe that they were similar or dissimilar in background to the model. The high-similarity condition produced more modeled behaviors than the low-similarity condition. Rosenkrans's study supports the notion that models who are perceived by observers to be similar to themselves are more effective models.

Schunk (1987), in reviewing the literature on model effectiveness, recognizes that when it comes to the question of how many models are needed, more are better. Studies have shown that multiple models increase the likelihood that observers will perform the model behavior. (This is a form of response facilitation, which we examined earlier.) But why should an increased number of models increase resp-onse facilitation effects? Schunk reasons that increasing the number of models in-creases the likelihood that observers will see themselves as being similar to at least one of the models.

Spence (1984) reviewed research to determine what influence the sex of the models had on observational learning. Spence concluded that the sex of the model seems to affect performance more than it does learning. Children learn behaviors from models of both sexes; they also judge the sex-appropriateness of those behaviors. Because some behaviors are judged more appropriate for members of one sex or the other, students who observe an opposite-sex model may

perceived similarity An observer's perception of similarity between himself or herself and the model.

Chapter 8 Social Learning 265

The assumptions are derived from the theoretical principles of educational psychology that inform classroom practice. In order to help students learn those principles and how they can be used to enhance the teaching–learning process, we have incorporated several instructional features in the design of each chapter.

FEATURES OF THE BOOK

The instructional features of this text have been designed to help learners integrate the theory of educational psychology with classroom practice and, consequently, to enhance their understanding of the teaching–learning process. These instructional features are described briefly below. The features and a strategy for their use are discussed in greater detail in Chapter 1.

Teacher Chronicle. Each chapter begins with a *Teacher Chronicle*, a brief, unresolved case based on actual classroom events. The case provides a practical context and a rich source of examples for the key theoretical concepts and principles presented in each chapter. Each *Teacher Chronicle* introduces an issue or problem that a teacher has faced in a real classroom.

A *Teacher Chronicle* opens and closes each chapter, presenting a single case drawn from real-life classroom experience. The case is referenced throughout the chapter to help relate topics in the text to actual practice.

Focus Questions follow each *Teacher Chronicle* and are designed to help students anticipate how the content of the chapter relates to the teaching–learning process that is represented in the *Teacher Chronicle* case.

The *Teacher Chronicle Conclusion* at the end of each chapter shows how the teacher addressed the problems or issues described in the *Teacher Chronicle.* Because the teacher's course of action is not given until the end of each chapter, students have the opportunity to reflect on the theoretical concepts of the chapter in an attempt to anticipate how the teacher solves the problem.

FIGURE 10.8

Metaphors of Management, Leadership Styles, and Value Orientations Placed on a Continuum of Use of Teacher Power

TEACHER Chronicle Conclusion

REFLECTING ON RANDY

Jean Oxford doesn't come up with a solution for working with Randy until the following weekend. Looking at the list again she links his love of reading, his orderliness (the appeal of cleaning up), and his interest in being in charge of things. She has been planning on setting up a class library with all of the books she has collected over the summer. Why not make Randy the class librarian?

Ms. Oxford and Randy discuss the library and his responsibilities. He takes to being librarian like a bear to honey. He gets up whenever his work is finished and checks in returned books. He has a valid context for washing his hands. He is "in charge" in a positive way, making sure that books are checked out properly. He straightens the books and organizes them by title.

Over time, Randy's behaviors change; the frequency of his interruptions decreases, his interaction with his peers improves, and although his confrontations with Ms. Oxford do not disappear entirely, they do diminish significantly. The overall atmosphere of the room improves. And Ms. Oxford no longer feels like a broken record repeating "Randy" over and over again.

Chapter 10 Leading Learning-Oriented Classrooms 349

The *Teacher Chronicle Conclusion* is followed by *Application Questions*, the final component of the Teacher Chronicle feature. *Application Questions* refer specifically to the events in the *Teacher Chronicle* and allow students to reinterpret those events through the application of key concepts from the chapter.

Insights on Successful Practice. The text not only encourages reflection, but models it as well. *Insights on Successful Practice* are the reflections of expert teachers — many of them are State Teachers of the Year — on how theories of educational psychology are used to teach effectively. There are multiple *Insights on Successful Practice* in each chapter. Each "insight" gives students the opportunity to study how an expert teacher uses chapter concepts and principles to enhance the teaching–learning process in his or her classroom.

Here's How. As an aspiring teacher, one of the questions that students should ask constantly as they read is, "How can I use this theoretical concept to enhance my classroom practice?" In each chapter, they will find a number of *Here's How* lists that can help them answer that question. Each *Here's How* list presents specific suggestions for classroom practice that are based on the research and theory of educational psychology. After a discussion of Gardner's Theory of Multiple Intelligences, for example, students encounter "Here's How to Engage Multiple Intelligences in Teaching Science and Math Concepts." *Here's How* lists are action plans for enhancing the teaching–learning process in a variety of classroom situations.

Key Concepts and Margin Notes. Key concepts throughout the book are printed in boldface. The key concepts are defined in the text itself and in a running glossary that appears in the margins of the text. The concepts are also listed alphabetically at the end of the chapter as a study aid and in a Glossary at the back of the book.

Margin notes appear throughout the entire text. These notes annotate the text and are designed to provide students with additional opportunities to reflect on the knowledge base, develop their views of the teaching–learning process, and discover conceptual connections to other portions of the text. The categories of margin notes include the following:

- Point — reminders of the basic assumptions of this text, statements of main ideas, and statements of key principles in educational psychology.
- Reflection — questions that help students reflect on their assumptions and values and to relate chapter content to their prior experiences.
- Example — additional illustrations of chapter concepts and their applications in practice.
- Critical Thinking — questions that help students link and apply chapter concepts and develop practical problem-solving strategies.
- Connection — cross-references to related concepts and information in other sections or chapters.
- Try This — active learning opportunities that students can undertake to expand their knowledge and apply that knowledge in authentic situations.
- Insights — questions that invite students to respond to the commentaries of the expert teachers featured in *Insights on Successful Practice.*

Each chapter includes *Insights on Successful Practice* presenting the responses of two to four teachers to questions linking theory and research. Special *Insights* annotations in the margins encourage critical thinking about the teachers' responses.

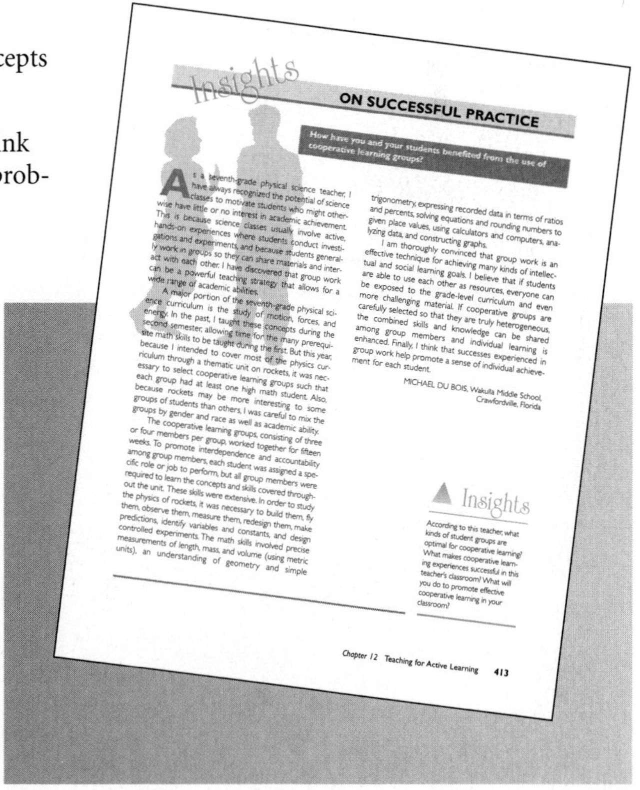

Insights ON SUCCESSFUL PRACTICE

How have you and your students benefited from the use of cooperative learning groups?

As a seventh-grade physical science teacher, I have always recognized the potential of science classes to motivate students who might otherwise have little or no interest in academic achievement. This is because science classes usually involve active, hands-on experiences where students conduct investigations and experiments, and because students generally work in groups so they can share materials and interact with each other. I have discovered that group work can be a powerful teaching strategy that allows for a wide range of academic abilities.

A major portion of the seventh-grade physical science curriculum is the study of motion, forces, and energy. In the past, I taught these concepts during the second semester, allowing time for the many prerequisite math skills to be taught during the first. But this year, because I intended to cover most of the physics curriculum through a thematic unit on rockets, it was necessary to select cooperative learning groups such that each group had at least one high math student. Also, because rockets may be more interesting to some groups of students than others, I was careful to mix the groups by gender and race as well as academic ability.

The cooperative learning groups, consisting of three or four members per group, worked together for fifteen weeks. To promote interdependence and accountability among group members, each student was assigned a specific role or job to perform, but all group members were required to learn the concepts and skills covered throughout the unit. These skills were extensive. In order to study the physics of rockets, it was necessary to build them, fly them, observe them, measure them, redesign them, make predictions, identify variables and constants, and design controlled experiments. The math skills involved precise measurements of length, mass, and volume (using metric units), an understanding of geometry and simple trigonometry, expressing recorded data in terms of ratios and percents, solving equations and rounding numbers to given place values, using calculators and computers, analyzing data, and constructing graphs.

I am thoroughly convinced that group work is an effective technique for achieving many kinds of intellectual and social learning goals. I believe that if students are able to use each other as resources, everyone can be exposed to the grade-level curriculum and even more challenging material. If cooperative groups are carefully selected so that they are truly heterogeneous, the combined skills and knowledge can be shared among group members and individual learning is enhanced. Finally, I think that successes experienced in group work help promote a sense of individual achievement for each student.

MICHAEL DU BOIS, Wakulla Middle School, Crawfordville, Florida

Insights

According to this teacher, what kinds of student groups are optimal for cooperative learning? What makes cooperative learning experiences successful in this teacher's classroom? What will you do to promote effective cooperative learning in your classroom?

Chapter 12 Teaching for Active Learning 413

ACKNOWLEDGMENTS

There is no question about where to begin the pleasurable task of thanking those who contributed to this book. Our families deserve top billing. Nona, Christopher, and Sara McCown; Robin Driscoll; Connie, Sterling, and Heidi Roop deserve more thanks than we can express here. They listened to us, shared ideas, prodded, cajoled, understood, and kept things in perspective when they threatened to get out of whack. Without their love, their spirits, and their gifts of time, their unflagging support and devotion, the partnership would not have succeeded.

The following master teachers shared their insights and their success as teachers, showed their enthusiasm for teaching, and demonstrated their commitment to bringing new teachers into the profession. Their voices ring true because they know students, value learning, and continually challenge themselves to develop professionally. We value them as teaching colleagues and acknowledge proudly their contributions.

COLLEAGUES AND CONTRIBUTORS

Dianne Bauman, Pittsburgh, Pennsylvania • **Michael A. Benedict**, Pittsburgh, Pennsylvania • **Lella Theresa Gantt Bonds**, Statesboro, Georgia • **Chuck Bowen**, Pekin, Illinois • **Don Daws**, Cedar Rapids, Iowa • **Delia Teresa De Garcia**, Boulder, Colorado • **Michael Du Bois**, Crawfordville, Florida • **Cindy Farren**, Indianapolis, Indiana • **Louvenia Magee Gafney**, Washington, D.C. • **Nancy Gorrell**, Morristown, New Jersey • **Lynda F. Hayes**, Gainesville, Florida • **Linda K. Hillestad**, Brookings, South Dakota • **Gregory Holdan**, Pittsburgh, Pennsylvania • **Carol Jago**, Santa Monica, California • **Steve Korpa**, Pittsburgh, Pennsylvania • **Maureen F. Logan**, Westerly, Rhode Island • **Jason D. Lopez**, Westminster, California • **Edna Loveday**, Sevierville, Tennessee • **Peter Olesen Lund**, Nashua, New Hampshire • **Wilma F. Mad Plume**, Browning, Montana • **Nanci L. Maes**, Wautoma, Wisconsin • **Pamela Maniet-Bellerman**, South Orange, New Jersey • **Jenlane Gee Matt**, Modesto, California • **Jennifer McGuire**, Appleton, Wisconsin • **Sue Misheff**, Canton, Ohio • **Virginia L. Pearson**, Detroit, Michigan • **Jean Sunde Peterson**, Coralville, Iowa • **David W. Purington**, Nashua, New Hampshire • **Leo Armando Ramirez, Sr.**, McAllen, Texas • **Connie B. Roop**, Appleton, Wisconsin • **Dorothy Sawyer**, Gladstone, Oregon • **William D. Smyth**, Charleston, South Carolina • **Edward Valent**, Milwaukee, Wisconsin • **Barbara Vinson**, Michigan City, Indiana • **J. Brock Vinson**, Michigan City, Indiana • **Gerald E. Walker**, Livingston, New Jersey • **Patricia Woodward**, Fort Collins, Colorado • **Linda Wygoda**, Lake Charles, Louisiana • **Betsy F. Young**, Honolulu, Hawaii

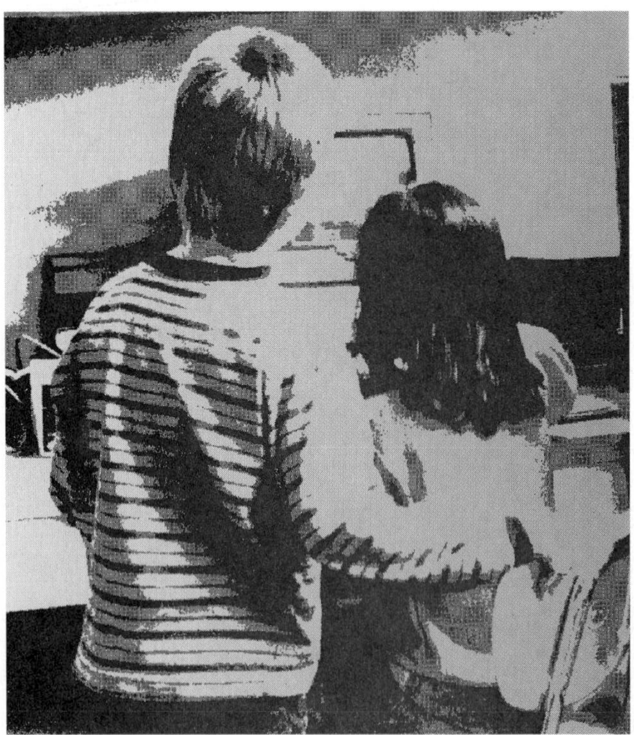

Among the myriad rewards of a teaching career are the colleagues who celebrate the accomplishments of their students and share the joy they find in learning. We say thanks to Rick's colleagues at Duquesne University who offered advice when asked, references when sought, and a sympathetic ear or kind word when needed. They suffered through his obsessive periods with understanding and good humor. They are not only colleagues, they are also friends. Rick especially thanks Wil Barber, Sue Brookhart, Carol Brooks, Bill Casile, Kathy Gosnell, Mary Fran Grasinger, Jim Henderson, Joe Kush, Susan Munson, Bernie Smith, Horton Southworth, and Laurel Swenson. Rick owes a tremendous debt to his undergraduate students at Duquesne, who have taken what they learned with him and reached out to others, especially Bob Aglietti, DaVaun Barnett, Michelle Bryan, Rachel Czarnecki, Carolyn Fodor, Michelle Frontera, Jamarr Jackson, Davi Katherisan, Heather King, Lisa Klein, Michelle Klingensmith, Chad Pysher, Heather Thiel, and Harold Turner. To his co-learners in the Interdisciplinary Doctoral Program for Educational Leaders, Rick expresses his appreciation for their understanding and their unqualified support, especially his doctoral advisees who — despite seeing him only sparingly during the past nine months — have remained supportive colleagues: Barbara Barnes, Roberta DiLorenzo, Linda Buchek Hippert, Doug Masciola, Walt McMillan, and Steve Vanucci.

We thank Marcy's colleagues — especially Walter Dick, Bob Reiser, Walt Wager, and Ann Shore — for their support, encouragement, and occasional gentle reminders when her program and professional responsibilities took a back seat for too long. Marcy expresses her appreciation to the many undergraduate and graduate students for their willing feedback and tales of experiences in the classroom, all of which helped to keep her grounded in reality. To her doctoral advisees and the students with whom she has worked closely in the last nine months, Marcy owes a special debt of gratitude, because they got the short end of her and yet did what they could to ease her load. These include Janette Hill, Nancy Gilbert, Terri Buckner, Cyndi Slocumb, Dan Gerson, David Lebow, Kurt Rowley, Robin Colson, and Elizabeth Kirby.

Peter especially thanks his current colleagues Judy DeShaney, Jean Wallace, Jane Anderson–Wood, Sara Born, and Terri Woodkey for sharing their insights into students and learning. Tom Loveall, Peter's principal for fifteen years deserves special recognition for helping him realize his potential as an educator. The following friends and educators, in late night talks and compelling conversations, contributed to this book in ways they will never know: Martha Turner, Marti Hemwall, Gary and Mary Finman, Bob Goldsmith, Laura Burrow, and John Peterson. Students, too numerous to name here, also aided in the creation of this book. Peter would like to thank all

Student Annotations include Key Concepts and Margin Notes, questions encouraging deeper thinking, connections to the *Teacher Chronicles*, and ideas for reflective writing exercises. *Try This* margin notes also provide concrete suggestions for learning.

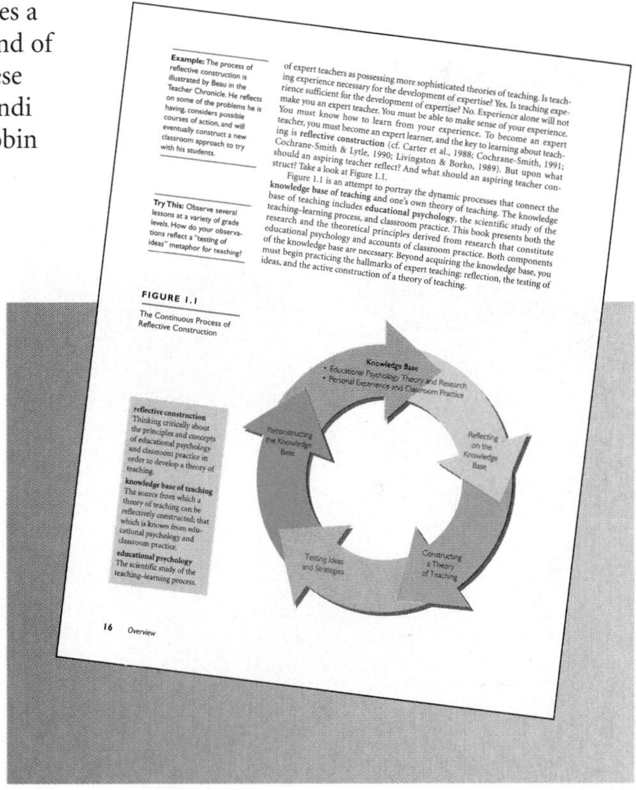
Example: The process of reflective construction is illustrated by Beau in the Teacher Chronicle. He reflects on some of the problems he is having, considers possible courses of action, and will eventually construct a new classroom approach to try with his students.

of expert teachers as possessing more sophisticated theories of teaching. Is teaching experience necessary for the development of expertise? Yes. Is teaching experience sufficient for the development of expertise? No. Experience alone will not make you an expert teacher. You must be able to make sense of your experience. You must know how to learn from your experience. To become an expert teacher, you must become an expert learner, and the key to learning about teaching is **reflective construction** (cf. Carter et al., 1988; Cochrane-Smith, 1991; Cochrane-Smith & Lytle, 1990; Livingston & Borko, 1989). But upon what should an aspiring teacher reflect? And what should an aspiring teacher construct? Take a look at Figure 1.1.

Figure 1.1 is an attempt to portray the dynamic processes that connect the **knowledge base of teaching** and one's own theory of teaching. The knowledge base of teaching includes **educational psychology**, the scientific study of the teaching–learning process, and classroom practice. This book presents both the research and the theoretical principles derived from research that constitute educational psychology and accounts of classroom practice. Both components of the knowledge base are necessary. Beyond acquiring the knowledge base, you must begin practicing the hallmarks of expert teaching: reflection, the testing of ideas, and the active construction of a theory of teaching.

Try This: Observe several lessons at a variety of grade levels. How do your observations reflect a "testing of ideas" metaphor for teaching?

FIGURE 1.1

The Continuous Process of Reflective Construction

reflective construction Thinking critically about the principles and concepts of educational psychology and classroom practice in order to develop a theory of teaching.

knowledge base of teaching The source from which a theory of teaching can be reflectively constructed; that which is known from educational psychology and classroom practice.

educational psychology The scientific study of the teaching–learning process.

16 *Overview*

of his students, present and past, who have been his tireless teachers for over two decades. Their parents, too, deserve thanks for their active participation in their children's schooling and support of Peter's teaching.

REVIEWERS

We are grateful to those who provided developmental and expert reviews of the manuscript:

Kay Alderman
University of Akron

John R. Bing
Salisbury State University

Kay S. Bull
Oklahoma State University

Michelle Comeaux
Gustavus Adolphus College

Richard Craig
Towson State University

Bryan Deever
Georgia Southern University

Gail C. Delicio
Clemson University

Peter R. Denner
Idaho State University

Janice Fauske
Weber State College

Kathleen Elizabeth Fite
Southwest Texas State University

Mark Grabe
University of North Dakota

Marlynn F. Griffin
Georgia Southern University

Herbert Grossman
San Jose State University

Sharon Lee Hiett
University of Central Florida

David S. Hill
Keene State College

Vernon F. Jones
Lewis and Clark College

Fintan Kavanagh
Marywood College

Suzanne MacDonald
University of Akron

Susan Magliaro
Virginia Polytechnic Institute and State University

Gollam Mannan
Indiana University-Purdue University at Indianapolis

Hermine H. Marshall
San Francisco State University

Catherine E. McCartney
Bemidji State University

Barbara McCombs
Mid-Continent Regional Educational Laboratory

Raymond B. Miller
University of Oklahoma

Sarah Peterson
Northern Illinois University

Richard Purnell
University of Rhode Island

Neil H. Schwartz
California State University-Chico

Robert E. Simpson
Western Kentucky University

Douglas J. Stanwyck
Georgia State University

Michael P. Verdi
Grand Canyon University

Barry J. Wilson
University of Northern Iowa

Their hard work made us work harder and better than we would have otherwise. We are grateful for the improvements their work has brought to this book.

We owe a special debt to Marlynn Griffin of Georgia Southern University and Gwen Quinn of Florida State University who created the *Assessment Package* that accompanies the text. Their understanding that assessment is an integral part of the teaching–learning process, their willingness to question our draft manuscripts, their persistence in an effort to "get it right" have contributed materially to the text as well as to the assessment package. We thank also Vicky Zygouris-Coe of the University of Florida for her insightful treatment of the text in the student *Study Guide* that supplements the text.

It is gratifying to have completed this second edition with our original publishing house, Allyn & Bacon. We are grateful to Bill Barke, President, for brushing off the welcome mat a second time. Under his distinctive leadership, this venerable old house just keeps getting better. Much credit goes to the Editor-in-Chief for Education, Nancy Forsyth. Her support, encouragement, and enthusiasm for the project was instrumental in bringing the second edition into reality. Her belief in the project and in the partnership has changed what was initially appreciation of her leadership skill into respect for her judgment and warm regard for a friend. It's good to be back again among other old friends at the house, people such as Sandi Kirshner, Ellen Mann, and Ray Short, who have not wavered in their belief in this project since it began in 1988.

There is one more person at the house who deserves our thanks. Mary Ellen Lepionka. Between the manuscripts produced for the first two editions of this text, we have written well over half a million words, but finding the right words to express our thanks to Mary Ellen is among the most difficult writing tasks we have undertaken. There are two reasons why this is so. First, she is an editor who demands the best from her authors, who challenges them to do better when they thought they had done their best, who is unwavering in her pursuit of excellence. She is an editor with remarkable knowledge and insight, a professional through and through. Second, she has shared with us her extraordinary spirit. Her passion extinguished our fatigue. Her love of learning inspired us. Her tenacity gave us confidence. Her sincere concern for each of us cemented a friendship that will endure. The authorship of this book may comprise only three people, but the team has four members. We are proud to be Allyn & Bacon authors and proud to call Mary Ellen Lepionka our Editor.

We end, as we always will, with a deep bow to our academic family. We hope this effort honors the values and traditions of that family, including our siblings and cousins: Mark Grabe, Ray Miller, Sarah Peterson, Neil Schwartz, and Gary Shank who helped launch this project. We hope especially to honor the generation that charted our course, particularly Don Cunningham, Mike Royer, and Uncle Ray Kulhavy. We are lucky to be among the stars.

Rick McCown
Marcy Driscoll
Peter Geiger Roop

1 Views of Teaching and Learning

CHAPTER OUTLINE

TEACHER Chronicle

TEACHER TALK

Beau and Loni greet each other in the teachers' lounge one day after school. They are members of an interdisciplinary team at a middle school. Both teach seventh grade. Beau, in his first year, teaches social studies and Loni, in her twelfth year, teaches math and science. They get together daily in their team to discuss student performance and student behavior. The third team member, who teaches language arts, hasn't yet arrived.

"What a day!" begins Beau. "I knew I was in trouble when Jamie challenged me during third period. First, she put her head down on her desk, and I thought she was just going to zee out for awhile. But then she deliberately ignored my directions to work out the problem in their groups, and it was a real battle to keep her on task."

"I know what you mean," agrees Loni. "Jamie can be a real handful. She needs a tight rein."

"Well, by fifth period, I thought I had been thrown to the lions. Sabrina kept punching Bucky in the arm. Mary wouldn't talk to the other members of her group. And Jayson . . . he was just being himself, I guess. He kept waving his hand and if I didn't call on him right away, he left his group and started disrupting the groups working around him. Why can't these kids cooperate with each other?"

"They will in time," reassures Loni. "Have you done any team-building activities with the students?"

"No." Beau looks blankly at her.

"How did you determine the groupings?"

"It was more or less random, I guess. I did think about personalities a little. I figured that putting Matt and Dana together would be like lighting the fuse to dynamite."

Loni laughs. "Yes, that would be an explosive combination all right. They're both strong-minded individuals. How often do you change the groups?"

"I haven't thought of that," Beau replies.

"Well," Loni suggests, "you have some more planning to do. When you put students into groups, you have to remember that it takes time for them to learn how to be a group. And just as some students take longer than others to work out a problem or understand a concept, so do some groups take time to mesh. I remember one group last year that just couldn't seem to get it together. I can't recall now what got them moving smoothly, but the results were dazzling. They worked out a system for generating hypotheses, systematically testing them, and keeping track of the results. Each member of the group took a specific role that determined what tasks he or she would perform. I've read research since that says assigning roles within a group is a good strategy for achieving cooperation. And my four students, whom I'd about given up on, connected it all up for themselves."

"So teaching is kind of like flying a kite," Beau says finally. "You have to let out the string enough to let each group find its own wind. Say, do you have some material on cooperative learning that I could take a look at?"

FOCUS QUESTIONS

1. How can teaching and learning be conceptualized as an integrated process?

2. What is Beau's theory of teaching? How will his theory affect his professional development as a teacher?
3. What are Beau's metaphors for teachers and learners? What are his assumptions about teaching and learning?
4. What knowledge base and thought processes will allow you to become an expert teacher?

WHAT ARE TEACHING AND LEARNING?

Teaching v. Learning

Beau and Loni are talking about teaching and learning, which are the subjects of this book. **Teaching** is action taken with the intent to facilitate learning. **Learning** is change in thought or behavior that modifies a person's capabilities. Although these statements are simple, their implications could fill several books.

Point: One of the basic assumptions of this book is that *teaching and learning are aspects of the same process.*

Note that the definition of teaching subsumes the definition of learning—that is, teaching results in change in thought or behavior that modifies a person's capabilities. Because you intend to teach, it is crucial that you conceive of teaching in terms of learning. Entering the teaching profession means intending to change the thought and behavior of students to enhance their capabilities. Imagine a person who considers his or her teaching to be independent of learning. After delivering an unsuccessful lesson, this person might explain the outcome by saying, "I taught that, but they didn't learn it." The error in this explanation is the assumption that teaching and learning are separate, distinct processes. No one would accept a salesperson's statement, "I sold the item, but the customer didn't buy it" (cf. Postman & Weingartner, 1969). If an item has to be bought in order to be considered sold, we should consider that knowledge and skills are taught only if they have been learned. Just as effective selling results in buying, so does effective teaching result in learning. When a teacher's efforts fail to produce learning, he or she does not accept the situation, but tries again.

Point: Loni's reflection is an indication of her teaching expertise. A basic assumption of this book is that *reflective construction is necessary for the development of teaching expertise.*

Teaching and learning are integrated. When we discuss either teaching or learning in this book, we are simply choosing to focus on one of two aspects of the same process: the **teaching–learning process.** Consider, for example, the shared reflections of Loni and Beau in the Teacher Chronicle. Although they are discussing teaching, they have a lot to say about student learning. Recall that one of the primary reasons they meet daily in the teachers' lounge is to discuss student performance and behavior. Beau seeks advice from Loni that might help him improve the cooperative efforts of his students. In essence, he seeks to teach differently in an effort to enhance the performance of his students. Loni reflects on a class in which her students were having difficulty working in cooperative learning groups. She describes how her students discovered that by taking specific roles, their learning improved. Loni also mentions having read research that supports the assignment of roles to individuals working in cooperative learning groups. In the Teacher Chronicle, both teachers view their teaching in light of student learning. Also, both teachers are themselves learners. They learn from their own teaching experiences. That teaching is a source of learning for both students and teachers is an important insight for those who aspire to teach (McLaughlin & Talbert, 1993).

Try This: Interview a practicing teacher in order to discover what and how teachers learn from their teaching.

teaching Action taken with the intent to facilitate learning

learning Change in thought or behavior that modifies a person's capabilities.

teaching–learning process The process of taking action to produce change in thought or behavior and subsequent modification of capabilities.

The teaching–learning process operates under all kinds of conditions and in all kinds of settings. Teaching occurs not only in schools but also in homes and hospitals, churches and child care centers, museums and meeting rooms, camps and clubs, garages and garbage trucks. Teaching also occurs across time and distance in the form of print, art, technology, and mass media. In some cases, the learner is also the teacher. For example, a person who studies independently takes actions that he or she believes will result in a modification of his or her capabilities. Independent learning, therefore, can be viewed as self-teaching. In other cases—when students engage in cooperative learning, for instance—learners teach each other. Teaching is a universal human activity. It occurs among and between humans of all cultures, in and across all times and places.

Connection: The techniques for facilitating cooperative learning are examined in Chapter 12, Teaching for Active Learning.

All of this is not to say that teaching always produces learning. The definition of teaching includes "the intent to facilitate learning," and even the best intentions do not always produce positive results. Have you ever observed or experienced teaching that failed to facilitate learning? Why does some teaching succeed while other teaching fails to enhance—or even diminishes—a learner's capabilities? Why are some people more capable of facilitating learning than others? How can one become a better facilitator of learning? How can you become, in the true sense of the word, a teacher? Not just someone who holds a position on a school's payroll, but someone who facilitates learning. And not just someone who facilitates learning, but who continually learns and improves as a facilitator of learning?

Classroom practice that reflects an understanding that teaching and learning are aspects of the same process is a hallmark of expert teaching. A conceptual integration of teaching and learning is necessary for teaching expertise. This book is based on the following basic working assumptions:

- Teaching and learning are aspects of the same process.
- Your view of the teaching–learning process affects your classroom practice.
- Reflective construction is necessary for the development of teaching expertise.

Reflection: What experiences have led you to seek a career in teaching? How have those experiences shaped your beliefs and values about teaching? Why do you want to be a teacher?

This chapter explores these basic assumptions, which are foundational to our view of teaching. Additional assumptions that we point out in this book build on these basic working assumptions and are based on our knowledge of the theory and research of educational psychology; our knowledge of classroom practice; and our reflections on theory, research, and professional practice. The assumptions underlie our descriptions, explanations, and predictions of the phenomenon called teaching. They are part of our **theory of teaching**. What is your theory of teaching and how will your theory affect your growth as a teacher?

Try This: Start a journal that will describe your development from aspiring teacher to practicing teacher. The first entry in the journal could be your images of teaching and learning.

HOW CAN YOU DEVELOP A THEORY OF TEACHING?

theory of teaching
Description, explanations, and prediction of action staken with the intent to facilitate learning.

What is the first thing that comes into your mind when you hear the word *teaching*? What images are evoked by the word *learning*? Do the images of teaching imply that someone is learning?

Your vision of teaching and learning will guide your actions as a teacher. Your vision will influence how you plan your lessons, what instructional and assessment strategies you implement in the classroom, and how you reflect on your teaching experiences. Your reflections will be based partly on your expectations according to your prior experiences. Aspiring teachers often think a great deal, for example, about what their ideal classroom will look like. Some choose to become teachers because they are convinced that teaching and learning can be

Insights ON SUCCESSFUL PRACTICE

What suggestions do you have for novice teachers on applying principles of educational psychology to better understand students and classroom events?

Building your own theory of teaching is essential to your success as a teacher, no matter what grade level you teach. When you face your first class, you will have a foundation of educational psychology on which to build your personal teaching. Over the years, experience will become another cornerstone of that theory. The melding of educational psychology and your experience will become your personal theory of teaching.

What do you need when you face your first class?

A thorough knowledge of the developmental stages through which humans pass is vital to your understanding students. An attention-getting routine that works with six-year-olds, like flicking the classroom lights, must necessarily be adapted to work with fifteen-year-olds, where placing your attendance book on a tall stool might be just as successful. The concept remains the same, but the application varies. Likewise, an abstract science lesson about fossils in a science book for seniors might be as effective as a hands-on fossil-hunting field trip for fourth graders. In both cases, information is being taught, but at the conceptual and physical level appropriate to the students' developmental stages.

Knowing how students develop socially is a key factor to better understanding classroom events. Providing second graders with five minutes' time to talk with one another at the beginning of the day helps them "move" from home to school, enabling them to share things foremost in their minds before an academic lesson begins. A thought-provoking quote that students can discuss for five minutes might serve the same function for tenth graders, mentally "moving" them from one class to another. Both strategies allow for social interaction at an age-appropriate level while setting the scene for the upcoming lesson.

As a student, you encountered master teachers who appeared to have an intuitive sense of teaching. They not only instructed but also managed a roomful of students with remarkable ease. Such intuition is based on a thorough knowledge of how students think, develop, and interact; the principles of educational psychology.

My advice for a beginning teacher: Think about your students. Think about your practice. Reflect on what works or doesn't work in your classroom, and why. The answers will strengthen your personal theory of teaching.

Most importantly, have patience with yourself in your own development as a teacher.

PETER ROOP, McKinley Elementary School,
Appleton, Wisconsin

---

vastly different from what they experienced as students in elementary, middle, and high school. However, many beginning teachers have not reflected enough on their views of teaching and learning. When asked "What is *your* theory of teaching?" they are stumped. Only by actively reflecting on your implicit views and making them explicit can you consider adopting alternative views (cf. Unger, Draper, & Pendergrass, 1987; Cunningham, 1987). Unfortunately, there is ample evidence to suggest that many teachers have not devoted time and thought to developing—to any serious degree—their views of teaching. They simply teach as they were taught, without reflecting on the effectiveness of those methods (Huling-Austin, 1994).

According to this teacher, in what ways is educational psychology a foundation for teaching practice? Why are self-knowledge and knowledge of students the bedrock of this foundation?

Reflection: How many of your teachers in school taught in similar ways. How many of your classrooms were arranged in the traditional "teacher in front" manner?

Critical Thinking: Why should simply observing teachers influence the way one views teaching?

Whether they have reflected carefully on their views of teaching or not, all prospective teachers have implicit assumptions about the nature of learning and what it means to teach. These assumptions are formed through experiencing more than 10,000 hours of teaching and learning during their school years. The wealth of images and impressions from this long observational experience contributes to the tendency to teach the way one was taught (Feiman-Nemser, 1983). In order to develop a theory of teaching, in other words, it is important to make explicit your assumptions and examine them for the implications they hold for classroom instruction. A useful way of discovering your assumptions is to consider possible metaphors for teaching and learning and to decide which of the metaphors reflects your ideal classroom.

Discovering Metaphors for Teaching and Learning

Lakoff and Johnson (1980) argue that **metaphors** reflect the very essence of thought, that "the human conceptual system is metaphorically structured and defined" (p. 6). In other words, we represent and talk about our experiences in terms of other more familiar or more commonly shared events that seem comparable. If you listen carefully to conversations among people, you will hear metaphors implicit in almost every sentence. Reread the Teacher Chronicle at the beginning of this chapter, for example. What metaphors does Beau use in describing problems with student behaviors in his classroom? What is Loni's metaphor for cooperative learning? What metaphor expresses Beau's theory of teaching?

skip metaphors

Examining the metaphors that teachers use when they talk about their experiences in the classroom is an approach to understanding their professional knowledge (Munby, 1987; Munby & Russell, 1990). The notion is that teachers have particular conceptualizations of teaching and learning that become evident in the language they use to describe events in the classroom. In a recent study, for example, interview transcripts of two teachers (Alice, an eighth-grade English teacher with five years of experience, and Bryn, an eighth-grade American history teacher with eight years of experience) revealed that both teachers used a travel metaphor in describing their classes. Alice, who used the metaphor extensively, employed the following phrases in describing her students and lessons: "I just went ahead," "these kids need a push in every direction," "if he's lost . . . he's just going to get further behind," and "they like to get off of the subject onto different topics" (Munby, 1987, p. 384). Statements such as "they're going to pick up on that" also suggested that Alice viewed learning as students gathering up information as the lesson travelled by them.

Reflection: Reflect on several of your teachers who made either positive or negative impressions on you. What metaphors would you ascribe to their teaching?

Because metaphors can structure our thinking, they can also affect our behavior (cf. Munby, 1987; Munby & Russell, 1990; Tobin, 1990; Marshall, 1990). Teachers' metaphors can guide the roles they choose to take, the ways they interact with students, and the approaches they take to solving problems in the classroom. In one case, for example, a high school science teacher conceived of his classroom management role in terms of a ship's captain. He emphasized whole class activities where he was in charge of the class, he called on nonvolunteers to make sure that all students were paying attention, and he acted assertive and goal-directed in class (Tobin, 1990).

metaphor A way to represent and talk about experiences in terms of other, more familiar, or more commonly shared events that seem comparable.

By contrast, another teacher in Tobin's study saw herself as a comedian. She believed that "students will be captivated by charm, humor, and well-organized

What might be this teacher's metaphors for teachers, learners, and the teaching–learning process? How might understanding these metaphors help this individual become a better teacher?

presentations, which they will find enjoyable and easy to learn" (Tobin, 1990, p. 124). Unfortunately, students responded to this teacher with aggressive and uncooperative behavior. Despite her beliefs in the teacher as a facilitator of learning, her classroom was not an environment conducive to learning. There seemed to be a mismatch between the teacher's expressed view of the teaching–learning process and her behaviors in the classroom. The results of Tobin's study suggest two conclusions. First, when teachers act in accord with various metaphors, different classroom cultures can emerge. Second, the cultures that emerge may not always reflect what teachers expect. Consider, for example, the teacher who thought her comedic approach to teaching would create an enjoyable and captivating atmosphere. Her behaviors, however, did not yield an effective learning environment. As a result, students in her classroom did not act as she expected.

Connection: The nature of "classroom cultures" will be examined in various parts of this book, including those dealing with student diversity, classroom dynamics, instructional planning, and assessment.

Analyzing Metaphors in Teacher Problem Solving

Discovering and reflecting upon their metaphors for teaching and learning can help teachers understand problems occurring in their classrooms. Examining a metaphor in light of classroom reality can also suggest possible solutions to problems. Recall how in the Teacher Chronicle Beau realized that his teaching behavior, based on a battleground metaphor, did not match his hopes and beliefs about the teaching–learning process. Making metaphors explicit and then reflecting on the metaphors to discover classroom implications is one way in which teachers can learn from their classroom experience and the classroom experiences of others. These discoveries can lead to beneficial changes in how teachers relate to students and organize and implement lessons. Consider, for example, this reflection of a student teacher:

> When my cooperating teacher referred to my view of teaching as "constant companion" I realized I was taking on more than I could be to my kids. I had been having lots of problems with management because I found it so hard to call anyone down—because I wanted everyone to know that I liked them the same, and I very much wanted them to like me. I wanted them to know I would be there for them. Part of me still wants that very much, but that conversation certainly clarified for me that I would lose any hope of winning anyone over if the classroom turned to chaos. (Carter, 1990, p. 114)

Try This: Interview a student teacher to discover the way he or she thinks about relationships with students and whether the student teacher's view has changed based on his or her student teaching experience.

Insights ON SUCCESSFUL PRACTICE

How did your experience working with a mentor help you to become a more effective teacher?

Finally, I had my own classroom, and after only a few weeks I was afraid I was becoming the teacher I swore I'd never become: arbitrary, gruff, and cynical. Enter the mentor. She taught down the hall from me. The same children who were making me crazy seemed to be transformed under her influence.

One evening, drained and in doubt, I walked down to her room and started drawing from her the first of many real-life lessons. She gave me some suggestions for working with Jackie, who had some serious learning problems. They were good ideas. As the year went on, she shared tips on organization, demonstrated a positive approach to discipline, and could even help me find a teacher's manual when I needed one. It meant a lot that year to have someone to listen, suggest, role model, and support.

I've been teaching for nearly twenty years now, and I just do not remember all the little things she shared with me. But it occurs to me now that those on-the-job lessons I got from her were not the most important things that she gave me. What were the important things? First, the knowledge that I wasn't alone in my work. She helped me see how I could work with other staff members, parents, and children for our common ends. Second, she managed to transmit her belief in children and their possibilities: she *knew* they were going to succeed in her class. Finally, she modeled respect for our children, the kind of respect that gets children in touch with the good things in themselves. Respect that demands the best work from students. Respect that is not afraid to challenge failings, but never attacks the person.

I think that the early positive, practical support I got has helped give me attitudes that allow me to love my work now. Connectedness, confidence, and respect are powerful shapers of success for teachers as well as students. New teachers all have to find personal paths to these things, and a mentor can help show the way.

EDWARD VALENT, Gilbert Stuart Elementary School, Milwaukee, Wisconsin

What are the benefits of mentors for beginning teachers? What steps might you take to develop a mentor relationship as you begin to teach?

reframing Rethinking an event or problem in terms of metaphors in order to gain a new perspective.

Analyzing metaphors is a problem-solving strategy; that is, **reframing** an event or problem in terms of metaphors provides teachers with novel ways of "seeing" professional puzzles (Munby & Russell, 1990). Insights gained in this way help teachers to resolve issues or problems in their teaching.

Exposing implicit beliefs about teaching and learning also helps teachers to detect inconsistencies in their metaphors. Beginning teachers, especially, often have stated beliefs about learning that are not reflected in their actions in the classroom. Recall Beau's comments in the Teacher Chronicle. Although he stated a belief in cooperative learning and shared knowledge construction, he initially described events of the day in terms of metaphors that conflict with these beliefs. Statements such as "Jamie challenged me" and "she threw down the gauntlet" suggest a *conflict* or *war* metaphor, in which the teacher and student are on opposite sides. The words "I was trying to get across . . ." suggest the notion that knowledge is a *commodity* to be handed from teacher to student.

Loni, in contrast, uses the metaphor of the well-oiled machine, which is consistent with a view of group dynamics in which students learn to work well together and each student plays an important part.

Teaching and learning can be viewed from many different metaphorical vantage points. Researchers and theorists often employ metaphors in an attempt to describe and explain teaching and learning. One example is the agricultural metaphor: a view of teaching and learning that focuses on student growth (see Table 1.1). As you can see from Table 1.1, every metaphor has certain consequences for what happens in the classroom—who defines the problem or task, the resources to be studied, how and with whom the work is accomplished, and with what anticipated outcomes. As you read each metaphor in Table 1.1, try to visualize what is happening in the classroom that is consistent with the metaphor.

Example: Additional illustrations and discussions of teachers' metaphors can be found in a special issue of the journal, *Theory Into Practice*, vol. 29 (2), Spring, 1990.

TABLE 1.1 A Sample of Metaphors Used by Teachers to Express Their Views of Teaching and Learning

Teacher Metaphor	Expression of Metaphor
Teacher as forest ranger	"I see myself as a protector of the learning environment. A protector takes care of everyone's common property, for the benefit of all."
Teacher as air traffic controller	"There are so many decisions to make in teaching. It's hard to get one thing settled before another plane full of passengers is ready to land."
Teacher as flood control director	"Things don't always work in teaching. Or maybe they don't work the way you expect. Sometimes, you do something that just opens the floodgates, and you have to wait for the flow to subside before you can redirect it."
Teacher as bird-watcher	"I try to be vigilant for the rare birds who can create such chaos in a classroom. But I have to be careful that spotting only that special species will make me miss lots of other birds in flight."
Teacher as gourmet chef	"I was coming in every day trying to serve up the most delicious instructional activities, and I was growing increasingly angry that the students weren't appreciating my delicious academic treats."
Teacher as scientist	"I'm experimenting all the time, trying different things to see how they work. I try to figure out what happened."
Teacher as traffic cop	"I'm trying to change my view of discipline, because I realized seeing myself as a traffic cop puts all the responsibility on me and assumes that students will be trying to break the law."
Teacher as preacher	"I lecture in class, because I think an important part of my role is taking the opportunity to share what I know."
Student Metaphor	**Expression of Metaphor**
Student as pathfinder	"At the beginning of the term, Ashley seemed so lost all the time. Now, she's beginning to find her way."
Student as scientist	"You pose a problem and the students have to try to hypothesize how to solve the problem. They look at all the variables and then go about doing their experimenting."
Student as plant	"With some kids, you really don't have to provide much structure. I just water them and they grow."
Student as detective	"Learning is like solving puzzles. Students have to find all the clues and then put them together in the right way to find the answer."
Student as sponge	"Some subjects—math is an example—just require more soak time."

Source: Some of the metaphors in this table were suggested by aspiring teachers at Florida State University; others were discussed in articles appearing in the special issue of *Theory Into Practice*, "Metaphors We Learn By," 29 (2), Spring 1990.

Consider the following aspects of classroom operation:

- how a teacher might deliver a lesson
- what classroom rules might be in place
- how much student–teacher and student–student interaction might take place
- what kinds of assessment techniques might be used
- what sorts of learning outcomes would be valued

Some teachers, for example, see themselves as captains whose role is to lead the troops into battle. They see themselves as being in charge, issuing directions, and providing relevant information. The role of the student, then, is to follow orders and to use the information as directed. Learning is a matter of conquering problems and overcoming barriers that may stand in the way of performance and achievement. Regardless of which metaphor of the teaching–learning process you adopt, there are consequences for the role of the learner, the role of the teacher, and the types of instructional strategies deemed most appropriate for helping students learn.

Reflection: Which of the metaphors in Table 1.1 is most attractive to you? Why?

So, how can you, an aspiring teacher, develop your view of the teaching–learning process? The first step is to make explicit your own metaphors of teaching and learning and to reflect on them. Your general metaphor is the foundation of your theory of teaching. It influences your description, explanation, and predictions about teaching. As a consequence of studying the theory, research, and practice presented in this text, your theory of teaching—and the metaphor on which it is based—will probably change. Your next step is to examine other metaphors to consider their contributions to your understanding of teaching and their implications for classroom practice. Your job will be to consider those implications as they apply to learners, learning tasks, learning environments, and learning contexts—such as students' cultural backgrounds—in which the teaching–learning process occurs.

The research on metaphorical reasoning, particularly on the metaphors used by teachers, suggests strongly that aspiring and practicing teachers can improve by explicating and examining their metaphors of teaching. In the Teacher Chronicle, Loni, the veteran teacher, commented on how her view of teaching changed when she reflected on both her experience in her classroom and research she had read. Even though she has considerable teaching experience, her theory of teaching continues to change. This is true of all expert teachers. Even so, the thinking of expert teachers differs in some significant ways from the thinking of novice teachers. What are these differences and how can such differences help aspiring teachers prepare to enter the profession?

HOW CAN YOU LEARN TO THINK LIKE AN EXPERT TEACHER?

Teaching the way you were taught might be satisfactory if the nature of schools and the society they serve did not change and if the teaching practices of days gone by were uniformly effective. But society has changed. The responsibilities given to schools and to teachers have changed. Fenstermacher (1990) likens the changes in the demands of teaching to changes in aviation:

> Thirty or forty years ago, much of what is known as . . . aviation was a matter of skill with stick and rudder, dead-reckoning navigation, and carefully nurtured seat-of-the-pants instincts. These relatively simple skills and instincts still form the core of flying, but no one can fly in heavily trafficked airways with just these skills. The crowding of modern airports, the amount of airplane traffic, and the horrible consequences of aviation accidents have resulted in the development of complex requirements and skills for flying. (pp. 139–140)

Connection: The changing nature of schools has implications for classroom dynamics and is discussed in Chapter 10.

The conditions of teaching and learning in schools have grown so complex that educators are experimenting with major changes in the way schools are organized, the way they are administered, and the way the teaching–learning process is implemented. You will enter the teaching profession at a time when the old paradigms of teaching and learning are being cast off in favor of efforts to reform and restructure education. As schools continue to respond to the complex problems of our society, it will be necessary for teachers to continue learning throughout their careers (Huling-Austin, 1994). The complexity of teaching requires that those who pursue it as a profession accept the challenge of continuous learning.

Try This: Consult local newspapers, your local school district office, or the local education association or teachers' union. Ask for brochures and other documents that describe efforts to restructure schools.

Not only has teaching practice changed, but so has our understanding of teaching. The recognition of teaching as a complex activity has spawned research designed to investigate how novice teachers differ from expert teachers. The rationale for such research is that if we can determine how teaching expertise develops, it may be possible to facilitate that development. How do expert teachers think? What do they think about? What do they see in classroom behavior that novice teachers can't see?

expert v. novice

Differences between Expert and Novice Teachers

Expert teachers see classrooms differently than do novices. The reason they see different things is that they know different things. The knowledge that expert teachers bring with them into their classrooms allows them to infer accurately and efficiently, to determine relevant from irrelevant information, to comprehend the meaning behind classroom activity. Experts can read classrooms better than novices (Swanson, O'Connor, & Cooney, 1990).

An experienced teacher was asked what novice teachers need to know in order to become successful teachers. The teacher responded, "I think what you have to learn is how to deal with mental jumbling. You have to learn how to manage the . . . excuse the term . . . 'mental mess' provided by all the action you see in the classroom and how to stay in control of yourself and the situation in such a way that it continues to be a productive learning environment" (Carter, 1987, p. 5). This teacher's advice is consistent with much of the research on the differences between expert and novice teachers.

Much of the research on expert–novice differences in teaching indicates that expert teachers are more able to comprehend complex classroom phenomena. This research has often compared the perceptual abilities of experts, novices, and postulants—people who are planning to become teachers after a midcareer shift (Berliner, 1986; Carter, Sabers, Cushing, Pinnegar, & Berliner, 1987). In one study, experts, novices, and postulants viewed a series of approximately fifty slides taken in either science and math classes and were asked to discuss their reactions (Carter, Cushing, Sabers, Stein, & Berliner, 1988). The sequence in which the slides were shown portrayed a classroom session from beginning to end. Subjects were free to stop the sequence at any point to comment on any slide.

Critical Thinking: Try to anticipate the reason expert teachers have better perceptual abilities than novices. As you read the results of this study, try to offer your own explanation. Soon you will be able to compare your explanation with that of the authors of the study.

The results of the study indicated that experts were better able than novices or postulants to determine what was important and unimportant information. Experts were better able to form connections between and among pieces of information. Experts were also better at identifying both instructional problems and classroom management problems. An additional finding from this study was that experts, to a much greater degree than either novices or postulants, agreed among themselves. Whenever one expert commented on one part of the classroom sequence, other experts tended to comment on the same part. This was true for slides taken at the beginning, the middle, and the end of the classroom session. Furthermore, the nature of the comments among experts was similar. For example, the following comments were made by three different expert teachers in response to the fifth slide in a sequence:

> "It's a good shot of both people being involved and something happening."
> "Everybody seems to be interested in what they're doing at their lab stations."
> "Everybody working. A positive environment." (Carter et al., 1988, p. 30)

Other findings supported the similarity among expert responses. Recall that the procedure used in the study allowed the subjects to interrupt a sequence of fifty slides at any time in order to comment on what they had seen and that the slides were in a reasonable but imperfect chronological sequence. Novices and postulants made no comments about the chronology of the sequence. Experts, however, noticed several instances of slides out of sequence. For example, one expert commented, "See here's everybody; this is everybody sitting back down again. Obviously, this is not in sequence with the other pictures" (Carter et al., 1988, p. 30).

The investigators, while photographing a math class for slides to show to subjects, noticed a student who seemed very unhappy. At one point during the class, tears appeared in the student's eyes. The student was inattentive and did not interact with any other students or with the teacher. This student was more noticeable in the slides near the end of the sequence than in earlier slides. Only one subject, an expert, was able to discern from the slide sequence what the investigators had seen in person. The expert made the following comments: "I feel kind of sorry for the one girl in the front. It doesn't appear that she is part of the group. . . . There is definitely a problem there . . . she's having problems other than what's going on with the classroom" (Carter et al., 1988, p. 30).

Reflection: What kind of information do you think you could gain from observing a classroom in person that could not be gained by viewing photographs or slides of the same classroom?

The differences Kathy Carter and her associates found between expert teachers on the one hand and novice and postulant teachers on the other were not attributable to attitudes alone. All novices eligible to participate in the study had been judged competent, and of those, only the novices who were judged by their superiors to have the greatest potential to develop into excellent teachers were selected. Assuming that novices who are "good" beginning teachers have good work habits and positive attitudes toward teaching, then the differences between them and the experts must be attributed to other causes.

Critical Thinking: Why are the qualifications of the novice teachers an important aspect of this study?

Chances are, you have a high level of confidence in your ability to teach. People entering teacher education programs generally do have high levels of confidence in their abilities to teach (Brookhart & Freeman, 1992). If you are a male, you might be more confident than your female classmates (Book & Freeman, 1986; Kalaian & Freeman, 1990; Knight, Duke, & Palcic, 1988). And if you entered your teacher education program as a freshman, you might be less confident than those who entered as juniors (Brookhart, Miller, Loadman, & Whordley, 1990). All those entering teacher education report high levels of confidence and high levels of commitment to the teaching profession. However, research shows that the way you feel about teaching and your abilities to teach, your affective responses, are not the major difference between you and expert teachers. The major difference is *cognitive;* that is, expert teachers *think* differently than do novices.

Try This: Use your journal to reflect on your level of confidence at present. Has it changed since you started your teacher education program?

Teachers' Thought Processes

Carol Livingston and Hilda Borko (1989) conducted an analysis of differences in the way expert teachers and novice teachers think. They compared the planning, the actual interaction with students while presenting a lesson, and post-lesson reflections of both experts and novices. The authors explained the expert–novice differences they found in terms of cognitive schemata (Anderson, 1984). **Schemata** are theoretical knowledge structures that contain information, facts, principles, and the relationships among them. For example, you probably have a restaurant schemata that contains facts about menus, waiters, checks, and how those aspects of eating at a restaurant are related. Furthermore, you can use this restaurant schemata to interpret new experiences. The next time you eat at an unfamiliar restaurant, notice how much of the experience you are able to predict or anticipate based on your prior knowledge. Teaching schemata include mental representations of teaching experiences. The teaching schemata of expert teachers are, predictably, richer collections of facts, principles, and conceptions of teaching than the teaching schemata of novices. Livingston and Borko describe the difference as follows:

Connection: The concept of schemata is discussed in several places in the text, including cognitive development in Chapter 2 and cognitive views of learning in Chapter 7.

> [The] cognitive schemata of experts typically are more elaborate, more complex, more interconnected, and more easily accessible than those of novices. . . . Therefore, expert teachers have larger, better-integrated stores of facts, principles, and experiences to draw upon as they engage in planning, interactive teaching, and reflection. (1989, p. 37)

Critical Thinking: How could the concept of schemata be used to explain the differences between experts and novices in fields other than teaching?

According to research on expert and novice teachers, what might be some differences in awareness and attitudes between this experienced teacher and a novice? Are there also differences in the ways beginners and experts think?

schemata Theoretical knowledge structures that contain information, facts, principles, and the relationships among them.

Insights ON SUCCESSFUL PRACTICE

What roles have professional reflection and collaboration played in your development as a teacher?

The teachers I remember fondly and who had great impact on my development are those who taught me not only the required subjects but also how to care for others. It was those teachers who taught me the important qualities necessary for a teacher. I was fortunate to work with Geraldine Lynn, who was named teacher of the year by the Indiana Federation Council for Exceptional Children for her contribution to the teaching profession. Later, I was honored to be a recipient of this award.

I have taught children with disabilities from preschool through high school. I have also been involved in a program to educate young parents in the care and stimulation of infants at risk to facilitate their readiness for school, and I have served as a resource teacher for students with learning disabilities.

My students bring with them different learning problems, but most have feelings of low self-esteem brought on by years of failure and frustration. My main goal is to emphasize their strengths and set them up for success so that they gain the self-confidence they need to reawaken their desire to learn. I also work with their general education teachers to help them understand the children and work with them in the classroom. We work as a team to create a positive learning environment for all the children.

As a school psychologist, I assess children's intellectual ability, academic achievement, social skills, self-help skills, physical and motor development, and personality and emotional development. As an education professional, reflection and collaboration play major roles in my work. I consult with teachers, parents, administrators, school counselors, school nurses, therapists, and community agencies to meet the needs of children. And I am also a teacher. Working with others, I teach them about testing, what it does and does not tell us. I teach about child development and what can be expected of children at different stages. I also work directly with children and youths, individually and in groups, to help them understand themselves.

BARBARA VINSON, school psychologist,
Michigan City Area Schools, Michigan City, Indiana

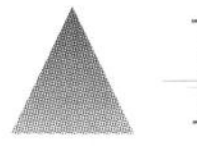

Insights

Who are your role models for being a teacher? What does professional reflection mean? Why are collegiality and collaboration so important in becoming a teaching professional?

The authors reported that experts described extensive mental plans for the lessons they delivered. The mental plans included a general outline of the content to be covered and the processes by which learning was to occur. The experts' plans did not include specific details such as how much time would be spent in any particular learning activity or the specific problems or examples to be covered. Rather, the specifics were determined in class as reactions to student questions or responses. However, the mental plans of two of the three experts studied included specific actions that would be taken, depending on the reactions of students.

Basing their interpretation on the notion of schemata, Livingston and Borko described experts' planning as matching existing information from their knowledge structures—information about instructional activities, the content to be learned, typical student behaviors—with the needs of a particular lesson. Experts were able to make these matches, and thus construct their plans, very efficiently.

Novices do not have the extensive information that experts have, nor can they access what information they do have as readily. In constructing their teaching plans, novices often have to interrupt the process in order to build or modify their teaching schemata. One way to think about these findings is that for experts, schemata facilitate the construction of plans, whereas for novices, planning facilitates the construction of schemata.

Reflection: Might this reasoning also explain why student teaching requires a great deal of mental effort?

Another advantage enjoyed by experts in the Livingston and Borko study is their ability to discriminate what is relevant to their planning and interaction decisions from what is irrelevant. For example, experts are better able than novices to compare student questions, concerns, or behavior with appropriate schemata to determine what should be taken into account in deciding the next step and what can be safely ignored. Because experts deal only with information that is relevant to decisions that must be made while teaching, they consider only information that is relevant to teaching decisions in their post-lesson reflections. Novices, however, cannot automatically discriminate relevant from irrelevant information. Just as the process of planning is disrupted because schemata need to be modified, so can a novice teacher become confused or thrown off by a student's question. Imagine a novice teacher who is attempting, without prior experience, to respond to a student who says, "I don't understand anything we've been talking about the whole period." The novice teacher, who wants very much to address the student's frustration, might feel lost and think, "Should I start over? Are they confused because I'm not sure of the content? Have I made a mistake in explaining a concept? Did I mix up that crucial distinction? Did I go too fast? Is this student just trying to frustrate me?" The novice, not sure of the appropriate way to respond, must evaluate all of the possibilities in order to make a decision. The expert, in contrast, has probably responded to that student question innumerable times. Through experience, the expert may have developed a routine of questioning that helps the student (and the teacher) get closer to the source of the student's confusion. Instead of considering many possible courses of action, as was the case with the novice teacher, the expert begins probing the student's confusion without hesitation.

Try This: Ask a practicing teacher how he or she responds to students who say, "I don't understand anything we've been talking about."

Novices' schemata do not contain routines developed as a consequence of responding to numerous similar teaching situations. Because they lack experience, their schemata do not include routine approaches to many of the situations they encounter early in their teaching careers. Novices must consider more information than experts both while planning and while making interactive decisions (Livingston & Borko, 1989). The comparative complexity and richness of expert schemata account well for the differences between experts and novices reviewed here. The richness of expert schemata also explains how experts are better able to use their interpretations of classroom activity to make instructional and classroom management decisions (Berliner, 1987, 1988; Borko & Shavelson, 1990; Carter et al., 1987; Leinhardt & Greeno, 1986; Peterson & Comeaux, 1987).

The Processes of Reflective Construction

The schemata of expert teachers allow them to describe, explain, and predict teaching and learning phenomena better than novices. Thus, one way to conceptualize the difference between expert and novice or aspiring teachers is to think of expert teachers as possessing more sophisticated theories of teaching. Is teaching experience necessary for the development of expertise? Yes. Is teaching experience sufficient for the development of expertise? No. Experience alone will not make you an expert teacher. You must be able to make sense of your experience. You must know how to learn from your experience. To become an expert teacher, you must become an expert learner, and the key to learning about teaching is **reflective construction** (cf. Carter et al., 1988; Cochrane-Smith, 1991; Cochrane-Smith & Lytle, 1990; Livingston & Borko, 1989). But upon what should an aspiring teacher reflect? And what should an aspiring teacher construct? Take a look at Figure 1.1.

Example: The process of reflective construction is illustrated by Beau in the Teacher Chronicle. He reflects on some of the problems he is having, considers possible courses of action, and will eventually construct a new classroom approach to try with his students.

Figure 1.1 is an attempt to portray the dynamic processes that connect the **knowledge base of teaching** and one's own theory of teaching. The knowledge base of teaching includes **educational psychology**, the scientific study of the teaching–learning process, and classroom practice. This book presents both the research and the theoretical principles derived from research that constitute educational psychology and accounts of classroom practice. Both components of the knowledge base are necessary. Beyond acquiring the knowledge base, you must begin practicing the hallmarks of expert teaching: reflection, the testing of ideas, and the active construction of a theory of teaching.

Try This: Observe several lessons at a variety of grade levels. How do your observations reflect a "testing of ideas" metaphor for teaching?

FIGURE 1.1

The Continuous Process of Reflective Construction

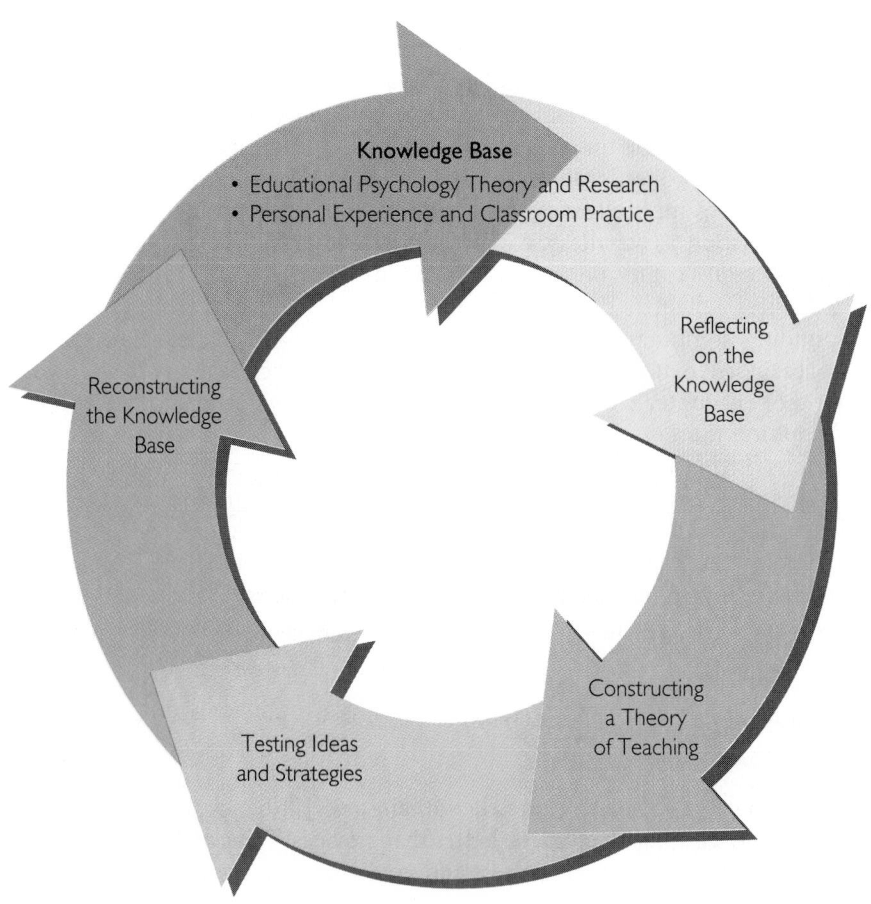

reflective construction Thinking critically about the principles and concepts of educational psychology and classroom practice in order to develop a theory of teaching.

knowledge base of teaching The source from which a theory of teaching can be reflectively constructed; that which is known from educational psychology and classroom practice.

educational psychology The scientific study of the teaching–learning process.

In the Teacher Chronicle at the beginning of the chapter, Beau was engaged in reflection. He thoughtfully considered his own practice in light of his purposes and goals. Loni contributed to his reflection by sharing her knowledge of pertinent research and some of her own classroom experiences. The product of Beau's reflection was a set of ideas of how the teaching–learning process would work in the context of his classroom. What his reflection produced was a change in his theory of teaching with regard to the use of cooperative learning tasks. Beau's description of cooperative learning was different, his explanation of cooperative learning changed, and his predictions of the outcomes of cooperative tasks were altered because he reflected—with the help of an expert.

The ideas that are tested by teachers come from their theories. If a teacher tries an idea in his or her classroom, the resulting experience augments the knowledge base. As long as a teacher tests his or her ideas, the knowledge base available for reflection will continue to expand. As long as a teacher continues to consult the research and principles that are generated by educational psychologists, the knowledge base will grow. And as long as the knowledge base continues to expand, a teacher will always have an opportunity to reflect on new knowledge and thus to construct and reconstruct an ever-evolving theory of teaching.

A career in teaching is a career in learning. You may not be an expert teacher by the time you leave this course, and you may not enter the teaching profession as an expert, but you can begin the process of reflecting on the knowledge base that you will encounter in this book. You can begin constructing a theory of teaching. The importance of reflective construction is our third basic assumption about teaching: Reflective construction is necessary for the development of teaching expertise.

Point: It was mentioned earlier that expert teachers are expert learners. This theme will recur in this book. One of the themes in Part 5, Effective Instruction, is that *teachers and students are both learners.*

ON WHAT THEORY OF TEACHING IS THIS BOOK BASED?

To answer this question directly, the theory of teaching you will encounter in this book is the theory that we, the authors, have constructed through reflecting on the research and principles of educational psychology, on the classroom experiences of dozens of other teachers, and on our own teaching experiences.

In this chapter we have stated our three basic assumptions about teaching.

1. Teaching and learning are aspects of the same process.
2. Your view of the teaching–learning process affects your classroom practice.
3. Reflective construction is necessary for the development of teaching expertise.

These are the foundations from which our theory of teaching derives. That theory, which has evolved from our understanding of educational psychology and classroom practice, yields other working assumptions. These are all assumptions we continue to work from and continue to test in our own teaching and research and continue to reflect on in the teaching and research of others.

Working Assumptions about Teaching and Learning

The book is organized into six parts. The working assumptions that underlie our theory of teaching and, therefore, our understanding of the knowledge base of teaching and learning are listed below. These statements represent the main themes of this book.

Reflection: Evaluate the main themes of the book against your current views of the teaching-learning process. Do any of the themes surprise you? If so, why?

Part I Development (Chapters 2 and 3)
- Development is complex and multifaceted.
- Development affects learning.
- Life conditions affect development.

Part II Diversity (Chapters 4 and 5)
- Learners are diverse.
- Students' diversity and individuality affect their learning.
- Inclusive classrooms provide learning opportunities.

Part III Learning (Chapters 6, 7, and 8)
- Learning is shaped by the learner's environment.
- Learning is a function of complex mental activities.
- Learning is active construction in social contexts.

Part IV Motivation and Classroom Dynamics (Chapters 9 and 10)
- People are naturally motivated to learn.
- Needs and values affect motivation.
- Classroom management is a shared concern.

Part V Effective Instruction (Chapters 11 and 12)
- Teachers and students are both learners.
- Teachers coordinate the context for learning.
- Instructional technologies support teaching and learning.

Part VI Evaluation (Chapters 13 and 14)
- Assessment serves multiple purposes.
- Assessment improves teaching and learning.
- Authentic activity provides a basis for assessment.

Understanding the teaching–learning process means understanding the factors that can influence it. The factors that influence the teaching–learning process are implied by the assumptions stated above. In this book, we have attempted to integrate the principles of educational psychology and the experiences of classroom practitioners for the purpose of helping you develop a theory of teaching that can be tested in your own classroom.

That integration of theory and practice will come from your own "systematic inquiry of teaching, learning, and schooling" (the primary context in which your theory of teaching will be tested) (Cochrane-Smith, 1991, p. 283). The features in this text have been designed to help you conduct that systematic inquiry.

The Teaching Approach of This Textbook

This book may not be the only learning resource at your disposal, but we have assumed that it is an important one. In writing it, we have incorporated a number of instructional features that are designed to help you acquire and use the knowledge base of teaching. This preview will serve as a basis for a learning strategy that you can employ as you study this book.

Teacher Chronicle. There are four components of the Teacher Chronicle feature. The Teacher Chronicle at the beginning of this and every chapter serves as a focal point for the ideas presented. Teacher Chronicles are events in teaching practice. These events are discussed in the body of a chapter and are concluded or resolved at the end. After reading this chapter, for example, you can find out how Beau modifies and retests his theory of teaching.

Focus Questions following the Teacher Chronicle are designed to help you anticipate how the content of the chapter relates to the teaching–learning process that is represented in the Teacher Chronicle event.

The Teacher Chronicle Conclusion at the end of each chapter is followed by Application Questions, the final component of the Teacher Chronicle feature. Application Questions refer specifically to the events in the Teacher Chronicle and allow you to reinterpret those events through the application of key concepts from the chapter.

Connection: When you discover how Beau modifies his view in the conclusion to Teacher Talk, compare his new approach with the metaphors in Table 1.1.

Insights on Successful Practice. Earlier in this chapter we identified classroom practice as part of the knowledge base of teaching. In addition to the Teacher Chronicles, descriptions of classroom practice are provided in three or four features called Insights on Successful Practice that are found in each chapter. The sources of the Insights are practicing master teachers. Many of them have been recognized as their state's Teachers of the Year. These expert teachers wrote essays in response to specific questions we asked that relate to the chapters in which the essays appear.

The essays are opportunities for you to share the experiences of expert teachers and to broaden the classroom practice portion of your knowledge base. These accounts of how experts use the principles and concepts of educational psychology to handle practical situations are potential solutions to the problems you will encounter in your teaching. Further, the master teachers who share their insights on classroom practice are models for developing your theory of teaching. What better way to begin the journey toward expertise than by studying the practice of experts? Opportunities to reflect on the insights of expert teachers are provided through Insights margin notes, which also invite you to think critically about the views presented.

Reflection: Think back to your own school experiences, and describe a teacher you would wish to model. Describe a teacher you would not wish to use as a model for your own teaching.

Here's How. Learning about the knowledge base of teaching is the beginning of your journey toward teaching expertise. Your goal should be to use the knowledge base to reflectively construct a theory of teaching and, ultimately, to add to your knowledge base by testing teaching ideas and strategies. To help you construct your theory of teaching and test ideas, we present features in every chapter called Here's How. These features list specific actions teachers can take in situations that all teachers face.

Try This: Use the Here's How lists as bases for entries in a journal of teaching ideas. The entries should address the conditions under which you would use the practical tips in the list.

What might be this teacher's assumptions about students and the teaching–learning process? How might these assumptions influence teaching practice?

Here's How features also list steps you can take to turn a theoretical principle or concept into classroom practice. These lists are action plans for teaching and learning. The Here's How that concludes this chapter, for example, is an action plan for using this book as a resource for your professional development.

Point: The assumption that *reflective construction is necessary for the development of teaching expertise* requires that your reading be active rather than passive. Passive attempts at learning are rarely successful. Reading and responding to margin notes will ensure that you bring your own thoughts, values, and experiences to bear on the material you will learn.

Key Concepts and Margin Notes. Key concepts throughout the book are printed in boldface. The key concepts are defined in the text and in a running glossary that appears in the margins of the book. The terms are also listed alphabetically at the end of the chapter as a study aid.

We hope you have been reading and responding to the margin notes in this chapter. You will encounter margin notes throughout the entire book. These notes annotate the text and are designed to provide additional opportunities to reflect on the knowledge base, construct your theory of teaching, and discover conceptual connections to other portions of the text. The categories of margin notes include the following:

- Point—reminders of the basic working assumptions of this book, statements of main ideas, and statements of key principles in educational psychology.
- Reflection—questions that help you reflect on your assumptions and values and to relate chapter content to your own prior experiences.
- Example—additional illustrations of chapter concepts and their applications in practice.
- Critical Thinking—questions that help you link and apply chapter concepts and develop practical problem-solving strategies.
- Connection—cross-references to related concepts and information in other sections or chapters.
- Try This—activities and field experiences you can undertake to expand your knowledge base and apply your learning in authentic situations.
- Insights—questions that invite you to respond to the commentaries of the expert teachers featured in Insights on Successful Practice.

We conclude this chapter with suggestions for using this book and its features. You may have already begun thinking about how you might use the text features in your learning. As with all the Here's How features in this book, we encourage you to test the ideas in the following list and to modify and improve those ideas.

here's how

Here's How to Use This Book

- **Preview/Question.** Use the Chapter Outlines at the beginning of each chapter to speculate on the issues of teaching and learning that will be addressed in the chapter. The major headings within each chapter are questions that will be addressed. As you read those headings in the Chapter Outline, think about your experiences as a student, your teachers, your assumptions about teaching and learning. The Teacher Chronicle and Focus Questions at the beginning of each chapter and the Chapter Summary at the end of each chapter can also be used to preview additional questions that you hope to answer as you study the chapter. Check the Insights on Successful Practice, for example, to see what questions the expert teachers who are featured in the chapter have addressed. Check also the Application Questions at the end of the chapter and questions in the margin notes.
- **Read/Relate/Reflect.** Make your reading of each chapter active. Relate the events in the Teacher Chronicle to the principles and concepts you encounter. Seek to answer your own questions as you read, using the features and margin notes to prompt reflective construction. Read each chapter with the goal of discovering relationships between theory and practice.
- **Share.** Share with classmates or colleagues your questions, insights, and developing theory of teaching. Share your interpretations of Teacher Chronicles, reactions to Insights on Successful Practice, and answers to Application Questions. Discussing with others how the material in a chapter informs your views is part of the social construction of knowledge.
- **Test Ideas.** Knowing is not the end of learning. Test the knowledge you acquire through reading, reflecting, and sharing by applying Here's How features and Try This margin notes. Try This is a source of ideas for additional learning activities such as teacher interviews, field observations, journal writing.

Try This: To remember easily the steps in this study strategy, notice that the steps are in alphabetical order. You might wish to remember the study strategy as PQ3RST.

TEACHER Chronicle Conclusion

TEACHER TALK

A few days after their conversation in the teachers' lounge, Loni and Beau arrive early for a faculty meeting after school.

"How are your groups faring?" asks Loni.

Beau smiles. "Much better. I realized that I was asking students to work cooperatively when they really didn't know how. And without adequate guidance on my part, I was pushing them out of the plane without a parachute. No wonder they were acting out.

The more I thought about your story and my experience and looked at the material you gave me, the more I realized that my actions in the classroom weren't very consistent with sound professional practice and my own beliefs about teaching. I really believe that kids can take responsibility for their own learning and that they learn by exploring their environment. But I acted as though teaching is telling. I told them what to do and expected them to learn it."

Loni nods. "As you gain more experience, I think you'll find that your theory of teaching shifts over time. I know mine did, and my beliefs are still evolving."

APPLICATION QUESTIONS

1. How does Teacher Talk reflect the idea that teaching and learning are two aspects of the same process?
2. How do the events in Teacher Talk support the three basic assumptions that serve as the foundation for the theory of teaching espoused in this book?
3. How do Beau's metaphors for teaching and learning change?
4. How do Beau's and Loni's thinking reflect known differences between expert and novice teachers?
5. How do Beau's schemata for teaching change?
6. On what parts of the knowledge base does Beau draw to reconstruct his theory of teaching?
7. In what ways do you expect this textbook to provide a knowledge base for you to develop a theory of teaching through reflective construction?

CHAPTER SUMMARY

WHAT ARE TEACHING AND LEARNING?

The definition of teaching (action taken with the intent to facilitate learning) subsumes the definition of learning (change in thought or behavior that modifies a person's capabilities). One of the assumptions on which this book is based is that teaching and learning are aspects of the same process: the teaching–learning process.

HOW CAN YOU DEVELOP A THEORY OF TEACHING?

Developing one's theory of teaching starts by becoming aware of one's metaphors for the teaching–learning process. Exposing and examining one's metaphors help to focus one's views of teaching and to identify inconsistencies between beliefs and practice. Various metaphors of the teaching–learning process are examined for their instructional implications. Research on metaphorical reasoning and on teachers' metaphors is presented.

HOW CAN YOU LEARN TO THINK LIKE AN EXPERT TEACHER?

Research on the differences between expert and novice teachers is discussed. The differences between expert and novice teachers are explained by the comparable richness and complexity of the schemata of expert teachers. Expert teachers interpret classroom situations differently than novices and, for that reason, can operate more efficiently and effectively than novices.

To become an expert teacher, aspiring teachers must become expert learners. Aspiring teachers must approach the knowledge base of teaching—including both educational psychology and classroom practice—through a process of reflective construction.

ON WHAT THEORY IS THIS BOOK BASED?

The authors' theory of teaching is described by presenting basic working assumptions of the text. In addition to viewing teaching and learning as integrated, two other basic assumptions are made. First, it is assumed that your view of the teaching–learning process will affect your classroom practice. Second, it is assumed that reflective construction is necessary for the development of teaching expertise.

The instructional features of the text and a strategy for using those features to enhance your study of the text are presented.

KEY CONCEPTS

- educational psychology
- knowledge base of teaching
- learning
- metaphor
- reflective construction
- reframing
- schemata
- teaching
- teaching–learning process
- theory of teaching

PART I

Development is complex and multifaceted

Human development includes physical growth and maturation; the development of cognitive capabilities for thinking, learning, remembering, and problem solving; and social and emotional development, which includes developments in moral reasoning. All these areas of human development continually interact. In the developing child, for example, learning to use language is a continuing process that is simultaneously physical, cognitive, and social.

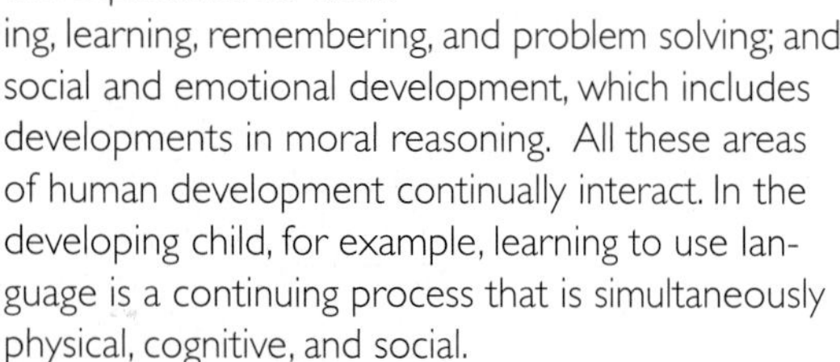

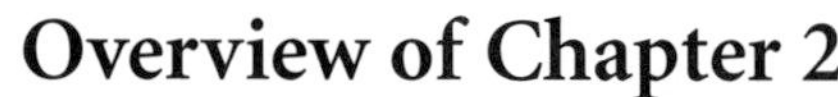

Overview of Chapter 2

Cognitive development is the first of two chapters on human development. Personal, social, and moral development are addressed in Chapter 3. After considering the nature of developmental change, we examine Piaget's view of cognitive development, introducing not only the stages of development but also the experiences and mental processes that are associated with this development. We then present Vygotsky's theory of cognitive development, which emphasizes social and cultural origins. Basic processes involved in human thinking, such as attention or memory, are the focus of information-processing theory, which is discussed next. Finally, because many classroom experiences depend on language, and teachers must understand the cognitive and linguistic capabilities of their students, we include a section on language development as it relates to cognition.

The chapter concludes with a discussion of how you, as a teacher, can accommodate the developmental differences and needs of your students in your instruction.

Development

Development affects learning

Teachers need to know the developmental characteristics and capabilities of their students, because development has profound effects on learning, behavior, social adjustment, and academic achievement. The strategies you develop for providing an appropriate education will depend on your students' levels of development as well as their individual needs and capabilities.

Overview of Chapter 3

Knowing how students develop a sense of self and how their interactions with other people influence that development is critical knowledge for a teacher. Self-concepts are influenced by social interaction, and school can be a place of intense social interaction. In the chapter Personal and Interpersonal Growth you will encounter theories that explain how students develop their sense of identity, how they develop a sense of right and wrong, and how social factors can become obstacles to that development. Finally, you will examine a model of classroom practice that can enhance the personal and interpersonal development of your students.

Life conditions affect development

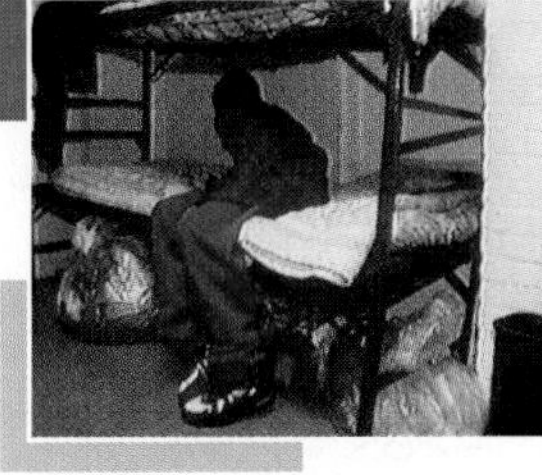

Individual development is shaped by complex environmental factors both within the school and in the larger social contexts of family, community, and culture. Children and adolescents face both developmental challenges and social problems, such as risks to health, safety, and material well-being. The strategies you develop for helping each student to succeed will depend on your knowledge of life conditions that affect the development of children and youths.

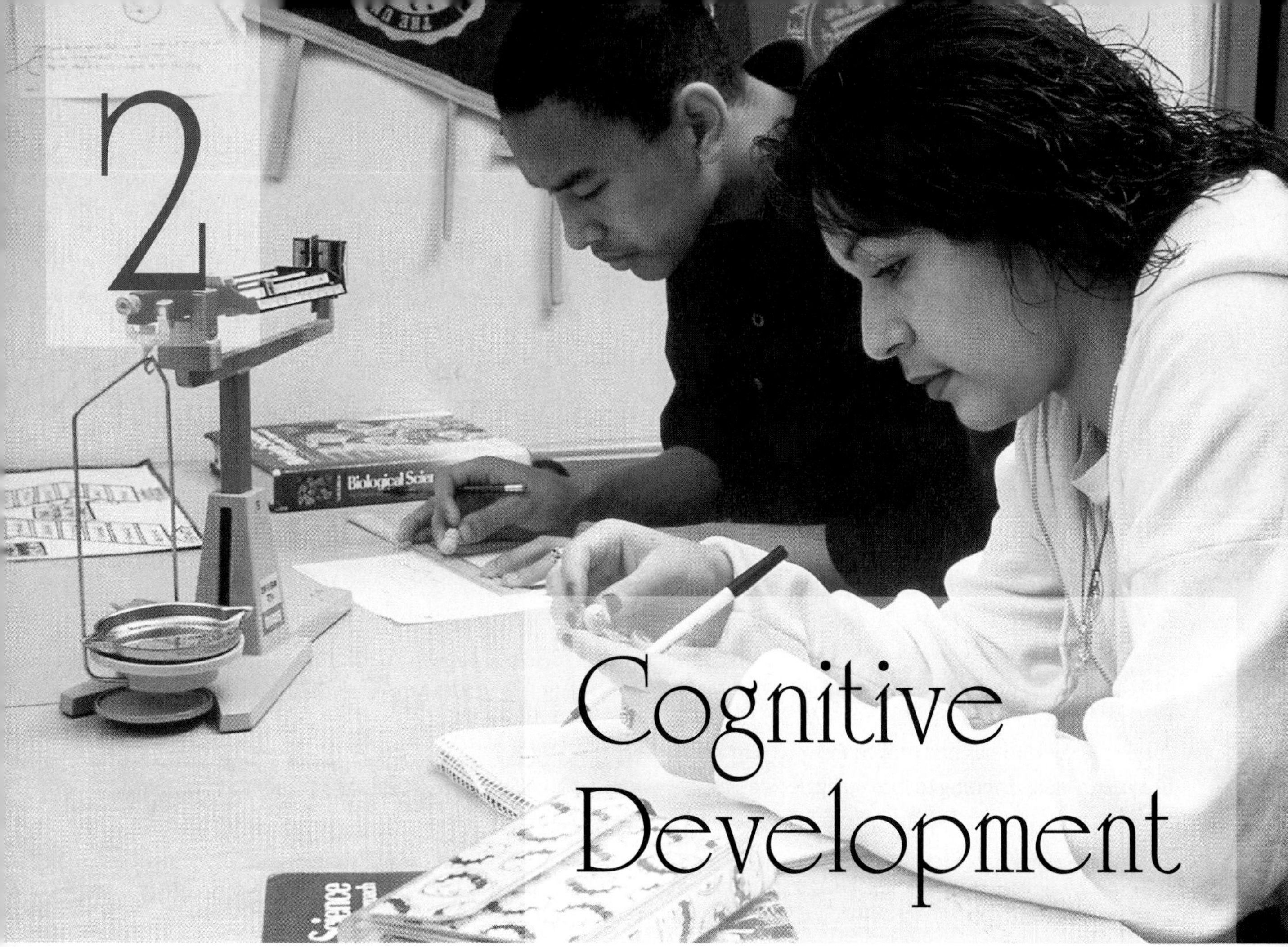

2 Cognitive Development

CHAPTER OUTLINE

TEACHER

Chronicle

CRACKING THE CODE

As she instructs, Marcia Frick constantly seeks clues from her third graders: weighing their reactions to her instruction, looking for puzzled faces, seeking signs of Eureka!, and finding frustration levels.

This morning she is introducing secret codes to her eight- and nine-year-old students in preparation for a lesson on George Washington. She has planned an easy message for her class to decipher, one that she feels most of the children will be able to crack. Her only worry is Ernesto, a Spanish-speaking boy who has just moved to town. She had heard him read, listening to him struggle as he tried to pronounce certain English words. He also had difficulty putting English in proper order.

Marcia made a game out of correcting him. For example, if he said, "I don't want nothing" instead of "I don't want anything," she responded by holding her hands out empty. Ernesto, who realized the difference between Spanish phrasing and English but did not consistently apply the rules, seemed to enjoy Marcia's special signals.

This morning, Marcia makes a mental note to watch him closely for signs of frustration as they work on the codes.

Before class she wrote on the board:

19 26 10 10 2　　25 18 9 7 19 23 26 2
20 22 12 9 20 22　　4 26 8 19 18 13 20 7 12 13

There is an immediate buzz as the students notice the numbers on the board.

"We can't read it," Eric complains. "It isn't letters."

"It's just bunches of numbers all mixed up," Jolene says.

Marcia listens to their questions, comments, and thoughts, but she only responds with a nod of her head and a smile. After she takes attendance and lunch money, she begins the lesson.

"What can you tell me about the numbers on the board?" she asks.

"They're all mixed up," Marcus shouts.

Marcia pulls on her ear. Marcus recognizes his special signal to answer more quietly.

"They are not in any order," Sheng says.

"They don't add up to anything," Sean observes.

Marcia pauses and asks, "Do you see anything the same?"

"Some numbers are up twice," Carlene says.

"What else do you notice?" Marcia glances at Ernesto whose knitted eyebrows signal intense concentration.

"You are not counting by twos or threes or fives," he suggests. "The highest number is 26."

"Hmmm, that's interesting," Marcia says. "Do you know anything else that has 26?"

"26 desks in our room?"

"26 rooms in the school?"

"26 books in Jeremy's desk?" A knowing giggle goes round the room.

"26 alphabet letters?" chips in Ernesto. There is a buzz of excitement as his statement sinks in.

Marcia nods.

"It's the alphabet in numbers!" Renita bursts out.

"That's right," Marcia tells them. "Any other observations about these particular numbers?"

The answers flow even faster.

"They're in groups!"

"Groups like words are!"

"Right again," Marcia encourages.

"They are words written in numbers!" Eric exclaims.

"Now let's see if we can figure out what they mean," Marcia asks.

Carlene immediately says, "A must be 1. B must be 2."

"Let's try it and see," Marcia tells them as they grab their pencils.

FOCUS QUESTIONS

1. What factors are likely to influence Ernesto's intellectual development?
2. How do students mentally organize their experiences in an adaptive way?
3. How does a student's mental representation of his or her environment change during development?
4. Why might the age of students be a factor in what they are capable of learning? What are the stages of cognitive development?
5. Can cognitive development be accelerated?
6. How might experience influence learning and development?
7. How might Ernesto's acquisition of English relate to his cognitive development?
8. What is developmentally appropriate teaching practice?

WHAT ARE THE DIMENSIONS OF HUMAN DEVELOPMENT?

Connection: Social, personal, and moral development are the subjects of Chapter 3.

How will you know when your students are capable of doing what you will ask them to do? How will you help each student realize his or her potential? *Developmental psychology* is the study of how humans grow toward their potential and of the capabilities that accompany that growth. Physical, cognitive, and social development are three dimensions of human development. **Cognitive development**, the subject of this chapter, is the growth in our capabilities as learners. *Cognitive development theory* attempts to explain how humans acquire and construct knowledge of themselves and their world.

p. 28-33

*

cognitive development Changes in our capabilities as learners by which mental processes grow more complex and sophisticated.

As humans develop, *what* they are capable of knowing changes, but so does *how* they are capable of knowing. What infants can know, for example, is probably limited to the world immediately surrounding them, and they come to know this world through physical interaction and manipulation of it. What do infants do with any object presented to them? They put it in their mouths, of course. This is an infant's primary means of learning about his or her world. Adults, in contrast, are capable of learning a great many things and have available to them many ways of doing so.

Theoretical descriptions of development are based on observations of change from inability to ability. For example, suppose that Cassie is unable to swim in June. But in August, she is observed swimming competently. Why did this change occur? Was Cassie physically capable of swimming in June but unable to because she did not know how? Or was she physically incapable of swimming in June but matured enough over the summer to be able to swim in August? Is this a matter of development or of learning?

Development theories differ from learning theories in that development focuses on human capabilities, whereas learning focuses on the realization of these capabilities. So in the example above, maturation enables Cassie to become capable of swimming, but learning provides the means by which she can transform the capability into proficient performance. The difference between development and learning has important implications for teaching. If teachers understand the capabilities—the potential abilities—their students bring to the classroom, they can do a better job of helping them realize those capabilities.

Development Capabilities

Although humans all develop cognitive abilities in generally the same way, the specific capabilities they acquire will be unique to them as individuals. No two people have precisely the same knowledge of the world, for instance. Nor do any two people think and learn in exactly the same way. Genetic inheritance combined with life experience produces tremendous variability in individuals. Children the same age as Cassie in the swimming example may already know how to swim in June or may never become proficient swimmers. Therefore, as you study the models of development presented in this chapter, you should be aware that, because of individual variability in development capabilities, the models will not always apply to every student in your classroom.

Point: *Development is complex and multifaceted.* The instructional decisions you make in planning developmentally appropriate instruction will depend upon your knowledge of a great many things about your students.

Not only will students naturally vary in their developmental capabilities, some will show signs of disability or exceptionality. They may have difficulties or special talents (Hallahan & Kauffman, 1994). Students are considered exceptional learners when they "require special education and related services if they are to realize their full human potential" (Hallahan & Kauffman, 1994, p. 7).

Influences on Development

Development is influenced by factors both internal and external to the individual. In the swimming example, physical maturation influenced the development of Cassie's ability to swim. This is an internal, or innate, factor. Physical growth occurs at a different rate for everyone, and everyone reaches a different endpoint of physical development. These differences will affect a person's individual capabilities. One of the authors, for example, will never be capable of world-class basketball because she is only five feet tall. On the other hand, she is not limited by her physical development in a sport such as sailing. Factors outside the individual also influence development. For instance, the active experience of manipulating objects influences the cognitive development of infants; they develop knowledge and capabilities through this interaction.

Reflection: Describe something that you learned easily and something that was difficult to learn. Were the breakthrough and the difficulty due to development or learning?

Developmental psychologists differ in the emphases they place on the roles of *nature* (internal factors) versus *nurture* (external factors) in human development. As you will see, emphasizing one over the other also has implications for the design of instruction and teachers' interactions with students in the classroom. Development is believed to be influenced by four factors: (1) maturation, (2) active experience, (3) social interaction, and (4) cultural and situational contexts.

Try This: Observe children in a playground, noting the ages at which they play different games. How do maturation rates help account for your observations?

Maturation. Some people mature more quickly than others. Two children of identical age may differ in size, athletic skill, reasoning ability, intelligence, and emotional reactions. Differences in the rate of maturation lead to the differences—physical and psychological—that you will see among the students in your classroom. Because students usually reach puberty during their middle school years, middle school teachers often witness the greatest variability in development. In a single seventh-grade class, for example, there may be girls who have reached their full adult height and boys whose voices have not yet begun to deepen. *Maturation*, or "the unfolding of inherited potential" (Wadsworth, 1984, p. 29), establishes the limits of human development throughout the stages of growth.

Active Experience. *Active experience* refers both to manipulating objects in one's environment and to reorganizing one's thought patterns. An adolescent can figure out the parts of a carburetor by handling one—turning it over and peering into it. By thinking about the carburetor, the adolescent can also think about its function in a new way. As development proceeds, students become increasingly able to reorganize their thoughts without the prior necessity of physically manipulating objects in their environments.

Social Interaction. *Social interaction* comprises the experiences people have with others in their environment, including the exchange of ideas. At a very basic level, people negotiate the meanings of things in their world through their interactions with each other. For example, a boy grasps at an object that is just outside his reach. His mother interprets his behavior as pointing and responds by giving him the object for which he was reaching. Gradually, as the boy apprehends the same meaning for the gesture as his mother does, he will deliberately use it to mean pointing (Vygotsky, 1978).

Reflection: How does the way you talk with children of different ages reflect your beliefs about children's levels of cognitive development?

People also exchange and negotiate ideas through conversation. Consider the example of a girl who is given a dog for her birthday. She plays with, pets, and feeds her dog. She also talks with her parents about the concept of "loyalty," which reminds her of her experiences with the dog. The social interaction with her parents actually gives meaning to the girl's experience with the dog. It is through this social interaction that she gains her knowledge of loyalty.

Cultural and Situational Contexts. "What does it mean [for development] to grow up in one cultural milieu and not another?" (Bruner, 1973, p. 20). The cultures in which people live make specific and unique demands on individuals that influence the capabilities they develop. For example, an ongoing study of Mexican families living in Tucson, Arizona, reveals that children are full participants in household activities, because their participation is often essential to the family's survival and well-being (Moll, Tapia, & Whitmore, 1993). In one case, the adolescent boys share in caring for their four-year-old sister, play musical instruments in the expectation of joining their father's band, and serve as English translators in helping their parents understand school notices and deal with government agencies. The family maintains close and frequent contact with relatives and friends in order to develop and share their "funds of knowledge" in coping with their environment.

Connection: Cultural diversity and the role of cultural beliefs and values in learning are discussed in Chapter 4.

Situational context influences development in a similar fashion. Saxe (1990) studied how different children in Brazil developed mathematical competence. Children who sold candy on the streets developed different mathematical understandings than their non-candy-selling peers. They developed a variety of procedures for making currency exchanges, whereas the non-candy-sellers acquired a mathematical symbol system for doing calculations on paper. The different situations in which the students were operating led to the development of different capabilities.

As individuals develop cognitively, their attention spans increase, they become able to reason about complex ideas, they acquire language, and they construct knowledge about the world around them. The Swiss biologist Jean Piaget (1896–1980) developed a theory of cognitive development that provides a comprehensive description of the cognitive changes people experience during development and the cognitive structures that come with development. The Russian scientist Lev S. Vygotsky (1896–1934), who was influenced by Piaget's work, offered a theory for understanding cognitive development as a process of learning as it is affected by the sociocultural environment of the child. This chapter explores these and other theories of cognitive development and their implications for teaching.

HOW DO INDIVIDUALS' COGNITIVE ABILITIES DEVELOP?

Piaget is best known for his extensive accounts of how children think at different times in their lives. Watching his own children at play, he wondered how children adapt to their environment, how they acquire knowledge of the world, and how that knowledge changes as they grow. The difference between children and, say, snails, he mused, is that humans can make use of their intellects to adapt to environmental changes. A person's intellectual progress is a matter of constructing increasingly adaptive knowledge of his or her environment. The important question that Piaget posed is, "By what means does the human mind go from a state of less sufficient knowledge to a state of higher knowledge?" (Piaget, 1970, pp. 12–13).

Organizing and Adapting Mental Constructs

Organization is the human tendency to arrange experiences, thoughts, emotions, and behaviors into a coherent system for constructing meaning. Piaget believed that people use their intellect to make sense of their environment and to form useful mental representations of it. For example, suppose you are handed a small, roundish, red object, the likes of which you have never seen before. It is hinged in the middle, and when closed into a half-moon shape, it has a small handle on one end and what appears to be a spout on the other. What is it? In order to make sense of this object, you must use your logical powers and prior knowledge. What *are* the mental processes and structures you might use to make sense of this experience?

Schemes. A small child is likely to approach this mystery object actively by feeling it, putting it in the mouth, shaking it, hitting another object with it, or throwing it. You might do some of the same things, such as feeling it and opening

Example: Schemes change continually as a person gains experience with his or her environment. When a child uses the "dog" scheme to understand the experience of seeing a cow, he or she is actively constructing meaning. Once interpreted, the new item becomes part of the scheme that was used to interpret it.

Example: Infants are born with the reflex to grasp objects placed in their hands. If you have ever placed your finger in the palm of an infant's hand, for example, you have observed that the infant will automatically grasp your finger. Infants are also born with the reflex to suck. They have schemes for grasping and sucking. After some experience grasping some objects, infants begin to grasp an object and then move the object to their mouths. The grasping scheme and the sucking scheme become coordinated in a new scheme.

schemes In Piaget's theory, generalized ways of acting on the world that provide the basis for mental operations.

assimilation In Piaget's theory, a process through which new experiences are incorporated into existing cognitive structures such as schemes.

accommodation In Piaget's theory, a process of modifying existing cognitive structures or creating additional ones as a result of new experiences.

and closing the hinge. Piaget proposed that **schemes** are generalized ways of acting on the world, and they provide the basis for mental operations (cf. Gruber & Voneche, 1977; Wadsworth, 1984; Siegler, 1986). In other words, from your actions you would derive some knowledge about this object, such as it's made of hard plastic, the hinge allows it to be opened flat, but the two sides of the hinge cannot be put back-to-back.

Schemes have also been described as modes of organization (cf. Brainerd, 1978), such that acting on the world results in like objects or events being organized together into larger mental structures, such as concepts. With respect to the mystery object, then, your physical actions, which are very rudimentary schemes, probably would not produce enough information to allow identification of the object. Other, more abstract schemes must therefore be used, perhaps relating to the possible uses for such an object.

Assimilation. Suppose you have seen or experienced things similar to the mystery object. Perhaps you observed a relative using something like it in preparing to serve tea. If so, you would immediately recognize our mystery object as an example of a previously known concept. One way in which mental constructs, such as schemes, change is to simply incorporate new experiences into existing structures. Piaget (1952) called this process **assimilation.**

Fitting the new experience into an existing scheme builds the overall cognitive structure, but it does not change the scheme's essential nature. For example, people who eat frog legs for the first time often comment that frog legs taste like chicken. They have organized their perceptions of taste according to their previous experiences. Therefore, having eaten chicken a great deal, they have a cognitive representation, their "taste of chicken" scheme, that allows them to understand the new experience of eating frog legs. Thus, they perceive the experience of eating frog legs as similar to that of eating chicken.

The ability to assimilate new experiences increases our sense of understanding our environment. Mistakes can occur, however, when we change the nature of an experience in order to preserve our current understanding. When a high school chemistry student refers to a colloid as a solution, he or she is assimilating the new experience incorrectly into an existing scheme. The process of assimilation can be the line of least resistance. If we can fit our experiences into ways of understanding that already exist, the job of understanding the environment is less complex or difficult. Much of what happens in schools, however, is designed to change students' cognitive structures.

Accommodation. Not all new experiences can fit easily into existing schemes. The mystery object is probably still a mystery to most of you, because no prior knowledge comes readily to mind that will help you understand what the object could be. **Accommodation** is the process Piaget identified by which we modify existing cognitive structures or create new ones as a result of experiences that cannot be easily assimilated. In such situations, the person's way of understanding is forced to change to fit the new experience. Together, assimilation and accommodation account for intellectual adaptation (cf. Piaget & Inhelder, 1969).

What about experiences that cannot be assimilated or accommodated very well? If a student experiences an event that is so unfamiliar that it cannot be filtered through existing schemes, then neither assimilation nor any subsequent accommodation will occur. For example, if a teacher were to begin writing meaningless symbols on a chalkboard, students may respond by trying to make sense

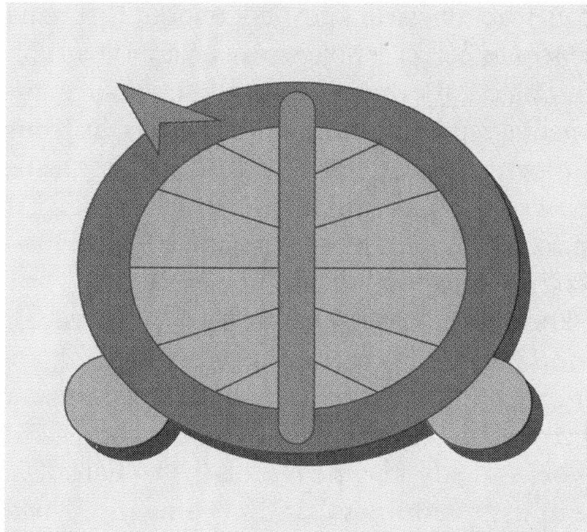

FIGURE 2.1

A Mystery Device: Kitchen Device Used for Squeezing Lemon Wedges

of the symbols. If they are unsuccessful in doing so, they will probably stop trying to organize the information. Likewise, after trying unsuccessfully to make sense of the mystery object, you might simply give up. Under these circumstances, guidance may be required to assist learners in constructing appropriate schemes. In the previous example, the teacher would have to provide guidance to help the students make sense of the unknown symbols. In the example of the mystery object, someone may have to demonstrate that it is a device for squeezing lemon wedges, shown in Figure 2.1.

Equilibration. What causes a child to seek experience and interaction that lead to significant reorganization in the child's thinking? How are new experiences integrated with what the child already knows, resulting in new knowledge? For Piaget, the answer is **equilibration**, a process that regulates other influences on cognitive development and governs how people organize knowledge to adapt to their environment. Assimilation and accommodation are both necessary for development, but a balance between them is as necessary as the processes themselves. Equilibration is the self-regulating process through which people balance new experiences with what they already know.

If new experiences do not fit into an existing scheme, then *disequilibrium* results. The physical changes accompanying puberty, for example, may cause disequilibrium in boys and girls who must adjust to new images of themselves. Any event—through active experience, social interaction, and cultural context—can cause disequilibrium in a child's thinking. Changing the existing scheme to accommodate the new experience is a way of achieving equilibrium. Our continual attempt to achieve equilibrium is what leads to adaptive changes in our cognitive organization.

Point: *Learning is shaped by the learner's environment.* Instruction is often an attempt to develop new ways to understand and interact with the environment. Assimilation contributes to cognitive development by providing greater experience and thereby strengthens an existing scheme. Changing the ways in which we understand our environment requires accommodation and equilibration.

equilibration The self-regulating process in Piaget's theory through which people balance new experiences with present understanding.

Constructing Knowledge through Active Experience

The experiences that people assimilate and/or accommodate influence the kinds of knowledge they construct. Piaget distinguished among three types of knowledge that people construct about their environments: physical, logico-mathematical, and social-arbitrary (Piaget, 1969; Driscoll, 1994).

Physical Knowledge. Children construct **physical knowledge** about their environment through the use of their senses to perceive object properties. When children see, hear, smell, taste, or touch objects, they experience physical, perceptual qualities that enable them to form mental representations of the objects. Listening first to a clarinet and then to a trumpet, a student might say, "I like the clearer, stronger sound the trumpet makes. The clarinet sounds too gushy to me." The physical experience of the sounds gave the student ideas—mental abstractions—of the sounds, which are reflected in the words used to describe them.

The process of constructing knowledge based on physical experience is called *empirical abstraction. Empirical* means "of or relating to observation and experience." Children observe various physical properties of objects encountered in the environment and abstract the qualities of these properties. For example, playing with wooden blocks yields knowledge of their "hardness," picking apples provides knowledge of their "shininess," and smelling roses yields knowledge of their "sweet" scent.

Example: When students move magnetized letters around on a board, they discover that the letters stick to the board; they abstract the magnetic property of the objects they are handling. Other physical qualities can probably be abstracted as well. Perhaps a student will put a letter in his or her mouth to form an idea of how magnet letters taste.

Logico-Mathematical Knowledge. When people construct knowledge that goes beyond physical experience and depends on inventing and reorganizing patterns of ideas, they are developing **logico-mathematical knowledge.** For example, Newton is said to have formulated the notion of gravity while pondering apples falling from a tree. His construct was not built on an empirical abstraction of the properties of apples—it didn't matter if they were red or rotten or shiny. Rather, it was his thinking about apples in another sense that led to a new idea. The same is true when students first learn the concepts of addition and subtraction. Whether they learn using pennies, or cookies, or oranges, the result is the same. Physical properties of these objects do not contribute to knowledge of addition and subtraction. But manipulations of them and mental operations—forming and re-forming patterns of ideas—do. Logico-mathematical knowledge is generated through the process of *reflexive abstraction. Reflexive,* using Piaget's definition, means "turned back on itself." Thus, in reflexive abstraction one is thinking by means of purely mental operations.

Example: Another example of a logico-mathematical experience would be discovering, while reading Shakespeare, that *anon* means "now," "immediately," or "even as we speak."

Example: In the Teacher Chronicle: Cracking the Code, Marcia's students were also able to see numbers as a code for letters and to mentally substitute one for the other.

Empirical and reflexive abstraction differ with regard to their sources of knowledge. They also differ in that empirical abstraction requires some object in the environment. Reflexive abstraction can be triggered by something in the environment, such as a falling apple, but it is also possible for reflexive abstraction to occur in the absence of concrete objects. Children can acquire the ability, for example, to add and subtract numbers mentally, without using concrete objects to carry out the operations.

Social-Arbitrary Knowledge. The knowledge that people acquire through their interactions with other people in their own social and cultural groups is what Piaget termed **social-arbitrary knowledge**. People are the source of this knowledge, which includes values, moral rules, language, and cultural symbol systems. For example, even though mathematics is generally regarded as a culture-free subject matter, the truth is that children learn different systems of counting depending on their cultures. Anglo-European children learn to count using numbers, whereas many children in Asian cultures may learn to count using an abacus. Similarly, children from certain southern African cultures learn to count using parts of their body (each finger, palm, backside of hand, inside of wrist, etc.). Knowledge of these symbol systems can be acquired only through interaction with people who already know them; they are culturally transmitted.

physical knowledge In Piaget's theory, any knowledge about objects in the world that can be gained through experiencing their perceptual properties.

logico-mathematical knowledge In Piaget's theory, knowledge that goes beyond physical experience and depends upon inventing or reorganizing patterns of ideas.

social-arbitrary knowledge In Piaget's theory, knowledge gained solely by one's interactions with other people within one's cultural group.

How do physical, logico-mathematical, and social-arbitrary knowledge develop?

Piaget's Stages of Cognitive Development

Piaget's account of the processes, experiences, and structures involved in cognition describes how people come to know about their world. The experiences we have and the schemes we use for understanding those experiences change as we mature. A seventh grader not only knows more things than a second grader but also knows things in a different way. The seventh grader has developed cognitive capabilities that are not yet in the repertoire of the second grader.

What are the capabilities of students who have reached different levels of cognitive development? All teachers need to know what the cognitive capabilities of their own students are. Teachers of younger children also need to know the capabilities of older children in order to understand the direction that their students' development should be taking. Likewise, teachers of older students need to understand the capabilities that their students developed earlier. The development of new capabilities builds on earlier ones. Moreover, not all behaviors reflect a student's highest level of functioning. Any experienced teacher can tell you that just because a student is capable of complex reasoning doesn't mean that the student will always reason that way.

From his observations of children, Piaget formulated four stages of cognitive development that reflect the dominant schemes of thinking children use and the ages at which they use them to organize and interact with their environment. Piaget's stages are summarized in Table 2.1. Piaget (1952) saw development as a process of successive, qualitative changes in children's thinking. The changes that children undergo at each stage derive logically and inevitably from the cognitive structures of preceding stages. New structures do not replace prior structures. Instead, they incorporate prior structures, which results in the qualitative change. Let's take a look at the benchmarks associated with each stage of development.

TABLE 2.1 Summary of Piaget's Stages of Cognitive Development

Stages	Approximate Ages	Nature of Schemata*
Sensorimotor	0–2	Sensations and motor actions
Preoperations	2–7	Illogical operations; symbolic representations; egocentric; self-centered
Concrete operations	7–11	Logical, reversible operations; decentered; object-bound
Formal operations	11–Adult	Abstract—not bound to concrete objects

*It is important to remember that the stages are cumulative. The adaptive characteristics of earlier stages are present in later ones.

Source: From *Piaget's Theory of Cognitive Development,* second edition by B. J. Wadsworth Copyright ©1979 by Longman Publishers. Reprinted with permission.

Critical Thinking: A junior high math teacher switched to teaching at the first-grade level. She learned that junior high and primary grade students have very different understandings of the concept of time. The first graders, while knowing the words *hour* and *half-hour,* had no concrete understanding of what those lengths of time meant. They constantly asked when recess would begin. The frequent interruptions decreased when the teacher compared a half-hour with the amount of time it took the students to watch a popular TV program. Explain this teacher's experience.

Point: *Development affects learning.* Piaget believed that the dominant schemes of thinking associated with a given stage made students ready to learn some things but precluded them from learning other things.

Example: The names of the stages describe the nature of the schemes at each stage. For example, the schemes of the typical fourth grader allow the child to perform concrete operations.

stages

Try This: Repeat the test for object permanence with young children of different ages. Can you pinpoint the approximate age at which it occurs? Why do you think young children love the game of "peekaboo"?

Try This: Observe young toddlers, perhaps in a day care center. Try to distinguish *imitation* from *deferred imitation* in the children's behavior. What are the implications of deferred imitation for teachers of young children?

Critical Thinking: A kindergarten teacher built a tepee in her classroom as a place for silent reading. After reading a story about Native Americans and buffalo, children began an elaborate game, which they played intensely for weeks. They became Native American parents and children, hunters and horses, buffalo and bears. Is this an example of imitation or deferred imitation?

Sensorimotor Stage (birth to approximately 2 years). Infants obtain knowledge at the **sensorimotor stage** through physical experience with the environment. Infants use their senses to experience the environment and their physical or motor actions to interact with it. The reflexes that newborns use to build schemes are the starting point for cognitive development, and the intellectual changes that occur during the sensorimotor period are quite dramatic. For teachers, the two most significant benchmarks of the sensorimotor stage are object permanence and imitation.

Think back to a time when you may have played with an infant. Can you recall playing a version of hide-and-seek in which you hid an object from the child's view and she, rather surprisingly, failed to search for it? What occurred in this case was, quite literally, out of sight, out of mind. A child who exhibits *object permanence* understands that an object can continue to exist whether or not he or she perceives it.

Object permanence is an important foundation for later development. The concept that objects have an existence that is separate from the child and permanent enables children to conceive of objects and actions that are not in their immediate environment.

Imitation, the other benchmark of the sensorimotor stage, is the ability to copy behaviors, and it begins with behaviors that are already part of the child's repertoire. For example, very young children open and close their hands, a behavior which is related to the grasping reflex. If a parent, playing with the child, begins opening and closing a hand, the child will likely imitate the behavior. The adult's action prompts the child to perform the same action. Many of the games that parents and infants play together are forms of imitation.

Imitation continues to become more complicated as the child's repertoire of behaviors increases. Toward the end of the sensorimotor stage, toddlers begin to display novel behaviors that are often not especially recognizable to the adult. Ask them what they are doing, and the likely response will be, "I'm being an airplane," or "I'm being a monkey." In deferred imitation, pretending to be something or somebody does not require prompting. A child does not need to see the mother combing her hair before combing a teddy bear's head, for example. The pretending and dramatic play-acting that preschool, kindergarten, and primary grade teachers see in students have their roots in deferred imitation.

Acquiring the capabilities of object permanence and imitation prepares the child for symbolic thinking, a benchmark of the next developmental stage. However, because students develop the capacity for symbolic thinking does not mean they no longer need to handle objects and observe models. The need for tangible objects, models, analogies, and concrete examples never disappears. Students always need concrete examples of the increasingly complex and abstract ideas that they are asked to learn.

sensorimotor stage The earliest stage in Piaget's theory of cognitive development, during which infants learn about their environment through their senses and motor actions.

preoperational According to Piaget, the stage at which children learn to mentally represent things.

Preoperations Stage (approximately 2–7 years). Piaget used the term *operations* to refer to actions based on logical thinking. The actions of a child at the preoperations stage are based on thought, but the actions do not always seem logical from an adult perspective. Thus, the child's thinking is considered prelogical or **preoperational**, because illogical thinking does not prevent youngsters from mentally representing or symbolizing. Preschoolers can easily pretend that a wooden building block is a car or a baby in a carriage or a piece of cheese. Symbolizing of this kind is based on imitation. This capability to replace one object with another or to use words to talk about actions and experiences is called symbolic representation.

Symbolic representation is the process whereby children learn to create their own symbols and to use existing symbol systems to represent and operate on the environment. The most important symbol system is language, which grows tremendously during the preoperations stage. Children's vocabularies increase several thousand percent. The complexity of their grammatical constructions also increases dramatically. From a developmental point of view, using language enhances the capability to think about objects that are not present. Remember, however, that using language to symbolize objects does not mean that children can think logically about them.

Connection: The process by which children acquire language is discussed later in this chapter.

The other benchmarks of the preoperations stage are cognitive characteristics that actually prevent logical thinking: perceptual centration, irreversibility, and egocentrism.

If you have ever witnessed a child responding to one of Piaget's classic conservation tasks (e.g., conservation of number, of volume, of mass), then you have probably seen dramatic evidence of perceptual centration. In conservation tasks, children are presented with two identical objects. One is then transformed in some way and the child is asked whether the objects are now the same or different. *Perceptual centration* occurs when the child tends to focus on or perceive only one aspect of an object or problem to the exclusion of other salient features. In the conservation task for liquid, for example, children are shown two identical beakers of water. The water from one beaker is then emptied into a tall, slender cylinder. When asked to judge whether the cylinder and the remaining beaker contain the same or different amounts of water, preoperational children will consistently say that the "taller one" contains more water. Their perceptions focus on the height of the liquid in the containers to the exclusion of width, circumference, and volume. Although the preoperational child may see an equal amount of water being poured back and forth between the short beaker and the tall cylinder, the child is unable to perceive another aspect of the problem.

Try This: Perform a conservation task with kindergarten and first-grade students. Look for evidence of perceptual centration and irreversibility. How does preoperational thinking limit learning?

Irreversibility, a characteristic of the preoperations stage, refers to a person's inability to mentally reverse actions. A second grader who is preoperational may know that 4 plus 2 equals 6 but may not be able to solve the subtraction problem of 6 minus 2. Likewise, a preoperational child who recognizes her doll as an old plaything believes she has a new toy when the doll is dressed in new clothes.

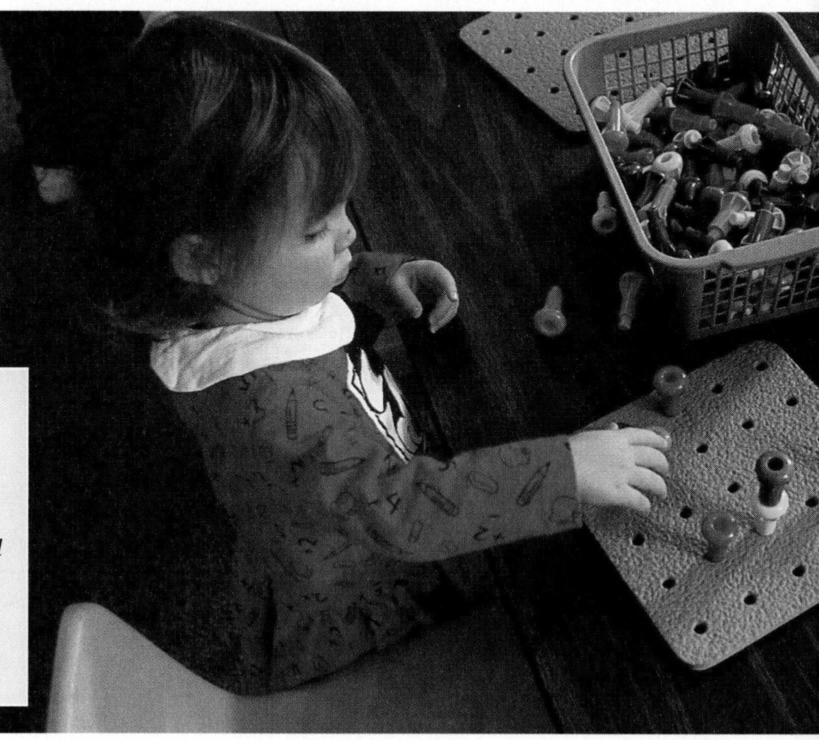

Children at the preoperational stage of cognitive development have not yet acquired the principle of conservation of number. This child will not understand, for example, that, given ten pegs, the number of pegs remains the same whether collected in a container or placed in the holes. Even when told or shown that the number is the same, the child will insist that there are more pegs when they are in the holes than when they are in the container.

Finally, children who are preoperational assume that everyone's experience of the world is the same as their own and that they are, quite literally, the center of everything. Piaget called this tendency *egocentrism*. Consider, for example, the case of the young girl seated at the dinner table who feels called on to "translate" her parents' conversation:

Father: Would you please pass the potatoes?
Child: Mommy, Daddy wants you to pass the potatoes.
Mother: Here, do you need the salt and pepper?
Child: Daddy, Mommy wants to know if you need the salt and pepper.
Father: Yes, please.
Child: Mommy, Daddy wants the salt and pepper.

Example: Picture a family on a long drive. The preoperational child in the back seat is listening through earphones to a song. (One lyric is "Jeremiah was a bullfrog. . . .") Egocentrically, the child asks a parent in the front seat, "What did that singer say Jeremiah was?"

Another form of egocentrism can be seen in parallel play and the collective monologue. In parallel play, children play near one another using similar materials, but they do not interact or attempt to influence each other. The collective monologue refers to the phenomenon of children talking in groups without having a conversation. One child may be talking about the colors in his painting, another child may be asking if there is applesauce for today's snack, and a third child may be arguing for a game of tag when playground time comes. Each child addresses the others, but no one responds. Very little linguistic interaction occurs, owing to the egocentric nature of each child's communication.

Because preoperational children develop the capabilities to create and use symbols—language and other symbolic representations—adults begin to consider them thinkers. Teachers should remember, however, that preoperational thinking is not logical. A child who insists that one, and only one, perspective is correct, who talks but doesn't listen, who monopolizes social situations, who refuses to consider all aspects of a problem, is not so much a troublemaker as a child functioning at the preoperations stage.

Critical Thinking: A first-grade teacher could not understand why Myra, a bright student, was having difficulty learning to read and was also so demanding of attention. Myra had appropriate language skills, but couldn't sit still or concentrate for longer than five minutes. In her teacher's words, "She's driving me crazy." Myra was falling behind her classmates. When the teacher checked Myra's birth date, she understood the problem. Myra had turned six only three days before school started; she was nearly a year younger than the majority of her classmates. Why would Myra's age make such a difference in her ability to learn how to read?

Concrete Operations Stage (approximately 7–11 years). **Concrete operations** is the first stage of operational or logical thought in which schemes become organized into operations that can be used to reason about the world.

concrete operations
Piaget's first stage of operational thought during which children develop skills of logical reasoning, but only about problems that are concrete.

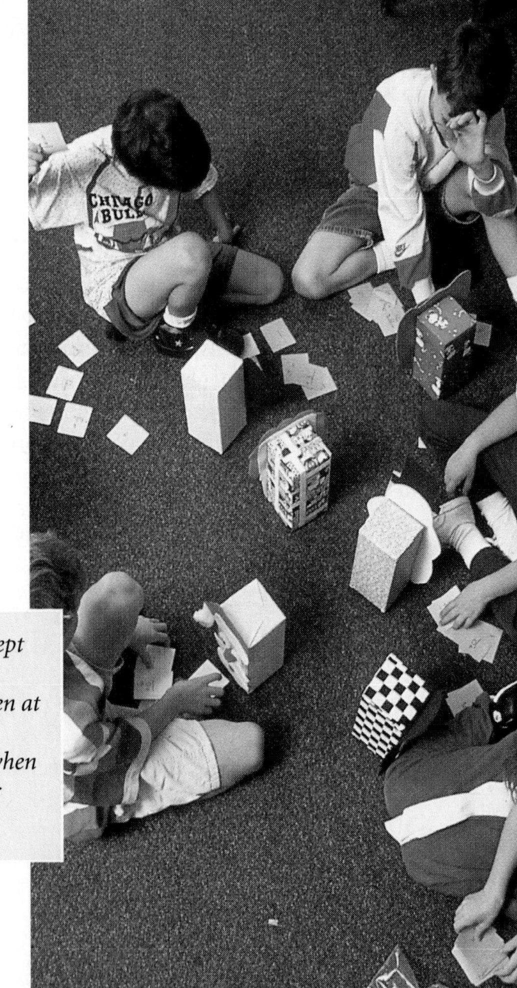

Students in this class are learning the concept of estimation through the use of math manipulatives. Research shows that children at the concrete operational stage of cognitive development learn abstract concepts best when those concepts are represented by objects or direct experiences.

Because logical operations are still new at this stage, students can best use them when considering problems that are concrete in nature. Many educators refer to the concrete operations stage as the hands-on period of cognitive development. Although the child can reason, the ability to reason is based on tangible objects and direct experiences.

Benchmarks of concrete operational thought include reversibility and decentration, which contribute to understanding the principles of conservation and the ability to perform multiple classification.

When children enter the concrete operations stage of development, usually around second grade, they become able to mentally reverse events, such as the steps of the amount-of-water problem. Students at this stage can imagine the results of pouring the water back and forth between containers of different shapes and sizes. *Reversibility* is also evident in students learning the related processes of multiplication and division. Given the numbers 12 and 6, for example, they can supply the answer "2" as the number that when multiplied by 6 equals 12 *and* that when divided into 12 equals 6. Their ability to reverse mathematical operations indicates that students are at the concrete operations stage.

Try This: Interview elementary teachers to collect ideas for hands-on activities. How are those activities developmentally appropriate for students at the concrete operational stage?

Children in this stage have also acquired the capability of *decentration*, which means that they can consider more than one aspect of an object or problem at a time. Doing multiplication and division, for example, requires that students can think about a number in two different ways: as a multiplier and as a divisor. Students capable of concrete operations can solve problems that have more elements and that are significantly more complex than those that preoperational children can solve.

Together, reversibility and decentration allow concrete operational students to perform conservation tasks that stymie preoperational children. *Conservation* is the ability to recognize that properties do not change because form changes. By applying logic, operational students understand that the amount of water does not change when the shape of the container holding it changes.

Example: Roll one of two equal-sized balls of clay into a long, skinny "snake." Concrete operational learners will realize that the amount of clay in the thin piece is the same.

Reversibility and decentration are also the basis for *multiple classification*, an important reasoning skill that allows children to organize objects according to more than one characteristic. Suppose a student is presented with several cardboard cutouts in shapes of circles, squares, and triangles. The cutouts also vary in color and size: red, yellow, and blue; small, medium, and large. Asked to classify these objects, a preoperational child would depend upon only one dimension, perhaps putting all the red ones together, all the blue ones together, and all the yellow ones together. The concrete operational child would use more than one dimension to classify the objects. The operational child may form groups of small red triangles, large blue squares, and so forth, indicating a more developed classification scheme.

Example: The concrete operational child may be able to classify animals into separate groups of carnivores and herbivores and also to classify both carnivores and herbivores as belonging to another group called mammals.

Concrete operations is only the beginning of logical reasoning. Students still have difficulty thinking about hypothetical problems, such as "If people could know the future, would they be happier than they are now?" (Siegler, 1986). Instead, they need to see things, touch things, experiment with things. They can reason when given concrete objects and experiences to reason with, but abstract reasoning doesn't develop until the final stage of cognitive development—formal operations.

Formal Operations Stage (approximately 11 years through adult). **Formal operations**—the final stage in Piaget's theory—begins roughly around eleven or twelve years of age and continues into and throughout adulthood. Abstract reasoning is the primary benchmark of formal operations.

formal operations According to Piaget, the stage of development in which the abilities to reason abstractly and to coordinate a number of variables are acquired.

Abstract reasoning is the ability to think logically about intangibles. Students who reach the stage of formal operations can begin to deal with possibilities. They can think in terms of a hypothesis: If X, then Y. They can see beyond the here and now. They can verbalize the mental rules they use in solving problems. The logical operations of the concrete operations stage can now be performed outside of the presence of concrete objects.

Connection: Problem-solving processes and strategies for teaching problem-solving skills are presented in Chapters 7 and 12.

For example, imagine you are standing directly in front of a chair. As you look at the chair, imagine a lamp to the right of it, a table to the left of it, and a rug behind it. Now imagine yourself standing in a new position so that the chair is behind the table. In this position, where is the lamp? A concrete operational student would have trouble with this problem, unless he or she could stand in proximity to the objects or symbolize them on paper. Being able to reason through this problem in the abstract is a characteristic of formal operations. (If you have difficulty working out this problem, do not fear for your stage of cognitive development. As Piaget noted, the ability to operate formally in one situation does not guarantee that the person operates formally in all situations.)

Inhelder and Piaget (1958) created a reasoning problem that illustrated the difference between concrete operational students and those in the formal operational stage. To solve the problem, students were supplied with objects to use in testing a principle of physics—that the length of a pendulum influences its speed.

The length of the pendulum could be shortened or lengthened; the weight at the end of the pendulum could be changed so that it was lighter or heavier. The height from which the pendulum was released could be changed, and the force with which the pendulum was pushed could be changed. Given these four variables, students were asked which of the factors influences the speed at which the pendulum would swing.

Their findings indicated that a student who is formally operational approaches the problem in a very systematic fashion, generating and testing various hypotheses. To illustrate, a formal operational student might choose one weight and one length, and push the pendulum at constant force, while varying the height from which the pendulum is released. Discovering that the height does not influence speed, the student would then proceed to manipulate other factors one at a time in an effort to eliminate possible solutions to the problem. A concrete operational student, by contrast, is likely to approach this task in a haphazard or much less systematic way, sometimes re-testing a hypothesis that has already been discarded. Figure 2.2 shows an analogous experiment. In this case, how might you determine if students are using formal operational reasoning to solve the problem?

Critical Thinking: In terms of what teachers need to know about their students, what are some strengths and weaknesses of Piaget's stage theory of cognitive development?

Piaget's stages paint human cognitive development in broad strokes. Teachers must remember that an individual student's thinking does not progress in neat, unambiguous steps according to a precise timetable. This is especially true for students who come from diverse cultural backgrounds. Cross-cultural research on development has generally revealed that children from different cultures progress through more or less the same stages but not at the same rates (cf. Siegler, 1986). There are gaps in the experiences of every individual that affect development within and between stages. Students do not advance from one stage to the next overnight, and even those students who seem firmly established in a stage may regress to the previous one.

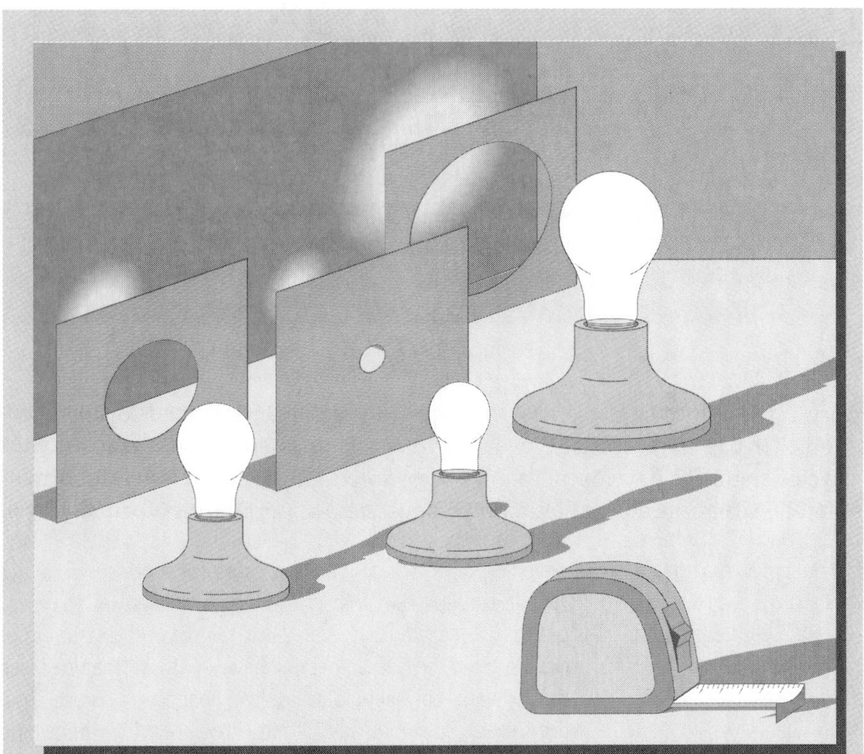

FIGURE 2.2

Objects for a Test of Formal Operations: What Affects the Distance Visible Light Travels?

WHAT IS THE SOCIAL BASIS FOR COGNITIVE DEVELOPMENT?

Think for a moment about your own experiences in learning to read. Did your parents or an older sibling read aloud to you? Did you read to them, with their guidance as you stumbled over words that were unfamiliar? Do you recall reading in groups or with a teacher at school? Although current theories of reading acquisition tend to focus on the individual processes of the reader, some researchers argue that "acquiring the ability to read is most decidedly *not* an individual process" (Cole & Engestrom, 1993, p. 23). Rather, it is thought to be a joint meaning-making activity between teachers and students, between students and their parents or siblings, and among groups of students.

Connection: Teaching approaches based on the social mediation of learning are presented in this chapter and in Chapters 8 and 12.

Reading is not the only capability whose development is thought to be influenced by the social environment of the child. Vygotsky believed that the social environment is critical to cognitive development (1978, 1987). In fact, he claimed that all capabilities acquired by children actually appear twice, first among people in the child's cultural environment and then within the child; that is, social processes enable the development of personal psychological processes. Let's examine how this occurs.

Insights ON SUCCESSFUL PRACTICE

How do the developmental characteristics of your students influence your interactions with them as their teacher?

Three messages have been on the walls of every classroom in which I have taught for the past twenty years. One is in the form of a poster showing ten runners ready to burst from their blocks at the sound of a starting gun. The caption reads: "You have failed only if you have failed to try." The other two messages are handmade signs. The words have faded over the years, but their meanings are clear: "SUCCESS Lies Not in *BEING* the Best, but in *DOING* Your Best," and "THINK POSITIVE!" I teach these messages to my students.

Each child is the product of countless and immeasurable influences, whether they be biological, social, economic, or political. To teach each child, therefore, means I must first learn from the child before he or she can learn from me. I have to learn who the child is. I cannot come with preconceived notions about the student and what he or she is capable of. Rather, I have to listen and reflect on the many confusing and contradictory messages the child gives and gear my efforts to these often subtle signals. I realize that the understanding I have of the student today will be invalid tomorrow, next week, next month, or next year. If life changes for all of us, it never changes so rapidly as it does for a child.

It is often said that students must trust us if we are to be successful teachers. I rather think it is the other way around. As a teacher, I have to trust that my students want to participate in the learning process, that they want to grow and master their environment, and that they will give me clues as to how I might help them reach their individual potential. I believe that if I listen to my students and respect them, I might become the teacher who makes a difference in their lives.

PAM MANIET-BELLERMAN,
South Orange, New Jersey

What are some examples of influences upon development? How might principles of cognitive development help you interpret children's messages? How will you find out about your students' individual capabilities?

Acquiring Tools to Understand the Environment

According to Vygotsky, people use tools to engage and understand their environment. Think of what an infant learns about the environment by wielding a small wooden block with which a satisfying noise can be made by hitting it against the high chair or with which peas can be reduced to a pile of mush. Alternatively, imagine what students learn who use computers to access large databases of information or to simulate complex scientific processes. But tools do not always have to be material things. They can also be psychological, such as language and mathematics. Words are tools used to converse and to exchange ideas with one another, and mathematical symbols are tools used in logical operations.

Material tools, then, are those that mediate between people and the natural world (cf. Strauss, 1993). *Mediate* means to "come between and meet halfway, or help to reconcile." So material tools are things that people produce to help them accomplish some task or purpose, such as driving a nail into two boards to bind them together. A variety of tools, some more efficient than others, might enable one to succeed in doing this task

Psychological tools, by contrast, mediate between individuals in their social interactions. These are signs, symbols, and conventions that have been socially negotiated. For example, putting up a hand is a sign to the teacher that a student wishes to speak. Likewise, turning the lights on and off when students are engaged in cooperative group activities is a sign to them that the teacher wants their collective attention. The happy faces that some teachers use on student papers are symbols of approval and sometimes humor.

Psychological tools can also form coherent systems of signs, such as language. Children must acquire not only individual tools but also the rules by which the individual tools relate to each other and are used. How do children acquire psychological tools and rules for understanding their use in the environment? How do they learn to use material tools in an appropriate fashion? For Vygotsky, the answers are found in human cultural activity and in the process of internalization. What is important is not the tools themselves but how they are used.

Human Activity Systems. People play an important role in the development of others by the activities in which they engage as part of a cultural community (Vygotsky, 1987; Newman, Griffin, & Cole, 1989; Cole & Engestrom, 1993). Human activities, or activity systems (Leont'ev, 1978, 1981), are historically conditioned systems of relations between individuals and their environments. In their homes, for example, people might engage in activities such as cooking, cleaning, gardening, and entertaining. Each of these activities requires that they assume certain roles and use certain tools in particular ways. One would not use a gardening hoe in the kitchen, for instance, any more than a teaspoon would be used to dig holes for installing a fence in the backyard. Similarly, the manner of greeting a guest is likely to differ from the casual interactions of family members around a board game.

Point: *Life conditions affect development.* Socioeconomic status, for example, affects activity systems as well as access to material and psychological tools for thinking.

In their interactions, parents guide their children in the appropriate use of material tools, as well as their development of appropriate psychological tools and rules. The same is true of teachers in school. By the activities in which you engage children, you help them develop the capacity to use material tools (such as word processors or calculators) and psychological tools (such as mathematical symbols and language) in appropriate ways. "Appropriate ways" are defined by the surrounding culture, which, it is important to note, is constantly changing and evolving as people interact with each other. Math teachers often have students use calculators in some activities (e.g., where computation is subordinate to the intended goal, such as problem solving) but not others (e.g., estimating). But using calculators in schools at all is a relatively recent development in Western cultures.

Critical Thinking: How would Vygotsky (whose theory is discussed in the section, What Is the Social Basis for Cognitive Development?) regard Piaget's social-arbitrary knowledge?

Activity systems provide the basic structures for social contact in which children acquire the tools of their culture. Internalization is the process by which these social and cultural understandings become personal understandings.

Internalization. "Any higher mental function necessarily goes through an external stage in its development because it is initially a social function" (Vygotsky, 1981, p. 162). Remember the example of pointing given earlier in the chapter. The gesture takes on its meaning only through the social interaction between the child and his or her mother. Pointing at an object in the absence of the mother (or another person) would have had no effect. Likewise, if the mother had ignored the gesture, the child would be unlikely to reproduce it when he or she wanted some other object. *Internalization* occurs, then, when the child appropriates the gesture for pointing and uses it in other situations and contexts.

Vygotsky believed that the process of internalization provided a reasonable explanation for the egocentric speech Piaget observed in preoperational children. Remember that preoperational children hold conversations that are really collective monologues. Each child speaks, as though to himself or herself, but no one responds. Is this evidence of egocentric patterns of thinking where children cannot understand the perspectives of their peers? Piaget thought so, but Vygotsky believed that collective monologues could be evidence of internalization of complex cognitive skills, such as self-monitoring. Children speak to themselves as a means of self-guidance and internalize this external speech as thought processes.

To test this hypothesis, Vygotsky conducted a series of experiments in which children worked alone, in cooperative groups with deaf children or children speaking a different language, and in situations where it was difficult to hear vocalizations. In each case, children talked less to themselves than when they worked with other children who could hear and understand them. Vygotsky concluded that egocentric speech showed "a developing abstraction from sound, the child's new faculty to 'think words' instead of pronouncing them" (1962, p. 135). With ensuing development, then, egocentric speech is internalized as private speech and becomes entirely inner-directed and subvocal.

Reflection: When do you use private speech? On what kinds of learning tasks or problem-solving tasks is private speech most helpful to you?

In recent years, other studies have been conducted that support Vygotsky's findings (Berk, 1994). Children tend to use private speech when working on difficult tasks or when confused about what to do next (Berk, 1992). For learners of any age, using private speech can lead to improved performance on tasks (e.g., Bivens & Berk, 1990).

Vygotsky's Zone of Proximal Development

Critical Thinking: How might manipulatives such as magnetized alphabet boards help teachers to provide instruction appropriate to a child's ZPD?

zone of proximal development (ZPD) In Vygotsky's theory, the gap between actual and potential development—that is, between what a child can do unaided by an adult and what he or she can do under the guidance of an adult or in collaboration with more capable peers.

On the one hand, Piaget posited specific stages of cognitive development through which children progress, and he described what children are capable of doing at each stage. Vygotsky, on the other hand, sought to understand how children develop by studying "those functions that have not yet matured but are in the process of maturation" (1978, p. 86). Vygotsky distinguished between the *actual* development of the child and the *potential* development of the child. Actual development is determined by what a child can do unaided by an adult or teacher. Potential development, in contrast, is what a child can do "through problem solving under adult guidance or in collaboration with more capable peers" (Vygotsky, 1978, p. 86). This area of potential development Vygotsky termed the **zone of proximal development (ZPD)** (Figure 2.3).

To better understand the ZPD, consider the experiences of first graders in learning to read. Most students in first grade are beginning to read, but some have difficulty making the connections between sounds and written letters. These students exhibit the potential for acquiring prereading capabilities, but reading is still beyond their zone of proximal development.

What is important about the ZPD? For one thing, it helps teachers realize that two children who are capable of the same performance now may not achieve the same level of performance six months from now. By observing how students perform on problems when they are assisted, teachers have a better indicator of potential performance than they do by considering just what students can do on

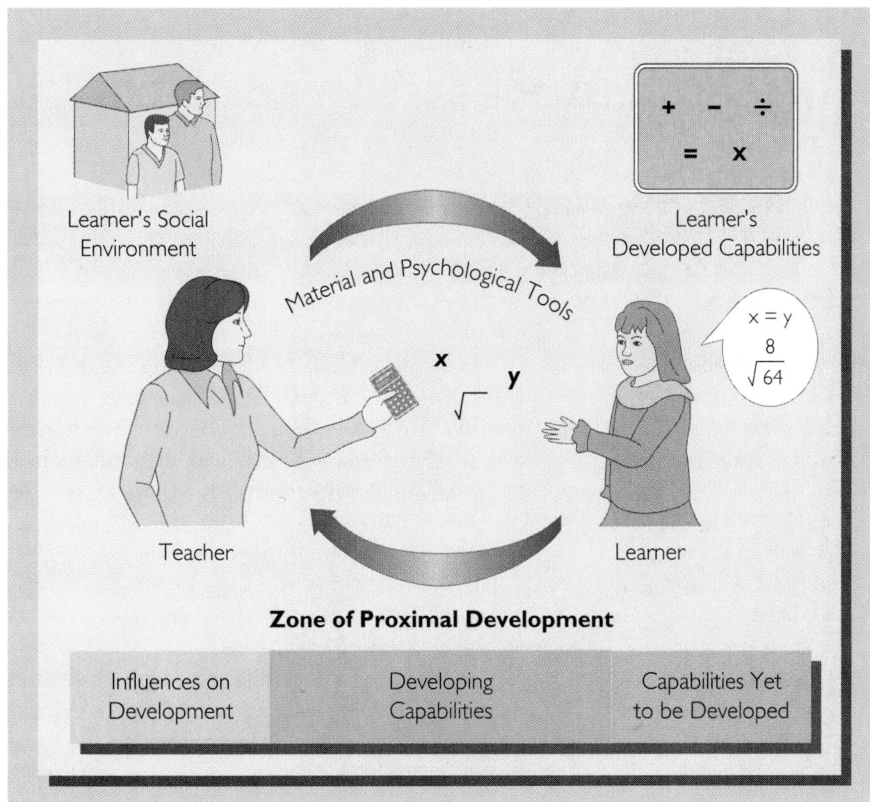

FIGURE 2.3

Vygotsky's Zone of Proximal Development: Areas of Opportunity between One's Actual and Potential Cognitive Development

unaided tests. Armed with this knowledge, teachers are better able to determine just what experiences will best support the development of their students.

Another important implication of the ZPD is the emphasis it places on social interaction for facilitating development. When students do much of their work in school by themselves, their development may be slowed (Gage & Berliner, 1992). To develop fully, students must work with more skilled partners who can systematically lead them into more complex problem solving. Through successive turns of talk and action, students negotiate new meanings with their partners that they appropriate and internalize for their own subsequent use. A consequence of this process is that students learn to self-regulate.

Point: *Teachers and students are both learners.* In scaffolding, a teacher may assume the role of the more knowledgeable partner, but he or she must learn what skills the student possesses in order to provide the most appropriate types of learning supports.

What are the conditions for effective social interaction between learning partners? Two characteristics that seem to be important are scaffolding and intersubjectivity.

scaffolding The process in Vygotsky's theory whereby a more advanced partner changes the degree and quality of support provided to the less skilled partner as he or she becomes more proficient.

Scaffolding. Scaffolding, a term coined by Jerome Bruner, is a process in which the more advanced partner changes the amount or kind of support provided to the less skilled partner as he or she becomes more proficient in the skill (Wood, Bruner, & Ross, 1976). The use of scaffolds in building construction is the

Insights ON SUCCESSFUL PRACTICE

What advice can you give novice teachers about using scaffolding as an instructional method?

Standing in front of my class of thirty-five mostly limited-English-proficient students, I quickly realized communication between myself and this pre-algebra class would be strained. Even the ability of communication among the students themselves would pose a challenge. The learning process seemed to go from challenging to nearly impossible, and given the communication challenge and diversity in this one class, I could not help wondering, what hurdles would my other five classes pose?

It was clear to me that I alone could not give all the students the learning opportunities they needed. I remember thinking that I needed a teacher for each of them. This is when I began to change the way I perceived the students. Rather than see them solely as individuals in need, I realized they represented a wealth of resources. By simply pairing the students into learning teams, I would, in fact, be providing a teacher for each of them.

Through trial and error, I discovered that the trick to pairing the students was to arrange partners who were sensitive to or suited to each other's needs, based on each student's areas of strength and weakness. These arrangements guaranteed a balance of leading and following in the partnership.

Teaching became even more motivating to my students than learning. Enabling the students to achieve success as leaders solidified their understanding of the content, and it also encouraged both partners to embrace the teaching and learning paradigm. A scaffolding process took place in which students supported each other's learning as needed, while I supported the learning of each team. I believe that in today's increasingly diverse and inclusive classrooms, scaffolding will be a necessity for the repertoires of tomorrow's teachers.

JASON D. LOPEZ, La Quinta High School, Westminster, California

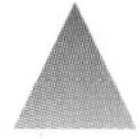 Insights

Why is effective communication a challenge in teaching and learning? How does scaffolding change the roles of teachers and learners? What is needed to make a scaffolding approach work?

intersubjectivity In Vygotsky's theory, the process in which learning partners negotiate a mutual understanding of the task and how to proceed with its solution.

metaphor for this process. To scaffold appropriately, the more knowledgeable partner must know the needs of the less advanced partner, because "information presented at a level too far in advance of the child would not be helpful" (Tudge & Rogoff, 1989, p. 24). Quite often, the teacher serves as the more knowledgeable partner in instruction. But sometimes you will find that other students are best at scaffolding instruction for individual students.

In the Teacher Chronicle, for example, Ernesto requires assistance in putting English words in the proper order. Although Marcia supplies this assistance by responding to the actual rather than the intended meaning of his words, Ernesto could be as easily helped by his English-speaking classmates. As Ernesto becomes more proficient, then the assistance can be gradually withdrawn.

Intersubjectivity. The intersubjectivity that exists between learning partners is also an important characteristic of social interaction that advances cognitive development. **Intersubjectivity** occurs when learning partners negotiate a mutual understanding of the task and how to proceed with its solution. They depend on each other in solving problems and accomplishing tasks. Thus, the teacher or more skilled peer does not dominate the interaction or simply demonstrate a solution to the problem. This would be like Marcia telling Ernesto what

Cognitive development and learning are enhanced through social interaction between learning partners. In scaffolding and intersubjectivity, for example, students are stimulated to grow intellectually through interaction with teachers and more skilled peers.

he should say instead of helping him to figure out the error in his choice of words. The more advanced partner adjusts his or her perspective to that of the student and then attempts to draw the student into a more advanced approach to the problem (Rogoff, 1990).

Using Learning to Facilitate Development

For Vygotsky, learning occurs in the zone of proximal development and actually *pulls* development along; that is, a capability that has already developed does not need to be learned and therefore does not benefit from instruction. For example, once students comprehend the abstractness of numbers, using manipulatives to work regrouping problems is no longer so valuable. Beyond the upper bounds of one's ZPD, however, learning will be fraught with difficulty. Students who do not understand how numbers work will be frustrated in learning if teachers use only abstract examples.

Try This: Determine how you might scaffold instruction to support a student's acquisition of a skill you plan to teach.

Learning is most effective when it occurs within the zone of proximal development with those capabilities that are in the process of developing. This view stands in contrast to Piaget's that learning cannot occur until certain capabilities have been developed. For Vygotsky, learning pulls development, but for Piaget, development pushes learning. This difference in views leads to different implications for teaching. According to Vygotsky, teachers should tailor their instruction to each child's ZPD, because that's where it will be be of greatest benefit in furthering the child's development. Vygotsky's view suggests a more "aggressive" approach than Piaget's in helping students reach beyond their current capabilities: Cognitive development can be accelerated.

Point: *Learning affects development.* According to Vygotsky, the more children learn, the more they become capable of learning.

HOW DOES THE ABILITY TO PROCESS INFORMATION DEVELOP?

Piaget and Vygotsky were similar in their beliefs that development depends on children's active interaction with their environment. Piaget attempted to describe universal changes in cognition that occur with development, whereas Vygotsky emphasized social and cultural origins of cognitive development. Neither theorist, however, had much to say about how thought and learning occur in the brain. One theoretical model of what happens in the brain is *information-processing theory*, which describes how children and adults operate on

Connection: The information-processing view of learning is examined in more detail in Chapter 7.

different kinds of information. How do people *code, store,* and *retrieve* information for later use?

Information-processing theory derives not from the work of a single individual but from a school of thought that applies a computer metaphor to human thinking. As computers have evolved in complexity, so has information-processing theory. Initially thought of as a linear process, information processing is now conceived in terms of multiple and simultaneous linkages, or neural networks, that develop during learning and account for memory. Primarily a theory of learning, information-processing concepts can be applied to classroom practice.

Increasing Attention

Attention is the process used to focus on one or more aspects of the environment to the exclusion of others. When a teacher notices a student looking out the window and says, "Will you *please* pay attention to what's going on here?" the teacher is asking the student to focus on what the teacher is doing to the exclusion of the activity outside. There are four ways that attention can change as children mature (Flavell, 1985).

First, the ability to *control* attention increases with age. Control refers to the length of time a child can attend to a stimulus—sometimes referred to as the attention span—and the ability to concentrate. The attention span increases because the child also becomes less distractible. If every new sound, sight, or smell pulls the child's mind away from the task at hand, his or her attentional control is poor.

Second, the ability to *match task demands* increases with age. This refers to the child's ability to focus on several task variables at once and is similar to Piaget's concept of multiple classification. Suppose, for example, that a map-reading problem requires a student to focus on both the location and elevation of a place as it relates to a river. An older child is better able than a younger child to attend to the location and elevation variables.

Third, the ability to *plan* attention increases with age. Older students are better able to determine what is important to focus their attention on. They can interpret cues that tell what is important and, therefore, where they should direct their attention. High school students, for example, often become expert at reading teacher cues for determining what is important, such as writing on the board or repeating information.

Try This: Observe children of varying ages in learning contexts. What differences do you detect in their abilities to pay attention? As their teacher, how would you accommodate these differences?

Fourth, the ability to *monitor* attention increases with age. With increases in attentional control, task matching, and planning comes a greater ability for students to monitor themselves and to notice when they need to pay more or less attention. For example, older students are more likely than younger students to notice that they are daydreaming instead of focusing on the learning task.

Acquiring Knowledge

Theories of cognitive development, such as Piaget's and Vygotsky's, focus on mental and social processes. In theories of cognition, such as information-processing theory, memory structures and processes are the focus. Information processing and memory are taken up in more detail in Chapter 7.

attention The process used to focus on one or more aspects of the environment to the exclusion of other aspects.

As they develop, children's ability to store, remember, and use information changes. They can solve increasingly complex problems involving more operations to be kept in mind. Case (1984, 1985, 1993) attributes improvement in problem solving to qualitative rather than quantitative changes in memory capacity—that is, the total amount of space available does not increase as children mature; what changes is how the space in memory structures is used.

One stage of information processing, **short-term memory**, holds the information a person is working on at any point in time—the information residing in a person's consciousness. An important characteristic of short-term memory is its limited capacity. A person can only deal with a limited amount of information at any given moment, but this capacity increases during cognitive development.

The space available in short-term memory can function as either *operating space*, where the necessary operations to solve a problem are executed, or *storage space*, where additional problem information is stored (Figure 2.4). Young children who are just learning to solve particular kinds of problems must use all their capacity to execute the required operations. As they gain experience with the problems, the operations used require less and less memory capacity. This means that more space is available to store problem information, so that problems with more steps or operations can now be tackled. **Automaticity** is achieved when an operation can be executed without conscious effort. Automaticity reduces the amount of operating space necessary to solve problems. When operating space is reduced, storage space increases. Children attain automaticity through repeated practice on problems requiring the same operations.

Example: To relate automaticity to operating space, think about the difference between a child who knows multiplication tables and a child who has not yet mastered multiplication facts. When each child encounters the problem, "9 times 3," the former responds "27" automatically, without effort. The child who is unable to respond automatically must use memory capacity to carry out mental calculations to get the answer.

By practicing operations to the point of automaticity, students can increase their efficiency. A second way to do this is to discover shortcuts. Most students look for ways to simplify the steps they must take in order to solve a problem. Older students are better at finding shortcuts than are younger students. They discover more efficient ways of processing information, but they keep the necessary steps in mind. The older student is also better able to keep track of the elements of a problem. This monitoring capability, which we discussed in relation to attention, also plays a role in memory. Younger students often overlook crucial steps. They oversimplify problems (Case, 1985).

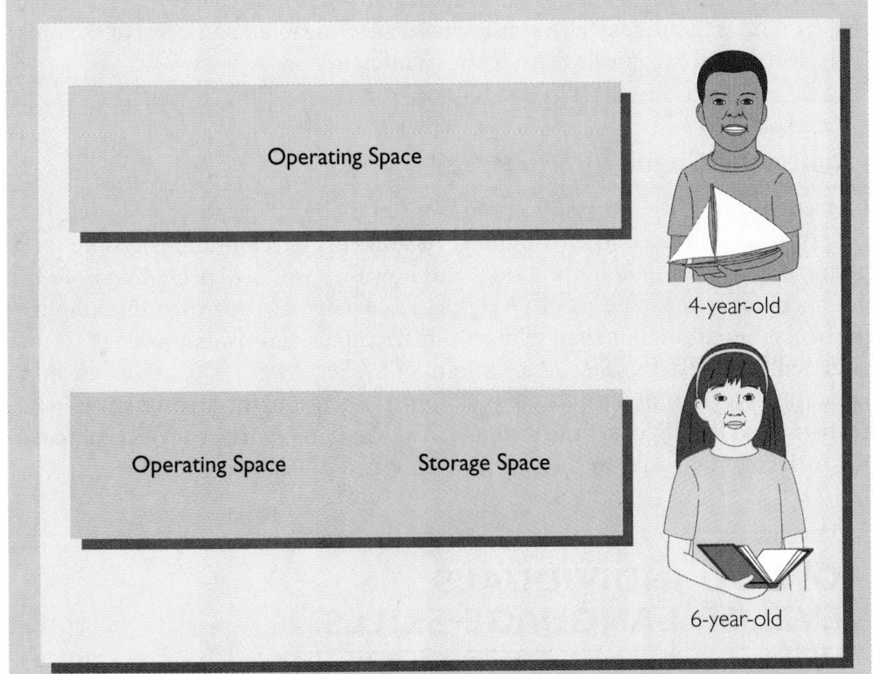

FIGURE 2.4

Memory Capacity in Two Stages of Development

short-term memory The phase of processing at which a limited amount of information is stored for a limited time.

automaticity The point at which a mental operation can be executed without conscious effort.

Reflection: Reflect on the shortcuts you discovered and the shortcuts you were given by teachers. Which shortcuts were more effective in your learning?

Oversimplifying a problem can be due to failure by young children to encode certain aspects of the problem. *Encoding* is a process of relating new information to prior knowledge so that it can be later retrieved and used. Siegler (1983, 1984, 1986) has found that younger students tend to overlook features of a problem that are critical for solving it, similar to the perceptual centration that Piaget described in preoperational children. Siegler attributed this tendency to the limited content knowledge of children and to their strong preferences for simple rules. With tutoring and practice, he discovered, children can learn to consider all relevant aspects of a problem.

In addition to automaticity, encoding, and the discovery of shortcuts, biological maturation of the brain contributes to "operational efficiency" (Case, 1984). The biology of the brain is a factor over which teachers have no control, but teachers can use automaticity, shortcuts, and encoding of relevant problem features to help students process problem-solving tasks more efficiently.

here's how

Here's How to Address a Student's Difficulties with Problem Solving

- Observe the student carefully. Is the problem a lack of automaticity in some critical operation, oversimplification of the task, or both?
- If a lack of automaticity seems to be the student's problem, provide appropriate practice.
- If the problem seems to be oversimplification of the task,
  a. determine what the student is leaving out;
  b. emphasize the missing step or steps by demonstrating how the oversimplification does not work;
  c. demonstrate a set of operations that accomplishes the task; and
  d. break down the task into discrete steps and have the student practice each one. In this way, the student learns to encode and use relevant aspects of the problem as well as to make these actions automatic.

Example: Younger students oversimplify problems. They tend to focus on one aspect, such as calculating the amount of water by observing only its height in a container.

Monitoring Cognitive Processes

Metacognition is the capability to monitor one's own cognitive processes. It is, simply, one's thinking about thinking. As students develop, they become more aware of their own thought processes and how they work (Meichenbaum, 1985). Younger students can be taught to apply knowledge of their own thinking in a particular situation, but they seldom transfer metacognitive knowledge to new situations (Forrest-Pressley, MacKinnon, & Waller, 1985). The ability to think about one's own thinking aids the planning of attention, the attainment of automaticity, and the discovery of shortcuts in solving problems. Strategies for teaching metacognitive skills to students are presented in Chapters 7 and 8.

Connection: Metacognition is examined in relation to information-processing views of learning in Chapter 7.

metacognition Knowledge about thinking and the capability to monitor one's own cognitive processes, such as thinking, learning, and remembering.

HOW DO INDIVIDUALS DEVELOP LANGUAGE SKILLS?

Language accounts for much of the communication that occurs in classrooms. Teachers and students talk. Words, phrases, and sentences are written on the board. Textbooks are read. But not all communication is done in a spoken or written language. Students raise their hands, furrow their brows, slump in their chairs. Teachers raise their fingers to their lips, lift their eyebrows, and shake their heads at slumping students. A language comprises symbols, sounds, meanings, and rules that govern the possible relations among these elements. Language is also arbitrary. Why do we call a cow a cow? Why do we associate the letter *R* with the sound "errrr" instead of "sssss"? Why do you recognize those sounds even though they are ink marks on a page? How do children become capable of using language to communicate?

Linguists, those who study the structure and function of language, identify the *grammar* of a language as a system of implicit rules that relate sounds to meaning (Clark & Clark, 1977). Grammatical rules operate on three major elements of language. The first is **phonology**, the sounds of a language and the structure of those sounds. When writing a poem, for example, you may look for words that rhyme. When you do, you are concerned about phonology, how the words will sound in the poem. The second is **syntax**, the way the words of language form sentences. When you convert a passive sentence to its active form, you are changing the syntax. The third is **semantics**, the meaning underlying words and sentences. Although "the man was a bore" is the same syntactically and phonologically as "the man was a boar," they have quite different meanings. The second sentence must also be understood metaphorically, in the sense that the man is similar to a boar (a wild pig) in some way.

Critical Thinking: How would Vygotsky explain these examples of communication in the classroom?

There is one other element of language, pragmatics. **Pragmatics** refers to the contexts in which language is used and the way language can be used to create contexts. For example, "the man saw a cow in his undershirt" is an ambiguous sentence without the appropriate context for interpreting it. Either the man was in an undershirt when he saw the cow, or he saw a cow that was wearing his (the man's) undershirt. The latter interpretation could be appropriate if the cow got loose from its pasture, ran under a clothesline, and managed to hook the man's undershirt. Similarly, a single sentence can take on different meanings depending on the context in which it is said, the tone of the speaker's voice, and the intention of the speaker. A linguist who focuses on pragmatics studies intonation, gestures, the conventions by which conversations occur, the meanings of pauses, the intention of a writer or speaker, and the like.

Connection: Limited English proficiency and bilingual education are discussed in Chapter 4.

The most dramatic language developmental changes occur before a child reaches school age. The early stages of language development are presented in Table 2.2 on page 52 (LeFrancois, 1991).

The stages of grammatical development reflect changes in phonology, syntax, semantics, and pragmatics. Grammatical development occurs rapidly. This is especially true of phonology, the sounds of a language. The majority of English-speaking children can pronounce properly most of the sounds of their language by the time they reach school. The speech sounds that take the longest to develop are *s*, *z*, *v*, *th*, and *zh* (Rathus, 1988). The "lisping" quality in the speech of children in the primary grades can be traced to the lack of development of these sounds. Let's look briefly at some benchmarks of development in the other areas of language, especially those pertinent to school-age children.

phonology The study of the sound system of a language and the structure of those sounds.

syntax The grammatical arrangement of words in sentences.

semantics The study of the meanings of words and sentences.

pragmatics An area of language that refers to the effects of contexts on meaning and the ways to use language to create different contexts.

Syntax

Children use adultlike sentences by approximately age four (Wood, 1981). However, these are very basic forms: simple declarations and questions.

TABLE 2.2 The Stages of Grammatical Development

Stage*	Characteristics: Middle of Age Range (years)	Characteristics: Grammatical Capabilities
Sounds	less than 1	Phonological experimentation; crying, cooing, babbling
Holophrases	1	Single words carrying sentential meaning; inflections
Telegraphic utterances	1½	Two-word "sentences"; key word modified; declarations, questions, imperatives, and negatives used
Short sentences	2–2½	Real sentences, subjects and predicates; tense changes
Complex sentences	3–4	New elements and clauses embedded; use of parts of speech in various ways
Adultlike structures	4	Structural distinctions made

*The descriptors are relative. Remember that the developmental changes outlined in this table occur before most children enter school.

Source: From *Children and Communication: Verbal and Non Verbal Language Development* by B.S. Wood. Copyright ©1981 by Allyn & Bacon. Reprinted by permission.

Although early elementary school–age children tend to use simple syntax when they speak, they are capable of understanding more complicated forms, such as the passive voice. For example, they are more likely to say "Mary threw the ball," but they can understand "The ball was thrown by Mary." The complexity of the forms they produce increases as they form compounds, learn to use conjunctions, add relative clauses, and master tenses. It is important that elementary school teachers recognize that students can understand forms that they do not use yet. When thinking about syntactic development, the rule of thumb is that comprehension precedes production (cf. Clark & Clark, 1977).

Try This: Document the sentence constructions of children of various ages. Read a complex sentence aloud to the children and ask them to repeat it back to you to observe the changes they make in syntax. How do your observations reflect stages of grammatical development? What are the implications of this effect for teaching?

Semantics

One aspect of semantics is vocabulary. A child begins to use his or her first words around the time of the first birthday. Once the child learns to use words, a single word is often used to communicate a variety of messages. For example, *milk* can mean "I want milk," "The milk is all gone," "That is milk," or "The milk fell" (Bates, O'Connell, & Shore, 1987; Snyder, Bates, & Bretherton, 1981). It takes approximately three to four months for the first ten words to appear. Once the child has acquired approximately ten words, he or she adds another word to the vocabulary every few days. A typical eighteen-month-old child has a vocabulary of approximately forty to fifty words. The average twenty-four-month-old child knows approximately 300 words and by age six, a child may know upwards of 14,000 words (Carey, 1977; Templine, 1957). Reading and other language-based activities that occur in the early grades may contribute to the roughly 5,000 additional words the child gains by age eleven (cf. Berger, 1986).

Aside from the development of a vocabulary, a benchmark of semantic development is the capability to understand complex language functions. For example, many children and some adolescents have difficulty with metaphors, similes, sarcasm, and facetious remarks. Teachers who like to joke and kid with students must be careful when speaking with those whose semantics do not embrace these complex structures.

Example: A high school English teacher who, when asked for the four-thousandth time, "How long does the paper have to be?" responded sarcastically, "The paper must be 4.23 pages long." The next day an anxious student asked, "How do you figure out how long .23 of a page is?"

Pragmatics

Pragmatic development occurs as a child becomes capable of using his or her grammatical competence to communicate in a variety of contexts. A collective monologue may contain grammatically correct language, but it is not communication. By adolescence, students have learned the conventions of conversation and can use them to gain information.

Using language to gain information is just one aspect of pragmatic development. Language can also be used poetically, persuasively, humorously, artistically, tactfully. The language experiences provided by teachers influence pragmatic development throughout a student's career.

Example: In the Teacher Chronicle, Ernesto's metalinguistic awareness helped him think effectively about cracking the code. Why was that awareness less effective when he attempted to read or communicate in English?

HOW CAN YOU ACCOMMODATE THE DEVELOPMENTAL DIFFERENCES AND NEEDS OF YOUR STUDENTS?

In this chapter, we have looked at patterns of cognitive development and the development of language. At the least, you have probably reached these three conclusions:

1. Your students are likely to think very differently from the way that you think.
2. Your students are likely to use different forms to communicate than you use.
3. There will be great variability in the thinking and communication of your students.

What can you do, then, to accommodate your instruction to the developmental differences and needs of your students? Let's explore some possibilities.

Assessing Student Thinking

Knowing that students think differently from you and that their thinking changes as they mature suggests the importance of assessing student thinking during instruction. To begin with, you will need to know something about your students' stages of cognitive development and ZPDs relative to your goals in order to appropriately tailor instruction. Following are some suggestions for finding out about their ZPDs.

Point: *Assessment improves teaching and learning.* The more you can find out about the capabilities of your students through assessment, the better prepared you will be to plan appropriate instruction.

Insights ON SUCCESSFUL PRACTICE

How have you used whole language in your classroom to foster developmentally appropriate instructions?

I have considered myself to be a whole language teacher for the past nine years. Adopting the whole language philosophy has forced me to continually reexamine my understandings of how children learn and perhaps more importantly, what motivates them to learn. As I reflect on my teaching and my interactions with students, I ask myself, "Is this activity meaningful to students? Do they see a real purpose for the activity? Are the children immersed in whole texts and invited to participate as readers, writers, speakers, and listeners?" In answering these questions, I am evaluating activities to determine whether or not they will motivate students to learn.

As a kindergarten teacher for five years and a first-grade teacher for four years, I have discovered that inviting children to participate as readers and writers motivates them to *become* readers and writers. By providing support and accepting their approximations, children are intrinsically driven to *actively* participate in the reading and writing processes and seek to make sense of the rules governing written language.

Rather than telling children what and how to read and write, I encourage them to choose their own personally meaningful topics for writing and their own books for reading. In addition, I support my students as they use available strategies to make sense of text and to record their messages. I help children become consciously aware of what it is they know and can do.

It was as I watched Becky become a reader that I realized how powerful invitations can be. Each year I invite the children in my first-grade class to choose their own books to learn to read. One year Becky chose *Green Wilma* as her goal. This was November and Becky was just beginning to acquire a sight vocabulary and was also just beginning to learn about sounding out words. Most first-grade teachers (including myself) would never have thought that Becky would be able to successfully learn to read this book. The vocabulary was difficult, there were few picture clues, and only a subtle rhyming pattern to support her predictions of the text. So why would Becky choose this book for independent reading? Ted Arnold, the author and illustrator of *Green Wilma*, had just visited our school and spent an hour talking with the children about his stories and pictures. The children were captivated as he read his favorite stories to them. Becky spent thirty minutes a day for the next four weeks actively studying the words in her book. During this time I questioned whether or not spending four weeks on one book would make a significant impact on Becky's growth as a reader. As a whole language teacher, I knew I needed to follow her lead. I provided support when she "got stuck" on a word and encouraged her to continue working toward her goal. At the end of four weeks she not only learned to read *Green Wilma*, but she was also on her way to becoming an independent, fluent reader.

We can learn so much from watching children, extending invitations, supporting their efforts, and following their leads. Children *want* to become readers and writers, and if we allow them, they will show us *what* they want to read and write. Many times what they show us unexpectedly exceeds our expectations!

LYNDA F. HAYES, P. K. Yonge Developmental Research School, Gainesville, Florida

Insights

What is the whole language philosophy? How does it relate to the idea that people are naturally motivated to learn? How does it relate to the idea that learning takes place actively in real situations?

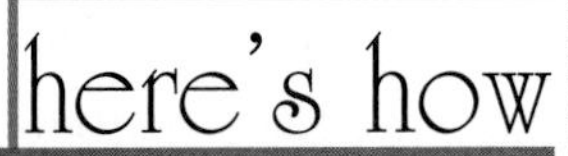

Here's How to Discover Student's Zones of Proximal Development

- Observe students during class activities. Regular observations of your students will help you become aware of their developmental levels and the types of instructional activities that might best meet their needs.
- Interview students in one-on-one sessions. Through questioning, you can probe a student's reasoning behind an answer or action and discover his or her constructions of knowledge. Some constructions might represent misconceptions or lack of understandings that require additional instruction or a different kind of instructional activity.
- Conduct formal assessments of students' capabilities. Formal assessments can help you to determine just what students are capable of doing on their own, which can serve as a foundation for further learning.

Questions that help you assess the level of your students' thinking can serve another purpose. For learning to pull development along, instruction should push students' current competencies to their limits. Questions can do this by guiding students to make new discoveries and to become aware of conflicts or inadequacies in their ways of thinking. Bruner (1960) called these **medium-level questions** after an experienced teacher of mathematics expressed the following point:

> Given particular subject matter or a particular concept, it is always easy to ask trivial questions or to lead the child to ask trivial questions. It is also easy to ask impossibly difficult questions. The trick is to find the medium questions that can be answered and that take you somewhere. This is the big job of teachers and textbooks. (p. 40)

Understanding and making students aware of the need for conceptual change is a hallmark of **developmentally appropriate instruction**. Students need a basis for deciding to give up naive beliefs or simple rules in favor of more accurate and useful ones. For example, young children's experience of the earth is that it is flat and stationary. When a teacher attempts to teach them that the earth is "round like a ball," they are likely to assimilate this contradictory information by constructing a representation of the earth as "round like a pizza" (Vosniadou, 1988). When you ask questions that lead students to conflicts or inconsistencies in their thinking, you prepare them to adopt new conceptions. Piaget and Vygotsky would agree that asking questions that throw the students out of equilibrium within their ZPDs can cause them to equilibrate (assimilate and accommodate) until an answer is reached.

medium-level questions
Questions that guide a learner to new discoveries or to conceptual conflicts and inadequacies in his or her ways of thinking.

developmentally appropriate instruction
Instruction that is child-centered and provides activities appropriate to the developmental level of the student.

Providing Concrete Experiences

Throughout the chapter, there have been examples of how experiences with concrete objects and real problems facilitate development, especially for children in stages from sensorimotor to concrete operations. Children who miss working with manipulatives at an early age may later experience difficulty in learning abstract concepts and operations. This is true in subject areas from mathematics to science to language arts. But even high school students, who are presumed to be formal operational thinkers, can benefit from instructional activities that provide them with concrete experiences and material representations of concepts.

Whenever you anticipate that students will know very little about a subject matter or skill that you intend to introduce, begin by making instruction concrete. In a beginning course on computers, for example, adult students had such difficulty understanding how the computer worked that the instructor built a board with slots that represented addresses in computer memory. Students moved index cards into and out of slots to represent, and therefore understand, the functions of input and output (Driscoll, 1994).

One of the benefits of providing concrete experiences to students is that they don't need you to provide feedback. They can obtain feedback from their own actions. The young child who mashes peas with a wooden block, for example, does not need to be told that the block is a tool capable of this task. The child sees the evidence in the pile of mush. Similarly, students investigating the pendulum problem described earlier do not need the teacher to tell them that the length of the pendulum influences its speed. They have evidence from the trials they conducted in which they varied different elements of the problem.

Using Authentic Activities

Point: *Authentic activity provides a basis for assessment.* As you plan authentic activities for your students, consider how these activities might also be used for assessment purposes.

Experimenting with tools and investigating phenomena are examples of authentic activities. **Authentic activities** are instructional tasks that provide culturally and situationally relevant contexts for learning and development. Based on Vygotsky's notions of human activity systems, an authentic activity for acquiring arithmetic competence, for example, might entail shopping for the best buys at a supermarket in order to stay within a particular budget. This is typical of an ordinary dilemma that arises in the context of everyday situations. Presenting students with real-life dilemmas to solve helps them to internalize the competencies and tools of their culture.

How do you devise and appropriately scaffold an authentic activity? Here are some guidelines derived from recent research (e.g., Cognition & Technology Group at Vanderbilt, 1991, 1993; Driscoll & Rowley, in press).

here's how

Here's How to Scaffold an Authentic Activity

- Select an activity that provides a motivating reason to learn the knowledge and skills involved in it. For example, middle school students can learn a great deal about friction by designing objects to run down a ramp.
- Help students determine and define subgoals necessary to be solved before the larger goal can be attained.
- Teach subordinate skills as they become needed in the solution of subgoals.
- Help students begin to regulate their own problem solving by gradually withdrawing task assistance and providing feedback on students' task management skills.

authentic activities
Instructional tasks that provide culturally and situationally relevant contexts for learning and development.

The Kamehameha Elementary Education Program (KEEP) is a good example of the use of authentic activities and scaffolding (Gallimore & Tharp, 1990).

In KEEP classes, students work on meaningful goals for which the teachers provide a variety of scaffolds:

- *Modeling*, to introduce children to unfamiliar skills.
- *Instructing*, to direct children toward the next specific act they need to learn in order to move through the ZPD.
- *Verbal feedback* (or reinforcement), to let children know how well they are progressing in relation to reasonable standards of performance.
- *Questioning*, to encourage children to think about the task.
- *Explaining*, to provide strategies and knowledge necessary for thinking in new ways. (Berk, 1994, p. 259)

Encouraging Student Interaction

Both Piaget and Vygotsky believed that children's interactions with their peers is an important source of cognitive development, but Vygotsky took a step further in describing the kinds of interactions that are most likely to advance development. When you encourage interaction among your students, you enable them to accomplish two goals. First, students are forced to confront the views of others. This helps them to become able to approach an issue from various perspectives and to understand a view that contradicts their own. Second, students learn to express and defend their own understandings and beliefs. Argumentation that was once social becomes personal and available for regulating their future thoughts and actions.

A useful strategy you can use to encourage interaction among your students is cooperative learning (e.g., Slavin, 1991). Cooperative learning, which is discussed in more detail in Chapter 12, means more than simply putting students to work in groups. For **cooperative learning** to be most effective, students must be dependent on each other to achieve a learning goal, they must be responsible for both their own work and for the group product, and they must know how to cooperate. You can effectively implement cooperative learning in your classes by following these guidelines.

Point: *Learning is actively constructed in social contexts.* Cooperative learning can help to provide a classroom structure in which students can explore the views of others at the same time they develop their own views.

Connection: Cooperative learning is examined in relation to motivation in Chapter 9 and as a support for active learning in Chapter 12.

here's how

Here's How to Organize Cooperative Learning Activities

- Choose complex tasks that require several students working together in order to be achieved. In middle school science, for example, groups can be assigned to develop, build, and test a rocket that will reach certain heights or trajectories.
- Assign roles to students within a group (e.g., primary investigator, hypothesis generator, time manager). Having different roles means that students will become the more advanced learning partner with respect to the tasks and competencies involved in their role. When you rotate the roles on subsequent assignments, students can serve as models to those newly assigned to their roles.
- Provide a set of norms or rules that govern the behavior of students in groups—for example, group members must help any member who requests it, all group members must have the same question before the teacher can be consulted, only one member of the group interacts with the teacher.
- Prepare students for the new norms that come with cooperative learning by role-playing these norms through games and exercises (cf. Cohen, 1986).

cooperative learning An instructional strategy whereby students work in cooperative groups to achieve a common goal. Conditions that promote effective cooperative learning include positive interdependence among group members, face-to-face interaction, clearly perceived individual accountability to achieve the group's goals, frequent use of interpersonal skills, and regular group processing to improve the group's functioning.

Using Many Sign Systems

As children acquire symbolic thinking around the age of two, they create their own symbols, and they begin to use the symbol systems of their culture, such as language. Vygotsky believed that language is most important in developing higher cognitive functioning, and it is certainly true that language dominates as a mode of communication in school. However, different subject areas have different language structures that must be mastered for content understanding to occur. When you and your students mean different things by the words you use, you are likely to talk at cross-purposes, as occurred in a study of a high school class in earth science (Lemke, 1988). The teacher meant one thing by "light" and "heat," but the students understood another.

Another aspect of language predominance in schools is that students from minority group cultures may be disadvantaged by language habits that differ from their teacher's. Although this will be discussed in greater detail in Chapter 4, it suggests that you should consider language difficulties as a possible source when your students exhibit misconception or misunderstanding. This is also true with respect to classroom pragmatics. You may take for granted that students know they should line up to leave the classroom or raise their hands to be recognized. But these typical (and often unstated) rules may be unfamiliar to students from diverse cultural backgrounds. You should not automatically assume, therefore, that their failure to follow the rules is a sign of either willful disobedience or lower levels of cognitive functioning. The most effective teachers use a variety of alternative sign systems in their instruction.

TEACHER Chronicle Conclusion

CRACKING THE CODE

As she observes her students trying to break the code, Marcia soon sees many looks of puzzlement. Some students continue to scribble letters and numbers on their papers; others have put down their pencils and stare at the board.

Marcia moves to the front of the room and waits until everyone is looking at her.

"Well, what did you come up with?" she asks. She waits until a hand is raised.

"Eric?"

"If A is 1, then the first word is 'szjjb'. I've never heard of that before."

"Me, either."

"If A is 26 what happens?" Ernesto asks, looking at Marcia for a clue as to if he is right. She tries not to smile and give it away, but she can't hold back any longer.

"A is 26," he shouts.

A flurry of pencils scratch across paper. Ernesto calls, "19 26 10 10 2 means 'Happy.'" A big smile spreads across his face.

Eric quickly finishes what he is writing. "Ernesto's right," he says, looking at his neighbor with new respect.

Shannon, who is normally a quiet observer of all that goes on, calls out next, "25 18 9 7 19 23 22 means 'Birthday.' "

Within minutes the entire message is translated, "Happy Birthday, George Washington."

"Now, can we try it?" Renita asks. "Can we write to each other in code?" Seeing the interest and sensing the excitement, Marcia decides to postpone the social studies lesson on George Washington until later.

APPLICATION QUESTIONS

1. Was Ernesto's bilingualism a factor in his breaking the code? Why or why not?
2. How does prior knowledge help students gain new knowledge? How does this concept apply in the code-breaking lesson?
3. Use the concepts in this chapter to explain how Marcia's students were constructing knowledge.
4. At which Piagetian stage of cognitive development might most of these third graders be? Would code-breaking work with younger students? Why or why not?
5. What teaching strategies did Marcia use to achieve her instructional goals? What roles did sign systems and student interaction play?
6. Why might a student become a better learner if he or she developed metacognitive skills? At what age do you think most students become aware of metacognition?

CHAPTER SUMMARY

WHAT ARE THE DIMENSIONS OF HUMAN DEVELOPMENT?

The study of human development involves assessing the capabilities we possess as we grow into and develop our potential. There are several areas of human development that have been identified for the purpose of study: cognitive development, personal development, and social development. This chapter has focused on cognitive development and the development of information-processing and language capabilities.

HOW DO INDIVIDUALS' COGNITIVE ABILITIES DEVELOP?

Piaget's theory of cognitive development is comprehensive in its description of universal capabilities that children acquire through four stages of development, from birth to adulthood. Although everyone passes through these stages in the same way, there is considerable diversity in the rates at which individual development proceeds. Piaget emphasized the role of active experience in the child's construction of knowledge about the world, and he demonstrated how children's thinking is qualitatively different at different points in their lives.

WHAT IS THE SOCIAL BASIS FOR COGNITIVE DEVELOPMENT?

Vygotsky's theory of cognitive development highlights the central role of the social and cultural environment of the child. Higher cognitive functions develop from the child's social interactions with more knowledgeable others in everyday situations. Learning, and consequently instruction, is most effective in the child's zone of proximal development, where it supports capabilities in the process of development.

HOW DOES THE ABILITY TO PROCESS INFORMATION DEVELOP?

As children mature, their attention spans grow longer, they are able to make better use of limited memory space, and they encode additional elements of complex problems that they once ignored. With maturation, students are also better able to monitor their own thought processes.

HOW DO INDIVIDUALS DEVELOP LANGUAGE SKILLS?

A language is a set of grammatical rules covering phonology (sounds), syntax (structure), semantics (meaning), and pragmatics (context). Grammatical abilities develop rapidly. Children can use relatively complex structures by the time they reach school. Pragmatic development continues indefinitely.

HOW CAN YOU ACCOMMODATE THE DEVELOPMENTAL DIFFERENCES AND NEEDS OF YOUR STUDENTS?

Five strategies were presented and discussed that can help you accommodate your instruction to the developmental differences and needs of your students: (1) assessing student thinking, (2) providing concrete experiences, (3) using authentic activities, (4) encouraging student interactions, and (5) using many sign systems in instruction.

KEY CONCEPTS

accommodation
assimilation
attention
authentic activities
automaticity
cognitive development
concrete operations
cooperative learning
developmentally appropriate instruction
equilibration
formal operations
intersubjectivity
logico-mathematical knowledge
medium-level questions
phonology
physical knowledge
pragmatics
preoperational stage
scaffolding
schemes
semantics
sensorimotor stage
short-term memory
social-arbitrary knowledge
syntax
zone of proximal development

language not important

3 Personal and Interpersonal Growth

CHAPTER OUTLINE

TEACHER Chronicle

LOOKS CAN DECEIVE

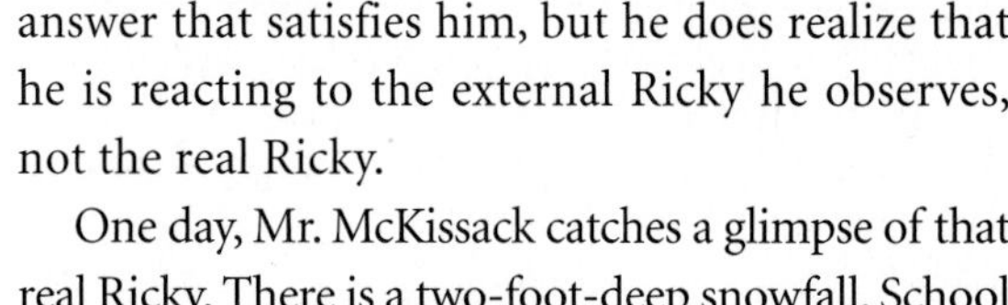

Mr. McKissack is pleased to see Ricky Chavez's name on his class list. He had noticed him around the middle school last year, and while he behaved like a typical sixth grader, his clean-cut appearance and handsome looks indicated to Mr. McKissack that he must be a model student, too.

This impression carries over through the first weeks of school. Ricky is attentive in class, asks questions, and does average work on his tests. In cooperative groups he shines, always willing to pitch in and help another student who is having difficulties. But by the end of the second quarter, Mr. McKissack realizes something about Ricky: He discovers that he doesn't really like him.

Mr. McKissack prides himself on being able to reach most kids, even the ones who try to get him to dislike them on purpose to get his negative attention. Yet every so often he finds himself, for no apparent reason, not liking a student. Disliking a student does not fit his image of a professional.

Ricky does nothing to antagonize Mr. McKissack. He has many friends, is a star of the swimming team, and is a member of the Student Council. He seems to enjoy his role as the model student. One day, Mr. McKissack takes a long walk after school and tries to sort out his feelings about Ricky. Is it his good looks or excellent behavior that bothers him? Is it his academic achievement or the high esteem in which his peers hold him? Is it that he is just too nice, too perfect? Mr. McKissack cannot come up with any answer that satisfies him, but he does realize that he is reacting to the external Ricky he observes, not the real Ricky.

One day, Mr. McKissack catches a glimpse of that real Ricky. There is a two-foot-deep snowfall. School doesn't close, but getting around presents challenges. When Mr. McKissack calls for the homework assignments the day after the snowfall, Ricky is the only student who doesn't have his completed. This is a first. Mr. McKissack is surprised, especially when Ricky doesn't offer an excuse and accepts the zero for the assignment.

When Ricky doesn't come back after school to discuss the zero (the way any other student would have done), Mr. McKissack begins to wonder if something is wrong.

FOCUS QUESTIONS

1. How does Mr. McKissack judge Ricky's self-esteem?
2. Is positive self-esteem a prerequisite to learning?
3. Should a teacher be aware of a value system different from his or hers? How could such a difference impact that teacher's interactions with a student?
4. In what ways do Ricky's peers affect his actions?
5. Is a teacher's perception of a student important to the student's learning? Success or failure in school?
6. In what ways are teachers role models?

HOW DO INDIVIDUALS DEVELOP SELF-CONCEPTS AND SELF-ESTEEM?

Students' personal and social development are as important as their cognitive development. Teachers understand intuitively that it is important for students to think well of themselves, to have a positive rather than a negative self-concept. Experienced teachers have seen students who can't wait to try new things, who welcome opportunities to interact with adults and peers, who radiate confidence in themselves. (Ricky Chavez in the Teacher Chronicle is such a student.) Teachers have also seen students who are hesitant to embrace both academic and social challenges. More important, teachers can influence the feelings students have about themselves. To prove the point, ask a few classmates, a roommate, or friends to join you in reflecting on the teachers you had in elementary, middle, and high school. Did a teacher ever say or do something that influenced, positively or negatively, your feelings about yourself? Chances are one did. Ask the group if a teacher ever gave them confidence. Ask if a teacher ever made them feel inadequate or "invisible." Analyze your own experiences and those of your friends. Do you think that, in all cases, those instances of influencing a student's feelings were intentional on the part of the teacher? Probably not.

As a teacher, however, you need to be aware of your influence on students' beliefs about themselves, their self-perceptions. Much of what students learn about themselves comes from their interactions with others, including teachers. Conversely, the interactions students have with other people are influenced heavily by their self-perceptions (Marsh, 1984). Given the influence that teachers can have on a child's or adolescent's self-perception, therefore, it is important for aspiring teachers to understand how self-perceptions are formed.

Connection: The nature of values and how they are acquired will be examined in Chapter 4.

Development of Self-Concept

self concept v. esteem

Teachers, parents, and administrators recognize the importance of students' self-perceptions. It is not surprising, therefore, that the way students view themselves is the subject of much discussion in educational circles. These discussions are often difficult because terms are thrown around and used indiscriminately. A prime example is the confusion between the terms *self-concept* and *self-esteem*. The terms are often used interchangeably, but there is an important difference between them (Beane & Lipka, 1980; Marshall, 1989). **Self-concept** is a person's description of himself or herself in terms of roles, attributes, or characteristics (Beane & Lipka, 1986; Berk, 1994). **Self-esteem**, which will be examined shortly, refers to a person's evaluation of his or her self-concept and the feelings associated with that evaluation. Two people may describe themselves as possessing the same attribute—stubbornness, for example—but one person may judge stubbornness as being positive while the other judges stubbornness as being negative, depending on their values.

self-concept One's description of self in terms of roles and characteristics.

self-esteem One's judgments about self and the feelings associated with those judgments.

The way in which people describe themselves changes with age. For instance, when preschoolers think about themselves and are asked to describe themselves, they tend to focus on concrete characteristics (Berk, 1994). Although such descriptions include characteristics of physical appearance and favorite possessions, research has shown that the most frequent type of description among preschoolers is typical behaviors (e.g., Keller, Ford, & Meacham,

1978). Examples of typical behaviors described might include the following statements: "I can dress myself," "I go to church," and "I play with Shana." Note that these statements, as well as descriptions of physical appearance and possessions, are observable attributes.

One question to raise about such early research is whether the concrete descriptions are the only types of descriptions of which preschoolers are capable. More recent research on the self-concepts of preschoolers has attempted to use other techniques to probe self-concept. One example is the presentation of pictures that depict children either succeeding or experiencing difficulty with tasks (Harter & Pike, 1984). Another technique is to present descriptions and then to ask preschoolers if they recognize the statements as being true of themselves. Recognizing descriptions of self is easier than generating those same descriptions. Using this technique, researchers have shown that children as young as three-and-a-half years old are capable of consistent self-descriptions. These descriptions go beyond observable characteristics to descriptions of typical emotions and attitudes (Eder, 1989, 1990). Examples of statements of emotion or attitude might include, "I don't like going to the library," "I am happy when I'm with my teacher," or "I feel like being quiet when I get mad."

Try This: To gather information about your students, develop statements that indicate students' feelings about various aspects of classroom activity and then ask students to identify those statements that descibe themselves.

Connection: Self-descriptions or attributions can be used to understand motivation, which is the subject of Chapter 9.

Evidence that self-concept is a developmental phenomenon can be seen in the shift that occurs in self-descriptions between the ages of eight and eleven. You might recall that in Piaget's theory of cognitive development this is roughly the period of concrete operations when children begin to think logically and to classify hierarchically (Marshall, 1989). Data suggest that children are able to apply these capabilities to their conceptions of self. The descriptions of characteristic attributes, behaviors, and internal states typical of preschoolers are, as children reach intermediate grades, categorized into dispositions or personality traits (Berk, 1994). When given the opportunity simply to describe themselves, school-age children are less likely to describe typical behaviors than preschoolers and more likely to emphasize competencies. The self-description of a fourth grader, for example, might include statements such as "I am good at arithmetic" or "I can play the piano" (Damon & Hart, 1988). Self-descriptions at this age also contain comparisons of self with peers, for instance, "I can ride a bike better than Joey" (Damon & Hart, 1982; Ruble, Boggiano, Feldman, & Loebl, 1980). Finally, self-descriptions during this period of development include generalizations of personal qualities or traits such as "I am smart," " I have a temper," or "I am kind to others."

The transition from childhood to adolescence is a time of dramatic changes in a person's life. The changes include self-concept and are discernible in the self-descriptions of adolescents. The categories that elementary-age children use in their self-descriptions are qualified as they enter adolescence and the middle or junior high grades. The self-categorization of "I am kind to others" by a fourth grader becomes "I am kind to most people, most of the time" in the seventh grade. The self-descriptions of adolescents indicate that their self-concept takes into account the situations they have experienced (Barenboim, 1977). One's response to others depends on many factors that change from situation to situation. Consequently, what an adolescent learns about him- or herself is that he or she is generally kind to others, but there are situations in which kindnesses are not easily given. The general sense of self that develops during adolescence is evidenced in self-descriptions that emphasize social virtues—such as kindness or cooperativeness—as well as concern for how one is viewed by others (Rosenberg, 1979).

From the preschool years through high school, what students learn about themselves culminates in a sense of identity. One's sense of identity is the extent to which one enjoys a sense of well-being, a feeling of knowing where one is going, and an inner assuredness that one will receive social recognition from those who count. Whether one develops a sense of identity depends on the overall nature of social interactions. As we will see in our examination of Erikson's theory of psychosocial development, identity is the positive resolution of the developmental crisis of adolescence. Negative resolution at this stage results in confusion about where one fits into the social fabric, a lack of a sense of identity.

The changes in self-descriptions described above can be viewed as representing three levels of self-concept: situational, categorical, and general (cf. Beane & Lipka, 1986). Preschoolers describe themselves in terms of concrete characteristics, activities, or emotions that are situationally specific. Elementary-age children create categories from the specific descriptions, thus their self-descriptions include statements of competencies. The change in self-concept from preschoolers to elementary students is a move from the specific toward the general. This pattern continues into adolescence. The self-descriptions at this stage include statements of a general sense of self. The statements, although very general, are likely to be qualified.

Point: Changes in self-descriptions suggest that students are learning to view themselves in different ways, which is one way in which *development affects learning.*

An important aspect of the development of self-concept is that as self-descriptions or perceptions change from specific to general, they also become more stable. Another way to think about the development of self-concept is that the self-perceptions of a ninth grader are more resistant to change than those of a second grader. Keeping in mind that self-concept refers to the way in which a person describes him- or herself, this means that a high school student's sense of self is not easily changed. Whether a student's sense of self is in need of change depends, of course, on whether the student views him- or herself in a positive or negative way. This evaluative aspect of a student's sense of self is what is referred to as self-esteem.

Cultural Diversity and Sense of Self

Self-esteem is one's evaluation of one's concept of his or her characteristics and competencies. A person whose self-concept includes the characteristic "solitary" may judge that characteristic to be positive or negative. Whether a person judges a characteristic to be positive (thus enhancing one's self-esteem) or negative (thus lowering one's self-esteem) depends on the personal value placed on that characteristic. Some people might value solitariness highly. Others might place no value whatsoever on that characteristic. The point is that one's self-esteem is based on his or her values; judgments about self are value judgments.

Children's self-concepts and sense of self-esteem develop in social contexts. These social contexts are influenced profoundly by cultural norms, beliefs, and values as expressed in the family and community that together define an individual's social environment.

Reflection: What personal characteristics do you value? Did you ever have a teacher who valued personal characteristics that you did not? How did that influence your relationship with that teacher?

Values are acquired from the culture in which you are raised. You will likely encounter cultural diversity—differences among people of varying cultural backgrounds—in the classrooms in which you teach. Consider, for example, the experience of Jason Lopez as he taught in his high school classroom in East Los Angeles, a classroom in which the cultural backgrounds of his students were highly diverse. Most of Jason's students valued assertiveness as a personal characteristic. One manifestation of that characteristic was direct eye contact. Jason himself had learned that teachers should make direct eye contact with students and did so with most of his students. There was one group of students in his class, however, with whom he was unable to make direct eye contact: female students of Asian heritage whose families were recent immigrants. After much effort and no success, he discussed the situation with both female and male students of Asian heritage. What he learned was that assertiveness in general, and direct eye contact in particular, were not culturally valued for females. If his female students of Asian heritage were to make eye contact, they would have felt as though they were defying his authority. Out of respect for his authority, they did not meet his eyes (Lopez, 1994).

Researchers have found that some children judge their own competencies in relation to other children. They establish their self-esteem through social comparison (Stipek & McIver, 1989). Children who use social comparison to judge their own worth place value on their standing compared with others. To illustrate, many children from the U.S. mainland use social comparisons in their self-descriptions, such as "I'm the best skater in my class," but children from Puerto Rico almost never describe themselves in relation to others (cf. Damon & Hart, 1988). As a group, Taiwanese students exhibit higher academic achievement than American children. However, American children possess higher self-esteem than the Taiwanese. In Taiwan, competition in classrooms is extremely intense; there is great pressure to achieve. Although students in Taiwan do achieve highly as a group, they also compare themselves with their classmates. Given the high level of competition, very few Taiwanese students will compare favorably with their classmates and consequently do not hold themselves in high esteem (Chiu, 1992–1993).

Reflection: What cultural values shape your self-concepts and measures of self-esteem?

The values of a child vary not only from country to country but also from cultural group to cultural group within the same country, and even within cultural groups. Because your students will not all value the same personal characteristics, and because self-esteem is based on value judgments, it will be important for you to understand the values each student brings to your classroom. Understanding cultural diversity is necessary for effective teaching as the diversity of students in our schools will continue to increase into the twenty-first century.

Connection: Learning about oneself often happens through experiences with others. Acquiring self-knowledge is examined again in Chapter 7 in relation to Bandura's concept of self-efficacy.

The Development of Self-Esteem

A person's self-concept can be clear or vague, accurate or inaccurate, realistic or unrealistic, comprehensive or incomplete (cf. Beane & Lipka, 1986). These dimensions focus on how well a person's self-concept is formed. They do not indicate whether a person feels good or bad about him- or herself. Self-esteem is a person's evaluation of his or her self-concept and, more particularly, the feelings associated with that evaluative judgment. Self-esteem is usually discussed using terms such as *high self-esteem* and *low self-esteem*. What do these phrases mean in terms of a student's feelings about him- or herself? Students with high self-esteem are basically satisfied with themselves, even though they may recognize faults or weaknesses that they hope to overcome (Rosenberg, 1979). Students with low self-esteem are not satisfied with themselves as persons; they judge their worth as a person as low.

Children begin at a young age to show their feelings about themselves; they smile when they succeed at a task and frown and might avoid eye contact with adults when they fail (Stipek, Recchia, & McClintic, 1992). Also, children often act bored if they cannot perform a task. Given the obvious relationship between self-concept and self-esteem, it is not surprising that the pattern of specific to general development of self-concept seems to hold for the development of self-esteem as well. Preschoolers make judgments about various characteristics and competencies. In essence, they form separate self-esteems that are integrated only later into a general evaluation of self (Harter, 1990). Although children develop an overall sense of self-worth, the development of self-esteem is characterized by increasing numbers of dimensions of self.

One way of investigating the self-esteem of young children is to make statements and then ask if the children agree with those statements. The difference between using this technique to investigate self-concept and self-esteem is that the latter uses statements that focus on self-evaluation. Examples of such statements include, "Most kids like me," and "I am good at homework" (Harter 1982, 1986). The results of this research suggest that children under seven years of age judge their social acceptance by how well they are liked by others and their competence by how well they can do things. If young children are questioned using pictures to supplement the verbal statements, evidence suggests that children's self-esteem is subdivided even further (Marsh, Craven, & Debus, 1991).

Around seven or eight years of age, about the time that children develop the classification capabilities associated with Piaget's concrete operations, at least three dimensions of self-esteem have developed. These dimensions include academic, physical, and social self-esteem. As children continue to gain developmental experience, these dimensions of self-esteem are refined even further. For example, a child's sense of academic self-worth may be differentiated by content areas. A child's sense of social self-worth may be judged separately in relation to peers and adults. During this period when the dimensions of self-esteem are expanding, children are also forming an overall self-evaluation (Harter, 1990). Two dynamics seem to be operating at once: A child's self-esteem is being differentiated into multiple dimensions and, an overall estimate of self-worth is being formed. The results of the operation of both dynamics during this period and the hierarchical structure of self-esteem are presented in Figure 3.1.

Critical Thinking: What are the characteristics of concrete operational thought that allow students to develop continually more refined dimensions of self-esteem?

Other dimensions are added to self-esteem as children become adolescents. Adolescents become concerned with the complexities of close friendships, same-sex, and opposite-sex relationships. Academic self-esteem becomes complicated by issues of career decisions. Physical self-esteem is influenced by physical maturation and an increased emphasis on one's appearance and attractiveness to others (Berk, 1994). Gender differences become more apparent in these and other areas during adolescence. Later in this chapter, we will encounter Gilligan's theory of moral judgment, which suggests that females and males use different criteria to evaluate right and wrong.

Example: Given what you know of Ricky Chavez in the Teacher Chronicle, how would you descibe his self-esteem, taking into account the dimensions of academic, social, and physical self-esteem?

A student's academic self-esteem is a powerful predictor of achievement and motivation (Marsh, Smith, & Barnes, 1985). Students with high social self-esteem are liked better by their peers than students with low social self-esteem (Harter, 1982). A student's self-esteem can have a significant impact on the quality of a student's experience in and out of school. In the next section, we examine how interactions with others shape one's view of self.

Reflection: How did you view yourself in elementary school with regard to academic, social, and physical dimensions? How did you view yourself in high school?

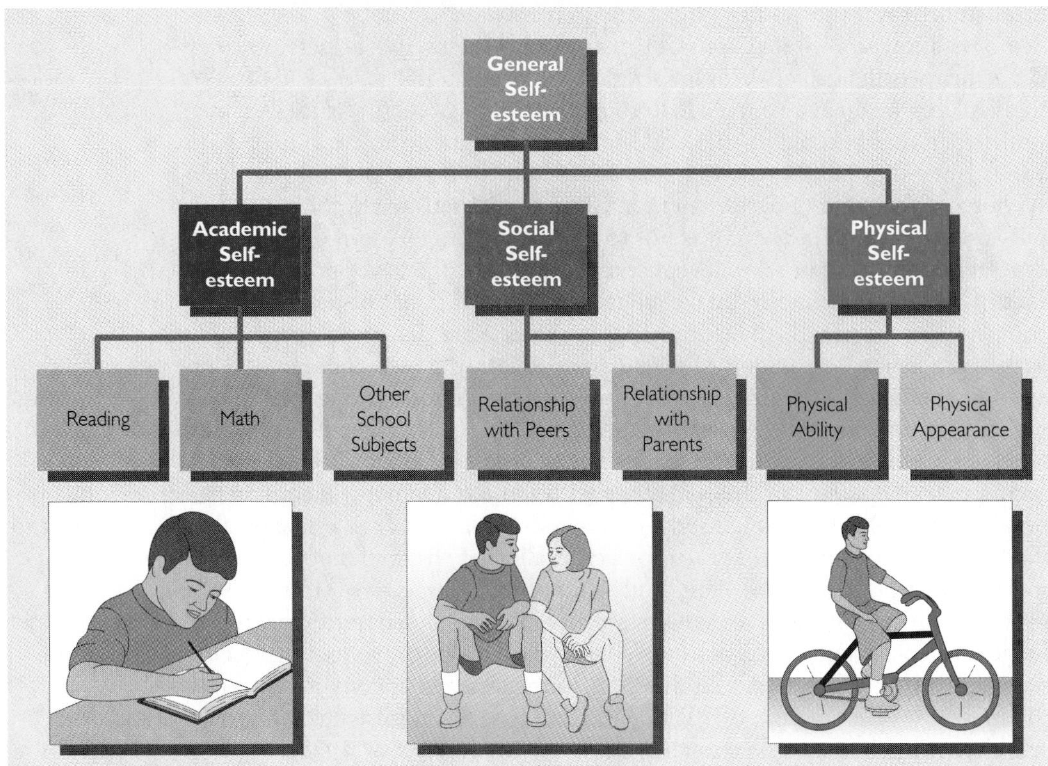

FIGURE 3.1

Hierarchial Structure of Self-Esteem for Children in Intermediate Grades
Source: From "Self-Concept: Validation of Construct Interpretations" by R. Shavelson, J.J. Hubner, & J.C. Stanton, 1976, *Review of Educational Research*, 46, 407–441. Reprinted by permission.

Connection: One's social environment—other people—provides potential models. The perceived competence of the models can influence one's self-esteem. This relationship is described in detail in Chapter 7.

Reflection: Identify messages other people communicate to you that make you feel good about yourself. How might you use similar messages to support the self-esteem of your students?

HOW DOES SOCIAL INTERACTION INFLUENCE PERSONAL GROWTH?

The hierarchical structure of self-esteem grows more complex as students grow older. One reason for this increase in complexity is that development is accompanied by an expanding social environment. Very young children have a fairly small social environment. When a child starts preschool, day care, and eventually, school, the social environment expands. As children get older and become adolescents, peers become more and more important. The interactions with the other people that constitute one's social environment provide challenges and experiences that influence one's self-esteem. Indeed, the development and/or the enhancement of one's self-esteem cannot be accomplished in isolation. As Damon (1991) puts it: "One cannot 'find' self-esteem in isola-

Insights ON SUCCESSFUL PRACTICE

What approaches have you used successully to help students improve academic achievement through positive self-image and higher self-esteem?

To promote the building of self-esteem among my second graders, I have used a "Student of the Week" program. At the beginning of the year, I assign each child a special week. A letter goes home to the family explaining what the special week means. Children look forward to it, and meanwhile the child and his or her family can be making plans for each day of that week.

During his or her special week, the student leads the class in morning exercises, posts the calendar date, conducts "Show and Tell" and "Daily News," and serves as "Line Leader," "Messenger," and classroom assistant for distributing materials. The Student of the Week has a special bulletin board to decorate with baby pictures and family photographs and has the opportunity to tell the class about the photos. The student also has a special table set aside on which to display and demonstrate favorite toys, souvenirs, collections, hobbies, or crafts. During the week, the student is encouraged to read one of his or her favorite books to the class, play a favorite record-book, and tell favorite jokes or riddles.

Students of the Week can make arrangements to bring pets to school to show the class and tell all about them. The children can also invite visitors to the classroom—family members, friends, or neighbors—to tell about their jobs or show slides or demonstrate a craft or hobby.

Students of the Week can bring a treat to pass out to the class and are encouraged to bring treats that they and their family have made together. This year, I added a new component to the program. I take the Student of the Week out to lunch.

In my twenty years of teaching, I have found that this program has always done a lot to increase each child's self-esteem, not only during the special week but also in the anticipation and planning stages and in the involvement of the family.

NANCI MAES, Riverview Elementary School
Wautoma, Wisconsin

tion from one's relations to others because it does not exist apart from those relations" (p. 17). Other people have a powerful influence on our sense of self. One way to think about this is to say that one's psychological development is affected by one's social environment.

What other benefits might "Student of the Week" have for students in inclusive, culturally diverse schools? How might this activity be integrated into the curriculum and used in assessment?

psychosocial development According to Erikson, the process whereby relationships with others influence one's search for his or her own identity.

Erikson's Theory of Psychosocial Development

Erik Erikson developed an important theory about the impact of one's social environment on one's psychological development. His theory of **psychosocial development** emphasizes how relationships with others influence one's search for his or her identity. By virtue of our cultural traditions, teachers occupy a potentially important position in the lives of young people. Teachers not only establish relationships with students but also influence the environment in which relationships between students are established. Erikson's theory gives us

TABLE 3.1 Erikson's Eight Stages of Psychosocial Development

Stages	Approximate Age	Important Event	Description
1. Basic trust vs. basic mistrust	Birth to 12–18 months	Feeding	The infant must form a first loving, trusting relationship with the caregiver, or develop a sense of mistrust.
2. Autonomy vs. shame/doubt	18 months to 3 years	Toilet training	The child's energies are directed toward the development of physical skills, including walking, grasping, and sphincter control. The child learns control but may develop shame and doubt if not handled well.
3. Initiative vs. guilt	3 to 6 years	Independence	The child continues to become more assertive and to take more initiative, but may be too forceful, leading to guilt feelings.
4. Industry vs. inferiority	6 to 12 years	School	The child must deal with demands to learn new skills or risk a sense of inferiority, failure, and incompetence.
5. Identity vs. role confusion	Adolescence	Peer relationships	The teenager must achieve a sense of identity in occupation, sex roles, politics, and religion
6. Intimacy vs. isolation	Young adulthood	Love relationships	The young adult must develop intimate relationships or suffer feelings of isolation.
7. Generativity vs. stagnation	Middle adulthood	Parenting	Each adult must find some way to satisfy and support the next generation.
8. Ego integrity vs. despair	Late adulthood	Reflection on and acceptance of one's life	The culmination is a sense of acceptance of oneself as one is and feeling fulfilled.

Source: From *Psychology* (4th ed., p. 350) by L. A. Lefton, 1991, Needham Heights, MA: Allyn & Bacon. Copyright 1991 by Allyn & Bacon. Reprinted by permission.

a way of understanding how the relationships young people build influence their sense of identity.

critical periods Each one of Erikson's eight stages of psychosocial development; each stage identifies the emergence of a part of an individual's personality.

developmental crisis According to Erikson, there is a conflict faced at each stage of psychological development. The way the crisis is resolved has a lasting effect on the person's self-concept and view of society in general.

Erikson's theory of psychosocial development focuses on the tasks our culture sets before an individual at various points along the continuum of development. The eight stages postulated in Erikson's theory are summarized in Table 3.1.

Erikson's stage theory describes and explains the development of the human personality. Erikson viewed psychosocial growth as consisting of **critical periods** when the "parts" of the individual's personality develop. It is these critical periods that define Erikson's eight stages of psychosocial development. Each stage identifies the emergence of a part of an individual's personality.

Each stage in Erikson's framework is structured as a dichotomy (e.g., trust versus mistrust, intimacy versus isolation), indicating the positive and negative consequences for each stage. Each dichotomy defines a **developmental crisis**, a psychosocial issue that will be resolved in either a positive or negative way. The resolution of each developmental crisis will have a lasting effect on the person's view of him- or herself and of society in general. What follows are brief descriptions of the developmental crises associated with the different stages in Erikson's theory.

Stage 1: Trust versus Mistrust (birth–18 months). If the interactions infants have with the other people in their environment are positive, then the infant will learn that people in their environment can be trusted. According to Erikson (1963), an outcome of trust is the result of consistent experiences over time. If the constancy of interaction between the infant and others meets the basic needs of the infant, then trust is developed. If, however, the interactions lack warmth and caring and the basic needs of the infant go unsatisfied, the developmental crisis is resolved in a negative way. The infant will learn to mistrust those around him or her.

Critical Thinking: Compare the concept of critical periods with Vygotsky's zone of proximal development (ZPD), described in Chapter 2. Would knowledge of a student's stage of psychosocial development help you identify that student's ZPD? Why or why not?

Stage 2: Autonomy versus Shame and Doubt (18 months–3 years). The developmental crisis at this stage occurs as the child enters toddlerhood. It is important for the toddler to explore his or her environment in an effort to establish some independence from parents. The toddler, who is now less dependent on others, seeks to develop a sense of independence and freedom through such exploration. If the child is encouraged to discover what is inside the book on the shelf, if his or her attempts to dress are uninterrupted, if the mess made while pouring cereal is tolerated, the crisis will more likely be resolved in the direction of **autonomy**, a sense of independence. If the toddler's exploration and attempts to be independent are discouraged, he or she will likely feel ashamed of these efforts, and develop doubts about his or her ability to deal with the environment. A parent or caregiver who is unable to allow the toddler to make mistakes, to persist, and to make further mistakes manifests the kinds of interactions that lead to a negative resolution of the developmental crisis of learning autonomy at this stage.

Try This: Observe the behavior of primary grade students. See if you can infer from their behavior those who have a sense of industry and those who have a sense of inferiority. Share your observations with the teacher in order to check the accuracy of your impressions.

Stage 3: Initiative versus Guilt (3–6 years). During this stage, children are attempting to develop a sense of initiative, that they are operators on the environment. According to Erikson, **initiative** "adds to autonomy the quality of undertaking, planning, and attacking a task for the sake of being active and on the move" (1963, p. 225). The child's imaginative play often allows the child to imitate adults in performing various tasks. If you have ever seen a child pretend to read or "fix" a clock or "nurse" the family dog, you have seen evidence of the child's attempt to undertake grown-up tasks. It is during this period that children typically learn to identify and imitate same-sex models. Exploration in play during this period is as important as it was during the previous stage. Given the increased linguistic abilities of preschool children, their explorations often take the form of questions to adults. If their interactions and explorations during play are encouraged, if their questions are recognized and answered sincerely, positive resolution of the developmental crisis is more likely. If the child's efforts to explore or his or her questions are treated as a nuisance, the child may feel guilty about "getting in the way."

Stage 4: Industry versus Inferiority (6–12 years). As the child enters school and advances through the elementary grades, the developmental crisis focuses on the child's ability to win recognition through performance. The notion that elementary students need generous encouragement and praise for their accomplishments is consistent with Erikson's view of psychosocial development at this stage. People in education know the importance of early success in school. The child who is encouraged to complete tasks and who receives praise for his or her performance is likely to develop a sense of **industry**, an eagerness to produce. If the child does not experience success—if his or her efforts are treated as unworthy and intrusive—the child will develop a sense of inferiority.

autonomy Independence. Autonomy versus shame and doubt marks Stage 2 of Erikson's theory of psychosocial development.

initiative The quality of undertaking, planning, and attacking a new task. Initiative versus guilt characterizes Stage 3 of Erikson's theory of psychosocial development.

industry An eagerness to produce. Industry versus inferiority typifies Stage 4 of Erikson's theory of psychosocial development.

During the industry-versus-inferiority stage of psychosocial development, children need to gain self-confidence through successful performance. Self-confidence grows through others' recognition of successes based on personal effort, productivity, and persistence.

Reflection: Which of Erikson's stages of psychosocial development best describes you?

Point: Erikson's view of psychosocial development supports the point that *development is complex and multifaceted.*

identity A sense of well-being, a feeling of knowing where one is going, and an inner assuredness of anticipated recognition from those who count. Identity versus role diffusion characterizes Stage 5 of Erikson's theory of psychosocial development.

role diffusion The negative outcome of Stage 5 of Erikson's theory of psychosocial development, whereby an adolescent is unable to develop a clear sense of self.

intimacy The state of having a close psychological relationship with another person. Intimacy versus isolation is Stage 6 of Erikson's theory of psychosocial development.

isolation Failure to establish a close psychological relationship with another person leads to this feeling of being alone. The negative outcome of Stage 6 of Erikson's theory of psychosocial development.

Stage 5: Identity versus Role Diffusion (adolescence). The developmental crisis of adolescence centers on the youth's attempt to discover his or her identity—to identify those things about himself or herself that are unique. For Erikson, **identity** "is experienced merely as a sense of psychosocial well-being . . . a feeling of being at home in one's body, a sense of 'knowing where one is going,' and an inner assuredness of anticipated recognition from those who count" (1968, p. 165). An important aspect of an adolescent's sense of identity is his or her choice of occupation (Marcia, 1980). Reflect on the groups, or cliques, from your own high school. Did not most members of any particular clique share similar aspirations about careers, if not about identical occupations?

Another important contributor to the adolescent's sense of identity is his or her emerging sexuality (Marcia, 1980). Adolescence is the period of puberty, dramatic physical maturation, and an increase in relationships with those of the opposite sex. If the nature of the adolescent's interactions supports the sense of who he or she is, the resolution of the developmental crisis is positive. A positive resolution instills a sense of self-confidence and stability; whether fulfilling the roles of friend, child, student, leader, boyfriend, or girlfriend, the adolescent feels at ease. Negative experiences that do not allow a student to integrate his or her various social roles into a unitary, stable view of self lead to a sense of diffusion. The adolescent who feels torn apart by what he or she perceives as inconsistent expectations exhibits **role diffusion.**

Stage 6: Intimacy versus Isolation (young adulthood). The young adult's personality—stemming from his or her sense of self—is influenced by efforts to establish an **intimacy**, a close psychosocial relationship, with another person. Typically, this is the period when a young adult who has just finished his or her education or training strikes out on his or her own to begin work and establish a life away from the childhood family. Among young adults, the need for intimate relationships can be seen at any number of places: work, health clubs, singles bars, church functions, athletic teams, recreation groups. Many young adults who are interviewing for jobs in a new town take into account the town's supply of eligible partners. Failure to establish a close relationship with another leads to a sense of **isolation**, a feeling of being alone.

Stage 7: Generativity versus Stagnation (young adulthood–middle age). Erikson identifies **generativity** as a concern for future generations. Childbearing and nurturing occupy the thoughts and feelings of people at this stage in the life span. Many people who decide against having a family and raising children are concerned with questions about their role regarding future generations. The classic career-versus-family decision reflects the developmental crisis that epitomizes this stage. Unsuccessful resolution leads to a sense of stagnation, the feeling that one's life is at a dead end.

Stage 8: Integrity versus Despair (later adulthood–old age). According to Erikson, **integrity** is a sense of understanding how one fits into one's culture and accepting that one's place is unique and unalterable. An inability to accept one's sense of self at this stage leads to despair—the feeling that time is too short and that alternate roads to integrity are no longer open.

This summary of Erikson's stages has highlighted the dichotomies that make up each developmental crisis. Although each dichotomy describes well the nature of the crisis to be resolved, it is a mistake to assume that each crisis will be resolved in favor of either the positive or negative qualities of the dichotomy. A student's personality contains positive and negative qualities. Positive resolution of any developmental crisis simply means that the positive quality of that stage is present to a greater degree than the negative quality.

Marcia's Work on Identity Statuses

James Marcia's work on the different types of identity—called **identity statuses**—is among the best known work derived from Erikson's own. Marcia was interested in conducting empirical research based on Erikson's theory. During interviews with male adolescents, Marcia explored concerns and opinions regarding occupational choice, sexuality, religion, and personal value systems (1967). As a result of his analysis of these interviews, Marcia proposed four identity statuses:

1. Identity diffusion types
2. Moratorium types
3. Identity achievement types
4. Foreclosure types

Identity Diffusion. A young person who is unable to commit to decisions and who is unable to postpone decisions by declaring a psychosocial moratorium may seek another solution to the developmental crisis—a solution that Erikson (1968) called a negative identity, an aspect of **identity diffusion.**

> The loss of a sense of identity is often expressed in a scornful and snobbish hostility toward the roles offered as proper and desirable in one's family or immediate community. Any aspect of the required role, or all of it—be it masculinity or femininity, nationality or class membership—can become the main focus of the young person's acid disdain. (pp. 172–173)

Young people who adopt a *negative identity* are often those who rebel against authority—parents and teachers. According to Marcia, identity diffusion also describes adolescents who avoid thinking about life-style decisions. Typically,

generativity A sense of concern for future generations, expressed through childbearing or concern about creating a better world. Generativity versus stagnation marks Stage 7 of Erikson's theory of psychosocial development.

integrity A sense of understanding how one fits into one's culture and the acceptance that one's place is unique and unalterable. Integrity versus despair marks Stage 8 of Erikson's theory of psychosocial development.

identity statuses Different types of identity, as identified by Marcia.

identity diffusion To Marcia, adolescents who avoid thinking about life-style decisions and are unable to develop a clear sense of self.

Try This: Interview college students to discover if they experienced a period during which they adopted a *negative identity.* What were the social ramifications? Academic ramifications? What can you infer about respondents' identity statuses?

they are disorganized; they act impulsively; they are not goal-oriented. They often avoid commitment to schoolwork or to interpersonal relationships.

Moratorium. The urgency of identity decisions can overwhelm some young adolescents. Rather than deal with life-style decisions they are not prepared to make, they enter a state Erikson called psychosocial **moratorium.** A psychosocial moratorium is a suspension of any decisions that commit the adolescent to a certain occupational or social role. The adolescent buys time. A moratorium period that is used to gain new experiences, to taste adventure, can often contribute to sound decisions when the moratorium ends.

According to Marcia, moratorium types have given thought to identity issues but have not reached any decisions. Their relationships are often intense but usually short-lived. They seem distracted a good deal of the time. It is not unusual for moratorium types to try on a negative identity for a short time before adopting the status of identity achievement.

Identity Achievement. **Identity achievement** is ascribed to those who have made life-style decisions, although not in all areas. For example, a young woman might decide, against the advice of her parents, to pursue a medical career. The same young woman may still be confused about sexuality, but she is determined about her occupational choice. The decisions made by identity achievement types are their own; they have not simply followed the advice of parents, teachers, or counselors. Identity achievement types may not have all the answers, but they have made some decisions that give their development direction.

Point: Emotional baggage influences a child's behavior, self-esteem, and motivation in the classroom, which supports the point that *development affects learning.*

Foreclosure. Adolescents who adopt a **foreclosure** form of identity avoid crises by simply accepting the decisions made for them by others. Often, the decisions they accept were made by their parents. It is typical of foreclosure types to make—or perhaps more appropriately, adopt—their decisions early. With no decisions to make, the crises of identity are averted.

moratorium According to Marcia, adolescents who have given thought to identity issues but have not reached any decisions.

identity achievement According to Marcia, adolescents who have made life-style decisions, although not in all areas.

foreclosure According to Marcia, adolescents who simply accept the decisions made for them by others. These decisions are often made by their parents.

The Significance of Developmental Crises for Teachers

A teacher who is knowledgeable about developmental crises will be alert to the kinds of emotional baggage students might carry into the classroom. Imagine that a fifth-grade teacher learns through a parent conference that one of her students never receives encouragement at home, that the child is viewed as a bother. The teacher might then observe the child carefully for a sense of inferiority, hypothesizing that the child needs to experience success and to receive praise to offset that effect.

Some research suggests the use of caution when interpreting a student's psychosocial well-being in terms of Erikson's stages. One reason is the suggestion that Erikson's stages are better descriptions of personality development in males than in females. During the industry-versus-inferiority period, for example, females appear to be concerned not only with achievement but also with interpersonal relationships (cf. Marcia, 1980). Carol Gilligan (1982) suggests that during adolescence, young women deal with the crisis of intimacy as well as with the crisis of identity.

Another point to keep in mind when making judgments based on Erikson's stages is that the crises that begin in toddlerhood and continue through the preschool, elementary, and middle school years are quite similar. The crises of autonomy, initiative, and industry all stress the need for independence and encouragement. Classroom tasks that allow students to succeed and that result in recognition for accomplishment are as critical for sixth graders who are working through the crisis of industry as for preschoolers who are working through the crisis of initiative.

Critical Thinking: Some students may be perceived as experiencing negative resolutions, which raises the question, "Is a teacher's perception of a student important to the student's learning?"

In summary, Erikson's theory suggests several ways in which teachers can facilitate healthy psychosocial development in their students. The suggestions listed in Here's How are possible actions that teachers might take.

here's how

Here's How to Help Students Develop Positive Self-Concepts

- Use the dichotomies as a basis for interpreting your observations of students. For instance, does a child's behavior indicate a lack of industry? A sense of inferiority? Confusion about his or her future?
- Look for or design opportunities that encourage independent action on the part of students. For example, you might have students interview other students, parents, other teachers, and/or friends outside of school on some appropriate topic.
- Reward independent efforts. Using the interview example, even if the interview is not particularly fruitful, you can praise the effort it took to conduct the interview. While discussing reasons why an interview was not successful, you can point out that the student's efforts have provided a learning opportunity that would not have existed.
- Recognize that gender differences may exist. Specifically, keep in mind that research suggests that females may be as concerned with interpersonal relationships as they are with achievement. This difference should be taken into account when interpreting observations of student behavior.
- Use parent conferences to determine whether and in what ways students are encouraged at home.

The Importance of Parental Involvement

Current efforts to reform or restructure schools include ways to work with families in the education of their children (Elam, Rose, & Gallup, 1992). Schools in the twenty-first century will not be places for only students and teachers. Parents and community members will be involved as well. Other adults can be a tremendous asset to teachers, especially in their efforts to enhance the self-esteem of their students.

Although school is an important part of a student's social environment, home and community must be considered just as important. If family members can be recruited as coworkers in an effort to enhance a student's self-esteem, the probability of success increases significantly. How then, can you recruit parents to join the effort?

Insights ON SUCCESSFUL PRACTICE

What do you do to create a social environment in which students can develop positive self-concepts and positive peer relations?

As the former director and teacher of a program for gifted high school students, I learned that many very bright, sensitive, talented students struggle academically, socially, and emotionally. School was not necessarily an enjoyable place to be for these students, some of whom developed serious personal problems, failed their courses, or dropped out.

I developed a program to motivate the underachievers and to help the achievers deal with the stress that comes from their own and others' high expectations of them. I set up noon-hour discussion groups to bring them together—achievers and nonachievers, affluent and low-income, the ever-popular and those who struggle socially. They met in groups of ten to discuss the "burdens of capability."

The program was a success. Discovering their commonalities, the students could drop their adolescent facades, break down stereotypes, and share personal and school issues as mere human beings. They could relate to and learn from each other. They gained skills in articulating personal concerns, learned to support each other, achieved greater self-awareness, and at the same time affirmed their gifts. I believe we all left each meeting feeling more motivated, and more at peace with ourselves.

JEAN SUNDE PETERSON, Retired,
Coralville, Iowa

Why should teachers be concerned about students' affective and social needs? What other student groups might benefit from discussion groups of this kind? What else might you do to help students develop positive social relations?

Try This: Brainstorm specific ways of learning about students at the grade level you plan to teach.

One way to approach parent recruitment is to be proactive. Garlett (1993) argues that proactive teachers will make certain that "parents know (1) the curriculum being taught and the methods being used to teach; (2) the class rules and regulations, including the consequences of breaking class rules; and (3) the value that the uniqueness of each child adds to the classroom." The last of the three pieces of information will be the most difficult to provide. It may be difficult for some teachers to provide because it requires reflection and careful writing, or because some teachers have difficulty finding the special delights of each student. Recall the teacher's response to Ricky Chavez in the Teacher Chronicle at the beginning of this chapter. In similar cases, teachers must find opportunities to learn more about those students. Persistence in such instances will help you find the special qualities of each student. Once found, those qualities can become the building blocks for enhancement of self-esteem. Opportunities to learn about students come to teachers in a variety of ways, many of them unexpected.

If values are the basis of self-esteem and if families are the primary shapers of values, then teachers who want to know the values of their students should get to know their students' families. Visiting the homes of your students is an excellent way to learn about their values. In many instances, however, such visits may prove impractical. If you can't go to the parents or caregivers, then invite them to school. Many parents do not visit schools, even though teachers issue an invitation. However, persistence and explicitness can improve parent participation. Use letters, phone calls, and face-to-face conferences or meetings to say something like the following to parents:

- "Visit our classroom on your way to work."
- "Have lunch with us in the cafeteria."
- "Come join us for our music rehearsal."
- "Check out library books with us when we visit the library." (Garlett, 1993)

Parents or caregivers can be invited to class presentations, either as observers or assessors. Parents can be invited to serve as academic coaches, career consultants, volunteer aides, tutors, field trip or other class activity chaperones, or class videographers, for example.

If parents or caregivers gain knowledge about your classroom, they can better help their children function there. If you meet parents or caregivers, you can better understand the values that your students use as the basis for their self-evaluations. Understanding how students judge themselves will help you structure activities that will contribute to increased self-esteem.

Key Socioemotional Issues at Different Grade Levels

Groups are different from individuals. Remember Ricky Chavez in the Teacher Chronicle at the beginning of this chapter. Before he walked into Mr. McKissack's class, the teacher had already formed an opinion of him. Mr. McKissack's knowledge of Ricky was stereotypic. A *stereotype* is the impression one has of a person based on that person's group. If we look closely enough, all students turn out to be different from our stereotypes of them. Knowing what is typical of a group of students does not inform a teacher about the unique qualities that each individual brings into the classroom. Nevertheless, knowledge of what is considered typical is helpful. By understanding the types of social and emotional issues that your students are likely to encounter, you will be more effective in facilitating their personal and interpersonal growth. As you read, keep in mind that students encounter issues as individuals. Helping students deal with developmental issues requires more than knowledge of their developmental stage. To help, teachers must know their students as individuals.

Reflection: Reflect on the ways in which you have used stereotypic knowledge in dealing with people.

Gender Roles in the Elementary Grades. The primary grades offer the child a number of challenges: achieving in school, establishing new peer relationships, and developing a new independence from family. With their new roles, primary graders are broadening their self-concepts.

An important social issue for young students is meeting the expectations of society. One area in which society communicates its expectations, for better or for worse, is how one's gender should influence one's behavior. Students acquire these expectations through a process called gender role socialization. The socialization process yields knowledge of society's expectations regarding gender-appropriate behavior. The knowledge students acquire is called **gender role stereotypes.** Research indicates that primary-grade children typically have acquired knowledge about society's expectations for the roles of each sex (Wynn & Fletcher, 1987).

gender role stereotypes Commonly held expectations about the roles of each sex.

Parents have taught their children behaviors that are appropriate for boys and for girls before these children reach the primary grades (Grossman & Grossman,

1994). One way parents teach is through the toys they give their children. Parents tend to provide their children with gender-appropriate toys (Sidorowicz & Lunney, 1980). Parents also interact with their children in ways that communicate their aspirations for their children. Parents encourage achievement, independence, competition, and control of emotions in boys. Daughters are encouraged to be warm, dependent, and nurturing (Bempechat, 1990; Block, 1983; O'Brien & Huston, 1985).

Try This: Visit a day care center or preschool to observe young children at play. What evidence of gender role stereotpyes can you infer from behavioral and verbal interaction?

Other children reinforce gender role stereotypes. Gender role stereotypes are often reflected in cooperative play. Preschoolers are likely to praise and to join in their peers' sex-appropriate behavior and to criticize what they perceive as sex-inappropriate behavior (Eagly, 1987; Fagot, 1977, 1985; Langlois & Downs, 1980; Shepherd-Look, 1982).

Elementary students are well versed in the language of gender role stereotypes. Whether these stereotypes will continue to be reinforced or not depends, in part, on teachers' responses to student behavior. For example, gender role stereotypes suggest that girls are more likely to request assistance than boys (Brutsaert, 1990; Stewart & Corbin, 1988). A teacher who wishes to combat stereotypes will take care to provide assistance to girls only when it is truly needed. Responding to requests from a female student who is quite capable of completing a task on her own reinforces dependence. Here's How provides some additional ideas for correcting stereotypical beliefs held by students (Grossman & Grossman, 1994).

here's how

Here's How to Encourage Gender Equity

- Reward young students for playing with toys and engaging in activities that are nontraditional. (Example: Praise boys for playing with dolls and girls for building models.)
- Expose students to nonsexist roles and instructional materials. (Example: Avoid materials in which women are portrayed only in stereotypic roles or in which they are "invisible.")
- Use nonstereotypic role models as guest speakers. (Example: Invite female engineers and male nurses to speak with your students about their careers.)
- Design units that allow students to participate in nonstereotypic ways; at the secondary level, recruit students into courses in nontraditional patterns. (Example: Encourage males in a food and nutrition unit and females in a mechanics unit.)
- Reduce the documented dominance of males over females in mixed-gender groups (see Scott, Dwyer, & Lieb-Brilhart, 1985; Women's Educational Equity Program, 1983). (Example: Use cooperative learning groups in which the rights and obligations of each member are clear and in which roles are not stereotypically assigned. For instance, the group recorder role should be shared by males and females.)

growth spurt A dramatic increase in height and weight that signals the onset of puberty.

puberty The time of physical change during which individuals become sexually mature.

Puberty and Peer Relationships in the Secondary Grades. Toward the end of the elementary grades, the **growth spurt**, a dramatic increase in height and weight that signals the onset of **puberty**, begins to occur (cf. Dusek, 1987). The social implications of this growth spurt, which may occur in some students as early as fifth grade, reverberate through the junior high grades and into high school.

Because girls mature more quickly than boys, and because, in both sexes, there is considerable variability in physical maturation, some junior high students appear quite mature while others do not. Because appearance is an important aspect of social and emotional experience, the wide-ranging differences can cause problems for students in these grades.

As suggested in Chapter 2, an issue that some junior high school students face is the social consequences of early or late physical maturation. Most girls complete their growth spurt around the seventh grade. The growth spurt for boys is usually not completed before the eighth or ninth grade (Tanner, 1978a, 1978b). Within each sex, there is a wide variation in maturation rates. Early-maturing girls, therefore, can be as much as four or five years ahead of late-maturing boys.

Because early and late maturation have significant effects on the social life of students, teachers should be prepared to help students deal with some of the problems they will face. This is especially true for early-maturing females and late-maturing males. How might teachers be helpful?

- Avoid using physical characteristics (such as height) to group students for activities.
- Expose students to role models who demonstrate that physical size, maturity, or lack of physical disabilities is not a prerequisite for accomplishment.
- Use cooperative learning techniques that stress contributions to the group instead of individual performance. (This item is addressed later in the chapter in relation to the integrative model of moral education.)
- Encourage students to participate in the establishment of classroom rules and procedures that address people's sensitivities to being treated as different.

Reflection: How does your body image affect you? How did you view yourself as an adolescent? A child? In what ways might you be sensitive to your students as they develop physically and mature?

Critical Thinking: Sarah towered above her middle school classmates. Although she was well liked, she felt awkward and uncomfortable. Her work and attitude began to slip. Then a long-term substitute teacher—a very tall woman—took over Sarah's math class. As Sarah spent time talking with the new teacher, her grades picked up and the smile returned to her face. Why did Sarah's contact with this teacher help?

WHAT SOCIAL PROBLEMS AFFECT STUDENTS' SCHOOL LIVES?

Many of the social problems that exist in our society place students at risk of failing in school. Some of those problems deny students the measure of security and comfort that most of us need to pursue our goals. Other problems threaten our health and safety. For teachers to understand the needs of their students, they must first understand the problems their students face. Consider how the problems discussed below might affect the behavior of students who face those problems.

Risks to Security and Comfort

The number of adolescents who experience family stress has increased. Family stress is introduced by many conditions, such as separation, divorce, and remarriage; single parenthood; birth of a sibling; illness, disability, or death of a family member; loss of income; and poverty. At a time when the adolescent is struggling to develop a sense of identity, turmoil within the family can make the task more difficult.

Consider the circumstances of a student who is temporarily living in a shelter for homeless persons. Now, compare the homeless student with another student who lives in an affluent suburb. Which of the two students is most likely to succeed in school? Which is most likely to experience difficulties? Because there are more factors that augur against success for the homeless student, we could say that the homeless student is at risk. **Students at risk** is a phrase much used by educators and the general public, but it is not clearly defined. Generally, the phrase "refers to students who perform or behave poorly in school and appear likely to fail or fall short of their potential" (Hallahan & Kauffman, 1994, p. 21). Just as a person who smokes too much, avoids exercise, and eats too much saturated fat is at risk of a heart attack, so too is a student who has no home, receives inadequate nourishment, and suffers from bouts of depression at risk of failing in school.

Connection: Students at risk are discussed in Chapter 5.

Therefore, some of the factors that place students at risk of failure are the circumstances of their lives, such as homelessness, poverty, or a dysfunctional family. Poor life circumstances often deny children and adolescents opportunities to develop and grow normally. In some cases, however, life circumstances can cause more than just developmental delays. Imagine a dysfunctional family, rich or poor, in which the parents are addicted to crack cocaine. A child born to an addict of crack cocaine (a "crack baby") faces problems ranging from neurological damage to organ dysfunction to general irritability or distractability. Severely detrimental life circumstances can lead to physical or psychological disability.

Critical Thinking: How might Erikson have defined students who are at risk?

The accommodation of disabilities in the learning environment is an important aspect of teaching and one to which we will return shortly. Physical disabilities, include hearing or visual impairments, traumatic head injury, spina bifida, and acquired immunodeficiency syndrome (AIDS), among others. Psychological disabilities include emotional or behavioral disorders, communication disorders, mental retardation, and learning disabilities.

Connection: Students with special needs and exceptional learners are discussed in Chapter 5.

There are also temporary situations that might place a student at risk of performing or behaving poorly, at least for the short term. Think about a student whose family moves to a new city, a new neighborhood, a new school. Starting at a new school can be traumatic for a student. Although the student will likely adjust to the new setting, eventually make new friends, and begin to feel comfortable in his or her new surroundings, it may take some time. Until the student has adjusted, however, the student is at risk.

It is important to remember that students who live in the best of circumstances and who have no disability can also be at risk of performing or behaving poorly in school, even if they are at risk for only a relatively short period. Every experienced teacher knows that events in their students' lives can influence their actions and accomplishments in the classroom.

Consider the case of Charlie, a nine-year-old who had to change schools in the middle of the academic year (Brodkin & Coleman, 1994). Charlie's father lost his job, and his family had to sell their home and move in with relatives. His new teacher expected Charlie to have some difficulties just after his arrival, but as time went by, he isolated himself from the other students more and more. At the same time, he made very little effort to complete his schoolwork. Charlie was clearly at risk. If his father remains unemployed and the family is unable to get back on its feet, then Charlie's circumstances might persist. If, however, circumstances change and Charlie's family becomes independent once again, this episode will be transitory. Either way, Charlie is at risk now and his teacher is looking for ways to help him in this period of transition.

students at risk Students whose life circumstances make them more likely to fail in school

Adele Brodkin and Melba Coleman (1994) suggest several ways in which Charlie's teacher might be able to help him. Some of the suggestions for helping Charlie include those listed in the following Here's How.

here's how

Here's How to Help Students when They Are at Risk

- Enlist a buddy—the teacher can assign a classmate, who can be relied upon, to be Charlie's buddy, to include Charlie in games on the playground, and generally "show Charlie the ropes."
- Empathize out loud—the teacher can let Charlie know, in a casual way, that he or she understands how hard it is to leave friends from his old school. The teacher might also reassure Charlie that he will soon make new friends and that the teacher is already one of those new friends.
- Assign responsibilities—the teacher can give Charlie jobs, such as playground helper, safety guard, or ball monitor.
- Cooperative learning—the teacher can take this opportunity to form new cooperative learning groups so that Charlie will not work alone and will share with classmates the experience of assimilating into a new group and learning the group's norms.
- Parent involvement—the teacher should take care not to infringe on the family's privacy or to offend their pride, but the parents can be informed of opportunities for them to become involved at school. The parents can be invited to share their hobbies with the class, tutor individuals or a small group, or accompany the class on field trips. Charlie's parents can be invited to help other parents coach sports teams, assist in the computer lab or library, call the parents of absent students, or help with school beautification projects.
- Selected book lists—the teacher can consult with the school librarian to generate a list of books and resources for Charlie's parents that would help them understand how their son's problems have placed him at risk. One such book is *My Daddy Don't Go to Work* by Madeena Spray Nolan (published by CarolRhoda, 1978).

Try This: Find and read several of the "Kids in Crisis" columns in *Instructor* magazine. What are the causes of the crises faced by the students profiled? What conditions placed the students at-risk? How did teachers and others help the students overcome their difficulties?

Although there are special education programs available for some students, you will need to consider ways of helping all students in your classroom through tough times. A common sentiment expressed by many experienced teachers is, "Every student is at risk at one time or another during the school years."

Risks to Health and Safety

There are other risks to school success that derive from physical conditions or injury. Some of these conditions are caused at the hands of others (e.g., an abusive adult), and some are self-imposed.

One physical condition that has reached high proportions is traumatic head injury (Bigge, 1991). The most frequent causes of traumatic head injury are automobile accidents, in many of which young children were not properly restrained or in which older passengers did not wear seat belts, and motorcycle and bicycle accidents, in many of which the cyclists were not wearing protective headgear. Tragically, violence—including gunshot wounds and child abuse—is another major cause of traumatic head injury (Hallahan & Kauffman, 1994).

Point: The risks to security, comfort, health, and safety that affect students' lives illustrate the point that *life conditions affect development.*

The disabilities that result from traumatic head injury vary from temporary to permanent and from mild to severe. The symptoms most associated with traumatic head injury include cognitive difficulties such as inability to focus or maintain attention, inability to remember information or learn new information, and inability to organize and think abstractly. These cognitive difficulties often make it hard for injured students to re-establish social relationships. The effects of traumatic head or brain injury are not always immediately seen. In some cases the effects may not become apparent for months or even years after the initial injury (Allison, 1992). Of those who receive serious traumatic brain injury, about half will require special education programs. The half that returns to the general classroom will likely require special accommodation if they are to succeed (Mira & Tyler, 1991).

While traumatic head injury is one effect of child abuse, other conditions can be traced to this altogether too common social problem. Public Law 93-247 defines child abuse and neglect as "physical or mental injury, sexual abuse, negligent treatment, or maltreatment of a child under the age of 18 by a person responsible for the child's welfare under circumstances which indicate that the child's health or welfare is harmed or threatened." The consequences of abuse include permanent neurological damage, skeletal and facial deformity, sensory impairment, or death. The intensity with which such injuries are inflicted inevitably causes psychological disorders as well (Hallahan & Kauffman, 1994).

The life circumstances of many children and youths are associated with patterns of abuse and neglect. It has been estimated that in as many as half of all cases of serious child abuse or neglect, the adults responsible for the child have problems with substance abuse (Murphy, Jellinek, Quinn, Smith, Poitrast, & Goshko, 1991). Thus, students who come from families in which a parent abuses alcohol or drugs are at risk of being abused or neglected.

Teachers are in a unique position to detect and report child abuse. Indeed, in every state of the United States, teachers have a legal responsibility to report suspected cases of child abuse or neglect (Chadwick, 1989). The methods and procedures for reporting suspected cases of abuse or neglect vary from state to state, district to district, and sometimes from school to school. In some cases, teachers report to school administrators and in other cases to public health officials. Because failure to report child abuse or neglect is professionally irresponsible, and because it may result in your being held liable in a court of law, one of the first things to do after securing a teaching position is to determine the procedures you are to use in reporting suspected cases of abuse and neglect.

Try This: Call social service agencies that deal with cases of child abuse. Identify yourself as a future teacher and ask for information on the identification and reporting of child abuse.

Unfortunately, students who are already at risk by virtue of other disabilities are at greater risk of abuse or neglect than nondisabled students (Zirpoli, 1986). There are several reasons why this may be so. Students with disabilities may be more vulnerable, parents of children with disabilities may experience greater stress, or disabled children and youths may exercise poor judgment in their dealings with adults. Whatever the reasons, individuals with disabilities in your classroom are more likely to be abused or neglected than your nondisabled students. Part of your responsibility as their teacher will be to report cases in which you expect child abuse or neglect. You can recognize abuse and neglect by the following signs (Berdine & Blackhurst, 1981):

- evidence of repeated injuries or new injuries
- frequent complaints of abdominal pain
- evidence of bruises, especially newer and older bruises

- evidence of welts, wounds, burns—especially those with well-defined shapes
- clothing that is inappropriate to the weather
- poor skin hygiene or body odor
- unprovided health services, eye glasses, dental work
- consistent sleepiness in class, frequent absence, chronic tardiness

Tragically, the problems faced by students are sometimes perceived to be so devastating and so intractable that suicide is considered as an alternative. Suicidal students, those who threaten or attempt suicide, are likely to give many clues. It is critical that teachers recognize these clues. Suicidal symptoms include the following:

- mention of suicide (80 percent of suicidal people discuss their intentions)
- significant changes in eating or sleeping habits
- loss of interest in prized possessions
- significant changes in school grades
- constant restlessness or hyperactivity
- loss of interest in friends

Every teacher should know what referral process for suicidal students is available in his or her school district. Teachers should also mentally rehearse what actions can be taken from various locations in the school in an emergency situation. In the event that you discover that one of your students is suicidal, it is critical that you remain with the student. Suicidal individuals remain suicidal for limited periods of time. *Do not leave the student alone!* (cf. Bell, 1980; Meyer & Salmon, 1988).

HOW DO INDIVIDUALS DEVELOP MORAL REASONING?

The social problems faced by students influence the way they see the world. Their experiences can influence their judgments about what is right and what is wrong. But maturation also influences the way in which students make moral judgments. These judgments change with age. A student may behave in one way at age six and in a very different way at age sixteen. In both instances, the student may consider him- or herself as behaving in the right way. Let us begin our study of moral development by examining how judgments of right and wrong change as people grow.

Piaget's Framework of Moral Reasoning

Piaget loved to observe children as they reacted to their environment. As a way of eliciting certain reactions, he made up the following pair of stories and asked children of different ages to discuss them.

> There was a little boy called Julian. His father had gone out and Julian thought it would be fun to play with father's ink-pot. First he played with the pen, and then he made a little blot on the table cloth.

A little boy who was called Augustus once noticed his father's ink-pot was empty. One day when his father was away he thought of filling the ink-pot so as to help his father, and so that he should find it full when he came home. But while he was opening the ink-bottle he made a big blot on the table cloth. (Piaget, 1948, p. 118)

Piaget questioned children about these stories. "Who was the naughtiest?" "Were Julian and Augustus equally guilty?" Piaget began to formulate a description of how **moral judgments**—judgments about right and wrong—develop, based on the variety of responses children of different ages gave and the consistency of the responses among children of similar ages.

Piaget concluded that there are general types of moral thinking. The first type—**morality of constraint**—describes judgments made by children up to approximately age ten. The second type of moral thinking—**morality of cooperation**—refers to the moral judgments of older children.

Try This: Adapt the story about Julian and Augustus to reflect a contemporary situation. Then ask the same questions of a variety of students. How might responses be classified in terms of Piaget's model?

Morality of Constraint. Morality of constraint is sometimes referred to as moral realism. Rules define what is right and what is wrong and come from some external authority. Because these rules are established by authoritative people—those who know—the rules should be obeyed. For students in early elementary grades, rules are sacred. There is no allowance made by the young realist for the context in which events occur. The intention of a person, for example, is not taken into account when judgments of right and wrong are made. Furthermore, the seriousness of a crime is determined by its consequences (cf. Lickona, 1976; Piaget, 1965).

Augustus made a bigger blot on the tablecloth than did Julian. Therefore, Augustus was more guilty than Julian.

Morality of Cooperation. Older children practice the morality of cooperation, alternatively called *moral relativism* or *moral flexibility*. The older child is a relativist; rules are not "carved in stone." A hallmark of cognitive development is decentration. As applied to moral judgments, it is evident in older children's awareness that others may not share their perceptions of rules. Rules, as older children understand them, provide general guidelines. It is inappropriate to follow rules blindly without considering the context in which they are applied. Rules should be obeyed not just because some "authority" has established them, but because they guard against violation of the rights of others. A person with good intentions who causes an injury or damage is not as culpable as a person with premeditation who commits a wrongful act (cf. Lickona, 1976; Piaget, 1965).

Older children who apply the morality of cooperation judge Julian to be more guilty than Augustus, who was attempting to do something nice for his father when he stained the tablecloth.

moral judgments Judgments about right or wrong.

morality of constraint According to Piaget, a type of moral thinking made by children under ten years of age; rules come from some external authority and strictly define what is right and wrong.

morality of cooperation According to Piaget, a type of moral thinking made by older children; rules provide general guidelines but should not be followed blindly without considering the context.

Kohlberg's Stages of Moral Development

Lawrence Kohlberg, during his graduate studies, became fascinated with Piaget's views on moral development. He followed Piaget's lead in using stories as a vehicle for investigating moral reasoning. Kohlberg wanted to apply his Piagetian-informed ideas on moral thinking to all ages, through adulthood. As a consequence, Kohlberg's stories were more elaborate and afforded a deeper analysis of an interpreter's reasoning. The stories Kohlberg created have become well known as "moral dilemmas." The following is a classic example that has been used by Kohlberg and others in research on stages of moral reasoning.

> In Europe a woman was near death from cancer. One drug might save her, a form of radium a druggist in the same town had recently discovered. The druggist was charging $2,000, ten times what the drug cost him to make. The sick woman's husband, Heinz, went to everyone he knew to borrow the money, but he could only get together about half of what it cost. He told the druggist that his wife was dying and asked him to sell it cheaper or let him pay later, but the druggist said "No." The husband got desperate and broke into the man's store to steal the drug for his wife. Should the husband have done that? Why? (Kohlberg, 1969, p. 376)

By classifying the reasoning his subjects used to respond to this and other moral dilemmas, Kohlberg formulated six stages of moral reasoning. Kohlberg's stages are divided into three levels: preconventional morality, conventional morality, and postconventional morality. Each level subsumes two stages. The levels and stages are presented in Table 3.2.

Reflection: How would you respond to Kohlberg's dilemma of Heinz and the drug?

Preconventional Morality (birth–9 years). **Preconventional morality** refers to judgments made before children understand the conventions of society. Children at this level base their reasoning on two ideas. First, one should avoid punishment, and second, good behavior yields some kind of benefit.

- *Stage 1: The Punishment–Obedience Level.* The child behaves in order to avoid punishment. Bad behavior is behavior that is punished; good behavior, therefore, is behavior that is rewarded. For example, children who do not talk without seeking permission do so because authority, the teacher, deems the act of talking without raising one's hand as punishable. Consider the moral dilemma Heinz faced and the question, "Should Heinz have stolen the drug?" A typical Stage 1 answer is, "No, he could get arrested for stealing."
- *Stage 2: The Instrumental Exchange Orientation.* This stage represents the beginnings of social reciprocity; the thinking here is, "You scratch my back and

Try This: Observe children in a school or neighborhood playground. How do the children decide about taking turns in the games they play? What stages of Kohlberg's model do their decisions reflect?

TABLE 3.2 Kohlberg's Stages of Moral Development

Level I Preconventional Morality
Stage 1: Punishment and Obedience Orientation
Stage 2: Instrumental Exchange Orientation

Level II Conventional Morality
Stage 3: Interpersonal Conformity Orientation
Stage 4: Law-and-Order Orientation

Level III Postconventional Morality
Stage 5: Prior Rights and Social Contract Orientation
Stage 6: Universal Ethical Principles Orientation

Source: From *Psychology* (4th ed., p. 326) by L.A. Lefton, 1991, Needham Heights, MA: Allyn & Bacon. Copyright 1991 by Allyn & Bacon. Reprinted by permission.

preconventional morality Rules of conduct of children (birth–9 years) who do not yet understand the conventions of society. This is Level 1 of Kohlberg's theory of moral reasoning.

I'll scratch yours." The moral judgments that children make at this stage are very pragmatic. They will do good to another person if they expect the other person to reciprocate or return the favor. In response to the Heinz question, a typical Stage 2 response is, "He shouldn't steal the drug and the druggist should be nicer to Heinz."

Conventional Morality (9 years–young adulthood). Conventional morality refers to judgments based on the rules or conventions of society; behaviors that maintain the social order are considered good behaviors. The reasoning at this level is based on a desire to impress others. Peer relationships become very important during this period.

- *Stage 3: The Interpersonal Conformity Orientation.* Reasoning about morality focuses on the expectations of other people, particularly the expectations of people in authority and peers. In order to create and maintain good relations with other people, it is important to conform to their expectations of good behavior. By being nice or good, approval from others is likely. A typical Stage 3 response to the Heinz question is, "If Heinz is honest, other people will be proud of him."
- *Stage 4: The Law-and-Order Orientation.* The conventions of society have been established so that society can function. Laws are necessary and, therefore, good. The moral person is one who follows the laws of a society without questioning them. A typical Stage 4 response to the Heinz question is, "Stealing is against the law. If everybody ignored the laws, our whole society might fall apart."

Postconventional Morality (adulthood). Postconventional morality is typified by judgments that recognize the societal need for mutual agreement and the application of consistent principles in making judgments. Through careful thought and reflection, the postconventional thinker arrives at a self-determined set of principles or morality.

Reflection: What does your own response to Kohlberg's dilemma tell you about your moral judgment?

- *Stage 5: The Prior Rights and Social Contract Orientation.* At this stage, laws are open to evaluation. A law is good if it protects the rights of individuals. Laws should not be obeyed simply because they are laws but because there is mutual agreement between the individual and society that these laws guarantee a person's rights. A typical answer to the Heinz question is, "Sometimes laws have to be disregarded, for example, when a person's life depends on breaking the law."
- *Stage 6: The Universal Ethical Principles Orientation.* The principles that determine moral behavior are self-chosen; they unify a person's beliefs about equality, justice, ethics. If a person arrives at a set of principles, the principles serve as guidelines for appropriate behavior. A typical Stage 6 response to the Heinz question is, "An appropriate decision must take into account all of the factors in the situation. Sometimes, it is morally right to steal."

conventional morality Rules of conduct of older children (9 years–young adulthood) based on the conventions of society. This is Level 2 of Kohlberg's theory of moral reasoning.

postconventional morality Rules of conduct of adults who recognize the societal need for mutual agreement and the application of consistent principles in making judgments. This is Level 3 of Kohlberg's theory of moral reasoning.

Criticisms of Kohlberg's Theory

Kohlberg's theory is a landmark in the scientific literature on moral development. A good scientific theory is one that generates new research. In this regard, Kohlberg's theory has proven very successful. Much of the research done in response to Kohlberg's theory has raised questions about the theory's utility. A discussion of some of those questions follows.

The Question of Stages. Kohlberg (1971) shared Piaget's view about the ordinality of stages; that is, Kohlberg held that all people progress through the stages of moral development in sequence. There is evidence, however, that calls into question Kohlberg's assumption of ordinality. For example, Holstein (1976) found that responses to moral situations did not consistently and unambiguously place subjects at a particular stage. Holstein also found that females and males differed systematically in their judgments. Other researchers have found that the level or stage of a person's moral reasoning is dependent on the particular moral dilemma that the person responds to (e.g., Fishkin, Keniston, & MacKinnon, 1973).

Although Kohlberg assumed ordinality, he did not assume that all people arrived at Stage 6—the universal ethical principles orientation. After others began to question the validity of his stages, Kohlberg went back and reexamined some of his original data (Colby & Kohlberg, 1984) and subsequently discounted the sixth stage in his theory (cf. Kohlberg, 1978).

The Question of Applicability. Very often, teachers need to reason with a student about the student's classroom conduct. If a teacher knows how a student reasons when confronted with a decision about what's right and what's wrong, the teacher can encourage the child to make a change in behavior in terms he or she will best understand. If classroom rules are central to students' decisions of what is right and wrong, for example, then a simple reference to classroom rules by the teacher is likely to be effective. With older students, a teacher might use the approval of parents or peers to encourage appropriate behavior.

Critical Thinking: The way a student reasons in response to a hypothetical dilemma may or may not be the way in which that student will behave in real-life situations. Why is this the case?

Direct attempts by teachers to facilitate moral development in students have resulted primarily in group discussions of moral dilemmas. Moral dilemmas can be of the type used by Kohlberg in his research, hypothetical situations that require a judgment about what is the correct or incorrect action to take in that hypothetical situation. There can also be real-life situations in the classroom or school (e.g., Reimer, Paolitto, & Hersh, 1983). Real-life dilemmas can deal with episodes of aggressive behavior, cheating on tests, copying homework, or abusing rules.

One technique used to enhance moral reasoning is called plus-one matching (Lockwood, 1978). In using this technique, the teacher determines a student's stage of moral development and then presents conflicting views that are consistent with the next higher stage. The goal of plus-one matching is to create some disequilibrium in the student so that he or she is encouraged to entertain other points of view on the issue under discussion.

The Question of Generalizability. For Kohlberg, moral development culminates in the recognition of individual rights and individually generated ethical principles. It is not surprising that Kohlberg, having grown up in a Western culture, would emphasize the Western value of individualism. The question is whether Kohlberg's stages would apply to cultures that prize the good of the group or of the family more highly than the good of the individual. Attempts to apply Kohlberg's scheme to other cultures have met with mixed results (e.g., Hwang, 1986; Vasudev & Hummel, 1987).

Critical Thinking: To what extent does Kohlberg's theory represent values of Anglo-European origin? To what extent do you think cultural values play a role in determining individual responses to moral dilemmas?

Gilligan's Theory of Gender-Based Morality

Another question of generalizability refers to gender differences (Gilligan, 1982; Holstein, 1976). Kohlberg developed his stages based on a longitudinal study of males. In other studies classifying males and females according to Kohlberg's stages, a disproportionate number of women have been placed in Stage 3 as compared with Stage 4. One explanation is that women are generally more empathetic and compassionate toward others and more sensitive to social relationships than men (Gilligan, 1977; Holstein, 1976). Based on these and other studies, Gilligan has developed a stage model of moral development.

Gilligan's theory, presented in Table 3.3, comprises three levels and two transitions. The first level of Gilligan's theory, **individual survival**, identifies selfishness as its primary concern. The transition from individual survival to self-sacrifice and social conformity leads to the realization that caring for others rather than just caring for oneself is good. Gilligan's second level, **self-sacrifice and social conformity**, is similar to Kohlberg's Stage 3. Brabeck (1986) identifies the second level as "the conventional view of women as caretakers and protectors" (p. 70). The transition from the second to the third level involves a growing realization that in order to care for others, one must also take care of oneself. Note the different motives for self-care in this second transition as opposed to the motives in the first transition. The third level of Gilligan's theory is the **morality of nonviolence**. The ethic of this third level is the equality of self and others: It is wrong to serve oneself at the expense of others.

Try This: Test Gilligan's theory by presenting dilemmas to male and female students separately. How much and in what ways does gender seem to influence moral judgment?

Brabeck (1986) has compared Kohlberg's view on moral development with Gilligan's. Brabeck labels Kohlberg's theory a "morality of justice" that stresses rights, fairness, rules, and legalities. Gilligan's theory, by way of comparison, is called a "morality of care and responsibility." This theory stresses relationships, care, harmony, compassion, and self-sacrifice. Some researchers regard Gilligan's model as a theory of female moral development. Perhaps a better way to think about Gilligan's theory is that it stresses different values than Kohlberg's. Support for this view comes from a study by Walker, deVries, and Trevethan (1987). These

individual survival The first level of Gilligan's theory of moral reasoning, in which selfishness is identified as the primary concern.

self-sacrifice and social conformity The second level of Gilligan's theory of moral reasoning, in which there is a realization that caring for others rather than just caring for oneself is good.

morality of nonviolence The third level of Gilligan's theory of moral reasoning, in which there is a realization that it is wrong to serve oneself at the expense of others.

TABLE 3.3 Gilligan's Stages of Moral Development

Stages	
1	Individual Survival
1A*	From Selfishness to Responsibility
2	Self-Sacrifice and Social Conformity
2A*	From Goodness to Truth
3	Morality of Nonviolence

* Marks a transition stage.

Source: From "Moral Orientation: Alternative Perspectives of Men and Women" by M. Brabeck, 1986, in *Psychological Foundations of Moral Education and Character Development: An Integrated Theory of Moral Development* (p. 71) by R.T. Knowles and G.F. McLean (eds.), Lanham, MD: University Press of America. Copyright 1986 by University Press of America. Adapted with permission.

Identity formation and moral development during adolescence are influenced by the emergence and validation of self-image, sexuality, expectations for adulthood, and life-style choices. Research has raised questions about differences between males and females in habits of thought and the origins of those differences in biology or culture.

researchers asked children and adults to describe personal experiences that involved some kind of moral conflict. The descriptions indicated that some subjects valued justice while others valued caring, but the values were not tied to the gender of the subject.

Gilligan's theory presents us with a new perspective to consider. It is not confined to moral reasoning (i.e., cognitive judgments of right and wrong) but stresses affect (i.e., feelings, attitudes, emotions).

Critical Thinking: In what ways does Gilligan's theory integrate affect and cognition?

While Kohlberg's framework informs us about how children think, we must remember that there is more to moral development than cognition. Peters (1977) characterizes Kohlberg's theory as cognitive, with little or no attention paid to affective feelings and attitudes. Peters argues that any attempt to facilitate moral development should address not only how to think but also how to feel. Among the attitudes that accompany sound moral decisions, Peters places caring for others at the top. Gilligan's framework introduces affect into the mix and certainly emphasizes caring as an important element of morality. Even so, the question is whether a student's reasoning and his or her attitudes are applied consistently in all situations that require a moral judgment.

Critical Thinking: An Honor Council president cheated to get a passing grade in English. After he was caught, he explained, "I knew that one way or the other—either failing or getting caught cheating—I would be off the council." How do you think the other members of the council responded to the president's explanation?

Lickona's Integrative Model of Personal and Interpersonal Development

In a classic study, Hartshorne and May (1930) found that for many children moral behavior is situation specific. Children who are generally honest and trustworthy will, under certain circumstances, cheat, especially if the stakes are high enough. Lickona (1976) concluded that, "variations in the situation produce variations in moral behavior" (p. 15). Lickona added, however, that there is evidence to suggest that some children are more morally integrated or consistent than others. What appears to be needed is educational practice that does not rely solely on reasoning exercises but that integrates cognition, affect, and behavior. We will return later in this chapter to the notion of integrative classroom practice. Before doing so, we examine some of the issues that students encounter in the social environment of schools.

skip to end

Insights ON SUCCESSFUL PRACTICE

What advice do you have for novice teachers about dealing with ethical or moral issues in daily classroom life?

In today's increasingly unstructured world, one thing most teachers agree on is that children need to be responsible for the consequences of their actions. Thus, guiding children toward taking this responsibility has become a purpose all teachers share. To help accomplish this purpose in my classroom I have compiled a core of teaching principles that help me lead children toward more responsible behavior.

My core of principles derives from what seems to me to be a universal wisdom that recognizes affection, courage, honesty, generosity, justice, tolerance, kindness, compassion, and self-reliance as essential attributes in a decent society. I use these attributes as my personal behavior templates. They have become the mental bumper stickers that flash through my mind while I am engaged in the process of building significant relationships with the children in my charge.

My core of principles based upon these attributes provides me with an economy of ethics, enabling me to respond quickly and consistently without starting from scratch to construct a moral position for every dilemma that arises in my classroom. Just a sampling from my code of principles would include the following three:

1. It is my responsibility to meet the learning needs of my students, not the students' responsibility to meet my ego-centered needs.
2. It takes a courageous, determined adult to see through irresponsible behavior without rejecting the student. Teacher and student must find a better way.
3. There is no third state or condition in the teacher-learner reciprocal relationship. Either both parties are in it or they are not.

Applying my core of personal principles to use in the classroom requires the design and implementation of a strategy. My design is based on the concept that reciprocity is essential to all constructive relationships. A successful learner–teacher relationship depends on a *quid pro quo* agreement that recognizes that learning is a transaction.

On the first day of a class, I claim the authority to establish the first rule: "Listen to me when I speak." I justify this first rule by agreeing to listen to any student who wishes to speak. Then I present the concept of reciprocity and discuss the nature of the teacher–learner agreement.

My core principles act as my compass as I guide the group to collectively compose a short list of principles that we all agree to live by while we are in class. The agreement is posted for everyone in class to see and may be amended as the need arises. When dilemmas arise, I refer students to the agreement and ask if we can find a solution.

Thus, I use my set of personal principles to establish my relationship with the students and lead them to establish a set of principles of their own in the form of an agreement by which we can all live in mutual respect. Such an agreement allows those "instants" of teacher–student reciprocity to occur. Those instants are the essence of learning.

STEVE KORPA, Carrick High School
Pittsburgh, Pennsylvania

What does it mean to say that teaching and learning involve a *quid pro quo* agreement? What kinds of moral dilemmas might you face in your classroom? Through what ethical principles might you guide your students, and how would you do so?

The Council for Research in Values and Philosophy, a group of scholars concerned with the moral dimension of education, share a view of moral development, an **integrative model** that combines cognition, affect, and behavior. The integrative view postulates moral development as occurring along two dimensions, vertical and horizontal. The *vertical dimension* refers to growth as an increased ability to coordinate the perspectives and needs of others, to discriminate values that advance the human condition from values that do not, to make principled decisions, and to be aware of one's moral weaknesses (Knowles & McLean, 1992; Ryan & Lickona, 1987). Vertical growth is the kind described by Kohlberg and Gilligan as advancement to higher levels of cognition and affect.

The *horizontal dimension* of moral growth refers to the application of a person's moral reasoning and affective capacities to an increasingly wider range of real-life situations. Horizontal growth requires that a person not only think and feel but also act in accordance with his or her cognitive and affective capacities. Suppose that a business executive reasons that laws must be determined through agreement and, at the same time, protect the rights of individuals (Stage 5 in Kohlberg). Suppose further that our executive decides to eliminate a company policy of job sharing without consulting employees. The lack of consistency between the executive's moral capacity to reason and the actions taken reveals weak horizontal development. (Note that the notion of horizontal development could be used to explain the classic Hartshorne and May findings: Good intentions do not always mean moral actions.)

Example: Lickona's model has also been called an "integrative model of the moral agent," in which each person is a moral agent

An integrative model of character education requires that attention be paid to vertical growth issues: reasoning, clarifying values, pursuing moral principles. It means also that students should use their thinking and feelings in a wide variety of ways; that is, that they pay attention to horizontal development.

Thomas Lickona presented an integrative model of character education in *Character Development in Schools and Beyond* (Ryan & McLean, 1987). Lickona's model specifies four processes that need to operate in classrooms if teachers are to influence the developing character of their students: (1) building self-esteem and social community, (2) encouraging cooperative learning and helping relations, (3) eliciting moral reflection, and (4) effecting participatory decision making (see Figure 3.2). Keep in mind that Lickona's model is aimed at both vertical and horizontal development.

Critical Thinking: Starratt (1987) reports a small group exercise in which each student writes his or her name at the top of a sheet of paper. The paper is passed to the next student who writes something likable about the student named on the page. The page continues around the circle until each student has named something likable about every other student in the group. Why has this technique proved effective?

Building Self-Esteem and Social Community. This process involves building a child's self-esteem, a sense of competence and mastery, in the social community of the classroom. This process also requires that students come to know each other as individuals, respect and care about each other, and feel that they are members of and accountable to the group.

As suggested in Chapter 2, self-esteem can be fostered in the classroom in a number of ways. Lickona reports a third-grade teacher's practice of learning something special about each student at the beginning of the school year. The teacher asks each student to tell her of an award, a skill, or something else he or she is proud of. In the teacher's words, "I then make this something important to me. I stress to the child how important it is to me and it's something just the two of us share" (p. 185). The teacher values each student, and each student tends to value himself or herself more highly.

integrative model A view of moral development that combines cognition, affect, and behavior; method of lesson presentation that combines inductive skills, deductive skills, and content in one model.

FIGURE 3.2

Lickona's Model of Moral Education

Source: From "Character Development in the Elementary School Classroom" by T. Lickona, 1987, in *Character Development in Schools and Beyond* (p. 183) by K. Ryan and G. McLean (eds.) New York: Praeger Publishers. Copyright 1987 by Praeger Publishers. Reprinted by permission.

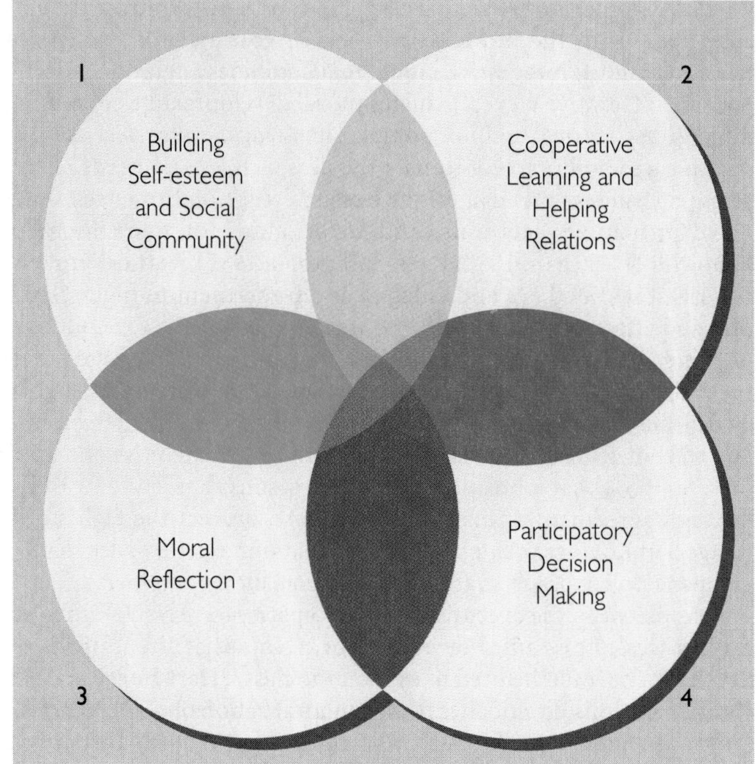

One sixth-grade teacher who felt that too many of her students viewed themselves negatively decided to write a note to each child. In each note, the teacher mentioned a characteristic in the student that she admired. The notes also invited the students to write back to the teacher, telling her about characteristics they admired in themselves. The teacher reported that following the note exchange, the students more frequently displayed in class the characteristics identified as positive. This kind of affirmation exercise has also been reported as effective in a high school classroom (Starratt, 1987).

Any sort of public effort to share personal feelings and perceptions can contribute to a sense of community. In developing this sense of community, it is important that each student feel that he or she is being listened to with respect.

Cooperative Learning and Helping Relations. The spirit of cooperation and the skills to realize that spirit are essential to adult living (Wynne, 1987). Cooperative learning—students learning from and with each other—can be fostered in classrooms at any grade level. Furthermore, research on classroom learning indicates that cooperative efforts result in higher self-esteem than competitive or individualistic efforts (Johnson & Johnson, 1989, 1992, 1994; Slavin, 1991).

Try This: Observe a cooperative learning activity and identify student behaviors that promote and those that subvert cooperative efforts.

For example, a third-grade teacher, teaching a unit on measurement, assigned pairs of children to collect physical measurements. The children were given the tasks of measuring the length of their jumps on a sidewalk, how far they could spread their feet, how high they could reach on the building, and so on.

The teacher suggested that when one partner jumped or reached, the other partner should mark the effort. The teacher reported that children enjoyed the active nature of the exercise and the interaction with their partners.

Establishing cooperation and helping as an integral part of one's classroom is not always "sweetness and light." In many cases, children who have not been in highly cooperative classrooms before will unintentionally subvert cooperative efforts by reverting to the skills required in classrooms emphasizing individual effort and achievement. One way of making cooperation easier for students is to help children learn to support each other socially. One fifth-grade teacher, attempting to establish cooperative learning, instituted a daily "appreciation time." At the end of the day each student could speak about something that another student did that day that the speaker appreciated. Appreciation time became the favorite classroom activity. Such acknowledgments allowed students to value helpfulness and thoughtfulness; it also gave students practice in delivering and receiving compliments.

Critical Thinking: What might be some advantages and disadvantages of using a thematic curricular approach rather than Kohlberg-type dilemmas in fostering moral development?

Moral Reflection. The third process in Lickona's model is moral reflection, which focuses on the cognitive aspects of moral development. It might involve reading, thinking, debate, and/or discussion.

A fifth-grade teacher in New York City organizes her whole social studies curriculum around the theme of the Middle Ages. The classroom is turned into a "Scriptorium," enabling students to approximate the experience of monks. They work on artistic ornamentation and calligraphy in the manuscripts they produce, which requires slow, painstaking effort. These efforts give the students "a great sense of achievement and appreciation of the artist monk" (Frey, 1983, p. 33). The medieval theme is carried through in the historical fiction that the students read. Reading and discussing good literature, which engages the mind and the heart, can go far beyond a contrived moral dilemma in eliciting moral reflection.

A teacher who attempts to pursue goals of moral education must be alert to the real-life moral situations that arise in every classroom. Lickona tells the story of a second-grade teacher whose class was incubating chicken eggs. One day, the teacher suggested that it might be instructive to open one egg each week as a way of studying embryonic development. Later that day, one of her students objected to the suggestion because it seemed cruel to him. The teacher saw the opportunity to engage the class in meaningful moral reflection. The class discussed the merit of the objection; alternative, though less satisfying, ways of finding out about chick embryos; and even questions about whether the embryos were really live chickens. Here was a moral dilemma that required reasoning, a clarification of feelings, and ultimately, action.

Try This: Interview a practicing teacher regarding his or her efforts to involve students in participatory decision making or to establish a more democratic classroom.

Participatory Decision Making. The fourth process in Lickona's model of moral education is participatory decision making, which holds students accountable for decisions that influence the quality of classroom life. This process is not simply a matter of having students participate in defining classroom rules; it is also a matter of establishing a sense of responsibility and genuine participation in the welfare of the classroom community. The process, when practiced well, yields a set of norms that guides students' behavior.

If students have participated in establishing class rules, the sense of collective responsibility will facilitate the development of norms. Suppose that a class meets to discuss some problems: for example, too much noise during seat work or too little help during cleanup. These problems are not treated as isolated issues, and the students involved in them are not singled out for special attention. The issues are considered by the class as a whole. The theft of one student's lunch money needs to be solved by the whole class. Helping a transfer student make friends and figure out the school's routine is a problem the class has to solve. In effect, the teacher can ask students to identify problems that they would like others in the class help them solve.

To make his point, Lickona relates the experiences of a young substitute teacher. She was asked to take over the class of a teacher who found the children incorrigible and had taken a six-week mental health leave. The substitute was greeted with an announcement from the class that they were the worst class in the school. The substitute immediately brought the class together to decide what rules were needed and why they were necessary. The discussion went on for some time and ended with consensus on one last student-generated rule: "Care about each other" (Lickona, 1987, p. 200).

Reflection: Reflect on the teachers in your own experience as a student who practiced participatory decision making and those who did not. What were your experiences in those classrooms? Did those teachers influence your personal and interpersonal growth differently?

The meetings continued on a daily basis. Caring for each other became the class ethic. When the substitute left at the end of six weeks, the students asked her to teach the returning regular how these class meetings worked. The substitute advised the regular teacher that the class meetings had had a wonderful effect on the class. The regular chose not to continue the meetings, and by all accounts, the class reclaimed its dubious reputation.

The four processes of Lickona's model are not effective in isolation. If the classroom sense of community is weak, it will be difficult to generate the kind of discussion and debate that makes useful reflection possible. If students do not participate in establishing the rules and norms of their community, it is less likely that a truly cooperative environment will develop. The Likona model has been applied successfully in a variety of classrooms. But its application requires a teacher who believes deeply in the value of moral education, a teacher who will persist through rocky beginnings and find a way to develop the sensitivity necessary to help students find character.

TEACHER Chronicle Conclusion

LOOKS CAN DECEIVE

Mr. McKissack asks Ricky to see him after school. Ricky nods with the same resigned look he had when he didn't turn in his homework assignment. When everyone has left, Ricky approaches Mr. McKissack's desk.

"Ricky, is something bothering you?" Mr. McKissack asks. "I've never seen you act this way before."

"No, nothing's wrong," Ricky replies, his eyes down.

"Well, you know that zero on your homework the other day will ruin your A average. You've never missed an assignment before."

"I know."

Dragging the words out of him is like pulling up a sequoia stump.

"Could you please tell me why you missed the assignment?"

Ricky hesitates, then looks at Mr. McKissack. "You know that snowstorm we had?"

Mr. McKissack nods.

"Well, you see, I'm supposed to shovel Mr. Walker's sidewalk for him. He has a bad heart and my family has known him for years and I've always cleaned his sidewalk for him. The day of the snow I went over to David's house to play video games and I forgot about Mr. Walker. He had to go to the store and began shoveling his sidewalk. He had a heart attack doing it. We spent the night at the hospital and so I didn't do my work." Tears well up in Ricky's eyes.

"How is he doing?" Mr. McKissack asks.

"He's okay now, but it was close for a while."

"And you think it was your fault that he had a heart attack?"

Ricky nods.

"Ricky, you don't know that. He could have had a heart attack climbing stairs. You can't blame yourself."

"But he wouldn't have been shoveling if I had remembered to come do it for him."

"Ricky, we all forget things. Your life is especially busy with all of the school things you do. Certainly Mr. Walker won't blame you."

"You don't think so?"

"Ricky, he is a dear friend of your family's. I'm sure he appreciates all the shoveling you've done more than he can tell you. Why don't you skip tonight's homework assignment and go see Mr. Walker. He needs you more than any old homework does."

Ricky hesitates.

"Don't worry," Mr. McKissack continues. "You will still get an A."

APPLICATION QUESTIONS

1. In what stage in Kohlberg's moral development scheme would you place Ricky? In what stage would you place Mr. McKissack? Explain your choices.
2. Evaluate the teacher's thoughts and feelings about Ricky. How might they be accounted for? Is it unprofessional for a teacher to dislike a student?
3. Have you ever had a teacher dislike you? If so, how did this affect your classroom performance?
4. Evaluate the teacher's response to Ricky's dilemma. If you were Ricky's teacher

would you have acted differently? Why or why not? Explain how the relationship between the teacher and student might change after this incident.

5. Analyze Looks Can Deceive from the viewpoint of Erikson's stages of psychosocial development. What stage is Ricky in? What stage do you feel you are in now, according to Erikson's model? According to Marcia's model of identity statuses?
6. In what specific ways would knowledge of your students' personal and interpersonal growth help you be a more effective teacher?

CHAPTER SUMMARY

HOW DO INDIVIDUALS DEVELOP SELF-CONCEPTS AND SELF-ESTEEM?

Self-concept is the way in which a person describes him- or herself. Self-esteem is related to self-concept in that self-esteem is one's evaluation of his or her sense of self. The feelings that one has about self come from self-evaluation. Because one's self-esteem requires a value judgment, the values one learns from one's culture can influence self-esteem.

HOW DOES SOCIAL INTERACTION INFLUENCE PERSONAL GROWTH?

Erikson proposes eight stages of psychosocial development. Each stage's developmental crisis is identified as a dichotomy of qualities, positive and negative. If the social experiences during that period are generally positive, positive qualities result. If experiences are generally negative, the crisis is resolved negatively.

James Marcia extended Erikson's work as it applied to adolescents' search for identity. He identified four identity statuses. Identity diffusion types are confused, disorganized, and avoid commitment. Moratorium types (not to be confused with Erikson's psychosocial moratorium) have given a great deal of thought to identity issues but have not yet arrived at any conclusions. Identity achievement types are those adolescents who have made life-style decisions on their own. Foreclosure types do not experience a crisis of identity; they simply adopt decisions made for them by others.

If a teacher uses Erikson's theory to make decisions about a student's psychosocial needs, he or she should keep in mind the evidence that suggests that Erikson's framework is a better description of males than of females. There is also a good bit of overlap in the stages: Crises that begin in toddlerhood and continue through the middle school years are quite similar.

WHAT SOCIAL PROBLEMS AFFECT STUDENTS' SCHOOL LIVES?

Minor social problems—such as the developmental crises in Erikson's theory—are faced by all students. Some students, however, are at risk of failing in school because the social problems they face go beyond those faced by students who are raised in safe environments. Social situations that result in risk to students' security, safety, and health place a special responsibility on those students' teachers.

HOW DO INDIVIDUALS DEVELOP MORAL REASONING?

Piaget distinguishes between the moral reasoning of younger and older children. Younger children follow the morality of constraint; they follow rules without question. Older children, who follow the morality of cooperation, take into account the context of behaviors in order to judge whether an action is right or wrong.

Kohlberg based his framework on Piaget's views. Kohlberg identified stages of moral reasoning that exist at three levels. At the first level, preconventional morality, reasoning about right and wrong is based on the idea that correct behavior is that which avoids punishment and yields some kind of reward. The second level, conventional morality, is based on respect for authority and a desire to impress others. The third level is postconventional morality. The reasoning at this level recognizes the need for societal agreement and the consistent application of moral principles. Gilligan's theory extends Kohlberg's work to suggest that moral judgment is gender based.

Lickona identified four overlapping processes that should occur in classrooms where moral education is addressed. The first process focuses on building healthy self-esteem through social support and a sense of belonging to the community of the classroom. The second process operates to establish cooperative learning; the emphasis is on students learning to help each other. The third process, moral reflection, is similar to Kohlberg's—and more similar to Gilligan's—moral reasoning. The final process encourages participatory decision making on questions of behavior in the community of the classroom.

KEY CONCEPTS

- **autonomy**
- **conventional morality**
- **critical periods**
- **developmental crisis**
- **foreclosure**
- **gender role stereotype**
- **generativity**
- **growth spurt**
- **identity**
- **identity diffusion**
- **identity statuses**
- **individual survival**
- **industry**
- **initiative**
- **integrative model**
- **integrity**
- **intimacy**
- **isolation**
- **moral judgments**
- **morality of constraint**
- **morality of cooperation**
- **morality of nonviolence**
- **moratorium**
- **preconventional morality**
- **postconventional morality**
- **psychosocial development**
- **puberty**
- **role diffusion**
- **self-concept**
- **self-esteem**
- **self-sacrifice and social conformity**
- **students at risk**

PART II

Learners are diverse

Today's classrooms reflect growing American cultural diversity. Individuals' cultural and ethnic identities, beliefs and values, and experiences as members of culturally defined groups shape the broader context within which their classroom learning takes place. Cultural awareness is, therefore, a critical part of teachers' self-knowledge and knowledge of students.

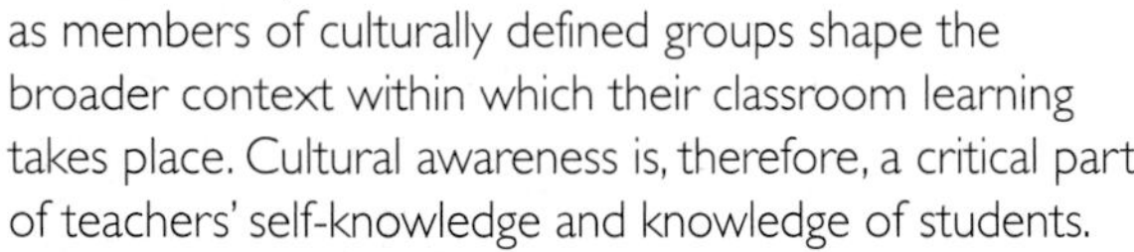

Overview of Chapter 4

The two previous chapters have described what is true of students as part of a general population at various periods of development. In the next two chapters, we examine how students as individuals differ from one another.

There are a number of ways to think about the differences among students. One is to consider the students' capacities and dispositions to learn, which is the subject of Chapter 5. In Chapter 4, "Cultural Diversity and Values in the Classroom," however, we discuss the different attitudes, beliefs, and values that reflect students' cultural backgrounds. As our society grows more multicultural in nature, teachers face classrooms full of students whose backgrounds vary widely from one another. There are boys and girls of different ethnic groups, different races, different socioeconomic backgrounds, and different religions. All of these differences affect the attitudes and beliefs students bring with them into the classroom. The chapter concludes with a discussion of how you can create a multicultural classroom that respects—indeed, thrives on—the differences among students.

Diversity

Students' diversity and individuality affect learning

Students are also diverse in their individual capabilities and characteristics as learners. Kinds of intelligence, preferred ways of learning, and areas of exceptional ability or disability, for example, further define students as unique individuals. The professional teacher's knowledge base includes ways of finding out about and responding to each learner's strengths and needs.

Overview of Chapter 5

The cultural values of your students make them different from one another. There are factors that make students unique. Chapter 5, "Individual Variability in the Classroom," examines how students vary in intelligence and, at the same time, how views of human intelligence are changing to the point that educators often speak of a student's several intelligences. Students also differ from one another in the ways they think and in the styles of learning they develop. Some students are unique because they are disabled in some way. Other students need specialized programs to reduce the risk of their failing in school. This chapter helps you to serve the variety of needs your students bring to your classroom.

Inclusive classrooms provide learning opportunities

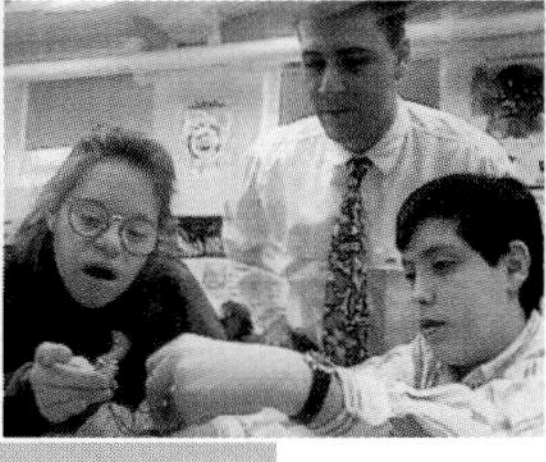

Today's classrooms reflect greater individual variability among learners, which is a source of both enrichment and challenge for all. In inclusion or mainstreaming, students with special educational needs are integrated and supported within the general education classroom environment. For general education teachers, therefore, knowledge of students' special needs, awareness of instructional adaptations, and skills in professional collaboration are increasingly important.

4 Cultural Diversity and Values in the Classroom

CHAPTER OUTLINE

TEACHER

Chronicle

GRANDMA TALES

Kevin is the star storyteller of Ms. Walker's eighth-grade English class. He tells stories that captivate his listeners, stories with strong beginnings, intriguing middles, and powerful endings. He tells stories about his older brother the basketball star, his Native American tribe, his aunt, his peers, and his recent trips. Kevin is proud of his heritage and frequently refers to it.

However, Kevin's reading skills are weak, and he constantly struggles with written work. He seems unable to organize his thoughts on paper. He cannot write the stories he tells so well. There seems to be no way to head off an F at report card time.

One day his class is discussing tall tales in preparation for a writing assignment. Students share the tales they had been given as a preparatory reading assignment: Paul Bunyan, Pecos Bill, Captain Stormalong, and Joe Magarac.

Near the end of the period, Amy notes, "You know, there aren't any tall tales about women."

Kevin pipes up, "You mean you haven't heard about my Grandma digging the Great Lakes?"

Sensing student interest in Kevin's question, Ms. Walker tells him to go ahead.

"Many years ago," he begins, "where the Great Lakes are now, there was an open prairie. Grandma came along, saw the prairie, and decided to make her garden there. She reached inside her leather pouch and took out five seeds: the long green bean seed, the fat pumpkin seed, the flat squash seed, the hard maize seed, and the round eye of the potato. Then she took her hoe and began to dig the right hole for each seed: a long skinny hole for the green bean, a fat hole for the pumpkin, a flat hole for the squash, a hole in granite for the hard corn seed, and a potato-shaped hole for the potato. She took all the dirt she dug and threw it to the west where she made the Rocky Mountains. Then, just as she got ready to drop in the seeds, along came this huge thunderstorm. It rained and rained for more days than Grandma could count. She stayed under her hoe to keep dry. Well, finally it stopped raining and Grandma looked out. The five holes were filled to the brim with water. And that's how Grandma dug the five Great Lakes and why they are shaped the way they are."

An appreciative silence follows Kevin's story until Luthien asked, "Is that a story the Menominees tell?"

Kevin shakes his head. "I just made it up," he beams.

"Do you know any other Grandma tales?" Brent calls out.

"I could tell you about the time Grandma made the Earth from an old basketball."

Ms. Walker glances at the clock and says, "We'll have to save that for tomorrow."

As the students hop up to leave, someone asks Kevin, "Did Grandma make the Atlantic Ocean?"

"Oh, sure, but it took her a little longer than making the Pacific because the ground is harder."

FOCUS QUESTIONS

1. In what ways might Kevin's cultural background influence his learning?
2. How might Kevin's storytelling skills relate to his cultural background?

3. How might Ms. Walker's cultural background be different from Kevin's? How might cultural background differences affect her teaching?
4. What strategies might Ms. Walker use to build on Kevin's storytelling skills? For example, how might Ms. Walker use Kevin's storytelling ability to help him improve his writing skills?
5. How might Kevin's cultural identity increase his classmates' awareness of diversity?

WHAT ARE SOME SOURCES OF DIVERSITY?

Point: *Learners are diverse.* In this chapter, many sources of diversity are examined that affect teaching and learning in the classroom.

Example: The U.S. Bureau of the Census predicts that school-age children who are members of racial or ethnic minority groups or who are native speakers of languages other than English will comprise 38 percent of the population by 2020.

In recent years, enormous demographic changes in the United States have diversified the makeup of American classrooms. The U.S. Bureau of the Census reported in 1990 that the numbers of ethnic minorities in this country had increased substantially within the previous decade. The largest increase, nearly 108 percent, was for Asian Americans. Hispanic groups accounted for a 53 percent increase, while Native Americans increased by 38 percent and African Americans by 13 percent. Among other groups, Arab Americans account for approximately 1 percent of the U.S. population (Bennett, 1995). It is estimated that nearly 40 percent of the school-age population will be ethnic minorities by the year 2020. As a teacher, you are likely to face a roomful of students who come from many different cultural backgrounds, ethnic heritages, and socioeconomic classes. You will face girls and boys, students with exceptional abilities, and students with disabilities. These differences among students influence the skills, knowledge, experiences, values, and strengths that they bring with them into the classroom. Understanding such differences can tell you how some students are likely to learn, make friends, interpret social messages, and approach school work.

Cultural Diversity

Culture, broadly speaking, is a way of life in which people share a common language and similar values, religion, ideals, habits of thinking, artistic expressions, and patterns of social and interpersonal relations (Lum, 1986). Some have suggested that people live in five intermingling cultures:

Universal—humans are biologically alike

Ecological—peoples' location on earth determines how they relate to the natural environment

National—people are influenced by the nation in which they live

Local and Regional—local, regional differences create cultures specific to an area

Ethnic—people reflect their ethnic heritages (Baruth & Manning, 1992)

A shared national culture is considered a **macroculture**, representing the core values of a society. Because public schools are embedded within the macroculture, schools tend to emphasize particular values. Cultures exist at other levels as well, however. These smaller groups are called **microcultures** (Banks, 1994a), and they share many, but not all, of the dominant values. Religious practices can define a microculture. People from similar economic backgrounds can form a microculture. Even a single school or classroom can represent a microculture in which people learn a set of values, beliefs, and behaviors valued by the teacher.

culture A way of life in which people share a common language and similar values, religion, ideals, habits of thinking, artistic expressions, and patterns of social and interpersonal relations.

macroculture A larger shared culture representing core or dominant values of a society.

microcultures Groups within cultures that share particular values, knowledge, skills, symbols, and perspectives.

Cultural diversity is a complex matter, more so when the focus narrows from the cultural values, beliefs, and behaviors of a group to those of an individual student. To begin with, the extent to which individuals identify with a particular microculture varies greatly from person to person. Moreover, individuals identify themselves in relation to a number of different microcultures; they are not just Native American or Asian American, male or female, poor or wealthy, hearing or deaf, Catholic or Jewish. Because all of the microcultures with which people identify will have some influence on their belief systems, understanding and responding appropriately to the needs of a particular student in your class can be challenging indeed.

Critical Thinking: Why do students approach learning tasks differently? How do cultural differences contribute to diversity in learning styles among students?

Although race is frequently used to differentiate among groups of people, it is an artificial category based upon *biological* differences, not cultural differences. For example, individuals can be labeled as African American by the color of their skin, but this tells us nothing about whether they identify with an African American culture. "The concept of race today still has a significant social meaning," but it "contributes few insights to cultural understanding" (Baruth & Manning, 1992, p. 11). Teachers must be very cautious not to assume cultural differences on the basis of skin color and other physical traits. These are cultural characteristics only insofar as people misidentify themselves as members of social groups on the basis of physical traits alone.

What are characteristics or categories of diversity commonly identified as important for education? In the sections that follow, we discuss racial and ethnic identity, language and culture, social class, and cultural identification based on gender, sexual orientation, and exceptionality.

Racial and Ethnic Identity

As indicated, racial identity is not, in and of itself, a good predictor of cultural difference, but as you will see, it is sometimes a component of **ethnicity**. People from the same **ethnic group** derive a sense of identity from their common national origin, religion, and sometimes, physical characteristics (Baruth & Manning, 1992). They share common values, beliefs, language, customs, and traditions. Major ethnic groups in the United States are as follows (U.S. Bureau of the Census, 1990):

Critical Thinking: To what extent are special values shared by people of particular ethnic groups?

Approximate percentage of the total U.S. population

Anglo European Americans	71%
African Americans	12%
Hispanic Americans	9%
Asian Americans	3%
Native Americans	1%
Other ethnic Americans	4%

It is important to remember, however, that these groups are themselves characterized by diversity. A considerable number of tribes make up the Native American population, which also includes Eskimos and Aleuts. Hispanic groups include people from Mexico, Puerto Rico, Central and South America, Cuba, and other Spanish-speaking countries. African Americans trace their ancestry largely to Africa but may be West Indian and Haitian as well. Asian Americans are Chinese, Japanese, Korean, Filipino, Vietnamese, Pacific

ethnicity A term used to describe the cultural characteristics of people who identify themselves with a particular ethnic group.

ethnic group The people who derive a sense of identity from their common national origin, religion, and, sometimes, physical characteristics.

Reflection: What cultural groups do you identify with? How does your identification with these groups affect your behavior? Your learning?

Islander, Cambodian, Thai, and Laotian, to name a few. Among other identified ethnic groups, Arab Americans include people from around the world who have their cultural origins in the Arabian Peninsula and the Arabic language, including Muslim, Christian, and secular Arabs. Finally, Anglo Europeans have ethnic backgrounds that include Italian, German, English, Czech, Dutch, and Scandinavian.

What is important for teachers to know about these ethnic groups? How are they different or similar to one another? Much research has been done on racial and ethnic differences, with some interesting results. Historically, Native American children raised in traditional tribal settings, for example, typically learned through story telling, oral history, and observation (remember Kevin and his story telling). Honored elders were their teachers. Sharing, living in harmony with nature, and respecting the rights and dignity of individuals are important values communicated from one generation to the next (Lewis & Ho, 1989; Banks, 1987). These qualities can, however, come into conflict with school practices that emphasize competition among students or familiarity between students and the teacher.

Point: *Students' backgrounds and individual characteristics affect learning.* The values and habits of thinking shared by members of a culture influence how students interpret and react to experiences at school.

Many Hispanic American and African American students share the characteristic of living in extended families or "kinship" communities. They have developed close ties with significant others who participate in child care and other family responsibilities. Interdependence and cooperation are principles learned early by these children (Lum, 1986). A difference between stereotypical African American and Hispanic American families is that African American families tend to be matriarchal, whereas in Hispanic American families, males tend to hold positions of respect and authority.

Hispanic American children (particularly in border states such as California, Arizona, New Mexico, and Texas) are apt to be bilingual, and their families may exhibit a strong commitment to Spanish as their native language. This can present difficulties when students are expected to speak English at school and Spanish at home. Using a student's first language as a learning resource to overcome such difficulties is discussed later in the chapter.

Although Asian Americans are a tremendously diverse group of people—they comprise twenty-nine distinct subgroups with different languages, religion, and customs (Hartman & Askounis, 1989)—their overall successes in American schools have led to the stereotype of "model minority" (Banks, 1987). However, it pays teachers to remember that Asian American students have as many special needs as any other students.

Finally, even though members of ethnic groups may display some of the characteristics most stereotypically associated with their ethnicity, not every member of a racial or ethnic group will necessarily behave in the same way or hold the same beliefs as the majority in that group. Furthermore, being different is not the same as being deficient.

Try This: Interview a teacher regarding the teacher's knowledge of his or her students' cultural identities as they affect teaching and learning.

Racism is "often defined as the domination of one social or ethnic group by another," and it remains all too evident in the United States (Baruth & Manning, 1992, p. 159). These acts of domination lead to inequalities in access to education, wealth, and political power. Racism is built upon a belief system that regards one's own group as inherently superior to others, whether the differentiating factors are ethnicity or some physical distinction (such as skin color). Carl's story illustrates this well:

Carl teaches social studies and coaches basketball in a midwestern middle school where students are of predominantly European ancestry. Carl, whose grandparents are German, feels very comfortable in this situation. However, an increasing number of Hmong families from Laos are moving to town. At first, Carl tried to just look past these new students, ignoring their questions and punishing them more frequently. As the community became more mixed, Carl's classes became more diversified.

One day Carl's daughter in fourth grade brought home a book written by two local teachers. The book provided information about the Hmong through history, folktales, cooking, and art projects. Carl's initial reaction was negative when his daughter asked him to read it.

Yet when he did read the book, he realized just how little he had actually known about his Hmong students and their rich and ancient culture. Many of their fathers and grandfathers had fought side by side with American soldiers in Vietnam. They had rescued downed American pilots and attacked enemy supply lines. When the war was over, the communists destroyed the Hmong villages, forcing them to flee to Thailand and then go to the United States. The more Carl read, the more he realized just how discriminatory he had been, consciously and subconsciously. And he was a social studies teacher! Armed with the information in his book, Carl began looking at his Hmong students in a different light. As he changed his response to them, he found his Hmong students opening up more to him and sharing aspects of their culture with his classes. Reflecting on this, Carl realized his own ignorance fed his discrimination. He became determined to learn more about his newest neighbors and students.

Language and Culture

Many students come to school speaking either a language other than English or a dialect that is considered nonstandard English. Their language or dialect links them to particular ethnic microcultures; language, as an important form of communication, is the primary medium through which ethnicity is shared. When microcultures do not share many of the values prized by the cultural group that is dominant in the local public schools, the stage is already set for potential conflicts. When teachers and students are also linguistically different, there is the additional potential for communication difficulties to occur. These may cause a student to experience academic problems or to withdraw from the school's society (Banks, 1994a). Let's examine two sources of language differences: bilingualism and dialect.

Bilingualism and Biculturalism. The term for the ability to speak fluently in two different languages is **bilingualism**. In rare cases, bilingual persons can read, write, speak, and think as well in one language as the other. This occurs when they have grown up using both languages in natural social settings for practical, communicative functions (Williams & Snipper, 1990). More often, however, bilinguals favor one language over the other, having acquired their first language in the social setting of home and the second language in the formal setting of school.

Competence in two languages appears to influence academic achievement in three ways (Banks, 1994a). **Additive bilingualism** enhances academic achieve-

Example: Factors such as limited English proficiency, low family income, homelessness, drug abuse, HIV infection, child abuse, or racial discrimination increase the likelihood that students may experience difficulties in school, be referred for and placed in special education programs, and drop out of school.

bilingualism A term used to describe the ability to speak fluently in two different languages.

additive bilingualism A form of bilingualism in which students have achieved complete literacy in two languages. Because of conceptual interdependence between languages, learning in one aids achievement in the other.

Students with limited proficiency in both English and the language of the home are at the greatest disadvantage in school. However, research suggests that fully bilingual children have great metalinguisitic awareness that can enhance academic achievement.

ment due to the complete literacy of the speaker in the two languages. Because of conceptual interdependence between languages, a concept learned in one language means that it is also learned in the other language. Additive bilinguals appear to enjoy an advantage over monolingual children in a number of specific cognitive tasks. For example, they appear better able than monolingual students to step back and reflect on the structure and function of language (Bialystok & Ryan, 1985). Being fluent in more than one language gives them a broader perspective. The ability to think about one's own knowledge of language is called ***metalinguistic awareness.***

Connection: Metalinguistic awareness relates to the concept of metacognition, which is discussed in detail in Chapter 7.

Dominant Bilingualism. **Dominant bilingualism,** by contrast, has neither a positive nor a negative effect on achievement (Banks, 1994a). In this case, bilinguals are fully competent in their first language and nearly so in their second. **Subtractive bilingualism** exerts a negative influence on achievement. These students, although conversationally competent in both languages, have not developed the thinking skills necessary for full literacy in their first language. Without those skills available for transfer to the second language, achievement in the second language suffers (Banks, 1994a).

Some students have **limited English proficiency**, which means that their first language is not English, and they depend primarily on their first language for communication and understanding. Their English language skills are limited, and they find it difficult to communicate in the dominant language of the classroom.

It is important for teachers to recognize that bilingual students or those with limited English proficiency might be set apart from their classmates in more than language differences. Because cultural differences usually accompany language differences, these students may feel conflict or confusion about their cultural allegiances. For example, a recent immigrant from Mexico to California said of his ninth-grade classmates:

> There is so much discrimination and hate. Even from other kids from Mexico who have been here longer. They don't treat us like brothers. They hate even more. It makes them feel more like natives. They want to be American. They don't want to speak Spanish to us, they already know English and how to act. (Olsen, 1988, p. 36)

These students must learn to operate not only in two languages but in two cultures as well. It is also interesting to note that one group attempts to establish its "native" recognition by discriminating against others from the same ethnic group.

metalinguistic awareness The ability to reflect on one's own knowledge of language.

dominant bilingualism A form of bilingualism in which students are fully competent in their first language and nearly so in their second.

subtractive bilingualism A form of bilingualism in which students, although conversationally competent in both languages, are not fully literate in either one; this has an adverse effect on achievement.

limited English proficiency A phrase used to describe students whose first language is not English and who depend on their first language for communication and understanding.

Dialects and Regional Culture. A **dialect** is a distinctive version of a language or a variation within a language. The differences among dialects may be in pronunciation, "yard" in the Midwest is "yahd" in New England; grammar, "I be going" in one neighborhood is "I'm fixing to go" in another; or vocabulary, "mash the button" in an elevator in Tallahassee is "push the button" anywhere else. Dialects differ in other ways as well, and factors other than location define dialect groups. People who share dialects often share an ethnic heritage, geographic regional culture, or a particular social and economic background.

Like language itself, all dialects enable their speakers to create meanings and express understandings. Teachers should respect the cognitive abilities of students who speak in nonstandard dialects, because these students will span the same range in other abilities as students who speak standard English. This does not mean that a teacher should accept nonstandard dialect in all settings. The physician who addresses a professional meeting of the American Medical Association speaks in one way. When she addresses her children she speaks in a different way. The language she uses on the basketball court is different still. She can shift her codes to suit the situation. What of the students who know only a nonstandard dialect? Unless these students learn the standard form of English, the situations that call for it are likely to remain out of bounds.

Today, Banks (1994a) recommends that teachers view students' languages or dialects as a source of strength and a resource for learning standard English. Rather than placing linguistically different students in separate language programs, he suggests that they be accommodated in regular classrooms. In cases where a large number of students speak the same language, a bilingual teacher may be a feasible option. Otherwise, monolingual English-speaking students or more proficient bilingual students can help classmates with limited English proficiency or with nonstandard dialects to learn standard school English, a practice that benefits tutors as much as tutees.

Critical Thinking: A disproportionate number of students from culturally and linguistically diverse backgrounds are in special education classes. Is this an example of discrimination in schools?

Try This: Interview a teacher regarding his or her approach to language skill development. How does the presence of bilingual students, or students with limited English proficiency, and students with regional dialects affect his or her teaching?

Here's How to Build on the Language Skills of Your Students

- Become familiar with the dialects and language skills of your students. You will be better able to detect when miscommunication or misunderstanding occurs.
- Use reading materials with predictable and familiar text structures. Knowing the text schema will help students better comprehend the text and figure out the meanings of unfamiliar words.
- Use visual aids to supplement printed and audio materials. Using multiple modalities to express a concept will facilitate student comprehension.
- Have students make up stories and conversations using different dialects and speech styles. Discuss with them the situations and contexts where each style would be appropriate.

Socioeconomic Status

Just as students reflect racial, ethnic, and language diversity, they also come from families differing widely in socioeconomic status. **Socioeconomic status**, a family's relative standing in society, is measured by a number of variables including income, occupation, education, access to health coverage and community

dialect A distinctive version or variation of a language in pronunciation, grammar, vocabulary, and usage.

socioeconomic status Relative standing in society as measured by variables such as income, occupation, education, access to health coverage and community resources, and political power and prestige.

Example: In the United States, 20 percent of children under the age of eighteen are poor, and it is estimated that their numbers have grown by more than two million in the past ten years. The majority of poor Americans are of Anglo-European ancestry and lives in rural areas. Over 25 percent of children living in inner cities are poor.

resources, and political power and prestige (Macionis, 1994). The unfortunate truth is that American schools already serve more than 15 million children who live in poverty, and this number is projected to grow to over 20 million by the year 2020 (Pallas, Natriello, & McDill, 1989). This means that one in four children under the age of eighteen will be poor.

Although more poor students come from Anglo European families than from families of other ethnic origins, the percentages are greater for students from ethnic groups such as African American, Hispanic American, and Native American. Thus, the overall poverty rate for children in the United States is approximately 20 percent (Macionis, 1994). However, the rate for Hispanic American children is 36 percent and for African American children, 44 percent. The majority of poor children live in rural areas.

Children in poverty face hardships on a daily basis that can be difficult to understand for a teacher who comes from a different background. For example, families living in poverty experience low wages, un- or underemployment, little property ownership and no personal savings, and lack of food resources (Baruth & Manning, 1992). It is not uncommon for children from these families to come to school not having eaten breakfast and without money for lunch. In some schools that serve a largely poor constituency, 80 percent or more of the student population might qualify for the federally funded free lunch program.

The effects of poverty can include students "at a high risk for dropping out of school, experiencing academic failure, and engaging in antisocial behavior" (Banks, 1994a, p. 36). Feelings of helplessness, dependence, and inferiority can also affect children from families living in poverty (Baruth & Manning, 1992).

However, it would be a mistake to assume that feelings or experiences associated with low social class alone necessarily lead students to lowered ambition or a lack of desire to improve themselves. In a review of nearly 140 studies conducted between 1960 and 1990, no evidence was found to support several commonly held assumptions about the achievement motivation of African American students (Graham, 1994). Contrary to the beliefs that initiated this line of research, "African Americans appear to maintain a belief in personal control, have high expectancies, and enjoy positive self-regard," regardless of social class (p. 55).

Gender and Sexual Identity

Many individuals in our society mistakenly associate *sex* and *gender*. Sex is a biological difference that is relatively fixed at birth. Gender, however, is a social construct that refers to the thoughts, feelings, and behaviors that have been labeled as predominantly "masculine" or "feminine." Actions that are sometimes identified as gender-specific might, in fact, be generated by ethnicity, socioeconomic status, or the expectations of one's context. Moreover, males and females behave differently in same-sex versus mixed-sex groups. Once again, it must be noted that not all males and females will behave in gender-stereotypic ways. "Even in situations in which people tend to behave in a gender-stereotypical manner, their actual behavior cannot be predicted on the basis of their sex alone" (Grossman & Grossman, 1994, p. 3). Therefore, you should consider the generalizations discussed here as broad characteristics that do not necessarily hold for all of your students. Nevertheless, they can alert you to anticipate how your students might react when their actions are based upon gender stereotypes.

Insights ON SUCCESSFUL PRACTICE

What strategies do you use with students in your classroom to promote acceptance of cultural differences?

Several weeks ago, a linguistics professor from the university came to my class to talk about her country, China. The children seemed to enjoy the visit as much as our guest. When I brought the thank-you notes written to her by my students, she told me, "Your students were very attentive. They showed a great interest. You must be doing something right—they seemed to have a great respect for other people's cultures."

Walking back to my car, I began to think, what is it that I've supposedly done right? All of a sudden, many memories began to cross my mind. I remembered the two-year project we did about Native Americans. Before we began our project I realized that I could not talk to my students about Native Americans. I didn't know what important information needed to be transmitted. I also realized that the students needed a role model. They needed to see me learn from other people, from other cultures, and to respect other points of view. During those two years our students heard several guest speakers talk about legends, computers, weather, tepees, laws, buffaloes, medicine, family, beliefs, and languages. All the speakers were from different Indian tribes. Some were parents from our school; others were members of our community.

Why is it so important to show our students we value other people's customs and traditions? Because our students are part of their own customs and traditions. They need to feel they are being respected for what they are so they can begin to respect others. Being a bilingual teacher, I want to model respect toward one another at every moment. If a child laughs about the sounds other languages make, the students and I discuss the issue. We talk about language, cultures, and differences right then and there. Languages are made out of many different sounds. There are many different groups of sounds, and they come from many different groups of people from all over the world.

Our role as teachers is to bring knowledge to our students about the world and its people, not to say who is better than whom but to appreciate their strengths and struggles. With this knowledge the students will become aware of differences and similarities among all of us. They won't be afraid of differences—on the contrary, they will be sensitive toward others. This is what it means to me to prepare students for the future. Hmmm, maybe I am doing something right.

DELIA TERESA DE GARCIA, University Hill Elementary School, Boulder, Colorado

"In general, females have a lower dropout rate than males. They also are less likely to get into trouble for behavioral problems, less likely to be disciplined by their teachers or suspended from school, and less likely to be placed in special education programs for the learning disabled, behavior disordered, or emotionally disturbed" (Grossman & Grossman, 1994, p. xi). Many gender differences seem to surface at different ages. Infants and toddlers, for example, show few gender-related differences in behavior, but by the time they have reached preschool age, they typically demonstrate marked differences in how they prefer to play. Girls tend to prefer structured activities where they assign specific roles, such as teacher, student, and bus driver in playing school. Boys, by contrast, tend to prefer more unstructured play activities with few rules.

How would you describe what this teacher is "doing right?" How does her story illustrate the principle that teachers and students are both learners?

Research has raised questions about the sources of differences in the way boys and girls learn. Sources might include cultural values and expectations, sex-role socialization, gender bias in the classroom, and the biopsychology of males and females. Are these girls more likely than boys to avoid disobedience, conflict, and competition?

In school, boys and girls exhibit differences in their emotions, their relations with others, and their communicative styles. Girls are more likely to be cooperative and to share their thoughts and feelings, whereas boys are more likely to be competitive and to express anger (Grossman & Grossman, 1994). In a recent study on how fourth- and fifth-grade students reason about important issues that arise in their reading, Waggoner, Chinn, Yi, and Anderson (1993) discovered interesting differences between girls and boys. They first had students read *Stone Fox*, a story about a boy named Willie whose grandfather is ill and can't pay taxes on their farm. To raise money for the taxes, Willie enters a dog-sled competition and leads most of the race. Ten feet from the finish line, Willie's dog dies from exhaustion. Stone Fox, a Native American who usually wins the race and needs the money to buy back land originally belonging to his people, is running in second place. The researchers then posed this question to the students: Should Stone Fox win the race himself or let Willie win?

Example: Studies show that when gender and race interact, African American and Hispanic girls experience the greatest discrimination.

Critical Thinking: A disproportionate number of male students are in special education classes. Is this an example of gender discrimination in schools?

The boys who participated in the discussion tended to argue from a rule-based position—that is, Willie's dog died so there is no way for him to win the race. In that case, Stone Fox should go ahead and collect the prize. The girls, in contrast, showed empathy for Willie and argued that Stone Fox should help him. They searched for ways to get around the indisputable fact that Willie's dog had died, and they related personal experiences of similar events to engender sympathy for Willie. These differences in argumentation between boys and girls reflect general differences in communicative styles, where girls are more apt to avoid conflict, preserve harmony, and promote egalitarian roles than boys (Grossman & Grossman, 1994).

Try This: Observe a class to see how boys and girls communicate verbally and nonverbally. Are there differences in styles of communication or discussion? How do these differences affect the teaching and learning in the class?

Do these differences between girls and boys stem from biology or culture? It is certainly true that boys and girls are treated differently from birth. Parents tend to play more roughly with their sons than their daughters, reacting positively to assertive behavior in boys and to emotional sensitivity in girls (Lytton & Romney, 1991). Despite parents' best efforts to raise their children in the absence of gender-role stereotypes, it is virtually impossible to completely avoid them. Department stores offer tools and trucks for boys, but dolls and cookware for girls. The differentiation also extends to gendered names for the same toy; girls play with *dolls* while boys play with *action figures*.

Connection: At the end of the Stone Fox story, Stone Fox picks up Willie's dead dog and carries it across the finish line of the sled race, thus making himself and Willie both winners.

As for learning and preference for certain types of instructional activities or learning environments in school, gender differences are complex and not clearly understood. For instance, it is well documented that boys begin to outpace girls in science achievement during middle school (e.g., Haertel, Walberg, Junker, & Pascarella, 1981; Zerega, Haertel, Tsai, & Walberg, 1986), but the reasons for this are speculative at best. The achievement difference could be a function of gender difference, or it could as easily be a consequence of cultural upbringing in which boys are expected to achieve in science and girls are not. It is also the case that girls and boys have different experiences in science from the early grades through high school. Results of a recent study revealed that boys carried out more science demonstrations and handled more laboratory equipment than girls (Sadker, Sadker, & Klein, 1991). During the same period, the attitude of girls toward science declined (American Association of University Women, 1992).

Try This: Observe a class and focus on how the teacher pays attention to the boys and the girls. Does the teacher call on one group more than the other? What does the teacher do to assure equal participation by boys and girls?

There is also evidence of a gender gap in mathematics achievement, but the gap appears to be closing (Hyde, Fennema & Lamon, 1990) and is less evident when males and females take the same math courses during high school (Linn, 1991). For teachers, achievement differences between males and females on large-scale assessments of this sort should not be used to predict learning in individuals.

Example: Teachers should also consider differences in sexual orientation. As many as 10 percent of students are homosexual and are often the targets of ridicule, discrimination, and hate crimes. They may be placed in special education programs intended for students with emotional and behavioral disorders. More than one-third of deaths by suicide involve homosexual youths.

In class, males and females differ in their preferences for instructional activities, with males preferring to work independently and with active learning tasks. Females, by contrast, tend to prefer working in cooperative groups or under the direct supervision of the teacher. Boys tend to demand more attention from the teacher than girls, often by calling out answers that prompt a teacher's response (Bailey, 1993). Whether or not this is always the cause, teachers generally pay more attention to boys, asking them more questions and giving them more feedback. Even when teachers are aware of the difference and try to call equally upon girls and boys in class, they still tend to pay more attention to boys, especially in science classes (Kahle & Meece, 1994). The unfortunate effect of these differences in attention is that by the time girls reach college age, they have received an average of 1,800 hours less instruction (Sadker et al., 1991).

The findings about gender differences suggest that teachers should try to be aware of how they interact with boys and girls. On the one hand, teachers should consider gender differences in structuring their class to meet the needs of both boys and girls. On the other, they should not discriminate against either girls or boys, and they should avoid perpetuating gender stereotypes that get in the way of effective learning.

Here's How to Create a Gender-Fair Classroom

- Examine your own attitudes and behavior for possible gender bias. Teachers can inadvertently communicate gender-role expectations and stereotypes.
- Model the behavior you want students to adopt, and reinforce students for behaving in nonstereotypical ways.
- Expose students to a variety of gender roles, illustrating both women and men in nonstereotypical roles. Choose curricular materials with a balance of gender roles, and select a variety of role models for guest speakers, tutors, and mentors.
- Encourage students to use nonsexist language, and help them to identify linguistic bias in the materials they read or the programs they view.
- Use a variety of instructional strategies to meet students' individual needs and to help them develop strengths in areas where their skills are weak. For example, although girls are generally able to work cooperatively better than boys, both can benefit from

Try This: Interview a teacher regarding his or her strategies for creating a gender-fair classroom.

instruction on how to function effectively in a cooperative setting. Similarly, help girls to function effectively in a competitive role when the situation calls for it.

- Encourage students to consider nontraditional careers and occupations. (Grossman & Grossman, 1994)

Exceptional Ability and Disability

Exceptional students are those who require special education or special services to reach their full potential. They may have mental retardation, learning disabilities, emotional/behavioral disorders, communication disorders, impaired hearing, visual impairment, physical disabilities, or special talents. In Chapter 5, we describe the nature of these exceptionalities and the types of accommodations that teachers can make to help these students reach their full potentials. When exceptional students identify with others who share their ability or disability, they form a kind of microculture. For example, students with hearing impairments, who often communicate in ways that make it difficult for hearing students to join their conversations, form a "deaf culture." A good illustration of the deaf culture can be seen in the events that occurred in 1988 at Gallaudet University in Washington, DC, which is dedicated to educating the deaf.

Before 1988, Gallaudet had never had a deaf person as its president. Two of the three candidates the board of trustees had considered were deaf, but the person they chose to appoint as president was not. To the students, the appointment represented the will of the hearing majority, and they felt cheated. They wanted a role model. One student expressed the frustration of being a deaf person in a hearing world: "I want to be equal. Why do deaf people have to be treated lower than hearing people? Deafness is not a handicap. It's a culture, a language." After weeks of protest, the students finally won and one of the two original deaf candidates was selected as president. In his words, "We showed the world that the only thing deaf people can't do is hear."

The important point to this story is that the differences among students attributable to their exceptionalities should not lead to discrimination against them. Teachers must take care to provide exceptional students, like all other students, with learning opportunities that take advantage of their capabilities and enable them to reach their full potential.

HOW CAN CULTURAL CONFLICTS ARISE IN YOUR CLASSROOM?

Reflection: What value orientations of the home influenced your attitudes toward school?

Cultural differences become most obvious in school when problems arise from mismatches between the students' beliefs and values and those of the teacher or larger school culture. Teachers must be alert for such mismatches and be prepared to provide experiences that may be more compatible with students' backgrounds.

Cultures of the School and Home

Students learn cultural values and behaviors at home that may or may not prepare them for the expectations of the school. Why, for example, are "an inordinate number of success stories coming from Asian American students, especially in the areas of math and science" (Reglin & Adams, 1990, p. 143)? A descriptive study of cultural differences between Indochinese families who had recently immigrated to the United States and their non-Asian American counterparts revealed three notable differences. Indochinese parents wanted their children to do well in school, and students responded to this influence. The Indochinese students tended to put off until their late teens activities that could interfere with studying, such as dating, watching television, or participating in after-school athletics. Finally, the Indochinese students spent more time doing homework than their non-Asian counterparts. In many Indochinese families, parents and older siblings also help students with their homework, making homework time a nightly ritual in the family (Caplan, Choy, & Whitmore, 1992).

The value that Asian parents place on student motivation is another factor that may contribute to the success of many of these students in school. In a comparison of Chinese, Chinese American, and European American mothers' beliefs concerning their children's math performances, Chinese mothers were more likely to attribute failure to a lack of effort than Chinese American mothers, who were, in turn, more likely to cite lack of effort than were European American mothers (Chih-Mei & McDevitt, 1987).

It is not true, of course, that all Asian American students do well in school. Sometimes the pressure of living up to parents' expectations causes frustration and conflict in adjusting to the culture of American schools. According to one Cambodian immigrant, "My parents will not let me stay after school to play soccer. They say I have to study. I study and I study and I study. . . . If I don't have homework, still I study. They make me do it over and over again. They really want me to do well, but they don't understand about schools here" (Divoky, 1988, p. 221). Similarly, a Chinese American girl says about her cultural conflicts that "I don't know who I am. Am I the good Chinese daughter? Am I an American teenager? I always feel I am letting my parents down when I am with my friends because I act so American, but I also feel that I will never really be an American" (Olsen, 1988, p. 30).

Connection: Identity formation is discussed in detail in Chapter 3.

Learning Styles and Classroom Organization

Another source of potential cultural conflicts occurs when the organization of classrooms or the instructional strategies used by teachers does not match the learning styles of students. This can be a problem for any student, not just members of ethnic groups, but cultural differences are often so subtle that they are difficult to recognize. In teaching Middle Eastern and Asian students, for example, one of the authors has often felt frustrated in trying to elicit their own opinions on a topic; their tendency is to quote extensively from other authors. After working closely with an Asian American and an Iranian American student, she has come to realize that their cultures call for people to greatly respect scholars and teachers. It is honorable to quote from respected masters of a discipline because the student's words are a poor match by comparison. The author has now adopted strategies to help students see the value in developing their own opinions.

Critical Thinking: In what kinds of instructional situations might a teacher need to accommodate students' cultural backgrounds?

Many American classrooms, despite the increasing adoption of cooperative learning structures, are organized so that students work individually and learn alone (Cushner, McClelland, & Safford, 1992). Grading on the curve still promotes

Insights ON SUCCESSFUL PRACTICE

What strategies have you found work best for increasing parental involvement?

For several years one of our building-wide goals has been an effort to improve parental involvement and communication in the school community. In order to facilitate this discussion, the staff met with a group of interested parents. While we had a solid core of very involved parents, we knew we needed to expand our base to include more parents.

With this in mind, we first brainstormed the things we currently did to involve parents in their children's education: regular and invitational conferences, monthly newsletters, notes about class activities, parents as field trip volunteers, workers in the library, parents as listeners for our reading incentive program. The list went on. We were pleased to see just how much involvement was already happening.

Next we listed (with the parent committee's input) what areas we could expand: more parents on school committees (budget, technology, school improvement) informal lunches or breakfasts with teachers and students, parental help in the classroom on projects, a phone message system to update parents on classroom activities, parental sharing of individual expertise, help with drama productions, creating a school calendar of events, help in the computer lab. This list grew longer and longer as we talked.

Our school is composed of teams with three to four teachers per team. After the all-staff discussion the teams met individually and put into place their strategies. For example, our team now begins the school year with a special open house for just our parents, during which we introduce ourselves and explain our program. We emphasize our open door policy in which parents are invited any time to drop in and see what's happening. We now send home a weekly note for each student highlighting successes and, if necessary, indicating be-havior difficulties. Almost weekly we have parents in sharing cultural heritage, occupations, or hobbies. (This month, for instance, one parent shared his hobby of raising iguanas, another her expertise at quilting, another her life in Laos, another the traditions of Hanukkah.) We call home when a student does something exceptionally well. We have a team calendar focusing on what we are teaching during the month and what events are happening. We post messages on the informational phone computer.

As we worked toward our goal, we realized that we needed to open more lines of communication. It is one thing to ask parents to become more involved and quite another to actually involve them. We are experimenting and learning. We have more ideas now: businesses providing release time so that working parents can come to school, a goal of requesting two hours of school time per month for parents to help, broadening our outreach to include parents of former students and others in the school community. This list grows and grows.

One of our cornerstones now is that it takes the whole village to educate each child. Our village partnership of parents and teachers is becoming a reality.

PETER ROOP, McKinley Elementary School,
Appleton, Wisconsin

Why is parental involvement important for students' success in school? What forces make it difficult for families to be involved? What other strategies can you think of for increasing parental involvement?

competition in some classrooms, and many are teacher centered, with activities that call for students to provide one right answer (Eggen & Kauchak, 1994). Contrast this classroom organization with the predominantly cooperative learning styles of many ethnic groups, such as some Native American and some African American groups. Conflict might occur not only because members might be uncomfortable with individualistic or competitive learning situations but also because other students are unaccustomed to working in cooperative groups when these are used in the classroom. When teachers become aware of cultural conflicts between the learning styles of their students and the instructional styles of the classroom, they can incorporate a variety of alternative instructional strategies. Teachers can examine the classroom's cultural norms and modify them to better match the cultural diversity of the students.

here's how

Here's How to Create a Culture-Fair Classroom

- Look for ways to present diverse perspectives, experiences, and contributions. Present concepts in ways that represent diverse cultural groups.
- Include materials and visual displays that represent members of all cultural groups in a positive manner.
- Provide as much emphasis on contemporary culture as on historical culture, and represent cultural groups as active and dynamic.
- View your instruction holistically, so that multicultural aspects will permeate all subject areas and all phases of the school day.
- Draw on your students' experiential backgrounds, daily lives, and experiences.
- Make sure all students have equal access to instructional resources, including computers and special programs as well as yourself. (Adapted from Baruth & Manning, 1992, pp. 175-176)

Try This: Interview a teacher regarding his or her strategies for creating a culture-fair classroom.

Communication Styles

Students and teachers can experience communication difficulties when they are culturally dissimilar, because either may misread the verbal and nonverbal cues of the other. Consider, for example, the findings of a study that compared the interactions of school counselors with students who were culturally similar or dissimilar (Erickson & Schultz, 1982). In conversation, the culturally dissimilar students did not acknowledge the individual counselor's comments; the culturally similar students did. The acknowledgment difference was due to the fact that the culturally dissimilar students did not want to interrupt the counselor when he or she was speaking. The counselors interpreted this lack of acknowledgment as a lack of understanding. Counselors repeated their messages several times, simplifying them each time. After the conversations, the counselors judged the culturally dissimilar students as less bright than students who were culturally similar to themselves. The culturally dissimilar students reported that the counselors made them feel stupid. Neither the students nor the counselors seemed to understand the subtle cultural differences that affected their judgments of each other.

Critical Thinking: How might a teacher find out about communication values to enhance students' participation in classroom interactions?

Try This: Observe students' verbal and nonverbal communication in and out of classrooms. What differences in communication styles might relate to cultural differences? What effect might these differences have in the classroom?

Problems can also occur in instruction when teachers expect students to actively participate in discussions and students are not accustomed to these interactions. Some Asian American and Native American students may sit quietly during discussion, even when they know the answer or are called upon to respond (Yao, 1985; Villegas, 1991). When students are accustomed to a particular type of interaction at home, they may find it difficult to adjust to alternate demands in the classroom. Likewise, teachers can feel frustrated by what they perceive to be a lack of response to their teaching efforts. Recognizing that cultural differences in communication styles exist can enable teachers to better understand their students and to help them feel comfortable with the interactive styles used in class.

WHAT ARE THE DIMENSIONS OF MULTICULTURAL EDUCATION?

Multicultural education currently means many things to many people (Banks, 1994b; Sleeter & Grant, 1987). Views of diversity and the impact it should have on teaching and school curricula reflect different ideologies about the nature of ethnicity and its place in modern societies such as the United States (Banks, 1994a). Some believe that too much emphasis on diversity denies the importance of the larger, national culture and might cause divisiveness in society. Others have argued that ethnic diversity provides strength to democracy and should be an integral part of education. These two positions reflect the assumptions of ideologies at two ends of a continuum, assimilation at one end and pluralism at the other. Multiculturalism, as a basis of school reform efforts, is most closely aligned with the pluralist end of the continuum. Let's examine each of these approaches to diversity.

Education for Integration and Assimilation

The ideologies of integration and assimilation might best be understood through the melting pot analogy, which has been used to describe U.S. society and culture. In the melting pot, individual ethnic groups merge into a single, shared culture; this is **integration**. Although some characteristics of the original cultures maintain, they blend in support of the new whole. They are coequal in contributing to the national culture, but they do not coexist with it. Just as the ethnic cultures change in response to the national culture, so does the national culture subtly change each time a new ethnic group is added to the mix.

Conversely, with **assimilation**, different ethnic groups learn the ways of the dominant culture and become one with it. A hierarchy of values is assumed where those of an incoming ethnic group are subordinate to those of the national culture. According to assimilationists, the national values of the United States are "embodied in the American Creed and in such documents as the United States Constitution and the Declaration of Independence" (Banks, 1994a, p. 125; cf. Ravitch, 1990). It is expected, then, that people from different cultural groups will adopt and live by these values. They are neither coequal with the national culture nor allowed to coexist with it. "Difference" in this case becomes "deficit."

In education, an integrationist or assimilationist view is characterized by the assumption that living in a common culture requires certain universal skills that must be attained by everyone. To support this goal, curricula should be geared to such skills in order to prepare all students for participation in and commitment to the national culture. The effect on ethnic groups of this educational plan

integration A view of diversity in which individual ethnic groups merge together to form a single, shared culture.

assimilation A view of diversity in which a hierarchy of values is assumed so that members of ethnic groups are expected to adopt and live by the values of the dominant culture.

depends on whether they are viewed as coequal with the national culture (as in integration) or unequal (as in assimilation). When educators expect socialization practices of some ethnic groups to have put members of those groups at an early disadvantage, and they recommend compensatory programs to help these students catch up, they adhere to a **deficit**, or unequal, **model** (Banks, 1994a); that is, some groups are deficient in skills that they must make up in order to contribute to the national culture. Students without these skills are considered to be at risk, likely to drop out of school if they are not quickly brought to the same level of skill as other students.

Another form of compensatory education has been offered in the recommendation that disadvantaged ethnic minority groups should study ethnic content. The reasoning is that "members of ethnic groups who have experienced discrimination and structural exclusion have negative self-concepts and negative attitudes toward their own racial and ethnic groups" (Banks, 1994a, p. 108). Negative self-concepts and low achievement strivings must be some of the reasons for the characteristically lower academic achievement of minority group children (Graham, 1994). Therefore, studying ethnic content should enhance the self-concepts, thereby raising the achievement levels of these groups (Assante, 1991). Evidence now suggests, however, that these assumptions are not entirely true.

Reflection: Examine your own beliefs about diversity. Are they most similar to assimilation, integration, or pluralism? What is the basis for your beliefs?

For one thing, comparisons among members of ethnic groups have revealed no systematic differences in their self-concepts or aspirations (Graham, 1994). For another, all students, not just ethnic minorities, can benefit from an approach to education that helps both teachers and students understand cultural differences. As Banks (1994a) put it, "the school should be a cultural environment in which acculturation takes place: both teachers and students should assimilate some of the views, perceptions, and ethos of each other as they interact" (p. 116).

Education for Cultural Pluralism

As the term suggests, **cultural pluralism** is a view of diversity that embraces cultural differences. From this perspective, it is important for individuals to develop ethnic attachments, because participation in the larger society is done from the ranks of the ethnic group. A salad bowl analogy has been used to describe pluralism. All the ingredients that go into the salad are equally important to the final product, so they are coequal. But they also coexist in the final product; each contributes something to the salad, but each maintains its integrity and uniqueness. According to the pluralist, society works in a similar manner. Ethnic groups are assumed to have independent norms, values, and beliefs. Oppressed ethnic minorities must build their strength from within in order to compete in the wider society, which is typically controlled by a dominant group. The ethnic group provides both psychological support and a sense of identity, which protect the individual from discrimination likely to be experienced in the broader society (Banks, 1994a).

In education, two consequences of cultural pluralism arise. First, it is assumed that students from different cultural groups will have unique learning styles and therefore different learning needs. This is the **difference model**, which suggests that curricula should be revised to be more consistent with the experiences of different cultural groups. They should reflect students' different learning styles, cultural histories, and present experiences. In addition, the goal of such curricula is to help students develop strong attachments to their ethnic groups,

deficit model The assumption that students who are members of ethnic minority groups are deficient in knowledge and skills required to contribute to the national culture.

cultural pluralism A view of diversity that embraces cultural differences.

difference model The assumption that students from different cultural groups will have unique learning styles and therefore different learning needs.

Critical Thinking: Consider the problem in the Teacher Chronicle in terms of assimilationist and pluralist views of diversity. If Ms. Walker believes in the deficit model, how would she be likely to interpret Kevin's problems with writing? What strategies might she use to help Kevin? If Ms. Walker identifies with cultural pluralism, how might she respond to Kevin's writing problem?

so that they will be able to function effectively within those groups. This is quite different from the goals of assimilationist curricula.

Both assimilation and cultural pluralism have their problems when taken as a basis for responding to cultural diversity in schools (Banks, 1994a). With assimilation, which has been the predominant response to diversity in education, ethnic groups have had to make all the accommodations. Moreover, the assimilationist assumption of universal learning styles does not seem to be completely true, and to the extent that research is conducted with members of the dominant culture only, we will fail to determine just what cultural differences are important for education. Yet, concentrating on the differences among cultural groups to the exclusion of what groups face in the common culture, as cultural pluralism would have us do, ignores the fact that people participate in a variety of subcultures at different levels. According to Banks (1994a), "the pluralist has not adequately conceptualized how a strongly pluralistic nation will maintain an essential degree of societal cohesion" (p. 127). In Banks's view, multiculturalism must be defined in such a way that cultural differences are both acknowledged and considered to be sources of strengths for building a common national culture.

Multiculturalism: Different Is Not Deficient

The society envisioned by multicultural theorists is an open one where individuals are free to associate with racial, ethnic, or gender groups and to participate in the wider, national culture. In fact, national ideals are assumed to be the unifying elements of society, even as groups maintain some form of microcultural identity. **Multiculturalism** recognizes that "even though the ethnic group and ethnic community are very important in the socialization of individuals, individuals are also strongly influenced by the common national culture during their early socialization, even if they never leave the ethnic community or enclave" (Banks, 1994a, p. 130). This is consistent with the notion of **multiple acculturation**, which Banks believes best describes how the general culture of the United States formed and continues to evolve. Thus, the common U.S. culture changes as some elements of various ethnic, racial, and religious cultures come to be an important part of it. The separate identities of these groups, however, take on a distinctly American flavor.

What implications for education does a multicultural ideology suggest? Learning is assumed to be influenced by the unique characteristics of students that they owe to their cultural heritage and gender, as well as by the characteristics they share in common with other students. The multicultural theorist believes that curricula should both respect cultural differences of students *and* reflect the shared national culture. This often means viewing cultural differences as an opportunity for learning. Students can learn about one another, and ethnic- or gender-specific materials may help some students perform better in school and enable them to be more successful in society later on. From this perspective, not only must teachers be skilled in applying theories and research on learning, but also they should be knowledgeable about and sensitive to the cultural differences of their students.

multiculturalism A recognition that ethnic groups make up and contribute to a national culture while they maintain an individual identity.

multiple acculturation The reciprocal idea that the general culture of the United States changes with the entry of each new ethnic and cultural group, which is itself changed by the national culture.

When responses to diversity become institutionalized, they typically take the form of special programs, curriculum reform, and school restructuring. For example, bilingual programs are offered for students with limited English proficiency, and summer math and science institutes are designed to enhance the achievement of girls in these subjects. In school reform, efforts are generally undertaken to change parts of the curriculum to reflect multicultural concerns or to change the very norms and values of the school itself.

Try This: As a teaching resource, develop a contact list of selected local, state, and national professional organizations for multicultural education, bilingual education, and the education of students at risk.

Bilingual-Bicultural Education

Special programs designed to teach English-language skills to students with limited English proficiency fall into the realm of **bilingual education**. Educators are of two minds on how and when students should be taught English. According to one view, the student's native language should be used initially as the main vehicle of communication and the primary means for acquiring other academic skills. In Maintenance: Native Language (MNL) programs, students become fully literate in their home languages before English is introduced. Therefore, they study all subject areas in the home language until they have mastered listening, speaking, reading, and writing. With mastery of these basic skills in the home language, it is expected that students will be readily able to transfer them into English (Banks, 1994a; Willig, 1985).

In programs known as Transitional: English as a Second Language (TESL), however, students begin studying English immediately, usually by being pulled out of their regular classes for some period each day. Instruction for other subjects is done in the regular classroom. **Language immersion** programs are an intensive form of TESL in which students are immersed in the English language arts for extended periods of time. Once they have learned to listen and speak in English, they work on reading and writing. When basic language skills in English have been mastered, students then return to their regular classes for instruction in other subject areas (Banks, 1994a).

Try This: Visit several schools in your area. What types of bilingual programs are being used in these schools? What was the reason for implementing an MNL or TESL approach?

Immersion programs seem to work best when they are begun very early in a child's schooling. Young children learn a second language quite easily (cf. Lenneberg, 1967; McLaughlin, 1984), and it makes sense from a curriculum standpoint. The social and experiential emphasis in kindergarten lends itself to language learning. Furthermore, a child who is taught in his or her native language for several years and then switched to an immersion program may suffer from the necessary disruption in the curricular sequence.

Immersion programs also seem to work well for native-English-speaking students who are learning another language through immersion. Participants in an immersion program learned to understand and produce the new language quickly and proficiently (in both oral and written form; cf. Genesee, 1985). However, how do immersion programs fare for students with limited English proficiency attempting to learn English?

In general, TESL programs (including immersion) have been found to teach students with limited English proficiency a functional level of English more quickly than MNL programs. However, long-range academic achievement and educational development have been shown to be greater for students in MNL programs than those in TESL programs (Willig, 1985). The reason for the difference seems to be that TESL programs do not teach skills for critical thinking, such as hypothesizing, predicting, and inferring, whereas the very premise of MNL programs is to make sure students are fully literate in their home language so that critical thinking skills will transfer to English. As Banks (1994a) points out, TESL programs are compensatory, viewing lack of English proficiency as a deficit that students must overcome. This is consistent with the notion in society that English has greater value (Landry, 1987). In con-

bilingual education The teaching of English language skills to students with limited English proficiency. Two approaches are taken to bilingual education: Maintenance: Native Language (MNL) programs, in which students become fully literate in their home languages before studying English; and Transitional: English as a Second Language (TESL) programs, in which students begin studying English immediately.

language immersion A form of bilingual education in which students study the English language intensively for extended periods of time.

Insights ON SUCCESSFUL PRACTICE

What advice can you give novice teachers for helping their students with limited English proficiency to succeed?

Once a child said to me, "Last year was so hard. If it hadn't been for Mrs. B., I would have dropped out of school."

"What did Mrs. B. say or do to you?" I asked, and the child replied, "She cared about me."

"How do you know that?"

"I noticed when I talked to her I knew she was really really listening. She would say, 'Hi, how are you?' every time she would see me sad or lonely."

So that's the magic wand, I thought. Show the students you care for them and they will care about themselves. Probably they would think it's worth the trouble to go to school if we let them know we value the time we spend with them.

I strongly believe that we, the teachers, need to show our students we honestly care for them. How can we do that? It takes time and effort. There are many ways: a glance, a smile, an honest look into their eyes, an ear, a shoulder, a laugh, respect, and belief. When you have a bilingual class, where half of the students speak one language and half of them speak another language, self-worth is a must. How can you show you care for students when you can't speak their language? They feel it. They know if we are serious about them.

One of my students used to hide during meeting time. He would hide behind the small sofa while everybody else was sitting in a small group in the center of the classroom.

"José, sit in the meeting area. I need you."

He would look at me as if he would be saying, "Need me? For what?" Every day I had to call him to sit in the meeting area.

"José, you're very important in this class. You are part of it."

Yes, as you guessed, it worked. Soon he would sit right in front of me as if he were ready to assist me with his learning. But it worked because I noticed he needed to know how important and how much a part of the class he really was, not just during meeting time but throughout the day. I ask him for small favors, sit next to him during assemblies, smile at him if I happen to see him during recess or lunch time, give him time to tell me his adventures.

I came to the realization that in order to show honest caring for every student, I needed to think about them—think about what makes each one unique and valuable. As I said before, the students feel if we are being honest. Wouldn't it be nice if every student had a Mrs. B. every school year?

DELIA TERESA DE GARCIA, University Hill Elementary School, Boulder, Colorado

Why did this teacher's strategy work for José? In what other ways will you let your students know that you care? How will you plan to work with students whose language of the home is not English?

trast, in MNL programs the lack of English proficiency is seen as a temporary condition. When literacy is achieved in the home language, it can serve as solid basis for acquiring English, thus making additive bilingualism possible.

Multicultural Curricula and School Reform

Multicultural education is still undergoing change as a concept. To many people, multicultural education has signified a reform effort designed to improve the schooling only of African Americans, who have a history of racial prejudice to overcome (Banks, 1994b). However, "a consensus is developing among scholars that an important goal of multicultural education is to increase educational equality for both gender groups, for students of diverse ethnic and cultural groups, and for exceptional students" (Banks, 1994b, p. 16; cf. Banks & Banks, 1993; Sleeter & Grant, 1988). Going further, most scholars agree that multicultural education should prepare all students—including European American students—to live in a society that is growing ever more culturally diverse. A third aim of multicultural education is **global education**, or helping students to understand that all peoples living on earth have interconnected fates (Banks, 1994b; Becker, 1979).

What do multicultural curricula look like that are designed to meet these goals? Several different approaches have been used, always with the aim of reforming curricula and each with different results. In the *contributions approach* (Figure 4.1), teachers conduct activities to celebrate holidays or other cultural observances of ethnic groups. For example, in addition to Christmas or Hanukkah celebrations, a school might offer special programs during African American History Month or to celebrate Kwanzaa. In the *additive approach*, multicultural concepts and themes are added to an existing curriculum without changing its basic structure, goals, or functions. This occurs when a unit or course on multicultural studies or on a particular cultural group is added. What is important to note about both the contributions and additive approaches is that neither challenges the status quo of the existing curriculum. In fact, as Banks (1994b) has noted,

> [W]hen these approaches are used to integrate cultural content into the curriculum, people, events, and interpretations related to ethnic groups and women often reflect the norms and values of the dominant culture rather than those of cultural communities. . . . Thus, Sacajawea is more likely to be chosen

global education An aim of multicultural programs that helps students to understand that all peoples living on earth have interconnected fates.

The Transformation Approach
The structure of the curriculum is changed to enable students to view concepts, issues, events, and themes from the perspective of diverse ethnic and cultural groups.

The Social Action Approach
Students make decisions on important social issues and take actions to help solve them.

Curriculum Reform

The Contributions Approach
Focuses on heroes, holidays, and discrete cultural elements.

The Additive Approach
Content, concepts, themes, and perspectives are added to the curriculum without changing the structure.

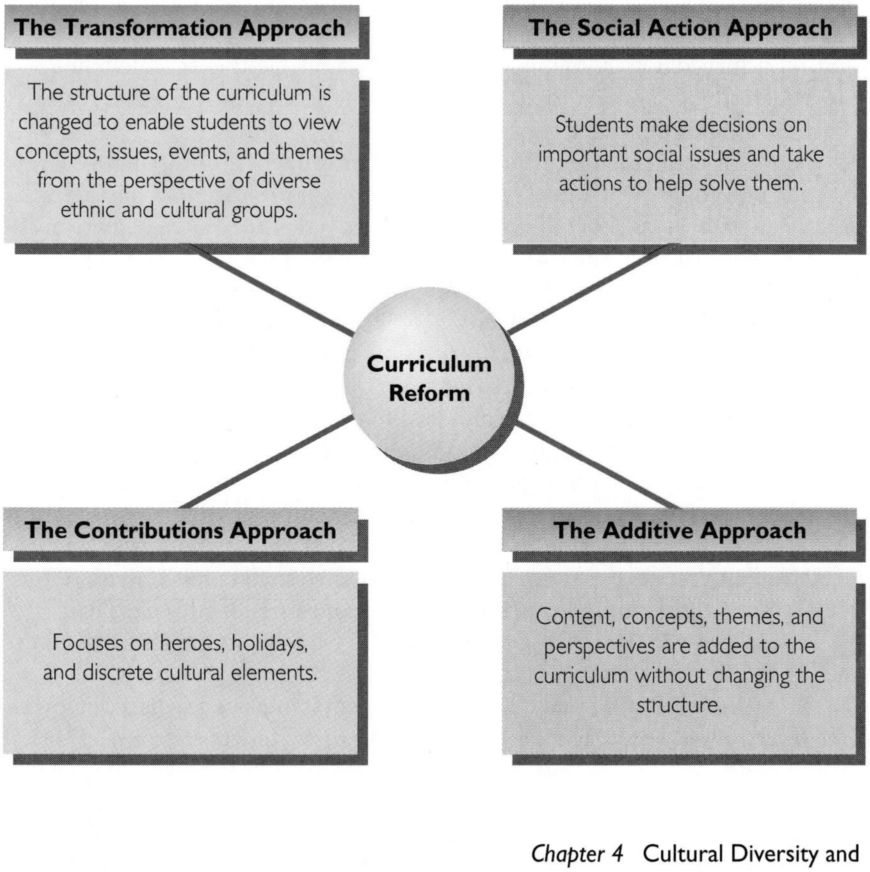

FIGURE 4.1

Approaches to Multicultural Curriculum Reform
Source: Adapted from "Approaches to Multicultural Curriculum Reform," by James A. Banks in *Multicultural Leader,* Vol. 1, No. 2, Spring 1988, 1–3.

> for inclusion than Geronimo, because she helped Whites to conquer Indian lands. Geronimo resisted the takeover of Indian lands by Whites. (p. 26)

By contrast, a *transformation approach* results in major changes to curricula, enabling students to experience the perspectives of different cultural groups. Through this approach, for example, the discovery of North America by Christopher Columbus takes on new meaning. After all, it wasn't uncharted territory for everyone, because Native Americans were already living there. Finally, a *social action approach* extends the transformative curriculum. Students may decide to pursue projects that build on the issues and problems they have studied previously, projects likely to result in personal, social, or civic action (Banks, 1994b).

These approaches to reforming curricula are consistent with five dimensions that Banks (1994a) has defined for multicultural education. The dimensions themselves can serve as the primary foci of curricula and school reform efforts that benefit all students. They also provide a means of interpreting and evaluating existing educational programs that purport to be multicultural. Banks' five dimensions of multicultural education are presented in Figure 4.2:

1. content integration
2. the knowledge construction process
3. prejudice reduction
4. an equity pedagogy
5. an empowering school culture and social structure

Try This: Examine a textbook you might consider using in your classroom. Are there examples of culturally diverse people portrayed in a meaningful, nonstereotypical way? Are various social classes portrayed? Are women, people with disabilities, or elderly people included? What would you conclude about the extent to which this book is bias free?

Education for Cultural Awareness. To help students learn about and appreciate cultural perspectives other than their own, teachers use content and examples in all subject areas that reflect both genders, diverse cultures, and different social classes. The extent to which they do this determines the degree of **content integration** achieved. Often, the first step toward implementing this guideline is in the selection of bias-free textbooks and other teaching–learning materials (Baruth & Manning, 1992).

Materials can have a tremendous impact on student attitudes both by what they include and by what they omit. For example, some textbooks have depicted Asian American students as excellent students but show Native Americans as warlike and Hispanic Americans as poor and violent (Klein, 1985; Gollnick & Chinn, 1990). These images can perpetuate inaccurate stereotypes just as surely as when images of women or elderly people are omitted from textbooks. With omissions, some groups are virtually invisible in textbooks, which has the effect of devaluing these groups in U.S. society.

The content of textbooks can also lead to distortions or unbalanced impressions of various cultural groups. For example, a single point of view presented on a controversial topic may be technically correct but misleading, failing to present the other side. Bias-free materials, then, include culturally diverse images, provide multiple perspectives on complex social issues, and use nonsexist language.

Multicultural perspectives can be integrated with all content areas, not just social studies or literature, with which they are most frequently associated. Multicultural views are also valid and important to examine in the sciences, mathematics, health, and physical education (Baruth & Manning, 1992).

Once the content of multicultural perspectives is in place, teachers can investigate the **knowledge construction process** with their students (Banks, 1994a). In

content integration The degree to which teachers use content and examples in all subject areas that reflect both genders, diverse cultures, and different social classes.

knowledge construction process A process by which knowledge is socially and culturally constructed.

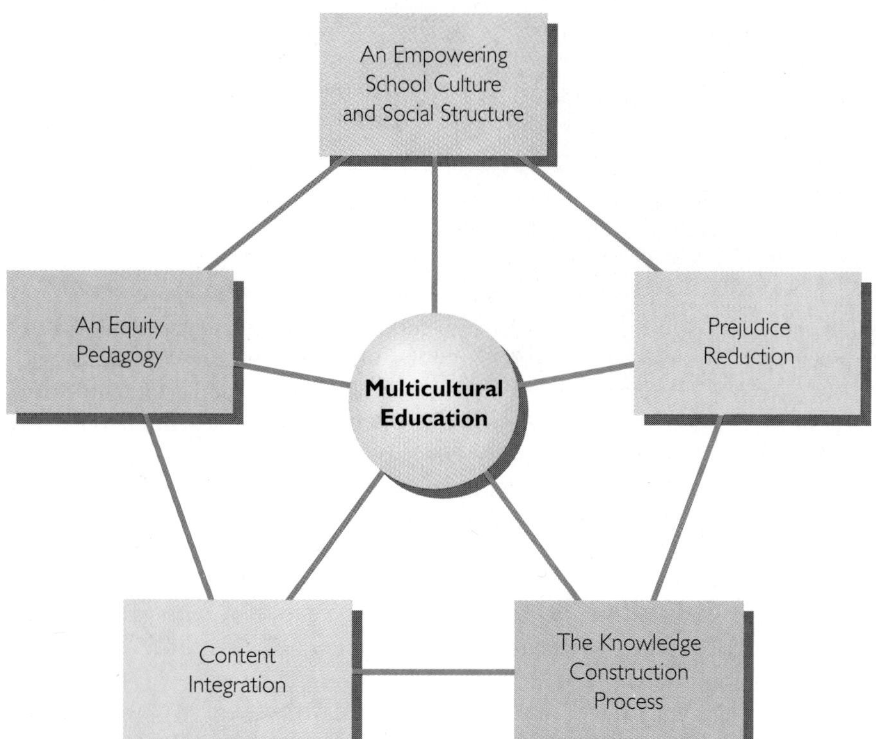

FIGURE 4.2

The Dimensions of Multicultural Education
Source: From *Multiethnic Education,* by James A. Banks, 1994, Needham Heights, MA: Allyn & Bacon

the Western tradition, knowledge is often taught to students as a body of truths that are not to be questioned or critically analyzed. However, even the most apparently objective experiment is influenced by the scientist's prior conceptions and personal biases. Teachers can help students understand how implicit cultural assumptions and perspectives influence the construction of knowledge by juxtaposing conflicting interpretations of the same event. In exploring these interpretations, students should consider which point of view the interpretations represent and why one interpretation may have become the dominant account in history.

Connection: Knowledge construction from a constructivist viewpoint is discussed in Chapter 7.

When students weigh evidence and think critically about how knowledge is constructed within a cultural context, they participate in a transformative curriculum. Whether reading or listening, they become able to "consider the author's purposes for writing or speaking, his or her basic assumptions, and how the author's perspective or point of view compares with that of other authors" (Banks, 1994a, p. 10).

Education for Equity. "An equity pedagogy exists when teachers modify their teaching in ways that will facilitate the academic achievement of students from diverse racial, cultural, ethnic, and gender groups" (Banks, 1994a, p. 13). To do this, teachers must know the cultural characteristics of students that significantly influence their performance and achievement in school. Instructional strategies can then be developed that will be effective in accommodating those

The aims of multicultural education include teaching cultural awareness and acceptance of diversity, promoting educational quality for all students, reducing prejudice and social disharmony, and transforming the culture of schools.

characteristics. We have already discussed how students are diverse in race, ethnicity, social class, and gender, and how general characteristics associated with these microcultures may influence student learning. What can teachers do to implement an equity pedagogy?

To begin with, teachers can get to know their students as individuals, rather than classifying them into stereotypical categories (Tyler, 1989). Just because a student is female and Islamic does not mean she will automatically identify with these microcultures or exhibit characteristics commonly associated with them. However, one must be alert to the possibility that she could. Coming to know students as individuals helps a teacher identify their unique needs and makes instructional accommodation possible.

Example: Consider the student whose parents would not allow him to exchange valentine cards at school. His teacher, not wanting him to feel left out, devised a unit that included Valentine's Day letters, but revolved around the workings of a post office. Activities such as making stamps and mailing and delivering letters kept him involved but did not require that he exchange valentines. Note how the teacher respected the parents' wishes without disrupting a traditional activity.

An instructional strategy that has proven useful with different cultural groups is cooperative learning. When cooperation and sharing are cultural traits of a group, members of the group tend to benefit from cooperative learning activities. Evidence has mounted in favor of using cooperative learning with Native Americans, Hispanic Americans, African Americans, Asian Americans, and girls (Sharan, 1990). Girls also seem to perform better in all-female groups than in groups where boys are mixed with girls. Not only has cooperative learning been shown to improve the achievement of students who work cooperatively, it also appears to improve relations among multicultural-multiethnic students (Sharan, 1985; Slavin, 1995).

Teachers must communicate clearly and fully the rules of the classroom and expectations regarding school activities and performance, taking into consideration students with limited English proficiency. Teachers may use communication signals that are different from those used by culturally different groups; it is essential, therefore, for teachers to develop communication styles that avoid confusion and respect students' linguistic or cultural differences (Bowman, 1989).

Education for Social Harmony. This dimension of multicultural education concerns helping students overcome racial prejudices and develop more democratic attitudes and behaviors. Prejudice is "an emotional, rigid attitude . . . toward a group of people . . . in the mind of the prejudiced person" (Simpson & Yinger, 1985, p. 21). A prejudiced person categorizes a group of people based on some perceived attribute. Racial and cultural prejudices have very complex causes that are not yet well understood. However, they are likely to include personality variables (aggression, insecurity) and sociocultural variables (norms, traditions, power structure). These and other variables also influence the extent to which individuals act on their prejudices and discriminate against others.

Reflection: Have you ever experienced discrimination on the basis of your race, sex, ethnicity, or religion?

From the research conducted thus far, Banks (1994a) concludes that "systematic experiences must be structured to reinforce and perpetuate the desired attitudes" (p. 245). Once again, cooperative learning can be a means to help combat racist attitudes.

here's how

Here's How to Use Cooperative Groups in Support of Social Harmony

- Arrange for heterogeneous groups where students can work with others who come from different cultural backgrounds and where no one group predominates.
- Maximize cooperation within heterogeneous groups, and minimize competition between cultural groups.
- Ensure equal status of all members of a cooperative group. Rotating roles of group members is a way to make sure every student has the opportunity to take on what might be perceived as a high-status role (such as group leader).
- Provide support for students to develop norms and skills associated with working in a cooperative group.
- Select learning tasks and goals that have the potential to extend beyond the immediate situation, encourage mutual disclosure of information, and extend tasks over a period of time.
- Change the composition of groups after a period of time, so that students will gain exposure to the diversity of backgrounds and views that are represented in the class. (Adapted from Stephan, 1985)

In the following excerpt of a practicing teacher, try to identify these principles in the actions and decisions of the teacher.

> When Shirley began her second-grade unit on family history, she had no idea how the unit would echo throughout the year. Her main goal was for students to realize where their ancestors had come from. She had her students ask their parents for information about their families: where had their grandparents been born, what customs did they celebrate, what special foods did they make at home. As a culminating activity, the students were to draw a self-portrait, research and "dress" their portraits in "cultural" clothes, and place their portraits on a large ship symbolic of a ship arriving in America.
>
> Looking at her class, Shirley knew she had students of Asian, African, and European ancestry. When the students returned with their family trees listing their grandparents' birthplaces, she suddenly realized that she had left out Native American students. To her surprise, three of her students had Native American ancestors. Looking at the ship she had already cut out and placed on the hall wall, she was reluctant to take it down and start all over again.
>
> As the students were sharing their information and researching their ethnic costumes, Shirley pondered her problem. Overhearing a student conversation provided the answer.
>
> "If your grandfather is a Chippewa, then how did he get here on the ship?"
>
> "His ancestors did not come on a boat. They were the ones who met the ship when it got here."

Shirley had her solution. Place the three Native American students greeting the other arrivals. Throughout the year, Shirley often turned to her Native American students to help dispel prejudice, to increase student awareness that "Indians" are not all dead and long gone, that Native Americans gave the world potatoes, tomatoes, canoes, snowshoes, hammocks, and a variety of other items.

Try This: Visit a model school in your area or state. What do you notice about the bulletin boards, school decorations, cultural composition of the faculty and administrative staff? Is there evidence of a commitment to multiculturalism?

Education for Accountability. In order for students from diverse cultural groups to experience equality, Banks (1994a) and others contend that schools themselves must be conceptualized as cultural systems with values and norms that support multiculturalism. Each of the previous four dimensions deals with an aspect of the school and school culture. But viewing the school holistically provides a unifying framework for examining not just teaching practices but counseling programs, sports activities, attitudes and behavior of school staff and administrators, and even what goes on in the school cafeteria (Banks, 1994a).

Table 4.1 shows eight characteristics proposed for multicultural schools (Banks, 1994b). Many of these have already been discussed in this chapter but several deserve particular mention.

The explicit curriculum of a school comes primarily from curriculum guides and other official documents that provide the framework and direction for what teachers are supposed to teach. It is therefore expressed in the goals and objectives that teachers adopt and in the instructional strategies and assessment procedures they use to teach and test for goal attainment. The **hidden curriculum**, however, comprises lessons and messages that, although not explicitly taught by teachers, are nonetheless learned by students. For example, the well-meaning teacher who puts Bible verses above her classroom door each week sends a message to students about religion and which religion is valued.

TABLE 4.1 The Eight Characteristics of the Multicultural School

1. The teachers and school administrators have expectations for all students and positive caring attitudes toward them. They also respond to them in positive and caring ways.
2. The formalized curriculum reflects the experiences, cultures, and perspectives of a range of cultural and ethnic groups as well as both genders.
3. The teaching styles used by the teachers match the learning, cultural, and motivational styles of the students.
4. The teachers and administrators show respect for the students' first languages and dialects.
5. The instructional materials used in the school show events, situations, and concepts from the perspectives of a range of cultural, ethnic, and racial groups.
6. The assessment and testing procedures used in the school are culturally sensitive and result in students of color being represented proportionately in classes for the gifted and talented.
7. The school culture and the hidden curriculum reflect cultural and ethnic diversity.
8. The school counselors have high expectations for students from different racial, ethnic, and language groups and help these students to set and realize positive career goals.

Source: From *An Introduction to Multicultural Education*, by James A. Banks, Needham Heights, MA: Allyn & Bacon, 1994.

hidden curriculum The tacit lessons and messages taught to students by the way teachers and schools operate.

Attitudes of the school as a social system are conveyed in myriad ways, from the pictures posted on bulletin boards to the way students are grouped for assemblies, to the representation of diverse cultures and both sexes on the faculty. In a multicultural school, these attitudes are regularly examined to be sure that messages of diversity are conveyed to students rather than messages of racism or sexism.

Similarly, assessment and testing procedures are scrutinized for potential bias against ethnic, racial, or gender groups. For many years now, companies developing standardized tests, such as the Educational Testing Service, have followed procedures during test development that are designed to minimize the likelihood that test items will be biased against particular groups. These procedures include asking representative members of cultural groups to review items for potential bias and comparing performances of different groups on individual items. Items answered incorrectly by a disproportionate number of students from a particular cultural group are eliminated from the item pool.

Even when such precautions are taken, however, using standardized tests for placement purposes can result in low-income and minority students' being overrepresented in some programs (e.g., those for people with learning disabilities) and underrepresented in others (e.g., those for the gifted) (Patton, 1992). Employing a variety of testing formats to assess students' talents and achievements is likely to be more equitable and more accurate, because students do not perform equally well on all formats (Shavelson, Baxter, & Pine, 1992). Assessment methods such as performance tests, long-range projects, and portfolios developed over a semester can provide greater sensitivity to both student diversity and the wide range of curriculum activities that students experience during the school year (Berliner, 1992).

Connection: The construction and use of performance tests and portfolio assessment is discussed in Chapter 13

Achieving the eight criteria for a multicultural school that are listed in Table 4.1 requires taking a *systems approach* to school reform because the school is a complex system of many interconnected variables. Unless these variables are all considered in the context of school reform, it is unlikely that the norms of the school will change. For example, teachers may begin to use culturally sensitive materials in their classes, but if practices continue to exist in the school that discriminate, however subtly, against certain groups, then no real change will be effected. Becoming a truly multicultural school takes the collaborative efforts of the teachers, administrators, students, and parents (Comer, 1988).

HOW CAN YOUR KNOWLEDGE OF DIVERSITY ENHANCE TEACHING AND LEARNING IN YOUR CLASSROOM?

Teachers who are effective in a multicultural environment first learn to know themselves. You, like your students, will come to the classroom with your own cultural experiences and perspectives, as well as possible stereotypes and misperceptions. As a teacher, you are the mediator of messages and symbols that are communicated by the curriculum to your students. You are also a role model for your students. Therefore, it is important for you to be aware of your own personal and cultural values and identity and how these affect your actions in the classroom. This is at the heart of being an effective multicultural teacher (Figure 4.3).

In addition, effective multicultural teachers both understand the complex nature of diversity and feel a commitment to a multicultural ideology (Banks, 1994a). This means that you accept cultural diversity in your students and help them to accept diversity in each other. Effective multicultural teachers have the ability to view events in their classrooms from various cultural perspectives and the skills to accommodate their instruction to the differences they perceive.

Accepting Student Diversity

Point: *Teachers and students are both learners.* In a multicultural classroom and school, students and teachers together learn to accept diversity by examining their own beliefs and values and becoming aware of others' beliefs and values.

Often without thinking about it, people assume that their own cultural ways are the right ways and universally appropriate to others. When the cultural lens through which they view the world extends to evaluating other cultures by their own cultural standards, then **ethnocentrism** is the result. People who have strong ethnocentric beliefs can find it difficult to accept diversity or to understand cultural perspectives that are different from their own. They tend to perceive the traits of other cultural groups as odd or inferior in some way (Baruth & Manning, 1992). You can help students to reduce their ethnocentrism first by recognizing and accepting their diversity. This entails recognizing cultural stereotypes as well.

FIGURE 4.3

Characteristics of an Effective Multicultural Teacher
(Derived and adapted from Banks, 1994a)

ethnocentrism The assumption that one's own cultural ways are the right ways and universally appropriate to others.

here's how

Here's How to Help Students Accept Diversity in Others

- Instill in children and adolescents the idea that cultural differences should not be considered right or wrong, superior or inferior.
- Arrange teaching–learning situations (cooperative learning and cross-age tutoring) whereby learners of varying cultures can have firsthand experiences with each other.
- Model acceptance and respect for all people.
- Respond appropriately to statements indicating a lack of understanding or acceptance of cultural differences.
- Encourage respect for *all* differences—cultural and ethnic, socioeconomic, handicapped conditions, gender, and other characteristics which contribute to diversity among individuals. (Baruth & Manning, 1992, p. 157)

In facilitating students' acceptance of diversity, remember that change comes slowly. You are challenging long-held beliefs that may have been taught or encouraged at home.

Using Multicultural Teaching Strategies

Regardless of the grade level or subject matter, there are many teaching strategies you can use to support the goals of multicultural education. In your school, start a resource file of ideas and materials that you and other teachers have used and found effective. Some ideas to try are presented in the following lists.

Strategies for School-Wide Cultural Awareness

1. Take a cultural census of the class or school to find out what cultures are represented; let students be the ethnographers.
2. Form a multicultural club.
3. Select a theme to tie various multicultural activities together; hold school programs with art, music, and dramatic presentations; hold a multicultural fair or festival featuring music, art, dance, dress; adopt a multicultural theme for existing activities.
4. Hold a school cross-cultural food festival.
5. Have multicultural celebrations and teach-ins with school-wide activities in all classes.
6. Decorate classrooms, hallways, and the library media center with murals, bulletin boards, posters, artifacts, and other materials representative of the students in the class or school or other cultures being studied. Posters and other information are available from foreign government travel bureaus and education agencies, private travel agencies, consulates, the United Nations, or ethnic and cultural organizations, for example.
7. Designate a permanent bulletin board for multicultural news and displays.
8. Hold a video film festival dealing with various cultures and multicultural issues.
9. Feature stories in the school newspaper on multicultural topics; publish a multicultural newspaper or newsletter.
10. Hold mock campaigns and elections based on multicultural issues.

Insights ON SUCCESSFUL PRACTICE

What steps do you take to ensure that your students are receiving a gender-fair education?

Most teachers I know are kind and well intentioned, working for the success of their students in many general and specific areas. Let's say that *I* am such a well-intentioned teacher.

Nevertheless, after reading about the years of research done by Myra and David Sadker concerning the unfair treatment of girls in our schools and the AAUW (American Association of University Women) report *How Schools Shortchange Girls*, I began to look into my own practices. What I discovered was that even though I was aware of what not to do, I was still doing it. These practices had become habit. I took a Gender/Ethnic Expectation and Student Achievement (GESA) course that utilized peer observation. I found out that I called on boys while girls waited endlessly, justifying it by saying this helped keep the boys in line. My interaction with the boys in my class was consistently more thorough than my interaction with the girls. Among other things, I talked to the boys in more in-depth and encouraging ways. I even *stood* by the boys more.

So . . . I got creative and tried to become a more equitable teacher. I thought of new ways to line up and group my students (kids with velcro shoes, kids with short sleeves). I learned what to look for in my own interactions with students. I began to guide this hidden curriculum as carefully as the posted curriculum. To counter the absence of girls from story books, history books, math examples, etc., I searched out books that showed girls' adventures and women's accomplishments. I began providing my own examples as I read in the content areas. "Astronauts are men who begin their careers by . . ." now becomes "Astronauts are women and men who begin their careers by. . . ." I believe it is vital to send that subtle message to the girls. To leave it out sends a subtle message of a different sort.

Becoming more equitable—looking at old habits—was tough at times. I just couldn't bring myself to give a dumb part in a play to a boy. Funny, I didn't wince when I gave a boring part to a girl. I'd think, "She won't mind," and usually she didn't. Was she used to getting the leftovers?

I also learned to use the talking turn-sticks. This is a can of craft sticks with a student's name on each stick. During most discussions I do not call on volunteers. I use the sticks, pulling one out and giving that student a chance to share or answer. Their stick then goes into the "had a turn" can. When everyone has had a turn we begin again. This way the same kids aren't always being called on. I tell the kids in my class what I'm doing and why. "Research says that we **all** learn best if. . . ."

The Sadkers' research continues to find that our expectations are different for girls and boys, our methods are different, and our interactions are different. In effect, girls and boys are receiving very different educations even as they sit side by side in our classrooms. One result is how few women astronauts, surgeons, Ph.D. candidates, senators, etc., we have. Somehow girls are not getting the message to GO FOR IT that their male classmates are. As I work toward becoming a more equitable educator, I notice benefits for all of my students.

JENNIFER MCGUIRE, Edna Ferber School, Appleton, Wisconsin

In what ways might teachers unintentionally discriminate against male or female students? Has this ever happened to you? What other measures might you take to ensure that your students are receiving a gender-fair education in your classroom?

Strategies for Cultural Awareness in the Classroom

1. Have students write to foreign consulates, tourist bureaus, or minority organizations for information and decorative materials.
2. Supplement textbooks with authentic material from different cultures taken from newspapers, magazines, and other media of the culture. Such materials are available from state departments of education.
3. Use community resources: representatives of various cultures talking to classes; actors portraying characters or events; musicians and dance groups, such as salsa bands or bagpipe units.
4. Work with the library media center for special bibliographies, collections, displays, and audio-visuals.
5. Hold a mock legislature to debate current or historical issues affecting minorities and cultural groups.
6. Hold oratorical, debate, essay, poster, art, brain brawl, or other competitions with a multicultural focus.
7. Develop a radio or television program on multicultural themes for the educational or local community access channel.
8. Study works in science, literature, and fine arts of various cultures, focusing on the contributions of minority individuals.
9. Have students write short stories or essays on multicultural topics.
10. Have student debates, speeches, and skits on multicultural topics, and present them to classes, PTOs, nursing homes, and other community groups.
11. Study the provisions and freedoms of the Constitution as they relate to minorities.
12. Compare and contrast other cultures with that of mainstream America.
13. Discuss the issues and personalities involved in various cultures from a historical, political, and literary standpoint.
14. Have students of other cultures, or their parents, share native songs with classmates; have students share instruments or recordings of their native cultures.
15. Take field trips to local multicultural sites, such as a neighborhood, ethnic recreation/social center, workplace, historical site, museum, restaurant, grocery.
16. Establish pen pals or video exchange programs with students from other cultures.
17. Focus on the everyday artifacts that differentiate the way people behave in various cultures, such as greetings, friendly exchanges, farewells, expressing respect, verbal taboos, ways of using numbers, body language and gestures, gender roles, folklore, childhood literature, discipline, festivals, holidays, religious practices, games, music, pets, personal possessions, keeping warm and cool, cosmetics, fashions, health and hygiene practices, competitions, dating and courtship, transportation and traffic, sports, radio and television programs, hobbies, foods, family mealtimes, snacking, cafes and restaurants, yards and sidewalks, parks and playgrounds, flowers and gardens, movies and theaters, circuses, museums, vacations and resort areas, careers.
18. Discuss what it means to be a member of a minority or different cultural group.

Strategies for Cultural Equity

1. Be sure that assignments are not offensive or frustrating to students of cultural minorities. For example, asking students to discuss or write about their Christmas experiences is inappropriate for non-Christian students. Instead, let students discuss their similar holidays.
2. Help students develop the skills needed to locate and organize information about cultures from the library media center, the mass media, people, and personal observations.
3. Use skills and information from various disciplines (math, social studies, geography, language arts) to compare population, economy, politics, lifestyle, culture, and other data about different cultural groups in the United States during different historical periods and as they are today. Discuss the meaning of the differences.
4. Discuss the relevance of the Constitution and government in dealing with today's problems that relate to minorities and cultural diversity.
5. Focus on geography skills and knowledge in geography courses as part of related courses.
6. Discuss the importance of international trade and the skills needed to be employed in that area.
7. Discuss what it means to be a responsible American citizen.

Strategies for Accountability

1. Make newcomers feel welcome through a formal program.
2. Form a school-wide planning committee to address the implementation of multicultural education.
3. Contact your district curriculum coordinators for ideas and assistance.
4. Let faculty knowledgeable about multicultural topics present in-service workshops for others or teach their classes occasionally.
5. Make reminders during daily announcements about multicultural activities. (Adapted from Baruth & Manning, 1992, pp. 211-214)

TEACHER Chronicle Conclusion

GRANDMA TALES

As Ms. Walker made her lesson plans for the next day, she reflected on Kevin and his storytelling ability. How could he use his skills to become a better writer? she asked herself. Could his telling stories orally replace written assignments?

The next day Ms. Walker met Kevin at the classroom door.

"Kevin," she asked, "Do you tell many stories at home?"

"Oh, sure. We tell stories all the time. My aunt says that telling stories to the whole family is much better than reading."

"Why?" Ms. Walker asked.

"She says that when you tell a story, everyone gets to be part of it. But when you read a story, only one person hears it."

"How would you like to tape-record your stories so that you could share them at school and home, too?" Ms. Walker asked.

"Can I really?" Kevin said.

"Yes, and then with a partner's help you can write them down for your written work. I think that your writing will improve, don't you?"

Kevin smiled. "Then maybe I might pass English?"

"Yes."

APPLICATION QUESTIONS

1. Rewrite the conversations between Kevin and Ms. Walker for a different ending.
2. What other strategies might Ms. Walker have used to capitalize on Kevin's strengths?
3. Is tape-recording an appropriate strategy? Why or why not?
4. Will writing the stories after telling them help Kevin's writing abilities?
5. What other cultural insights might Ms. Walker have gained in understanding Kevin better?
6. How might Ms. Walker become a more effective teacher in dealing with other students whose cultural backgrounds differ from hers?
7. How does culture influence learning?
8. How does culture influence teaching?
9. If Ms. Walker shares Kevin's stories with a math teacher, how might that teacher use this knowledge to aid in Kevin's math instruction? Geography? Science?

CHAPTER SUMMARY

WHAT ARE SOME SOURCES OF DIVERSITY?

As American society continues to diversify, so do American schools. Students come from many different racial, ethnic, and socioeconomic backgrounds. They speak many languages and dialects in addition to standard English. They come with a variety of abilities and disabilities that can become cultural traits to the extent that students identify with others having the same exceptionality. All of these characteristics influence how students learn and interact in the school environment.

HOW CAN CULTURAL CONFLICTS ARISE IN YOUR CLASSROOM?

When your students come from different backgrounds and experiences, there is a potential for conflict. You may organize your classroom, use instructional strategies, or communicate in ways that are either unfamiliar to your students or conflict with the values with which they were raised. It is important for you to examine your own values and beliefs in relation to those of your students and consider ways in which you can best meet their needs.

WHAT ARE THE DIMENSIONS OF MULTICULTURAL EDUCATION?

Traditional responses to diversity in education include compensatory programs, where students from various ethnic groups are expected to catch up on presumably lacking skills needed for society. This deficit model stems from an assimilation ideology, which assumes that ethnic groups must adopt and live by the values of the dominant society. More recent approaches to multicultural education are based on the pluralist assumption that all ethnic groups contribute equally to American society. They both define and are defined by the greater national culture. The current purposes of many multicultural programs include enhancing cultural awareness, increasing educational equity, and overcoming racist attitudes. To do this, a systems (or school-wide) approach to multicultural education is recommended.

HOW CAN YOUR KNOWLEDGE OF DIVERSITY ENHANCE TEACHING AND LEARNING IN YOUR CLASSROOM?

By becoming familiar with the diversity of your students, you can help them to be more accepting of cultural differences in one another. You can also use a variety of multicultural teaching strategies to facilitate cultural awareness, educational equity, and social harmony.

KEY CONCEPTS

additive bilingualism
assimilation
bilingual education
bilingualism
content integration
cultural pluralism
culture
deficit model
dialect
difference model
dominant bilingualism
ethnic group
ethnicity
ethnocentrism
global education
hidden curriculum
integration
knowledge construction process
language immersion
limited English proficiency
macroculture
metalinguistic awareness
microculture
multiculturalism
multiple acculturation
socioeconomic status
subtractive bilingualism

CHAPTER OUTLINE

TEACHER Chronicle

MY NAME IS ROBO

Mrs. Bernstein is preparing her first-grade room in anticipation of the beginning of the school year. It is new student visiting day, and parents and students are dropping in to meet her.

"Good morning, Mrs. Bernstein. My name is Dr. Kotre and this is my son, Heath. We just stopped by to say a quick hello."

Heath buzzes past Mrs. Bernstein and heads straight to the play corner. Picking up a toy robot, he begins manipulating its arms, saying in a mechanical voice, "My name is Robo. I am model 2005." Dropping the robot, Heath grabs a shell from the science table and howls into it. "WHOOOOOOOO!" Seconds later, he is building a tower with wooden blocks.

Mrs. Bernstein quickly tries to recall what she had learned about Heath from his cumulative record folder. He has an IQ of 145, is already selected for the gifted and talented program, is not yet a reader, and is thought by his kindergarten teacher to be highly creative.

Dr. Kotre smiles. "He's going to love your room, Mrs. Bernstein."

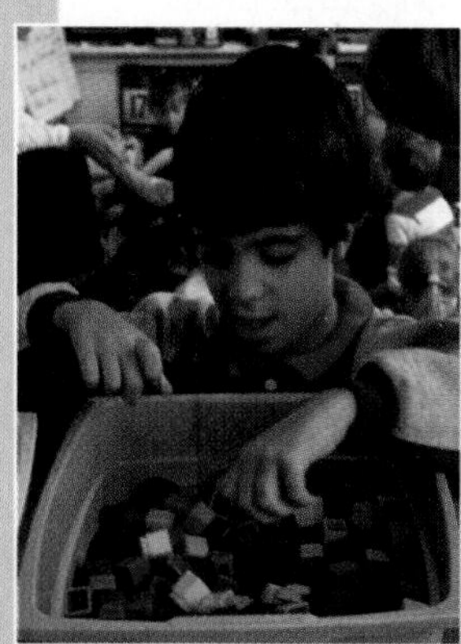

"I hope so," she says. "If he's happy here, I can teach and he can learn."

Heath had stacked the blocks and was running a toy fire truck into them.

"Okay, Heath, it's time to go," says Dr. Kotre as the blocks tumble down.

"No," he answers defiantly.

"Yes, Heath, I have an appointment."

"NO!" he shouts.

Dr. Kotre looks at Mrs. Bernstein.

"Heath, you will have plenty of time to play with those toys when school starts next week."

Heath bangs the blocks together and starts crying. "I'm not through yet."

"Yes you are," Dr. Kotre says, frustration creeping into her voice. She takes him by the arm, but he pushes away.

"No!" he screams.

Mrs. Bernstein remembers another comment from Heath's kindergarten teacher. Heath was recommended for observation by the teacher for emotionally disturbed students.

After several embarrassing minutes, Heath is finally coaxed with a bribe into leaving.

"Yes, Heath, I will buy you that new transformer toy," Dr. Kotre says. On the way out, her eyes meet Mrs. Bernstein's with a look that says "Good luck."

FOCUS QUESTIONS

1. In what ways did Heath exhibit the intelligence suggested by his high IQ score? Other than the robot, what are Heath's manipulation skills? Are these skills a sign of intelligence? Are there gaps in his intelligence? If so, what are they?
2. Consider the ways in which you think Heath would learn best. How would you characterize his preferred style of learning? What factors might place Heath at risk of failing in school? What evidence supports your choice of factors?
3. In preparation to consult with other professionals concerning Heath's needs, what behav-

iors should Mrs. Bernstein document from her classroom observations? Will interactions with other students provide important information? How can information about Heath's relationships with other children be communicated without invading his or other students' privacy?

4. Would you predict that Heath can be helped through behavioral training? Will medication be necessary? What role would Mrs. Bernstein play in such decisions? If medication is prescribed, what responsibilities would fall on Mrs. Bernstein?
5. What kind of special program might be established to help Heath? Are there legal requirements for such a program? Who should participate in its development? Why?
6. Do you think Heath's behavior might prove disruptive for other students? How? What strategies should Mrs. Bernstein use to make Heath feel included in the class? What strategies should she use to help him learn? How should she assess Heath's learning?

HOW DO STUDENTS VARY IN INTELLIGENCE?

Heath, in the Teacher Chronicle, presents a unique challenge for his teacher. But so will every other student in Mrs. Bernstein's class. Ultimately, the question for Mrs. Bernstein, and every other teacher, is "How can I adapt the teaching–learning process to meet the unique needs of each individual student? " The first step in solving this problem is to recognize the importance that individual student characteristics play in learning. The next step is to acquire an understanding of the ways in which students differ from one another.

An analysis of research data on relationships among variables thought to influence school learning shows that student characteristics are among the most important variables (Table 5.1) (Levin, 1993; Wang, Haertel, & Walberg, 1993). Student characteristics include demographics and academic placement histories as well as social, motivational, cognitive, and affective characteristics.

It is important for future teachers to recognize that the characteristics of their students will vary and how those characteristics influence students' learning.

In this chapter we focus on the key factors that determine the individual characteristics of your students and, therefore, their learning. We begin by examining a student characteristic that has long been linked to success in school, intelligence.

TABLE 5.1 Ranking of Variables Found to Influence School Learning

1. Student characteristics
2. Classroom practices
3. Home and community educational contexts
4. School demographics, culture, climate, policies, and practices
5. State and district governance and organization

Source: Adapted from "Toward a knowledge base of school learning" (Table 3, p. 270), by M. C. Wang, G. D. Haertel, & H. J. Walberg, 1993, in *Review of Educational Research*, 63 (3), 249–294.

The Definition and Measurement of Intelligence

Reflect: How do you define intelligence? How does that definition help you explain differences among people?

Although we examine several variations, the term **intelligence** is generally defined as one's capacity to learn. Intelligence is included on most permanent records of students. Indeed, in many school districts, the measured intelligence of a child is used in concert with other information to make instructional decisions concerning that student's future.

The measurement of intelligence yields an index called an intelligence quotient (IQ). A person's IQ is typically represented by a single number. For example, someone with an IQ of 102 is considered to have average intelligence; an IQ of 120 is considered above average. In and out of educational circles, when we talk about a person's intelligence, we usually think of it as a unitary thing that can be reflected in a single number. Incidentally, while we usually talk about IQ as a single value, it is more accurate to speak of the probable range of a person's IQ. The measurement of intelligence will be discussed in Chapter 14. In this section, we examine the meaning of the term *intelligence* rather than its measurement.

There has been a long and animated debate among psychologists as to the meaning of *intelligence.* Intelligence is a **construct**, an idea devised by a theorist to explain something else. Intelligence, for example, has been used to explain why some students graduate from law school and others can't finish high school; why some complete tasks with ease and others struggle; why some succeed and others fail. It is a measure of differences among students. Some psychologists suggest that there is a general overriding mental ability that can be referred to as a person's intelligence. Others take the view that there are multiple intelligences.

Cultural Views of Intelligence and Student Performance

Beliefs about intelligence vary with culture. In a study of parents whose children all attended the same school in California, researchers asked parents to characterize an intelligent first grader (Okagaki, Sternberg, & Divecha, 1990). Okagaki et al. found that Cambodian, Filipino, and Vietnamese families rated noncognitive attributes, such as motivation for school tasks, self-management, and social skills, as more important than cognitive skills, such as problem solving and verbal skills. This conception of intelligence as a strong motivational element was particularly strong for the Filipino and Vietnamese parents. This finding is similar to a study of Japanese and Chinese mothers (Stevenson & Lee, 1990). For these parents, an intelligent child is one who exerts effort in pursuit of goals. This conception of intelligence differs considerably from that of Anglo American parents, who view intelligence as a function of innate cognitive abilities. Hispanic parents rated cognitive and noncognitive as equally important aspects of intelligence. Of the noncognitive factors, however, social skills were particularly important to their concept of intelligence. If one assumes for a moment that the culture of schools in the United States reflects Anglo American norms, it comes as no surprise that Okagaki and Sternberg (1991) found that "the more important parents believe that social skills are to a child being an intelligent individual, the lower children's scores" (p. 11).

Connection: Beliefs about intelligence can contribute to one's self concept and self-esteem, as discussed in Chapter 3.

Cultural norms influence not only parents' concepts of intelligence but also the types of intellectual abilities that are likely to develop. Anglo-European-American culture tends to emphasize logic-mathematical and linguistic intelligences. The Anang people of Nigeria, in contrast, emphasize musical intelligence.

intelligence A personal capacity to learn, often measured by one's ability to deal with abstractions and to solve problems.

construct An idea devised by a theorist to explain observations and relationships between variables.

Children raised in the Anang culture are expected to be able to sing hundreds of songs by the age of five. They are also expected to play several instruments and to perform complicated dances (Hetherington & Parke, 1993).

Children's beliefs about their own intelligence can also influence their performance in the classroom. Children who believe that intelligence is incremental—that is, something that can be developed—view their performance in terms of improving their skills and abilities. In contrast, children who believe intelligence is a fixed entity view their performance as a test of ability. When faced with failure, children with an incremental belief tend to adopt a mastery orientation; those who hold entity beliefs tend to feel helpless (Cain & Dweck, 1989; Dweck, 1989). Such beliefs may also be related to observations that some children tend to cope well with criticism of their work, while for other children criticism damages their self-images (Heyman, Dweck, & Cain, 1992).

Critical Thinking: Why would a belief that intelligence is incremental rather than fixed yield a different orientation toward mastery?

Three Traditional Theories of Intelligence

The nature of intelligence has been debated since the earliest days of scientific psychology. Francis Galton (a cousin of Charles Darwin) was an early participant in the debate and one of the first to measure intellect directly (Gardner & Hatch, 1989). The result of the debate has been a multitude of definitions of the construct and, by implication, a considerable degree of disagreement among the experts in the field (Hetherington & Parke, 1993).

Three views of intelligence are presented that illustrate the variety of perspectives that psychologists have traditionally taken. Piaget's view of intelligence is based on his concern with explaining cognitive development. In the course of explaining the way in which cognitive capabilities grow and change, Piaget addressed the construct of intelligence. David Wechsler's view illustrates the general position that intelligence is most usefully considered as a single mental capacity. A third view, J. P. Guilford's multifactor view, represents the school of thought that intelligence is best seen not as a single entity but as a range of separately identifiable factors.

Piaget's Dynamic View. In Piaget's view, a person's intelligence is dynamic—that is, it changes as a person's interaction with the environment changes. Recall Piaget's stages of cognitive development, discussed in Chapter 2. Each stage defines a person's intelligence. According to Piaget, an infant organizes his or her environment into sensorimotor schemata; he or she is using sensorimotor intelligence to understand the environment. As the infant accommodates and assimilates new experiences, he or she constructs new types of cognitive structures, called preoperational schemata. Development proceeds through concrete operational schemata and formal operational schemata. The type of schemata a person uses defines the type of intelligence a person has. Because schemata change throughout the course of a person's cognitive development, a person's intelligence is dynamic. In Piaget's view, cognitive development is the development of new forms of intelligence.

Connection: Piaget's stages, described in Chapter 2, identify essentially different ways of thinking.

Piaget's dynamic view suggests that there are dangers in thinking about intelligence as some intellectual "substance"—such as the ability to reason abstractly—that students should acquire in greater quantities as they proceed through school. To use only one yardstick to measure intelligent behavior is to deny the differences in cognitive capabilities that exist among students at different stages of intellectual development.

Wechsler's Global View. David Wechsler became well known as a developer of IQ tests. Although he died in 1981, one of the most respected IQ tests for children remains the Wechsler Intelligence Scale for Children (the abbreviation is WISC-III). From his work, he developed a global view of intelligence: "Intelligence is the aggregate or global capacity of the individual to act purposefully, to think rationally, and to deal effectively with the environment" (1958, p. 7). Wechsler viewed people's intelligence as an overall ability to deal with the world around them.

Wechsler's view, derived as it was from concerns about testing the construct, suggests that a test of spatial ability, a test of mathematical computation, or a test of verbal reasoning may tell us very little about a student's overall ability to deal with the world. Intelligence, from the global view, is more than the sum of its parts.

Guilford's Multifactor View. While Wechsler focused his efforts on defining intelligence as a single entity, Guilford worked to establish a definition of intelligence that recognized a range of factors that constituted it. Guilford sought some way of organizing appropriate factors into a framework. The result of his efforts was the "three faces of intellect" model, which organized intellectual capabilities along three dimensions, or faces (Guilford, 1967; see also 1980, 1985).

The first face in Guilford's model describes the types of operations a person performs. An operation is a kind of intellectual activity or process, such as knowing, remembering, making judgments. The second face in Guilford's model is the *content* of the operation. Content refers to the nature of the information being operated on, such as images, and abstract systems of codes, such as numbers or words. When a person operates on some kind of content, a *product* results. The information that defines the content is transformed through processing into independent items of information, sets of items that share properties, and ways of organizing information. Guilford's model gives us a way of thinking about what mental operations students perform, what content they operate on, and what mental products they generate.

Try This: Using one kind of operation and one type of content, try to predict what type of product would be generated.

Gardner's Theory of Multiple Intelligences

Piaget, Wechsler, and Guilford represent perspectives that have been part of the debate on intelligence for several decades. In the 1980s, two new intelligence theorists arrived on the scene. The work of Howard Gardner and Robert Sternberg has captured the imagination of many educators. Although there are critical differences between the two formulations, both theorists have caused educators to reexamine the relationship between learning and intelligence.

Gardner's **theory of multiple intelligences** sprang, as many theories do, from discontent. In Gardner's case, the discontent was twofold. First, Gardner's own research in the area of cognitive development (1975, 1979, 1982) ran counter to Piaget's notion that the use and interpretation of various symbol systems were all aspects of one intellectual function. Gardner (and his colleagues) supported the notion that discrete psychological processes are used for linguistic, numerical, pictorial, and other types of symbol systems (Gardner, Howard, & Perkins, 1974; Gardner & Wolf, 1983). The second part of Gardner's discontent came from his observation of the types of symbolization processes that were—and in many cases still are—typical in schools: linguistic symbolization and logico-mathematical symbolization. Although these two forms of symbolization are important for most

theory of multiple intelligences Howard Gardner's theory of seven distinct intelligences or talents.

The capacity to use symbol systems, such as language, math, and logic, is a common indicator of intelligence. Defined more broadly, intelligence is the ability to solve culturally valued problems or to create culturally valued products.

of the tasks required of students in school and are the symbol systems that underlie most items on intelligence, aptitude, and achievement tests, there are other symbol systems that are important to learning and performance both in and outside of school (Gardner & Hatch, 1989).

As Gardner contemplated the importance of additional symbol systems in human cognition, he realized that he was extending traditional notions of human intelligence. For this reason, Gardner theorized that there are autonomous human intelligences. Thus, Gardner's definition of intelligence is applied to seven different forms of thinking: "the capacity to solve problems or to fashion products that are valued in one or more cultural settings" (Gardner & Hatch, 1989, p. 5). In the Anang culture in Nigeria, for example, the capacity to perform songs is highly valued and is considered a sign of intelligence. Gardner has also established criteria that determine what is and what is not a human intelligence. Of particular significance in Gardner's definition is the recognition of cultural values as an important element in human intelligence(s). We return to the educationally important connection between culture and intelligence before concluding our examination of intelligence. First, however, we examine the product of Gardner's discontent and subsequent contemplation, his seven intelligences.

Reflection: Why should culture be an important aspect of one's view of intelligence? How does your cultural background influence your view of intelligence?

The Seven Intelligences. Gardner's seven intelligences are presented in Table 5.2. The core components of each intelligence provides an essential description of the abilities, capacities, and sensibilities of each type of intelligence. The "endstates" are typical occupations associated with each intelligence. Although the end states can serve as instructive examples, it is important to recognize that real people represent a blend of intelligences. A skilled surgeon, for instance, must possess both the spatial intelligence necessary to recognize the correct point and length of incision as well as the bodily-kinesthetic intelligence needed to wield the scalpel. A religious leader, whose intra- and interpersonal intelligences afford insight into the spiritual nature of humans, also needs the linguistic intelligence to communicate that insight (Gardner & Hatch, 1989).

The theory of multiple intelligences predicts that individuals will differ in their particular profiles of intelligence. A preschool study illustrates the kinds of data that have been collected in support of the theory of multiple intelligences. The performances of children in ten different activities were assessed. The activities included story telling, drawing, singing, music perception, creative move-

Point: This research supports one of the basic assumptions of this book: *Learners are diverse.*

TABLE 5.2 Gardner's Seven Intelligences

Intelligence	Core Components	End States
Logico-mathematical	Logical or numeric patterns; long chains of reasoning	Scientist, mathematician
Linguistic	Sounds, rhythms, meanings of words; different functions of language	Poet, journalist
Musical	Rhythms, pitch, timbre; forms of musical expression	Composer, violinist
Spatial	Visual-spatial relationships; transform perceptions	Navigator, sculptor
Bodily-kinesthetic	Control of body movements; object manipulation	Dancer, athlete
Interpersonal	Moods, temperament, motivations, desires of others	Therapist, salesperson
Intrapersonal	Own feelings, strengths, weaknesses, desires, intelligences	Person with detailed accurate self-knowledge

Source: From Gardner, H. & Hatch, T. (1989) "Multiple Intelligences Go to School: Educational Implications of the Theory of Multiple Intelligences." *Educational Research, 18* (8), 4–10. © 1989 by the American Educational Research Association. Reprinted by permission of the publisher.

ment, social analysis, hypothesis testing, assembly, calculation and counting, and number and notational logic. Using statistical comparisons, the twenty children in this study were classified as below average, average, or above average on each activity. Above-average performance was taken as an indication of strength; below-average performance was taken as an indication of weakness. An analysis of the performances indicated that fifteen of the children had a strength in at least one area. Twelve of the children's performances indicated one or more weaknesses. Only one child performed in the average range on all activities—and her performances varied considerably within the average range. The particular strengths and weaknesses revealed in this study were not similar across children, indicating distinct profiles (Gardner & Hatch, 1989).

Try This: Using Table 5.2, try to determine how all of the intelligences might manifest themselves in the life of a surgeon. What about the life of a musician? A politician? A teacher?

Gardner's Theory in Practice. Recent efforts by Gardner and his colleagues have focused on the development of appropriate assessments and on instructional materials and activities that support the forms of thinking represented by the seven intelligences. One such effort, called "Project Spectrum," has developed curriculum materials, activities, and assessments that have a student-centered learning focus (cf. Malkus, Feldman, & Gardner, 1988; Krechevsky, 1991; Ramos-Ford & Gardner, 1990). The study of preschool children described in the previous section was part of Project Spectrum.

In Project Spectrum, each activity is designed to tap one or more of the seven intelligences. Project Spectrum classrooms are supplied with materials that invite manipulation and experimentation. As students work and play with the materials, teachers are afforded the opportunity to observe unobtrusively the strengths and interests of students.

Try This: Interview teachers to discover if any is familiar with the theory of multiple intelligences. If they are, ask how the theory has influenced their teaching.

The Key School, an elementary school in Indianapolis, used the theory of multiple intelligences to design special classes and activities that encouraged students to discover their intellectual strengths and develop the full range of their intelligences (Olson, 1988). Over the course of the school year, each student engaged in a number of projects, which were videotaped. Researchers developed criteria for assessing the videotaped presentations.

At the junior and senior high school level, Gardner and his colleagues have collaborated with the Educational Testing Service and the Pittsburgh Public Schools on a project called Arts PROPEL (Armstrong, 1994; Magee & Price, 1992; Wolf, 1989; Zessoules, Wolf, & Gardner, 1988). The project yielded a series of modules called domain projects, which focus students' efforts on exercises and activities in music, creative writing, and the visual arts. The products generated by students, including early drafts or preliminary sketches, are collected in portfolios that are assessed by both teacher and student. This type of assessment allows students to reflect on their own work and on the feedback they receive; the portfolios also provide an opportunity for feedback from external evaluators, which can provide extra incentive for students to do their best work.

Critical Thinking: According to Gardner, what type(s) of intelligence(s) represents Heath's strengths in the Teacher Chronicle? His weaknesses?

Gardner's theory of multiple intelligences is significant for aspiring teachers because it provides an understanding of the variety of talents that students might bring to the classroom, talents that may or may not be seen easily in the context of traditional school learning. Consider the cases presented in Table 5.3. Gardner studied the highly accomplished people portrayed in the table—some would call them geniuses—in an attempt to discover the connection between their intelligences and creativity. These cases of exceptional creativity are taken

TABLE 5.3 Creativity and Success in School

Name	Childhood Characteristics	Degree of School Success
Sigmund Freud	Avid reader, articulate, self-learner, well-behaved	Very high
Albert Einstein	Spoke late, loner, loved to build and manipulate objects, usually quiet but capable of tantrums and disruptive behavior	Low in early grades, high in middle and later grades
Pablo Picasso	Loved to observe people and patterns, learned to read and write with difficulty, suffered in arithmetic, school-phobic, socially dependent on father, cheating	Very low
Igor Stravinsky	Privileged life-style, surrounded by adult intellectuals, early interests in painting and theater, preferred improvisation on the piano, disinterested in formal schooling, self-learner	Low
T. S. Eliot	Affluent family of considerable accomplishment in religion and education, sensitive,observant, when very young generated sounds—not words—in the rhythm of sentences, fascinated by sensory impressions	Very high
Martha Graham	Mother was strict, daily prayers, church-father entertained Martha by singing; close to her father—who caught her in lies by reading her body language; quiet but respected by classmates	High
Mohandas Gandhi	Born into a family with high ethical and moral standards, advised and mediated adult conflicts, pondered social and ethical issues of everyday life, not physically robust	Average

Source: Based on Gardner, H. (1993). *Creating Minds: An Anatomy of Creativity Seen through the Lives of Freud, Einstein, Picasso, Stravinsky, Eliot, Graham, and Gandhi.* New York: Basic Books.

by Gardner and other proponents to be evidence in support of the theory of multiple intelligences.

Reflection: Think about your own aspirations when you were a child. How do you think they may have influenced your thinking and learning in school?

For teachers, an important aspect of the theory of multiple intelligences is the connection between intelligence and thinking. The various types of intelligence define forms of thinking. The way a person thinks and the types of questions, problems, and issues about which a person thinks are, perhaps, the most defining feature of that person. Whether a child grows up to be a composer, physician, mechanic, engineer, or teacher; whether a child becomes an environmental advocate, patron of the arts, volunteer firefighter, community fundraiser, or president of the local PTA depends greatly on what occupies his or her thinking and how he or she thinks.

Teachers need to find ways of encouraging the use of all kinds of intelligences, not just the linguistic and logico-mathematical intelligences that are tapped by typical academic tasks. How can teachers tap the talents that are less obviously related to academic learning? How can they facilitate learning with students in whom such talents are predominant? How can bodily-kinesthetic, inter-, or intrapersonal intelligences, for example, be used to teach abstract concepts in math or science? The following ideas are based on lessons developed by Thomas Armstrong (1994).

Here's How to Engage Multiple Intelligences in Teaching Math and Science Concepts

- When teaching multiplication tables (for the fours, let's say), have students count to forty. Have students stand or clap on every fourth number. [bodily-kinesthetic intelligence]
- When teaching the function of an unknown *x* in algebraic equations, have students act out an equation. For example, using the equation $4x - 3 = 9$, arrange a group of four students next to a student wearing a mask to represent the unknown *x*. Then place a student representing subtraction, a group of three students, one student representing equals, and a group of nine students on the right side of the equation. As the class takes steps to solve the equation, students in the equation leave or join groups in an effort to isolate *x* and thus determine *x*'s value. [interpersonal, bodily-kinesthetic]
- The concept of an algebraic unknown could also be addressed by asking students to reflect on the mysteries—the unknown *x*'s—in their own lives and to discuss how they solve for *x* when handling personal issues. [intrapersonal]
- When teaching Boyle's law (when mass and temperature of a gas are fixed, pressure is inversely related to volume) in a high school physics class, have some students act as individual molecules of air. The molecule students move at constant rate (temperature). Other students confine the molecules in a corner of the room by stretching a string that becomes one boundary of the container. The students holding the string begin to move toward the corner (reducing volume). As the volume decreases, the molecules will begin bumping into each other (pressure) more frequently. [interpersonal, bodily-kinesthetic]
- Boyle's law could also be addressed by having students discuss how they feel when they are under lots of pressure in their personal lives. Have them discuss the sense of personal space they feel when under pressure and when they feel very little pressure. [intrapersonal]

Insights ON SUCCESSFUL PRACTICE

How do you accommodate students' individual differences in the ways they learn best?

I teach a mixed-ability fifth-grade class. I have to be on my toes to keep the interest of such a diverse group. I have begun some of my lessons by running into class wearing my jogging suit and a bronze medal. My entrance caught their attention. The students' reading lessons at the time were about sports figures; they were eager to bring in their own trophies and medals to share with the rest of the class. It seemed that from then on, I had created an environment In which they were much more willing to learn.

Another activity I have used is having students read how-to books and then bring in homemade projects based on their readings. Their projects have included ecology boxes, stationery, and doll houses. The students are proud of their accomplishments, and we display them in the main hall of the school so other students can enjoy them as well.

I have also asked students to complete a unique kind of book report: a hanging mobile! I am usually amazed at the creativity they display in these assignments. One child read the mystery, *Ten Little Indians.* His report consisted of a bow from which he suspended each of the characters from the story.

English grammar can be taught in a multisensory way. For example, my students were having difficulty with complex sentences. I made signs that read "main clause" and "conjunction" and "subordinating clause." Then I chose three students and made up an elaborate story about the "main clause" being so independent. Each student became a part of the sentence through a comical identity. Through the hilarity, the students were able to learn and enjoy English grammar.

All ages benefit from experience rather than lecturing. In the elementary years, the subjects taught are more readily learned and accepted when creative activity accompanies the lesson. Hands-on teaching also creates a classroom with fewer behavior problems.

DIANNE BAUMAN, Burkett Elementary School, Pittsburgh, Pennsylvania

Sternberg's Triarchic Theory of Intelligence

What is meant by teaching in a multisensory way? How did this teacher use humor and hands-on activities to help all her students reach their full potential in her class regardless of their abilities?

Gardner's theory of multiple intelligences is important for teachers because the theory helps us recognize that the talents students bring to our classrooms come in a variety of forms. Although this is a valid reason for examining Gardner's theory, it has also been raised as a criticism. Robert Sternberg, who joins Gardner as a major contemporary figure in the study of intelligence, argues that Gardner's theory of intelligences is, in reality, a theory of talents (Sternberg, 1989). To distinguish talent from intelligence, Sternberg provides an illustrative comparison between a person who is tone-deaf, and thus lacks some aspects of musical talent, and a person who lacks the cognitive ability to plan ahead. The former is capable of functioning quite well in the world—many of us have done it for years; the latter might very well require substantial assistance or resident care to carry out everyday functions. "Intelligence is general: without it we cannot function independently. Talents, however, are specialized" (Sternberg, 1989, p. 42).

Sternberg's approach to the study of intelligence focuses on how it functions in everyday life. He views intelligence as a kind of mental self-management.

Critical Thinking: What would be the difference between a theory of intelligence and a theory of talent? How could you test Gardner's theory to determine if Sternberg is correct?

Mental self-management has three elements that form the basis of his formal definition of intelligence. Sternberg's definition is that intelligence is "purposive adaptation to, selection of, and shaping of real-world environments relevant to one's life and abilities" (Sternberg, 1989, p. 65).

Sternberg identified three kinds of intelligence: componential, experiential, and contextual, hence the name, triarchic ("ruled by three") theory. The triarchic theory is presented in Figure 5.1.

componential intelligence Part of Sternberg's theory of intelligence, referring to a person's ability to reason abstractly, process information, and determine the kind and sequence of operations required for a task or problem.

Componential Intelligence. **Componential intelligence** identifies the mental components of what we call intelligent behavior. Components are mental processes that underlie behavior and are classified by the function they serve. *Metacomponents* are processes that identify problems, determine goals, plan strategies, and monitor and evaluate performance. *Performance components* are processes that are used to execute the plans or to carry out the tasks that have been selected. *Knowledge acquisition components* are the processes by which new learning occurs (Sternberg, 1986).

To illustrate componential intelligence, consider a student—perhaps this happened to you as well—who is working on a word problem in science or math. The

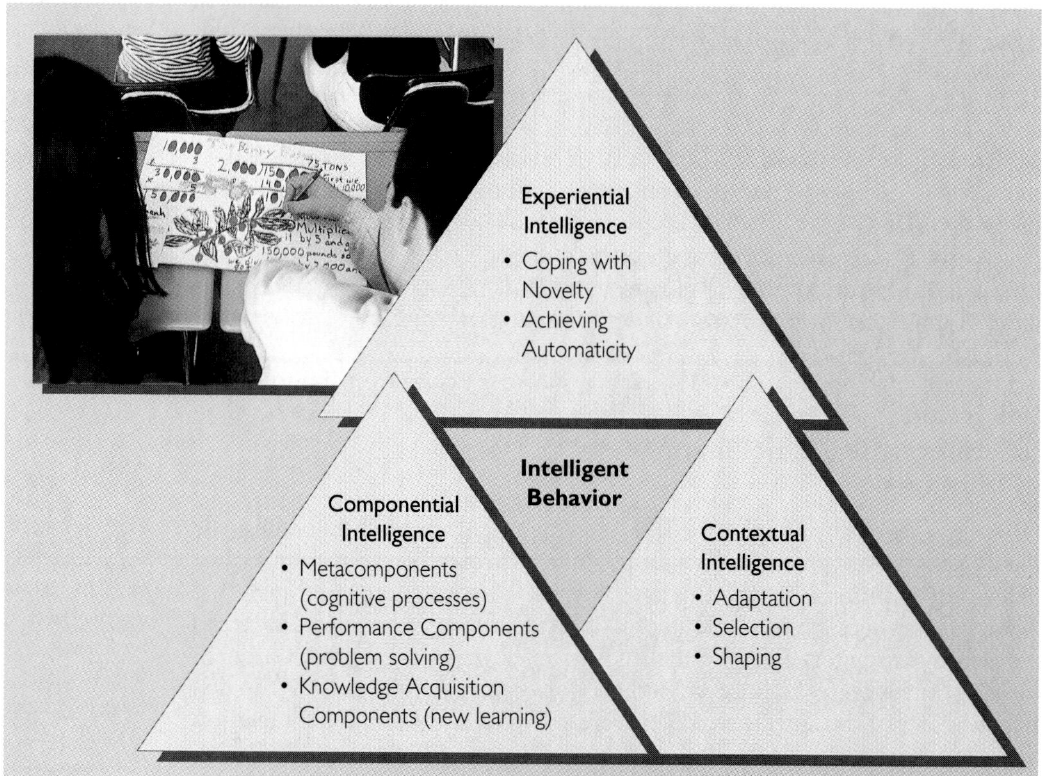

FIGURE 5.1

Sternberg's Triarchic Theory of Intelligence
Source: Based on R.J. Sternberg (1989). *The Triarchic Mind: A New Theory of Human Intelligence.* New York: Penguin Books.

student reads the problem to determine its nature, how to solve it, what information is required, and what information is irrelevant. This aspect of problem identification and planning is a metacomponent function. The student then begins carrying out the appropriate calculations, a function of performance components, to solve the problem. Along the way, the student discovers that there is a calculation needed that he or she does not know how to perform. This discovery halts work on the problem and serves as feedback to the metacomponents. This feedback allows the metacomponents to determine that what is required is to learn the procedure needed to continue work on the problem. The new procedure is learned (through knowledge acquisition components) and is performed (through performance components) as the student continues toward the goal of solving the problem.

Connection: How do the metacomponents described here relate to the notion of metacognition described in Chapter 2?

Try This: Observe children or adolescents solving problems. After observing, interview the students to see if you can document their use of componential intelligence.

Experiential Intelligence. The second part in the triarchic arrangement is experiential intelligence. **Experiential intelligence** explains how intelligence is related to novel tasks or new ideas in one's environment. Learners who exhibit a high degree of experiential intelligence are those who deal effectively with novel situations. This type of intelligence allows a student to analyze new tasks and to access knowledge and skills that will allow completion of the task. After several encounters with a new task or problem, those high in experiential intelligence will have automated the procedures required to complete the task. If a set of procedures becomes automatic, those procedures can be carried out with little or no effort, which, in turn, frees cognitive resources for other activities. An individual with little experiential intelligence is less capable of automating procedures and must, therefore, reason through a particular kind of problem each time it is encountered.

Try This: Find difficult historical situations for your students to study. Have your students brainstorm ways of adapting, selecting, and shaping the environments to improve the situations.

Contextual Intelligence. **Contextual intelligence** is reflected in one's ability to adapt, select, or shape one's environment to optimize one's opportunities. An implication of this type of intelligence is that measuring it requires judgments of the quality of one's existence within his or her environment. Sternberg (1986) provides a cross-cultural example to illustrate what he means by contextual intelligence and why he feels that the measurement of intelligence behavior must be sensitive to the context in which it occurs.

Suppose that a traditional intelligence test developed in North America were used to assess the intelligence of an African Pygmy. The type of intelligence tapped by North American tests is not likely to be the type of intelligence that allows a Pygmy to survive and flourish in his or her everyday environment. While the North American tests used in this hypothetical situation might measure something, it would not be contextual intelligence. The test would serve little purpose unless, of course, the Pygmy had as a goal adapting to North American culture.

Reflect: What ingenious adaptations have you displayed to disguise an inability?

If adaptation to an environment is a form of intelligent behavior, consider the intelligence displayed by the mentally retarded student who was incapable of telling time. The student spent part of each day in a work program away from the school. Because the student had to catch a bus back to school, it was important that he keep track of the time. Every day, the teacher wondered if the student would miss the bus back to school, but he never did. The teacher discovered that at work the student wore a watch, something he never did at school. More important, the watch was broken. Whenever the student needed to know the time he would look at his watch and then say to someone, "Excuse me, but my watch is broken. Could you tell me the time, please?" His practice of putting on a nonfunctional watch on arriving at the work program was an adaptation to his new environment, and a rather ingenious one at that.

experiential intelligence
Part of Sternberg's theory of intelligence, describing a person's capacity to deal with novel tasks or new ideas and to combine unrelated facts.

contextual intelligence
Part of Sternberg's theory of intelligence, relating to one's ability to adapt, select, or shape one's environment to optimize one's opportunities.

Ingenious adaptations are contextually intelligent behaviors. Students—and adults in the work force—who can't read but find ways to get by demonstrate contextual intelligence. Students who find shortcuts or exploit loopholes to avoid classroom work also demonstrate this type of intelligence.

People who exhibit contextual intelligence may not always adapt to an environment; sometimes the most intelligent move is to select an environment. Selection is a second form of contextual intelligence that is related to an individual's ability to find an appropriate environment. Consider, for example, those who chose to leave or deselect the environment of Nazi Germany rather than to remain and adapt to it. Another example of selection comes from a book entitled *Whatever Happened to the Quiz Kids?* (Feldman, 1982). The Quiz Kids, who all had very high IQ scores, appeared on radio and television in the 1940s and 1950s. A follow-up study of the Quiz Kids found that only those who found work that interested them and who persevered in that field had successful careers. The less successful Quiz Kids were unable to find a niche for themselves and, despite their high IQs, exhibited little contextual intelligence.

A third form of contextual intelligence is shaping. There are times when adapting to an environment or selecting a new environment is not possible. In such instances, contextual intelligence can still be used to shape or change the environment rather than the person. Oskar Schindler, whose story was portrayed in the movie *Schindler's List*, shaped his environment in Nazi Germany rather than adapt to or deselect it. Schindler was an industrialist who employed Jewish workers and bribed Nazi officials, thus saving many Jewish people from the death camps during the Holocaust. Shaping environments occurs in many less dramatic or historically significant contexts as well. A person whose talents are unrecognized or undervalued by a company might propose a new position or division that would match more closely his or her strengths.

Recent research and theory on the nature of human intelligence, particularly the work of Howard Gardner and Robert Sternberg, have broadened the concept of intelligence from the traditional views. The new views have emphasized that intelligence needs to be understood in context, including the context provided by cultural norms. The notions of multiple intelligences and multiple components of intelligence suggest that there are different ways in which students can exhibit intelligent behavior (Bransford, Goldman, & Vye, 1991). If this is so, teachers and parents should look for and acknowledge students' strengths—not just in the traditional academic areas, but in other areas as well. Teachers can also help students broaden their views of what intelligent behavior is. If students who have not experienced success on traditional academic tasks can learn to see themselves as intelligent, their self-esteem should be improved. As we learned from Chapter 3, enhancement of a student's self-esteem is critical to facilitating psychological growth. Intelligence is one characteristic that contributes to variability in classrooms. Another source of variability is the way students prefer to think.

Critical Thinking: What other historical figures have demonstrated contextual intelligence by shaping their own environments?

Try This: Interview a teacher to discover the methods by which he or she determines the strengths and weaknesses of students.

HOW DO STUDENTS VARY IN THE WAYS THEY THINK AND LEARN?

Watch your classmates as they discuss a question, read their textbooks, listen to a presentation, or prepare a lesson plan. How do they engage in these activities? What are the differences in preparation? Do their study outlines look different? Do some incorporate drawings? Are some of the textbooks read by your colleagues highlighted heavily? Do some of your fellow learners ask a lot of questions in discussion? Offer lots of suggestions? Speak only infrequently? Do they persist in the face of difficult problems? Do some have difficulty getting organized on projects? Any group of students, including the groups you will teach, represents a variety of dispositions and preferences for thinking and learning.

Thinking and Learning Dispositions

Thinking is central to the teaching–learning process and is, therefore, a consistently recurring theme in this book. In this section, we examine thinking as a source of individual variability. There are at least two ways that thinking varies among students. The first is thinking skills. Some students think better than others because they have better thinking skills. The development of thinking skills was addressed in our examination of cognitive development in Chapter 2 and will be addressed further in Chapters 7, 11, 12, and 13. The second way in which thinking varies among students—and the one on which we focus in this section—is in the ways students are disposed to think. **Thinking dispositions** are mental habits, inclinations, or "abiding tendencies in thinking behavior exhibited over time and across diverse thinking situations" (Tishman Perkins, & Jay, 1995, p. 37).

People have all kinds of behavioral inclinations or dispositions. Some people are inclined to eat too much, to be kind, to rise early, or to sleep late. People also are disposed to think in various ways. Some people think by asking lots of questions, some are persistent when they think about a problem, some routinely take multiple perspectives. As we saw in the last chapter, one's cultural background and home environment influence what behaviors are considered appropriate and, therefore, what are valued. For instance, a student raised in a home where family members routinely consider points of view other than their own is likely to develop that disposition in his or her own thinking. Likewise, a student who is raised in a family that dismisses as wrong all viewpoints that differ from his or hers will likely be close-minded in his or her thinking.

Reflection: Did you see any evidence in the Teacher Chronicle that Heath might have been influenced by his mother's thinking? If so, how?

It would be possible, of course, to speculate endlessly on different ways in which people are disposed to think. Some dispositions, however, are obstacles to learning. A student who is inclined to ignore instructions, for example, is not likely to become a competent problem solver.

Try This: Give this idea to a teacher. See if the teacher is willing to try it in his or her classroom and if you can observe.

Rather than speculating on all of the thinking dispositions that might exist, Shari Tishman and her colleagues (1995) from Harvard have focused on identifying dispositions that foster learning. Tishman and her colleagues suggest that good learners tend to exhibit curiosity, flexibility, precision, organization, and patience in their thinking. To understand the dispositions in context, assume that a seventh-grade class has been challenged by their teacher as follows: "Water is a precious natural resource. As good citizens, we have a responsibility to conserve it. What is our class going to do to conserve water? This is not a paper assignment. We are going to take some actions that conserve water. Now, what are we going to do?"

thinking dispositions Mental habits, inclinations, or tendencies in thinking behavior exhibited over time and across diverse thinking situations.

For each disposition, general descriptions are followed by examples (in italics) of thinking dispositions that would contribute to solving the water conservation problem.

- Curiosity: Curious thinkers ask questions, look for additional information, probe, and reflect. *We should find out if there other groups who have taken steps to conserve water and find out what they did. Maybe we could get some stuff from the Water Department or even interview some of their experts.*
- Flexibility: Flexible thinkers take alternative points of views, venture new ideas, are open-minded and playful. *Maybe we should divide into teams and let each team brainstorm a bunch of ideas. One of the things we might want to think about is whether water is the best resource to conserve.*
- Precision: Precise thinkers seek clarity, are thorough, and take care to avoid errors. *Do we have to think of things that only we can do, or can we teach other people to help conserve? If we are going to teach others, we had better try out our ideas on ourselves first.*
- Organization: Organized thinkers are orderly and logical, they plan ahead, and work methodically. *I think we should figure out how much water we need to conserve and then think about how we are going to measure water that won't be used. That will take some thought.*
- Patience: Patient thinkers are willing to give themselves time to reason and are persistent in their efforts. *This should be a big project. I think we should do it, but if we are really going to do this, let's make sure we will have enough time each week to work on it* (cf. Tishman et al. , 1995).

Tishman and her colleagues do not claim that this is an exhaustive list; other positive dispositions surely exist. However, these are considered to be the "bottom-line" dispositions that support classroom learning. If curiosity, flexibility, precision, organization, and patience are benchmarks, then they can be used to gauge the degree to which a student is disposed to good thinking. How can the benchmark dispositions be used by a teacher to determine variability among the individuals in his or her classroom?

here's how

Here's How to Gauge the Thinking Dispositions of Students

- Give students opportunities to display their thinking dispositions. This means setting up tasks, such as the water conservation challenge, that require students to initiate investigations, make decisions, solve problems. We have a colleague, for example, who challenges his students to find the best chili recipe in the world (Shank, 1995).
- Have students document their own thinking. As students work on the thinking challenges you give them, have them stop from time to time to talk about, write about, or otherwise record how they are thinking. Our colleague has students keep a journal of their investigations of the best chili recipe in the world. The younger students' thinking might be documented through checklists or interviews that determine, for example, what questions students have asked, their attempts to clarify a problem, or their persistence (Woditsch & Schmittroth, 1991).
- Ask students to critique demonstrations of your thinking. Set up a thinking challenge for yourself and then perform a thinking scene for your students. Your thinking scene could take place in the library, at a computer, or with other thinkers. First, display poor thinking dispositions: Make guesses instead of asking questions, take only one point of view, give up on difficult parts. Then, using the same challenge, act the scene again, but this time display the benchmark dispositions. Ask students to identify the differences between the first and second scenes. Use stu-

dents' responses—which could be either written or oral—to gauge thinking dispositions (see Woditsch & Schmittroth, 1991).

- After small group or class discussions, ask students to identify ways in which the group's thinking might be improved in future discussions. Have students focus on the group's thinking processes rather than on any specific product of the discussion. Monitor the discussion to ensure that all students have a chance to evaluate thinking processes and that, as a consequence, you have a chance to note those students who do and do not display the dispositional benchmarks suggested by Tishman et al.
- Allow for a variety of observations over a reasonable period of time. Keep in mind that thinking dispositions are "abiding tendencies in thinking behavior exhibited over time and across diverse thinking situations" (Tishman et al., 1995, p. 37). Judgments made on the basis of one observation may or may not represent a student's tendencies.

Learning Styles and Cultural Differences

The work on thinking dispositions reported here builds on several decades of what is referred to as "learning styles" research. However, the bottom-line thinking dispositions account well for the findings of this earlier research. For example, Guilford's (1967) three faces of intellect model suggests a distinction between convergent and divergent styles. Convergent thinkers tend to react to instructional materials in conventional ways. Divergent thinkers tend to respond in unconventional or idiosyncratic ways. This distinction can be understood in terms of the flexibility disposition presented earlier. Thinking flexibly (including divergently) contributes to learning.

Another example of earlier research on learning styles distinguishes impulsive or reflective styles of learning (Kagan, 1964a, 1964b). Impulsive students tend to answer questions quickly; reflective students take their time, preferring to evaluate alternative answers. Reflective students are more concerned with being accurate than with being fast. From the perspective of thinking dispositions, these learning styles can be interpreted in terms of the bottom-line dispositions of patience and curiosity. These dispositions indicate that reflectivity supports learning to a greater extent than impulsivity.

Dispositional differences among students vary. The thinking dispositions postulated by Tishman and her colleagues (1995) have an advantage over earlier research on learning styles, which attempted to categorize and test for specific learning styles (Dunn, Beaudry, & Klavas, 1989). Although the reliability and validity of many of these tests have been questioned, the tests have been used to categorize students. Once learners were categorized, specialized instructional programs were developed for learners in the various categories. Programs were developed that focused on visual styles, auditory styles, and left-brain and right-brain styles. There is a danger in this approach to the teaching–learning process:

> People are different, and it is good practice to recognize and accommodate individual differences. It is also good practice to present information in a variety of ways through more than one modality, but it is not wise to categorize learners and prescribe methods solely on the basis of tests . . . The idea of learning styles is appealing, but a critical examination of this approach should cause educators to be skeptical. (Snider, 1990, p. 53)

Try This: Ask practicing teachers why it is dangerous to categorize students.

The danger of categorizing students is further complicated by some research findings suggesting that there are learning-style differences among various groups of people. Some researchers have investigated whether a person's cultural or ethnic heritage might predict one's learning style. For example, Hispanic American students have been shown to prefer socially oriented learning, while some Native Americans prefer learning individually (Garcia, 1992; Vasquez, 1990). Some research on African American students suggests that visual thinking is preferred to verbal thinking (Bennet, 1995). Although there has been little research on Asian Americans, a stereotype exists that students belonging to this ethnic group are persistent in their learning efforts but socially passive (Suzuki, 1983).

Studies of learning-style differences among groups have been criticized for at least two reasons. First, as mentioned earlier, the tests used to determine a person's learning style have questionable value. Second, research that stereotypes people fosters instructional practice that reinforces stereotypes rather than addressing the learning needs of each individual (Gordon, 1991; Yee, 1992).

Connection: Do you think that Heath, in the Teacher Chronicle, will be categorized? How might that influence his progress in school?

Categorizing learners by ethnic group ignores differences that exist among individuals within that group. Likewise, categorizing individuals according to tests of learning style ignores the different ways an individual can think. The bottom-line thinking dispositions are not categories into which students are sorted. They are standards of thinking that support learning. Individuals may differ in regard to which dispositions they use, but knowledge of such differences fosters teaching that addresses each learner's needs.

HOW DO STUDENTS VARY IN ABILITIES AND DISABILITIES?

Connection: Recall the discussion of students at risk in Chapter 3.

The needs of individual students are a function of their life circumstance abilities. Some students need special attention because they are raised in difficult circumstances; others because they have exceptional abilities. In the Teacher Chronicle at the beginning of this chapter, Heath has a very high IQ, and comes from a family that has at least one parent who is a professional and also interested enough to come to school for a meeting. If we stop there, Heath's profile would suggest that he should do well in school. However, the events in the Teacher Chronicle also allow inferences about Heath's behavior and emotions that suggest he may be at risk of performing or behaving poorly in school.

Programs designed to help students at risk of school failure because of their life circumstances include early intervention, prevention, and compensatory education. In addition, "full service schools" offer an increasingly comprehensive array of social services for students and their families.

Exceptional Learners

The needs of some students require special accommodations in the classroom. Special needs students—called **exceptional learners**—are either impaired by mental retardation, learning disabilities, emotional/behavioral disorders, communication disorders, hearing loss, visual impairment, physical disabilities, or they are gifted. In both cases, such students require special instruction and services to reach their full potential (Hallahan & Kauffman, 1994). Recent figures indicate that 10 percent of school-age children are disabled to such an extent that they need special instruction or services. An additional 3 percent to 5 percent require special attention because they are gifted (U. S. Department of Education, 1989).

Formal recognition of the special needs of exceptional students came in the form of legislation passed by the U. S. Congress in 1975. Public Law 94-142 is the Education for All Handicapped Children Act. A key phrase in the legislation refers to a least restrictive environment, an instructional environment that is as similar to the regular classroom as possible. It is from PL 94-142 that the practice of mainstreaming, the inclusion of students with special needs in regular classroom instruction, began. Mainstreaming is one way to meet the requirements of the least restrictive environment. PL 94-142 also requires that instruction be designed to meet the needs of each exceptional student. The plan for instructing an exceptional student is called an individualized education program (IEP).

Since PL 94-142, two other pieces of landmark legislation have been enacted. In 1990, the Individuals with Disabilities Education Act (IDEA) and the Americans with Disabilities Act (ADA) were passed by the 101st Congress. The IDEA (sometimes called PL 101-476, i.e., the 476th public law passed by the 101st Congress) amended PL 94-142 and assures the rights of all children and youths with disabilities to a free and appropriate public education. The ADA (PL 101-336) prohibits discrimination against people with disabilities regardless of age or the nature and extent of a person's disability. The ADA ensures the civil rights of persons with disabilities in areas of employment, public accommodations, telecommunications, transportation, and state and local government.

Try This: Contact your local school district and inquire about their procedures for generating IEPs.

The IDEA and the ADA are complementary laws. Both laws anticipate that people with disabilities "will enjoy equal opportunity to fully participate in the life of the community and will have equal opportunity to live independently and achieve economic self-sufficiency" (Turnbull, 1993, p. 24). PL 94-142 uses the term *handicapped* in its title; the IDEA and the ADA refer to *disabilities.* The difference is more than simply a change in vocabulary, there is substance to the distinction that is critical for aspiring teachers to understand.

Reflection: Did you ever experience a time when a disability became a handicap? What were the circumstances? How did you handle it? How did you feel about it?

Most types of exceptionality stem from a disability. The terms *disability* and *handicap* are often used interchangeably in everyday language. Even so, the terms are distinctive, and the distinction is important for teachers to understand. "A **disability** is an inability to do something, a diminished capacity to perform in a specific way. A **handicap,** on the other hand, is a disadvantage imposed on an individual. A disability may or may not be a handicap, depending on the circumstances" (Hallahan & Kauffman, 1994, p. 6, emphasis added). In your classroom, you will encounter students who are disabled in some way. Their disabilities may or may not be handicaps, depending on the accommodations you make in your classroom.

exceptional learners Learners who have special learning needs and who require special instruction.

disability A diminished capacity to perform in a specific way.

handicap A disadvantage imposed on an individual.

Insights ON SUCCESSFUL PRACTICE

In your experience, what strategies work best in promoting the academic success of student at risk?

At risk. Who isn't at risk?! During my eleven years of teaching I have seen many children who were and are at risk. Here are just a few problems that I dealt with. To me they are heartbreaking. Mary's father is in prison. She loves him very much and truly believes in him. Audrey reminds me of myself when I was a little girl. She has a mother who has been abused by her father. I wonder sometimes what the future holds for her. Trevor needs a father. Curtis needs a mother. Being born out of wedlock is what is hurting a lot of children. Children need to feel a belonging to someone. Michell, the one who was quiet and very bright, had a grandfather who committed suicide in their home. Holli's only shot himself. Mom and Dad couldn't cope with it so they turned to drinking. Stephen, the one who was always in trouble, had some severe mental problems because of being mentally abused by a family member. These are not happy experiences you enjoy talking about. Every year I and many other teachers have had to experience working with these types of students.

What helps me is that I have lived through some of these experiences. I understand when some students come to school and want to be understood and to feel loved, protected, and secure.

Many of the high risk problems have to do with alcohol, violence, or drugs. The traumas are real and it often makes you wonder if the child will ever survive to be a mentally healthy adult.

My main strategy in working with these students is to establish trust. Listen and talk to them. Talk without criticizing the problem, but understanding them with sincere words and attention, gestures, and verbal praise (this helps them to feel confident). Expecting them to work harder at school helps them to keep their mind off of what might be going on outside the classroom. Help them feel good about succeeding in their academics and not failing. This also teaches them to be more responsible people.

It helps the student to give them the hope that receiving a good education will someday get them through some stressful times in their life. Although a child's memory can't ever erase bad memories, teachers can inspire a child to succeed in life with love and understanding, so that children may strive for the best.

WILMA F. MAD PLUME, Vina Chattin School,
Browning, Montana

Who are students at risk? What special educational needs might these students have? What are some other strategies you might use in your classroom to increase the academic success of students at risk?

Exceptionality and Diversity

Understanding the impact of cultural diversity is especially important for teachers of exceptional students because of the disproportional representation of some minorities in exceptional populations. According to the U. S. Department of Education (1992), approximately 65 percent of high school students in the United States are Anglo-European-American, approximately 12 percent are African American, and approximately 8 percent are Hispanic American. African American youths, however, account for about 25 percent of all students with disabilities.

Cultural diversity can be viewed as a strength in a classroom, as an expanded opportunity for learning (cf. Banks, 1994). Research on cooperative learning, for example, shows that heterogeneous groups achieve better than homogeneous groups (Johnson & Johnson, 1994). Heterogeneity provides a richer source of experience to a learning group than homogeneity, in which every member of the group brings a similar background and experiences to the work of the group.

Because some students with disabilities suffer from low self-esteem, and because cultural differences sometimes lead to conflicts of values, it is particularly important for teachers to attend to students' self-concepts. Charles Jones taught in a self-contained classroom of twelve disabled students. All of the students were African Americans. The students had negative self-images and denigrated their own heritage. Ethnic name-calling was common among members of the class. In an effort to improve the situation, Jones had his students create an "Ethnic Feelings Book." Students worked together and individually to learn about their heritage, discussed negative terminology and stereotypes, listened to African Americans from the community who visited the class, participated in role playing, and focused on the positive attributes of relatives and community leaders. They documented what they learned in the book. The result of the project was a substantial decrease in name-calling—including peer reprimands—increased enthusiasm, and cooperative behavior (Ford & Jones, 1990).

Connection: Think back to Lickona's model for moral education in Chapter 3. In the context of that model, how is diversity in a classroom an opportunity for learning?

At the heart of the matter of cultural diversity, exceptionality, or any other source of variability of students is the importance of recognizing the individual needs of students. Heward & Orlansky (1992) ask the following question: "If a student cannot speak, read, or write English well enough to progress in the school curriculum, does it make any difference whether the limited English proficiency is caused by cultural differences or by a disability?" (p. 491). Yes and no. No, in the sense that, in either case, the student and teacher face a problem: The student is at risk of performing poorly. Yes, in the sense that the instructional solution to the problem depends greatly on the origin of the problem.

Try This: Consider creating an Ethnic Feelings Book for your students during practice teaching. Seek the advice of your cooperating teacher and your supervisor.

Students with High-Incidence Disabilities

Categories of exceptionality are general descriptions. Students who enter your classroom with a particular disability or who are gifted will differ from one another in the same way that nonexceptional students differ from one another. As you prepare yourself for the variety that exceptional learners will introduce to your teaching situation, there is an important point to keep in mind. The point, which we will examine more closely later in the book, is that good teaching practice serves the individual needs of learners, regardless of the label they have been given.

One aspect of exceptionality to recognize is that some types of exceptionality are much more common than others. You can expect to teach many more students from the high-incidence exceptionalities described in the following discussion than students from the low-incidence exceptionalities described in the next section.

Reflection: Think back to your days as a student. Did you ever know an E/BD student? What kinds of behaviors did he or she display?

Emotional and Behavioral Disorders. Emotional/behavioral disorder (E/BD) is a disability that has proven difficult to define in a widely accepted way. Despite the lack of a generally accepted formal definition, E/BD students are easily noticed in a classroom (Hallahan & Kauffman, 1994). Through advanced statistical analysis, researchers have identified patterns or dimensions of disordered behavior (e.g., Achenbach, 1985; Quay, 1986; Quay & Peterson, 1987).

emotional/behavioral disorders A disorder in which people have difficulty controlling their feelings and behavior.

One broad category of disordered behavior is externalizing—that is, acting out against others. Acting out in the form of classroom disruption—showing off, fights, temper tantrums—is a particular kind of externalizing called *conduct disorder.* Experienced teachers recognize that these behaviors occur in normal

In today's inclusive classroom, general education teachers, special education teachers, and other professionals collaborate to meet all the students' educational needs.

students as well as in E/BD students, the difference being that E/BD students cry, scream, and fight much more impulsively and with much greater frequency. Acting out that occurs in the company of others is called socialized aggression. The aggressive, illegal, and disrespectful behavior of gangs is an example.

Another broad category of disordered behavior is internalizing—that is, behavior that reflects emotional problems, such as depression or debilitating anxiety. More specific types of internalizing are immature or withdrawn behaviors. Students who exhibit immaturity tend to have shorter attention spans, are easily distracted, and answer questions impulsively. Behaviors symptomatic of withdrawal include embarrassment, self-consciousness, sadness, and anxiety (Hallahan & Kauffman, 1994).

Specific Learning Disabilities. **Learning disabilities** is a generic term referring to a disorder in cognitive processing. It emerged as a field of study for educational researchers in the early 1960s. Since that time, eleven different definitions of learning disabilities have, at one time or another, been embraced by a significant number of researchers (Hammill, 1990). At present, the most popular definition is the one endorsed by the U. S. government:

> "Specific learning disability" means a disorder in one or more of the basic psychological processes involved in understanding or in using language, spoken or written, which may manifest itself in an imperfect ability to listen, think, speak, read, write, spell, or do mathematical calculations. The term includes such conditions as perceptual handicaps, brain injury, minimal brain dysfunction, dyslexia, and developmental aphasia. The term does not include children who have learning problems which are primarily the result of visual, hearing, or motor handicaps, of mental retardation, of emotional disturbance, or of environmental, cultural, or economic disadvantage. (*Federal Register,* 1977, p. 65083)

Nearly half of all children with disabilities are identified as having learning disabilities (U. S. Department of Education, 1989), making it important that teachers know the "official" definition of the term. It is even more important for teachers to know what students with learning disabilities are like, how they see themselves, and how they understand their disabilities. For our description of this exceptionality, we present an excerpt from a remarkable book entitled *"L. D." Does NOT Mean Learning Dumd!* The book was written by students of Pamela Maniet-Bellermann. They wanted to pass along their experiences in hopes of helping other students recently identified as having a learning disability. The

learning disability A generic term for disorders in cognitive processing that interfere with learning.

book has also proved helpful to parents of children who are entering programs for students with learning disabilities.

> A person with a "disability" has difficulty doing things that most people can do easily. A person with a "visual" disability may not be able to see well or at all. A person who has a "hearing" disability may be deaf or able to hear only a few sounds. "Physically" disabled people may have trouble using their arms, legs, and other parts of their body. The "learning" disabled person has difficulty with learning. "Mentally" disabled or retarded people also have trouble with learning but having a learning disability is not the same as being retarded. Sometimes people have called us retarded or dumb and that makes us feel bad because we know they just don't understand us! AND when we have so much trouble learning something, we get mad at ourselves and begin to feel like we ARE dumb! Miss Maniet has to remind us many, many times that we are not dumb. We've needed a lot of convincing!! (p. 11–12)

The types of experiences described in *"L. D." Does NOT Mean Learning Dumd!* suggest different kinds of learning disabilities. Subcategories include developmental learning disability and academic learning disability. Developmental learning disabilities affect those skills that are necessary for academic achievement, such as attention, memory, perception, thinking, and oral language. Academic learning disabilities refer to problems encountered in learning skills and content that are part of the traditional academic curriculum, such as reading, math, handwriting, spelling, and written expression (Kirk & Chalfant, 1984; Lerner, 1993).

Try This: Interview a student with a learning disability-perhaps there is one in your class. Find out what kind of disability he or she has and how the disability has affected him or her.

Communication Disorders. **Communication disorders** fall into two major categories: speech disorders and language disorders (American Speech-Language-Hearing Association, 1982).

Speech disorders include articulation, voice, and fluency problems. Sounds are sometimes omitted, substituted, added, or distorted. Voice quality problems, such as abnormal pitch, loudness, or quality, also fall into the category of speech disorder. A lack of fluency in the flow of verbal expression—stuttering—is another form of speech disorder. Stuttering can begin in childhood and persist into adulthood. However, stuttering is chiefly a childhood disorder. With the help of a speech therapist, most children stop stuttering by the end of adolescence.

Language disorders are problems in using symbol systems to communicate, resulting in difficulty in understanding or generating messages. Language disorders may involve phonological impairment (see Chapter 2); they may also be experienced by students who use a nonvocal system of symbols such as American Sign Language (ASL). Children who experience communication disorders do not necessarily experience other types of challenges, though it is quite possible that they will experience other types of disorders, including cerebral palsy, mental retardation, and learning disabilities.

Point: That communication disorders might require special instruction supports a basic assumption of this book: *Students' background and individual characteristics affect learning.*

Communication is basic to social interaction and to our intuitive judgments of a student's general intellectual ability. It is important to remember that although a student's ability to send and receive messages may be impaired, that impairment does not necessarily mean that the student's intellect is also impaired.

communication disorder Speech (voice) and language (symbols) disorders.

Students with Low-Incidence Disabilities

You can expect to have students with high-incidence disabilities in your classes frequently throughout your career. Depending on the particular certification you seek and on the type of district or school in which you will teach, you will probably encounter students with the types of disabilities described here less frequently.

Mental Retardation. The AAMR (American Association on Mental Retardation) provides the most widely accepted definition of mental retardation.

> **Mental retardation** refers to substantial limitations in present functioning. It is characterized by significantly subaverage intellectual functioning, existing concurrently with related limitations in two or more of the following applicable adaptive skills areas: communication, self-care, home living, social skills, community use, self-direction, health and safety, functional academics, leisure, and work. Mental retardation manifests before age 18. (AAMR Ad Hoc Committee on Terminology and Classification, 1992, p. 5)

Mental retardation is not an all-or-none phenomenon. The AAMR system of classification lists four levels of mental retardation: mild, moderate, severe, and profound. Mild mental retardation is by far the highest incidence of these four categories.

Instruction for mildly retarded students (or students with cognitive disabilities) focuses on developing readiness skills in the early elementary grades. Readiness skills include sitting still, following directions, discriminating sounds and visual stimuli, self-help (e.g., dressing, using the rest room), and working cooperatively with peers. Instruction in later elementary grades addresses functional academics. Mildly and moderately retarded students are taught to read ads in the newspaper, the telephone book, and labels at the supermarket rather than social studies or fiction. The purpose of such a reading program is to allow them to function independently. Junior high and high school instruction encourages the development of community living and vocational skills (Epstein, Polloway, Patton, & Foley, 1989). The major instructional goal for severely and profoundly retarded students is independent behavior. Practical skills, such as eating, dressing, and personal hygiene, are emphasized.

Try This: Volunteer some time with a local agency that serves people with mental retardation. Use your time to observe and reflect on the challenges faced by people with mental disabilities, and do some research on the programs designed to help them reach their goals.

Sensory Disorders. **Sensory disorders** refer to disabilities in using sensing information from the environment. Hearing and visual impairment are sensory disorders. Hearing impairment includes students who, on one end of the continuum, are hard of hearing and, on the other end, are deaf. Students who have hearing impairments can, with the aid of special amplification devices, use their sense of hearing to good advantage. Deaf children must be instructed through other senses. Because a child with a hearing impairment may have difficulty speaking or understanding speech, he or she is often assumed to have below-average intelligence. Language deficits are not deficits in intellectual ability.

Many hearing-impaired students need only amplification devices and articulation therapy. Others must learn special communication techniques. In addition to auditory training, which can help students make use of whatever hearing they possess, the techniques include speech reading, finger spelling, and true sign languages. Speech reading is a more accurate name for what most people call

mental retardation Significantly subaverage intellectual functioning, usually present at birth, resulting in or associated with impairments in adaptive behavior and manifested during the developmental period.

sensory disorders Disorders such as hearing and visual impairments.

lipreading. Speech readers use not only visual cues from the speakers' mouths but also gestures and body language cues. Finger spelling is a way of translating spoken English and differs from a true sign language (Figure 5.2).

A true sign language has its own grammar and, contrary to the opinion of many, can be used to convey abstract ideas (Sacks, 1989). The communication techniques used by those with hearing impairments make it difficult for those who do not have hearing loss to join them in a conversation, and vice versa. Because communication plays a critical role in social interaction, deaf people socialize with those who share their disability to a greater extent than do people in other exceptional categories (Hallahan & Kauffman, 1994).

Critical Thinking: What is the difference between a language and a translating system?

Visual impairment is legally defined by a person's acuity and field of vision. A legally blind person is one whose acuity is 20/200 or less. (A person with 20/200 vision sees at twenty feet what a person with normal vision sees at 200.) Field of vision refers to the width, measured in angles, of a person's peripheral vision.

Educators define visual impairment in terms of the method of reading instruction a student with visual impairment requires. A child with low vision is able to read print through the use of magnification technology; a child who is blind must use braille or audio tapes. These and other technological advances make it possible

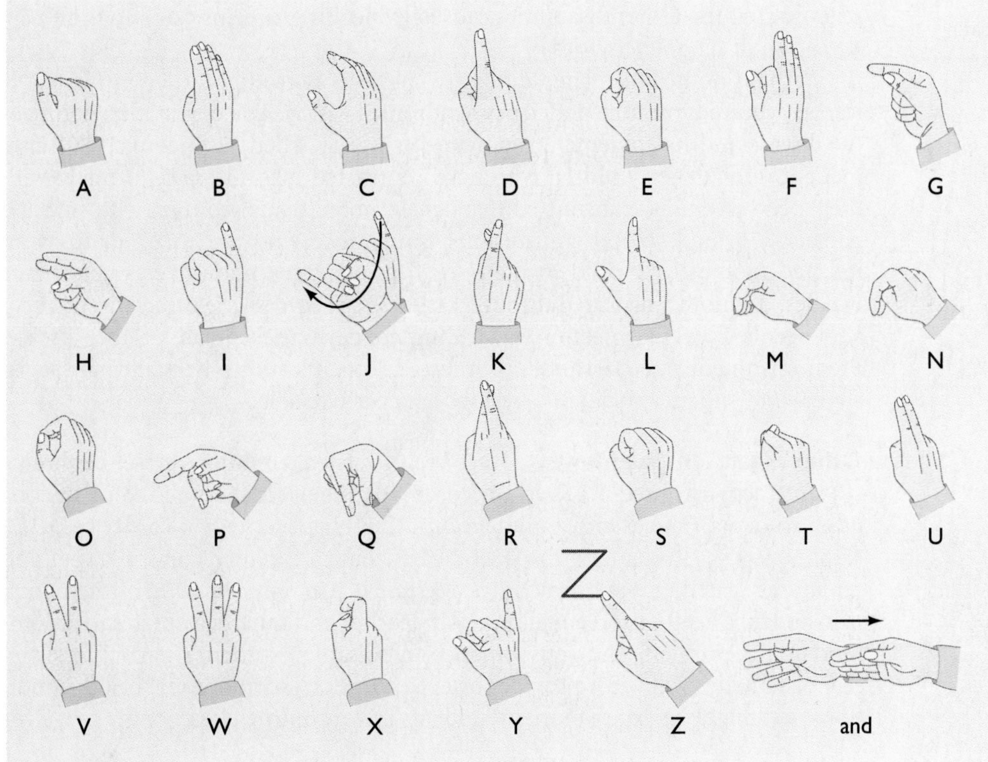

FIGURE 5.2

Finger Spelling Alphabet

Source: Exceptional Children (5th ed., p. 284) by D.P. Hallahan and J.M. Kauffman, 1991. Copyright 1991 by Allyn & Bacon. Reprinted by permission of the National Association of the Deaf.

to teach students with visual impairments in regular classrooms. In addition to using devices that enlarge viewing material or vocalize printed matter, students with vision loss may need aids, such as guide dogs or sensor devices, to move about.

Physical Disabilities. **Physical disabilities** include disorders of the skeleton, joints, and muscles or health conditions that interfere with students' educational performances. Some physical disabilities, such as cerebral palsy and epilepsy, are due to neurological impairments. Cerebral palsy is not a disease in the proper sense of the word. It is neither contagious, remittable (with periodic relief from symptoms), nor progressive (although poor treatment can cause complications). It is a syndrome that includes motor and/or psychological dysfunctions, seizures, behavior disorders, or any combination of symptoms due to brain damage.

Epilepsy is a condition that periodically causes abnormal amounts of electrical activity in the brain, resulting in seizures. Seizures vary in duration, frequency, and intensity. Some seizures last only a few seconds; others may last for several minutes. Some children with epilepsy have seizures every few minutes, others have them only once a year. The most intensive seizures involve major convulsions, which can be frightening to an observer. Minor seizures, a common indicator of which is rapid eye blinks, sometimes go unnoticed.

Try This: Contact your local school district and ask to receive materials that explain the district's policies and procedures for accommodating students or staff who are HIV-positive. The American Red Cross has several publications available. Contact your local Red Cross Office or write AIDS Education Office, 1730 D St. NW, Washington, DC 20006. Useful information is also available by writing for the *NEA AIDS Booklet,* NEA Communications, 1201 16th St. NW, Washington, DC 20036.

Skeletal/muscular disabilities, such as muscular dystrophy and arthritis, can limit a student's movement and, as a result, his or her participation in some school activities. Other disabilities caused by health problems can also limit participation in school activities.

Perhaps no health-related disability has been so readily turned into a handicap as acquired immune deficiency syndrome (AIDS). The devastating nature of the disease and its epidemic proportions (Church, Allen, & Stiehm, 1986) have made it difficult for children who have contracted it to interact normally with their peers. AIDS is transmitted through intimate sexual contact with infected partners, through blood transfusions from those who are infected, from an infected mother to a child in utero, or from using contaminated hypodermic needles. It is not transmitted through casual social contact. Sex education to help adolescents prevent infection is helping to curb the spread of the disease. Programs to educate classmates of infected students and to help alleviate social stigma and enhance social interactions are also available.

Other Health Impairments. Other health-related conditions can either limit a student's activity or require special accommodation by teachers and sometimes by other students. One example is attention deficit–hyperactivity disorder (ADHD) (Hohn, 1995). Students with ADHD often have difficulty concentrating and remaining seated and are sometimes aggressive. An understanding of the nature of a student's health problem allows both teacher and other classmates to accommodate the problem and thus enhance the disabled student's participation in school activities. Table 5.4 provides brief descriptions of additional health conditions that might be experienced by students in your future classrooms.

physical disability
Disorders of the skeleton, joints, and muscles, or health conditions that interfere with students' educational performances.

gifted and talented
Students who are able to meet academic challenges better than the majority of their peers in any number of areas.

Students Who Are Gifted and Talented

Gifted and talented students are able to meet academic challenges better than the majority of their peers in any number of areas. Renzulli (1982) distinguishes between "academic" giftedness and "creative" giftedness. Students who

TABLE 5.4 Additional Physical Conditions

Condition	Description
Asthma	Chronic respiratory condition characterized by repeated episodes of difficulty in breathing, especially exhalation
Cystic fibrosis	Inherited disease characterized by chronic respiratory and digestive problems, including thick, sticky mucus and glandular secretions
Diabetes	A hereditary or developmental problem of sugar metabolism caused by failure of the pancreas to produce enough insulin
Nephrosis and nephritis	Disorders or diseases of the kidneys due to infection, poisoning, burns, crushing injuries, or other diseases
Sickle-cell anemia	Severe, chronic hereditary blood disease in which red blood cells are distorted in shape and do not circulate properly
Hemophilia	A rare, sex-linked disorder in which the blood does not have a sufficient clotting component and excessive bleeding occurs
Rheumatic fever	Painful swelling and inflammation of the joints (typically following strep throat or scarlet fever) that can spread to the brain or heart
Tuberculosis	Infection by the tuberculosis bacterium of an organ system, such as lungs, larynx, bones and joints, skin, gastrointestinal tract, genitourinary tract, or heart
Cancer	Abnormal growth of cells that can affect any organ system

Source: Hallahan, D. P., & Kauffman, J. M. (1994). *Exceptional children: Introduction to special education* (6th ed.). Boston: Allyn & Bacon. Reprinted by permission.

are academically gifted are able to learn quickly and easily. They generally score well on tests of intelligence, aptitude, and achievement. Creatively gifted students tend to solve problems in new and effective ways. Interestingly, academically gifted students tend, as a group, not to be any more or less successful in later life than the general student population, whereas creatively gifted students are more likely to achieve later success.

There are underachieving gifted students. Schoolwork that does not challenge gifted students is considered a major reason for underachievement (Hallahan & Kauffman, 1994). Gifted underachievers often have negative attitudes toward school and toward themselves (Delisle, 1982; Ribich, Barone, & Agostino, 1991). One approach to working with underachieving gifted students involves observing carefully their performances and behaviors in various instructional situations, sharing those observations and hypothesized causes for underachievement with the students, and developing a partnership with the students (and their parents, if possible) aimed at solving the problem (Whitmore, 1986).

Historically, federal legislation has assumed that between 3 and 5 percent of students in schools are gifted and talented. For this reason, gifted and talented is usually considered among other low-incidence exceptionalities. There are, however, experts who believe that a much larger percentage of students—perhaps 15 to 25 percent—could benefit from programs for gifted and talented students (Hoge & Renzulli, 1993; Renzulli and Reis, 1991).

Reflection: Think back to your classmates in high school who did very well in school. Try to identify characteristics that would allow you to infer whether they would have been considered academically or creatively gifted.

Try This: Interview a principal or a director of special education services. Ask his or her opinion of the claim that 15 to 25 percent of students could benefit from programs for the gifted and talented.

WHAT PROVISIONS ARE MADE FOR THE EDUCATION OF STUDENTS AT RISK AND EXCEPTIONAL LEARNERS?

Exceptional learners and those whose life circumstances place them at risk are served through educational programs that augment the regular instruction in classrooms. These programs fall into three categories: compensatory education, early intervention, and special education. Compensatory education programs are designed to remediate the delayed development that occurs when students are denied opportunities because of difficult life circumstances. Early intervention programs are designed to prevent developmental delays and thus eliminate the need for later remediation. There are other types of intervention programs—such as drop-out prevention—that may not start until the elementary or middle grades, but most interventions are designed to be preventative and are, therefore, begun in early childhood. Special education programs serve students who have disabilities, either physical or psychological, that are relatively long term.

Compensatory Education

Compensatory education programs were started to counteract the presumed effects of poverty on school performance. It was assumed that children raised in poverty were often denied the kind of stimulation that fosters readiness to achieve in school. Research has since confirmed the assumption (Kennedy, Jung, & Orland, 1986). Compensatory education programs, such as Head Start and Follow Through, are designed to combat the effects of poverty and thus prepare students for success in school.

The largest compensatory education program came from Title I of the Elementary and Secondary Education Act of 1965. This legislation was part of President Lyndon Johnson's war on poverty. Title I programs became part of Chapter 1 of the Education Consolidation and Improvement Act of 1981. Now called Chapter 1, these compensatory programs operate in over 90 percent of the school districts in the United States (Birman, Oraland, Jung, Anson, Garcia, Moore, Funkhouser, Morrison, Turbull, & Reisner, 1987). Schools must use the money for no other purpose than to improve the academic achievement of poorly performing students from disadvantaged homes. Only those schools in very disadvantaged neighborhoods—those in which 75 percent or more of the students qualify for the free lunch program—may use Chapter 1 funds for general school improvement. One common approach taken by school districts or schools that provide Chapter 1 services is to hire a teacher whose primary responsibility is the Chapter 1 program.

Try This: Find a Chapter I teacher in a local school district. Ask if you can shadow him or her for a day. Keep a diary of the day to share with colleagues.

One of the models for delivering Chapter 1 programs is referred to as "pull-out programs." The pull-out model requires students to leave the regular classroom to receive special assistance. However, research on pull-out programs suggests that there may be better ways to meet the needs of disadvantaged students. One study compared disadvantaged students who remained in the regular classroom without Chapter 1 services with students who received the services through a pull-out program. The results indicated that students who remained in the regular classroom performed as well, and in some cases better, than those students in the pull-out program (Glass & Smith, 1977). Other research has found that pull-out programs

compensatory education Educational programs designed to combat the presumed effects of poverty on school performance.

ON SUCCESSFUL PRACTICE

What do you do to help both your low-ability and your high-ability students succeed academically?

One way that I accommodate learners of varying abilities is by using contemporary literature. The short fiction of writers such as Jamaica Kincaid, Donald Barthelme, Isabel Allende, and Gabriel García Márquez forces all readers to reexamine their preconceptions about text. These authors break with so many narrative traditions that every student, gifted and challenged, must struggle to understand the work. Fortunately, these writers are such extraordinary storytellers that the struggle is hardly painful.

In Kincaid's short story "Girl," for example, an Antiguan mother lectures her daughter on how to behave. In the two-page diatribe, the daughter only gets to pipe up twice to defend her behavior. Talking about the story, students immediately respond to the conflicting directions parents so often give them: Be independent, think for yourself, do as I say. They are reminded of how their own mothers beat them up with instructions for living. When I ask students to write a similar piece, modeling Kincaid's style but itemizing the warnings they've heard, they jump to the task.

One student wrote, "Serve from the right, clear from the left. Don't look for love. It will find you. This is how to balance a checkbook. Be a designated driver. Keep your head up, shoulders out. Don't slouch." Like Jamaica Kincaid's girl, theirs could only speak out twice. Like her, theirs were dismissed out of hand. "Don't give me those looks." The imitations helped students understand the literature they had read. They didn't need a lesson or quiz on tone; they felt what Kincaid had done with language in their bones.

Often less confident, less well-read readers are put off by the demands of traditional literature. When asked to navigate Herman Melville's waters, they flounder, and their failure becomes the more evident in comparison with well-prepared students. Reading contemporary texts, all students face the same challenges. No one, not even the teacher, has privileged information. The class unlocks the text's meaning and discovers its richness together.

CAROL JAGO, Santa Monica High School,
Santa Monica, California

---

suffer from lack of coordination between the regular classroom teacher and the Chapter 1 teacher. Johnston, Allington, and Afflerbach (1985) discovered that approximately half of the Chapter 1 teachers they studied were unable to name the reading textbook series being used by their students. Approximately two-thirds of the Chapter 1 teachers were unable to name the specific textbook being used. This lack of coordination can be especially devastating to students. Students who have already fallen behind in school are probably poorly equipped to handle the demands of learning from teachers who use very different approaches (Meyers, Gelzheiser, Yelich, & Gallagher, 1990). The implication is clear: If you have students who are receiving Chapter 1 assistance, it is imperative that you consult with the Chapter 1 teacher to coordinate your efforts.

Coordination and communication between teachers is critical. Recent studies indicate that delivering Chapter 1 services in class is now more common than the pull-out model. Although some schools combine pull-out programs with in-class strategies, there was a 50 percent increase in the number of districts using in-class

Why was this teacher's literature-based approach successful in reaching all students in her mixed-ability class? In the subject area you plan to teach, what analogous approaches might you use to give all your students an equal stake in their learning?

Reflection: Think back to your own teachers in elementary and high school. How much coordination did you perceive among your teachers? Why do you think there was or was not sufficient coordination? What could be done to improve coordination?

instruction for their Chapter 1 programs (Millsap, Turnbull, Moss, Brigham, Gamse, & Marks, 1992). Other trends in the delivery of Chapter 1 services include the use of school-wide learning projects, parental involvement, and changes in assessment techniques (Wong, 1994). These and other aspects of current practice in Chapter 1 programs are indicative of the evolution of such programs toward collaborative efforts of teachers and other educational professionals who serve disadvantaged students. Other types of programs for exceptional learners and for learners at risk, such as intervention and prevention programs, also call for collaboration.

Intervention and Prevention Programs

Compensatory education programs were motivated by an effort to remediate the difficulties that placed students at risk. More recently, there has been an increase in programs designed to prevent the need for remediation through early intervention (cf. Slavin, Karweit, & Wasik, 1994). Programs for infants and preschoolers that provide stimulation, parent training, and other services have shown long-term positive effects on school performance (Berrueta-Clement, Schweinhart, Barnett, Epstein, & Weikart, 1984; Wasik & Karweit, 1994). One such program, called "Success for All," provides reading instruction, individual tutoring, family support, and other services. The goal of the program is that students from disadvantaged homes will not fall behind in the early grades. This goal is pursued tenaciously. When problems arise, changes are made quickly to solve the problem and maintain student achievement. As a result, students who experienced Success for All compare favorably to control students in reading performance throughout the elementary years (Madden, Slavin, Karweit, Dolan, & Wasik, 1993).

Connection: The instructional effects of individualized instruction are examined in Chapter 12: Teaching for Active Learning.

Another program designed to prevent learning problems through early intervention is called "Reading Recovery" (Clay, 1993, 1994; DeFord, Lyons, & Pinnell, 1991). The program focuses on first graders who are most at risk of failure to read. Teachers who work in Reading Recovery programs are specially trained in the program's instructional model and in the nature of teacher–student interactions during instruction. Students receive one-on-one tutoring for thirty minutes each day from the specially trained teacher. Research has shown impressive results for the program. First graders at risk from approximately two hundred school districts in Ohio participated in Reading Recovery. Of those first graders, 83 percent attained the average reading level for their grade (cf. Huck & Pinnell, 1991; Pinnell, 1989). Reading Recovery is a national program in New Zealand and has been widely used in the United States, Canada, and Australia.

Reading Recovery and Success for All are examples of intensive intervention programs. The professionals who work in these programs understand that failure to intervene early and decisively increases the risk that a child will fail. These programs demonstrate that intensive intervention can give students at risk a good start and that a good start in school can prevent many students from becoming academically disabled.

Special Education and Inclusion

special education Specially designed instruction and services to meet the needs of exceptional learners.

"**Special education** means specially designed instruction that meets the unusual needs of an exceptional student" (Hallahan & Kauffman, 1994, p. 14). Designing instruction to meet the needs of exceptional learners may require special materials, special teaching techniques, or special equipment or facilities. The instructional needs of a student with a hearing impairment, for example, may require that the teacher use sign language or closed caption video. Exceptional students may require related services—that is, services that allow students to participate in specially designed instructional activities. A gifted student may require transportation to a local college to take an advanced course. A student with a physical disability may require physical or occupational therapy to participate in job training. A student with an emotional disability may require counseling to work cooperatively with classmates. These services—both instructional and related—are provided by professionals and staff members in a variety of settings.

Try This: Conduct a survey of faculty in a school, college, or Department of Education. Try to find out what the faculty views are of GEI and of full inclusion.

The relationship between general and special education has been the focus of much policy making. One proposal to merge the two types of education is called the General Education Initiative (GEI), initially called the Regular Education Initiative. Most proponents of the GEI argue that general education teachers should take primary responsibility for students with mild or moderate disabilities. Special educators would be available to assist general education teachers but would serve as consultants. A more radical version of the GEI calls for the elimination of special education as a separate and distinct system. This version would have one system of education in which all students are viewed as special, each having unique needs, strengths, and weaknesses (Hallahan & Kauffman, 1994). Although the GEI remains part of the debate on educational reform, the initiative has attracted some informed criticism (Goodlad & Lovitt, 1993).

Another proposal that will continue to be debated for the foreseeable future is called full inclusion. **Full inclusion** is the position that all students with disabilities, no matter how profound or severe, should be educated in the general education classroom. Those who advocate full inclusion argue that the least restrictive environment clause has been used to separate students with disabilities from general education classrooms and peers (see Laski, 1993). Advocates of full inclusion argue also that labeling is harmful and that people with disabilities should not be viewed as a minority group. Not all educators are proponents of full inclusion. Opponents of full inclusion often argue that the needs of many exceptional students cannot possibly be met in general education classrooms: Some students need the special attention or care that is more readily available in the resource room or other settings.

Although it is unlikely that either the GEI or full inclusion will become the model of preferred practice in the immediate future, these proposals will continue to attract debate and experimentation, and classrooms will become more inclusive. As educators continue the trend toward professional collaboration and inclusion, proposals such as the GEI will influence the way professional teams deliver instruction.

HOW WILL YOU USE YOUR KNOWLEDGE OF INDIVIDUAL VARIABILITY TO ENHANCE TEACHING AND LEARNING?

There is an old story that has passed, in one form or another, from teachers' lounge to teachers' lounge for years and years. It is the story of the new history teacher and the old history teacher. Meeting for the first time, the old teacher asks the new teacher, "What are you going to teach this year?"

full inclusion The inclusion of all students in the regular classroom.

Insights ON SUCCESSFUL PRACTICE

What advice can you give novice teachers about successfully including students with disabilities in their classrooms?

Including students with disabilities into the classroom is no different than successfully including all students into the classroom. After twenty-five years of teaching high school English, I think I am finally beginning to learn this lesson. From *Multiple Intelligences* by Howard Gardner, *Gifts Differing* by Isabel Briggs Myers, and *Please Understand Me* by David Keirsey and Marilyn Bates, I learned that there are many different ways humans learn and relate to one another. I learned that the highest dropout rate in our country occurs among students who are active, hands-on learners. The kid who can't sit still for a lecture on *Romeo and Juliet* blossoms when we act out a scene. The student who won't write a fifty-word essay on anything will work and rework almost everything if she can use the computer.

So new teachers need to forget about teaching the way they were taught. Most of us went into teaching because we were successful in the average American classroom. Memorizing, comprehending what we read, and working alone were techniques that worked for many of us. But for the average American student, and most certainly for the student with a disability, these techniques don't work. Many students learn their literacy skills from the TV, not the tradebook. To judge a student's ability on *how* they learn is to doom many of our students to assignments and assessments in which they will seldom shine.

I learned this lesson from Mark, a special education teacher who worked right alongside me in an English 9 classroom. I learned that students with behavior disorders such as attention deficit disorder (ADD) are not intentionally trying to disrupt the classroom. I learned that graphic organizers help learning disabilities students understand a novel better than study questions. And most important, I learned that teaching can be a very isolated profession. We walk into our classrooms alone and retire thirty years later without ever having seen a colleague in action. I can't think of another profession so cut off from itself.

So the most important advice I can give novice teachers about successfully including students with disabilities in their classrooms is to seek out advice from other teachers, to open your classroom door, to volunteer for collaboration. We have so much to learn from one another.

Working in collaboration with special education teachers has opened my eyes to all my students. Appreciating their different gifts and their ways of knowing is the key to reaching all students.

MAUREEN F. LOGAN, Westerly High School
Westerly, Rhode Island

What were the keys to this teachers success with mainstreaming? What roles did expanding her knowledge base and working collaboratively play? What guidelines for teaching in inclusive classrooms can you derive from this example?

The new teacher responds enthusiastically, "World history." The new teacher launches into a long and nauseatingly detailed description of the content topics, the key historical events, and the important documents that students will study. The old teacher listens politely and without interruption. Finally, with pride and the satisfaction of having demonstrated impressive knowledge, the new teacher says, "And what are you going to teach?"

The old teacher smiles and says, "Students."

The point the old teacher in the story was making is that teaching is not simply covering the content. Theoretically, it would be possible for a teacher to cover the content in a classroom without students. Teaching is inextricably tied to the learning that results. How can a teacher say that he or she has taught if no student has learned?

Accepting Individual Differences

Modeling acceptance in your own interactions with students who are at risk or disabled is an important instructional strategy. There are, however, other techniques that you can employ in your classroom. One of these techniques is simulation exercises in which nondisabled students are artificially—and temporarily—disabled. An example would be to blindfold sighted students so they can experience visual impairment. Such simulations allow disabled students to teach the nondisabled students how to handle the demands of a disability. Another example of how acceptance can be enhanced is to invite successful adults with disabilities to meet and talk with students. Such models illustrate to disabled and nondisabled students alike that a disability does not prevent people from achieving success (Salend, 1994). There are also materials—films and books, for example—that portray protagonists with disabilities. Class discussions of these materials can enhance the acceptance of individual differences related to disabilities. Teaching techniques that allow nondisabled students to benefit from the work of disabled students, such as cooperative learning, can also be employed to advantage. Cooperative learning, which requires students to depend on each other in order to be successful, is described in detail in Chapter 12: Teaching for Active Learning.

Connection: The effects of modeling are discussed in Chapter 8: Social Learning.

Creating an Inclusive Classroom

The mandate of least restrictive environment and the movement for inclusion means that students with disabilities will be placed in regular classrooms. Simply placing students with disabilities in regular classrooms, however, does not guarantee that those students will feel a part of that classroom group. An inclusive classroom is one in which students are socially integrated, not just physically present.

The feelings of students toward one another (especially students with disabilities) can be influenced considerably by the interaction patterns and attitudes displayed by the teacher (Simpson, 1980). Thus, if a teacher models a positive attitude toward students with disabilities, regular students are more likely to interact positively with their disabled peers.

An inclusive classroom makes those present feel like part of a community. The teacher plays a critical role in creating a feeling of community in a classroom and making all of the students feel as though they are members of that community. The processes in Lickona's model (see Chapter 3) are an excellent source of ideas for building a sense of community in the classroom.

Adapting Instruction

Knowledge of the characteristics of students is necessary for effective teaching but so is concern that students' needs are met by the instruction that is delivered (Oser, 1994). The descriptions of individual variability in this chapter (and in Chapters 2, 3, and 4) are a good start on acquiring the requisite knowledge. The requisite concern must come from an attitude that student learning is the most important measure of teaching. Knowledge of the ways in which students differ and concern that the needs of students be met are both necessary if a teacher is to adapt his or her instruction to the needs of students.

Adapting instructional practices to the needs of individual students is something that good teachers do. But how can adaptions be made? Here are some ideas suggested by Maniet-Bellermann (1986).

here's how

Here's How to Adapt Instruction to Meet Individual Needs

- Present material on tape for students who do not read successfully.
- Allow students to tape-record answers if writing is difficult or their handwriting is illegible.
- Provide lots of visual reminders (pictures, maps, charts, graphs) for students who have trouble listening or attending.
- Break directions and assignments into small steps. Completion of each step is an accomplishment. Reward it.
- Give tests orally if the child has trouble with reading, spelling, or writing. Testing that demonstrates what the student knows, rather than language skills, gives you a clearer picture of the student's abilities.
- Emphasize quality rather than quantity of writing.
- Carefully establish routines so that students with disabilities do not become further handicapped by the confusion of unclear expectations.
- Arrange desks, tables, and chairs so every person can be seen easily and every word heard easily. Remember, students with hearing deficits need to see your face as you speak.
- Provide carrels or screens—an "office"—for students who are easily distracted.

Adaptations should emphasize the abilities of students rather than their disabilities. Because instructional adaptation is something that good teachers do, we will revisit the notion in Chapter 12: Teaching for Active Learning.

Using Alternative Assessments

Assessment is part of instructional practice. The methods you select to assess learning performance can themselves be positive learning experiences for your students. If instructional adaptation is part of good teaching practice, it makes sense that adaptations of assessment activities are also good teaching practice.

Traditional paper-and-pencil tests may be difficult for some disabled students to take. Accommodations might include giving the test orally or without a time limit. Such adaptations make sense. If a student who has cerebral palsy is incapable of writing answers, then it makes sense to give the test in a way that will allow for a fair assessment of what he or she has learned. The point is to find ways to assess fairly what students have learned. But this is the point no matter who the student is, no matter what strengths or weaknesses he or she has, no matter what his or her cultural background.

Connection: The use of alternative assessment is expanding in schools. We look closely at assessment techniques in Chapter 13: Assessing Classroom Performance.

In an effort to enhance the quality of information gained from classroom assessments, new approaches are being proposed and tested. These new approaches are referred to as alternative assessment, authentic assessment, and portfolio assessment. These new approaches to assessment attempt to make the assessment of learning more relevant and more descriptive of the capabilities of learners. Such assessment is appropriate for all learners and is examined closely in Chapter 13: Assessing Student Performance.

The individual characteristics of your students will influence profoundly the teaching–learning process in your classroom. Knowing your students as individuals will allow you to understand and honor how each is different from you and from each other. Knowing their individual characteristics will allow you to include them in the community of your classroom; to adapt your instruction to their needs; and to assess their abilities, not their disabilities. Each student displays intelligent behavior. Each student is at risk at some time. Each student is exceptional in some way.

Teacher Chronicle Conclusion

MY NAME IS ROBO

At the end of September, Heath's mother requested a special conference with Mrs. Bernstein to review Heath's progress.

On the positive side, he had already learned to read and now read at a second-grade level. He had created a comic strip, shared it with the class, and helped another student create her own. Every time an animal was mentioned in storytime he made that animal sound (something Mrs. Bernstein enjoyed and encouraged). He displayed a high degree of accuracy in his science drawings, frequently turning to reference books (and using the index) for more knowledge. In large group discussions he shared his knowledge on every topic from robots to the Latin names of jellyfish. His art-work was exceptionally creative and detailed.

On the negative side, he rarely followed the exact directions given by Mrs. Bernstein, as he always added his own wrinkle to his work. He never played with other children at recess. Instead, he just swung by himself, back and forth, for fifteen minutes and was frequently late coming in, as he ignored the bell. On impulse, he had hit three students one day with blocks. Each time he was placed in a cooperative group, it ended in his throwing a tantrum or the other children complaining about him. His impulsive behaviors of wandering around or focusing on something else interfered with his math instruction, and he rarely finished an assignment. He had no real friends with whom he played.

Mrs. Bernstein told Dr. Kotre that the teacher of emotionally disturbed children had made several observations of Heath and would be providing her with a report. She suggested they meet with the special needs teacher when the report came.

Dr. Kotre shook her head and thanked Mrs. Bernstein for her patience and understanding.

"Somehow I had hoped that this year would be better than kindergarten for Heath. Maybe I'm in over my head."

"I think we all are," Mrs. Bernstein said, "but we'll find the best way to keep Heath learning and to help him develop his social skills."

APPLICATION QUESTIONS

1. How would you characterize Heath's intelligence in My Name Is Robo? Which view of intelligence provides the best description of

Heath? Why? From what you have learned about student diversity, add to the list of Heath's strengths and weaknesses.

2. What aspects of Heath's situation place him at risk of failing in school? What steps, other than those indicated, should be taken by Mrs. Bernstein?
3. What strategies could Mrs. Bernstein use to encourage Heath to participate more fully in group activities?
4. How could you model acceptance of Heath in your classroom? What steps would you take to encourage Heath's classmates to accept him?
5. Could Mrs. Bernstein make any instructional adaptations that would help Heath be more successful? How would you build on Heath's strengths to encourage growth in his areas of weakness?
6. How might other professionals help Mrs. Bernstein and Dr. Kotre meet Heath's needs?

CHAPTER SUMMARY

HOW DO STUDENTS VARY IN INTELLIGENCE?

What is considered intelligent behavior depends on the view of intelligence being considered. Piaget's view assumes that intelligence changes as students develop cognitively. Wechsler assumes that intelligence is a global capacity. Newer views of intelligence, such as Gardner's theory of multiple intelligences and Sternberg's triarchic theory, expand the notion of intelligence beyond what is measured on traditional IQ tests to a consideration of talents and abilities to behave adaptively in one's environment.

HOW DO STUDENTS VARY IN THE WAYS THEY THINK AND LEARN?

Students are disposed to think in different ways. Research on thinking dispositions indicates that there are some bottom-line dispositions that contribute to learning. Variability in thinking has also been documented in research on learning styles. A dispositional approach to thinking establishes standards against which students can be compared. Categorizing students according to learning styles or identifying the predominant learning style of a group is seen as dangerous teaching practice.

HOW DO STUDENTS VARY IN ABILITIES AND DISABILITIES?

Students are sometimes placed at risk of failing in school. The factors that place students at risk often arise from conditions over which the student and the teacher have no control—for instance, the student's home environment. The factors that place students at risk may be temporary or permanent. Exceptional students require special help to learn effectively. Cultural minorities are disproportionately represented in exceptional populations. Emotional and behavioral disorders and learning disabilities account for the largest number of exceptional students. Other, low-incidence disabilities include students with mental retardation and students with communication disorders, sensory disorders (such as hearing and visual impairments), physical disabilities, and health-related impairments, such as AIDS.

WHAT PROVISIONS ARE MADE FOR THE EDUCATION OF STUDENTS AT RISK AND EXCEPTIONAL LEARNERS?

Students with special needs—because they are at risk or because they are exceptional—are served by a variety of educational programs. Compensatory education seeks to compensate for the effects of poverty. Intervention and prevention programs are designed to monitor at-risk students closely and provide special instructional interventions to ensure student success. Special education and inclusion programs provide the accommodations that exceptional learners need to succeed.

HOW WILL YOU USE YOUR KNOWLEDGE OF INDIVIDUAL VARIABILITY TO ENHANCE TEACHING AND LEARNING?

Knowledge of students as individuals is key to teaching. Recognizing that students are individuals with individual needs is the first step in accepting students and helping them to accept each other into the community of the classroom. Creating a classroom that includes all students regardless of ability or disability requires accommodating needs. Various ways of adapting instruction and assessment are discussed.

KEY CONCEPTS

communication disorder
compensatory education
componential intelligence
construct
contextual intelligence
disability
emotional/behavioral disorder
exceptional learners
experiential intelligence
full inclusion
gifted and talented
handicap
intelligence
learning disability
mental retardation
physical disability
sensory disorder
special education
theory of multiple intelligences
thinking dispositions

PART III

Behaviorism emphasizes the role that the environment plays in determining behavior. The environment provides stimuli that elicit responses; it also provides consequences to those responses. Throughout the chapter are possible applications of behavioral theory that you can use in your classroom.

Learning is shaped by the learner's environment

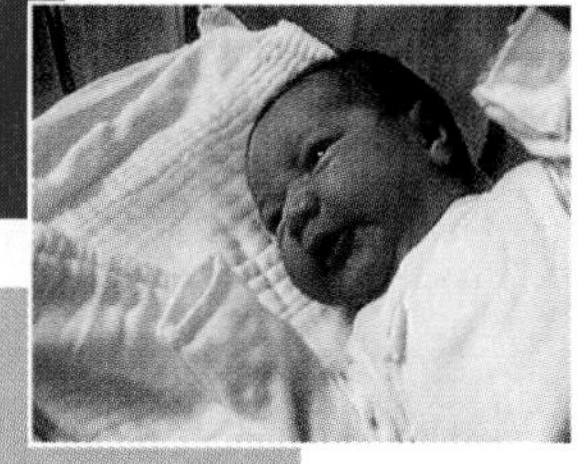

People learn through direct experience, responses to environmental stimuli, and the consequences of their actions. Through this kind of learning, individuals change their behavior, for example, by continuing or increasing behavior that is reinforced or rewarded. Principles of behavior learning support the teaching–learning process.

Learning is a function of complex mental activities

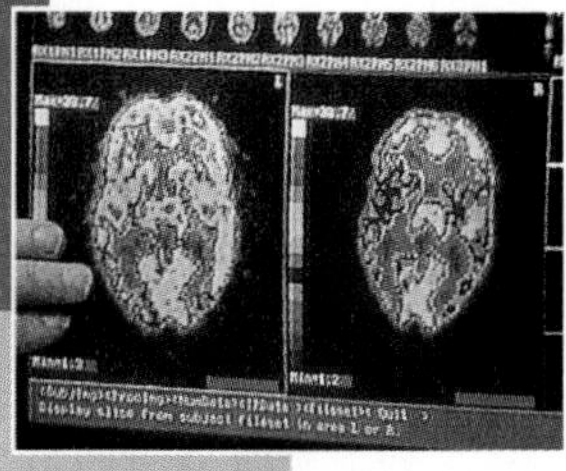

People learn through the mental structures and processes that are involved in cognition and memory. Many factors influence how individuals receive and process information, remember what they learn, and solve problems. These factors and metacognitive awareness—knowledge of one's own thought processes—are important enabling tools for both teachers and learners.

Overview of Chapter 6

Chapters 2 through 5 described aspects of student development and diversity. Our examination of students as learners continues in Chapters 6 through 8, focusing on how students learn, what they remember, and how they apply what they know. Environment and Behavior presents a behavioral approach to the subject of how students learn.

TEACHER Chronicle

OUT OF CONTROL

Becky Hoffman sits at her desk at the end of the worst day of her two-year teaching career. Her second-grade class is out of control and she knows it.

She is feeling manipulated by several students, most notably Leah. She is discouraged and wondering if teaching is really for her. As she reflects, she thinks about Sarah O'Dell's class next door where there is always a buzz of activity and excitement; the kids are talking quietly with each other, they're interacting with Ms. O'Dell individually and in groups, they're doing independent projects. When the time comes to shift to another activity, some kids put away the materials being used, while others are helping Ms. O'Dell get new materials out, all without apparent direction from the teacher. The kids never seem out of control. She makes it appear so easy, Becky thinks. But how? she wonders. What is *she* doing that *I* can't do? Why do her students seem so on task when mine are like a bunch of wild chimpanzees? Sarah has been so approachable . . . maybe she should ask her for some advice.

That evening Becky calls Sarah to discuss her situation. "Just when I have them settled and on task, Leah blurts out something. Then Jeremy joins in and pretty soon they're in charge. When it comes time to start another activity, I wind up doing all the cleanup. No matter what directions I give, I find myself running from one side of the room to the other—taking one thing away from Leah, telling Jeremy to get back in his area, trying to make sure that every table has the materials they need to get started."

"What have you tried to get them organized and on task?" Sarah asks.

"First I offered them extra free time if everyone finished their work. But then some finished early, got their free time, and the others wanted it and. . . ." Becky hesitates. "Then I tried punishing Leah every time she broke one of the rules. None of the punishments seem to matter to her anyway—losing recess, staying after school, seeing the principal."

"Have you given her time-out?"

"Yes, but she does so many distracting things that the others can't focus. I'm at the end of my rope."

"I tell you what. Tomorrow, I'll go to Mrs. Lucka and arrange for you to come observe me for a morning. You'll see more than I can possibly tell you about. And Becky, don't worry. I was in the same situation early in my career."

"Not you!" Becky exclaimed.

Sarah laughed. "Oh yes, and I was having so many problems I was almost fired."

"And last year you were District Teacher of the Year?"

"I had some mentors to help me along, and so now I want to continue the tradition. Then someday, you'll be Teacher of the Year."

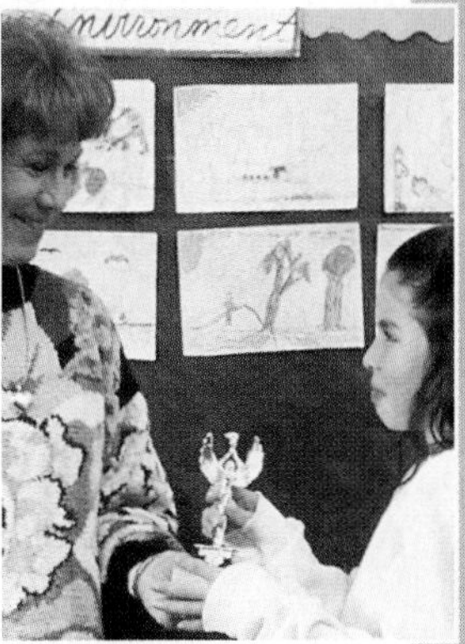

FOCUS QUESTIONS

1. How might a behavioral scientist approach Becky's problem?
2. What role does the classroom environment play in learning?
3. How are behaviors reinforced?

4. How can student behaviors be changed?
5. How is behavior learned?
6. What is a possible reason for the persistence of Leah's off-task behavior?
7. What principles should guide decisions about student behaviors?
8. Will your students perceive reinforcement or punishment the same way you do?

WHAT IS BEHAVIORAL SCIENCE?

When your first group of students walks into your classroom on your first day as a certified teacher, they will respond to you and to the classroom you have prepared for them. When you present a lesson, administer a test, lead a discussion, monitor study hall, ask and answer questions, review a test, organize a lunch line, or referee a scuffle in the hall, students will respond to you. How will they respond? Will they do what you ask of them? Will they ignore you? Will they defy you? Becky Hoffman's students in the Teacher Chronicle go off task when Leah and Jeremy interrupt a class activity, and they ignore her directions to put away materials when it is time to begin a new activity. What are her students responding to? Let's examine the principles of behavioral analysis as they apply to human learning, and see what answers they provide to these questions.

The **behavioral approach** to learning represents a school of thought in which learning is explained through observable aspects of the environment. Imagine, for example, that a student answers discussion questions at the end of a textbook chapter by taking notes on chapter content. On the chapter test, the end-of-chapter questions appear in a modified form as essay items. The student earns the highest possible score on the essays and, for all remaining reading assignments, takes notes based on the chapter discussion questions. What did this student learn?

A behavioral scientist would approach this question by first observing the student's behavior—taking notes from textbook chapters—and analyzing what happened to the behavior—it increased. The apparent reason for the increase in note-taking behavior is also an observable event. That is, the consequence of taking notes was a high score on the essay items. By linking the behavior with its consequence, the behavioral scientist infers that the student learned to take notes from textbook chapters. Although cognitive or mental processes may accompany the student's change in behavior, they are not thought to be important in understanding learning (cf. Skinner, 1987a, 1989). Thus, it doesn't matter what the student thinks about note-taking from textbook chapters as long as the behavior continues to result in high test scores. If that contingency holds, the note-taking behavior is likely to be maintained.

Critical Thinking: Give an example of the distinction between observable behavior and inferences based on observation.

behavioral approach A school of thought in which learning is explained through observable aspects of the environment instead of mental or cognitive processes.

reinforcement The process by which the consequences of behavior establish and maintain it.

The behavioral approach to learning offers strategies for classroom management and student learning and suggests ways to prevent and resolve discipline problems. (Incidentally, classroom management, as you will see in Chapter 10, is much more than student discipline. It involves managing the classroom environment and learning activities of students as well.) Behaviorism defines, for educators, the concept of reinforcement. **Reinforcement** refers to consequences of responses that establish and maintain desirable behavior. The high score on the essays served as reinforcement of the note-taking response.

The term *behavior*, when used in everyday conversation, comprises an immense body of activities. From a behavioral scientist's point of view, however, the term includes only observable behaviors. What students *think* is of relatively little concern to behaviorists; what they *do* is the focus of importance. In linking environmental events to behavior, the behavioral scientist also seeks to understand the cues prompting learners to act and the consequences determining whether learners will continue to act in the same way. These environmental cues and consequences govern whether a particular behavior is appropriate or inappropriate in a particular situation.

The appropriateness of behaviors is judged within the context of the environment in which they are displayed. In schools, teachers establish the environmental conditions that, in effect, control student behavior in their classrooms. Students learn to respond appropriately to teachers' cues so that they know, for example, when tossing an eraser at the teacher will earn them a smile and a chuckle or a scowl and detention.

Environmental events can come to control the behavior of those who find themselves in that environment. Important questions for any teacher to ask, and especially a novice teacher, are: How do I increase and maintain desirable student behavior and decrease undesirable behavior? How do I teach students self-management skills so that they control their *own* behavior? Principles of behavioral psychology help provide answers to these questions.

Principles of Classical Conditioning

Ivan Pavlov, who won a Nobel prize in 1904, conducted conditioning experiments that became classics in the history of psychology. Pavlov studied how a dog's salivation reflex might be conditioned—that is, brought under control of the environment. Pavlov's procedure began by simply presenting food to the dog. The dog salivated. The food is an unconditioned stimulus, a stimulus that automatically elicits a response. Salivation is an unconditioned response, an automatic reflex. Reflexes do not need to be learned or conditioned; they occur automatically in the presence of particular stimuli. People flinch when they see they are about to be hit. They blink when a puff of air hits an eye during a glaucoma test. They draw back in haste upon touching a hot surface, such as a burner on the stove.

In the case of Pavlov's experiments, the trick was not to get the dog to exhibit a reflex (salivating in the presence of food) but to get the dog to salivate predictably before food was presented. Pavlov conditioned the dog to salivate to a particular sound, a stimulus that does not normally elicit salivation. The sound, or tone, is the conditioned stimulus, a stimulus that is paired with an unconditioned stimulus. The tone preceded slightly the presentation of food. After several pairings of the conditioned stimulus (tone) with the unconditioned stimulus (food), the tone elicited salivation. Salivation elicited by the previously neutral tone is a conditioned response, a response to a conditioned stimulus. Figure 6.1 illustrates how Pavlov's **classical conditioning** works.

classical conditioning The process of bringing reflexes under control of the environment. Also known as Pavlovian and respondent conditioning.

operant behavior According to Skinner, behavior that is not a simple reflex to a stimulus but an action that operates on the environment.

Principles of Operant Conditioning

B. F. Skinner, after carefully analyzing Pavlov's work, became interested in behaviors that were not simply elicited reflexes but that operated on the environment to produce consequences (Skinner, 1938). Skinner called behavior that operates on the environment **operant behavior**. He believed that organisms are inherently

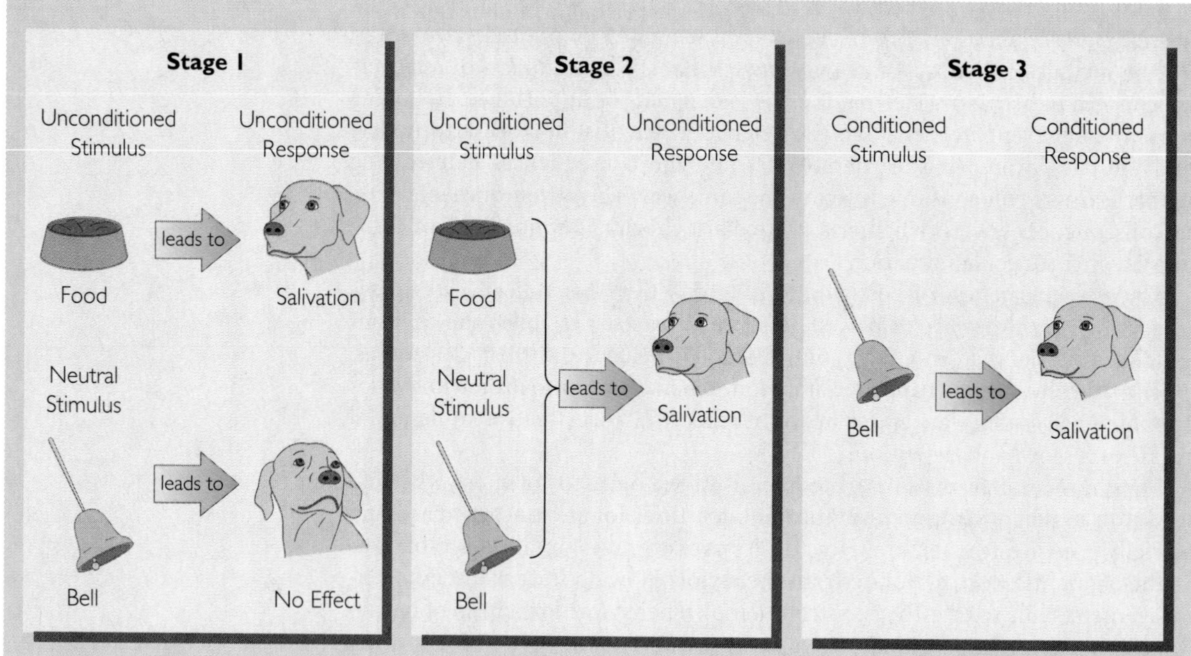

FIGURE 6.1

The Three Stages of Classical Conditioning

active in their environments, so that most behavior is of this type. Birds, for example, peck at things, perhaps looking for food or gathering twigs with which to build a nest. When Skinner put pigeons into an enclosed compartment with a recessed light (known as a key) and food hopper, they pecked randomly at the walls, the key, and the edge of the food hopper. When he systematically presented food after certain pecks—at the key, for example—these pecks became conditioned. Thus, the operant behavior of pecking the key resulted in the consequence of getting food. Because getting food was a desirable consequence for the pigeon, it pecked at the key more often. Through **operant conditioning**—learning through responses and consequences—the pigeon learned how to obtain food in the Skinner box.

Point: *Learning is shaped by the learner's environment.* The pigeon pecks in the Skinner box, randomly at first. When pecking the key results in food, this behavior is conditioned.

Through responses and consequences, students can learn how and when to raise their hands during a classroom discussion, how to write in a cursive style, how to operate the class computer, and other behaviors that support learning. Because operant behavior is the type most often encountered in classrooms, our examination of behavior and environment concentrates on operant conditioning.

HOW DOES REINFORCEMENT INFLUENCE BEHAVIOR?

operant conditioning According to Skinner, learning through responses and their consequences.

To understand why some operant behaviors are learned and others are not, Skinner (1953) argued that behavior should be studied in terms of its antecedents and its consequences. Antecedents refer to environmental events that come before a behavior and provide the context for it to occur. They are the cues that signal the availability of reinforcement for a given behavior. Consequences are what result from a behavior and, according to Skinner, determine whether the behavior ever occurs again. If a pigeon did not receive food for pecking at the key in the Skinner box, for example, it would peck at the key no more often than it pecked anywhere else in the box. When pecking at the key does result in food, then the pigeon pecks at the key much more often than it pecks anywhere else.

The concept of reinforcement is critical to Skinner's operant conditioning, and it was first expressed by E. L. Thorndike (1913) as the **law of effect**. According to Thorndike, when a response is made that results in a "satisfying state of affairs," the response becomes more likely to occur again. Conversely, when a response is made that results in an "annoying state of affairs," the response becomes less likely to recur. Two important relations between a behavior and its consequence are expressed in Thorndike's law. First, the consequence is *contingent upon* the response, which means that it occurs only when the response occurs. Second, the nature of the consequence, whether satisfying or aversive to the learner, determines its effect on the behavior. Satisfying consequences lead to a strengthening of behavior, whereas aversive consequences lead to a weakening of behavior.

The **contingencies of reinforcement**, or what Skinner (1969) called the learning principles based on the law of effect, can be identified in any learning episode by analyzing the episode for the three components of antecedent, response, and consequence. In Becky's class in the Teacher Chronicle, for example, the shift to a new activity appears to signal students to go off task; the consequence of this behavior is individual attention from the teacher, which acts as a reinforcer. This kind of analysis can be useful in helping teachers to identify problem behaviors and opportunities for new behaviors in their classes and to develop strategies for increasing desirable behaviors and decreasing undesirable behaviors.

Try This: Observe a student in a class. Record, in strictly behavioral terms, his or her behavior and the antecedent and consequent events. What can you infer about learning?

Antecedents of Behavior

Once the pigeon has learned that pecking a key results in food, the behavior of pecking can be brought under further control of the environment by making food available only when the pigeon pecks at a *lighted* key. The lighted key becomes a signal for when pecking will result in food. In a sense, the lighted key has acquired the ability to control the pigeon's behavior. It serves as a **discriminative stimulus**, which cues the learner that a particular behavior will be reinforced when it is present.

Suppose a teacher begins a discussion in a science class by walking around her desk and sitting on the edge nearest the students. She smiles and says, "Okay, let's see if we can figure out the concept of aerodynamics together." She then asks a question about the material. A student raises his hand, is called on, and answers the question. The teacher praises the student's response. The teacher's pattern of positive reactions is consistent for all students who respond, even when an answer is not what it should be. For instance, a teacher might ask the class how an airplane is able to fly. If a student responds, "By going real fast," the teacher may reinforce the attempt by saying, "Speed is a very important part of the answer. Your answer shows me that you are thinking. Keep it up, Sharon. Now, Sharon has identified speed as an important reason airplanes can fly. What are some of the other reasons?"

law of effect Thorndike's law of learning, which states that any action producing a satisfying consequence will be repeated in a similar situation. An action followed by an unfavorable consequence is unlikely to be repeated.

contingencies of reinforcement According to Skinner, learning principles based on the law of effect, the relationship between antecedent, response, and consequence.

discriminative stimulus A stimulus that is present consistently when a response is reinforced and comes to act as a cue or signal for the response.

By raising their hands, these students are exhibiting operant behavior. What discriminative stimulus are they responding to? What consequence will reinforce their behavior? How will their responses act as a contingent stimulus for the teacher's behavior?

The teacher's question, her smile, and her position on the desk are all aspects of the stimulus situation present during reinforcement of student responses. Asking the question, smiling, and being seated on the desk are potential signals, or discriminative stimuli, to participate in the discussion. Students may participate in future discussions even when the teacher is not seated on the desk, but the probability of "participation behavior" is enhanced by the presence of the additional discriminative stimuli.

Now, further suppose that the same teacher is in the habit of pacing quickly up and down the rows while asking drill-and-practice questions in a rapid-fire manner. The questions during drill and practice are factual questions. Quick recall is sought, but student responses are not praised or elaborated in the way they are during discussions. The teacher's smile is gone.

If reinforcement is delivered when the teacher is seated and smiling but not while she is pacing and stone-faced, the nature of the class participation will be different. Students will learn to discriminate between questions asked while she is seated and smiling and questions asked while she paces. The students may volunteer less frequently during drill and practice, causing the teacher to call on students who have not raised their hands. (This may be precisely what the teacher wants to have happen.)

Reflection: Recall *signals* used by your teachers. What effect did they have on your behavior and that of classmates?

Teachers are largely responsible for the environment in which students respond; they are a source of discriminative stimuli. If discriminative stimuli are *signals*, remember that students of all ages are enthusiastic readers of the signals that teachers give. You may even be sending signals of which you are unaware. An entire junior high health class once decided that quizzes always came the day after the teacher wore a particular blue dress. (Lest you doubt the ability of students to identify discriminative stimuli, think back to your days in junior and high school and the time you spent analyzing, critiquing, and in many cases, making fun of the dress, mannerisms, and behavior of some of your teachers.)

Example: A teacher might use a secret code as a discriminative stimulus, such as pulling the left ear as a signal for a student to stop an undesired behavior.

Let's now turn to Becky Hoffman's predicament in the Teacher Chronicle. What signals, or discriminative stimuli, might she be emitting inadvertently that trigger disruptive behavior? Despite her desire to have students put away their own materials at the conclusion of a class activity, perhaps her running around the room, taking materials away from some students and giving new materials to other students, tells them that she will do everything if they wait long enough.

Kinds of Reinforcers

Discriminative stimuli can exist as antecedents to behavior only when a consequence of the learner's response also exists. In the Skinnerian model of learning, the consequence of a response alters its probability of recurrence. The most common consequence is one that is satisfying, or *reinforcing*, to the learner and results in increasing the likelihood that the learner will repeat the response. However, consequences of behavior can also be aversive to the learner, with the result that the response becomes less likely to recur. For example, the student whose answers in class discussion are always met with a frown from the teacher is likely to participate less over time.

The use of reinforcement as a consequence of behavior is perhaps the most important management skill a teacher can possess. Understanding the effects of reinforcement entails recognition of the different types of responses that can serve as reinforcers.

Primary Reinforcers. A **primary reinforcer** is basic to biological functioning. Food, water, shelter, physical comfort, and affection are reinforcers that contribute to human functioning. Primary reinforcers can be used effectively in instructional settings (cf. Rachlin, 1991). Teachers find that some autistic children, for example, learn to make eye contact or to speak when rewarded for their behavior with small bits of food. Middle school students also cite gum and soda as favorite rewards for which they will behave appropriately in class. However, reinforcements used in classrooms usually involve conditioned reinforcers.

Conditioned and Generalized Reinforcers. A **conditioned reinforcer** is a neutral object, gesture, or event that acquires the power to reinforce behavior as a result of being paired with one or more primary reinforcers. Perhaps the most common conditioned reinforcer for humans is money. Pieces of paper, authorized as legal tender, have become associated with many of the necessities of existence. The potency of money as a reinforcer is extraordinary. Consider all of the behaviors people engage in to receive it in sufficient quantities. Money is sometimes used to reward students' academic progress, a practice that has met with criticism because progress tends to halt when the money stops (Kohn, 1993). However, Chance (1993) points out that, in many cases, no progress was made prior to the use of money as a reinforcer. He says, "If students show little or no interest in an activity, it is silly to refuse to provide rewards for fear of undermining their interest in the activity" (p. 789).

Some kinds of conditioned reinforcers are social in nature. A gesture of affection, a word of praise, a hand placed on a shoulder, a handshake, a physical threat, or a verbal reprimand are examples. Can you recall from your own childhood a teacher or other adult who could comfort you with a smile, or one whose look ignited terror? What is a reinforcing stimulus? This question is crucial for teachers; it is one that each teacher must answer for her- or himself. Furthermore, it is a question that each teacher must answer for each student; not every student is motivated by a good grade or a kind word. Becky, in the Teacher Chronicle, has not yet discovered effective reinforcers to motivate Leah. Perhaps this is because Becky has concentrated on punishing Leah's inappropriate behavior rather than looking for ways to reinforce her on-task and appropriate behaviors. We see later in the chapter that behavioral procedures are preferable that involve motivating students toward the achievement of positive goals, rather than away from aversive circumstances.

Reflection: What kinds of reinforcing stimuli do you prefer to use in the classroom? What means of communicating these stimuli are most comfortable for you as a teacher?

Critical Thinking: Why should a teacher attend to discriminative stimuli when testing possible reinforcers?

primary reinforcer Something that satisfies a basic biological need, such as food, water, or shelter.

conditioned reinforcer A neutral object or event that acquires the power to reinforce behavior as a result of being paired with one or more primary reinforcers, for example, money.

Self-Reinforcement. Skinner (1987b) proposed the simple idea that many reinforcers offer learners the opportunity to manipulate the environment successfully. What is the attraction of video games? Why do people bowl or play billiards? Why do people enjoy hobbies such as painting or gardening? Why do people engage in behaviors "just for the fun of it?" (Nye, 1979, p. 38). Perhaps because these activities allow them to manipulate and control a portion of their environments without having to rely on other people or other aspects of the external environment, people are using self-reinforcement.

Self-reinforcement is an important concept for teachers. When students learn to reinforce their own behavior, they begin to exert control over themselves and their immediate environments. Becky observed that Ms. O'Dell's students appeared to pick up and put away instructional materials without the teacher's apparent direction (or reinforcement) of this behavior. Students learn to self-reinforce when they understand the contingency between their behavior and its consequences and when they value or desire the consequences. Ms. O'Dell's students, for instance, may have learned the contingency between putting materials away and having an uncluttered work space. Alternatively, they may have learned that putting materials away leads to easy access of these materials in the future. If students value either an uncluttered work space or easy access, then putting materials away is a behavior they can use by themselves to add something desirable to their environment.

Principles of Reinforcement

When the consequences of behavior are examined for the potential effect they have on the behavior itself, specific principles of reinforcement result. These principles are shown in Figure 6.2.

The nature of the reinforcer refers to whether the consequence of behavior is satisfying or aversive. What makes a reinforcer satisfying or aversive is a crucial point for teachers who seek to influence students' behavior. A satisfying consequence is something the learner wants and will work to obtain. An **aversive** consequence is something the learner does not want and will try to avoid. In Figure 6.2, behavioral contingency refers to the relationship between a response and its consequence. A student behavior might lead the teacher to present a reinforcer or to terminate or remove a reinforcer.

Try This: Observe behavior during a lesson and identify all the contingencies of reinforcement.

Example: Correctly identifying the value of a consequence can be tricky. One teacher kept putting a disruptive student out in the hall, assuming that he would prefer to participate in class and would be persuaded to control his behavior. However, the student loved going into the hall, seeing the activity near the office, and talking with everyone who passed by. What might the teacher do to correct the situation?

aversive Undesirable.

Depending on the behavioral contingency and the nature of the reinforcer, then, there are four general principles that increase or decrease behavior. Positive reinforcement and negative reinforcement both serve to increase behaviors, and reinforcement removal and punishment both serve to decrease behaviors. Positive reinforcement occurs when a satisfying consequence is presented and results in strengthening the response. For example, a teacher rewards a student's participation in class discussions, which increases the student's participation. Negative reinforcement also strengthens behavior, but it does so through the removal of an aversive consequence. This means that something undesirable to the learner is removed to increase the desired behavior. Teachers who give weekly quizzes, for example, might exempt students who achieve a certain score on graded homework. The impetus to complete the homework is strengthened because it enables students to avoid the aversive consequence of weekly quizzes.

To weaken a response, punishment can be used to present an aversive consequence to the learner, such as assigning students to detention for fighting in

		Nature of Reinforcer	
		Satisfying	Aversive
Behavioral Contingency	Stimulus Presented Contingent on Response	**Positive Reinforcement** *Example*: Student turns in neater assignments when teacher praises neatness (Behavior Strengthened)	**Punishment** *Example*: Student is sent to detention for fighting (Behavior Weakened)
	Stimulus Removed Contingent on Response	**Negative Reinforcement** *Example*: Student is exempted from weekly quiz for exemplary homework (Behavior Strengthened)	**Reinforcement Removal** *Example*: Students lose earned free time for playing with lab equipment (Behavior Weakened)

FIGURE 6.2

Basic Principles of Reinforcement

Source: Adapted from *Psychology of Learning for Instruction,* by M. P. Driscoll, 1994, Needham Heights, MA: Allyn & Bacon. Copyright 1994.

school. Reinforcement removal also weakens undesirable behaviors, because it involves taking away reinforcers from students who behave inappropriately. For example, a student who has earned free time on the class computer may lose some of that time for interfering with other students' learning.

HOW CAN YOU DEVELOP STRATEGIES FOR CHANGING STUDENT BEHAVIOR?

In any classroom, students behave in ways that either support their own and others' learning or that get in the way of learning. Through behavioral analysis and the principles of reinforcement, you can strengthen desirable behaviors and weaken or eliminate undesirable behaviors.

Strengthening Desirable Behaviors

There are many behaviors that teachers wish their students would display more often in class. These might include, for example, turning in assigned homework, participating in class discussions, paying attention, putting away materials at the end of an activity, writing neatly, and behaving courteously toward other students. Students might already know how to do these things, but they just don't do them often enough or at the appropriate times. To strengthen desirable behaviors,

positive reinforcement The presentation of a satisfying stimulus, contingent on a response that results in strengthening the response.

teachers use positive reinforcement, the Premack principle (a special case of positive reinforcement that we will discuss shortly), and negative reinforcement.

Positive Reinforcement. **Positive reinforcement** occurs when a satisfying consequence is presented contingent upon some behavior, which results in strengthening that behavior. How can you use positive reinforcement?

here's how

Here's How to Use Positive Reinforcement

- Identify a possible reinforcer for the student whose behavior you wish to reinforce.
- Present it to the student each time the student exhibits the desired behavior.

Point: *Teachers and students are both learners.* To use positive reinforcement effectively, teachers must observe their students and learn what reinforcers are desirable to them.

A teacher who wants students to participate more in class may smile and nod each time a student offers a comment. Becky, in the Teacher Chronicle, was attempting to use positive reinforcement when she offered extra free time as a reinforcer for getting work done.

Critical Thinking: How do you know if a consequence is positive reinforcement?

Connection: How does the information on psychosocial development in Chapter 3 relate to this discussion on effective reinforcement?

Try This: In a class you observe, look for examples of procedures based on behavioral principles. How do teachers strengthen or weaken behaviors? Which procedures do they use most often and with what effect?

Premack Principle. David Premack (1959, 1965) reviewed the conditions under which positive reinforcement influences behavior. His analysis yielded what is known as the **Premack principle**: A high-probability behavior can be used to reinforce a low-probability behavior.

What is a high-probability behavior? If as a student you were given the choice between working on the computer or doing seat work, which activity would you choose? The activity you choose is your high-probability behavior. The Premack principle is like "Grandma's rule," the contingency millions of grandmothers have used to get kids to eat vegetables: "Eat your green beans and then you can have some ice cream." Given a choice, most kids would choose to eat ice cream rather than green beans. The high-probability behavior—eating ice cream—is promised to increase the incidence of the low-probability behavior—eating green beans.

Perhaps you have observed a classroom in which the teacher says something like, "Okay, we are going to have ten minutes of free time now so that we will be ready to concentrate on those verb conjugations during language arts." Assuming that using free time is a high-probability behavior, such an attempt misses the point of the Premack principle, because the free time is not used to reinforce verb conjugation. A better way for the teacher to proceed would be to say, "If we all work together on our verb conjugations in language arts, we can take ten minutes at the end of the period for free time."

Premack principle A special case of positive reinforcement in which a high-probability behavior is used to reinforce a low-probability behavior.

negative reinforcement An aversive stimulus is removed or terminated following a desirable response in order to strengthen that response.

Using the Premack principle increases a teacher's chance of selecting effective reinforcers. How do you select a reinforcer that will be effective for a particular student? Why not ask? Just as restaurants give their customers menus from which to choose, teachers can use a reinforcement menu to determine what students would like to receive as a consequence of their behaviors. What might happen, for example, if Becky asked Leah what should be the consequences of her (mis)behavior? Once you have identified high-probability behaviors, you can use those behaviors to reinforce other behaviors you desire for your students.

Insights ON SUCCESSFUL PRACTICE

What kinds of reinforcements have you used successfully to help your students improve their academic performance?

More than ten years ago, in response to an apathetic student's complaint, "English doesn't have anything to do with the real world," I devised a classroom management approach that does, in fact, emulate the philosophy and management style of successful businesses. I set up my classes to be run the way a large corporation is, complete with a board of directors (parents and school board members), personnel policy, salary schedule, job descriptions, incentives, and bonus trips for top producers.

In an effort to encourage adult, responsible behavior in a typical junior high, every academic grade was translated into economic terms. Instead of giving 25 points for a vocabulary quiz, I paid up to "$25." Rather than getting 100 points for an essay or test, a student could earn as much as "$100." Outstanding class participation, asking a good question, or exhibiting exemplary behavior could earn additional income. However, tardiness, disruptive behavior, sloppy work, or general "goldbricking" would result in a dock in pay.

Students were grouped into heterogenous "departments" of five or six "employees" and a supervisor, who had qualified, applied, and interviewed for the position. These students would work both individually and as a group to turn out high-quality work that would result in high "pay," bonus trips to a local country dinner playhouse, the respect and recognition of their peers, and the approval of their boss. Of course, students were not paid in real money, but with all the other "pay-offs," students enthusiastically accepted their nonnegotiable paychecks, which were then translated into traditional grades for the official records.

This system can be adapted quite easily to any content area with as little as or as much detail as the teacher wants to incorporate. The beauty of this approach is that it not only captures the imagination of the students but it also teaches responsibility, encourages creativity and initiative, and establishes a work climate that allows students to behave like adults.

PATRICIA WOODWARD, Lincoln Junior High School, Fort Collins, Colorado

Negative Reinforcement. **Negative reinforcement** occurs when an aversive consequence is removed or terminated following a desirable response to strengthen that response. Think about how car manufacturers prompt people to buckle their seat belts, and you will have a good example of negative reinforcement. A person who instantly buckles up (the desirable behavior) can avoid the sound of the buzzer (the aversive consequence) that begins when the car is started.

Negative reinforcement is sometimes called "escape conditioning" (see Sulzer-Azaroff & Mayer, 1986). Skinner (1987b) argued that our culture, in general, relies too heavily on negative reinforcement, when positive reinforcement is a better solution. Too many times we may do something just to keep a boss, a parent, or a teacher off our backs. In these cases, we're not motivated toward the behavior; we're motivated against the aversive consequence.

Which principles of behavioral psychology did this teacher use? How do incentive systems work? What do you think are some advantages and disadvantages of applying a business metaphor to classroom practice?

Weakening Undesirable Behaviors

Just as teachers want students to behave in some ways more often, they also want students to behave in other ways less often. Behaviors deemed undesirable are those that disrupt the class and interfere with students' learning. These could include, for example, talking out of turn or without being recognized, fighting in class, passing notes to a friend, and throwing food in the cafeteria. Teachers can deal with these behaviors by either presenting an aversive consequence or removing a desired consequence. The learner sees both responses as undesirable. In the Teacher Chronicle, the teacher views sending students to the principal as an undesirable consequence of inappropriate behavior, but the student clearly does not share this view, because being sent to the office did not change her behavior as the teacher expected.

Reflection: What is your view on the use of physical punishment in schools? On what knowledge and values is your view based?

Punishment. Weakening undesirable behaviors through **punishment** entails presenting an aversive consequence. This occurs, for example, when the gym teacher assigns extra laps to a student who misbehaves. Similarly, teachers might punish fighting or cursing by assigning students to detention after school or for some part of the school day. Punishment is most effective when a warning against misbehavior precedes it and when the punishment is used to communicate to students what behavior is not appropriate in particular situations (Azrin & Holz, 1966; Walters & Grusec, 1977). Punishment should be used sparingly, however, because it can have negative side effects, such as engendering fear or aggression in the transgressor. Although some states permit physical punishment, it is not recommended because of a host of potential harmful effects. The side effects of punishment are a serious concern when they result in running away or truancy. A student who is punished for doing poorly in school, for instance, may come to view school or home with anger and fear. If running away or staying out of school enables the student to avoid those feelings, then undesirable behavior is being inadvertently reinforced.

Try This: Interview a teacher to find out the types of behaviors that can and cannot safely be ignored.

Reinforcement Removal: Extinction. People sometimes ignore the wails of a child who has just been put to bed or denied something. By ignoring the behavior, thereby removing the reinforcement that was sustaining it (your attention), you succeed in eliminating the offending behavior. This is known as **extinction**. Teachers practice extinction on a daily basis when they ignore annoying, but not exceedingly disruptive, behaviors of students. The boy who wanders around the room, the girl who taps your elbow to get your attention while you work with another student, the child who fusses when it's time to come in from recess are all examples of situations in which teachers may withhold their attention from the student and ignore the annoying behavior.

Extinction works best when coupled with positive reinforcement for establishing more desirable alternative behaviors. Students can be distracted from misbehaving and then rewarded for behaving appropriately.

punishment The presentation of an aversive stimulus immediately following a response in order to weaken the incidence of the response.

extinction Removing reinforcement that is maintaining a behavior in order to weaken that behavior.

time-out The practice of separating a disruptive student from the rest of his or her classmates in order to decrease the probability of the response that precedes it.

Reinforcement Removal: Time-Out. **Time-out** removes reinforcement by separating a disruptive student from the rest of his or her classmates to decrease the disruptive behavior. The rationale for this practice is that if a child misbehaves to receive the attention of the teacher or other students, separating the child from his or her audience removes a desirable aspect of the environment.

here's how

Here's How to Use Time-Out Effectively in Your Classroom

- Use time-out to separate a child from sources of reinforcement, *not* from an aversive situation. For example, a child who is easily distracted by activities in a busy classroom might act out in order to be put in time-out, where it is quiet by comparison. In such a situation, the class can be seen as aversive and the time-out as reinforcement for disruptive behavior.
- Try to remove *all* sources of reinforcement. A corner of the classroom where students can still see and hear their peers would not work well as a site for time-out. In Becky's classroom, even when Leah was given time-out, she was able to distract her classmates.
- Keep the period of time-out relatively brief. Time-outs that are too long permit students to become acclimated to the environment, perhaps finding activities of interest to do there. A rule of thumb is one minute per year of the learner's age (Sulzer & Mayer, 1972; Sulzer-Azaroff & Mayer, 1986).

Try This: Interview a teacher who uses time-out as a consequence. Does the procedure work with all students? How does the teacher decide when and with whom to use time-out?

Reinforcement Removal: Response Cost. Like extinction and time-out, response cost results in the removal of reinforcement contingent on a behavior in order to decrease or eliminate that behavior. In **response cost**, however, the removal consists of taking away specified amounts of some previously earned reinforcer (Weiner, 1969)—that is, the individual must pay a fine for misbehavior. In society, response cost commonly occurs in the form of fines for overdue library books, exceeding the speed limit, and parking in restricted areas. It is important that the fine be high enough to deter the person from behaving in the same way again.

Response cost can work well in the classroom when students decide for themselves what the fines should be for behavioral transgressions. In a middle school in Florida, for example, students earn scrip (currency in the form of tokens or play money) that they can exchange for privileges such as free time or extra time on the school's computers. At the same time, they are fined in scrip for such misbehaviors as arriving late to class, appearing in the hallway without a hall pass, and being impolite to another student.

Critical Thinking: Why might an emphasis on aversive consequences in the classroom have a negative effect on the learning environment?

This child's banishment to time-out is designed to weaken an undesirable behavior by removing access to positive consequences (being with peers). What conditions will help to ensure the effectiveness of time-out?

response cost A fine is exacted from an individual as punishment for misbehavior.

Teaching New Behaviors

To this point, we have discussed how teachers change behaviors that are already in their students' repertoires. Sometimes you want to increase some of these behaviors and reduce or eliminate other behaviors. What do teachers do when they want students to behave in new ways?

To teach students new behaviors, teachers use shaping, fading, and chaining, among other methods. Some goals teachers have for students are rather like holes on a golf course. A golfer rarely makes a hole in one. Instead, the golfer starts by taking his or her best shot with a driver. The object of the initial shot is to get as close to the green as possible so that the next shot will carry to the general vicinity of the hole. As the golfer gets closer and closer to the hole, he or she needs to be more precise in selecting clubs to use and shots to make. So it is in a classroom. The behaviors that teachers set as their goals cannot be reached with one shot. Teachers must choose their environmental tools and make their shots with increasing finesse until they reach their goals: the change in students' behavior that they wish to effect.

Example: Using small steps to successively approximate behavior increases the likelihood of success and, therefore, reinforcement. Successively raising expectations and standards of performance has the same effect.

Shaping. The process of reinforcing successive approximations to a target behavior is called **shaping** (Reynolds, 1968: Skinner, 1954, 1963). Successive approximations are behaviors that, over time, come closer to some complex action. The first approximation of a forehand stroke in tennis is to grip the racket correctly.

Shaping behavior can be accomplished in a number of ways with a wide variety of behaviors. By simply paying attention to a child on the school playground, a teacher shapes the child's play on the jungle gym, encouraging various stages of proximity to the jungle gym, touching, climbing, and finally, extensive climbing—the target behavior (Harris, Wolf, & Baer, 1967). Skinner (1958) discussed shaping academic behaviors by using teaching machines, before the days of instructional computing. The presentation of material—either on audiotape, on a video monitor, or in a book—is called *programmed instruction*. Skinner described programs that provide reinforcement of correct responses and that gradually increase in difficulty. Small steps, or frames, that proceed from simple to complex help to ensure that students respond correctly and are reinforced as often as possible.

Critical Thinking: A teacher used bear-shaped note paper to send home her first graders' weekly reports. Good notes were written on the front and notes about negative behavior on the back. The teacher decided mid-year to stop writing the notes but did not tell the students. Much to her surprise, only two students asked why they weren't getting their bears anymore. Why didn't more students ask about the notes?

Shaping is necessary because many of the behaviors we desire of students are complex. If we waited for students to learn multiplication on their own or speak French spontaneously before we reinforced their learning behaviors, we might wait a very long time. So teachers have to take an active role in modifying behavior. In Chapter 8, we discuss how teachers (and other students) model behavior as a first step in the shaping process.

Connection: How is fading similar to the notion of scaffolding that was discussed in Chapter 2?

Fading. Recall that discriminative stimuli can exert a measure of control over behavior. Suppose Leah has learned to stay on task whenever Becky is walking around the room monitoring students. The monitoring aspect of the environment has come to control Leah's seat-work behavior. Becky is happy with Leah's effort but also wants her to work effectively on her own.

Using an approach called fading could accomplish Becky's goal. **Fading** is the gradual withdrawal of a discriminative stimulus while the behavior continues to be reinforced (Terrace, 1963a, 1963b). Becky could use fading to make Leah's seat-work behavior less dependent on her own behavior. Here's how she might do it.

shaping The process of reinforcing responses that are successively closer to the ultimate desired behavior.

fading The gradual withdrawal of a discriminative stimulus while the behavior continues to be reinforced.

Becky knows that Leah stays on task whenever Becky walks around the room monitoring students' work. Because Leah is working well, she is getting good

Insights ON SUCCESSFUL PRACTICE

How have you applied behavioral learning principles successfully in classroom management?

I taught a public school class for intermediate students with moderate cognitive disabilities. There were ten students in the classroom—nine boys and one girl. One student in particular, who had been referred by at least two teachers for emotional problems, was often in control of the classroom. His behaviors included making threats on the life of the teacher by imaginary uncles, kicking the wall, saying that absent students had been misbehaving, attributing behaviors to students who were incapable of performing those behaviors, and chanting.

I decided to use a form of response cost that emphasized good behavior for all the children in the classroom. In other words, I wanted to catch my students being good and then reward that behavior. The system was color coded, using green, yellow, and red tokens. At the beginning of the day, everyone started out in the "green." This meant that everyone had two smiley faces in the green, two in the yellow, and two frowning faces in the red. A child who exhibited a negative behavior was given a warning. If the behavior occurred again, the child lost a smiley face from the green and was sent to time-out for three minutes. At the end of the three minutes, if the child was calm, he or she was allowed to rejoin the class. If the child was not yet calm, the timer was reset for another three minutes. If, at the end of that time, the child was still not calm he or she was given a choice of being calm, or losing another smiley face. I explained to the child that although he or she had lost one smiley face, he or she was still in the green, but if he or she chose to continue the negative behavior, he or she would then be out of the green. Once out of the green, the child was reminded that he or she was still in the yellow.

At the end of the day, if a child was still in the green, the child was allowed to have popcorn while watching a movie. If the child was in the yellow, the child was allowed to watch the movie and still had tomorrow's recesses. If a child lost all of the smiley faces, then the child was in the "red," which meant no movie and no popcorn, but he or she could have recesses the following day. A child who had lost all of his or her frowning faces was no longer in the red and would lose recesses for the following day.

The color coding and rewards were combined with verbal feedback. For me, this feedback was the most important part. For example, if a child had an extremely bad day and was in the red at the end of the day, I would say to that child as he or she was leaving, "Tomorrow, you *will* have a good day." This technique resulted in a transference of external control to internal control. For example, eventually, as the students were leaving for the day, they would say, "Ms. V., tomorrow I ***will*** have a good day!" I would then praise them.

A problem with this technique occurred between the time the movie and popcorn were given and the time the school bus arrived. The problem student would display disruptive behaviors, knowing that he had received his reward for the day. I began passing out candy to those who were exhibiting desired behaviors. Those who acted disruptively were ignored. This technique was successful in reducing the negative behaviors prior to bus arrival.

The technique I used has proven to be successful in reducing negative behavior. It does need to be used with other strategies to maintain or increase positive behaviors. Also, it has not been found to be effective in increasing production or quality of work. However, it was successful in reducing the amount of time the child spent out of the classroom (e.g., in the principal's office). The best part of this approach is that I regained control of my class in a positive way.

J. BROCK VINSON,
Pine Elementary School
Michigan City, Indiana

Which principles of behavioral psychology did this teacher use? How do response cost systems work? What role did locus of control play in this teacher's strategy? Why might behavioral methods be appropriate for some students with disabilities?

marks on her papers. Becky could begin the fading procedure by spending less time next to Leah's desk as she strolls around the room. Each day, she could decrease her proximity to Leah, checking Leah's work carefully to ensure that she is still earning good marks. Becky must be careful to reinforce Leah's good work with laudatory comments on her papers or with verbal praise. She must also be careful to fade the discriminative stimulus slowly, because too great a change would have the reverse effect. If Becky finds that the quality of Leah's work suffers or that off-task behavior increases, then she must again increase the discriminative stimulus—her presence—until Leah's work improves. Fading a discriminative stimulus requires a delicate balance between supporting a student's efforts and requiring a little more self-direction at each turn.

Try This: Interview a teacher to find out how complex behaviors are broken down so that they can be successively approximated or chained.

Chaining. Sometimes complex behaviors must be learned that are made up of simpler, discrete tasks. **Chaining** occurs when these simpler behaviors are successively linked prior to the presentation of reinforcement. Driving a car is an example of a behavioral chain that consists of the following sequence of behaviors (once the person is behind the driver's seat of a car with automatic transmission): adjust seat, adjust rearview and side mirrors, insert key, turn key to start, put in gear, press accelerator. Reinforcement occurs at the end of the chain in successfully backing out of the driveway. Often, the simpler tasks are acquired through shaping, as when a driver learns how much pressure is required on the gas pedal to accelerate at a reasonable speed.

Connection: In Chapter 7, you will encounter a cognitive view of how information is committed to memory and motor performances are learned.

Other typical examples of behaviors learned through chaining include memorizing long passages of prose (sentences are added in succession until the entire passage can be recited without mistakes) and performing a dance (each discrete step is added until the entire dance can be performed).

HOW CAN YOU MAINTAIN NEWLY ESTABLISHED BEHAVIORS?

Consequences of behavior are contingent on changes in behavior. As we saw in the last section, the nature of the consequences that follow a response influences whether it is strengthened or weakened. The frequency of consequences also plays an important role. In practice, consequences of behavior do not always occur uniformly. Not every student who raises his or her hand to participate is called on. Not every smile from the teacher serves to reinforce. Not every misbehavior is reprimanded. A student doesn't have to make the correct response to every item on every test to be rewarded with an A. How, then, can you effectively maintain behaviors that have been newly established in your students?

chaining Successively linking together discrete, simpler behaviors already known to the learner in order to establish complex behaviors.

continuous reinforcement A schedule of reinforcement in which reinforcement is delivered after every correct response.

Continuous Reinforcement

When you provide reinforcement after every correct response, then you are using a schedule of **continuous reinforcement**. Continuous reinforcement is important when first establishing a pattern of correct responding. For example, in trying to encourage a reticent student to participate in class discussion, you might reinforce the student with praise or acknowledgment every time he or she joins

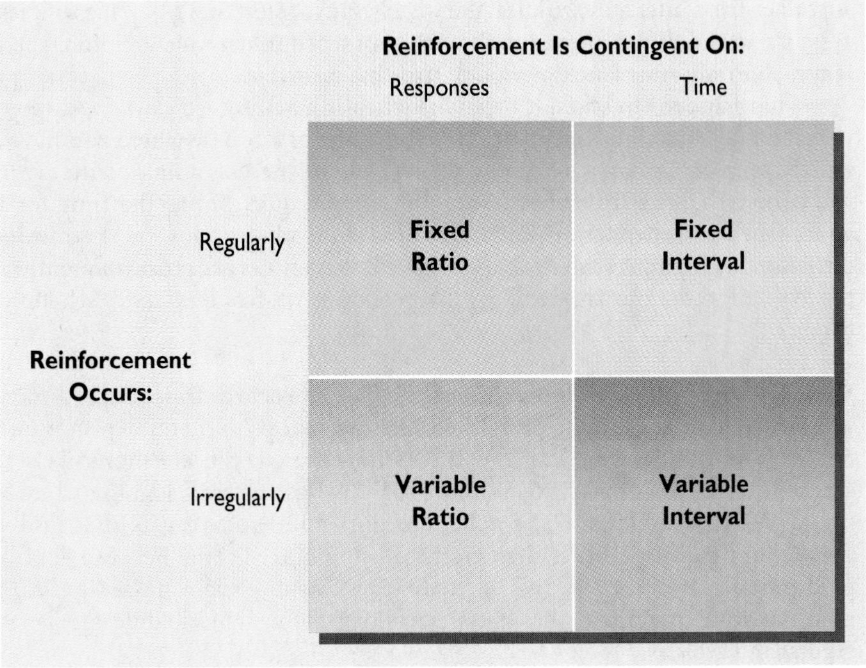

FIGURE 6.3

Types of Reinforcement Schedules

Source: From *Psychology of Learning for Instruction,* by M. P. Driscoll, 1994, Needham Heights, MA: Allyn & Bacon. Reprinted with permission.

Reinforcement Occurs:	Reinforcement Is Contingent On: Responses	Time
Regularly	**Fixed Ratio**	**Fixed Interval**
Irregularly	**Variable Ratio**	**Variable Interval**

in. The result of continuous reinforcement is a pattern of behavior that occurs at a steady, though not necessarily frequent, rate. A behavior that is continuously reinforced is also relatively easy to extinguish when reinforcement is stopped. To increase the overall rate of behavior, or to maintain it over time, then intermittent reinforcement should be used.

Intermittent Reinforcement

Intermittent reinforcement is contingent not on each response but on some schedule or combination of schedules (cf. Ferster & Skinner, 1957). For example, you might acknowledge or praise a student every other time the student entered a class discussion. In another situation, you might praise students for every ten minutes of remaining on task.

There are two types of schedules of intermittent reinforcements: interval schedules and ratio schedules. Interval schedules are based on time, so that reinforcement is available only after a certain interval of time has elapsed. Ratio schedules are based on the number of responses exhibited by the learner (Skinner, 1953).

Example: Piecework, such as being paid for each garment you sew, is an example of a ratio schedule.

In addition to conditions of time and number of responses, schedules of reinforcement are defined by the consistency with which reinforcement is delivered. Fixed schedules, whether they are interval or ratio, deliver reinforcement at a constant rate. Variable schedules deliver reinforcement at an unpredictable rate. Figure 6.3 identifies four schedules of intermittent reinforcement: fixed interval, variable interval, fixed ratio, and variable ratio.

intermittent reinforcement A schedule of reinforcement in which reinforcement is delivered on some, but not all, occasions.

Fixed Interval Schedules. A fixed interval schedule provides reinforcement for a correct response only after a certain period of time has passed. Classrooms are full of fixed interval schedules: the weekly spelling test on Friday, the unit test every six weeks, Friday afternoon films. All are schedules in which reinforcement is available only after a fixed period of time has passed.

What happens to student behavior when it is reinforced on a fixed interval schedule? Imagine your own study behavior in a course where you have a weekly quiz on Friday. Over the weekend and at the beginning of the week, you probably think little about studying for the quiz, but as the time for it approaches, you spend more and more time studying, perhaps even cramming on Thursday night. A scallop shape, where behavior occurs most frequently at the end of the time interval, is characteristic of fixed interval schedules (Figure 6.4).

Try This: Keep a journal reflecting on your own study behavior in classes where pop quizzes are given and in classes where tests are given on a predictable schedule.

Variable Interval Schedules. A variable interval schedule produces a more uniform rate of response than a fixed interval schedule. If you expect a quiz but are not told on what day it will be administered, you are more likely to study a little each day than to cram the night before. Overall, you might study no more than under a fixed schedule, but your studying is distributed throughout the week rather than crammed into one evening. Because distributed practice is more effective at facilitating learning than massed practice, many teachers prefer to administer pop quizzes than to schedule quizzes at regular intervals.

FIGURE 6.4

Cumulative Responses Under a Fixed Interval Schedule

Source: From *Theories of Learning* (5th ed., p. 180) by G. H. Bower, and E. R. Hilgard, 1981, Englewood Cliffs, NJ: Prentice-Hall. Reprinted by permission.

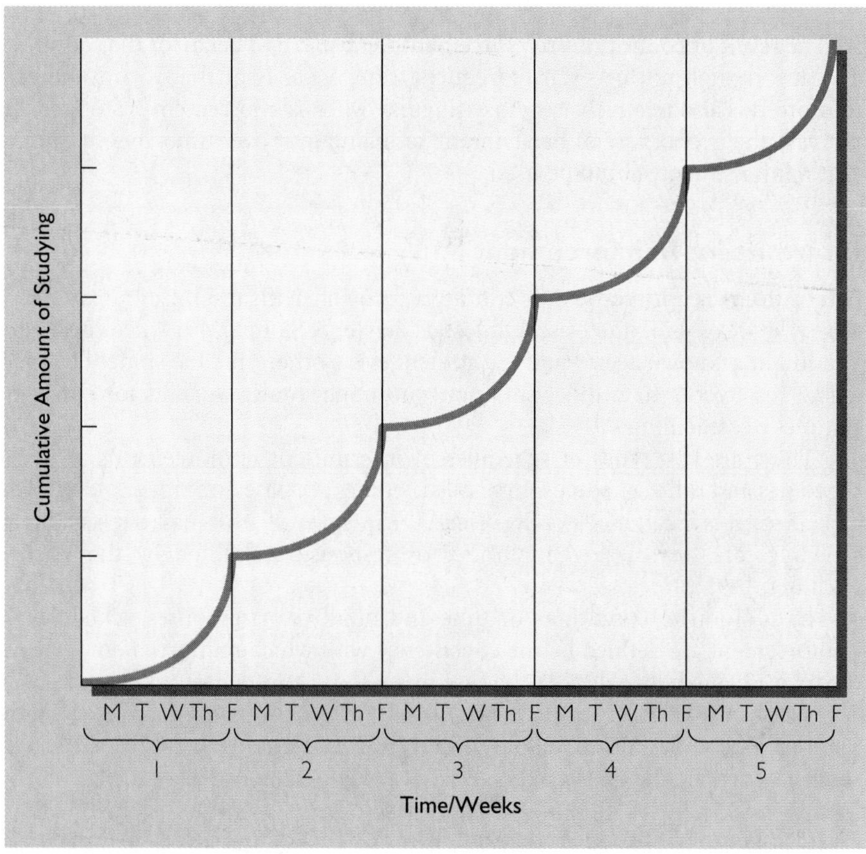

Fixed Ratio Schedules. A fixed ratio schedule provides reinforcement for a consistent number of responses regardless of how long it takes to produce these responses. A student working through a computer tutorial, for example, may have to answer five questions correctly before being permitted to advance to a new topic. Likewise, a student in reading may earn free time at the library for every three books read.

The fixed ratio schedule, like the fixed interval schedule, produces an uneven pattern of responses. Immediately after a reinforcement is delivered, the rate of response slows. It's as if the learner has taken a break to savor the reinforcement just received. So, for example, the student who has just finished reading her third book and received free time in the library may not begin a new book for several more days.

Variable Ratio Schedules. A variable ratio schedule provides reinforcement after a varying number of desired responses. This type of schedule produces a frequent and consistent pattern of responding.

One high school teacher wanted to use extensive practice to teach math concepts in her remedial classes. She faced a major problem in encouraging her students to complete their homework. She used a variable ratio schedule to solve her problem. For each homework assignment a student completed with at least 90 percent accuracy, he or she got some number of chances to spin the "wheel of fortune." (Some assignments were worth more spins than others.) The wheel contained each student's name. If the student's name came up on one of his or her spins, the student won points that could be used to exchange for certain privileges. The teacher found that homework performance improved dramatically and, consequently, so did test scores. The teacher's scheme is an example of a variable ratio schedule because the number of spins that led to winning varied.

Intermittent reinforcement, if there are sufficiently long intervals or ratios, can be a powerful controller of behavior. Behavior maintained using these schedules is more resistant to extinction than behavior that is continuously reinforced, with variable ratio schedules producing a behavior pattern most resistant to extinction. Setting up an environment and providing appropriate consequences is part of the teacher's job. The other part of the job is determining what responses should be reinforced and helping students to learn strategies for self-reinforcement.

HOW CAN BEHAVIORAL PRINCIPLES ENHANCE THE TEACHING–LEARNING PROCESS IN YOUR CLASSROOM?

Envision, if you will, a well-functioning classroom. Everyone's vision is probably a little bit different. For most people, however, a well-functioning classroom is one in which students know what they are supposed to do, work busily on task, and have facial expressions ranging from alert attentiveness to smiling satisfaction. The teacher may be working with one student, a small group, or the entire class. What does it take to achieve this vision?

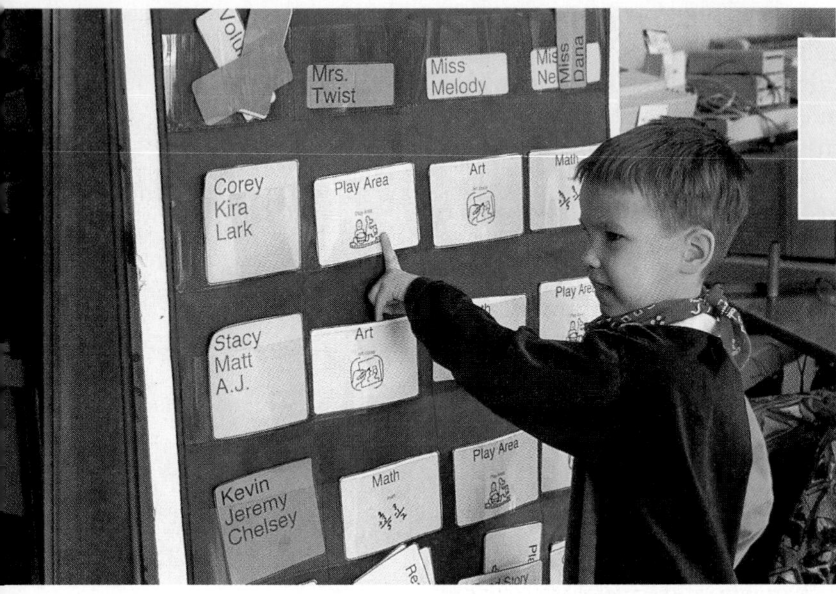

Often, the most effective reinforcers are those that individual students choose themselves. Wise teachers involve students directly in setting behavioral goals, customizing reinforcers, and monitoring progress.

From the examples so far provided in this chapter, you may have realized that problems in a class can come from a single individual who misbehaves or fails to behave in the desired fashion. Alternatively, problems can stem from a misunderstanding of what the rules are by the entire class. Either situation can wreak mayhem for the teacher as he or she attempts to solve the problem and get students back on task. The remaining sections of this chapter show how you can employ behavioral management techniques to solve individual or whole-class problems and design a learning environment that will facilitate all students' learning.

Point: *Teachers coordinate the context for learning.* By using behavioral principles, teachers can work with individual students, as well as the entire class, to manage their behavior and maintain an environment conducive to learning.

Working with Individuals to Change Behavior

Most teachers can tell you who, in their classes, are the "quiet ones," the "social ones," the "active ones," the "passive ones," the "immature ones," and so forth. These are the students about whom teachers are heard to remark, "I wish Nicole would participate in class more often. She has so much to offer the other students." Or "I wish Jonathan would take just a little more time to organize his work. He can be so impulsive." There are also students whom teachers identify as behavior problems, students whose disruptive behaviors interfere with class activities and students' learning. Whether you identify a problem behavior to eliminate in one student or a behavior you'd like to encourage in another student,

here's how

Here's How to Work with Students to Change Their Behavior

- Decide on behavioral goals.
- Determine appropriate reinforcers.
- Select procedures for changing behaviors.
- Implement the procedures and monitor results.
- Evaluate progress and revise as necessary (Driscoll, 1994; Sulzer & Mayer, 1972).

Set Behavioral Goals. To change a student's behavior, you must know how you want the student to behave. What is the student doing now that you want to reduce or eliminate? What should the student do to behave appropriately in your classroom that he or she is not doing now? By observing the student carefully in class, you can determine just how frequently the student engages in both wanted and unwanted behaviors. From this baseline, and by enlisting the student's participation, you can establish specific goals for decreasing an undesired behavior and increasing a desired behavior. For example, with one student, you may set a goal for reducing temper tantrums from two or three times per day to no more than once a week. With another, you might set a goal for increasing the neatness with which assignments are prepared from less than one a week to at least 90 percent turned in neatly. Knowing the baseline of behavior before you implement procedures to change behavior provides a basis for evaluating progress toward the goals you and your students have decided on.

Point: *Learners are diverse.* The reinforcers and contingencies of reinforcement that are effective with one student may not work for another.

Determine Appropriate Reinforcers. As we have indicated throughout this chapter, what is reinforcing to one person may not be for another. What you choose as reinforcers for a particular student should depend on careful observation of the student to determine likes and dislikes. A conference with the parents or student can also reveal wants or desires that can serve as potent reinforcers in a behavior change program. Alternatively, you can arrange for students to choose their own reinforcers. Often, the most effective reinforcers are those that individual students choose for themselves.

Reflection: Recall a situation in which you had a choice of reinforcers. How did your choice influence your behavior?

Select Procedures for Changing Behavior. Whether your goal is to increase or decrease a behavior determines the type of procedure likely to be most effective in reaching the goal. When increasing a behavior, using positive reinforcement and the Premack principle is the best choice because negative reinforcement is a form of aversive control. For teaching entirely new behaviors, you may decide to use shaping, fading, or chaining, depending on the behavior or task to be learned. When reducing or eliminating a behavior, some form of aversive control is probably necessary for at least a short time. However, by using a combination of procedures, you can emphasize the acquisition of desired behaviors as alternatives to those being eliminated.

Implement Procedures and Monitor Results. Once goals, appropriate reinforcers, and behavior change procedures are all determined, you and the student are ready to implement the plan. The most important aspect of implementing a program of behavior change is consistency. If you are not consistent, you are likely to inadvertently maintain behaviors you are trying to change. During the period of implementation, you should also observe the student's behavior carefully to determine whether the procedures you selected are having the desired effect.

Evaluate Progress and Revise as Necessary. The final step in working to change behavior is to evaluate whether the procedures implemented are indeed working as intended. Is the undesired behavior that was targeted for change actually occurring less often? Is the desired behavior you or the student wish to establish occurring more often, or is at least some progress being made toward its achievement? If the answer to these questions is no, then you should reexamine every aspect of the program. Perhaps the reinforcer being used with the Premack principle is not a high enough probability behavior to reinforce the desired low-probability behavior. Perhaps you have emphasized aversive control procedures without planning for positive reinforcement of alternative behaviors. Whatever the cause, you should make adjustments to the program and continue to monitor their effects.

Suppose, in contrast, that the program is effective. In this case, you should consider gradually changing the schedule of reinforcement, so that the student's behavior becomes more under his or her control and less affected by the external reinforcement. In the following episode, which took place in Peter Roop's classroom, can you detect the five steps to changing behavior? What were Peter's goals for changing Rodney's behavior? How did he enlist Rodney's participation in achieving these goals? Based on Peter's experience, what advice would you give to Becky in the Teacher Chronicle?

> Rodney was a handful in the classroom. If he could disrupt a lesson, he did. If he could hit someone, he did. If he could avoid work, he did. If he could cause trouble on the playground, he did.
>
> Nothing seemed to work in my attempts to manage his behavior. Not only did I want to control his outbursts and problems with others, I wanted him to eventually internalize some control over his own behavior.
>
> One day I discovered Rodney's desire to play football at recess. Not only did he want to play, he wanted to be the one to take the football out to the playground. At times, his need to take the ball superseded his wish to play. Once I finally saw his desire to have the ball, I used it in the classroom to effect a change in his behavior preceding recess. Together we decided that he could take the ball on those days when he was nice to others. For several weeks he took the ball on good days and couldn't play with it on bad days. Each morning he checked with me to see how he'd done, although he already knew ahead of time whether the ball would be his. Then a day came when he was good and forgot all about the ball as a reward. For the next two days, he behaved himself without needing the ball. After that, his behavior backslid and the football became necessary again—but only for the rest of the week. Unfortunately, we had a spell of rotten weather; with recess inside his behavior deteriorated. But as the weather got better, the football once again became an important tool for eliciting appropriate behavior.

Managing by Rules

The contingencies, or the rules, that students learn and that come to govern their behavior can be learned by responding in an environment. Behavior that is controlled by rules is called rule-governed behavior. When students enter school, they must learn what the rules are. After spending several years in school, however, many of the rules are givens. Much of the behavior you will expect of students in your classes is rule-governed behavior (cf. Rachlin, 1991).

For students to behave as you expect them to, they must know the rules. You can tell students what the contingencies are in the classroom environment or learning situation. You can also elicit students' input in determining what the rules of the classroom should be. When students have a hand in deciding rules (and possibly consequences), they exercise some degree of control over their environment. This is likely to bring them one step closer to self-reinforcement and the management of their behavior.

Reflection: Recall teachers you had whose actions did not match their words. How effective were these teachers?

Insights ON SUCCESSFUL PRACTICE

How have you used behavioral methods to increase student motivation?

It's vital for a young child entering school or preschool to build a positive self-concept and develop an enjoyment of learning as well as to become responsible. In order for young students to feel good about themselves, they need to become self-reliant. A clip system that I started about ten years ago and still use works beautifully with most young children. A successful positive approach to discipline makes both teaching and learning a joy in the classroom.

The classroom rules should be discussed thoroughly and should be posted so that the student is aware of rules, rewards, and consequences before the process begins. After the child is aware of what is expected, the classroom management begins. The child is responsible for picking up two clips (I use colorful plastic clothespins) upon entering the classroom each day. Anytime during the day if a school or class rule is broken, the teacher will ask the child for a clip and either remind the child of the rule, or better still, ask the child to state the rule or the reason for losing a clip. It takes only a few seconds to direct a student back on task with minimal interruption to the teaching procedure.

At the end of the day the student with one or two clips will be rewarded. One clip is exchanged for a sticker card, and an additional treat is given for the second clip. If the child loses both clips, he or she will be given a "You Can Do Better" sad clown stamp card. When ten stickers are collected the student may trade them in for something out of the class treasure chest.

A cooperative communication between home and school makes the system work much more successfully. The parents have already been notified of how the clip system works, have a copy of school and class rules, and have been asked to follow up by providing reinforcement at home. I have received positive feedback from parents through the years, adding a little more responsibility each time. This also keeps the system from becoming old hat to the students and helps them become more self-reliant.

Discipline was my greatest dread when I first started teaching, and I experimented with many different methods. This system has helped me tremendously by relieving a lot of pressure from me and has also improved my students' self-discipline. I have shared this system with other teachers in my school, my school system, and throughout Tennessee. Other teachers in day care centers, kindergarten classes, and first-grade classes are also using it. They have relayed to me that it makes classroom management a much more pleasant task.

EDNA LOVEDAY, Sevierville Primary School,
Sevierville, Tennessee

What were the goals of this teacher's response cost system? What role did parental involvement play? Why might behavioral models be appropriate for younger students?

Knowing rules and following rules, however, are two separate things. Following rules is something a person does, a kind of behavior. Rule-following behavior, like any behavior, is influenced by the consequences of the behavior. Whether or not your students follow the rules in your classroom, then, is determined by the consequences they experience and the consistency with which they experience these consequences.

here's how

Here's How to Encourage Rule-Following Behavior in Your Classroom

- Respond immediately. Although it is unlikely you can reinforce every student who is following a rule, you should respond immediately when any student breaks a rule.
- Be consistent. One teacher developed a system where he drops a yellow card on the desk of any student caught breaking a rule. The first yellow card is a warning. If the student earns a second yellow card, the student is to see the teacher after class or after school. For the third infraction, the teacher drops a red card on the student's desk, which means "Gather your materials quietly and report to the principal's office."
- Be fair. Breaking a particular rule should merit the same consequences whether the student is the class clown or the class leader.

When managing by rules in your classroom, remember the old teaching maxim: Practice what you preach and model appropriate or desired behavior. If you follow that rule, your consequences will be desirable.

Try This: Observe a token economy and interview teachers who use it. What are the strengths and weaknesses of this approach? Ask if the teachers have plans for stretching the ratio or fading.

Managing a Token Economy

Sometimes teachers develop token economy systems for managing rule-governed behavior. In a **token economy**, students earn objects (e.g., poker chips, marbles, stickers, play money) that they can redeem for reinforcers. Each reinforcer has a price. After students earn the requisite number of tokens through correct responses, they obtain the reinforcer. In many respects, token economies are fixed ratio schedules. The fixed ratio is different for each reinforcer: A dinosaur pencil may cost seven tokens, whereas thirty minutes of free time on the computer may cost twenty-four. For a particular reinforcement, however, the ratio of responses to reinforcer is fixed.

Token economies have been shown to work in a variety of settings, including with patients in mental hospitals (cf. Ayllon & Azrin, 1968). In a remedial classroom, a token economy was used effectively to help students stay on task and to ask questions (Wolf, Giles, & Hall, 1968). Bushell, Wrobel, & Michaelis (1968) demonstrated the effective use of a token economy with children in a regular classroom, who, as a result of their participation, increased their attention to task instructions and became quieter.

Token economies differ from simple token collection systems, such as those set up by libraries to encourage children to participate in summer reading programs. Typically, children are rewarded a star or a point or a sticker—which is displayed on a chart—for reading a certain type or number of books. After the children have completed the requirements of the program, they receive a certificate and have their names posted at the library. Similar systems are used in many classrooms: behavior charts, reading charts, multiplication charts, for example. In such systems, unlike the true token economy, collecting stars or checks does not allow the learner to choose a reinforcer. True token economies allow the learner some choice in determining reinforcement. In a token economy, the tokens acquire the status of conditioned reinforcer. Conditioned reinforcers can, of themselves, be powerful motivators of behavior.

token economy A behavioral program that allows students to earn objects for good behavior. The objects can be redeemed for desirable goods or privileges.

Token economies also permit the use of response cost that, together with positive reinforcement, helps to manage all sorts of rule-governed behavior. In a sense, the management system becomes something of a minisociety. Remember the Florida middle school mentioned earlier. Class or school rules are posted, with tokens earned for exemplary conduct or owed for rule transgressions. Students may not be happy about losing tokens when they break a rule, but they understand what they did wrong when you question them about their behavior and exact the fine.

Using Praise Effectively

Behavioral principles are so widely used to support rule-governed behavior of students in classrooms that we sometimes forget their usefulness in supporting other kinds of learning outcomes. Praise is a powerful reinforcer for learning more than rules or how to behave appropriately in various environments. It is also a powerful reinforcer for learning subject-related and self-management skills. Haven't you felt that glow of satisfaction when a teacher praised you for doing a good job or accomplishing a difficult task? Haven't you worked that much harder after a teacher praised your progress toward an instructional goal? Praise can affect a student's persistence at a task, strategies for learning, and confidence in achieving a goal.

Try This: Observe a classroom in which the teacher enjoys a good rapport with his or her students. How does the teacher reinforce desirable behavior?

Here's How to Use Praise Effectively in Your Classroom

- Praise students' accomplishments and progress during an instructional activity, not just their participation in it. For example, "I can see from your answers that your measurements are becoming more accurate. Accuracy is so important in conducting experiments."
- Praise students when they demonstrate self-management skills, such as monitoring their time in order to complete a task during an allotted period. A seventh-grade teacher is careful to praise students working in groups when they carry out their assigned roles in an efficient and cooperative fashion.
- Make praise truly meaningful. Don't give undeserved praise, either because the student hasn't earned it or because task accomplishment is too easy to be especially praiseworthy. In either case, students may begin to question whether they have the ability to earn genuine recognition (Woolfolk, 1995).

Making Behavioral Principles Work for You

No matter what behavioral principles you decide are useful for enhancing teaching and learning in your classroom, there are three important points you should keep in mind. First, behavioral strategies designed to change student behavior must be used responsibly. There are important ethical issues for you to consider when you use behavioral strategies. There is evidence to suggest, for example, that rewarding students for learning what they are already interested in will undermine their interest in learning (see further discussion of the undermining effect in Chapter 9). Some researchers are also concerned about the message of teacher control that is conveyed by behavioral strategies at a time when student autonomy in learning should be facilitated (Lebow, 1993). Finally, it is important to consider the effects of these strategies on individual students. A behavioral program involving reinforcement at home may backfire and lead to increased abuse if the student has experienced a history of being punished by parents for poor progress reports (Woolfolk, 1995).

Second, the actions you take to reinforce a student do not constitute positive reinforcement unless behavior increases. For reinforcement to occur, the consequence must be desirable to the learner. You cannot assume that verbal praise—or candy, free time, or high grades—is always desirable. Likewise, the punishment you mete out is only punishment if behavior decreases, which means that the consequence is undesirable to the student. One of the basic assumptions of operant conditioning is that the individual is the appropriate source of information about learning. Individuals differ in what they find desirable and undesirable.

Connection: What suggestions for effective reinforcement are offered by the developmental theories that were presented in Chapters 2 and 3?

Finally, you must be comfortable with the consequences you use in your classroom. There are any number of potential positive reinforcers. Many are tangible and obvious. An equal number are subtler: a smile, a nod, a casual comment (Nye, 1979). Moreover, there is the matter of the particular classroom environment and the group of students with whom you are working. In some schools, a teacher may be able to use a trip to the computer lab as a reward or to implement a token economy. In other schools, the school's structure and rules may not permit this. Knowing your strengths and weaknesses and what can and cannot be used as reinforcement in your particular environment allows you to offer students realistic choices among reinforcers. Finally, although students learn through the operation of behavioral principles, as you have seen in this chapter, they also learn through cognitive processes and social interactions, which are the subjects of Chapters 7 and 8.

TEACHER Chronicle Conclusion

OUT OF CONTROL

The following Monday, Becky spends the morning in Sarah O'Dell's classroom. Again she marvels at the control Sarah has without being overbearing. The students understand the room rules, they frequently monitor themselves without Ms. O'Dell's intervention, and when there is an occasional disruption, Sarah handles it quietly. While the children are working independently after a reading lesson, Sarah walks around the room, praising and questioning students.

Every so often Sarah drops a penny into a large bear-shaped jar on her desk. The students who see her do it smile at each other and get back to work. Twice before recess she drops in three pennies, once after all students had finished their work and once when three students cleaned their desks. At recess, Becky asks Sarah about the penny jar.

"That's the secret for this semester. When we discussed room rules at the beginning of the year, they all had their input." Pointing to the rules posted on the wall, she says, "See, none of them start with DON'T. They all are positive, like 'We will work quietly.' After we established the room rules, then we decided on how to enforce them. The solution is the penny jar. When I catch them being good as a class or individually, I quietly drop in a penny. Not every time, but frequently."

"What happens when the jar is full?" Becky asks.

"Two things. They get to choose extra gym time, extra free time, watch a video, or even have a party. Then we split the pennies, and I start all over again."

"I tried something similar with my kids," Becky says. "I put a piece of candy in a jar at the end of the day if they were good. That fell apart real soon."

Sarah laughs. "I tried that, too. But the more frequently I can reinforce the positive behaviors, the more involved they become in acquiring them."

"I can't tell you how much just watching you has helped," Becky says. "Now I think I can make it to Thanksgiving break!"

"You'll make it far beyond that," Sarah says, just as the kids rush back in.

APPLICATION QUESTIONS

1. What did Becky do to reinforce good behaviors?
2. What kind of reinforcement schedule did Sarah employ with the penny jar? Becky with the candy jar? Why did Becky's use of the candy jar fail?
3. Would the penny jar work with high schoolers? Why or why not? What would work?
4. Imagine if Becky tried the penny jar approach now. Why might it fail or succeed for her?
5. How important is it for students to have input into class rules?
6. How should Becky make Leah an ally, instead of an enemy?
7. Are rewards more effective if a person can choose the rewards for certain behaviors?
8. Imagine you are teaching a middle school English class. How would you involve the students in controlling their adolescent behaviors?
9. Write a set of classroom rules for first grade, sixth grade, ninth grade, twelfth grade. What similarities and differences do you find?
10. Will what works for one teacher work for every teacher? Work every year?

CHAPTER SUMMARY

WHAT IS BEHAVIORAL SCIENCE?

Behavioral science is an approach to learning that relies on the observable environment and observable behaviors. Skinner's model of operant conditioning came from his study of Pavlov's work with behaviors that were reflexes to environmental stimuli. Skinner's theories address behaviors that lead to environmental consequences and thus operate on the environment.

HOW DOES REINFORCEMENT INFLUENCE BEHAVIOR?

Skinner's basic model of learning involves three components: antecedent, response, and consequence.

Antecedents are aspects of the environment that, in the presence of reinforcement, come to signal and control behavior. Consequences of behavior influence the probability that a given response will reoccur. Teachers systematically design reinforcement contingencies to increase or decrease the behaviors of their students.

HOW CAN YOU DEVELOP STRATEGIES FOR CHANGING STUDENT BEHAVIOR?

Teachers strengthen desirable behaviors through positive reinforcement, negative reinforcement, and the Premack principle. Although it is possible to use primary reinforcers (such as food) to reinforce behavior, teachers generally use conditioned reinforcers, such as grades, praise, or other forms of recognition. To weaken undesirable behaviors, teachers can use aversive measures such as extinction, punishment, timeout, and response cost. For the most effective use of these procedures, teachers should pair them with more positive measures to reinforce alternative behaviors.

To teach entirely new, often complex, behaviors, teachers use shaping to reinforce successive approximations to a goal or chaining to link previously learned discrete skills into a more complex target behavior. Fading, the gradual withdrawal of discriminative stimuli while the response continues to be reinforced, is used to make student behavior less dependent on the teacher or other aspects of the student's environment.

HOW CAN YOU MAINTAIN NEWLY ESTABLISHED BEHAVIORS?

Once a behavior is established using continuous reinforcement, you can maintain it by gradually changing the reinforcement schedule so that the response is less dependent on external reinforcement. Eventually, behavior may come to be entirely self-reinforced. With interval schedules, the time is lengthened and varied until reinforcement is delivered. With ratio schedules, the number of responses required for reinforcement, regardless of the time it takes to produce them, is increased and varied.

HOW CAN BEHAVIORAL PRINCIPLES ENHANCE THE TEACHING–LEARNING PROCESS IN YOUR CLASSROOM?

To change the behavior of an individual student, you can work with the student to set a behavioral goal, determine appropriate reinforcers, select procedures to change behavior, implement procedures and monitor results, and evaluate progress and revise as necessary. To ensure that students follow class or school rules, consequences of following or violating the rules must be established and consistently applied. One means of doing this is through a token economy, where students earn objects as a result of appropriate behavior that they can use to buy reinforcers. Transgressions of the rules require paying fines by giving back previously earned tokens.

As a teacher, you must decide how and when behavioral principles will work best for you. Some teachers are opposed to the use of external reinforcers, whereas others do not feel comfortable using particular social reinforcers, such as jokes, with students. By understanding your own personal strengths and biases, as well as the effects of behavioral techniques, you will be in a position to make realistic decisions about the management of behavior and learning.

KEY CONCEPTS

aversive
behavioral approach
chaining
classical conditioning
conditioned reinforcer
contingencies of reinforcement
continuous reinforcement
discriminative stimulus
extinction
fading
intermittent reinforcement
law of effect
negative reinforcement
operant behavior
operant conditioning
positive reinforcement
Premack principle
primary reinforcer
punishment
reinforcement
response cost
shaping
time-out
token economy

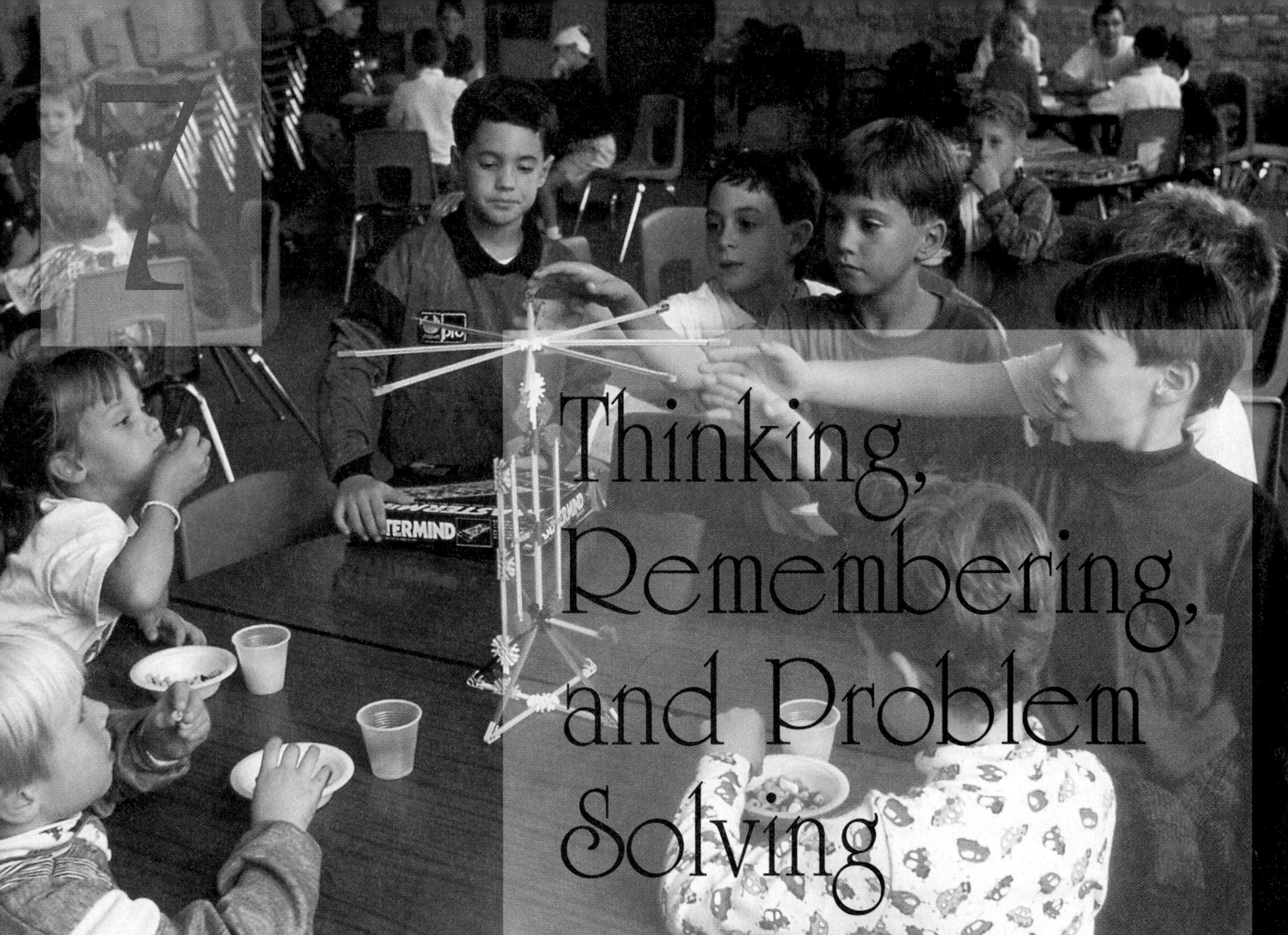

7 Thinking, Remembering, and Problem Solving

CHAPTER OUTLINE

TEACHER Chronicle

CHINESE PROVERB

Every day, Dan Lovely presents new information to his fourth graders: how to identify a bird of prey by its body shape, the difference between active and passive verbs, how to do long division word problems, what photosynthesis is.

Tonight he is correcting a test he gave on the human eye. Dan is disappointed in the results. While his students did fine on labeling the parts of the eye, they did poorly on how the eye functions.

Dan reflects on the lessons he has presented. He covered the material in the curriculum guide: cornea, iris, pupil, contraction, reversed images, expansion, retina, how the eye "sees" upside down. Most of the students seemed to be paying attention during the lessons. Why, then, hadn't they learned the material?

The next day as he is walking down the hall Dan notices a sign on another teacher's door.

> Tell Me, I Forget.
> Show Me, I Remember.
> Involve Me, I Understand.
> —Chinese Proverb

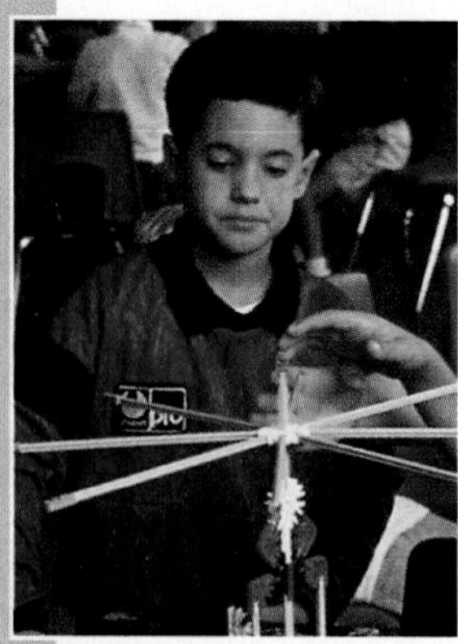

The words rattle in his head all day long. He had *told* his class about the eye and they had forgotten. He had *shown* them the parts of the eye through drawings on the board and they had remembered. But he realizes that he hadn't *involved* them. He makes new plans that night.

FOCUS QUESTIONS

1. How does Dan know if his students are learning?
2. What techniques can a teacher use to enhance student learning?
3. What difference does a student's previous knowledge about a subject make in learning?
4. Why is student application important in mastering new knowledge?
5. How might Dan use what his students already know to enhance their learning?
6. How can knowing how you learn as an individual be an important factor in your learning?
7. Why might sharing an experience or teaching another student improve learning?
8. What processes do students use to remember information?
9. What role do metaphors, analogies, and images play in remembering information?
10. How does one process new information?
11. Why might Mr. Lovely's students have done well on labeling and poorly on how the eye functions?
12. How does the amount of student attention affect learning new information?
13. How important is the relevance of a lesson to student mastery?
14. How much should teachers help students integrate new knowledge with what they already know?
15. In what ways should teachers simplify lessons to enhance student understanding?

WHAT IS INVOLVED IN THINKING, REMEMBERING, AND PROBLEM SOLVING?

You learned in Chapter 6 that behavioral scientists focus exclusively on the stimulus, response, and associated environmental changes that occur with learning. Although these may be accompanied by changes internal to an individual learner, behavioral scientists argue that such changes need not be investigated in order to understand learning. Learning is conceived in terms of changes in observable behavior. Cognitive learning theorists, in contrast, believe that events occurring within the learner are just as important for understanding learning as the environmental events external to the learner. The term *cognition* has to do with the act of knowing. Therefore, cognitive theorists conceive of learning in terms of the acquisition of knowledge.

Differing Views of Cognition

What does it mean to acquire knowledge? And how is knowledge a part of thinking, remembering, and solving problems? Cognitive theorists offer different answers to these questions. In this chapter, we examine several views of cognition. Information-processing theory is based on a computer metaphor that assumes humans can process information in much the same way as computers do. In this view, learning is a matter of inputting information from the environment, transforming it for storage in memory, and then retrieving it from memory to produce a response.

Critical Thinking: Sherlock Holmes once used the analogy of storing items in an attic to describe human cognition. Why might the computer analogy be more accurate?

Extensive research on the properties of memory have extended the information-processing view and demonstrated how important prior knowledge is to the comprehension and encoding of new knowledge. Students come to school already knowing a great many things. What they know and how they have organized this knowledge in memory will greatly influence what they are able to learn from the lessons you teach.

Finally, an opposing view of cognition is represented in constructivism. Based on a construction, or "mind as laboratory," metaphor, the constructivist view proposes that learning is a matter of constructing knowledge in a learning community. In this view, learning is a process not only of individual knowledge construction but also of enculturation into the practices of intellectual disciplines (Cobb, 1994). As you will see, all of these views have important implications for teaching.

Learning How to Learn

For students to develop the critical reasoning skills that are an essential part of thinking and problem solving, they must, in effect, learn how to learn. They must become aware of their own cognitive processes. They must become capable of regulating these processes in appropriate ways so that specific learning goals may be attained. And they must monitor their own learning, recognizing when particular strategies are ineffective and should be revised.

Connection: Learning how to learn is a process of developing metacognitive skills. This is discussed in Chapter 2 and later in this chapter.

It can be argued that learning how to learn is the most important outcome of schooling. A student who leaves school knowing how to learn has options that are not available to a student who does not learn well. Both the effective learner and the poor learner may possess basic reading and math skills, but the effective learner can use those skills to augment his or her opportunities. An effective learner is equipped not only to find and secure employment but also to improve and advance as an employee. One who knows how to learn is capable of continuously discovering opportunities and of critically analyzing those opportunities. The challenges that await our students when they have left our classrooms require that we help them develop their ability to learn. Being able to augment their knowledge and skill in any area they choose empowers them to identify and solve problems. For instance, an effective learner may not know upon graduation what opportunities exist in the field of outdoor recreation but will be able to reason, to apply strategic knowledge, and ultimately to discover what opportunities do exist or what opportunities might be created. Helping our students become able learners will allow them to pursue better jobs, better interpersonal relations, better educations, and better ways of living.

But learning how to learn is by no means easy. University professors regularly encounter students who study in ways that are ineffective or who tackle problems using strategies that are not appropriate for the particular problem at hand. In many cases, these students are not aware that their actions will not produce the desired result, and they are puzzled when this happens. "But I studied for *so* many hours!" they protest. As you will see in this chapter, learning comes about not only from being cognitively engaged but also from being engaged in particular ways. As you examine the ways in which cognition can be engaged effectively, compare your own cognitive activity to that discussed in the chapter. If you intend to use this chapter to improve your own learning, you must first reflect on your own cognitive efforts. How do you think about new material that you are supposed to learn? How do you go about trying to remember information that you need to know? How do you first define and then work on problems you are required to solve? After you have carefully considered the way you go about the work of learning, you will be in a position to experiment with some of the principles and techniques of learning that you will encounter in this chapter.

HOW CAN YOU TEACH IN WAYS THAT FACILITATE THE PROCESSING OF INFORMATION?

Developments in computer technology coincided with the growth of psychological research. Psychologists were among the first to use computers to help them in their work (particularly in conducting statistical analyses). These psychologists became knowledgeable about the ways in which computers processed information; they began to theorize that humans processed information in an analogous way (Hunt, 1971). Human **information-processing models** borrow heavily from the vocabulary of the computer with terms such as input, output, storage systems, capacity, encoding, retrieval, and executive control.

information-processing models Models of learning that rely on an analogy between the human mind and the computer to explain processing, storage, and retrieval of knowledge.

Much of the information students encounter in classrooms is coded information. Making sense out of written or spoken information is a matter of using a linguistic code. Using numerals and symbols to define and solve mathematical problems requires another code. How do students learn these codes? And, once learned, how do they use the codes to comprehend new information, understand concepts, and put to good effect what they have learned? The information-processing view assumes that certain types of mental structures form a mechanism by which information is acquired, comprehended, stored, and retrieved for later use.

Figure 7.1 shows a flowchart illustrating the human information-processing model. Most information-processing models can be traced to Atkinson and Shiffrin (1968).

Let's follow the flow of information through the various stages. Then we look more closely at the major stages of processing and the specific means by which information is transformed at each stage. These stages also provide ideas for strategies you can use to facilitate students' information processing. Refer to Figure 7.1 as you read.

Point: *Learning is a function of mental activity.* According to information-processing theory, this mental activity consists of encoding, storing, and retrieving knowledge.

The *environment* is the source of input into the information-processing system of the learner. Through sense *receptors*, humans take in stimulus information from the environment, which they see, hear, smell, taste, or feel. Receptors are the physical connection between the organism and the environment. Each receptor has a corresponding *sensory register*, where information is stored very briefly.

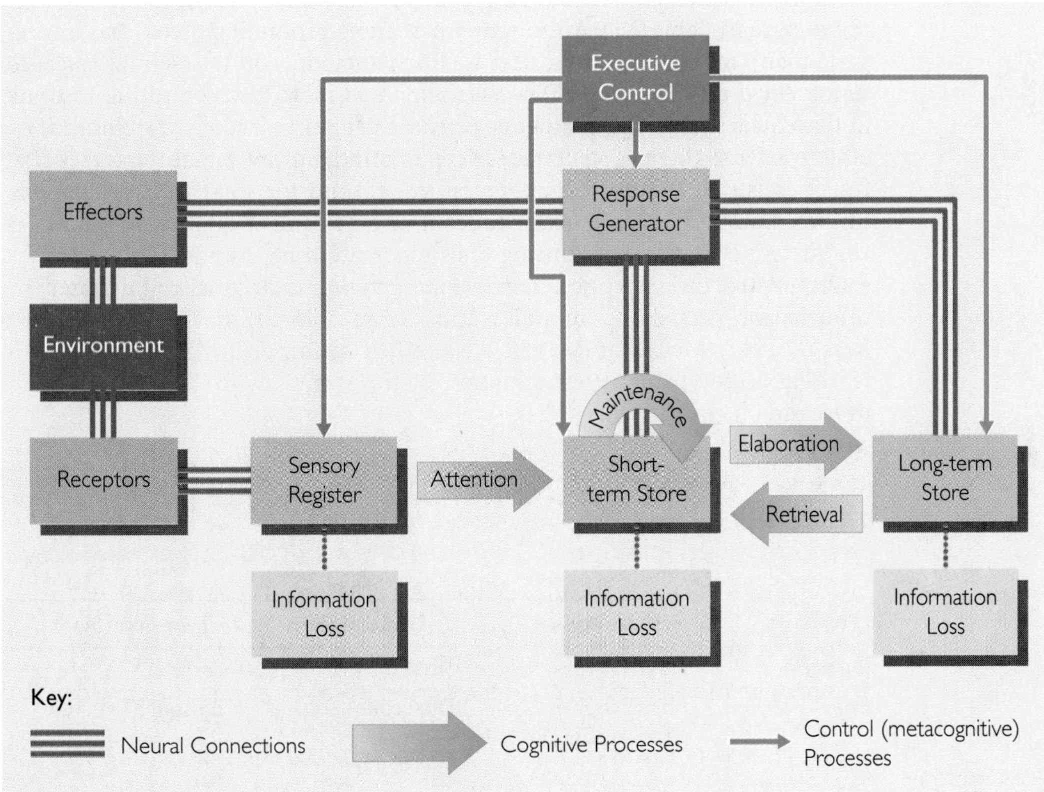

FIGURE 7.1

The Human Information-Processing Model

Source: From *Essentials of Learning for Instruction* (2nd ed., p. 13) by R. M. Gagné and M. P. Driscoll Copyright. ©1988 by Allyn and Bacon. Reprinted by permission.

From the sensory register, information that receives the learner's attention moves into *short-term store* (STS), where it meets one of four fates. Information may be lost, maintained in STS, used to make a response, or transferred by means of elaboration to long-term store.

Information reaching *long-term store* (LTS) can remain there, reenter STS through the process of retrieval, or be used to make a response. To generate a response, the learner converts cognitive information into neural messages that activate effectors. *Effectors* are the muscle systems that produce a response, such as speaking, writing, or moving in a specified way. The effectors are the physical means by which the learner operates on the environment.

Finally, *executive control* monitors the flow of information throughout the system. It governs the use of various processes to transform, store, and retrieve information. The monitoring and governing functions are executed by means of control processes.

Following the trail of information takes us from the environment (stimulus input), through the cognitive mechanism of the learner, and finally back to the environment (response output).

Information-processing theory is a stage theory, postulating that information goes through a series of transformations as it passes through the cognitive system (Table 7.1). Although information-processing theory has undergone many modifications since it was first introduced, its essential stages—sensory register, STS, and LTS—have remained intact. It is tempting to think of these stages as having analogous physical structures in the brain. Indeed, we tend to refer to them as structures. Keep in mind, however, that the stages represent constructs made up by theorists to account for what seems to happen to information as people learn. Indeed, as more and more brain research is conducted, evidence is mounting that information is processed in parallel by multiple structures at once, rather than serially as originally illustrated by information-processing models (Iran-Nejad, Marsh, & Clements, 1992; Kesner, 1991; McClelland, 1988). Nonetheless, important implications for teaching accrue from an examination of the stages involved in information processing.

TABLE 7.1 Summary of Memory Stages

	Stages		
Properties	**Sensory Register**	**Short-Term Store**	**Long-Term Store**
Capacity	Large	Small	Large
Code	Literal copy of physical stimulus	Dual code —verbal —visual	Episodic/semantic
Permanence	0.5 seconds	20–30 seconds	Permanent
Source	Environment	Environment and prior knowledge	Effective encodings from STS
Loss	Decay	Displacement or decay	Irretrievability

Transferring Information in the Sensory Register

The sensory register is the memory stage most closely connected to the information in the learner's environment. The sensory register stores information in a form that is very close to the physical stimulus, a literal copy of the input. For example, when you are listening to a friend speak, the information in your sensory register takes the form of sounds, not words. You turn those sounds into words at a later stage of processing.

Example: Information from the environment enters the sensory register, where it must be selectively attended to and perceived for it to be transferred to short-term store.

The information in the sensory register is not very durable. Information can reside in the sensory register for about one-half of a second (Houston, 1986), and it decays quickly unless further processing takes place.

Although the sensory register holds information in an undeveloped state for only the briefest period, its capacity is quite large. A lot of information from the environment enters the sensory register. At any time, an incredible amount of information is available for a learner to process. A student sitting in a classroom receives sensory information from the teacher, a neighbor's whisper, the chalkboard, the bulletin board, the ticking of the clock, the aroma from the cafeteria, the buzz in the lights, the breeze from the window, the clouds rolling by, the graffiti on the desk. All of that information enters the student's sensory register, but not all of it is being noticed by the student. It is only the information that is noticed that moves on to STS.

Gaining Attention. For students to process information further, they must pay attention to important aspects of the information. In the information-processing model, attention is a process that acts on information to transform it in some way. Attention determines which information is transferred from the sensory register to STS and which information is not. What causes a learner to attend to information?

Critical Thinking: A third-grade student is fascinated by large machines. One morning, a road crew begins drilling outside the school. The usually attentive student cannot concentrate and watches out of the window even during free time. What will the teacher do when he or she realizes that the machines are the explanation for the student's inattentiveness?

Attention can be engaged selectively or automatically. **Selective attention** is under the control of the learner. Learners have the ability to orient their cognitive effort toward a particular source of information in the environment. A student in a classroom can make a conscious effort to attend to the speech and actions of the teacher. A student can also direct his or her attention to other information available in the classroom environment.

Imagine, for example, that you are a member of a discussion group for the class in which you are reading this book (you may actually remember a similar episode to the one we describe). There are twelve discussion groups in the room, each consisting of between three and six people. The task is to develop recommendations for teaching based on the developmental theories discussed in Chapter 2. Each group is to examine recommendations for elementary, middle, or high school. You have unwittingly joined a group that is discussing elementary school, while you plan to teach high school. As a consequence, you pay less attention to the discussion than perhaps you should. You do at least look at the other members in the group as they speak, and from time to time, you nod in reaction to particular comments. You are allocating just enough attention to the discussion so that you can nod, but you are not really following what is being said. Rather, you are listening to a conversation that is occurring in the group adjacent to yours. A woman in the adjacent group is describing her recent experience trying out a lesson plan she developed for a high school history class.

selective attention The process of attention whereby the learner chooses to focus on a particular source of information from the environment.

You selectively attend to the high school teaching story at the expense of recommendations for elementary school teaching. Should a group member ask you for your opinion on a particular strategy, you would be at a loss for an answer. The reason is that selective attention, the gatekeeper of STS, uses up some of the limited capacity available in STS. Attending to some aspects of the environment precludes the processing of other information.

You continue your nodding at the elementary school discussion while attending to the high school story when, three groups over, you hear someone mention your name. Suddenly, you hear neither the elementary school discussion nor the high school story as you strain to hear what is being said in that faraway group. The switch of attention, a cognitive phenomenon, is almost a physical sensation. You can almost feel your ear growing in the direction of your name.

Why did you hear your name spoken? You have no idea what was said just prior to the mention of your name, but suddenly, you hear the conversation quite clearly. The explanation is **automatic attention**—processing information without effort.

The conversation occurring three groups away has been entering your sensory register. (Remember, sensory register has a large capacity.) Prior to the mention of your name, you were not attending to that conversation. Therefore, the conversation did not enter your STS. The mention of your name automatically drew your attention. The conversation thus became part of the information in your STS, a part of your consciousness. Information is transferred from the sensory register to the STS by means of the process of attention, which can occur in either a selective or an automatic fashion.

Try This: Interview teachers for the strategies they use to direct student attention. What are similarities and differences in their strategies? What effect do the strategies appear to have on students' learning?

Controlling, or at least guiding, the attention of students is something teachers attempt every hour of every school day. Reflect on the teachers whom you have had who were adept at keeping your attention focused on the content of the class. Reflect on those teachers who could direct your attention to themselves but not to the material you were supposed to learn. Reflect on those teachers who did not control your attention at all. Finally, consider the ways in which you control and direct your own attention. Effective learners employ a variety of strategies for attending to important aspects of instruction.

Perceiving Information. Gaining attention is a necessary condition of information processing but not a sufficient one. Students must also appropriately perceive information, recognizing familiar patterns that can serve as a basis for further processing. Children learning to read, for example, must be able to perceive the input *b* as the letter *b* and not the letter *d* in order to correctly interpret certain words. **Selective perception** is the process of selectively attending to specific features of the stimulus information in order to process it further. Perception is influenced by the nature of the stimulus itself, by the tendency of the cognitive system to organize and find meaning in stimulus inputs, and by the context in which a given stimulus appears.

To illustrate, examine the symbols shown below.

-    )   :

Chances are that you recognized, from their physical shapes, that these symbols represent a dash, a parenthesis, and a colon, respectively. Now look at the same symbols in the following rearranged format. What do you perceive?

:-)

automatic attention The process of attention that occurs without effort.

selective perception The process of selectively attending to important aspects or details in stimulus information in order to process them further.

Insights ON SUCCESSFUL PRACTICE

What strategies have you used successfully to help students process information and retain learning?

Every teacher encounters the problem of students not being able to remember what they learned last week, last month, last quarter, or last semester. It is a typical problem. Students remember what they need to recall for the next test and then promptly forget the material. Then when cumulative tests come, students fall apart. They do not seem to remember material they should readily have at their fingertips. Whether the test is a teacher-made exam or a national standard of measurement, students and teachers look bad.

There is a solution, however. It is a game called "Around the World" that teachers and students can enjoy. Played daily or whenever time permits, the game can be adapted to all subjects and age levels. There are virtually no limits to how the game can be employed.

Simply stated, the teacher calls out questions and students answer. Two randomly selected students seated next to each other begin. They stand and the teacher asks a question such as "What is the continent on which we live called?" The first of the two students to say "North America" wins and advances to the next student. That student stands to face the challenger. The teacher asks another question. If the student who previously won wins again, he or she advances to the third student. If not, that student sits down in the seat of the second student, and the second student advances. The game continues for several rounds or as long as time permits. Each student tries to go "Around the World" or around the classroom by defeating all the other students. A prize may be offered for doing so.

Competition requiring calculations takes students to the chalkboard. With chalk in hand, the two competitors listen to the problem and work it as quickly as possible. When they are finished, they step back and point to the correct answer. If neither is correct, the teacher might allow students to work the problem again. Normally, whoever finishes first with the correct answer challenges the next student. Variations could include letting one-half of the room challenge the other half. Points for right answers are tallied. Sometimes, points are awarded to both teams if students come up with correct answers within a certain time limit.

"Around the World" works beautifully with English grammar questions. A teacher might ask students to find the verb in the sentence "John walked to school" or the proper noun in the sentence "I asked Mary to come to the game." In science, questions could focus on scientific terms, body systems, parts of the universe, or animals and their habitats. Social studies is perhaps the easiest subject in which to formulate questions because there is seemingly no end to the number of geography questions a teacher can generate.

There really are no limits to this game. Teachers and students will see its advantages immediately and think up a number of variations. If played regularly, students will remember material from earlier classes and surprise themselves and test administrators with the knowledge they have accumulated.

WILLIAM D. SMYTH, Charleston County School District, Charleston, South Carolina

How does this teacher's "Around the World" game work to facilitate the retention of learning? Would this approach be appropriate for all kinds of learning? What might be some advantages and disadvantages of classroom competitions?

Arranged together in this way, the symbols appear to form a smiling face oriented sideways. Even though the physical stimulus inputs have remained the same, you perceived them differently. This demonstrates the tendency of the human cognitive system to form a *gestalt*, or a meaningful interpretation of physical patterns. Finally, the influence of context on perception can be seen in the following sentence.

> I love the month of March, because that's when
> the cold snows of winter give way to flowers in the
> the spring.

Did you detect the error in this sentence? Chances are you read right over the second *the* in the part of the sentence that reads "flowers in the *the* spring." Prior knowledge sets up expectations for perception, so that students perceive what they expect the stimulus information to be. This is why, for example, proofreading is such a difficult task. It requires paying attention to the stimulus input of letters, while at the same time ignoring the meaning their arrangement provides.

Critical Thinking: A kindergarten teacher begins each math session with a game. She asks certain students to stand up, choosing the students by a particular attribute: patterns in seating, initials, colors of clothing, eyes, hair, types of shoes. The other students guess why the students are standing. Why would this game help young students with mathematics?

To facilitate selective perception, teachers draw students' attention to particular features in the instruction that are important to process further. In reading, students learn to distinguish similar letters. They also learn to use contextual information to interpret the meanings of unfamiliar words in sentences or paragraphs. In science, students learn to perceive the units of measurement on graduated cylinders. In music, students learn to distinguish the sounds of different instruments, different scales, and different rhythms.

here's how

Here's How to Gain Attention and Facilitate Selective Perception

- Use gestures, voice inflections, and other signals to alert students and indicate important points in the lesson.
- Ask questions to stimulate curiosity and interest in the lesson.
- Tell students what they will learn in the lesson to establish an expectancy for learning. Help them to find relevance in the lesson to their own interests and goals.
- Compare and contrast similar features to help students focus on essential details.

Encoding Information in the Short-Term Store (STS)

working memory In some models, another term for STS because this is the stage at which a learner works on information from the environment.

encoding The process of converting a message from the environment to a cognitive code so that the information can be stored and later remembered.

In some versions of the information-processing model, STS is called **working memory** (cf. Bell-Gredler, 1986); STS is where the learner *works on* the information from the environment. In STS the learner encodes information: Sounds become spoken words, visual patterns on a page become written words.

To *encode* means to convert a message into a code. In information-processing theory, **encoding** is the process of converting a message from the environment to a cognitive code so that the information can be stored and later remembered (Kulhavy, Schwartz, & Peterson, 1986). Encoding is one kind of work done in STS, and from an instructional perspective, it is the most important. Making codes—constructing cognitive representations—is the primary business of the human cognitive mechanism. This is the work we want our students to do in our classrooms. The codes that learners create in STS allow them to say they understand or do not understand the material that has been presented to them. The codes also allow students to perform tasks of varying complexity.

As we have already discovered, information from the environment arrives in STS through the sensory register. The knowledge that allows us to encode sensory input is stored in LTS. Creating meaningful codes requires integration of information from the environment with the knowledge stored in LTS. STS is a busy place because it is where what students know comes together with the information they are to learn.

Example: The making of meaning occurs in STS. It is in STS that information from the environment is brought together with prior knowledge—that is, information from LTS.

Another reason why STS is such a busy place is that it has a limited capacity. If you have ever had thirty students all asking you questions at the same time, you know what limited capacity means. In his classic article, Miller (1956) identified the capacity of STS at about seven pieces of information. Pieces of information are known technically as "chunks." Chunks may not sound much like a scientific term, but it is a good descriptor. What follows is a row of numbers, fifteen pieces of information—DON'T LOOK YET. Study the digits for about ten seconds and then cover the list with your hand. Here are the fifteen digits you will be asked to remember in order:

Connection: Effective encoding depends upon prior knowledge, which is discussed in greater detail later in this chapter.

1 4 9 1 6 2 5 3 6 4 9 6 4 8 1

Now, with the list covered, see how many of the digits you can remember in order. (By the way, if you cheated and looked ahead at the digits, try this little experiment with a friend by reading the numbers to him or her.)

If you tried to process each digit separately, you were taxing the limit of your STS. As a result, you probably did not recall all of the digits. If you grouped the digits into two- or three-digit numbers (e.g., 149, 162), you probably recalled more of the information. Grouping the digits into numbers is an example of chunking (Miller, 1956; Simon, 1974). When the digits are chunked, the number of pieces of information to remember is reduced. The amount of information per se has not changed, but the limited capacity of STS has been used more efficiently. This is especially true if the chunks form a meaningful pattern. Can you detect a pattern in these numbers?

Reflection: In what ways do you chunk information to make it easier to learn? Are these strategies useful for teaching as well as learning?

An item of information in STS can last for approximately twenty to thirty seconds (Miller, 1956; Peterson & Peterson, 1959). Items may not last that long if they are displaced by new information arriving from the sensory register. Have you ever tried to take verbatim notes during a lecture? As you will see, there are a number of reasons why this isn't a good way to learn. In the context of STS, the problem with transcribing is that it taxes capacity. Unless you are a very fast writer, you are working on the new information that the lecturer is presenting while attempting to remember old information long enough to write it down on paper. We have all tried this kind of note taking at one time or another; most of us gave it up about the time we realized that we had very little idea of what the lecturer was trying to convey.

Try This: Observe students in middle and high school as they take notes in class. Are they attempting to take verbatim notes? What can you infer about their learning?

Items in STS can be maintained for longer than thirty seconds if they are rehearsed (Anderson & Craik, 1974). Rehearsing information in order to maintain it in STS has a positive side effect. Rehearsal can lead to the transfer of information from STS to LTS. Transfer is not guaranteed, but the longer information is rehearsed, the more likely it will be transformed to LTS (cf. Atkinson & Shiffrin, 1971; Jacoby & Bartz, 1972).

These students will remember their lines through maintenance rehearsal. At the same time they will encode key elements of the play, such as plot sequence and characterization. Based on this knowledge, their capacity for elaborative rehearsal will enable them to improvise if they forget their lines during a performance.

Maintenance Rehearsal. Maintenance and elaboration are the two process arrows that originate in STS (see Figure 7.1). **Maintenance rehearsal** maintains the availability of information in STS by keeping it activated. Repeating a telephone number over and over to maintain the information long enough to dial it is maintenance rehearsal. With enough rehearsal, it is possible to transfer the information to LTS. You've probably stored a lot of information in LTS simply because of repetition. Do you remember a poem you once learned in high school? Or portions of the Gettysburg Address? Through sheer repetition—maintenance rehearsal—the information may have been stored in LTS.

Example: To learn, it is necessary to remember information. However, memorization is not always the learning goal.

Maintenance rehearsal is a type of encoding that could be called brute force learning. Repeating information doesn't guarantee that information will be stored permanently, but it can lead to permanent storage. Information stored in this way, however, may not be all that meaningful.

Memory does not equate understanding. How many times have you memorized a formula or a definition of some concept that you did not truly understand? Maintenance rehearsal, or rote memorization, is helpful or necessary in many situations, both in and out of the classroom. For example, students can solve many types of arithmetic problems quickly and easily when they have committed the multiplication tables to memory. For most people, this requires maintenance rehearsal. Likewise, maintenance rehearsal is useful for learning spelling rules, the genders of French and Spanish nouns, and the dates of historic events. However, because many of the learning outcomes we seek for students are outcomes of understanding, another type of encoding is required, elaborative rehearsal.

Example: Elaborative rehearsal may take more effort than maintenance at the point of encoding, but in the long run it is a more efficient learning tactic.

Elaborative Rehearsal. **Elaborative rehearsal** is a type of encoding that relates new information to information already stored. The stimulus information becomes transformed because the learner elaborates it in some way (cf. Driscoll, 1994). A student, after reading a description of a concept, might generate an example of that concept. Another student might create a mental picture of stimulus information, such as the solar system in order to visualize the relative distances planets are from the sun. Stimulus information might be supplemented with additional information that aids recall—for example, learning to spell *arithmetic* by memorizing the sentence, "a rat in the house may eat the ice cream."

maintenance rehearsal Rote memorization, which does not guarantee understanding.

elaborative rehearsal A type of encoding that relates new information to information already in LTS.

Do you recall learning the names of the Great Lakes? Perhaps your teacher wrote the names of the lakes on the chalkboard:

Huron
Ontario
Michigan
Erie
Superior

Your teacher, after writing the names on the board, may have asked the class to look closely at the names. "Does anyone in the class notice anything about the names of the Great Lakes? Don't answer aloud, but does anyone notice something about the first letters of each lake? Look at the first letters and see if they form a word. What is the word?" Using the word HOMES to store the names of the Great Lakes is a form of elaborative rehearsal known as a **mnemonic device**, specifically an acronym.

Whether you, as a teacher, decide to use maintenance rehearsal or elaborative rehearsal in the classroom has important implications for the way students will encode information effectively. The teacher who asks students to continually repeat information takes on an additional burden: Drill and practice can be boring. Using maintenance rehearsal as an instructional technique makes it hard to maintain a high level of attention in the classroom. It is easier to keep students interested and on task if they are transforming information rather than merely repeating it.

Another implication of your choice relates to students' cognitive efforts. Both maintenance and elaboration require STS capacity, but the student who elaborates is doing more with information than the student who merely maintains. Maintenance rehearsal occurs in STS. Maintenance rehearsal may cause information to be transferred to LTS, but the encoding itself is an STS activity. Elaboration requires the use of knowledge in LTS. In order to integrate stimulus information with prior knowledge, prior knowledge must be transferred from LTS to STS.

Connection: Mnemonic devices are discussed in greater detail later in this chapter.

Reflection: Think about times you have used maintenance and elaborative rehearsal in learning. What was the result in each case? Which was more effective in helping you to achieve a learning goal?

Try This: Begin a list of all the means of elaborative rehearsal you have found effective in helping you learn. How might you employ these strategies with your students?

Retrieving Information from Long-Term Store (LTS)

LTS is considered to be the permanent store of the human information-processing system (Driscoll, 1994). LTS houses many different kinds of information: episodes that you have experienced in childhood, facts, abstract rules that allow you to understand language, strategies for solving problems, smells, sounds, tastes, feelings, and visual images. There is information in LTS that you may not know is there.

"How many windows were in the house or apartment in which you were raised?" Our guess is that no one has ever asked you for that information. Therefore you have never retrieved it from your LTS. The number of windows is not the kind of information you use every day, but let us see if we can find the information somewhere in the recesses of your LTS.

First, picture in your mind the house or apartment that you grew up in. Do you have the place in mind? If it had multiple stories, concentrate on the main floor. Now, imagine that you are inside your childhood home. Picture yourself just inside the front door. As you stand there, turn to your right. Now begin walking around the main floor. If there is a wall, follow it to an opening. If there are doors, open them and proceed slowly. Walk through all of the rooms on that floor and look out each window, keeping track of the number of windows you encounter. How many windows are there?

LTS contains much of what we learned intentionally and much that we never made a conscious effort to learn. As learners, we bring the contents of our LTS to

Critical Thinking: Why might feelings of anger, happiness, envy, or love help lock memories in LTS? What poems or phrases have you memorized, and what triggers bring them forth?

mnemonic device A technique for remembering that connects new information with prior knowledge.

school with us. Our experiences are represented there. Our knowledge is represented there. We call that knowledge and experience prior knowledge.

Retrieval. Retrieval is the process that transfers information from LTS to STS. It is the utilization of stored information. For information stored in LTS to be used by the learner, it must be brought into working memory. How is information stored in LTS brought to bear on stimulus information being encoded in STS? What can a teacher do to facilitate retrieval? Recall the teacher who used the word HOMES to help students elaboratively encode the names of the Great Lakes. At some later time, the teacher will be able to use HOMES as an effective retrieval cue. The cue—HOMES—is specific to the encoding of the names of the Great Lakes.

Another connection between encoding and retrieval is evidenced by the nature of the codes created during elaborative encoding. The prior knowledge a learner retrieves in order to make sense of incoming information influences the comprehension of the stimulus. For example, students use their general knowledge about war to interpret an account in the local newspaper about an armed conflict in a particular region of the world. Although the report may include no information about atrocities perpetrated by the aggressors, students are likely to believe that these acts took place nonetheless. They infer from previously learned information meanings that are not explicitly presented.

Example: Inferential comprehension, which involves reconstructive retrieval, is an important milestone in the development of fluent reading.

Try This: Identify a topic you anticipate teaching in your own classroom. Think about how you will conceptualize the topic. Describe from a student's point of view how he or she might process the information you give, allowing him or her to conceptualize the topic.

Reconstructive Retrieval. Although cues, such as the HOMES acronym, can make retrieval very efficient, some information in LTS is not so readily available. Earlier you were asked to retrieve the number of windows in your childhood home. The cues we provided to help you retrieve that information were not memory tricks (like HOMES) or something you inferred (e.g., that "aggressors perpetrated atrocities on their victims"). Instead, we suggested that you create a visual image of your home, which helped you to reconstruct the information you were asked to retrieve.

Retrieval of this sort can be viewed as a type of problem solving. The learner uses logic, retrieval cues, and prior knowledge to reconstruct information (Lindsay & Norman, 1977). Reconstructive retrieval is highly sensitive to the particular knowledge and experiences stored in a learner's LTS. In reading and remembering the details of a story set in Alaska, for example, students who live in Hawaii or Florida are likely to construct and retrieve understandings that differ from those of students who live in Maine.

Instructionally, when you help students solve the problem of accessing information you help them make sense of the material they are to learn, facilitating the process of retrieval. The knowledge students retrieve from LTS influences their understanding.

retrieval The process that transfers information from LTS to STS in order to be used.

prior knowledge Knowledge that has already been acquired and stored in long-term memory.

WHY IS IT IMPORTANT TO ACTIVATE STUDENTS' PRIOR KNOWLEDGE?

Prior knowledge—knowledge that has already been acquired—influences the quality and quantity of what students learn. Human beings intuitively understand that prior knowledge is useful in understanding new information. Recall a time in high school when you were listening to a teacher's explanation of some concept. If its meaning somehow eluded you, what did you do? You probably

Insights ON SUCCESSFUL PRACTICE

What memory games or mnemonic devices have you used successfully to help students remember information?

One of several junior high teaching positions that I have held was in a larger inner-city school. While the students were classified as mildly learning impaired, they were all from economically disadvantaged homes where learning was not valued. The students lacked motivation and seemed to be merely marking time until they were able to drop out. They offered a challenge to teachers to make learning opportunities not only meaningful but also exciting and memorable.

I relied largely on the use of mnemonics to make learning "stick" and found they were successful because the students enjoyed using them. Mnemonics are those wonderful devices that place memory tracers on essential but seemingly unrelated bits of Information. Just as metaphors are devices to make the unfamiliar seem familiar, mnemonics are devices to make the illogical seem logical. In whatever manner teachers make use of mnemonics, research has shown them to be very effective as teaching devices—not just for classrooms, but I use them personally. My favorite, which I use every time I have to replace a lightbulb or put a screw in a fixture is "Righty, tighty. Lefty, loosey." Another mnemonic I use regularly is one to help remember the spelling of *absence,* my own personal memory hurdle. I finally realized that "There is no *sense* in your ab*sence*."

In one of my junior high classrooms the students were relatively proficient in mathematics computation and enjoyed the challenges of multiplication. I soon noticed, however, that, without exception, when they had obtained the sum they would liberally sprinkle commas into the answer without order or meaning, as if they knew that all long figures required a few commas to be complete. I tried explaining the system for placement or commas, but without success.

One day I wrote a figure **1** on the far left side of the chalkboard, and then proceeded to follow that with zeros across three contiguous boards. I then gave each student a piece of chalk, had them line up behind me, and going from right to left we sang "One, two, three, a comma! One, two, three, a comma!," and marked commas as we conga-lined around the room. Never again did a single student misplace a comma in a computation answer. I would often notice students with heads bowed, softly saying "One, two, three, a comma!" as they counted off places in their answers.

VIRGINIA L. PEARSON,
College of Education, Wayne State University,
Detroit, Michigan

knitted your brow, raised your hand, and said something to the effect, "I don't understand what you are talking about. Could you give me another example?"

The prior knowledge learners bring to a learning situation influences their understanding of new information. Indeed, part of the understanding constructed by a student is due to his or her prior knowledge (Rumelhart, 1980; Leinhardt, 1992). Tobias (1982) argued that students' prior knowledge is the most important factor in determining the outcome of any instructional situation. Tobias suggested further that we should worry less about ability or other individual differences. Instead, we should concentrate on discovering methods of instruction that will best tap the learner's prior knowledge and capitalize on what a student brings to the lessons we are teaching.

What are mnemonic devices? According to this teacher, in what ways can they aid learning? What are some memory tricks you use to recall information? In the subject area you plan to teach, what memory aids will you teach your students?

What prior knowledge does each of these children bring to school? According to educational psychology theory and research, why is it important for teachers to ascertain students' prior knowledge?

It is important to remember that prior knowledge can inhibit learning as well as facilitate it. Have you ever tried to learn racquetball after years of playing tennis? Although both are racquet sports, the way in which the racquet is swung requires entirely different movements of the arm and wrist. As a consequence, it can be very difficult for a tennis player to learn the wrist movements required in racquetball. Leinhardt (1992) offers another example involving the use of base ten blocks (Dienes blocks) in teaching arithmetic.

Point: *Learners are diverse.* The students who come into your classroom will vary tremendously in the prior knowledge they bring with them.

Dienes blocks are very helpful in providing students with a concrete representation of regrouping in addition. When the concept of regrouping is later encountered in subtraction, those students with prior knowledge of Dienes blocks are better prepared than students without this prior knowledge. However, when students are asked to use Dienes blocks to represent decimals, their learning is often hindered. It is difficult to make the switch in meaning from a block representing, for example, one hundred to a new representation of the block meaning one-hundredth (Leinhardt, 1992).

When you begin planning lessons for your students, keep in mind this quote at the beginning of a book by Ausubel, Novak, & Hanesian (1978).

> If I had to reduce all of educational psychology to but one principle, I would say this: The most important single factor influencing learning is what the learner already knows. Ascertain this and teach him [or her] accordingly.

As a teacher you want your instructional messages to make sense to your students. If they are to do so, you must find ways to tap your students' prior knowledge, connecting the information you want them to learn with what they already know. Let's see how students mentally represent their prior experiences and examine ways teachers can build on them.

Episodic Memory

episodic memories Memories associated with specific personal experiences, including the time and place they occurred.

mental images Cognitive representations of, for example, pictures, sounds, and smells.

Episodic memories are those associated with a particular time and place or those connected with events (Tulving, 1972). The memory you have of a phone call you made this morning, the breakfast you ate, and the birthday gift you received when you were twelve years old would all be episodic memories.

Episodic information tends to be stored in the form of **mental images**. We usually think of these as visual representations (i.e., pictures in your mind), but they can be representations that involve any of your other senses as well. Can't you imagine the spicy smell of your mother's special recipe or the fumes of the school bus you used to ride?

Memories that are represented in images can also be represented verbally. For example, the memory of Shakespeare's *Macbeth* can be represented verbally, as in recalling that Lady Macbeth's "Out, out damn spot!" speech refers to blood she imagines she has on her hands and that she rubs over and over to get off. But if one sees the play performed, the speech is likely to be remembered as well in a vivid image of the experience.

The existence in memory of multiple codes is the essence of **dual-code theory** (Paivio, 1971, 1975, 1978). Two systems are assumed to represent information in memory, one for verbal information and the other for nonverbal, or imaginal, information. When both systems are used to represent a particular piece of information, as in Lady Macbeth's speech, memory for the event will be particularly strong.

Critical Thinking: A teacher begins a review session with the question, "Who can remember what we were doing when we talked about ellipses?" Why might this be an effective retrieval method for some students.

The organization of images in memory is based on the temporal and spatial relations of events. As evidence of these time and space relations around which episodic information is organized, imagine yourself in the following situation:

You are taking a multiple-choice test. You have gone through the exam, completing all of the items that you are sure of. Now you are contemplating an item that has two plausible alternatives: A and C. You ponder the alternatives, knowing that you read the pertinent information somewhere in the text. You try to recall exactly what you read. You can't seem to remember what you read, but you do know that it was located on the upper left-hand part of the page.

Why is it that you remember the location of the information, but not the information itself? You search memory in an attempt to find the specific information you need. What you recall is the location of the information you seek but not its content. Because the information is stored episodically, it is natural for the spatial nature of the information to be retrieved.

Reflection: Recall times when you reminisced with friends or family. Identify some of the images that were elicited by those remembrances. How important were those images in remembering?

Many episodic experiences follow a pattern (e.g., one family dinner is very much like any other family dinner). Because many events fit into the same pattern, the distinctiveness of each specific instance is lost. A departure from the pattern can make one episode very distinctive and therefore easily remembered. For example, people tend to remember where they were and what they were doing when they heard about history-making or catastrophic events.

Critical Thinking: How might a teacher use unusual experiences to teach material effectively?

To take advantage of episodic memory, teachers can include distinctive and interesting events in their lessons as a context for learning information and skills. In learning about geography, for example, students on an excursion who walked through the mud of a mangrove shore, waded in the sea, and tasted foliage for salinity remembered more than students whose guides merely pointed out geographic areas of interest (MacKenzie & White, 1982). Likewise, acting out scenes from *Macbeth* can enhance literature students' memory for aspects of the play, and designing a space station can provide a distinctive context for learning history, science, mathematics, and nutrition.

Semantic Memory

Semantic memories differ in nature from memories of specific episodes. Semantic memories make up one's general knowledge, for example, that "*i* comes before *e*, except after *c*" and that "what goes up must come down." When and where did you learn those rules? Most of us know many rules but have forgotten the exact circumstances in which we acquired them.

For the most part, we structure the memory of our experiences around certain patterns. These stored patterns tend to subsume the details of those experiences.

dual-code theory The assumption of two systems of memory representation, one for verbal information and one for nonverbal, or imaginal, information.

semantic memories Memories of facts and general knowledge but not including the time and place they were learned.

We can remember the general pattern, but we lose the autobiographical tags of these events. Each general pattern of experience is stored in memory as a knowledge structure. Just how knowledge structures are organized in memory, and how they are modified or used, has been a matter of some debate among memory theorists. Proposals for the structure of knowledge in memory have ranged from vast conceptual networks (cf. Anderson, 1983, 1990) to connections among subsymbolic units (called parallel distributed processing models; cf. McClelland, Rumelhart, & the PDP Research Group, 1986).

Two related structures in which knowledge is hypothesized to be organized are the schema and the mental model. The term *schema* is used in much the same way that Piaget used the idea of scheme. (For a review of Piaget's theory, see Chapter 2.) Concepts that we acquire as the result of various experiences are thought to be stored as schemata. Richard C. Anderson (1977) provides a clear description.

> A **schema** represents generic knowledge; that is, it represents what is believed to be generally true of a class of things, events, or situations. A schema is conceived to contain a slot or a place holder for each component. For instance, a Face schema includes slots for a mouth, nose, eyes, and ears. (p. 2, emphasis added)

Take as an example an event schema. By the time they graduate from high school, students have had considerable experience taking standardized tests. They know that no materials except pencils are permitted at the test site, that no talking is allowed, that a certain type of answer sheet is used, and that they will work on each subtest for a specified amount of time. If they were to appear for a test and find the desks arranged in groups of four, they would be surprised. Their expectations for standardized test taking would be violated.

Students understand new experiences and new information in terms of the schemas they already possess. What students understand as they read their textbooks, for example, depends on their text structure schemas, such as compare/contrast, cause/effect, and problem/solution (Armbruster, 1986). When information is presented in ways that fit students' expectations, their comprehension of the information is enhanced. To help students comprehend unfamiliar information, teachers can provide practice in recognizing and interpreting different types of text structures. Similarly, students solve arithmetic word problems more effectively when they access relevant schemas for particular problem types (DeCorte, Verschaffel, & De Win, 1985; Cooper & Sweller, 1987). Helping students to recognize and represent problem types in arithmetic leads to their greater ability to solve a variety of problems (Lewis, 1989; Fuson & Willis, 1989).

Try This: Interview students to construct a representation of their mental models of using a calculator (or word processor, or some other concept/principle of interest to you). How might you use their representations to inform your teaching of that concept?

schema A mental structure for organizing information and representing knowledge. Any set of objects, experiences, or actions that is consistently classified forms a schema.

mental model A schema-based representation of experience, including perceptions of task demands and task performances.

A **mental model** is a schema-based representation of experience, but it also includes a learner's perceptions of task demands and task performances. A mental model governs how a person approaches a learning task. You can see this in the following illustration of a mental model in action. Norman (1983) studied how people used handheld calculators and offered this description:

> One of the subjects I studied (on a four-function calculator) was quite cautious. Her mental model seemed to contain information about her own limitations and the classes of errors that she could make. She commented, "I always take extra steps. I never take short cuts." She was always careful to clear the calculator before starting the problem, hitting the clear button several times. She wrote down partial results even when they could have been stored in the machine memory. (p. 8)

Students approach learning tasks with mental models that are usually incomplete, idiosyncratic, and utilitarian. Remember the preference for simple rules that has been observed in young children (see Chapter 2). The same is true with mental models. Students will cling to understandings that have served them well in the past, even though these may contain contradictory, erroneous, or unnecessary concepts (Driscoll, 1994).

In order to build effectively on students' prior knowledge, teachers must ascertain the mental models they possess, which means getting in touch with the naive or informal knowledge students have about things (Prawatt, 1989). Armed with this information, teachers can help students to see inherent contradictions or errors in their naive theories by explicitly modeling and providing guided practice in more accurate conceptions (cf. Gagné & Glaser, 1987).

Critical Thinking: Give another example of an event schema and describe its contents.

Procedural Memory

Prior knowledge that includes knowledge of how to do things is called **procedural knowledge**. Procedural knowledge is thought to be stored as a series of stimulus–response pairings. Assume that you have procedural knowledge of how to ride a bike. It is difficult to explain the procedure verbally, but it is easy to demonstrate it. It is also difficult to engage in the correct bike-riding responses unless a bike is part of the stimulus situation. If you doubt this, put down your book and try to display bike-riding behavior without a bike.

The stimulus-response pairings stored as part of procedural knowledge allow learners to respond to certain stimuli automatically. You jump into water and start to swim (if swimming procedures are stored). Procedural knowledge is acquired through practice. With enough practice, the appropriate responses are stored permanently and can be retrieved automatically, without conscious effort.

Although procedural knowledge is a large part of motor skills, it is also involved in many cognitive tasks. For example, knowing how to multiply and divide are examples of procedural knowledge. Knowing how to construct grammatical sentences while speaking is another example of procedural knowledge. It is important for this type of procedural knowledge to become automatic. In speaking, for example, we want to concentrate on the meaning of what to say, not on how to say it. Similarly, when procedural knowledge in mathematics or other subject areas becomes automatic, it facilitates solving problems. Many experts cannot tell you how they solved a complex problem in their fields, but they know their solution is accurate.

Conditional Memory

Prior knowledge also includes knowledge of when and how to use certain schemas and/or procedural knowledge. A student may have the procedural knowledge that allows him or her to read fluently. But some reading tasks may require that a text be skimmed rather than read closely. Conditional knowledge allows a student to match procedures and semantic knowledge to the task at hand (Schunk, 1991).

This kind of regulation of knowledge and processes is referred to as **metacognition**, which means, literally, cognition about cognition (Flavell, 1985). One metacognitive function is the application of conditional knowledge. For example, a student who has learned to skim a textbook to locate desired information could skim the newspaper at home for information about his or her favorite sports team. Another function of metacognition is to monitor and

procedural knowledge Prior knowledge that involves knowing how to do something.

metacognition Knowledge about thinking, and the capability to monitor one's own cognitive processing, such as thinking, learning, and remembering.

Example: Students who are metacognitively aware can think critically and reflectively about what they know and the ways in which they learn.

evaluate thinking processes. Students who are metacognitively aware question their comprehension of ideas and make decisions about how to study based not only on the material to be learned but also on their own cognitive strengths and weaknesses.

Instructionally, metacognition is referred to as learning how to learn. Students learn specific strategies for controlling their own processes of attention, encoding, and retrieval in order to attain particular goals. A teacher interested in encouraging metacognition might have students read a humorous story or a set of instructions or listen to a lecture at the planetarium or a political debate. A discussion of purposes for listening or reading would precede the event (e.g., enjoyment, specific directions, concepts, decision making). When students can distinguish between reading for enjoyment and reading for making a decision, then these different concepts can be applied to other learning situations from which students will derive further benefit (Schunk, 1991).

here's how

Here's How to Facilitate Metacognitive Awareness in Your Students and Help Them Use Conditional Knowledge Effectively

- Demonstrate a variety of strategies to help students attend to, encode, remember, and retrieve information.
- Point out when, where, and why a given strategy is effective.
- Provide opportunities for students to practice using strategies. Complex or involved strategies may require extensive practice to be used effectively.
- Remind students to use strategies. Younger or less experienced students are less likely than older or more experienced students to use the strategies they know.
- Provide positive feedback when students use strategies appropriately. This serves to reinforce students and to enhance their awareness of when strategies will help them learn.

Try This: Observe a class to discover ways in which teachers encourage students to use metacognitive skills.

HOW CAN YOU HELP STUDENTS TO REMEMBER WHAT THEY LEARN?

Learning outcomes are the joint product of what students know when they enter a classroom and the instruction they encounter while they are there. What should this instruction be to make the most of what students already know? The answer depends on the desired outcomes. Are students supposed to simply remember information? Are they supposed to create concepts, solve problems, apply a procedure, or make judgments? We want students to acquire high-level outcomes that characterize skilled performance within a knowledge domain. In many cases, however, students must be able to remember information before they can pursue other goals.

Enhancing Imagery

Imagery is a form of elaborative encoding. Mental images are mental pictures, sounds, smells, and so on. We can retrieve mental images that are already in LTS, as in the exercise to count your windows that prompted you to conjure a mental image. We can also construct images during encoding to help us remember information better (see Corbett, 1977).

When students generate their own images to help them remember things, they are actively processing information. The more active students are in processing information, the more likely it is that they will retain and elaborate on that information. When using images for instructional purposes, it is important to keep in mind the distinction between interactive and noninteractive images.

Reflection: Identify a key concept or information that you anticipate teaching. What kinds of instructions might you give your students to help them generate images of the key points?

Let's suppose, for example, that a teacher begins a history lesson on the Wars of the Roses. Some children may create an image to represent these wars on their own. They may start with two visual symbols, a white rose for the Yorks and a red rose for the Lancasters. Picturing the roses separately would be a noninteractive image of the two symbols. An interactive image could have the Yorks' white rose to the north and the Lancasters' red rose to the south scratching England with their tangled thorns.

Although the generation of images by students is a more active form of processing, evidence suggests that images provided by a teacher can also be beneficial (Wollen & Lowry, 1974). Either their own or a teacher's images can help students make connections between the material to be learned and their prior knowledge. Most of the research on the use of imagery as a memory aid has dealt with fairly simple stimuli. Even so, there exists compelling evidence that interactive imagery is more beneficial as a retention aid than separation imagery and that both of these types of imagery seem to work better than no imagery at all (Houston, 1986).

The ability to generate images develops along with other cognitive abilities. Young children can benefit from images provided by a teacher for use during learning, but they cannot readily generate images of their own (Reese, 1977). As children develop, they become more effective in generating their own images than in using those provided by a teacher. The more cognitively advanced students become, the more likely it will be that images introduced by an instructor will interfere with the tendency to generate images on their own.

You might want to give your students practice in developing mental images. Have them select vocabulary words and draw pictures of what these concepts mean to them. In a seventh-grade science class, for example, students drew images of concepts such as mass, energy, and force, which facilitated their understanding when it came to applying these concepts in solving problems.

Using Mnemonic Devices

As mentioned previously, **mnemonic devices** are techniques that help us to organize or elaborate information we wish to retain. Mnemonics works by relating the information to be remembered to well-known or familiar information (Houston, 1986; Norman, 1968). Although we think of mnemonics as procedures that help improve one's memory, the word *mnemonics* also refers to the art of memory, which served an important function for the ancient Greeks. The art was taught to Greek scholars as a technique to help them remember long speeches. The mnemonic method used familiar locations as a way of organizing material.

Example: Classical scholars who developed philosophical arguments remembered them by placing key points of the arguments behind various pillars of the Parthenon.

FIGURE 7.2

Thinking, Remembering, and Problem Solving

Unlike imagery, mnemonic devices have been demonstrated to be useful for students of all ages, including preschool students (Levin, 1985; McCormick & Levin, 1987). There are at least five different types of mnemonic devices: rhymes, letter and sentence mnemonics, peg mnemonics, stories, and keyword mnemonics. Used alone, these devices have been shown to enhance memory, but imagine the effects of combining these techniques with imagery (Figure 7.2).

Rhymes. Many mnemonic devices make use of sound patterns or **rhymes.** Consider many of the memory aids you learned as a child: "Thirty days hath September, April, June, and November. . . ." "*I* before *e*, except after *c*." The rhyming pattern makes it easier to remember. Most people learn the alphabet by reciting it in a singsong manner. If you silently sing the alphabet song to yourself, you will discover that the song makes use of rhyme. The alphabet song also aids memory by virtue of its being a song (with a familiar rhythm and notes to sing). A fifth-grade teacher of our acquaintance uses the familiar theme to *The Flintstones* to teach her students the names of the countries in Central America. If you sing along, we guarantee you won't forget them either:

> Bel-ize. Guat-e-ma-la.
> Hon-duras. El Sal-va-dor.
> Nica-nica-ra-gua.
> Costa Rica and Pan-a-ma.

Example: The peg-word method is used to teach children their telephone numbers. Students also use number peg words as an aid in remembering the order of species along a phylogenetic scale. For double-digit numbers, the images are combined. For example, twelve is a "bun-shoe"; twenty-one is "shoe-bun." The visual image for twelve is a foot wearing a dinner roll. The visual image for twenty-one is a shoe inside a sliced roll, described as a shoe sandwich.

Letter and Sentence Mnemonics. A second type of mnemonics makes use of letters or sentences. The memory device we used to encode the names of the Great Lakes (HOMES) is an example of an **acronym,** or first-letter mnemonic. Another example is ROYGBIV (pronounced as a name, Roy G. Biv). This name stands for the colors of the spectrum of visible light: red, orange, yellow, green, blue, indigo, and violet. A technique very similar to the acronym is the acrostic.

An **acrostic** is a mnemonic that uses a sentence as a memory cue for information. For example, remembering the nine planets in order has traditionally been achieved by saying Men Very Easily Make Jugs Serve Useful New Purposes. Learning the notes represented by lines on a musical scale is easy when you remember the sentence, Every Good Boy Does Fine.

Peg Mnemonics. **Peg mnemonics** are mnemonic devices that make use of visual imagery. Peg mnemonics are organizational in nature. The learner uses known information as organizational pegs from which to hang new information. Some peg mnemonics require that the learner first learn the pegs and then use the pegs to remember additional information. One peg mnemonic is the method of loci mentioned earlier in reference to Greek scholars learning their speeches. (*Loci* is from the Latin word *locus*, which means "place.") The pegs used in the method of loci are familiar locations. For example, a student can be asked to remember the route he or she takes when walking home from school and to identify several distinctive landmarks along the route. With the well-known locations serving as pegs, new information can then be imagined and mentally stored. Suppose you wanted your students to learn the thirteen original colonies and the order in which they were established. The method of loci could be used to remember the names of the colonies. By placing the colonies along a familiar route, they could be recalled by mentally walking the route.

rhymes Words that are identical to others in their terminal sound.

acronym A word formed from the initial letters of a group of words (e.g., NASA).

acrostic A sentence used as a memory cue for information to be remembered.

peg mnemonics A strategy for memorization in which items of a list to be learned are associated with cue words and images.

A more direct application of the method of loci, as it was used by the Greeks, would be to store images that represent topics for an informational speech. The images would be stored in various locations around the student's home or even in the classroom in which the speech will be delivered.

Another peg mnemonic is called the peg-word method. The peg words are learned by the student for use in a variety of situations requiring sequential recall. Note that the peg words make use of rhyme.

One is a bun.
Two is a shoe.
Three is a tree.
Four is a door.
Five is a hive.
Six is sticks.
Seven is heaven.
Eight is a gate.
Nine is a line.
Ten is a hen.

Try This: Create a lesson in which you would use a mnemonic device (rhyme, acrostic, peg words, or story technique) to help students learn and remember information.

With the exception of *heaven*, the peg words are concrete. All of the peg words, however, can be easily imaged. By integrating new material with the familiar peg words, the new information can be more easily recalled. The value of this peg-word mnemonic is in remembering information in a particular sequence. The key to using this mnemonic is to learn the peg words themselves so that they can be recalled automatically.

Story Mnemonic. Another mnemonic technique that helps in recalling ordered information is the **story technique**, which combines the elements to be remembered in their correct order in a brief story. Suppose you wanted students to remember the order of the elements in a simple declarative sentence: subject, verb, object. "His best subjects in school were verbal. He hated using his hands to make objects."

Try This: Identify several key elements of a concept you expect to teach. Then generate a story that students could use in a classroom situation to aid them in remembering the information.

An even shorter "story" is as follows: "The subject verbed the object."

Using the word *verb* as a verb is a bit whimsical, but the elements serve their defined function. The passive voice might be illustrated this way as well: "The object was verbed by the subject."

Memory experts who present mnemonic techniques in business seminars or to the general public tout the story technique as a good way of remembering a list of chores or errands.

Try This: Consider using the keyword mnemonic as a way of remembering new vocabulary in this chapter.

story technique A memorization technique that helps in recalling ordered information by combining the elements to be remembered in the correct order in a brief story.

Keyword Mnemonic. Most mnemonics have been in use for quite a long time. The final mnemonic discussed here is of recent vintage. The keyword method was developed specifically for learning foreign language vocabulary (Atkinson, 1975; Atkinson & Raugh, 1975). The keyword method requires first that a known word be chosen from the learner's first language. The chosen word must sound similar to part of the foreign language word to be learned. The Spanish word for *letter* is *carta*. The English word *cart* becomes the keyword. The German word for *newspaper* is *zeitung*. The last syllable is similar to the English word *tongue*.

The second step is to generate a visual image combining the keyword and the meaning of the foreign word. To remember the word *zeitung*, the student might use an interactive image of a person reading a newspaper with his or her tongue stick-

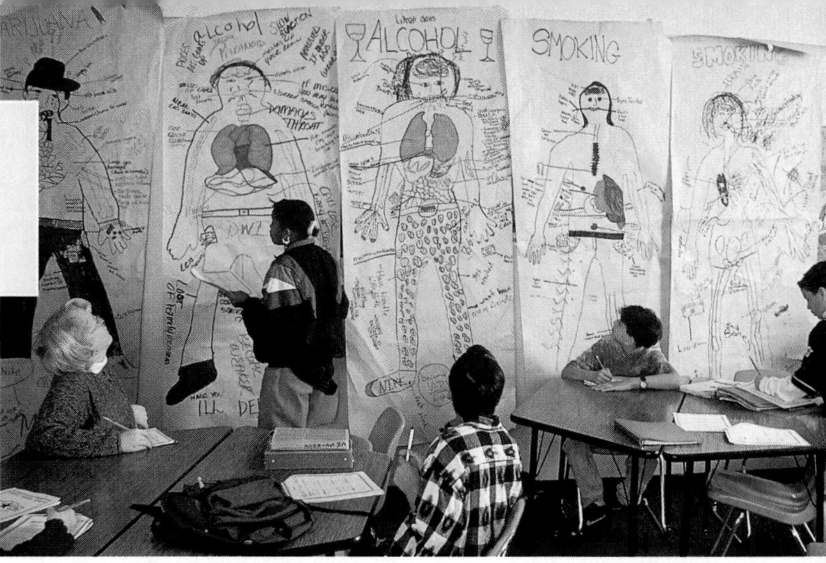

Imagery is a powerful tool in learning. How does imagery strengthen metaphors and analogies? Which mnemonic devices include the use of imagery? How is imagery used to represent a problem in problem solving?

ing out. Or a more bizarre image—giving the newspaper a tongue of its own—might be generated. What image would you create to remember the Spanish word *carta*?

The keyword method has been used in other content areas—for example, as an aid in absorbing data about U.S. presidents: chronological, biographical, and statistical information (Levin, Dretzke, McCormick, Scruggs, McGivern, & Mastropieri, 1983; McCormick & Levin, 1987). The keyword method has also been demonstrated to be an effective learning technique for students with reading difficulties and for students with learning disabilities (see Goin, Peters, & Levin, 1986; Peters & Levin, 1986).

Generating Metaphors and Analogies

In addition to using imagery techniques and mnemonic devices, you can help students make connections between new information and prior knowledge by using metaphors, analogies, and examples. Houser (1987) identified the role of analogy and metaphor by using an example. "When the teacher . . . says that the sun is the mother of the earth, the metaphor is intended to present an immediate object that the student would otherwise not associate with the sun and the earth, but which informs the student of something important about their relationship" (p. 272).

When learners are presented with concrete analogies, their retention of abstract information improves significantly. In a study conducted by Royer and Cable (1976), subjects read an abstract passage about the flow of heat or the conduction of electricity. Some readers were provided with a relevant physical analogy: The molecular structure of the conductor was presented as a Tinkertoy structure. In this way a connection was made between the students' knowledge of Tinkertoys and the new information about the way that heat or electricity is conducted through a solid object.

The connections between prior knowledge and new information can be made by the students (through the use of imagery or mnemonic devices) or by the teacher (through the use of examples, metaphors, or analogies). In either case, the integration yields lasting and organized representations that can then be retrieved and used for other learning tasks. The instructional goal of integration is not simply the retention of the new information; the goal is to make the new information available so that it enhances additional learning in the future.

Try This: Observe language arts classes to discover how metaphors and analogies in reading material are interpreted in class discussions.

Systematic use of imagery, mnemonics, metaphors, and analogies can help students remember a great deal of information, some of it apparently arbitrary and unconnected to larger bodies of knowledge. Spelling rules are an example. Although spelling is an essential part of language arts, the spelling of some words can only be memorized or the rule for spelling them memorized. Moreover, such

Insights ON SUCCESSFUL PRACTICE

What techniques work best for you in gaining student attention and activating their prior knowledge at the start of a lesson?

Getting the students' attention is essential if any learning is to take place. The teacher who makes any attempt at instructional delivery without first gaining student attention is doomed to fail and to promote student failure. Activating prior knowledge empowers the student to construct new learning around that which is already familiar. Thus, the student realizes that there is a relatedness to all learning and that no knowledge, skill, interest, attitude, or appreciation exists in isolation.

During the course of my teaching career I have found that using realia, using models, using illustrations, and raising questions that require reflective thinking have been successful in both getting the students' attention and activating prior knowledge. These techniques have been useful when used alone or in any combination. When teaching a lesson about the nature and cause of water pollution, for example, a container of polluted water can be placed before the students to get their attention. Their prior knowledge can be called upon in an introductory discussion of how the water may have become polluted. To introduce a lesson on mammalian characteristics, small mammal pets can be displayed to serve as an attention-getter. These are only two examples of bringing the real thing into the classroom to begin a lesson. The possibilities are limited only by teacher creativity.

Models serve as excellent attention-getters when the real thing is unavailable or when it simply is not feasible to bring in the real thing. When teaching the distribution of the earth's water, for instance, a globe can be used to show the amount of water compared to the amount of land on the surface. Model airplanes can be used to get the students' attention when the teacher begins a lesson on the principles of flight. Illustrations can be used to paint a picture in words, drawings, paintings, pictures, charts, graphs, or some other form. Illustrations enable students to get a picture in their minds that, when coupled with any prior knowledge or previous experiences on the topic, will make the new learning much more meaningful for them.

Certain questioning strategies set the scene for and orient the student to what is to follow. Rhetorical questions, such as "What is matter?," can be used to introduce a lesson and get students ready to explore matter and its behavior. Analysis, synthesis, and evaluation questions encourage a different kind of thinking and require reflection on the students' part. Reflection is quite an effective way of activating prior knowledge. When students are allowed time to reflect, whether they are faced with realia, models, illustrations, or questions, they are better able to link previous experiences to the current situation. This helps them to better attend to what they are learning and even to make predictions or develop hypotheses about some future action or occurrence.

LOUVENIA MAGEE GAFNEY, Birney Elementary School, Washington, D.C.

According to this teacher, what are good ways of engaging students' attention? In classes you teach, how might you introduce a lesson to arouse curiosity and activate prior knowledge?

knowledge is a necessary, but not sufficient, prerequisite to skilled performance in writing. But skilled performance in writing is an example of a desired high-level learning outcome. How can teachers make the most of their students' prior knowledge to help them reach these higher level-learning outcomes? One way is to make automatic the basic skills that comprise higher-level outcomes.

Encouraging Automaticity through Practice

As you saw earlier in the chapter, attention is a limited resource. Because of this, the teacher's task is to help students focus on critical features of the instructional environment while fostering the development of automatic processing (Grabe, 1986). Fostering **automaticity** helps the learner in several ways. The development of automaticity allows a learner to perform cognitive tasks without any cost in capacity. This is a crucial point for a teacher. Bloom (1986) called automaticity "the hands and feet of genius." He argued that automatization of basic skills, not simply mastery, would be a desirable objective in the primary grades.

Picture two students reading aloud. One is a skilled reader; one is a poor reader. How do their performances differ? On the one hand, the poor reader stumbles over words and uses little inflection to signify a deep understanding of the material. He or she expends a great deal of effort sounding out difficult or unfamiliar words. The poor reader has to devote much of his or her cognitive capacity to the task of word recognition and pronunciation, leaving little capacity for the business of constructing meaning. The good reader, on the other hand, recognizes words automatically and is able to devote the majority of attention to understanding what is read.

Critical Thinking: Beginning readers tend to sound out words. Why might sounding out words diminish readers' capacity to focus on their meaning?

In reading, as well as other content areas, component skills must be learned to the point of automaticity if learners are to be considered truly skilled or fluent (LaBerge & Samuels, 1974). Students learning a second language must acquire the ability to use rules of grammar automatically. Aspiring tennis players must be able to act automatically when they set up and serve a ball. Driver education students must learn to operate the car automatically while they attend to possible hazards in the road.

Try This: Interview teachers in the elementary grades for ways they employ to help students develop automaticity in basic skills. Do they use similar or different techniques for different skills (such as reading vs. math facts)?

Developing automaticity of basic skills such as reading is mostly a matter of practice (cf. Shiffrin & Schneider, 1977). Although component part skills can sometimes be practiced independently of the larger complex skill of which they are a part (as in memorizing the multiplication tables), others (such as driving) must be practiced in their entirety.

automaticity Automatic processing of information from the environment that results in the automatic execution of certain skills.

problem solving The activity of applying rules, knowledge, and cognitive strategies to move from the current situation, or initial state, to a desired outcome, or goal.

HOW CAN YOU HELP STUDENTS LEARN TO SOLVE PROBLEMS?

When students acquire a foundation of information, automatic basic skills, and an arsenal of metacognitive strategies, they have the essential tools for solving problems. **Problem solving** is defined as the activity of applying rules, knowledge, and cognitive strategies to move from the current situation, or initial state, to a desired outcome, or goal (Anderson, 1993; Eggen & Kauchak, 1994). For example, suppose you are invited to visit a friend or relative who lives in a different city. The goal is to reach that location at a specific time. Suppose the initial state is that you do not own a car (or any other means of transportation). The problem, then, is how to get from your home to the home of your friend or relative.

To solve this problem, you would bring to bear other knowledge of your initial state, such as how much money you have for public transportation and whether you know of anyone else driving in the same direction at the time you wish to go. You would also employ specific skills and knowledge to acquire train, plane, and/or bus schedules and fares. You might use rules of arithmetic to compare costs in money and time of alternate modes of transportation. And you might employ various cognitive strategies to generate other candidate solutions to the problem.

Reflection: Recall some of the problems you have solved in school. Were they well defined or ill defined? What ways did your teachers use to help you identify the nature of a problem?

This problem is relatively well defined, in that the rules to solve it are known and can fit into a simple algorithm specifying what steps to follow (Figure 7.3). Other problems, such as diagnosing a patient's symptoms when they match those of more than one disease, are complex and ill defined. Solving ill-defined problems may require a lengthy process of defining and redefining the problem, trying out and monitoring the success of candidate solutions. This is why solving problems is often a matter of creating or generating solutions, applying known rules in unique and insightful ways (Gagné, 1985; Woolfolk, 1995).

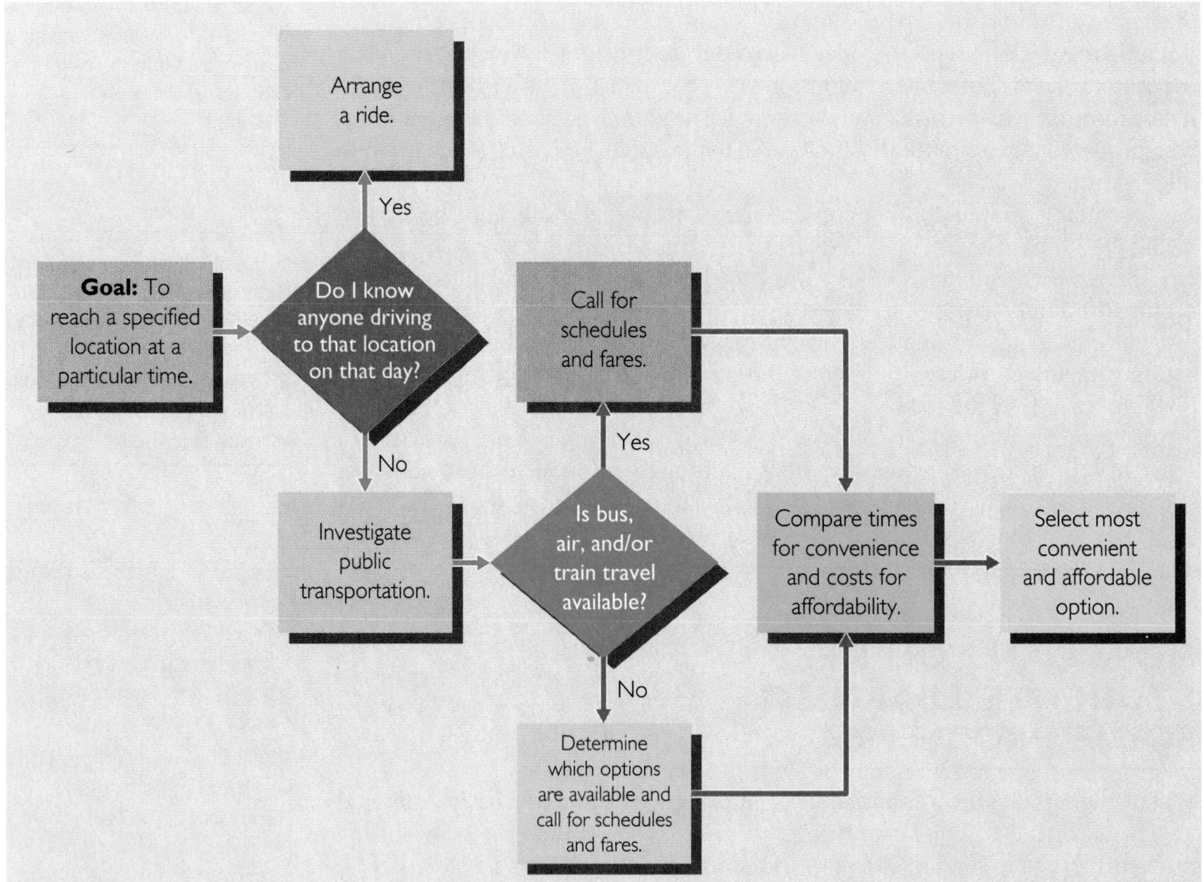

FIGURE 7.3

A Simple Algorithm for Solving a Transportation Problem

Strategic versus Tactical Problem Solving

Researchers who study problem solving have discovered that problems are typically approached on two levels. On a broad or *strategic* level, learners employ an overall approach to solving problems, such as breaking the problem into parts and determining subgoals that must be solved. Usually, subgoals are identified that, when solved, reduce the difference between the initial state and the desired end state. Most people are very reluctant to identify and solve subgoals that temporarily increase this difference or seem to take them in a direction away from their goal (Anderson, 1990).

Once a problem has been defined and subgoals identified, then *tactical* problem solving takes over; that is, learners apply domain-specific methods that depend on subject matter knowledge. In geometry, for example, proving that two triangles are congruent requires recognizing vertical angle configurations. In planning your trip in the preceding example, you know to check schedules and fares before making a decision about what mode of transportation to select. The specific steps taken to solve a problem, then, depend upon the subject matter domain to which the problem belongs. The more students know about a subject, the better able they are to think of divergent ways to solve a problem. Divergent thinking leads to greater success in problem solving.

Expert versus Novice Problem Solving

Experts in a subject area differ from novices in more than the actions they take to solve problems in the domain. They also differ in how they define and represent problems in the domain. Experts appear to understand a problem in terms of deeper features, whereas novices tend to focus on superficial aspects of the problem (Chi, Feltovich, & Glaser, 1981; Anderson, 1993). For example, experienced teachers and prospective teachers were asked to identify instructional problems from student comments such as, "Why do we have to learn this stuff?" and "I never figure out what we're supposed to do before the teacher moves on to the next chapter." Prospective teachers tended to interpret the problems in terms of surface features of a lesson, such as pacing. Experienced teachers, however, did not see pacing as the problem. Rather, they recognized that decisions about pacing are based on a teacher's awareness of student prior knowledge. Too fast a pace is a sign that the teacher misjudged the prior knowledge of students, assuming that they knew more than they actually did (Driscoll, Klein, & Sherman, 1994).

Experts in a subject matter are also more likely to ask questions and seek additional information to clarify the nature of a problem than they are to accept a problem as stated (Rowland, 1994). This means that their efficiency in solving problems is greatly enhanced compared to the novice, because in better defining the problem, they take fewer wrong turns to reach a solution.

Teaching Problem Solving

So how can novices become more expert at problem solving besides learning more about a subject matter? Listed in Table 7.2 are seven steps that constitute a general approach to solving problems that teachers can model with their students in any domain.

TABLE 7.2 Teaching Problem Solving

1. Identification: What is the problem in context?
2. Definition: Why is it a problem? What does it mean?
3. Representation: What does it look like? How can we visualize the problem?
4. Hypothesis formation or prediction: How might we solve it? What do you think is the solution?
5. Experimentation: What happens if we . . . ?
6. Evaluation of solution: Does this solution really work?
7. Reflection on problem-solving process: What did we do to solve the problem?

Source: Based on *The Ideal Problem Solver* by J. D. Bransford and B. S. Stein, 1984, New York: Freeman.

Identifying, Defining, and Representing the Problem. To begin with, students must determine what the problem is that they are to solve. This involves identifying the problem in context, determining why it is a problem, and finally, setting out all the parameters of the problem (including subgoals). For example, a seventh-grade teacher and his students arranged an experiment to investigate the effects of air pressure, amount of water in a two-liter plastic bottle, and rocket design on the height of the bottle's trajectory when it was launched as a bottle rocket. After comparing the data collected on a particularly windy launch day to data collected when the winds were calm, the students decided they had a problem: The wind affected both the bottle's trajectory and their measurements (*identification*). This was a problem because the wind introduced an additional, confounding variable (*definition*). And not only was the wind an additional and confounding variable, it was also unpredictable and uncontrollable (*representation*). Hence, the effect of the wind was likely to mask whatever true effects were caused by aerodynamic shape, pressure, and water.

These students represented their problem conceptually by describing the unanticipated variable (wind) and its projected effects on their experiment. However, problems and their elements can also be represented visually (or graphically). Producing a visual representation often helps students to better understand the nature of a problem.

An important aspect of identifying, defining, and representing a problem is ensuring the accuracy of the determination. In this case, students had to ask themselves whether the wind was the *only* difference between the two launch days that could account for the difference in the results.

Predicting Candidate Solutions. Once a problem has been defined as completely as possible, then predictions can be entertained as to what might be done to solve it. It is often useful to have students generate as many hypotheses as possible, no matter how farfetched they may seem. Then each prediction can be subjected to critique and analysis on its likelihood of success. In addition, advantages and disadvantages, or costs and benefits, of each candidate solution can be weighed. In the rocket example, the students discussed possible orientations for the rocket launcher to minimize the effect of wind. They considered their schedule and the possibility of launching only on calm days.

They noted the fact that seven teams were taking the same measurements from different vantage points during each launch and wondered whether calculating an average would conquer the problem—that is, a steeper angle of launch recorded by the team who viewed the rocket coming toward them would be offset by a shallower angle recorded by the team who viewed the rocket going away from them.

Trying Out and Evaluating Solutions. After the possible solutions that have been judged least likely to succeed have been winnowed out, students can try out those that remain and evaluate their success. In the rocket example, the teacher and students decided that launching only on calm days was not feasible. They reasoned that wind direction on any given day would be a constant for all launches, provided that the launcher remained in the same position, so they chose a single position facing away from the school. They also chose to average their measurements as a means of pooling errors caused by the wind. Since the same patterns were revealed in the data over different launch days, the students judged their solution to be reasonably effective.

A solution that does not work should be examined in terms of whether it was implemented as planned before it is judged unworkable. If no solution works, then you can encourage students to reexamine their definition and representation of the problem. Perhaps they overlooked an important variable or factor that had to be accounted for.

Reflecting on the Problem-Solving Process. When students have concluded an activity that involved solving problems, encourage them to reflect upon what they learned from the problem-solving process. What solution worked, and why did it work? Was their process of solving the problem efficient, and if not, why not? What else might they have done to improve the process? In the case of the rocket-launching experiment, the teacher held discussions with students on a regular basis to reflect on the process. As a consequence, some students built additional rockets at home that might be more impervious to wind effects, whereas others made suggestions to improve the design of the rocket launcher. Reflection of this nature helps students to become more metacognitively aware and makes it more likely that they will be successful in future problem-solving endeavors. This is especially true of ill-defined problems, which are typical of the problems students will face in the world outside school.

Here's How to Create a Context for Solving Ill-Defined Problems

- Look for broad, interdisciplinary problems with more than one right answer.
- Emphasize the importance of identifying, defining, and representing the problem. Ill-defined problems can often be defined and represented in several ways. How they are represented will affect the subgoals that are solved.
- Have students reflect upon their tactics and strategies throughout the problem-solving process. Sometimes they need to examine problems from a new perspective to make progress in finding a solution.

Insights ON SUCCESSFUL PRACTICE

What strategies have you found work best for your students in making learning meaningful?

If you provide children with trust, meaningful content, adequate time, choice, and an enriched environment, they will have the tools to be successful. Special needs children need to know that we will give them adequate time to finish work, take tests, and finish projects.

Academic content must be meaningful to children. One important approach to this is the integrated thematic instruction model. This teaching model enables a teacher to write his or her own curriculum so that it branches out to embrace the several learning modalities of children. The thematic model at our school relies on creating a theme that will integrate several subject areas. The theme and curriculum are broken down into learning components. Students and teachers identify key points that embrace the ideas of the components. Children show their knowledge of key points through inquiries—projects that show the students' knowledge and provide them with several options to apply their learning. For special needs children, thematic inquiry-based instruction is a welcome relief from reading books, memorizing information, and taking tests.

As a special educator, I have learned much from my general education colleagues. They are not bound by labels. They see each child as a potential learner, and the results usually indicate that their professional and personal intuition and initiative were right on target. Our students who came from self-contained special education classes obtained more IEP goals at a quicker rate in a general education setting than in self-contained classrooms. Special educators are the facilitators that break down the needs of each child, determine how those needs can be met in a general education setting, and provide the best service possible to those children. Our results have been phenomenal. We attend to reading discrepancies on an individual basis, but we also read to our students during class time to close the gap between students with and without disabilities. We give students tools to learn to study. We help them map out a timeline for an inquiry and the steps for completion. We adapt spelling tests by introducing the whole list phonetically, visually, and through stories about words. We teach them guided reading to help them read for content. We teach them to study what they have read and to store the information away until they need to connect it to other parts of the curriculum.

Inclusion has been the bridge that has allowed our children who learn differently to come home to the classroom and be at peace with themselves and others. The academic expectations are very high for them. We are building a great program based on an understanding of disabilities, a willingness to shift the teaching paradigm, and a strong conviction that children learn best when they are included.

CINDY FARREN, Amy Beverland Elementary School, Indianapolis, Indiana

According to this teacher, what roles do curriculum integration and thematic inquiry play in making learning meaningful? How are instructional adaptations and alternative assessments used to help students with special educational needs? What can you infer about teacher problem solving?

HOW CAN A CONSTRUCTIVIST APPROACH ENHANCE THE TEACHING–LEARNING PROCESS IN YOUR CLASSROOM?

What does it mean to "understand"? To "know"? There is a distinction between *understanding* as it is used in an everyday setting and *understanding* as it is used by cognitive psychologists (Royer & Feldman, 1984). The everyday sense of the word conveys a subjective experience of empathy or comprehension. If a friend tells you about his or her disappointment and anger at not being accepted in a graduate program, you might say, "I understand how you feel." When you use *understand* in this sense, you mean that you can empathize with your friend's emotional state.

Consider the use of the word *understanding* to denote comprehension. For example, "For best results, squeeze tube from bottom." After reading the sentence, you probably have a sense of what it means. However, consider this sentence: "The trip was delayed because the bottle broke" (Bransford & McCarrell, 1974). This sentence most likely leaves you with a sense of uncertainty. The words are familiar but you are not sure what they mean. As a message, the sentence is difficult to decipher. Many times, students have a sense that they follow a teacher's message and so they respond, if queried, that they understand the lesson. If Dan in the Teacher Chronicle had asked his students prior to the test if they understood the functions of the eye, they probably would have said they did.

From a cognitive perspective, understanding is the most important outcome of learning. However, understanding means more than comprehending or following the gist of an instructional message. When students have acquired information in a way that enables them to solve problems, serves as a foundation for mastering additional material, or motivates them to seek applications of what they know, only then has understanding been achieved (cf. Royer & Feldman, 1984).

Critical Thinking: A teacher was convinced that the key to understanding a subject was the ability to understand and use subject-appropriate vocabulary and the teacher hit on a fun way for students to learn new vocabulary. The teacher had them write jokes. Extra credit was given for jokes, and jokes regularly appeared on tests. Why might joke writing help in remembering and using subject-linked vocabulary?

To take an example, understanding the concept of *remainder* means more than being able to say "a remainder is the amount left over from the division of one number into another." The student who truly understands remainders should be able to use this knowledge to solve problems and interact successfully in the world. Unfortunately, only 23 percent of thirteen-year-olds nationwide could give the right answer to the following problem, despite the fact that 70 percent successfully performed the long division (Schoenfeld, 1988).

> An army bus holds 36 soldiers. If 1,128 soldiers are being bused to their training site, how many buses are needed?

What happened? Students failed to connect the computation of a remainder with its practical consequences in this problem. Almost a third gave the answer as "thirty-one remainder twelve." However, if soldiers are left over after the number of full buses is determined, then one more bus is needed to carry the remainder.

This example illustrates the problem of what constitutes necessary conditions for developing and displaying understanding. How do teachers know when their students have understood? Does the student who is able to work the problems at the end of a textbook chapter understand the chapter's material? Do students actually have to assign soldiers to buses in order for us to conclude that they understand remainders?

Finally, understanding involves reflection on alternative perspectives and commitment to one's own beliefs. The students who truly understand the concept of remainder will not be dissuaded from their belief that thirty-two buses are needed to carry 1,128 soldiers if each bus seats 36 people. An important part of learning is the consideration of alternative views and explanations and a rejection of those that are inconsistent with available data. Conversely, situations in which not all the facts are known call for a willingness to adopt a tentative explanation and remain open to the possibility that it will be wrong. This, too, is a part of understanding.

Point: *Learning is a function of mental activity.* In the constructivist view, this mental activity consists of constructing knowledge through experience.

In the remainder of this chapter, we present a view of learning that represents a paradigmatic shift from the information-processing and memory models discussed earlier. Although still cognitive in orientation, the **constructivist view of learning** stems from the assumption that knowledge is constructed by learners as they attempt to make sense of their environments (e.g., von Glasersfeld, 1988; Lave, 1988; Leinhardt, 1992; O'Loughlin, 1992). It implies the development of principled knowledge that is a function of the activity, context, and culture in which it is used (McLellan, 1993; Cognition and Technology Group at Vanderbilt, 1993); knowing cannot be separated from doing (Brown, Collins & Duguid, 1989).

Connection: How does the constructivist view of learning relate to Piaget's view of cognitive development? To Vygotsky's view?

Active Learning

A natural consequence of the idea that knowing and doing are inseparable is the belief that students must be actively engaged in the instructional task for learning to occur. The notion of **active learning** is not particularly new; we stressed earlier in the chapter that the more active students are in processing information, the more successful they will be in encoding and retrieving it. However, active learning from a constructivist perspective requires qualitatively different interactions between students and content than is achieved through more practice or more feedback (Semb & Ellis, 1994). Rather, active learning calls for students to engage in meaningful tasks in which they have *ownership* of content (Honebein, Duffy, & Fishman, 1994).

Example: Active learning is effective because students can construct a meaningful cognitive representation of an abstract concept, such as static electricity.

For example, elementary school students were asked to use LOGO (a computer language designed for children) to write a program that would teach fractions to students one year behind them in school. Although fractions are usually heartily disliked, these students tackled the project with great enthusiasm, learning not only fractions but also computer programming and instructional design in the process (Harel & Papert, 1992; cited in Honebein, Duffy & Fishman, 1994). Similarly, students who learned research methods by designing their own studies and collecting and analyzing data remembered these procedures for a very long time, more than ten years (Conway, Cohen, & Stanhope, 1991, 1992). Conway et al. (1992) attributed the findings to active learning, which "may have led to the creation of more stable long-term memory structures than did the *passive* learning characteristics of other parts of the course and, hence, the high level of memory performance for research methods" (1992, p. 475).

constructivist view of learning A cognitive view of learning whereby learners are assumed to construct knowledge in the context of the activity of the culture and knowing cannot be separated from doing.

active learning Students engaging in meaningful tasks in which they have ownership of content.

In a recent review of what students remember from knowledge taught in schools, Semb and Ellis (1994) concluded that instructional strategies that promote higher levels of original learning enhance retention over the short term, but only instructional strategies that involve active learning prevent forgetting over the long term. In summary, cognitive research clearly points to the conclusion that teachers who foster active learning enhance the outcomes of learning for their students. The question for teachers who seek to apply these research findings in their classrooms becomes, How do we establish instructional situations that foster active learning on the part of our students? From the constructivist perspective, the answer comes in two parts: the nature of the task and the nature of the interaction among learners. The issues of task and interaction are examined, in turn, in the last two sections of the chapter.

Authentic Activity and Situated Learning

An important issue in active learning is the type of activity in which learners engage. Many constructivist researchers argue that for students to learn the skills and knowledge of a given discipline, they should engage in activities that are *authentic* to the discipline. What makes a context for learning or a particular instructional activity authentic? Leinhardt (1992) summarized it well:

> A task can be **authentic** because it is part of the world outside of school (for example, a grocery store) or because it is part of the culture of a particular discipline (such as mathematics or chemistry). (p. 24, emphasis added)

Connection: Authentic tasks are also discussed in relation to cognitive development in Chapter 2 and in relation to student evaluation in Chapter 3.

The first sense of authenticity emphasizes the need for many skills and knowledge learned in school to be transferred to contexts outside of school. For example, arithmetic skills are needed to comparison shop in a grocery store or to balance the family budget. Likewise, learning to communicate well both orally and in writing is essential for participating in a debate on whether to ban the use of nets in commercial fishing. During the debate, one might be required to speak at a public forum or write letters to the local newspaper. When these kinds of activities can be incorporated into instruction, students see the relevance of certain knowledge and skills, and they practice these skills in appropriate ways.

Authentic tasks can also imply the activities performed by people who are proficient in their respective disciplines. Not only do we want students to be able to learn mathematics skills that can be applied in real-world contexts, but we also want them, in some degree, to think like mathematicians (or scientists or historians). To do this requires working on problems common to the discipline, where answers are not always known in advance and the teacher can take part in the problem-solving process. All too often, working on problems that can be solved relatively quickly leads to a belief that *all* problems can be solved quickly, if only one understands the material (Schoenfeld, 1988; Doyle, 1988).

Critical Thinking: Why do "experiments" attract students' attention so readily and facilitate learning so well?

When students work on complex and authentic problems, the teacher serves as a guide, modeling strategies and processes during class activities. For example, a teacher of American history decides to adopt the theme of *conflict* in units on the settling of America, the Revolutionary War, and westward expansion. In each case, students face the problem of how to represent and understand the conflict—who were the adversaries, why were they fighting, what conditions of the time influenced their actions, and so forth. The students examine the conflicts from retrospective and modern perspectives, including their own. The teacher provides resources to the students in the form of textbooks, historical novels, critical analyses of the events, and videotaped documentaries, but the students must make their own selections of information to access as their investigations proceed (L. Scott, personal communication, December 1994). The activities in which these students engage are authentic to the discipline of history; they represent what historians do in trying to understand an historical event.

authentic task An instructional task that is part of the world outside of school (e.g., comparison shopping) or part of the culture of a particular discipline (e.g., "exploiting extreme cases" in mathematics reasoning).

An approach very similar to authentic activity can be seen in the concept of **situated learning.** In situated learning, students are engaged in solving realistic or simulated problems that require the use of disciplinary knowledge and skills. For example, the Cognition and Technology Group at Vanderbilt (CTGV) has developed a series of interactive video lessons for mathematics called the *Jasper Woodbury Problem Solving Series* (CTGV, 1991). In paired lessons, Jasper experiences various adventure-related problems, and students are challenged to find an optimal way for Jasper to resolve them. In one lesson, they must figure out how Jasper can get home from a boat trip before sunset without running out of gas. The problem involves mathematical concepts of distance, rate, and time, and it requires students to determine a series of subproblems to be solved (CTGV, 1990, 1991, 1993). The goal of the series is to provide realistic and interesting ways for students to do and learn mathematics. Moreover, the lessons are paired in order to provide transfer of skills learned during one Jasper adventure to another, analogous one.

Point: *Instructional technologies support teaching and learning.* A wide variety of technology-based instruction is now available to teachers for use in their classes.

Evidence from the implementation of the Jasper series in the schools of several states suggests that it is effective in helping students see connections between the problems they solved with Jasper and everyday problems they encounter at home where mathematics could be applied (CTGV, 1993). In class, students also appear motivated to engage in problem solving and to persist in their efforts to solve Jasper's adventures (CTGV, 1991).

Try This: Interview teachers regarding ways they attempt to provide authentic activities in their instruction.

Besides computer simulations or microworlds (Rieber, 1991), hands-on projects, theme-based units, and complex scenarios and cases provide other means for implementing authentic or situated activity. We hope, for example, that the Teacher Chronicles used in this book, which come from the experiences of real teachers, will help you to learn and solve problems related to teaching in a more authentic way. Moreover, the cases involve more than one principle or idea, illustrating the complexity of the teaching–learning environment and enabling you to examine them from multiple perspectives (cf. Spiro, Feltovich, Jacobson, & Coulson, 1991).

Communities of Learning

Ms. McKay's students are working on a lesson in thermodynamics. They work in four-person teams, making predictions about what kinds of materials will keep baked potatoes hot and cold drinks cold. Myra, the Principal Investigator, is in charge of directing the team's experiments and keeping things going. Karl records predictions in his role of Hypothesizer. Abby, as Researcher, selects options on the computer simulation and reads out results as they appear on the screen. The students discuss the results of each trial, but Lena's job is to summarize the group's conclusion prior to their generating the next hypothesis.

"Okay," says Myra. "Let's start with potatoes at 150 degrees internal temperature. What do we use to keep them hot?"

"Aluminum foil. That's what my mom always uses," offers Abby.

"Good idea," agrees Karl. He writes as he says aloud, "Beginning temperature equals 150 degrees. Material is aluminum foil. What is it called—what we're doing?"

"Insulating, dumbo!" shouts Lena.

"Oh, yeah. Insulator is aluminum foil. Time for fifteen minutes. Predict no temperature change."

situated learning Students engaging in problem solving of realistic or simulated problems that require the use of disciplinary knowledge and skills.

Abby types in the group's selections and groans as she reads out the result. "Temperature loss: 25 degrees."

"That can't be right," exclaims Karl. "You must have typed something wrong. Do it again."

"No, wait a minute," says Lena. "Remember we talked in class about metals being good *conductors* of heat. Aluminum foil is a metal. It can't be a good insulator as well as a good conductor."

"But if that's true," insists Karl, "why do restaurants use aluminum foil to keep baked potatoes hot?"

Point: *Learning is active construction in social contexts.* The dialogue in which students engage with their teacher and classmates plays a critical role in their learning.

In this example, you see students confronting a misunderstanding that might have lain hidden and unquestioned without both the experiment and the exchange of ideas among students. In the constructivist view, learning is inherently a social process, because knowledge is distributed across individuals. For understanding to occur, students must accept or refute ideas proposed by their peers and teacher, offer interpretations and explanations of their own, and eventually build on or reconstruct the network of concepts and principles that make up their knowledge—that is, learning occurs in a community. "When students talk to each other, they rehearse terminology, notational systems, and manner of reasoning in a particular domain, thus reducing the individual burden of complete mastery of material while keeping the visions of the entire task in view" (Leinhardt, 1992, p. 24).

Connection: How does this episode exemplify cooperative learning as discussed in Chapters 2 and 12?

When students assume particular roles within a group, as they do in this example, they are often able to collaborate more fully, with each member contributing something essential to the success of the entire group. Another way of achieving such a learning community is offered by Brown and Campione (1990), who described a middle school science curriculum in which students also worked in research groups. However, these groups, like the elementary school students who designed computer programs to teach fractions, were responsible for becoming experts on a topic they would teach to the others in the class. Each group researched its topic and wrote a booklet they would use to teach the topic. Then the students were regrouped into teams made up of one expert from each of the original research groups, so that they could learn the other topics. Expertise was thus distributed throughout the classroom, and dialogue among students was an essential part of the learning process, as "students force each other to sort out their own misunderstandings" (Brown & Campione, 1990, p. 118).

A Constructivist Classroom

A primary goal of constructivist educators is to foster critical thinking skills, and they argue that this is best done through learning communities engaged in authentic, situated learning tasks. As Brown and Campione (1990) put it:

> The goal is reading, writing, and thinking, in the service of learning about something. Teaching is on a need-to-know basis, with experts (be they children or adults) acting as facilitators. Student expertise is fostered and valued by the community. A community of discussion is created with distributed expertise. This change from traditional teaching and learning practices results in significant improvements both in the students' thinking skills and in the domain-specific knowledge about which they are reasoning. (p. 124)

Point: *Teachers and students are both learners.* In constructivist classrooms, teachers do not know all the answers, and students can act as facilitators of learning as much as do teachers.

here's how

Here's How to Plan a Constructivist Classroom

- Choose themes or learning contexts that provide authentic activities for students to engage in. These are likely to span several weeks or months, involve complex problems with many possible solutions, and cross disciplinary boundaries to integrate aspects of different subject matters.
- Model the processes (such as defining a subproblem or managing the activities of a learning team) that you want students to learn.
- Support students' activity with helpful hints and instruction on an as-needed basis, but endow them with responsibility for task completion and learning.
- Provide ample opportunity for students to engage in meaningful dialogue, among themselves, with you, and with experts in the topics they are studying.

TEACHER Chronicle Conclusion

CHINESE PROVERB

As the morning science lesson gets underway, Dan Lovely walks to the window and closes the curtain.

"I want everyone to get a partner," Dan says, crossing the room to the light switch. There is a shuffling of chairs and a flurry of conversations as the students find partners.

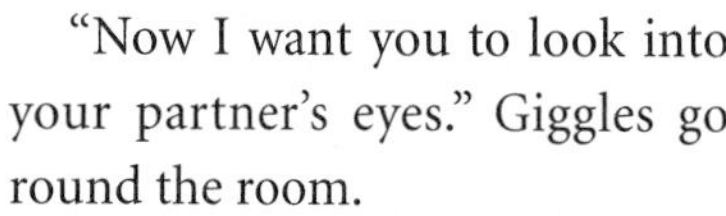

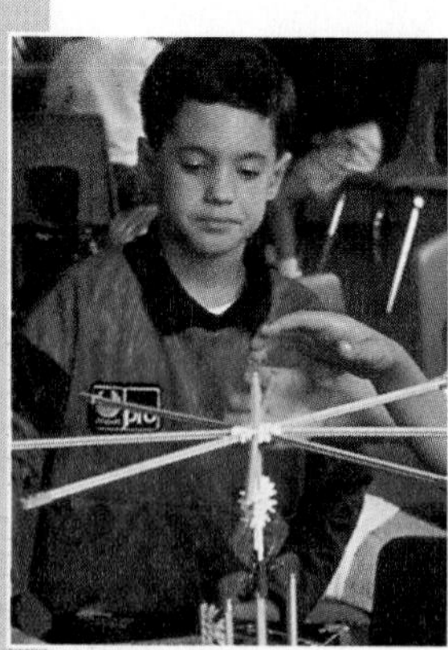

"Now I want you to look into your partner's eyes." Giggles go round the room.

"On the count of three," Dan continues, "I'm going to turn off the lights. I want you to observe what happens to your partner's pupils."

"What's a pupil?" Tim asks. Groans chorused around the room.

"You won't be one for long," Dan chides, " if you don't pay attention.

One, two, three." He hits the switch and the room darkens.

"Wow!"

"Cool!"

"Did you see that?"

"Now I'd like you to predict what will happen to your pupils when I turn the light back on," Dan says.

"Our pupils will be smaller," Sara says.

"They'll contract!" Sammy exclaims.

"Super answers," Dan encourages. "Sammy gave us the science word for what will happen. What word describes what just happened to your pupils?"

"They expanded," Susie says.

"Right. Now one, two, three." Dan turns the lights back on. Exclamations burst forth as the students observe the quick contractions of their pupils.

"Can you do that again?" Corey asks.

"Sure," Dan replies, flicking the lights off. Five more times that lesson he turns the lights off and on.

"I think I understand contraction and expansion now," Tim says.

"Me, too," a dozen voices concur.

"Will this work on my cat?" Leah asks.

"Try it tonight and see," suggests Dan, knowing he has connected.

APPLICATION QUESTIONS

1. Why did Mr. Lovely's experiment work better than lecturing about how the eye works? How did the experiment support elaborative processing and active learning?
2. Did students pay more attention during the experiment or the lecture? Explain your answer.
3. How did students' prior knowledge help them understand the light experiment?
4. How might student understanding of expansion/contraction be carried over into another lesson?
5. How might Mr. Lovely revise his test to better assess students' understanding of how the eye functions?
6. Describe a lesson you remember from elementary school, middle school, and high school. Why do you remember these lessons over others? Did they make use of imagery, mnemonic devices, or stories? Did they promote active learning? Did they involve authentic tasks?

CHAPTER SUMMARY

WHAT IS INVOLVED IN THINKING, REMEMBERING, AND PROBLEM SOLVING?

Cognitive theories of learning are built around the premise that events occurring within the learner are important for understanding the process of learning. Information-processing models of cognition rely on a computer metaphor to explain processing, storage, and retrieval of knowledge, whereas constructivist views propose that learning is a matter of constructing knowledge in a social environment. In both perspectives, learning how to learn—becoming aware of and regulating one's own cognitive processes—is essential for developing critical reasoning and problem-solving skills.

HOW CAN YOU TEACH IN WAYS THAT FACILITATE THE PROCESSING OF INFORMATION?

To help students process information during instruction, teachers gain and direct their attention to important aspects or details that are to be further processed. Attention can operate selectively, as when a student consciously directs his or her concentration to some stimulus information. Attention can also operate automatically, as when a learner is able to focus on information without conscious effort.

Further processing occurs through encoding, which is the process of integrating new knowledge with prior knowledge. Effective teachers prompt students to elaborate on new information, thereby forming many connections to prior knowledge and ensuring understanding.

WHY IS IT IMPORTANT TO ACTIVATE STUDENTS' PRIOR KNOWLEDGE?

The prior knowledge they bring with them to the classroom has an enormous influence on what and how students learn. Facts and concepts that make up a learner's prior knowledge can be organized as episodes (episodic knowledge) or as general knowledge of the world (semantic knowledge). Procedural knowledge is prior knowledge of how to do things, such as how to apply facts and concepts. Conditional prior knowledge is knowledge of when and under what conditions facts, concepts, and procedures should be used.

HOW CAN YOU HELP STUDENTS REMEMBER WHAT THEY LEARN?

You can help students use their prior knowledge in many ways to remember information. Imagery is the basis for many types of elaborative encoding, including the use of mnemonic devices. Mnemonics are processing techniques that make information more memorable. Metaphors and analogies are useful in helping learners to integrate their prior knowledge with the information they are asked to learn. Practice on component basic skills helps to make them automatic, so that learners can direct their attentional resources to more complex tasks.

HOW CAN YOU HELP STUDENTS LEARN TO SOLVE PROBLEMS?

Learners develop specific tactics for solving problems of particular kinds as they acquire knowledge of a subject matter. You can help students become effective problem solvers by teaching them to identify, define, and represent a problem; predict candidate solutions; try out and evaluate solutions; and reflect on the problem-solving process.

HOW CAN A CONSTRUCTIVIST APPROACH ENHANCE THE TEACHING–LEARNING PROCESS IN YOUR CLASSROOM?

According to the constructivist view, learning occurs by actively constructing knowledge in a learning community. Active learning is best facilitated with tasks that are authentic to the world outside school or to a subject matter discipline and with interactions among learners that prompt them to sort out their own understandings and misunderstandings.

KEY CONCEPTS

acronym
acrostic
active learning
authentic task
automatic attention
automaticity
constructivist view of learning
dual-code theory
elaborative rehearsal
encoding
episodic memories
information-processing models
maintenance rehearsal
mental images
mental model
metacognition
mnemonic devices
peg mnemonics
prior knowledge
problem solving
procedural knowledge
retrieval
rhymes
schema
selective attention
selective perception
semantic memories
situated learning
story technique
working memory

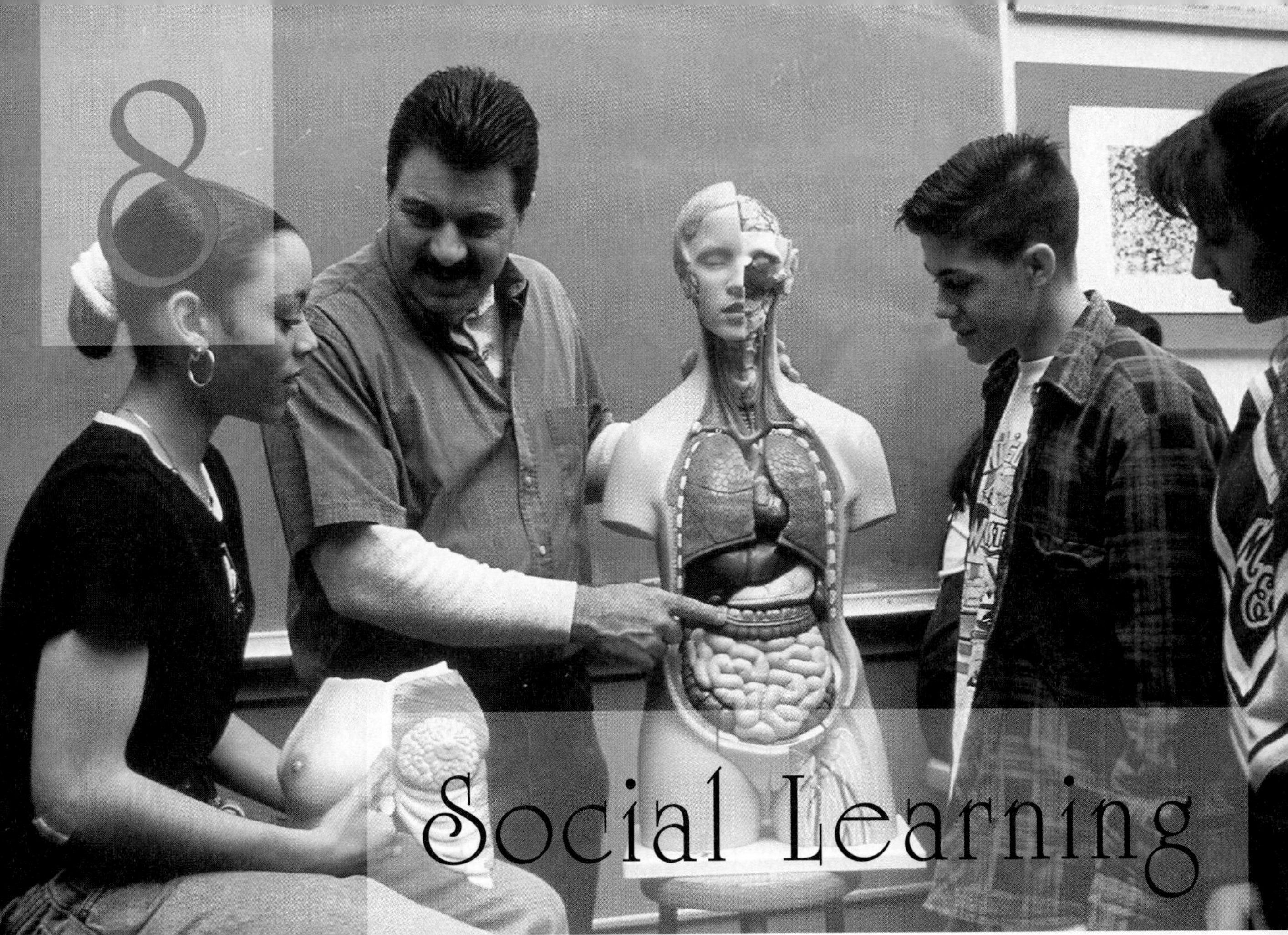

CHAPTER OUTLINE

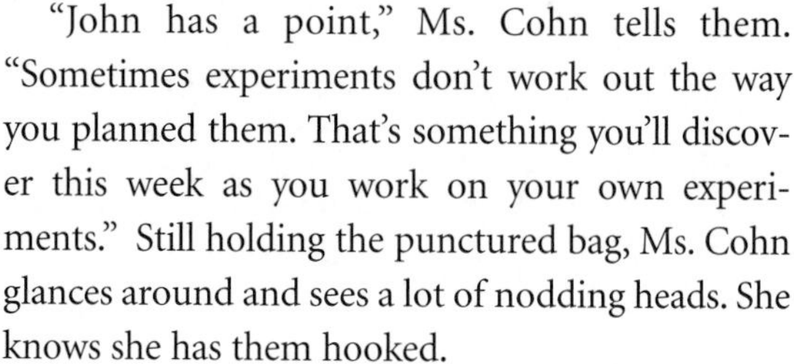

WIZARD WEEK

It is the start of Wizard Week, when each student in Ms. Cohn's ninth-grade class selects, demonstrates, and explains a scientific experiment. Dressed in a long white lab coat, Ms. Cohn stands in front of her sixth-hour science students, a water-filled plastic bag in her hand and a newly sharpened pencil in the other. She has everyone's attention as she prepares to jab the bag with the pencil.

"Don't!" Carey (in the front row) begs. Other students in the front prepare to move.

"What do you predict will happen when I stab the bag?" Ms. Cohn asks.

Hands pop up all over the room.

"The bag will explode."

"We'll get drowned."

"You'll ruin my new shirt and my mom will kill me."

"Are you sure it will pop?" Ms. Cohn asks.

"Yeah!" come shouts from all over the room.

With a quick jab, Ms. Cohn stabs the bag. The pencil passes harmlessly through the plastic. Not a drop of water drips out. Carey sags with relief. (Inside Ms. Cohn does, too. This experiment sometimes backfires.)

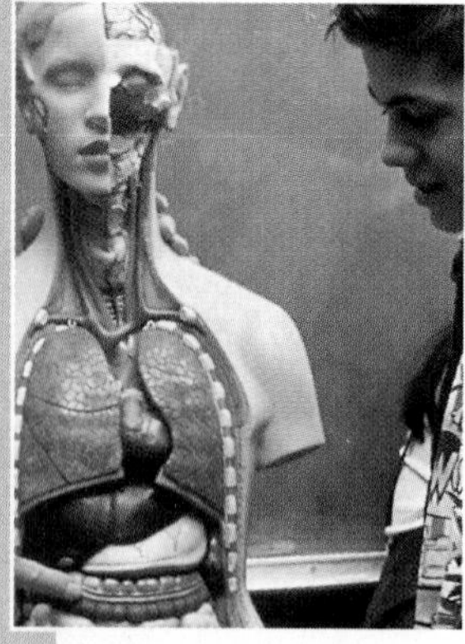

"Awesome!"

"Neat!"

The students are clearly impressed, even astonished. "How did you do that?" Andrea asks.

"Is it magic?" Enrico wants to know.

"No," Ms. Cohn says. "It's science. And tonight I want you to try this at home."

"No way," John exclaims. "My dad will hit the ceiling if it doesn't work right."

"John has a point," Ms. Cohn tells them. "Sometimes experiments don't work out the way you planned them. That's something you'll discover this week as you work on your own experiments." Still holding the punctured bag, Ms. Cohn glances around and sees a lot of nodding heads. She knows she has them hooked.

"Now let me tell you what I did to get ready for this particular experiment," says Ms. Cohn as she begins writing the steps on the board. "First, I looked through these books to find an experiment that I wanted to try. Then, I got my materials together and practiced the experiment at home to see if there were any unexpected problems. I also planned how I was going to explain it to you. Finally, I demonstrated the experiment to you. Now, before you start looking through these books for your own experiments, let's figure out why the bag did not pop."

FOCUS QUESTIONS

1. How did the students react to the teacher's demonstration? Do you think students will try the experiment at home? Do you think students were able to visualize themselves doing the experiment? Why is observing another person an effective way to learn?
2. How did the students' anticipation of the outcome of the experiment influence their attention? How closely did the students attend to the teacher's behavior? Do you think the students attended to the teacher's review of the steps she took in preparing the demonstration?
3. Will the students be able to perform the experiment on the first try? Will their observation be sufficient to perform the experiment? Will the students participate enthusiastically in Wizard Week?

4. Do the students in this class perceive Ms. Cohn to be an effective model? How did the demonstration influence the students' perception of the teacher? How will students feel about themselves and their own demonstrations during Wizard Week? How confident will they be?

WHAT ARE THE DIMENSIONS OF SOCIAL LEARNING?

Ms. Cohn performed a demonstration that captured the attention of her ninth graders. She also invited her students to reenact the activity that night at home. Given what you learned from reading the Teacher Chronicle, how would you answer the following questions?

- How many of her students do you think tried puncturing a plastic bag full of water that night?
- Did her students learn anything merely by observing?
- Will they learn anything else, if they try the experiment themselves?
- And finally, aren't you dying to put down this book and go stick a sharp pencil through a bag full of water? Or have you already tried it?

As Ms. Cohn prepared to stab the bag of water, she became a salient part of her students' social environment. As a consequence, her students observed the behaviors that she modeled. Models are a significant source of learning and motivation in and out of classrooms. In this chapter, we examine how people can learn by observing others. As we begin our examination of learning through modeling, reflect on your reaction to the Teacher Chronicle. Did Ms. Cohn serve as a model for you? Did her behavior motivate you to try the bag of water experiment?

Connection: The influence of the environment and the effects of reinforcement on learning are discussed in Chapter 6.

Models and Observers

Wizard Week illustrates principles of **social learning**. The theoretical perspective in which those principles are embedded is called social cognitive theory. Its major proponent, Albert Bandura, takes a broad view of learning. Bandura's (1986) **social cognitive theory** stresses concepts of operant conditioning (the environment and reinforcement) as well as the concept of mental activity or cognitive processes to explain learning.

Social cognitive theory has its origins in Bandura's early research on the phenomenon of observational learning (imitation). His investigations were partially motivated by a dissatisfaction with the operant-conditioning explanation of learning. Operant conditioning holds that a student learns by doing. Bandura felt that much of what humans learn they learn by watching what other people do.

In his early work (1962, 1965, 1971a, 1971b), Bandura investigated a number of variables that influence the outcomes of observational learning. In all of these studies, the learner is an **observer**. The stimulus is the behavior of another person, acting as a **model**. Bandura studied the effects of age, sex, and the perceived status and perceived similarity of the model. (An observer's perceptions of a model have important instructional implications; we examine those implications later in the chapter.) In addition to investigating the perceived characteristics of the model, Bandura also investigated the type of behavior that the model displayed, including displays of skills unknown to the observer, hostile and aggressive behaviors, and standards of reward that the model accepted.

social learning Changes in thought or behavior brought about through observation of or interaction with one's social vironemnt.

social cognitive theory A learning theory, originated by Bandura, that draws on both cognitive and behavioral perspectives.According to the theory, people learn by observing the behavior of others in their social environment.

observer The learner is an observer, according to Bandura.

model A person whose behavior acts as a stimulus to learning, according to Bandura.

In a series of classic investigations known as the "bobo doll" studies, children who observed models kick and punch a large inflatable doll (the bobo doll) demonstrated this aggressive behavior more often than children who did not observe such behavior (e.g., Bandura, Ross, & Ross, 1963; Bandura & Walters, 1963). Another early finding suggested that observers tend to imitate the types of moral standards exhibited by a model. If an observer sees a model behave in questionable ways, the observer is more likely to lower his or her standards of appropriate behavior.

To illustrate, picture yourself at a banquet or wedding reception, some kind of gathering where each table has a floral centerpiece. As the festivities wind down, a few people wonder aloud if it would be appropriate to take a centerpiece home. Conversations about the flowers take place at a number of tables. These discussions end with someone saying, "Well, if we don't take them home with us, they'll just be thrown out." Finally, one of the guests picks up a centerpiece and leaves. No one stops or even questions the flower-toting guest. A model is born. The observers, even some who initially questioned the correctness of taking the centerpieces, imitate the model.

Example: During a review of an exam, student A convinces the teacher that her answer should be considered correct. Student B reports that he used the same reasoning as student A. Most of the students join in the chorus, "Yeah, that's what I thought, too."

Another example of a model influencing an observer's standards of appropriate behavior might be found in the old notion, "Nobody gives his correct weight on his driver's license." How many of us have observed people in our immediate social environment model questionable behavior when it comes to the issue of reporting our weights?

Observational learning is not limited to aggression or questionable moral behavior; not all models beat up bobo dolls or cheat on their income tax. Many positive outcomes can be gained by observing models. If teachers are to find and use models to their advantage, they must first understand the cognitive capabilities that allow students to learn not only by performing activities but also by observing others perform.

Learning versus Performance

Bandura raised a key point with his research in the early 1960s: Learners need not experience punishment or reinforcement to learn what is and is not appropriate behavior in a given situation. Much human learning can be done vicariously, by observing another person responding in a situation. From Bandura's point of view, learners need not be behavers; they can be observers.

Reflection: Think of an activity, demonstrated in school, that you tried at home. What were the characteristics of the demonstration that prompted you to try it at home?

Bandura's early studies examined how the consequences of a model's behavior affected imitation by the observer. Behaviors that are rewarded instead of punished or ignored lead to a higher degree of imitation by the observer. You have already considered how many of the students in the Teacher Chronicle might demonstrate the plastic bag experiment to family or friends. Would they be as likely to experiment in front of friends and family if the teacher had tried repeatedly to insert the pencil and wound up being soaked each time? (Even if the teacher had failed miserably, the students may have tried the experiment out of curiosity, but probably in private, not in front of people as the teacher/model did.) Bandura (1971b) also examined the effects that various levels of motivation had on an observer's imitation of modeled behavior. In an interesting manipulation, Bandura (1982) demonstrated that regardless of whether the model's behavior is rewarded or punished, the observer's imitative performance increases in the presence of a reward. Bandura rewarded observers for imitating behavior for which the model was punished in order to see if the observer *could* imitate unrewarded behavior. In interpreting Bandura's findings, Bower & Hilgard (1981) stated,

"Thus it was found that the observer had learned the 'bad guy's' responses, even though he did not perform them until the incentive to do so was offered" (p. 463).

Bandura's research provides a basis for distinguishing **learning**—becoming capable—from **performance**—exhibiting a capability. In this respect, the social cognitive perspective differs from the operant-conditioning perspective. Operant-conditioning theory says that learning is behavior; social cognitive theory separates what observers learn from the behaviors they perform.

Bandura (1986) enlisted the concept of cognitive processes to explain how observers can learn without performing. As we will begin to see, the social cognitive theory of learning is a hybrid of behaviorist and cognitivist notions. The processes that Bandura postulated to explain observational learning are cognitive processes of the type found in information-processing theory that was examined in Chapter 7.

Point: The information-processing theory and the constructivist notions discussed in Chapter 7, as well as Bandura's theory, support one of the assumptions of this book: *Learning is a function of complex mental activity.*

Bandura's research has been truly programmatic. His research moved from issues of model effectiveness, reward of model, and reward of observer to consideration of the ways in which an observer's personal factors influence learning and performance (Bandura, 1986). Understanding the role that an observer's perceptions of a model, or of him- or herself, play in the learning process will make us more aware of issues of student motivation. Social cognitive theory is not only a hybrid of behaviorist and cognitivist learning theories, it also bridges the gap between issues of learning and issues of motivation.

As Bandura (1986) has pointed out, the technological age has provided observers with a multitude of models in a variety of communicative contexts. We observe models in our homes, churches, classrooms, and malls and on television and other media. The anecdote about Ms. Cohn, presented in the Teacher Chronicle, demonstrates that text can also be a medium for modeled behavior. The behaviors that we observe in others and the consequences of their actions are part of our social environment. Observing others can teach us a great many things about ourselves.

Critical Thinking: Although theories of motivation are addressed in Chapter 9, consider the following question: What is the relationship between learning and motivation? Does motivation always precede learning? How might learning enhance motivation?

Operant-conditioning theorists explained learning by focusing on the interaction between the environment and behavior. Cognition was considered an interesting phenomenon—something that might accompany behavioral change—but unnecessary for the explanation of learning. Social cognitive theory, however, treats human cognition as an essential concept in understanding learning. The importance of cognition in social cognitive theory can be seen in two ways: first in the distinction that is drawn between enactive and vicarious learning and second, in the way that cognition is thought to influence and be influenced by both environment and behavior.

Try This: List the ways in which a student's environment and behavior might influence his or her cognitive activity.

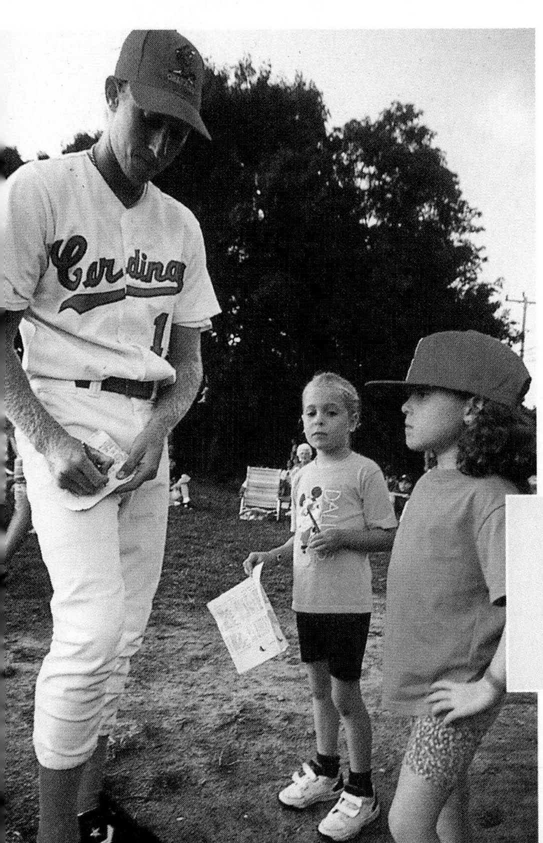

According to social cognitive theory, media characters and sports heroes are often effective models. Children learn the thoughts and behaviors of these models vicariously through observation.

learning Becoming capable.

performance Exhibiting a capability.

Vicarious Learning and Enactive Learning

From the perspective of social cognitive theory, "Learning is largely a [cognitive] processing activity in which information about the structure of behavior and about environmental events is transformed into symbolic representations that serve as guides for action" (Bandura, 1986, p. 51). Clearly, this definition implies that cognitive activity mediates learning and therefore is absolutely distinct from the operant-conditioning view described in the previous chapter. Enactive and vicarious learning are different modes of learning in social cognitive theory. It is important to keep in mind that both modes of learning are thought to involve cognition, because enactive learning may appear, at first, to be identical to operant conditioning. As we will see, it is not.

A student learns enactively by performing and learns vicariously by observing others perform. **Enactive learning** occurs when one learns from the consequences of one's behavior. Behaviors that lead to favorable consequences are retained by the learner and used again in similar situations. Behaviors that lead to unfavorable consequences are discarded. To this point, enactive learning sounds like operant conditioning. Indeed, the behavioral consequences are the same.

Connection: Look back at the consequences of behavior in Chapter 6.

The difference between enactive learning and operant conditioning is how the consequences of behavior function. "Social cognitive theory [of which enactive learning is a part] contends that behavioral consequences, rather than strengthening behaviors as postulated in operant theory, serve as sources of information and motivation" (Schunk, 1991, p. 103). Learners use the consequences of their actions to determine whether their actions are appropriate or inappropriate, correct or incorrect. Learners also evaluate the desirability consequences and seek to learn behaviors that lead to desirable outcomes. Enactive learning is learning by performing and then processing the information provided as a consequence of those performances.

Reflection: From your student experience, identify the most significant learning that occurred through the observation of another. Did you learn a concept? A skill? Both? What kinds of outcomes do you think are most likely to occur through vicarious learning?

Vicarious learning occurs when one learns by observing the performance of others without overtly performing oneself. Vicarious learning is a common mode of human learning, perhaps because it has significant advantages for the learner. Vicarious learning saves time. Imagine students trying to learn how to use a microscope or a new software program without a teacher demonstration or an instruction manual. Vicarious learning is adaptive because it prevents learners from learning about dangerous situations "the hard way." Having read, heard, or watched accounts of the devastating effects of tornadoes causes most of us to take precautions when a funnel cloud is reported. Fortunately, people do not always have to experience consequences to learn that some behaviors are not adaptive.

Try This: Observe a lesson and record instances of both enactive and vicarious learning. After the lesson, share your observations with the teacher, and discuss the importance of both kinds of learning.

While it is important to understand that enactive and vicarious learning are distinct modes of learning, it is critical to recognize that much of the learning in classrooms requires both. Observing models (usually, but not necessarily, teachers) explain and demonstrate a skill enhances learners', (usually, but not necessarily, students') first attempts at performing that skill. Ms. Cohn in Wizard Week was such a model. Think of all the skills that require some orientation and explanation for the learner to attempt performance: writing; reading; performing long division or algebraic manipulation; playing a musical instrument; operating tools; searching databases; using sewing machines, stoves, TV cameras; checking out library books. Now, consider the degree to which any of those skills would be learned if the learner was prevented from enacting what he or she had learned vicariously. How well can one learn to write by listening to someone explain

enactive learning Changes in thought or behavior that are a function of environmental consequences experienced by the learner.

vicarious learning Changes in thought or behavior through observing the behavior of others and the consequences of those behaviors.

writing or by reading about the mechanics of writing, the function of plot, and the purpose of character development? Teachers provide the modeling—via demonstrations, explanations, and presentations—that supports vicarious learning, and they provide the consequences, in the form of informative feedback and motivation, of student performance.

Example: Many people read magazines and books devoted to writing for publication. Unless they attempt to write, however, what they learn vicariously will never be enacted.

In the course of distinguishing enactive and vicarious learning, mention was made of multiple sources or media by which learners can observe the performance of models. Humans are capable of learning vicariously via live performances, written accounts, photographic or videographic presentations, and oral stories or reports. A discussion of the capability to learn through vicarious experience—as well as other human capabilities—follows shortly, after an examination of the relationships among behavior, environment, and personal factors, factors such as a learner's cognitive activity.

As mentioned earlier, the social cognitive point of view assumes that learning can be vicarious as well as enactive. By observing other people's behaviors and the consequences of those behaviors, we can learn what courses of action are and are not effective. Such observations allow us to build up our own store of knowledge and then to use our symbolizing capability to plan courses of action. The vicarious capability affords us a major advantage. Because we can learn by watching others make mistakes or succeed, we do not have to learn everything by trial and error. We do not have to spend as much time acquiring experience.

Reflection: Think of an instance when one of your classmates got caught engaging in inappropriate behavior. What was your reaction? How did the episode influence your behavior in that class?

Many skills and much knowledge in our culture could not be transmitted very efficiently without vicarious learning. What would happen if everyone had to learn to drive a car by means of trial and error—that is, through selective reinforcement of the correct responses? What would happen if medical students had to learn the techniques of surgery in a trial-and-error fashion? Indeed, what would happen if aspiring teachers had no models from whom to learn? Many complex skills could not be mastered at all were it not for the use of modeling. Children who had no models of linguistic behavior in their environments would be hard-pressed to develop the linguistic skills necessary to communicate with fellow members of their society.

Try This: Ask some students to identify characters from television or movies that influence the way they act. Ask them to give specific examples of behaviors and situations.

The technology of communication has increased the symbolic environments from which both children and adults learn vicariously. We learn not only ways of behaving but also patterns of thought, life-styles, values, and attitudes from television, film, and print media. We are able to learn from symbolic environments because we possess this vicarious capability.

Other Cognitive Capabilities

A basic assumption of this theory is that people have the following basic cognitive capabilities: symbolizing capability, forethought capability, self-regulatory capability, self-reflective capability, and vicarious capability, which we just discussed. Let's look at each of the other capabilities in turn.

Ability to Symbolize. People use symbols in virtually every aspect of their lives, as a way to adapt to and alter their environment. This capability results from a cognitive process that transforms the environment into some kind of cognitive representation. This perspective is shared by Bandura's social cognitive theory as well. Humans **symbolize,** or process symbols, that help us transform our experiences into internal or cognitive codes. These codes serve as guides to future action. Humans can cognitively play out scenarios of action by using prior knowledge

symbolize To form mental representations of modeled events.

and their power to symbolize. Playing out scenarios releases us from the need to perform all possible courses of action in order to decide which action to take. Testing ideas symbolically saves people from many mistakes. An illustration comes from the Teacher Chronicle. Prior to entering her classroom, Ms. Cohn played out the scenario of the plastic bag and pencil experiment mentally and decided the demonstration would work. On the basis of her cognitively generated scenario, she took the course of action we witnessed in the Teacher Chronicle.

Using symbols also helps people communicate with one another across great distances and even across time. Technological advances have taken advantage of this use of symbols. Essentially, the use of symbols assumes that people's behavior is based on thought. Behavior based on thought, however, does not mean that thoughts and the consequent behavior will always be rational. Rationality depends on the skills of the learner. An individual, for example, may not have fully developed the ability to reason, which is at the foundation of rationality. (We will see later in this chapter that social cognitive theory accounts for many of the cognitive developmental characteristics that we discussed in Chapter 2.)

Critical Thinking: How did Piaget, discussed in Chapter 2, describe the development of reasoning? Why should the development of reasoning be an important factor in the ability to symbolize?

Even if an individual is capable of sound reasoning—of logical reasoning—that individual will make mistakes because of faulty information. We may reason possible outcomes based on inadequate knowledge of a situation, faulty interpretation of events, or failure to consider all of the possible consequences of a particular choice of action. Suppose, for example, that a teacher assigns a student extra homework because the student was not paying attention in math class. The teacher takes the action because the student was unable to answer questions about the addition problems on the board. Two days later, the school nurse, in the course of a visual screening, informs the teacher that the child has poor eyesight. Symbolizing capability accounts not only for accomplishment but also for poor judgment, and even irrational behavior.

Connection: The importance of metaphors in the development of teaching expertise is discussed in Chapter 1.

Capacity for Forethought. Human beings do not simply react to their immediate environment but are guided by their past experiences as well. Using knowledge of the past, humans are capable of **forethought,** of anticipating the future. They can consider possible courses of action and anticipate the outcomes of those actions. People set goals for themselves and plan for what Bandura (1986) calls "cognized" futures, planned courses of action. Anticipating that one's goals will be met by following these plans provides the motivation to do so. The capability of forethought—the ability to plan, to carry out intentions, to achieve a purpose—is based firmly in symbolic activity.

We often use a metaphor or an analogy to represent our past experiences and imagine future events. Using these symbolic representations, we plan possible courses of action. For example, viewing one's job as *war* leads one to think about colleagues and/or competitors as either friends or foes. Our course of action would likely be a militant one. Viewing the job as a *public educational campaign* would lead to a different course of action. Our cognized futures can have a strong causal effect on our present action. A student might focus great effort on athletic training or academic study because he or she envisions a college scholarship. Our capability to think ahead, to imagine the future, serves as an impetus for present action.

forethought Anticipation of the future.

self-regulation The act of applying an internal set of standards and criteria to regulate one's own behavior.

self-reflection The act of thinking about one's own experiences and reflecting on one's own thought processes.

Self-Regulation and Self-Reflection. Bandura (1986) assumes that humans do not behave solely to please others in their environment, that they also behave in ways that please themselves; that is, people are self-reinforcing. To this end, they develop a technique of **self-regulation,** by applying a set of internal stan-

Insights ON SUCCESSFUL PRACTICE

What advice can you give novice teachers about helping students become reflective, self-regulating, self-advocating learners?

Soon after I began teaching, I became frustrated with students' lack of responsibility, so I developed a responsibility education program to solve the problem. The program's goal is to have children become responsible, independent learners. They learn to set goals, evaluate their progress, and use organizational skills to succeed.

To help students become independent learners, I designed a child-centered grading system. I feel that grades should make sense to children. How else can students evaluate progress toward their own goals? Unfortunately, we often use grading systems that were designed for adults' convenience instead of children's understanding. For example, to a child limited to Piaget's "concrete operational thought," abstractions such as weighted grades seem more like magic than useful, relevant information. Furthermore, issuing report cards weeks after the work is done compounds students' confusion. I solved the problem with a weekly grading system based on concrete operations that students can understand and use as independent learners.

The skills students learn in the responsibility education program allow them to grow beyond being merely responsible. They learn to be independent and to strive for excellence. The "payoff" comes when the students take over the class.

For example, one year my fifth-grade class designed. organized, and carried out a very successful read-a-thon for world hunger. The students used their skills to set goals and organize committees. They gathered information, arranged publicity, designed ways and means to implement the project, and handled the money they raised. Along the way they taught themselves lessons in geography, earth science, political science, nutrition, and English. To further educate themselves and others they obtained a speaker and arranged a school assembly. The students examined charitable agencies to compare how well each would use their contributions to help the hungry. And of course, each student read five hundred pages. In five weeks, the "500 For Food" read-a-thon raised about eight hundred dollars for world hunger.

As is demonstrated by the "500 For Food" read-a-thon, students can learn to be responsible, self-directed learners. It was designed, organized, and carried out by fifth graders who had learned not only to feel responsible for themselves and for others but also how to be responsible.

CHUCK BOWEN, School District 108,
Pekin, Illinois

dards and evaluative reactions to their own behavior. Through evaluative self-reactions, they are able to detect discrepancies between their performance and their internal standards of behavior. By taking particular actions and evaluating those actions against personal standards of performance, they are able to adjust their behavior. Although behavior is undoubtedly influenced by others in one's environment, Bandura assumes that self-produced influences also play a role. For example, junior high and high school students are under immense social pressure to follow the crowd, but not every adolescent bows to peer pressure.

People are capable of thinking about their own experiences and reflecting on their own thought processes. For Bandura, **self-reflection** leads to self-knowl-

According to this teacher, what is the key to helping students become independent learners? How do student-centered instruction and student-centered assessment contribute to this process?

edge—that is, knowledge about our effectiveness under certain circumstances and, more generally, knowledge about our ability to adapt to our environment. People gain an understanding of themselves, evaluate, and on the basis of that evaluation, alter their thought processes and enhance their future actions.

Point: A basic assumption of this book is: *Reflective construction is necessary for the development of teaching expertise.* The point here is that the substance of the reflection is also important.

The self-reflective capability, however, does not guarantee that future actions will always produce positive consequences. If we operate on faulty or mistaken beliefs, such beliefs can lead to erroneous thought, and therefore, erroneous action. Suppose, for example, that a teacher believed that fear was the only effective way to motivate students. Such a teacher might reflect on the methods he or she used to make students fearful: Were my threats taken seriously? Was the exam sufficiently difficult to scare them into studying harder? Could I have gotten Elizabeth suspended for her inadequate reading of the assignment? Our fear-monger is capable of self-reflection, but reflecting on ways to motivate solely through aversive consequences will not lead to sound instructional decisions.

Self-reflection leads to evaluative judgments about our own thought and action capabilities. Central among these judgments of self is a sense of **self-efficacy,** a person's judgment about his or her ability to deal effectively with tasks he or she faces (Bandura, 1986). Self-efficacy is an important concept in social cognitive theory, and it is important to teachers. The sense that students develop about their abilities to perform tasks influences their motivation and, ultimately, their learning performances. Several sources of information contribute to our self-judgments of efficacy. We look at those variables later in this chapter.

The human ability to use and generate symbols along with the ability of forethought, to cognize futures, allows us to set goals and plan courses of action. Because we can symbolize and anticipate, we are able to learn by observing others. We gather information about ourselves through direct and vicarious experiences. Our self-knowledge includes the set of internal standards by which we judge the effectiveness of our own thought and action and thereby regulate our own behavior. Self-regulation of behavior is one source of information that influences our all-important sense of self-efficacy. The capabilities reviewed here are clearly cognitive in nature and interrelated. For Bandura, these capabilities are a major part of what the observer contributes to learning outcomes. The capabilities of the learner are but one reason why humans learn and behave as they do.

Connection: The importance of prior knowledge—which is related to these capabilities—that learners bring to a learning task is discussed in Chapters 6 and 7.

Reciprocal Determinism

The capability for vicarious learning that Bandura (1986) ascribes to humans reveals his assumption that cognition plays a major role in determining behavior. Cognition that produces thoughts, beliefs, values, and expectations is subsumed into a category that Bandura called "personal factors." Noncognitive characteristics—the learner's size, sex, physical attractiveness, race, and social skills—are included in the category as well. Personal factors interact with the environment and with behavior to influence learning and performance. Both behavior and environment are modifiable. Each controls the other, to some extent. The relationship that exists among personal factors, environment, and behavior is called **reciprocal determinism.** The relationship has also been referred to as triadic reciprocality (Bandura, 1986; Schunk, 1991) to emphasize that each element is related to the other two elements. Bandura (1986) described the reciprocal determinism (depicted in Figure 8.1) as follows:

self-efficacy A human being's judgment about his or her ability to deal effectively with tasks that need to be faced.

reciprocal determinism In cognitive social theory, the three-way relationship that exists among personal factors, environment, and behavior.

> In the social cognitive view people are neither driven by inner forces nor automatically shaped and controlled by external stimuli. Rather, human functioning is explained in terms of a model of triadic reciprocality in which behavior, cognitive and other personal factors, and environmental events all operate as interacting determinants of each other. (p. 18)

We examine the reciprocal interactions by focusing, in turn, on the three sides of the triangle in Figure 8.1.

Links between Personal Factors and Behavior. To describe the interrelations, let's start from the top of the triangle with the personal factors at the apex. The personal-factors category influences and is influenced by behavior and environment. Personal factors (*P*) such as cognition, a sense of self, attitudes, appearance, and demeanor influence behavior (*B*) by means of basic human capabilities we've just discussed (*P*→*B*). Carey, one of the students in the Teacher Chronicle, because of her learning capabilities, can imagine herself doing the bag-and-pencil experiment. She is likely to try the experiment at home. Even if the experiment fails, she will likely persist because she has seen it done and believes herself capable of performing the experiment. Carey's personal factors influence her behavior.

Reflection: Think about the decisions you have made regarding your appearance and your demeanor. How have those decisions influenced your behavior? Give specific examples.

Behavior also influences personal factors (*B*→*P*). If Carey succeeds in carrying out an experiment of her own during Wizard Week, her success will translate into an enhanced sense of self-efficacy. Personal factors influence a learner's behavior. The behavior, once evaluated, influences personal factors.

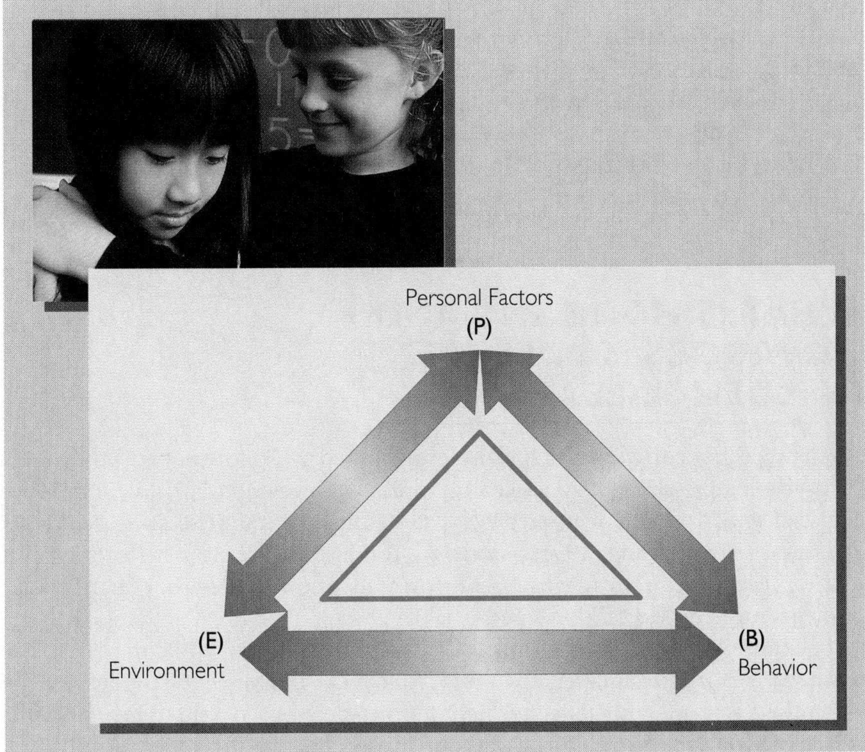

FIGURE 8.1

The Relationships of Reciprocal Determinism
Source: Reprinted with the permission of Simon & Schuster, Inc. from the Macmillan College text *Learning and Instruction* by Margaret E. Gredler. Copyright ©1992 by Macmillan College Publishing Company, Inc.

Try This: Interview a friend or colleague who is disabled. Ask for comments on the ways other people typically respond to his or her disability in professional situations and in social situations. Are there any differences? If so, how does your friend or colleague account for the differences?

Links between Personal Factors and Environment. In addition to cognition, other personal factors, such as physical characteristics, size, sex, and social attributes, influence (or activate) the reactions from the environment (*E*) (*P*→*E*). A friend of ours who is confined to a wheelchair tells us that many of the people she encounters in her daily travels ignore her presence. It is unusual for people she sees everyday to make eye contact or nod a casual acknowledgment as they pass in the halls where she works. She tells the story of how she was heading to the parking lot one day with her ambulatory office partner. Another employee said hello to the office partner and chatted about office matters for a couple of minutes. Not once during the chat did the employee acknowledge our friend's presence with a word or look. The environment responds to the personal factors one displays to the environment.

The social environment provides us with feedback that influences personal factors, such as thoughts and attitudes (*E*→*P*). Once activated by personal factors, differential social treatments from the environment influence personal factors. The environment informs an individual's perception of self, including a sense of self-efficacy that grows out of various social situations.

Links between Behavior and Environment. Behavior operates on the environment to produce certain consequences (*B*→*E*). For example, Ms. Cohn, in the Teacher Chronicle, changed the classroom environment by beginning the class dressed in a white lab coat, carrying a water-filled bag and a sharp pencil poised in dangerous proximity to one another.

Example: As an example of this point, consider the difference between learning how to whistle and learning the conditions under which whistling is or is not appropriate.

Environmental consequences influence the likelihood that a behavior will occur in similar environmental situations (*E*→*B*). Given the students' responses to the demonstration, it is likely that the teacher will use the demonstration to introduce other Wizard Weeks.

Reciprocal determinism reflects the social cognitive view that humans are neither driven wholly by inner forces nor controlled entirely by their environment (Bandura, 1986). Understanding learning from the social cognitive view means understanding not only the interrelationship between environment and behavior but also how cognitive and other personal factors influence and are influenced by environment and behavior.

WHAT IS MODELING AND HOW DOES MODELING INFLUENCE LEARNERS?

Modeling is a generic term in social cognitive theory (Bandura, 1986) that refers to psychological changes (e.g., changes in thought, action, attitude, emotion) that can occur when a learner observes one or more models (cf. Rosenthal & Bandura, 1978; Schunk, 1991). Modeling produces a variety of effects or outcomes. Teachers can, by means of their own attention to the task at hand, make students more or less task oriented.

modeling Learning by observing the behavior of others.

Because teachers and students acting as teachers are potential models for all learners, it is important that they understand the outcomes of modeling. Too often theorists and clinicians use the term *modeling* as a synonym for *imitation*. Modeling involves more than just mimicking behavior; the acquisition of new behaviors is just one type of change brought about through modeling.

According to social cognitive theory, individuals do not respond to environmental reinforcement alone but are self-reinforcing. People reflect on their own thoughts and experiences and exercise self-regulation.

Bandura (1986) has identified five categories of modeling outcomes: inhibitory and disinhibitory effects, response facilitation effects, environmental enhancement effects, arousal effects, and observational learning effects (Figure 8.2). A teacher who understands the distinctions between these outcomes can use modeling as an effective classroom tool.

Inhibitory and Disinhibitory Effects

Inhibitory effects strengthen previously learned inhibitions. By observing a model, an observer acquires information about the feasibility and probable consequences of modeled actions and in this way learns restraint. For example, suppose that student *O*, the observer, has recently acquired the ability to whistle loudly. Suppose also that another student, *M*, the model, in the class also possesses this ability and demonstrates this ability in response to a group presentation on branches of government. Student *M* receives glares from the presenters as well as an under-the-breath comment, "What a jerk," from a popular student in the class. By observing the consequences of whistling by student *M*, student *O* learns not to engage in that behavior. Student *O*'s whistling behavior is inhibited, but only in situations that are the same or similar to the model's situation. Student *O* may refrain from whistling in the classroom, but not on the way home from school.

Reflection: Recall a similar situation from your own student experiences. How did your classmates react to the inappropriate behavior? How did you feel toward the student who exhibited the behavior?

Disinhibitory effects occur when a behavior already known by the observer, but infrequently performed, increases as a result of observing a model. If, in our whistling example, the model had received reinforcement, or at least had not experienced discouraging consequences as a result of whistling in the classroom, our observer's whistling behavior would be disinhibited. The observer would be more likely to whistle as a result of observing the model.

inhibitory effects Consequences of modeling that reinforce previously learned inhibitions.

disinhibitory effects Consequences of modeling that increase a behavior already known but infrequently performed by the observer, by removing the inhibitions associated with that behavior.

response facilitation effects Consequences of modeling that promote previously learned behavior by introducing inducements to perform that behavior.

Facilitative and Environmental Effects

Response facilitation effects serve as social prompts for previously learned behavior. Bandura refers to response facilitation as "exemplification" (1986). Response facilitation effects are similar to disinhibitory effects. Both result in previously learned behavior being performed as a result of observing a model. The difference is that response facilitation increases behaviors not by lifting inhibitions, but by introducing behavior inducements. The simple observation of a model's behavior is often sufficient inducement for the observer to engage in the same type of behavior. Take, as an example, applauding in the middle of a speech given at a school assembly. If one student begins applauding, other students will likely join in. The modeled behavior cues a known response by the learner.

FIGURE 8.2

How do each of these scenes depict the modeling effect represented?

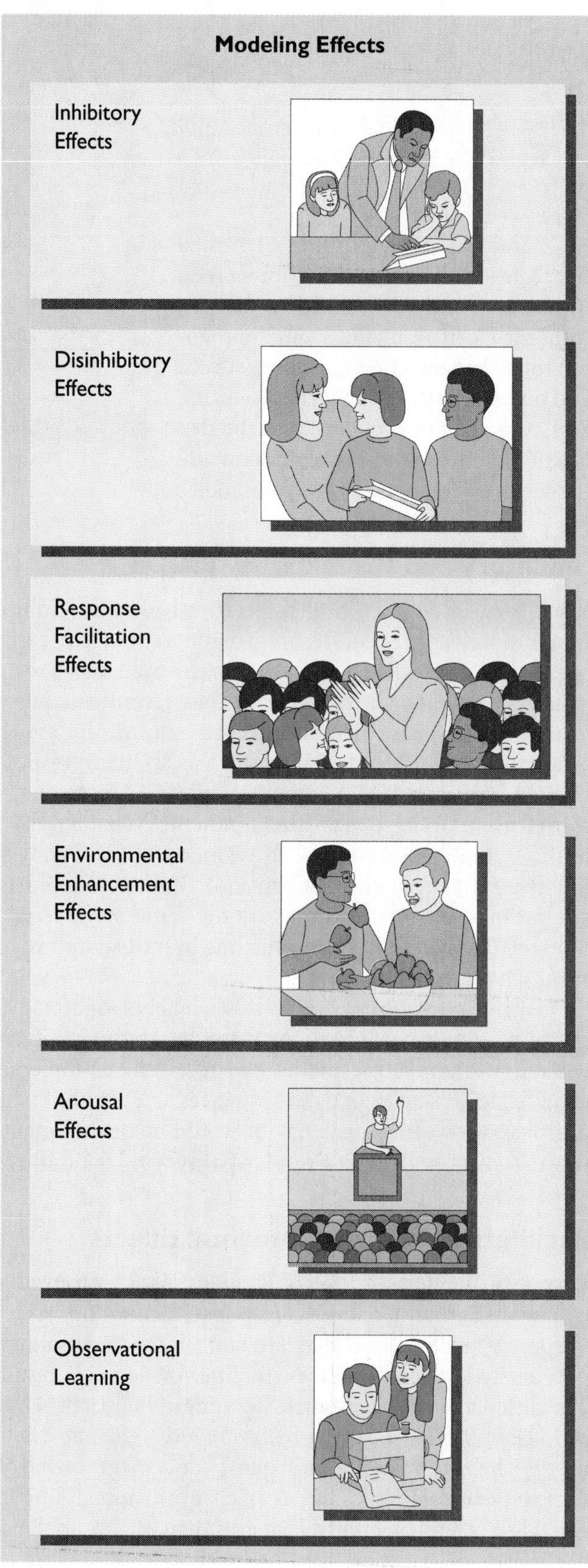

Bandura (1986) uses the example of one person looking up at the sky. Once one person looks up, others will imitate the behavior and look up, too.

Meaningful classroom behavior can also be facilitated or exemplified by models. Research has shown that models can activate altruistic behavior, conversation, discussion, questioning, and brainstorming (cf. Bandura, 1986). Schunk (1991) presents as an example of response facilitation a new display in a classroom. If the display causes one student entering the room to examine it closely, a group is likely to form around it. If the group begins discussing the display, other students will join the group even though they do not know why their schoolmates have gathered.

Try This: Interview a practicing teacher in an attempt to discover how he or she uses the response facilitation effect to generate student interest.

Environmental enhancement effects direct an observer's attention to certain aspects or objects in the model's environment. If a model's behavior includes the use of certain objects, an observer will focus more on those objects than on other objects in the environment. As a result of having their attention thus directed, observers are more likely to select those objects used by the model than other objects. This result holds true even if the observer uses the object in a different way or for a different purpose than does the model. Picture a student demonstrating her recently acquired ability to juggle. It is easy to imagine other students picking up one of the balls and tossing it, squeezing it, or bouncing it off the floor.

Arousal Effects

Arousal effects are changes in an observer's emotional level caused by a model's expressed emotion. Although an emotional model may cause an observer's emotions to be aroused, the observer may not display the same emotion that the model does. Recall or imagine a situation in which you observed two angry people arguing in public, perhaps in a store or a restaurant. As you observed the argument, you probably felt a surge of emotion, but the emotion you felt might not have been anger. It is more likely that you felt embarrassed by this public display. If the argument appeared to be on the brink of becoming an altercation, you might have felt anxiety or fear.

Try This: Observe a class for a period of time sufficient to allow you to identify class leaders. Observe the leaders in an attempt to determine if they facilitate the types of effects discussed here more than other students.

Positive emotions can also be aroused by models. The enjoyment that the teacher felt during the bag-of-water demonstration was translated into excitement from the students when they realized they, too, would have a chance to conduct the same or similar experiments as part of Wizard Week.

environmental enhancement effects Consequences of modeling that direct an observer's attention to certain aspects or objects in the model's environment.

arousal effects Consequences of modeling that change an observer's physical and psychological reactions caused by the model's expressed emotions and actions.

observational learning effects Consequences of modeling that lead to the acquisition of cognitive and behavioral patterns that had no chance of occurring prior to modeling.

Observational Learning Effects

Observational learning effects involve the acquisition of cognitive and behavioral patterns that, prior to modeling, had a zero probability of occurring. A model may teach an observer new behavioral skills, such as juggling, or cognitive competencies, such as long division. An observer may learn new standards of socially acceptable behavior or rules for generating such behavior. The observational learning effect includes new ways of organizing existing component skills. For example, when a student learns to pronounce a new word, he or she is learning to combine previously known sounds in a new way.

To summarize, modeling can result in cognitive, affect, and/or motor outcomes, depending on the context and consequences of modeled actions. Inhibitory or disinhibitory effects occur when a model plays a role analogous to that of either a subject in a research study or a test pilot. Response facilitation effects occur when a model serves as a prompter who cues certain behaviors. Environmental enhancement effects occur when the model serves as a prop

ON SUCCESSFUL PRACTICE

In your experience, how have strategies based on social learning theory benefited you and your students?

Education can be seen as a simple transaction between the knower and the learner. The goods labeled *knowledge* are packaged and passed unmodified from one person to another. Tidy as this model may seem, in my experience it just doesn't work. For learning to be meaningful, it must be interactive. Teacher and students together must wrestle with text, discover what it means in their worlds, and construct or create meaning for themselves. In this process, the teacher is primarily a catalyst, but she or he must also serve as model, resource, and manager of time and space. The goal is to create a total environment in which students learn how to learn.

Pleasure is a key ingredient in an interactive classroom: the pleasure of figuring out something for yourself, the pleasure of working with friends on a project, the pleasure of watching students encased in aluminum foil perform *The Idylls of the King*. I could fill a hope chest with the bed sheets that have been left behind from a decade of Caesar skits. Emotional responses to literature stay with us long after we've forgotten the characters' names. Learning that is attached to feeling lasts.

In my opinion, an outstanding teacher is one who is also a lifelong learner and who has developed strategies for helping students become the same. When I watch my students struggle together with a poem—matching wits, defending their views, finding meaning if not consensus—I feel that my classroom is a laboratory for the human experiment. I see growth.

CAROL JAGO, Santa Monica High School,
Santa Monica, California

What principles from social learning theory can be inferred from this teacher's essay? What role does social interaction play in meaningful learning? What does it mean to say "learning that is attached to feeling lasts?"

handler or tour guide who highlights certain objects or aspects of the environment. Arousal effects occur when the model serves as a cheerleader, a cheerleader charged with whipping up not enthusiasm but emotions. Observational learning effects occur when a model serves as an instructor or training demonstrator.

The outcomes examined here occur in classrooms because students observe and learn from models. Some of the models that affect classroom learning and performance are internal to the classroom. These internal models include the teacher, classmates, and fictional characters and historical figures encountered in assigned readings. Other models—such as television, movies, sports, and rock stars; cartoon characters; parents; and religious leaders—are external to the classroom. Any model, no matter who or what it is, is capable of generating one or more of the modeling effects described in these sections.

If a teacher is to use modeling as an effective tool, he or she must understand modeling outcomes. Teachers who understand the various kinds of information that models can convey understand the roles a model can play. Armed with such knowledge, teachers can select models to play the role or roles students need to observe. However, just because a teacher selects good models does not ensure that students will accept those models as their own. Knowledge of modeling outcomes is necessary, but not sufficient. Teachers need to know about the effects models can have, but they must also understand that it is the observers who must acquire the information, attitudes, and behaviors conveyed by these models. The cognitive processes of observational learning explain how an observer learns from a model.

Try This: Interview a teacher about the ways in which he or she uses models in the classroom. Who are the models? How are they selected? For what specific purposes are models used?

WHAT ARE THE PROCESSES OF OBSERVATIONAL LEARNING?

Bandura (1986) characterizes observational learning as a cognitive processing activity. Information from modeled events is transformed into symbolic representations that guide future action. There are four processes that operate as observers learn from models: attention, retention, production, and motivation (Figure 8.3).

Reflection: Who were your models in school? Why did those people become your models? Why did they attract and hold your attention?

Attention governs the aspects of the modeled event that learners observe or fail to observe. **Retention** converts modeled events into cognitive representations. **Production** allows the observer to organize his or her observations so that he or she may perform the modeled behavior. **Motivation** determines the likelihood that observational learning is turned into performance. Let us examine each process in turn.

attention The ability to observe modeled behavior.

retention The capacity to remember modeled behavior.

production The act of producing modeled behavior.

motivation The desire to produce modeled behavior.

Attention

Unless people pay attention to modeled events, they cannot learn much from them. This conclusion is consistent with the attention process as it is understood in the information-processing model. Attentional processes in observational learning allow the observer to determine which aspects of the modeled events are relevant and which are irrelevant. Selectively attending to aspects of the modeled event is an important subfunction in observational learning. There are a number of factors that influence the observer's selectivity. Some are properties of the model and the modeled behaviors; others are properties of the observer.

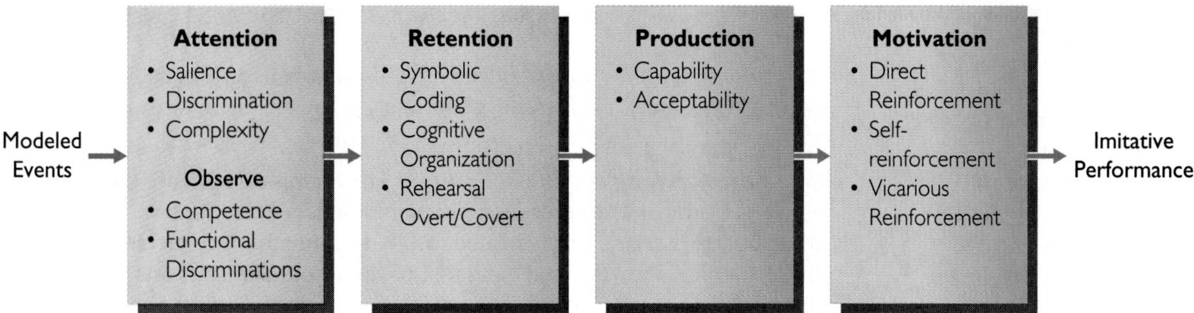

FIGURE 8.3

The Four Processes of Observational Learning

Source: From *Social Foundations of Thought and Action: A Social Cognitive Theory* (p. 52) by A. Bandura, 1986, Englewood Cliffs, NJ: Prentice-Hall. Copyright 1986 by Prentice Hall. Reprinted by permission.

Influence of Models on Attention. The quality and quantity of observational learning can be affected by the *salience* of modeled actions, the extent to which these actions stand out from other aspects of the environment. In a classroom filled with potential models, one classmate may behave in a highly conspicuous manner. The conspicuous model may jump up and sing the "Star-Spangled Banner." Such an event would likely be considered salient.

Example: Examples of what is meant by relevant aspects of behaviors can be found in various instruction manuals such as a book on how to improve your tennis game.

Relevance—the extent to which relevant and irrelevant behaviors can be discriminated—is another property of modeled events that influences the attention process. Suppose an observer is watching a professional tennis player on television. The observer may attend not only to the position of the racket prior to the swing and to the footwork of the professional player but also to the particular tennis clothing worn by that player. Attending to the position of the racket and the footwork of the player are relevant aspects of the model's behavior; such attention will allow the observer to better imitate the model's tennis stroke. Imitating the model's style of dress may occur as a function of observation, but the style of dress is irrelevant for imitating the model's tennis stroke.

An observer's attention can be influenced also by the *complexity* of the modeled events. Complex modeling requires that the observer acquire the rules for generating behavior rather than simply imitating the behavior itself. If an observer is to learn chess by observing a model, he or she must watch how the various pieces are moved and, from those moves, abstract the rules that govern each piece. If the observer is to acquire some level of competence, he or she must also abstract the strategies and tactics that govern a series of moves.

The salience, relevance, and complexity of modeled events affect an observer's attention. But remember that a basic assumption of social learning theory is reciprocal determinism: Aspects of the environment and personal factors determine each other. In terms of attention, this means that what is salient, relevant, and complex about a modeled event is influenced by the personal factors an observer brings to the modeled event. How can a teacher make modeled events salient, relevant, and appropriately complex?

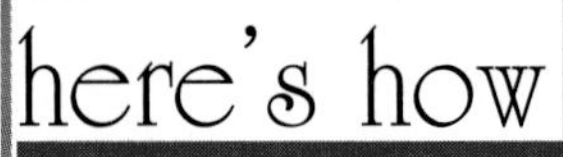

Here's How to Faciliate Attention to Modeled Events

- Ask or survey your students' interests. Find out what recreational activities they pursue, who are their favorite performers, what are their favorite books and movies.
- Use the interest surveys to select models. For example, if you are going to teach a science unit, select several scientists of both genders and various cultural backgrounds whose work is related to the unit. In addition to readings, select a film or a movie excerpt that is related to the topic. Give students options as to the resources they can choose to consult. Let them choose what is most salient to them.
- Ask students to help you determine what the outcomes of the unit should be. Should we take a test? Create a project? Teach other students through demonstration? Allow students to help make the work relevant.
- Create follow-up activities for students who desire to pursue a topic in depth. Don't stifle a student's interest in pursuing a topic at a more complex level.

Influence of Observers on Attention. The attentional process can be influenced by properties of the observer, in addition to properties of the model's behavior. An experienced chess player will attend to different aspects of a televised chess match than will a chess novice. As we saw in Chapter 1, expert teachers interpret classroom situations differently than novice teachers. The complexity of the modeled event is better appreciated by the expert observer because the expert observer has a knowledge base that allows him or her to make more critical discriminations of the actions taking place. Similarly, a chess master's cognitive competencies and prior knowledge influence what he or she sees as salient and relevant in the modeled activity. The cognitive competencies of the observer, therefore, influence the perception of the modeled events.

Observers make a determination of the functional value of modeled events. An observer who expects to function in an environment similar to that of the model will pay closer attention to the behavior of the model than will an observer who does not expect to function in such an environment. A junior high student who studies ballet may watch both ballet and gymnastics on television. The student will perceive the salience, understand the complexity, and make better discriminations of relevant and irrelevant behaviors of the ballet dancers than those of the gymnasts.

Connection: The effects of perceived relevance on motivation are discussed in the ARCS model presented in Chapter 9.

There is a developmental effect in observational learning that is associated with attentional processes. Bandura (1986) reports that young children cannot attend well to modeled events for long periods of time. Furthermore, they do not easily distinguish relevant aspects of modeled behavior from irrelevant aspects. Rather, it seems that salience is the most important factor, even though the most salient aspect of a modeled event may not be the most relevant. As children mature, they develop a more extensive knowledge base and are better able to make use of various memory strategies. Maturation influences the capacity for observational learning. As children develop cognitively, they get better at symbolically representing vicarious experiences.

Retention

Retention processes include symbolic coding, organization of what has received attention, and rehearsal. For the observer to form and retain a cognitive representation of the modeled behavior, it is necessary that he or she code and store observations. The cognitive representation that results is the basis for further action by the observer. Think of what students in Wizard Week stored in their memory from Ms. Cohn's demonstration.

Critical Thinking: Speculate as to which kind of rehearsal might be most effective in learning a skill. Are there learning activities that would facilitate one more than the other? Other activities that would enhance both?

In order to perform a modeled behavior, a student must form an accurate cognitive version of the model's behavior—what Bandura refers to as symbolic coding and organization. Retaining the information requires more than simply coding and organizing a model's behavior, however. Some sort of rehearsal is necessary if the observer is to perform. Bandura (1986) refers to two types of rehearsals: cognitive rehearsal and enactive rehearsal, also known as *covert* and *overt* rehearsal. Overt rehearsal is of the type that most of us think of as practicing. It usually involves a physical action. Imagine, for example, the prospective dancers who arrive at an audition for a Broadway show. Typically, the choreographer of the show brings the hopefuls to the stage and demonstrates a series of dance steps. Those auditioning are given the opportunity to briefly rehearse the dance steps in an overt fashion—that is, to actually do them. After being shown the steps, the auditioners go into the wings to await their turn to perform the steps for the director of the show. As the dancers wait in the wings for their opportunity to perform, they practice the dance steps. Because there is insufficient room in the wings for them to perform the series of steps fully, they tend to abbreviate their actions.

Try This: Talk with gymnasts, figure skaters, or ballet dancers. Ask them to describe if they use covert rehearsal. If so, ask them how they use it.

In some cases, you can see auditioners sitting quietly, perhaps with their eyes closed, dancing to themselves. This is covert rehearsal. Perhaps you have heard or read that Olympic athletes, especially gymnasts or figure skaters, who must perform a prescribed program of action, engage in a kind of covert rehearsal called imaginary practice (Bower & Hilgard, 1981). Reports by Olympic athletes indicate the effectiveness of such covert rehearsal. Greg Louganis, a gold-medal-winning diver, choreographed his dives to music. The music was not played aloud, but covertly, in his head. After much covert and overt practice, the music became part of his symbolic code. The dive could be covertly rehearsed by mentally playing the musical accompaniment. More formal evidence also exists to suggest that covert rehearsal is an effective way to improve actual performance (see Corbin, 1972; Feltz & Landers, 1983).

Production

After the observer attends to and retains modeled behaviors, he or she is ready to produce the behaviors. Production processes are influenced most immediately by the observer's physical capabilities. Later, production is influenced by the self-observation and self-feedback associated with the performance.

The cognitive component of production processes can be thought of as decisions that the observer must make. The first of these is whether or not he or she is physically capable of producing the modeled behavior. The second decision is whether or not producing the modeled behavior is socially acceptable.

Suppose you read about a teacher with an unusual way of energizing her students at the beginning of class. From time to time she dons a cape and runs into the classroom to the taped strains of a trumpet fanfare. As she reaches the front of the classroom, the taped music switches to a rock tune. She invites the class to stand and dance with her. After a minute or so of dancing, the music fades, and she removes her cape and begins the day's lesson.

Reflection: Would you use these particular tactics with your own students? Why or why not?

What would you do with this modeled event? Would you imitate the behaviors? You have two decisions to make. Am I capable of producing the modeled behaviors? If so, do I judge the behaviors to be acceptable? To make those decisions, you need to consult your knowledge of self. Having observed and judged your own past behavior, you can anticipate the consequences of modeling the caped dancer. The decision of capability is more than simply determining whether or not you are physically capable of the modeled behaviors. The question, Is this behavior acceptable? means deciding if you can bring yourself to display such behaviors. What if you tried the cape-and-music gambit and it led not to energy, but to embarrassment? The point is that decisions of capability spill over into decisions of acceptability. But what if students never tried new activities? What if their production decisions prevented them from taking small risks? How can you help your students make sound capability and acceptance decisions?

here's how

Here's How to Foster Good Production Decisions

- Establish an atmosphere where risk taking is encouraged. Students who feel they are unable to risk certain behaviors may never try new activities.
- Take risks yourself. Try to learn new skills and demonstrate your progress—mistakes and all—to your students. Show students that learning new concepts and skills can be all the more rewarding for the mistakes that are made along the way.
- Support effort. When students attempt to play a new song, sculpt for the first time, apply a new math concept, write their first haiku, you can reward the effort even if the product of that effort is flawed.
- Talk about decisions. Ask students to share their decisions of capability and acceptance. Help students reflect on their reasoning and encourage them to test their decisions. A student who chooses not to participate in a folk dance because he or she fears embarrassment can be encouraged to test his or her prediction.

Motivation

Motivation is the last component of Bandura's (1986) observational learning model. Motivational processes include three kinds of reinforcement: direct reinforcement, self-reinforcement, and vicarious reinforcement.

Direct reinforcement is provided by the external environment. If the production decisions are positive, the observer performs the modeled behavior. The observer's behavior yields an environmental consequence: direct reinforcement. If the students in the Teacher Chronicle perform the pencil-and-bag-of-water demonstration for friends or family members, they may receive direct reinforcement, just as Ms. Cohn received direct reinforcement from the students in the classroom.

Connection: The facilitation of self-regulation skills is examined later in this chapter.

Self-reinforcement is derived from the observer's evaluation of his or her own performance independent of environmental consequences. The caped teacher may perform her musical lesson staging simply because she enjoys it or because she feels competent doing it. Jugglers do not always need an audience—a source of direct reinforcement—to perform. Juggling is often performed in solitude because the juggler finds reinforcement in the act itself.

Vicarious reinforcement is derived from viewing a model engaged in the behavior. Vicarious reinforcement explains why you might stay up late to watch, for example, Harrison Ford movies. You may be neither capable nor particularly desirous of producing the behaviors you observe, but you do derive vicarious pleasure from watching Ford perform them repeatedly.

direct reinforcement Using direct consequences from the external environment to strengthen a desired behavior.

self-reinforcement Using consequences that come from within to strengthen a desired behavior.

vicarious reinforcement Using consequences derived from viewing a model engaged in a desired behavior to strengthen that behavior.

If students learn behaviors by observing others in their social environment, and if through the processes of observational learning they come to decisions about their capabilities and their efficacy in performing behaviors that they have learned, an important instructional question arises. What makes an effective model? Further, how can teachers provide and serve as effective models?

If we consider the questions developmentally, the most obvious candidates for potential models change as children change—as they grow older. For very young children, prominent adults in their social environment have an advantage as potential models. As children grow older, the influence of significant adults in their

Insights ON SUCCESSFUL PRACTICE

How do you use peer modeling in your classroom and with what results?

Another important aspect of morning business periods is our daily sharing. A particular kind of sharing is designed for each day of the week. Mondays are teacher's sharing days. This practice gives me an excellent opportunity to model and set standards indirectly. I share poems, books, current events, and teach songs.

The students share from Tuesday to Friday. Each student is scheduled so that he or she knows what and when to share during the month and can plan accordingly. The class is divided into five groups. Each group is scheduled to present in one of three categories—current events, poetry, or books—during the week.

When sharing current events, the students search for articles related to the science, social studies, or literature units of study. For example, last month the students had to apply their newspaper reading skills in selecting articles related to our science units on plants, animals, and ecology. The students prepare for the sharing by locating an appropriate article. reading it, and then writing a short summary. During their oral presentations, they point out the location of the incident discussed in the article on a map. These sharings bring additional real-life dimensions to our units.

What contexts for peer modeling has this teacher used? What are the advantages to students of learning in these contexts? In the subject area you plan to teach, what are some peer modeling activities you might use to advantage?

When sharing poetry, the students choose poems related to the social studies and science topics and literature themes. They also attempt to identify specific literary elements previously taught within the poem of their choice. For example, Malie chose a poem by X. J. Kennedy, "The Whale Off Wales," and demonstrated her recognition of personification and simile in this poem. In addition, the students' own understanding of personification and simile enhances their appreciation and comprehension of her piece. The students enjoy and appreciate the range of poems shared; these poems also serve as models for their own writing. Through exposures to poems on subjects about which they have done reading, they realize there are many ways to express ideas about a topic.

When sharing books, the students select books related to our study of literature and other social studies topics for the month. They read, prepare, and creatively present their books. For example, upon selecting and reading a myth or tall tale, each student pretended to be a director or a member of a cast of characters for a play based on the story. In the context of enjoyable book-sharing activities, the students analyzed the qualities of the characters and identified similar qualities among their classmates.

I have found that students extend their range of reading, expand the ways they "sell" books to others beyond the traditional book report, and stimulate their own perceptions when interpreting stories through these book-sharing activities. The *daily* integration, application, and modeling of content and communication areas has far-reaching benefits for my students by providing the necessary involvement and practice to help them internalize content and refine their communication abilities.

BETSY F. YOUNG, Liholiho Elemetary School, Honolulu, Hawaii

environment decreases. As children enter the intermediate elementary grades and proceed through junior high and high school, the importance of peers increases. Think of how important it was for you to feel accepted and supported by adults when you were very young and then by your classmates in junior and senior high.

HOW CAN YOUR KNOWLEDGE OF SOCIAL LEARNING MAKE YOU A MORE EFFECTIVE TEACHER?

Teachers who know the processes and outcomes of observational learning are better able to decide when and under what conditions models might prove useful. If, for example, a teacher wants to motivate students—to arouse some interest in an upcoming project—employing a model to demonstrate the project would be a reasonable plan. Think back to the arousal effects of the water-bag demonstration in Wizard Week. Making use of models in the classroom is not, however, simply a matter of deciding when to use a model. Decisions about the instructional use of models is complicated by the fact that not all models are equally effective.

Critical Thinking: Why should modeled events—such as the water bag demonstration in Wizard Week—more effectively arouse interest than a simple verbal preview?

Selecting Effective Models

In order to select the right model, a teacher must know what makes a model more or less effective. Effectiveness depends on the perceptions of the observer; model effectiveness is in the eye of the beholder. We now examine two types of observer perceptions, similarity and competence, and ways in which those perceptions relate to peer modeling.

Try This: Identify a particular outcome you intend for your students. List as many models as you can that might be used to help your students attain the outcome.

Perceived Similarity. Perceived similarity is an observer's perception of similarity between him- or herself and the model. As is the case with other characteristics of a model, the observer's perception influences the model's effectiveness.

Rosenkrans (1967) showed children a film of a model playing a war game. The children were then led to believe that they were similar or dissimilar in background to the model. The high-similarity condition produced more modeled behaviors than the low-similarity condition. Rosenkrans's study supports the notion that models who are perceived by observers to be similar to themselves are more effective models.

Schunk (1987), in reviewing the literature on model effectiveness, recognizes that when it comes to the question of how many models are needed, more are better. Studies have shown that multiple models increase the likelihood that observers will perform the model behavior. (This is a form of response facilitation, which we examined earlier.) But why should an increased number of models increase resp-onse facilitation effects? Schunk reasons that increasing the number of models in-creases the likelihood that observers will see themselves as being similar to at least one of the models.

Spence (1984) reviewed research to determine what influence the sex of the models had on observational learning. Spence concluded that the sex of the model seems to affect performance more than it does learning. Children learn behaviors from models of both sexes; they also judge the sex-appropriateness of those behaviors. Because some behaviors are judged more appropriate for members of one sex or the other, students who observe an opposite-sex model may

perceived similarity An observer's perception of similarity between himself or herself and the model.

Reflection: Make a list of the five most influential models you had in high school. How many were of the same gender? Were there any of the opposite sex? If so, identify the characteristics that most influenced you.

decide that the behavior is not, to use the term from the production process of observational learning, acceptable. The tendency to imitate behaviors performed by same-sex models can therefore be attributed to perceived similarity.

Perceived similarity is an important element of model effectiveness. If an observer sees him- or herself as being similar to the model and then observes the model succeeding in a particular situation, the observer is more likely to infer self-efficacy. Thus, perceived similarity means that the observer is likely to say to him- or herself, "If he (she) can do it, I can do it."

Perceived Competence. **Perceived competence** is an observer's evaluation of how expert a model is. Simon, Ditrichs, & Speckhart (1975) found that children are more likely to follow the behavior of models they perceived as being competent than they are to follow models they perceive as being less than competent in the displayed skill. This is especially true when they are learning a novel response.

A model who masters a situation is perceived as being competent. However, this competence can itself be perceived in at least two different ways. Suppose that a teacher brings in two published novelists to talk about creative writing. The first novelist reads a scene from her latest book and discusses her characters' motivations and their symbolic meanings. The second novelist brings in marked-up copies of his first five drafts of a scene and describes the frustrations involved in getting from the rough draft to the published version. Both models have mastered the skill of creative writing. The first novelist presents her mastery as an accomplished fact; she can be called a *mastery model.* The second novelist demonstrates how he overcomes problems on his way to mastery; he can be called a *coping model* (cf. Schunk, 1991).

Try This: Observe various classroom teachers. Identify those teachers who exemplify mastery models and those who can be classified as coping models. Which of the two types of teachers would you consider to be more effective? Explain your choice.

When learners are fearful about a particular situation, they are more likely to improve their performances and gain self-confidence when they observe coping models rather than mastery models. Coping models initially demonstrate the typical fears and deficiencies of the observers. A model who copes with a situation rather than mastering it instantly may be a model who helps observers enhance their sense of self-efficacy (Schunk, Hanson, & Cox, 1987).

There is one other aspect of perceived competence that merits mention here. Perceived competence can be influenced by an observer's perception of a model's social status. One attains high social status by distinguishing her- or himself from others in a field of endeavor. A well-known political figure has been elected ahead of others. A well-known movie actor has been cast in more leading roles than other actors. A professional athlete has been selected over other athletes. If a model has high social status, he or she is often given credit for competence outside his or her area of expertise. We buy breakfast cereals because they are endorsed by athletes, not nutritionists.

A teacher who is judged by students to be a really great teacher has attained high status within the school community. The teacher may have attained that status because he or she is a recognized authority in a particular academic field or is recognized as a teacher who fosters student success.

Using Cognitive Modeling as an Instructional Approach

perceived competence An observer's evaluation of how expert a model is.

One of the implications of the social cognitive view is that modeling expands instructional opportunities beyond the process of shaping (Ormrod, 1990; Schunk, 1991). Shaping, an instructional process based in operant-conditioning theory, begins by reinforcing existing behaviors and then selectively reinforces changes in those behaviors to bring about complex behavior. Modeling, however, is an instructional process by which new behaviors, concepts, and skills can be introduced, demonstrated, practiced, and reinforced. Consider, for a moment, how difficult it would have been for Ms. Cohn in the Teacher Chronicle to have used shaping as a way of inducing her students to conduct and present scientific experiments.

Teachers typically model cognitive skills that they want their students to acquire. The usual instructional sequence is for the teacher to explain and demonstrate the skill to be learned. After the skill is presented, students are given the opportunity to practice with guidance from the teacher. As the teacher monitors the students' practice, he or she checks for understanding and provides feedback to improve performance. If students experience severe problems, the skill is retaught, perhaps using a different explanation and demonstration. If students perform adequately during guided practice, they move to independent practice with only periodic checks by the teacher.

Connection: This aspect of cognitive modeling is related to the notion of fading, discussed in Chapter 6.

Cognitive modeling is an instructional approach that builds on modeled explanation and demonstration by augmenting the demonstration of the skill with model verbalization (Meichenbaum, 1977). As the model—usually the teacher—demonstrates the skill, he or she speaks aloud his or her thoughts, reasons, and decisions. To illustrate, imagine you are a student in a class in which the skill being taught is long division. The teacher writes the following problem on the board:

$$4\overline{)\,116}$$

As the teacher begins working on the problem, you hear the following verbalization: "Okay, let's see. First I have to decide what number I divide four into. I start with the first digit of the dividend, which in this problem is one. Four won't go into one, so I move to the right to see if it will go into that number. By moving one number to the right, I now have eleven. Four will go into eleven three? No, four times three is twelve and that's bigger than eleven. Four will go into eleven two times. So, my quotient begins with two, which I write above the eleven. Okay, the next step is to multiply two times four, which is eight. I write the eight under the eleven, subtract and end up with three. Now, I bring down the six that is left in the dividend . . . ." And so the verbalization goes. By modeling not only the skill but also the thoughts, reasoning, and decisions that accompany the performance of the skill, the teacher is modeling his or her cognition. This approach is consistent with the concept of thinking dispositions presented in Chapter 5.

Try This: Observe one-on-one tutoring. Make a note of the number of times the tutor uses these kinds of statements in working with the learner. After the tutoring session, share your notes with the tutor as you discuss the session.

Verbalization during cognitive modeling can also include statements that indicate the model's motivation. Statements that imply self-reinforcement, such as, "This is going well, " "I think I'm getting this," or "That looks like it was a good decision," show students that making progress on a problem or task has positive consequences. Sharing the positive feelings of success seems a worthwhile reason to use cognitive modeling, but what would happen if, while verbalizing, a teacher makes a mistake? After all, teachers who use cognitive modeling run the risk of revealing their own weaknesses, especially if they are working on novel problems or if they are truly attempting to discover a new understanding in partnership with students. The research on model effectiveness suggests that making mistakes is okay and that verbalizing one's difficulties may, in the long run, prove helpful to students who are struggling. If a teacher's verbalization acknowledges a prob-

cognitive modeling An approach to instruction that combines demonstration of skill with verbalization of cognitive activity that accompanies the skill.

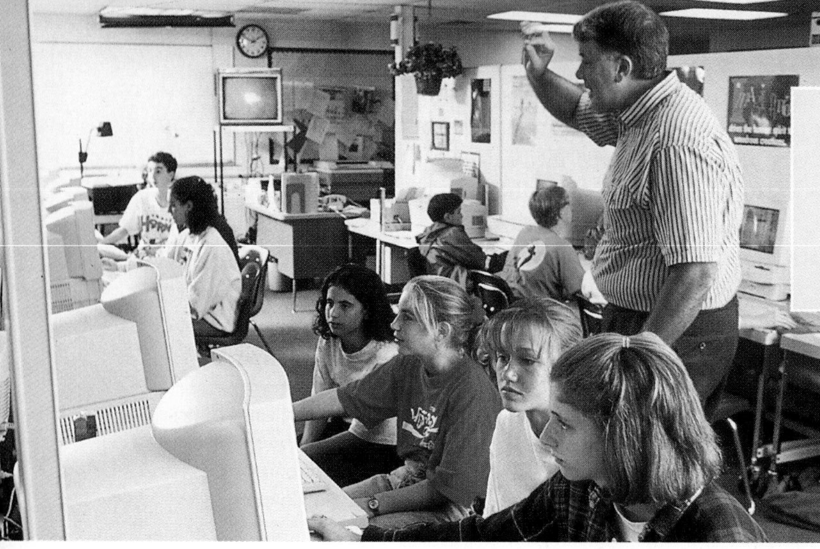

This teacher is engaging the processes of observational learning to model a thought process that will lead to mastery. What characteristics of the model will make this lesson effective? What cognitive processes of the observers will affect their observational learning?

lem, determines what steps he or she might take to solve the problem—including the possibility of rereading an assignment or consulting an additional source of information—and ultimately solves the problem, that teacher will probably establish him- or herself as a coping model. Recall that both coping and mastery models are perceived as competent, but the coping model is more effective (Schunk, 1991). So, what if you use cognitive modeling in your own class and you make a mistake? Acknowledge it. Determine how to correct it. Persevere until the correct solution is found. Modeling the process by which you learn from mistakes might be one of the most valuable lessons you will ever teach.

Reflection: Think back to a situation in which you worked with an expert. How did the experience influence your learning? What was the nature of the relationship between you as the apprentice and the master?

An instructional approach that is conceptually similar to cognitive modeling is called cognitive apprenticeship (Brown, Collins, & Duguid, 1989). In secondary and higher education, apprenticeships have usually taken the form of internships. Internships are opportunities for students to apply the knowledge and skills they have acquired in school to real work situations (Driscoll, 1994). Although most classroom teachers may not be able to establish internships, they can model skills and then structure learning activities that require students to apply those skills in meaningful and realistic ways (cf. Honebein, Duffy, & Fishman, 1994). Suppose, for example, that a science teacher assigned a project, the outcome of which was transforming the classroom into a science museum, complete with hands-on exhibits and guided tours for other students in the school, parents, and administrators. The exhibits could be developed on the basis of the units in the school's curriculum. The teacher could function as the director of the museum, while students functioned as other personnel—for example, members of exhibit teams, evaluators of other exhibits, guides, resource persons, brochure writers, exhibit caption writers, and publicists. This type of project allows the teacher to model skills, coach students, and evaluate student learning in ways similar to those used by the master in whose charge the apprentice was placed.

Helping Learners Build a Sense of Self-Efficacy

One of the most important outcomes that a student can acquire is the ability to learn. Bandura postulates the existence of a self-regulating system within the learner, which permits the learner to observe and evaluate his or her own performance. The judgments that the learner makes by means of self-evaluation influence his or her belief that he or she is capable of learning. Learning to learn is an outcome of instruction. To the extent that observational learning occurs in classrooms—and it occurs a great deal—self-efficacy is also an outcome of classroom instruction. Bandura (e.g., 1977, 1982, 1986) suggests four possible sources by which students can gain information relevant to their sense of self-efficacy: outcome of performance, vicarious experience, verbal persuasion, and physiological states.

The first source of information about self-efficacy is the outcome of performance. Successful performance on a given task enhances one's sense of self-efficacy.

A second source of efficacy information is vicarious experience. Students who observe models who attain success can use those observations to determine their own efficacy. If the role model attains success, the student will make judgments about the similarity between him- or herself and the model. The observer, seeing that the model has successfully completed the task, will also infer competence. If the competent model is perceived as being similar to the observer, the observer's sense of efficacy will be enhanced. If, however, the competent model is seen as being dissimilar, the observer may attribute the model's success to those qualities that he or she does not possess.

Try This: Ask practicing teachers if the success of one student has a ripple effect on the motivation of other students. Ask whether the "If he or she can do it, so can I" attitude is noticeable in the classroom. If it is, ask for examples. If it is not, ask why.

A third source of information that can influence self-efficacy is what Bandura refers to as "verbal persuasion." Other people in the learner's social environment—peers, teachers, parents—can persuade the learner verbally that they are capable of success at a particular task. Verbal persuasion by others is a substitute for the self-evaluation that occurs normally in observational learning. Verbal persuasion can occur internally as well, taking the form of what might be called positive self-talk.

Physiological states provide a last source of information about self-efficacy. Bandura refers to the gut feelings that convince a learner that he or she can or cannot achieve a goal. By taking into account factors such as perceived ability of the model and of self, the difficulty of the task, the amount of effort that needs to be expended, and aids to performance, students may experience physical sensations of increased alertness or excitement.

Teachers must try to provide the type of information that will enhance students' sense of self-efficacy. For example, suppose you were to respond to a sense of difficulty in your class by saying, "I don't understand why you people can't do this; the class last year had no problems." Such a response would require students either to perceive themselves as dissimilar to last year's class or to perceive themselves as less capable.

Reflection: Think back to an episode in which a teacher responded to your class in a way similar to that indicated here. How did the teacher's comments make you feel? Were they motivating? If so, how? If not, why not?

The degree to which a sense of self-efficacy has been developed is an outcome of observational learning (Driscoll, 1994). As there is with all learning and motivation issues, the relationship between self-efficacy and motivation is a strong one. Bandura (1977, 1982) argues that students with a sense of high self-efficacy will produce greater effort and persist longer in a task than students with a sense of low self-efficacy.

Motivational overtones are also seen in the relationship between self-efficacy and choice of activity. Bandura argues that self-efficacy influences a student's choice of activity. Students with low self-efficacy in a particular area take measures to avoid tasks in that area. In contrast, students with high-efficacy expectations toward a particular task tend to approach that task eagerly.

Point: Although the concept of self-efficacy is related to self-esteem, discussed in Chapter 3, there is an important difference. Self-efficacy is situation-specific.

Self-efficacy involves a belief that one can produce some behavior regardless of whether one actually can or cannot produce that behavior. Bandura (1977) proposes that the concept of self-efficacy is an indicator of both performance and achievement. He states that "individuals can believe that a particular course of action will produce certain outcomes, but if they entertain serious doubts about whether they can perform the necessary activities, such information does not influence their behavior" (p. 193).

Therefore, outcome expectations and efficacy expectations must be met before a person will enact a behavior that leads to an anticipated outcome (Figure 8.4). Efficacy expectations, which are predictions of how effective or competent one will be in his or her performance, differ from outcome expectations. Outcome expectations refer to a person's predictions about the likelihood that a given behavior will lead to particular consequences. In this sense, outcome expectations are the judgments that observers make about the functional value of modeled behaviors.

As we will discover in Chapter 9, the learner's expectations and the teacher's expectations of learners are important determiners of motivation, especially in classroom achievement situations. Goal setting is an important component of the self-regulation system and, therefore, an important determiner of a student's sense of self-efficacy.

Bandura (1977, 1986) suggests that when individuals set goals, they determine a desired standard against which they compare internally their present levels of performance. Bandura suggests further that delaying self-reward until goals are met increases the likelihood that individuals will sustain their efforts until the goals are attained. Bandura's observations have led to additional research on the practice of goal setting and its influence on the individual student's sense of self-efficacy.

FIGURE 8.4

The Relationship among Efficacy Expectations, Outcome Expectations, and Behavior

Source: From *Social Learning Theory* (p. 79) by A. Bandura, 1977, Englewood Cliffs, NJ: Prentice-Hall. Copyright ©1977 by Prentice-Hall. Reprinted by permission.

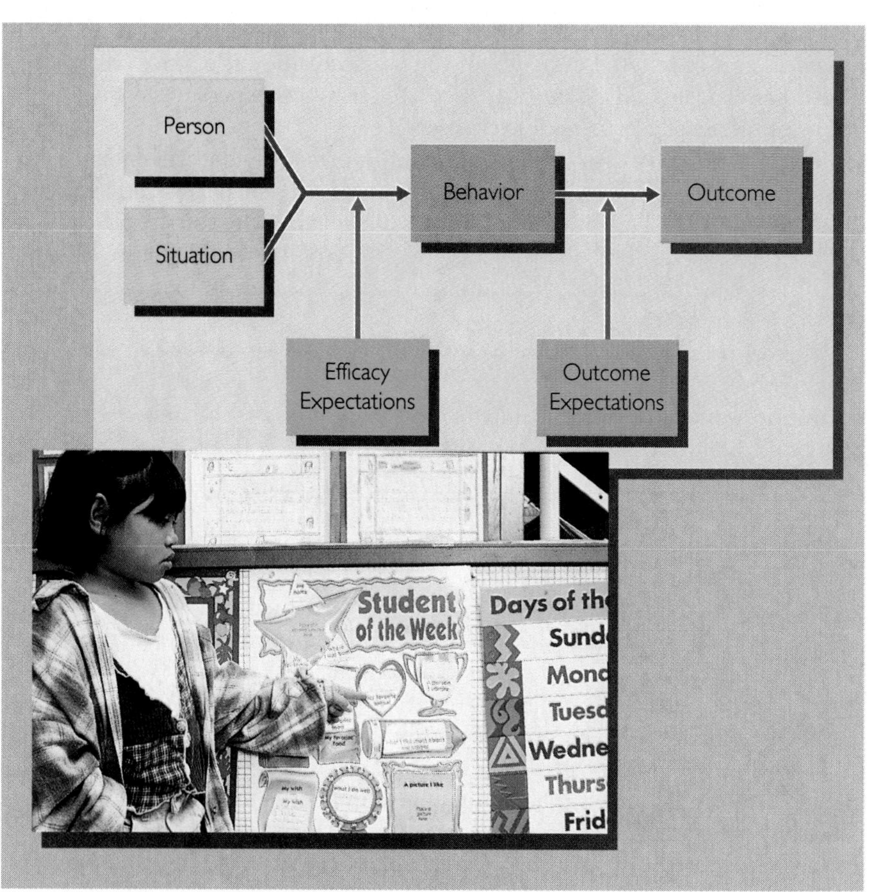

Teaching Goal-Setting and Self-Regulation Skills

Learners who are good at regulating their own learning activities are likely to set more realistic goals for themselves. Positive efficacy expectations motivate students to achieve (Schunk & Zimmerman, 1994). It is important to remember, however, that a sense of self-efficacy results from gathering information from the environment and from one's own performance. Because learners must gather and interpret so much information, they may make mistakes. Setting unrealistically high goals, for example, would be the result of erroneous beliefs or inaccurate observation of models. The same could be said for setting unrealistically low goals. Locke, Shaw, Saari, & Latham (1981) identify the properties of goals as being important to the goal-setting process. They note that setting goals using specific standards of performance is better than setting nonexplicit or general goals for improving performance. In addition, assuming that one is capable of performing the goal, setting more difficult goals tends to lead to better performance.

Goals can be long range or short range. Short-range goals are called *proximal* goals. Long-range goals are referred to in social cognitive literature as *distal* goals. Schunk & Gaa (1981) argue that it is better to set proximal goals than distal goals for improving self-motivation and performance. They suggest that the result is especially important for young children who may not be capable of cognitively representing distal goals. They also maintain that learners who set proximal goals may be promoting self-efficacy; as they observe their progress toward these goals, the quality of their performance increases. Successful performance helps children maintain their motivation and enhance their sense of self-efficacy.

Try This: Interview students in an attempt to discover their long-range goals and their short-range goals. Ask them if they consciously set goals for themselves. If so, how? If not, have they ever considered doing so?

The evaluation of one's own performance is part of the self-regulation system. Students can evaluate themselves in terms of the internal standards that are part of the self-regulation system. In a social environment, however, it is difficult for students to escape the reality of social comparison. Ruble, Boggiano, Feldman, & Loebl (1980) provided a developmental analysis of the role of social comparison in self-evaluation. They found that very young children make little use of comparative information when performing evaluations of their own performance. However, by the fourth grade, students utilize social information in evaluating their own competence. For example, a preschool child may not compare his or her drawing with those of other students before judging the drawing's quality, but a fifth grader would judge his or her drawing by comparing it with the drawings of others. This use of social information, according to Bandura (1986), can have a vicarious influence on self-efficacy.

Additional research on the relationship between goal setting, social comparison, and self-efficacy was undertaken by Schunk (1983). Schunk compared the effects of social comparative information against proximal goal setting. Four groups of children were studied. The first group was given comparative information about problems solved by other children in a division-skills program. A second group pursued the goal of a set number of problems in each session. A third group received both of the treatments. A fourth group served as the control, receiving neither treatment.

Critical Thinking: How might the results of this study be explained using the concept of scaffolding discussed in Chapter 2?

The third group, which operated with both information about the performance of others and a clear goal, demonstrated the highest perceived self-efficacy and achieved the highest skill level. These results indicate that the combined use of social comparison information and an internal standard leads to higher levels of self-efficacy. If the information from others and having goals can help performance, how can we teach our students to set goals?

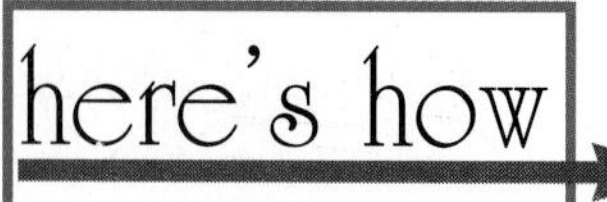

Here's How to Encourage Goal Setting and Self-Regulation

- Encourage students to compare their work and their products with each other and to discuss the standards they use in judging their work and the work of others.
- Encourage students to set both distal and proximal goals. After setting a long-term goal, have students work together to determine the steps that can be taken to reach that goal.
- Give feedback regarding not only the quality of student products but also the quality of the work process. Encourage students to think of ways they can improve their work habits and, thereby, improve the final outcome.
- Help students learn to judge their internal standards. A student who establishes unrealistic goals may do harm to his or her sense of self-efficacy.

Selecting Diverse Models

The research on the effects of perceived similarity on model effectiveness indicates that students are more likely to model someone whom they view to be like themselves. Given the cultural diversity and the inevitable gender differences that will exist in any classroom, not all of your students will perceive you to be similar to themselves. One answer to this problem is to provide multiple models for your students. Multiple models have been shown to be more effective with learners than a single model because, by providing a number of models, learners are more likely to perceive similarity between themselves and at least one of the models. The use of multiple models not only enhances the probablity of perceived similarity but also provides an opportunity to celebrate diversity.

Try This: To provide diverse models contact local organizations such as the NAACP or the office of a local Native American tribe, or ethnic Eurpean organizations, and ask if they have a speakers' bureau. Many organizations have speakers' bureaus and are happy to help teachers.

Women are underrepresented among science and math teachers. Men are underrepresented among English and art teachers and also among all elementary teachers (Grossman & Grossman, 1994). These patterns reinforce sex-role stereotypes. If the teacher is the only adult that students observe, and if the teacher does not attempt to expose students to other adults, the stereotypes will be perpetuated. One way to combat this problem is to seek out female scientists and male artists, those people who function successfully in nonstereotypic roles. Cultural groups are often also underrepresented on school faculties. Invite African Americans and Hispanic Americans, both male and female, who can model success in nontraditional occupations to share their experiences. Although little research has been done on the effectiveness of this approach, the research that has been done indicates that providing female students with female models improves their participation in math. Research has shown that same-sex models for boys enhance their achievement in a variety of academic areas (Brody & Fox, 1980; Mitchell, 1990).

Using Peer Models

peer models Models who are from the same social environment.

Peer models are people who are from the same social environment as the observer. In a classroom, students who model behavior for other students are peer models. The literature on peer modeling suggests that classroom peers can help in training social skills, enhancing self-efficacy, and remedying deficiencies in a variety of skill areas (Schunk, 1987). In another study of the effects of peer models,

Gresham (1981) examined the acquisition of social skills in children with physical disabilities. Those children who observed peer models engaging in a variety of social interactions showed enhanced social skills.

What is called *peer modeling* when seen from a social cognitive point of view becomes *peer tutoring* when put into practice in a classroom. The teacher who uses peer tutoring in his or her classroom should do so with an eye toward model effectiveness. A student chosen to tutor another student is a potential model; the student to be helped, the observer. Social cognitive theory holds that the observer's perceptions of the model determine the model's effectiveness.

Generally, research evidence suggests that peer tutoring works. Such evidence can be explained in terms of perceived similarity—a model who is a peer is likely to be perceived as being similar by the observer. Although peer tutoring has the built-in advantage of perceived similarity, the evidence on peer modeling suggests that coping models benefit observers as well. Finding a good match between students in terms of competence provides a reasonable basis for forming peer-tutoring pairs in the classroom.

Connection: Peer tutoring is examined in some detail in the context of cooperative learning techniques in Chapter 12.

Being a Model

Social cognitive theory provides us with an explanation of how observers learn from models. As instructional leaders, teachers are in a unique position to choose models for their students and to serve as models. As we learned earlier in this chapter, the perceived competence of a person influences his or her effectiveness as a potential model. When students walk into a classroom, the teacher is in a position of defined competence. What the teacher does with that status influences his or her ability to model behaviors for the students. Although social cognitive theory tells us that perceived competence makes for an effective model, it is important that we realize that our defined status of authority will not maintain our effectiveness. Students may attend to us initially because we are teachers. But unless we can maintain our status as competent models, students will soon stop attending to our behaviors. If the attention process is not supported by the model in the environment, then the retention, production, and motivation processes of observational learning will not occur.

Connection: Think back to the information-processing theory described in Chapter 7. Attention—either selective or automatic—is necessary for additional processing of information.

We are often told as teachers that we should model enthusiasm for the content we are going to teach. If teachers are not enthusiastic, then the students won't be either. But think back to your own elementary and high school experiences. Weren't there teachers in your classrooms who seemed to be enthusiastic yet who attracted little of your attention? One explanation is that their competence was mitigated by a lack of perceived similarity.

If we assume that as teachers we must serve as models, we must find ways of connecting with students. In Chapter 6, when we considered connections, we examined ways of connecting the content we teach to students' prior knowledge. Social cognitive theory requires that we look for ways to connect ourselves with our students. How can we be an effective model for Monica? For Jamal? Whether the outcome we seek for our students is discipline, understanding, or self-efficacy, making connections remains an important part of the job.

Reflecting on our characteristics as models is one way of pursuing avenues of connection. If our students experience difficulties, we can set ourselves up as coping models. If we show that we have or have had difficulties with material, and then provide examples of how we mastered the material in the face of those difficulties, we are more likely to be perceived as similar—and competent—by our students and therefore more likely to serve as effective models.

Point: Reflecting on our characteristics as models supports one of the basic assumptions of this book: *Reflective construction is necessary for the development of teaching expertise.*

Incidentally, if you were unsuccessful in getting the pencil through the bag of water, make sure the pencil is very sharp—or try a different brand of plastic bag. If you need a hint, the explanation involves "stretching molecules." Do you think you might use the demonstration in your own classroom someday?

TEACHER Chronicle Conclusion

WIZARD WEEK

At the end of Wizard Week the students share their experiments. Some students worked in groups, others prepared their experiments on their own. There are rockets blasting off, super bubbles being blown, crystals being grown, and a dozen other experiments being demonstrated. The class exudes enthusiasm and excitement.

Near the end of the hour, Neil raises his hand and Ms. Cohn calls on him. "Ms. Cohn, my little brother in the fourth grade thought my experiment was amazing. He asked me to help him learn it so that he could show it to his class. I was wondering if we could take our show on the road and visit his class with all of our experiments." "Yeah!" shout a number of students in agreement.

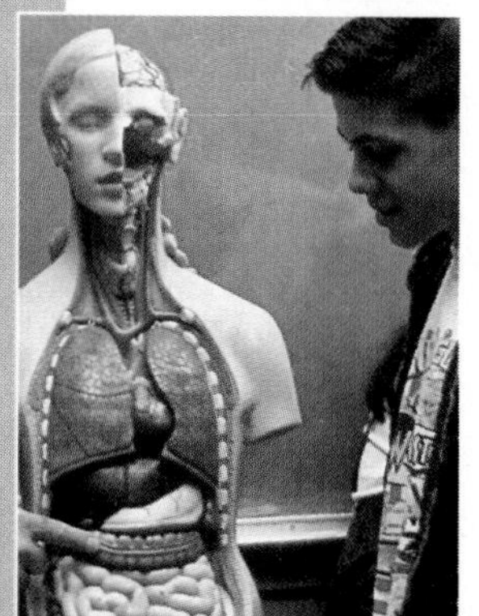

Ms. Cohn smiles and says, "I'll call Macintosh Elementary School this afternoon and set it up."

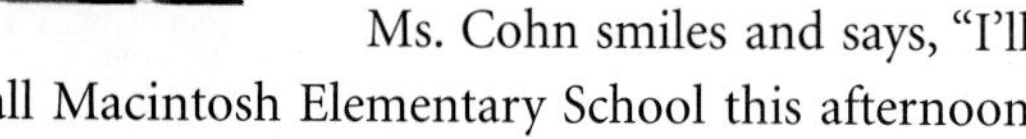

APPLICATION QUESTIONS

1. What would happen if Ms. Cohn's class took their show to a twelfth-grade class? How would the twelfth graders perceive the ninth graders? How confident would the ninth graders feel?
2. Suppose Ms. Cohn's pencil-jabbing experiment had backfired and the bag popped? If that had happened, what should she have done?
3. List the people after whom you model yourself. Defend your selections. How many of your models are teachers? If some are teachers, explain why. If not, why not?
4. Imagine that you are a fourth grader seeing the older students in Ms. Cohn's class coming into your room to perform their experiments. How would you feel? Would you pay more attention to them than to your teacher? Why or why not?
5. Is Ms. Cohn's relationship with her students a contributing factor to the success of Wizard Week? Did her relationship with her students change as a function of the Wizard Week activities?
6. To what extent do you think demonstrating their experiments for the other students in the class influenced preparation? Would the students have worked as hard if the experiments produced a written lab report? Why or why not?

CHAPTER SUMMARY

WHAT ARE THE DIMENSIONS OF SOCIAL LEARNING?

Social learning occurs when a learner observes a model. What the observer learns may or may not be performed. Social cognitive theory suggests that we need not engage in a behavior to learn that it is or is not appropriate in a particular situation. We can learn the consequences of behaviors by observing others. Vicarious learning is possible because humans have cognitive capabilities that allow them to symbolize, anticipate, and reflect. Social learning theory recognizes the relationship among behavior, personal factors, and the environment.

WHAT IS MODELING AND HOW DOES MODELING INFLUENCE LEARNERS?

The effects of observing models can cause an observer to engage in behaviors that are not normally performed or to refrain from exhibiting known behaviors. Observing a model can also highlight aspects of the environment that would not have been otherwise perceived. Observation of a model can also arouse emotions—either positive or negative—in the observer.

WHAT ARE THE PROCESSES OF OBSERVATIONAL LEARING?

Learning by observing others occurs when the learner attends to the model's behavior and undertakes overt or covert rehearsal to retain the observed behavior. Once cognitively represented or retained, the learner must decide whether the behavior can and should be exhibited. Reinforcement can be delivered by others in a learner's environment or by oneself, or it can be experienced vicariously through observation.

HOW CAN YOUR KNOWLEDGE OF SOCIAL LEARNING MAKE YOU A MORE EFFECTIVE TEACHER?

Social learning principles govern the properties that make models more or less effective. Perceived similarity and competence contribute to a model's effectiveness. Cognitive modeling—modeling not only overt behavior but also the cognitive processes that underlie that behavior—can be used as an effective instructional tool. Social learning principles also help teachers build self-efficacy, select models, and encourage relationships between model and observer.

KEY CONCEPTS

arousal effects
attention
cognitive modeling
direct reinforcement
disinhibitory effects
enactive learning
environmental enhancement effects
forethought
inhibitory effects
learning
modeling
motivation
observational learning effects
observer
peer models
perceived competence
perceived similarity
performance
production
reciprocal determinism
response facilitation effects
retention
self-efficacy
self-reflection
self-regulation
self-reinforcement
social cognitive theory
social learning
symbolize
vicarious learning
vicarious reinforcement

PART IV

People are naturally motivated to learn

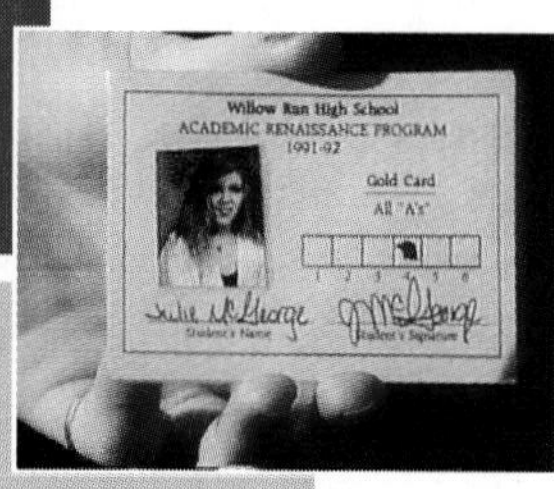

The teaching–learning process involves engaging, directing, enhancing, and maintaining motivation to learn through communication. Theories of motivation provide important insights into psychological factors that influence the thoughts, actions, and communications of teachers and learners. Research on those factors has yielded valuable motivational strategies for use in all learning contexts.

Overview of Chapter 9

In Chapter 9, we examine student motivation. Every student has unique interests, individual needs, and personal goals that become sources of motivation. Motivation that derives from within the student is intrinsic motivation. Motivation that comes from outside the student—from the teacher, for example—is extrinsic motivation. In addition to considering the distinction between intrinsic and extrinsic sources of motivation, Facilitating Student Motivation examines the effect of both students' and teachers' beliefs on motivation. Students' beliefs in their own abilities relate to their willingness to undertake and persist in learning tasks. Similarly, teachers' beliefs in their own abilities as teachers, as well as in their students' achievement abilities, influence their expectations of students and, hence, the motivational strategies they employ in instruction. We conclude the chapter with a discussion of ways that you can facilitate student motivation in the classroom and help students develop autonomy in managing their own learning.

Motivation and Classroom Leadership

Needs and values affect motivation

Motivation to learn is influenced by the satisfaction or frustration of basic human needs and of personal desires or goals. Attitudes, beliefs, and values—including cultural values—also have a profound effect on individuals' motivations. Because motivation affects learning, behavior, and achievement, teachers and learners need to understand the roles that these needs and values play.

Overview of Chapter 10

Some teachers lead, some direct, some boss. The way teachers view the role as classroom manager influences student learning. The relationship that you build with your students will depend, in part, on whose classroom you believe it to be. In Leading Learning-Oriented Classrooms, you will examine some of the skills and attitudes associated with classrooms in which discipline is established and then supports learning. You will also encounter several approaches to handling disruptive behavior and to maintaining the discipline that underlies learning.

Classroom management is a shared concern

Classrooms; the people who share them; the materials; time, and space they provide; and the routines and activities that take place in them comprise learning environments. Effective planning, organization, and management of the learning environment can be seen as a collaborative or negotiative process involving both teachers and students. Sound classroom management facilitates learning and reduces or prevents discipline problems. Effective models exist for dealing with discipline problems when they do occur.

9 Facilitating Student Motivation

CHAPTER OUTLINE

TEACHER Chronicle

GOLDEN OPPORTUNITES

Golden opportunities to reach a student appear at the most unexpected times. These moments often provide the best teaching of the day.

Marita Vasquez walks around her room observing her fifth-grade class writing. The board is covered with the results of a brainstorming lesson the class has just completed. Lists of words fill the board, connected by a web of lines linking one idea to another. The class is prewriting for an assignment on following directions.

All are intently punching their keyboards except Bronson. Bronson has his hand up for help. He followed the brainstorming session, but because of a minor speech impairment, he did not join in orally. He wrote his ideas down, however, and gave them to Marita to add to the board. Marita enjoys teaching Bronson. He has a super sense of humor and is an excellent reader. She often wishes she could help him overcome his embarrassment in front of the class when he stutters.

"Does the story have to be about something you make, or can it be what happens to food or something after it is made?" Bronson whispers as his teacher approaches.

"What are you thinking?" Marita asks, noticing that he has nothing on his screen.

"About what I do when I am served broccoli."

"You eat it, don't you?"

"No, I hate broccoli! Can I write about how I get rid of it?"

Marita thinks for a moment, considering the options. Her goal in the lesson is to have the class write a set of directions so that they make sense. If Bronson writes about the steps necessary to get rid of unwanted broccoli, he would be accomplishing the same objective, although from a different perspective.

"Sure," she tells him. "Remind me to tell you later how my sisters and I got rid of our spinach."

Bronson smiles and begins hitting the keys furiously. Marita thinks about Bronson's idea while she continues walking around. If the kids develop an interest in his writing about getting rid of broccoli, then she could use that idea for another story starter. She can't wait to hear his tale.

FOCUS QUESTIONS

1. What internal and external factors affect Bronson's motivation to learn? To participate in class? To complete the learning task?
2. How does Marita's lesson reflect her understanding of the importance of student motivation in learning?
3. In what ways do Marita's goals and Bronson's needs influence Bronson's motivation?
4. How might Bronson's self-concept and his explanations of success and failure influence his motivation to strive for academic achievement?
5. How might Marita's expectations and uses of reinforcement influence students' motivation?
6. What teaching strategies might Marita use to increase students' motivation to learn?

WHAT IS MOTIVATION TO LEARN?

Reading this chapter is a learning activity focused on the topic of student motivation. As you embark on this activity, consider your reasons for doing so. Are you reading this chapter now because your instructor assigned it? Are you reading the chapter because you have a quiz at the end of the week? Are you reading the chapter because you want to understand why students differ in their pursuits of academic achievement? Are you reading the chapter because you will be a student teacher soon and you are concerned about motivating your students? What motivates you to do what you're doing right now? What motivates you to continue reading a textbook when you find its subject matter uninteresting? What motivates you to learn new things even when you have no particular use for them at the moment?

When students develop a **motivation to learn**, they initiate learning activities, they stay involved in a learning task, and they exhibit a commitment to learning (Ames, 1990). These are all outcomes that we desire of students in school, and effective schools are those that help students acquire the goals, beliefs, and attributes that will sustain a long-term engagement in learning. In the Teacher Chronicle, for example, Marita wants to involve Bronson in the writing activity, and there are many ways she could go about doing this. As you will see in this chapter, however, some ways are more effective than others, especially when it comes to promoting an ongoing commitment to learning.

Point: *People are naturally motivated to learn.* Sometimes, however, the activities in which students have intrinsic interest to learn are not the same as those teachers want them to learn.

Intrinsic and Extrinsic Motivation

Why do students initiate or engage in some learning tasks and not others? One aspect of motivation to learn concerns the reasons students behave as they do. **Intrinsic motivation** occurs when learners work on tasks for internal reasons, such as pleasure or enjoyment in the activity, satisfaction in learning something new, or curiosity about and interest in the topic. The child who reads during recess, on the bus to and from school, and in the family car on vacation, for example, is said to be intrinsically motivated toward reading. Likewise, the student who is fascinated by trains and seeks out information about them is intrinsically motivated to learn about the subject of trains.

Extrinsic motivation occurs when learners work on tasks for external reasons. They may want to please a teacher or parent or avoid getting in trouble that would be certain to follow if they failed to complete the task. Students who engage in tasks for the sake of achieving some reward or anticipated outcome also are extrinsically motivated. For example, an aspiring teacher may take a particular course, not because he or she is especially interested in the subject matter but because it is required in order to obtain certification. Similarly, some students memorize the multiplication tables in order to achieve a good grade rather than for the satisfaction of learning math and becoming prepared for more complex problem solving.

What is important about the reasons students possess for learning is that two students may well engage in the same behavior but do so for quite different reasons. Whereas one is interested in the topic, the other may be working to achieve a certain grade. Their reasons have consequences for the quality of cognitive engagement in the learning task and, hence, the quality of learning that results. Different reasons also have different consequences for continuing motivation. The intrinsically motivated person is more likely to stay involved in and demonstrate a commitment to

motivation to learn A disposition of learners that is characterized by their willingness to initiate learning activities, their continued involvement in a learning task, and their long-term commitment to learning.

intrinsic motivation When learners work on tasks for internal reasons, such as pleasure or enjoyment in the activity.

extrinsic motivation When learners work on tasks for external reasons, such as to please a parent or to avoid getting into trouble with the teacher.

learning than is the extrinsically motivated person. For the latter, task engagement is likely to cease when the extrinsic reasons for learning no longer exist.

Reflection: Think about your motivation to learn in this class. Are you primarily extrinsically or intrinsically motivated? Why?

Internal and External Sources of Motivation

Student motivation is an extremely complex matter. Many sources of motivation arise from within the learner, but just as many come from the learning environment. Listed in Figure 9.1 are various sources of student motivation to learn. Identifying internal sources—such as a student's goals, beliefs about his or her ability, or willingness to take risks—can help you understand why students appear motivated or unmotivated to engage in certain learning tasks. Understanding these factors can also aid you in helping students to develop adaptive motivational patterns. For example, you could work with students to increase their self-confidence when they have the capability of achieving a goal but don't believe they can do it. Knowing how aspects of the learning environment can influence motivation enables you to arrange learning conditions to best support the intrinsic motivation of your students.

Different Perspectives on Motivation

The sources of motivation shown in Figure 9.1 are associated with different views of motivation that emphasize some factors over others. Recall the behavioral perspective on learning (Chapter 6), for example. Reinforcement was described as a process that increases the incidence of existing behavior and facilitates the establishment of new behaviors. If you consider motivation from a behavioral perspective, you can see that reinforcers serve as extrinsic motivators of behavior. To the extent that learners find a reinforcer satisfying or desirable, they will be motivated to engage in the behavior that leads to the reinforcer.

Critical Thinking: What are the sources of motivation according to behavioral learning theory (Chapter 6)? According to cognitive learning models (Chapter 7)? According to social learning theory (Chapter 8)?

FIGURE 9.1

Sources of Student Motivation

Within the Learner	From the Learning Environment
• Personal goals and intentions • Biological and psychological drives and needs • Self-concept, self-esteem, and self-confidence • Personal beliefs, values, expectations, and explanations for success or failure • Self-knowledge, prior experiences, and sense of self-efficacy • Personality factors, e.g., willingness to undertake risk, ability to manage anxieties, curiosity, and persistence in effort • Emotional states and levels of arousal	• Goals of teachers, parents, and peers • Classroom goal structures • Outcomes of social interactions • Social and cultural beliefs and values • Classroom reinforcements; incentive and disincentive systems • Instructional stimuli involving complexity, novelty, and ambiguity • Teachers' and others' expectations of the learner • Performance models • Instructional practices that attract attention, provide relevance, foster confidence, and lead to satisfaction

From a cognitive perspective, by contrast, the focus is on intrinsic motivation as influenced primarily by thoughts and beliefs. Learners hold beliefs about their abilities to accomplish tasks and achieve certain goals, which influence their motivation to undertake a task in the first place. Similarly, their thoughts about success or failure in achieving a goal will affect their motivation to continue a learning activity. Cognitive theorists are also concerned about the influence of the teacher's beliefs and expectations on student motivation.

Example: A fourth-grade student really wants to be in the top reading group but is not willing to work on his reading enough to make the top group. His parents offer him extra TV time in exchange for extra reading. This arrangement works for awhile. The boy makes progress but not enough to merit moving him into the top group. Then his parents hire him to read: They offer to pay him by the hour. Soon, he is reading far more than his parents expect him to do, and the teacher moves him into the top reading group. What elements of motivation are in action here?

A third perspective on motivation stems from humanistic theories, which focus on biological and psychological needs and drives. Examples of needs that influence motivation include the need to achieve, the need for self-fulfillment, and the need for autonomy. Humanists believe these needs propel learners to seek certain goals and to act in certain ways in much the same way that hunger causes you to seek food. In some of these theories, needs are arranged hierarchically; that is, basic needs such as safety and self-esteem must be satisfied first before learners can go about the business of satisfying growth needs such as knowing and understanding.

Finally, social learning theories integrate intrinsic and extrinsic sources of motivation as they focus on both the goals and expectations of learners and the consequences of reaching those goals. Expectancy *x* value theories, for example, regard motivation as a function of the learner's expectation of achieving a goal and of the learner's perceived value of that goal—that is, learners must expect to achieve a goal *and* they must value such achievement to be motivated and willing to take actions toward goal attainment.

This chapter provides a multidimensional picture of student motivation that draws from all four perspectives, so that you will be well prepared to understand and solve problems related to motivation in your classroom.

HOW DO STUDENTS' NEEDS AND WANTS AFFECT THEIR MOTIVATION TO LEARN?

Point: *Needs and values affect motivation.* Understanding the needs and wants of your students can help you plan lessons that will meet their needs and stimulate their interest in learning.

To help your students improve their motivation to learn in your classroom, you must understand the needs and wants of your students and how these influence motivation. What needs will your students bring to school? What do they want that they might work hard to attain? What are sources of motivation for academic achievement?

Maslow's Hierarchy of Needs

hierarchy of needs A theory proposed by Abraham Maslow in which human needs are arranged in a hierarchy from basic needs to self-actualization, or self-fulfillment.

Human beings need water to drink; they need food to eat; they need shelter and love. They need to feel safe, both physically and psychologically. Part of being human is the need to feel good about oneself. Part of being human is the need to understand the world around oneself. Different people have different needs, and their needs vary in degree. For some, the need for shelter is most important; for others, the need for food is the primary motivation. Individuals' needs change as well—during a day, a year, a lifetime.

The concept of human needs is basic to the theory formulated by Abraham Maslow (1943, 1954), known as Maslow's **hierarchy of needs** (Figure 9.2). At the

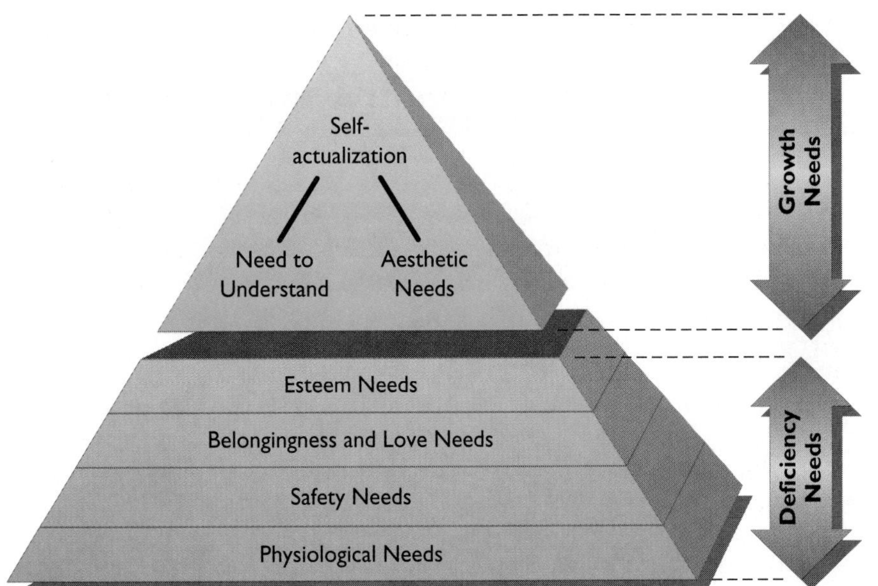

FIGURE 9.2

Maslow's Hierarchy of Needs
Source: From *Psychology* (4th ed., p. 406) by L. A. Lefton, 1991, Needham Heights, MA: Allyn & Bacon. Copyright 1991 by Allyn & Bacon. Reprinted by permission.

lower levels of the hierarchy are basic needs that humans require for physical and psychological well-being: **deficiency needs**. Deficiency needs must be at least partially satisfied before a person can be motivated to pursue satisfaction of higher-level needs. The higher-level needs, which, when satisfied, enable the human being to grow psychologically, are called **growth needs**. As growth needs become satisfied, a person is able to fulfill his or her personal potential and achieve **self-actualization**.

Connection: Principles of human development discussed in Chapters 2 and 3 relate to Maslow's theory.

As an example of how the hierarchy of needs helps explain motivation, consider a child who comes from an unhealthy, abusive home environment. Any student who comes to class from such a neglected environment has unfulfilled basic needs. Given his or her life circumstances, that student may not feel very safe. If a student has an unfulfilled need as basic as safety, it will be very difficult for that student to focus on higher-order needs, such as the need to understand. Parents play an important role in satisfying the deficiency and growth needs of their children. Parents who wish their children to become capable of pursuing growth needs must help their children satisfy the more basic needs of health, safety, belonging, love, and self-esteem (Nystul, 1984).

The same argument can be made for adult learners (Sappington, 1984). Teachers of adult learners must also help those learners satisfy basic needs before expecting them to be motivated to understand and to grow in other ways. For both children and adults, one basic need is an emotionally safe learning environment. Establishing a safe environment enables students to address constructively any fears they may bring to the learning situation. It also allows learners to take risks in the classroom, to participate more fully, and, thereby, to grow psychologically.

How can Maslow's theory provide a means for teachers to identify problems in students who appear to be unmotivated— that is, who appear to be motivated by goals other than academic achievement and who take nonacademic routes to their goals? Observe such a student and, starting at the bottom of the hierarchy,

deficiency needs According to Maslow's hierarchy of needs, the basic needs that humans require for physical and psychological well-being.

growth needs According to Maslow, the higher-level needs, the satisfaction of which enables human beings to grow psychologically.

self-actualization Fulfilling one's personal potential.

Insights ON SUCCESSFUL PRACTICE

What strategies have you used successfully to increase your students' motivation to learn?

Several years ago, I decided to experiment with the technique of improvisation as a method of "getting into" drama. I wanted my students to identify and empathize with the character, to get into the character's shoes, so that they might imagine the complexity of emotions, choices, and conflicts at the heart of the work. I developed a hypothetical office scene for my students to improvise that would parallel the critical office scene in the play, *Death of a Salesman*. My goal was to improve motivation (curiosity/enthusiasm), aesthetic appreciation, dramatic sensibility, and critical thinking.

I paired the students and gave them ten minutes to plan their improvisations. I told them to decide what office they were in, what characters they would be, and their respective roles. The results were highly successful. For students with no acting experience or ability, I was surprised and delighted with the ease and execution of this scenario. Students were immediately engaged in the conflict and fell naturally into the roles of the characters. They had no difficulty imagining an appropriate office setting. Ironically, several students created scenes similar to the parallel scene in *Death of a Salesman* during which the boss fires Willy. In their corporate office scenes, the boss either fires an incompetent employee or fires a woman employee who refuses sexual favors. Another improvisation scene that was successful involved a principal and student in a discipline office and the student being expelled.

Our improvisations provided a powerful anticipatory mood. My students were highly curious and eager to read the play. They were wondering how our improvisations related to *Death of a Salesman.* I told the class we had improvised a parallel scene and to look for that scene as we read the play. Our oral reading was no longer monotonous. Students intuitively felt the character and read with expression and emotion. When we arrived at the office scene, we acted it out in front of the class. Then we compared the scene with our improvisations. Students were amazed at the similarities.

Next I showed Dustin Hoffman's interpretation of the same scene. Students were struck by the heightened emotions. They were expecting anger, frustration, and desperation, but they did not anticipate the explosions they saw on screen. Here was true appreciation—the kind that comes from experience.

I knew our experiment had succeeded by the sustained interest and motivation of my students, their eagerness to read the play, their attention to detail, and their insightful comments when analyzing and comparing the scenes. They had gained a dramatic sensibility. I saw this when they performed their improvisations and when they acted as an appreciative audience.

NANCY GORRELL, Morristown High School, Morristown, New Jersey

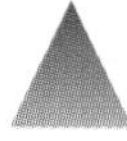 Insights

For this teacher, what was the key to increasing student motivation to learn? What roles did active learning, situated learning, and affective outcomes play in her experiment?

ask yourself some questions. Are the student's physiological needs being met? Is the student receiving adequate food and shelter? If physiological needs have been met, what about the safety of that student? Does the student feel physically safe at home and in school? An interview with the student might give you some clues about the student's feelings of safety. Next, what about this student's needs to belong to a group and to feel loved? In this regard, you can think about Lickona's model of moral education (examined in Chapter 3). Observing this student's social interactions can give you some clues about the extent to which his or her needs to belong and to be loved are being gratified.

If the student appears to have positive relations with peers, if he or she is not a social isolate, if the student exhibits a sense of community in the family and at school, and if the student seems to feel loved, then the next set of questions to ask should address the student's self-esteem and his or her sense of self-efficacy. You may want to assign tasks that you feel sure the student can perform successfully in order to gauge the student's views of his or her abilities. Finding out the student's expectations of efficacy could give you some clues about academic self-esteem.

Try This: On the basis of classroom observations, brainstorm with your classmates to define an *emotionally safe environment*. What elements contribute to such an environment?

The failure to gratify a need results in a related form of dysfunction or disturbance. If your observations reveal a dysfunction related to deficiency needs, some kind of action is needed. For example, safety, belongingness, and esteem needs might be gratified in a classroom that operates on the basis of Lickona's model (1987). For the most part, teachers can exert influence only at school. If problems related to deficiency needs cannot be met at school, a teacher must seek outside help. One of the first things a new teacher should do is learn the school district's referral system. Find out what student services and other professional help are available for students.

Reflection: As a student in elementary and secondary school, how did your unmet needs influence your experiences in school?

A student whose deficiency needs have been met is said to be growth motivated. Growth-motivated students have a need to understand and to know. They also have aesthetic needs. A student in physics might appreciate the beauty inherent in the phenomena of astronomy, for example. Another student might appreciate the rhythm of a sonnet or the elegance of a mathematical formula. Growth-motivated students tend to seek a tension that they find pleasurable, usually in the form of a challenge. Learners who attempt independent studies, for example, seek to solve problems of their own devising.

Connection: Lickona's model of moral education in Chapter 3 relates to the satisfaction of deficiency needs in Maslow's theory.

It is important to note here that students who are growth motivated tend to be self-directed. These students take the responsibility to satisfy their need to know and understand and their aesthetic needs. Recalling the earlier distinction between intrinsic and extrinsic motivation, we can see that growth-motivated students tend to rely more on intrinsic rewards than extrinsic rewards. Teachers who work with such students should provide them with opportunities to pursue self-directed learning and take care not to undermine their intrinsic motivation with unnecessary extrinsic rewards.

Example: Many of the problems encountered by growth-motivated students are problems they have devised themselves. The tension created by such problems is imposed by the student and hence becomes a source of pleasure.

A growth-motivated person has had his or her deficiency needs met and therefore seeks the challenge of meeting growth needs. This suggests that you should arrange learning situations students will view as challenging but not threatening. If students perceive your classroom as threatening, they are likely to play it safe. They will not take risks academically; they will not seek out the challenge. From Maslow's perspective, therefore, the best classrooms are those that maximize the opportunities for growth by reducing the possibilities for failure and embarrassment. Risk-taking behavior, in an academic sense, is to be encouraged.

The Need to Achieve

Achievement motivation is a desire or tendency to overcome obstacles and to accomplish some difficult task through the exercise of power. Achievement motivation can manifest itself as an attitude of competitiveness and willingness to take certain risks (e.g., McClelland, 1965).

achievement motivation A person's desire or tendency to overcome obstacles and to accomplish some difficult task through the exercise of power.

The level of the need to achieve that students project gives us an index of the amount of risk-taking behavior they are capable of and, to some extent, the types

According to Maslow's theory, what are every learner's basic human needs? How might the satisfaction or frustration of those needs affect a student's motivation to learn?

of goals that motivate them. In a classic study, McClelland (1958) asked children to play a ring-toss game. The children were allowed to choose the distance from which they would toss a ring over a peg. McClelland found that *high-need achievers* preferred to toss the ring from a medium distance. *Low-need achievers* tended to choose a distance either very near or very far from the ring. The interpretation that McClelland offered was that high-need achievers stand in the middle distances because the probability of success is estimated to be around 50 percent. This probability of success, balanced with the value of winning, maximizes the challenge of the game. A child who stands very near to the peg increases the probability of success, but such a success is easily won and does not present much of a challenge. When a child chooses to stand very far from the peg, he or she decreases the probability of success to such a point that the goal of tossing the ring onto the peg is not likely to be achieved very often. Success from a great distance is more a matter of luck than a matter of achievement.

Example: A ninth-grade math student always proclaims "I can't do that" whenever his teacher introduces new material. He often does have a difficult time mastering new material, especially when compared with his more math-oriented peers. This negative comment is always his first reaction. What purpose do repeated negative comments serve? How do they affect success as a learner?

How do people develop a need for achievement? McClelland believes that achievement motivation is a stable trait resulting from the home environment and how parents raise their children. Children who are permitted to solve their own problems and make their own mistakes are more likely to develop a high need for achievement than children whose parents intervene when they experience failure (McClelland & Pilon, 1983). Other, more contemporary theorists emphasize the effects of conscious beliefs and values and recent experiences in achievement situations on the development of achievement motivation (Stipek, 1993), suggesting that experiences in school as well as those at home can influence the need to achieve.

If we interpret McClelland's study in terms of academic goals, the children high in need to achieve appear to pursue goals that are at once challenging and realistic. This does not tell the whole story, however. Atkinson (1964) concluded that people have a need to avoid failure as well as a need to achieve. Depending on which need is stronger in a given situation, students can perceive a challenging situation as threatening instead. In that case, they may withdraw from the situation or play it safe by pursuing goals they know they can achieve. For example, consider two gymnasts preparing for an important competition. One, whose need to avoid failure is stronger than the need to achieve, practices an old routine that has served her in the past and that she is confident of performing well. The other, whose need for achievement outweighs any fear of failure, works on a new routine with difficult movements. Done well, this new routine is likely to win the meet for the team, but doing it is a risk, a risk the second gymnast is willing to take. Although they are in the same situation, the two gymnasts, with their differing needs, respond differently to the challenge (Woolfolk, 1995).

Critical Thinking: What is the relation between Maslow's growth and deficiency needs and the emotions of hope of success and fear of failure?

The Need for Autonomy

Can you recall a situation in which you offered help, perhaps to a younger friend or sibling, only to be told, "I want to do it *myself*" or "Let me do it *my way*"? Not only do people have a need to achieve and demonstrate competence, we also have a need to initiate and regulate our own actions. This is referred to as the **need for autonomy**, or self-determination (Deci & Ryan, 1985; Deci, Vallerand, Pelletier, & Ryan, 1991). According to Deci's self-determination theory, actions can be motivated by forces that fall on a continuum from external regulation to self-regulation. External regulation is itself a continuum. At one end is doing something because of an external contingency, such as behaving in class to avoid punishment by the teacher. At the other end is doing something because its outcome is valued, such as learning to use a computer in order to gain access to resources on electronic networks. **Self-regulation**, in contrast, occurs when a person is motivated to engage in an activity purely by choice and by virtue of his or her interest in the activity. So, for example, another gymnast on the team may learn a new routine, not to help the team win but simply because she wants to learn it for herself.

Motivation that is more autonomous in nature has been linked to positive educational outcomes, such as greater conceptual learning, better academic performance, and more enjoyment of school and academic tasks (Deci et al., 1991). According to Deci and his colleagues, teachers can support autonomy in the classroom by using a noncontrolling style of presentation in class, providing choices to students with information about the personal utility of various activities, and creating a climate of acceptance. A variety of means by which teachers can help students develop self-regulatory skills is presented later in this chapter.

Reflection: What have you learned recently purely because you wanted to learn it, and how did your motivation influence your learning? What conditions in the learning environment may have supported your need for autonomy?

Students' Goals

Whether students engage in learning tasks for intrinsic or extrinsic reasons affects the kinds of academic goals they willingly pursue. An aspect of goals related to student motivation is the distinction between performance goals and learning goals (Dweck, 1986; Elliott & Dweck, 1988; Dweck & Leggett, 1988; Ames, 1992). A **learning goal** is a goal through which a student seeks to increase his or her competence; it reflects a challenge-seeking, mastery-oriented approach (hence, a learning goal is sometimes referred to as a mastery goal). For example, you might have as a learning goal to "find and use effective strategies for gaining students' attention." A **performance goal** is a goal through which a student seeks to gain favorable judgment of his or her competence or to avoid negative judgment. A performance goal would be reflected in your statement that you "want to get an A in educational psychology."

Different types of goals promote different motivational patterns in students. Performance goals lead students who lack confidence in their abilities to avoid challenge and to display helplessness. For example, an undergraduate student who, when asked if he wishes to retake a quiz in hopes of raising his grade to an A declines and says, "Oh no, Ma'am. I'm not an A kind of guy." Offered the chance, students with performance goals might give up rather than persist in a learning task. Conversely, students confident of their own abilities react to performance goals by rising to the challenge, but only if they can avoid taking risks. For example, a student might choose to retake a quiz only if the score can result in a higher grade and not a lower one.

need for autonomy The need to initiate and regulate our own actions; self-determination.

self-regulation Motivation to engage in an activity purely by choice and by virtue of one's interest in the activity.

learning goal An aim of students who place primary emphasis on increasing competence.

performance goal An aim of students who place primary emphasis on gaining positive recognition from others and avoiding negative judgments.

Reflection: Recall courses you took in college in which your goals and the professor's goals did not match. How did these mismatches influence your behavior? Your motivation to learn?

With learning goals, however, students display a mastery-oriented pattern of motivation (Dweck & Leggett, 1988). They tend to seek challenging tasks and to demonstrate persistence in those tasks. In a recent study, Clark and Tollefson (1991) found that students with learning or mastery-oriented goals were more motivated to write, had greater confidence in their writing, and more positive attitudes toward writing than students with performance goals. Instead of thinking about their ability in relation to learning goals, students consider what strategies must be applied to achieve the goal. For example, consider the case of Kelly, who wants to learn how to sail a windsurfer. Although she has never done this before and does not see herself as especially athletic, she is determined to master boardsailing. Rather than question her ability to perform the correct movements, she concentrates on the instructor's directions, and when she falls numerous times, it is because "I didn't put my feet in the right place."

HOW DO STUDENTS' BELIEFS AFFECT THEIR MOTIVATION TO LEARN?

How long students will persist in their efforts to attain an academic goal depends to a large degree on beliefs they hold about their own abilities and about learning in general. This section examines those beliefs and the effects they have on student motivation.

Beliefs about Knowledge and Ability

Reflection: Reflect on your own beliefs regarding learning. How do your beliefs relate to the strategies you use to learn? How do your beliefs influence your actions when you are faced with a difficult or challenging task?

Recent studies investigating the epistemological beliefs of students reveal that academic performance and motivation are both related to what students believe about the nature of knowledge. Four possible beliefs are hypothesized (Schommer, 1990, 1993). The first is that knowledge consists of isolated facts, as opposed to integrated, complex systems of information. A student with this belief is likely to seek simple answers to questions and ignore connections across topics. The second belief is that knowledge is absolute. Students who believe in the certainty of knowledge are likely to accept the word of the teacher or the textbook as the authority and not question it. Students who believe that the ability to learn is innate—the third belief—view learning as unaffected by effort or strategic behavior. Finally, students who adhere to the fourth belief, that learning occurs quickly or not at all, tend to think that success is unrelated to hard work, so that concentrated effort is a waste of time.

Not all of these beliefs have yet been investigated with respect to motivation. However, there is evidence that children with a strong belief in innate ability tend to feel helpless when faced with a difficult task (Dweck and Leggett, 1988). Children who believe that ability is more malleable perceive the same task as a challenge. Moreover, performance goals, discussed earlier in the chapter, seem to promote a greater belief in fixed ability, whereas learning goals promote a greater belief in the possibility that ability can be changed. Mathematics educators have also pointed out that experience with problems that are easy and quick to solve promotes a belief in quick learning, so that students tend to give up when faced with lengthier, more complex problems (Doyle, 1988; Schoenfeld, 1988).

The relation between students' epistemological beliefs and their motivation to learn merits thoughtful examination. Schommer (1993) suggests that teachers may want to assess students' beliefs and consider how they may be influencing those beliefs during instruction:

> Do [teachers] test to teach facts or to understand concepts? Do they assign tasks that are quick to complete or do they give students challenging tasks that take time? Do all test items have only a single right answer or do some test questions allow for several possible answers? (p. 411)

Try This: Interview teachers as to their goals for students to develop sophisticated epistemological beliefs. What means do they employ to help students develop more sophisticated beliefs?

The answers to these questions can determine the teacher's role in motivating students to engage and persist in learning tasks and the subsequent effect on their academic achievement.

Beliefs in Self-Efficacy

When students observe their own successful completion of academic tasks, they develop a belief in their ability to continue such accomplishments—a belief called **self-efficacy** (Bandura, 1977, 1982). Students' beliefs about their own ability to perform successfully influence their motivation. From experiences with multiple-choice tests, for example, students may classify themselves as good or poor test takers. On future tests of this nature, students who believe they can't do well will not put forth the effort required to perform well. Subsequent poor performance then serves to reinforce the initial belief.

Reflection: In what areas do you feel you have a sense of strong self-efficacy?

Students develop expectations of self-efficacy from a number of sources. The first source of self-efficacy is simple self-observation. Past success leads you to expect you will succeed in the future on similar tasks; such success enhances your sense of self-efficacy.

Critical Thinking: How does social cognitive theory (Chapter 8) support this discussion on the development of self-efficacy?

A second source of self-efficacy is the observation of others. When you observe others whom you perceive to be similar to yourself, you attend to their behavior. You view yourself as being capable of achieving the same outcome they do. You say to yourself, "If that person can do it, I can do it."

A third source of self-efficacy is encouragement, usually in the form of verbal praise. Verbal encouragement may come from a teacher who says, "I know that you have the ability to accomplish this particular task and I'm confident that you will be able to perform well." Verbal encouragement can also come from within, an internal pep talk called positive "self-talk."

Try This: Observe teachers to discover how they use verbal encouragement and model positive self-talk.

A fourth source of expectation for self-efficacy is emotional arousal. Some kind of emotional event can spur your determination to attain a particular outcome. Perhaps you have experienced, in your own academic career, a teacher who expressed doubt in your abilities to do well in school. As a result of your indignance at the doubt expressed by the teacher, you set out to prove to him or her, to others, and to yourself that you are indeed capable of attaining what they thought was, for you, unattainable. If a student has expectations of efficacy, if a student believes he or she is capable of accomplishing a particular goal, the belief will serve as motivation. This is true even in cases where there are many obstacles to success.

Reflection: Recall teachers who made you want to prove yourself to them. What role did emotional arousal play in your decision to increase your efforts?

Some of your students will be physically, emotionally, or cognitively challenged in some way. When such students overcome obstacles and succeed in attaining the goals they've set, they can be assumed to harbor expectations of efficacy. Learners who persist, learners who believe in their abilities under certain conditions, and learners who exert an extraordinary amount of effort in pursuit

self-efficacy A learner's beliefs about his or her ability to successfully perform a task or attain a goal.

of a particular academic goal are motivated by their sense of self-efficacy. They use their capabilities in a focused way. The mental effort that a student exerts in pursuit of an academic goal can be an index of that student's motivation.

When students attain or fail to attain a particular goal, they explain their success or failure in ways that influence their sense of efficacy and their subsequent engagement in similar academic tasks. Looking at motivation from this perspective requires an understanding of attribution theory.

Attributions of Causes for Success and Failure

The explanations, reasons, or excuses that students give for succeeding or failing at tasks are called attributions. For example, a student who says, "I got a good grade on the test because it was easy," is attributing his success to the test, whereas the student who says, "I did well on the project because I worked really hard," is attributing her success to her own efforts.

Weiner's **attribution theory** of motivation is based on three dimensions of attribution: locus, stability, and responsibility (1980, 1986, 1992). The first dimension, locus, refers to the location of the cause of success or failure. A student may cite as the cause for his or her success or failure something that is internal or something that is external. For example, attributing success on a test to one's effort is an internal attribution, whereas attributing the same success to luck is an external attribution.

The second dimension, stability, refers to whether an attributed cause is consistent or inconsistent from one situation to the next. Effort is an unstable attribution because a student might exert a great deal of effort in studying for a history exam and little or no effort in preparing for a math exam. Ability, in contrast, tends to be stable in that, for instance, previous musical facility is likely to predict future musical facility.

Reflection: Think about your attributions for success and failure. Do you emphasize an internal or external locus of control?

The third dimension in Weiner's formulation is responsibility, that is, whether a perceived cause of success or failure is under the student's control. From the point of view of a student, effort is a controllable attribution; the difficulty level of a test is not. Therefore, depending on the reasons given for success or failure, the situation may or may not have been under the student's control. Weiner's dimension of responsibility is related to Rotter's (1954) locus of control, which was proposed as a generally stable trait concerning one's sense of control over life. People with an internal locus of control believe they are mostly in control of their own fates, whereas people with an external locus of control believe that what happens to them is mostly a matter of luck.

When Weiner's three dimensions are combined, the result is a set of attributions that is commonly used by students to explain their failure on a particular learning task (Table 9.1). Recall your own experiences as a student. Which attributions in Table 9.1 best reflect your own thinking? How did your thinking influence your motivation?

attribution theory The explanations, reasons, or excuses students give for their own successes or failures in learning.

Whatever reason is given for success or failure, a central assumption of attribution theory is that students will seek in their reasoning to maintain a positive self-image (Frieze & Weiner, 1971; Kukla, 1972; see also Aronson, 1972). Students who perform well on a standardized achievement test, for instance, are most likely to attribute success on the test to their own ability. The locus is internal. Students who perform poorly on such a test, however, are likely to attribute their failure on

TABLE 9.1 Weiner's Attribution Theory

Dimension Classification	Reason for Failure
Internal-stable-uncontrollable	Low aptitude
Internal-stable-controllable	Never studies
Internal-unstable-uncontrollable	Sick the day of the exam
Internal-unstable-controllable	Did not study for this particular test
External-stable-uncontrollable	School has hard requirements
External-stable-controllable	Instructor is biased
External-unstable-uncontrollable	Bad luck
External-unstable-controllable	Friends failed to help

Source: From *Human Motivation: Metaphors, Theories and Research* (p. 253) by B. Weiner, 1992, Newbury Park, CA: Sage Publications, Inc. Copyright ©1992 by Sage Publications. Reprinted by permission of Sage Publications, Inc.

the test to some external factor, such as the difficulty of the test or poor instruction by a teacher, or to something that is uncontrollable, such as illness during the test.

Particularly important for teachers to realize is that low achievers tend to attribute their failure to lack of ability (internal and relatively stable). They also, incidentally, tend to attribute their successes to luck (external). Failure-prone learners tend to be sensitive to indirect cues from the teacher that reinforce their low ability attributions. "Seemingly positive teachers' behaviors as praise for success at easy tasks, the absence of blame for failure at such tasks, and affective displays of sympathy or compassion can communicate to the recipients of this feedback that they are low in ability" (Graham & Barker, 1990, p. 7). High achievers attribute failure to lack of effort (internal and unstable) and so are not especially attuned to the teacher's behavior. This attribution leads them to try harder on subsequent occasions.

Reflection: Think of times when you rationalized outcomes in a way that helped you maintain a positive self-image.

Critical Thinking: For teachers, what is the value of attributional style as a tool for understanding the motivations of individual students?

Learned Helplessness

An ability attribution for failure provides learners with a negative self-perception. They have failed and the reason they have failed is that they lack ability, an internal, stable source. Students who fail consistently and attribute these failures to causes that are not under their control can develop a serious motivation problem called **learned helplessness** (Dweck, 1975; Seligman & Meier, 1967). Students who have a learned-helplessness orientation feel that nothing they do matters. They tend to attribute failures to reasons that are internal and stable. For example, "I do not succeed because I am dumb. Therefore, nothing I do will improve my situation. I will always fail."

Learned helplessness as a condition can also arise from teacher-mandated consequences that are inconsistent and therefore unpredictable. In such situations, the students cannot predict what sorts of behavior will bring about a particular consequence, such as a good grade or punishment for misbehavior. The environment operates on the students rather than the students being instrumental in bringing about changes in the environment. Perceiving themselves as being unable to alter events by their behavior, students develop low expectations, which cause deficits in future learning as well as motivational and emotional disturbances (Seligman, 1975).

Point: *Life conditions affect motivation.* Students who come from homes where they are constantly denigrated by parents or siblings may develop a learned-helplessness orientation.

learned helplessness A depressed state when a person feels that no matter what he or she does, it will have no influence on important life events.

Try This: Interview teachers about learned helplessness in students. How might teachers inadvertently contribute to this condition? What are some interventions teachers might try to overcome learned-helplessness in students?

Connection: The topic of learned helplessness relates to the education of children at risk, discussed in Chapters 3 and 5.

Learning to be helpless can influence not only students' perceptions of themselves, their self-efficacy and sense of self-esteem, but also the instructional treatment they receive in school. In a study of 164 children who had been referred to a school problems clinic, the primary cause of difficulty for 80 of them was identified as a lack of motivation (Landman, 1987). When the 80 "unmotivated" children were compared with the 84 who were perceived as "motivated," it was found that the unmotivated children were further behind academically and received less remedial help in school.

Attribution theory gives us a way to identify motivation problems that could have serious consequences. How can teachers respond to motivational problems in children? Possible answers to this question appear later in this chapter, which presents a variety of strategies teachers can use to enhance the motivation of their students toward academic goals.

Impacts of Cultural Beliefs and Values on Student Motivation

Do attributions as defined by Weiner and others exist across cultures? In a study of 140 school children from Sri Lanka and 149 children from England, the attributional dimensions of locus of cause, stability, and controllability were present, but there were differences in the frequency with which certain attributions were used (Little, 1987). Weiner's attribution theory identifies *luck* as a major attribution. For children from Sri Lanka, however, *luck* was not a frequent attribution, but *karma* was. This suggests that attribution theory should be used along classification dimensions that are consistent with the culture of the child rather than with the culture of the researcher (or teacher).

Connection: Review the discussion of cultural differences in Chapter 4.

Three dimensions of attribution theory—locus, stability, and responsibility—appeared to be useful in identifying differences between male and female children in the Philippines (Watkins & Astilla, 1984). For females in this study, on the one hand, attributions that are external and uncontrollable led to a preference for rote learning approaches. Males, on the other hand, tended more to internal and controllable attributions, which led to an emphasis on internalizing and approaches to study that resulted in higher achievement.

Critical Thinking: How can cultural differences influence motivation? Why is it important to know a student's background when attempting to understand a student's motivation?

These studies suggest that cultural background influences attributions. When you use a child's attributions to gauge motivation, you should take cultural differences into account. These studies indicate macrocultural differences (see Chapter 4), but it is possible that the microcultural differences in a classroom might also affect your judgment of student motivation.

HOW DO TEACHERS' BELIEFS AFFECT STUDENT MOTIVATION?

Imagine yourself in the classroom conducting a group activity. Some students are participating actively, others are sitting quietly but apparently paying attention to the comments of their peers, still others are staring out the window, doodling in a notebook, or wandering around the room. Based on their behavior and your knowledge of the students, you can make some reasonable predictions about who is motivated in this situation and who is not. You also know that many different factors can influence the motivation of students to participate in this particular task, or in learning activities in general. Now consider your expectations about whom you expect to succeed in the task and how much influence you believe you can have toward motivating those students who seem unmotivated. What effect might your beliefs have on your actions in the classroom? What effect might these beliefs have on student motivation?

Beliefs about Students

Teachers acquire a variety of beliefs about students from a number of sources. Have you had an older brother or sister precede you through school? The experiences your teachers had with your sibling created certain expectations that they probably applied, albeit unintentionally, to you. Many students go through school trying to live up to or live down an older sibling's reputation. Teachers also acquire beliefs about students from other teachers, from medical or psychological reports in school records, and from standardized test scores. To the extent that these sources enable a teacher to construct an accurate understanding of a particular student's characteristics and needs, there is no need for concern. A problem arises, however, when teachers maintain beliefs about their students that are inaccurate. This could happen because of stereotypes held by the teacher or because the teacher fails to adjust his or her perception of a student over time even though the student's behavior or performance has changed.

For example, teachers commonly believe that boys have more behavior problems than girls and that physically attractive students will achieve at higher levels than less attractive students (Woolfolk, 1995). Knowledge of ethnic background, language differences, and disability can also affect a teacher's beliefs about students. Even the students' behavior in class can be the source of inaccurate beliefs by the teacher about the students' motivation. For example, a middle school teacher realized that the fidgety behavior of her students wasn't always a sign of inattentiveness or lack of motivation. Sometimes, the students just needed to get up and move about after sitting still for a period of time.

The Impact of Teacher Expectations

The **Pygmalion effect** refers to one way teachers' expectations may influence the behavior of students. The term comes from the myth of a Greek sculptor, Pygmalion, whose expectations of a statue he created caused the statue to come to life. (George Bernard Shaw's *Pygmalion,* the story of the transformation of a cockney flower girl, Eliza Doolittle, into a refined lady of aristocratic demeanor, was the basis for the musical, *My Fair Lady.*)

The term *Pygmalion effect* was applied to teachers' expectations by Rosenthal and Jacobson (1968). Rosenthal and Jacobson measured the intelligence of children in the first through sixth grades in a school in San Francisco. After the test was administered, the teachers of certain students were told that the test predicted substantial intellectual gains for those students in the coming year. In reality, the students identified as potential achievers performed no better or worse than other so-called average children who took the test. At the end of the school year, the group of children took the intelligence test a second time.

The results of the second test showed that the potential achievers did in fact show significant gains in intelligence. The gains were attributed to the heightened expectations of the students' teachers. This result was labeled the Pygmalion effect. These and similar results have also been referred to as *self-fulfilling prophe-*

Pygmalion effect The influence that a teacher's expectations may have on the behavior of students. Also called the teacher expectancy effect and the self-fulfilling prophecy.

Reflection: How did self-fulfilling prophecies and teacher expectancy effects influence your motivation and performance as a student?

Example: A teacher has one of her best friend's daughters in class. Because the teacher already knows the student well, the teacher has high expectations for the child. In addition, the teacher does not want to disappoint her friend in terms of her daughter's accomplishments that year. Therefore, the teacher gives the student extra responsibilities and extra attention, in some cases bending the rules. One day the teacher overhears the student say, "I wish she would treat me the same as everyone else." How should the teacher resolve this situation?

cy and the *teacher expectancy effect,* terms that are still used to identify any situation in which the communication of expectations by a teacher is thought to influence student behavior.

Rosenthal and Jacobson's study was intensely scrutinized. Additional research studies directed toward the effects of teacher expectations were also undertaken. Close inspection of Rosenthal and Jacobson's results showed that the self-fulfilling prophecy operated in the first and second grades but not in the third through sixth grades. Some questioned the test used to measure IQ, arguing that better measures of IQ should have been used. Others pointed out that even the positive results in the first and second grades could not be construed as convincing evidence that negative expectations necessarily lead to low performance (cf. Wineburg, 1987).

The interest of researchers in teacher expectancy effects has remained high, and recent research has yielded important qualifications regarding the influence a teacher's expectations may have on student behavior. For one thing, self-fulfilling prophecies appear to operate in a three-stage process (Jussim, 1986). During the first stage, teachers develop expectations of individual students. In the second, teachers begin differential treatment based on those expectations. In the third, students behave in expectancy-confirming ways. However, it appears that, in the second stage, both the frequency and nature of teachers' interactions with low-achieving versus high-achieving students must be considered. In one study, teachers tended to interact more *frequently* with high-achieving and high-expectancy students, but they spent more *total time* waiting for and interacting with low-achieving and low-expectancy students (Leder, 1987). This suggests that if we balance our interactions with students, we interrupt the process by which self-fulfilling prophecies come to fruition.

Finally, the results of a recent study emphasize the importance of teachers' actions over teachers' expectations. In the cases of two students, year-end achievement was opposite that predicted and expected by the teacher. What happened? In one case, "the teacher had failed to take corrective action when she should have *because she had expected* [the student] to do well on her own" (Goldenberg, 1992, p. 539). In the other case, "*in spite of the teacher's low expectations* for [the student's] success, the teacher took actions that appear to have influenced [her] eventual first-grade reading achievement. . . . Low expectations were clearly evident, but they were irrelevant in determining the teacher's actions" (p. 539).

To the extent that we allow our expectations about students to influence our actions with them, we risk creating a classroom of haves and have-nots. If we are aware that expectancies can influence interactions in our classrooms we can guard against differential treatment.

Here's How to Avoid the Negative Effects of Teacher Expectations

- Examine your own beliefs and teaching practices for possible stereotypes and prejudices. Do you tend to give boys different tasks than girls? Do you call on or involve all students equally in a learning activity? Do the instructional materials you use show both genders and a wide range of ethnic groups? Try to ensure that your instructional materials and strategies, including evaluation and disciplinary procedures, treat all students fairly.

- Be careful about how you use information about students that comes from their personal records, standardized tests, and other teachers. Although these sources of information can be helpful in determining individual students' needs, they can also create expectations that do not hold true in the context of your classroom.
- Be prepared to change your expectations of students as they acquire and demonstrate new competencies.
- Monitor your verbal and nonverbal responses to students in your class. Try to ensure that all students have equal access to you—your critical feedback, your encouragement, your smiles as well as your frowns.

Reflection: What do you want to know about your students before they enter the classroom? What do you *not* want to know? Why?

Try This: Interview teachers about the ways they guard against teacher expectancy effects.

Beliefs about Teaching Efficacy

Just as students have beliefs about their own abilities that affect their motivation, so teachers have similar beliefs that can affect whether they employ effective motivational strategies with students in their classes. In recent years, the concept of self-efficacy has been applied to teachers' general beliefs about the influence of teaching on learning, as well as to their specific beliefs about their abilities to motivate students. **Teaching efficacy** refers to a teacher's belief that teaching, in general, will have an influence on students' learning. Personal teaching efficacy is the teacher's belief in his or her ability to motivate students (Ashton & Webb, 1986). For example, a teacher who largely agrees with the statement, "When it comes right down to it, a teacher can't really do much because most of a student's motivation and performance depends on his/her home environment" (Woolfolk & Hoy, 1990), is said to be low in teaching efficacy. However, a teacher who says, "I am confident I can get my students interested in learning," is likely to be high in personal teaching efficacy.

Reflection: What are your beliefs about the ability of teachers to influence the motivation and performance of their students? How might your beliefs affect decisions you make in the classroom?

Teachers who are high in teaching efficacy and personal efficacy tend to provide students with tasks that are challenging and opportunities to take responsibility for their own learning (Ashton & Webb, 1986). These teachers also tend to be more committed to teaching (Coladarci, 1992) and more likely to use effective motivational strategies with exceptional students (cf. McDaniel & McCarthy, 1989). Results of one recent study indicated that general and special education teachers with high personal and teaching efficacy were most likely to agree with general class placement of an exceptional student (Soodak & Podell, 1993).

teaching efficacy A teacher's belief that teaching, in general, will have an influence on students' learning.

By contrast, teachers who are low in teaching or personal efficacy are more likely to be authoritarian in style and less likely to try teaching strategies that might challenge their own capabilities. As a consequence, these teachers are also less

In what ways will your expectations of the students you teach affect their motivation to achieve? What beliefs and values as a teacher will contribute to your ability to enhance students' motivation to learn?

Insights ON SUCCESSFUL PRACTICE

What advice can you give novice teachers about the effects of teacher expectations on student motivation?

Motivation is undoubtedly the crux of the learning process. Encouraging love of learning remains our challenge, and if teachers examine their own motivations for teaching they might become more successful in enhancing students' motivation to learn. For instance, do you love both your subject and your students? Are you interested and excited by words, ideas, and concepts? Do you have faith in your students' innate yearning for knowledge and ability to recognize what is important? Do you have high expectations for them?

Are you willing to look for the particular key that will unlock this unique personality, that individual mind? Not every teacher will succeed every day with every student, because we are limited in our understanding of all that goes on in each of their lives. Nevertheless, we are given the charge not only to show the way but also to encourage the journey.

Once your students have embarked on the journey—shown an interest in the subject (however great or small the journey might be)—it is the teacher's responsibility to act as a guide. You become their mentor, encouraging them to continue their quest and strive for excellence. Because your students leave your classroom does not mean they leave your life—or that you have left theirs. Your influence continues. Your expectations for them be-come part of their expectations for themselves.

PATRICIA WOODWARD, Lincoln Junior High School, Fort Collins, Colorado

What questions should you ask yourself about your expectations of students in your classroom? What might be some short- and long-term impacts of your expectations on students' motivation to learn?

Critical Thinking: How are expert and novice teachers likely to differ on teaching efficacy? Why?

likely to find ways of helping students who experience difficulty in in their classes (Ashton & Webb, 1986).

How can teachers develop high teaching and personal efficacy? Probably in much the same way that students develop high self-efficacy toward specific learning tasks. You can imagine how successful experiences in teaching may build confidence in your ability to make a difference in students' learning. These experiences could occur in your teacher preparation program, in your student teaching, and in your teaching as a professional employed at a school. It has also been found that a healthy school climate directly relates to a positive sense of teacher efficacy (Hoy & Woolfolk, 1993).

HOW CAN YOU ENHANCE YOUR STUDENTS' MOTIVATION TO LEARN?

How can you enhance motivation in a systematic and effective way? This final section of the chapter presents an integrated model of motivational design that you can use to identify potential sources of motivational problems in your classes and to select motivational strategies to help solve those problems. Also discussed are ways you can arouse and maintain students' curiosity during learning, use reinforcement effectively, and help students attribute their successes and failures to motivational and learning strategy variables, viewing ability as something they can change.

Arousing Curiosity

Curiosity is a knowledge state caused by stimuli that are novel, complex, or in some way incongruous (Berlyne, 1965). Intuitively, you will recognize that curiosity is a strong source of motivation. Consider the following example of arousing curiosity in a classroom context:

> "Before we begin the next science chapter," the teacher said, "I'd like to tell you a story. Then," she added with a slight smile, "I'll ask you a question."
>
> The sixth graders looked at their teacher expectantly.
>
> "A man was out driving his car," the teacher began, "when he noticed something quite unusual. A truck stopped in the middle of a block and the truck driver got out with a baseball bat in his hands. He walked back to the center of the truck and suddenly hit the side several times with the bat. Then he got back in and drove on."
>
> Several children who had been somewhat indifferent when the teacher started now looked at her raptly.
>
> "As the man in the car followed the truck," she continued, "he saw the truck again stop after about three blocks and again the driver got out, beat his truck a few times with the bat, returned to his seat, and drove off."
>
> Every eye in the room was now riveted on the teacher.
>
> "Once more," the teacher went on, "the man in the car followed the truck and, sure enough, in another three blocks it stopped, the driver got out and banged away with his bat."
>
> The teacher paused and glanced around the room. Satisfied that she had the class's attention she continued. "The man in the car," she said, "was fascinated. He followed the truck for almost two miles trying to figure out what the truck driver was doing. Finally he gave up."
>
> The teacher again paused, scanning the intent faces in front of her.
>
> "The next time the truck stopped," she went on, "the man jumped out of his car, ran over to the truck driver, and said, 'Sir forgive me for bothering you. But I've been following you for almost two miles. Why on earth do you drive exactly three blocks, get out with a baseball bat, and hit your truck a few times?' The truck driver said, 'It's really very simple. I've got a two-ton truck and inside I've got three tons of canaries. So I've got to keep one ton of them in the air at all times.'"
>
> A few of the students looked puzzled, some seemed skeptical, and several laughed. As the teacher waited, the laughter gradually spread until the entire class was smiling.
>
> "Now," she said, "let me give you a question."
>
> Looking pointedly at the class, she said, "Was the truck driver stupid?"
>
> There was a sudden silence as the children pondered the query.
>
> "Yes," a sandy-haired boy said suddenly. "He still had three tons in his truck."
>
> The teacher remained silent watching her students. Then a bright-eyed girl in the corner of the room raised her hand shyly.
>
> "Beth."
>
> "He really wasn't being stupid," the girl said, "because if one ton was flying around inside the truck, they wouldn't add any weight."
>
> With this the teacher smiled and walked to the board. She then began a lesson on the principle of air support. (Rubin, 1985, pp. 129-130)

curiosity An eager desire to know caused by stimuli that are novel, complex, or strange or that involve fantasy and ambiguity.

Using novelty, as the teacher in the example did, is one way of creating the perceptual arousal that is one aspect of curiosity. Novel or incongruous situations alert students' attention. Consider what would happen, however, if the

Novelty, complexity, incongruity, and ambiguity are qualities of learning tasks that naturally stimulate students' curiosity. Curiosity—a state of mind of the learner—automatically increases motivation.

teacher telling the story of the canaries were to use such a story to begin every lesson. Would the novelty of such incongruous stories wear off? If so, would she be less likely to engage her students' curiosity? Curiosity, as a source of motivation, has a somewhat limited use in the classroom unless it can be sustained. How do teachers sustain curiosity?

here's how

Here's How to Arouse and Maintain Students' Curiosity in Learning

Try This: Observe classrooms to discover how teachers use curiosity to introduce lessons and maintain attention.

- Use fantasy to provide a meaningful context for learning. Students find it easy to augment a situation involving fantasy with their own imaginations (Rieber, 1991). For example, a unit on the solar system could be set in the context of space travel and preparing to explore "strange new worlds where no one has gone before" (cf. *Star Trek*).
- Use problem-based scenarios that require students to seek additional information in order to solve. Computer-based simulations (e.g., *Sim City, Sim Earth*) and technology-based instruction (e.g., the *Jasper Woodbury Problem-Solving Series* on videodisc) are good examples of this strategy. They provide complex problems to students along with numerous clues and information regarding their solution. Moreover, there are typically several ways in which the problems can be solved, which adds to the challenge and curiosity engendered in students.
- Give assignments to students that are somewhat ambiguous in nature to generate curiosity and prolonged task engagement (Woolfolk & McCune-Nicolich, 1984). For example, groups of students can be given the same set of oddly assorted materials in a science class and be told to "invent something" or "create a vehicle" or in a language arts class to "create a story involving these materials."

Using Reinforcement Effectively

undermining effect Consequence that an extrinsic reward can have on behavior that is intrinsically motivated.

The **undermining effect** is the result that external rewards can have on behavior that is intrinsically motivated (Deci, 1971, 1975; Morgan, 1984). For example, a student who begins reading biographies of World War II figures and who brings the subject to the attention of a parent or teacher may find the parent or teacher delighted with the student's new-found interest. As a function of this delight, the parent or teacher tells the student that for every new World War II biography read, the student will receive some sort of reward—either free time in the classroom to pursue a hobby or release from a household chore or some more tangible reward. According to Deci and other researchers, establishing external rewards in a situation like this might undermine the student's intrinsic motivation. The student might continue her reading not out of curiosity about the figures in World War II or a need to understand the events of that war but because of the rewards delivered from external sources—the parent or the teacher.

Critical Thinking: How might teachers inadvertently undermine students' motivation?

It is tempting for a teacher to encourage academic pursuits, especially in a student who has not demonstrated a keen interest in reading or writing or other cognitive activities. However, teachers should take care in identifying those areas in which students require motivation from external sources and to allow intrinsically motivated behavior to flourish on its own terms. The undermining effect appears to operate at all ages. The intrinsic motivation of young children is especially susceptible to being undermined by extrinsic rewards (see Lepper, Greene, & Nisbett, 1973; Sarafino, 1984).

Example: A teacher uses a system of plus and minus marks to monitor student behavior. At the end of the week, students with two pluses get a treat. This system works great with first graders. With sixth graders, however, it does not. Why?

You have learned from other chapters that reinforcement is a powerful teaching tool. Teachers should not, however, reinforce student behavior indiscriminately. To reinforce effectively, a teacher needs to know students' goals and their intrinsic motivations. Part of the reason is that such knowledge helps a teacher decide when to provide external sources of motivation and when to allow the intrinsic motivation of a learner to determine classroom activity.

Reflection: Recall an activity in which your motivation was undermined by external rewards.

Varying Classroom Goal Structures

Teachers can have a strong impact on student motivation to pursue particular types of goals by the classroom structures they create (e.g., Ames & Ames, 1984; Dweck, 1986). A classroom **goal structure** is the way in which teachers manage learning and evaluate and reward student performance. Johnson & Johnson (1987) described three types of goal structures: cooperative, competitive, and individualistic.

Connection: Cooperative goal structures also relate to models for active learning discussed in Chapter 12.

A **cooperative goal structure** is present when rewards are bestowed on a group based on their performance as a group, rather than to members of the group based on individual performance. As a consequence, students perceive cooperation as the best means for successfully attaining goals. If the group is given the task of publishing a volume of poetry, for example, then the anticipated group product—the volume of poetry—provides the basis for evaluation and subsequent rewards. One student cannot receive a higher grade than another student for his or her contribution to the book of poetry. In such instances, students are motivated to put forth their best efforts in cooperation with their group, not just to help themselves but out of a sense of obligation to the other members of their group.

goal structure A means by which teachers manage learning and evaluate and reward student performance.

cooperative goal structure A class management structure in which rewards for performance are given to a group, not to individuals within the group. As a consequence, students view attainment of goals as possible only through cooperation with members of their group.

Think back to your own high school experience. Perhaps you were in a group—the band, the cast or crew of a play, the French club, an athletic team, or the school yearbook staff. The success of the product or performance depended on cooperation. If you contributed to such an effort, part of your motivation was likely a sense of obligation; you may have worked harder because you didn't want to let the other people down. To be sure, you invested time and effort in the group because the group was doing something you liked. But there were probably times when you went above and beyond the call of duty.

Cooperative goal structures are effective for several reasons (Johnson & Johnson, 1987, 1990):

1. Group work requires discussion, promotes the discovery proccess, and leads to a higher level of learning.
2. Discussion promotes diversity of ideas, opinions, and positions. In arguing for a position, explanations are sought, repeated, and—through repetition—clarified. Comprehension and retention are enhanced.
3. Members in the group provide feedback and, because it is a group project, encouragement for each other.

In a cooperative goal structure, students attain the goal only if other students also attain the same goal. In a **competitive goal structure**, students view attainment as possible only if other students do not attain the goal. By definition, competitive goal structures ensure that some students will be unsuccessful. In general, students who experience a classroom managed by means of a competitive goal structure tend to have low expectations, show little persistence on achievement-oriented tasks, and, as just indicated, avoid tasks on which they have experienced little success (cf. Johnson & Johnson, 1987).

Critical Thinking: How might a competitive goal structure be focused on effort rather than ability?

Although students may show improvement in performance under a competitive goal structure, this improvement should not be interpreted as success. Students appear to reward their own behavior only if they win a competition (Ames & Ames, 1984). When they win, they tend to think of their success as due to ability, whereas when other students win, they attribute that success to luck. Competition also fosters social comparisons.

Are there any classroom situations in which a competitive goal structure is appropriate? Consider a spelling bee. In a spelling bee, there is only one winner. In order to attain the goal of winning the spelling bee, others must lose. Does this mean that spelling bees should be avoided? Not necessarily. If a class spelling bee were conducted at the beginning of a spelling unit, the competition would highlight the differences among learners in terms of prior skill or ability. If the spelling bee were conducted at the end of the unit when all students have had a chance to master the list, the results would be more easily attributed to effort. At the end of the unit, more students have a chance of winning. Failure for any one student is less likely because all students have mastered the material or are approaching mastery. The outcome of the game or competition is more in doubt and therefore more fun. In sum, competitive goal structures can be used effectively if the competition is based on effort toward mastery rather than on the ability levels the students bring to the learning situation.

competitive goal structure A class management structure in which students must compete for rewards so that they view attainment of goals as possible only if other students do not attain them.

individualistic goal structure A class management structure in which rewards are given on the basis of an individual's performance, unaffected by the performance of other students.

An **individualistic goal structure** is one in which rewards are provided on the basis of an individual's performance, unaffected by the performance of other students. An individual is not a contributor to a group performance nor are rewards available to only one or a few winners. An individualistic goal structure allows each student to compete against a criterion. If all students achieve the criterion, all students are rewarded.

Individualistic goal structures probably constitute the most common form of evaluating and rewarding student performance. Although students are judged and rewarded on the basis of their own work, they also learn, however, that there is no payoff for cooperation. In addition, some students may perceive an individualistic goal structure as competitive and exhibit competitive behavior even though such behavior is neither required nor desired.

The goal structures used in classroom learning situations can also orient students toward learning (or mastery) goals rather than to performance goals. At least six organizational variables in schools and classrooms affect student motivation: *t*ask, *a*utonomy, *r*ecognition, *g*rouping, *e*valuation, and *t*ime (Ames, 1990; Maehr & Anderman, 1993). These six variables are expressed in the acronym TARGET which refers to an approach being tried in schools to establish a greater task or learning focus while at the same time minimizing an ability or performance focus. Here's How outlines this approach.

Critical Thinking: What kinds of attributions would mastery-oriented students exhibit?

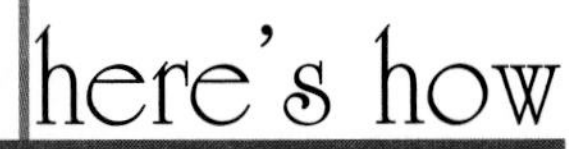

Here's How to TARGET Learning Goals in Your Classroom and Enhance Intrinsic Motivation

- Choose *Tasks* that are challenging, interesting, worthy of consideration, and meaningful to your students.
- Support *Autonomy* and responsibility in learning by providing choices to students along with the opportunity to set their own learning agenda.
- *Recognize* progress toward goal attainment, as well as student achievement of learning goals. Make sure the efforts of all students are recognized.
- In *Grouping* students (organizing them for instruction), provide opportunities for students to participate equally in decision making and other classroom roles. Create a climate of acceptance and encourage participation of all students.
- Use *Evaluation* practices that reduce emphasis on social comparisons among students and provide opportunities for students to demonstrate progress as well as their best work. Encourage students to evaluate their own work and help them to develop skills to do so.
- Schedule *Time* for interdisciplinary units and complex problems to facilitate lengthy student engagement in learning. (Adapted from Maehr & Anderman, 1993)

Try This: Observe a number of classrooms to identify the types of goal structures being used. How do differences in goal structures affect student motivation and learning?

Motivational Training

Besides organizing your classroom and your instruction to facilitate motivation, you can employ a variety of means with students to help them self-regulate. According to McCombs (1984, 1988; McCombs & Marzano, 1990) teaching students to become self-regulated learners is motivational training. This training should include attention to cognitive, metacognitive, and affective strategies. Thus, students must acquire motivation-related skills, such as setting realistic learning goals that interest them and using appropriate self-talk when they experience difficulty or failure in a learning task. Students must also acquire motivation-related will, which involves recognizing "the power of their choices—the power of the self as agent" (McCombs & Marzano, 1990, p. 64).

Setting Goals and Changing Attributions. Programs have been developed that help teachers address achievement motivation and attributions of their students. For example, several programs have been designed to help students at risk of dropping out of school (Alschuler, 1973). These programs focus specifically

Insights ON SUCCESSFUL PRACTICE

What do you regard as the most important aspect of your role as a teacher who influences students' motivation to learn?

If someone were to write a "teacher's epitaph" for me, I would want it to say, "She listened." As a teacher, the single most important activity for me is to listen *to* my students rather than listen *for* prescribed answers. By listening and by providing a student-centered learning environment, I contribute to my students' motivation to succeed academically.

A classroom that is student-centered will always be more conducive to the educational process than one in which student–teacher interaction is dependent on materials or instructional approaches alone. Student-centeredness is at the heart of trends toward literature-based curricula or whole language classrooms. What else are these approaches but attempts to get teachers to pay attention to the needs and interests of their students?

We know from research in response to reading programs that conditions intrinsic to the learner, which are part of the subjective nature of reading, are integral to reader engagement and understanding. This appears to be true in both narrative and expository text. When a student finds personal meaning in a lesson, this meaning becomes the key to sustained and continuing learning, the springboard for knowledge development. No number of workbook pages or computer programs or creative bulletin boards can substitute for the subjective response. For this reason, the human communication aspects of education are crucial, including my role as one who listens.

SUE MISHEFF, Malone College, Canton, Ohio

According to this teacher, why is student-centeredness the key to effective teaching? What are the hallmarks of student-centered instruction, and what part does intrinsic motivation play in student-centered learning?

attribution training Attempting to change the student's style of explaining his or her own learning successes or failures.

on the use of self-paced materials, games and activities intended to enhance the student's sense of personal responsibility for success and failure. In effect, the programs provide **attribution training**, attempting to change the attributional style of the student.

DeCharms's work (1976, 1980) provides the best known examples of attribution training. In his attributional training program, DeCharms uses the analogy of origins and pawns: Origins are people who are masters of their own fate, those who exhibit an internal locus of control; pawns are people who do not exert a control over the events in their environment but, rather, are controlled by them. The program focuses on treating the students as origins rather than pawns. Pawns have an external locus of control. Children in the DeCharms classic study were trained to become origins. They were taught to plan their actions, starting with the establishment of realistic goals—goals that are neither so difficult that they precluded successful completion nor so easy that success in completing them is perceived as meaningless.

DeCharms demonstrated that one way to combat the problem of the pawn syndrome or the characteristics of learned helplessness is to teach children how to set realistic goals. When these goals are learning goals, as opposed to performance goals, self-concept and an internal locus of control are also likely to be enhanced (e.g., Smith, 1986). Parents, teachers, and students should together seek opportunities for success, change attributions from external to internal reasons, and learn to use feedback in a positive manner (Greer & Withered, 1987). The keys to the success of this kind of program seem to be the establishment of adaptive goal-setting behavior; learning the difference between realistic and unrealistic goals; and, having established these goals, planning actions that will lead to their attainment. Attributional training programs that implement these suggestions have been found to be successful. For example, students trained in DeCharms's program attended school more regularly than those who did not participate in origins and pawns training. Participants in the DeCharms's program were also more likely than untrained students to graduate from high school. Attribution training has been shown to affect the motivation and performance of educationally at-risk children and of adults with mental retardation. Participation of students, their parents, their peers, and teaching and counseling professionals in such programs may also help to reduce informal (and possibly inaccurate) labeling of students by teachers and other professionals.

Try This: Develop a plan for attribution training that you could use with students you plan to teach. What goal-setting activities will you include?

Developing Self-Regulation. Attribution training, with its emphasis on students learning to control their own environment and their own learning, also supports self-regulation and the development of autonomy. But there are other ways as well to help your students become autonomous self-regulated learners.

here's how

Here's How You Can Help Students Become Self-Regulated Learners

- Model strategies for setting goals, planning actions, monitoring progress, and making appropriate attributions. Show students what they can expect as a result of applying these strategies to help them understand the personal utility of self-regulated strategies (Deci et al., 1991).
- Provide opportunities for students to make meaningful choices and decisions about their own learning with a minimum of pressure to respond in a particular way. For example, a seventh-grade history teacher collects a variety of resources to make available to students—including textbooks, reference books, historical novels, videotapes, and newspapers. From this extensive database, the students choose what they wish to investigate when the class studies an event or period in history.
- Convey expectations and confidence in students' ability to regulate their behavior. There is evidence that teachers who believe students will regulate themselves are more autonomy-supportive and less controlling toward those students. In contrast, when teachers think students have to be extrinsically motivated, they become more controlling and less autonomy-supportive (Pelletier & Vallerand, 1989).
- Acknowledge individual students' feelings and perspectives as valid and valued. Let students know that it's okay to feel confused during a difficult learning activity or resentful about limits placed on their behavior. Providing a context of socioemotional support for students is an important aspect of developing self-regulation (McCombs & Marzano, 1990).

Try This: Develop a plan from the Here's How strategies for helping students become self-regulated learners. How will you monitor your behavior in supporting autonomy and minimizing teacher control?

Applying the ARCS Model

Let's take a look at some of the conditions that should exist if achievement motivation is to develop within a student. The conditions can be referred to by the acronym ARCS. The **ARCS model** is a general model of motivation that was developed by Keller (1983, 1984, 1987a,b) and described by Driscoll (1994). There are four elements in this model of motivation, representing conditions that must exist in order for a learner to be motivated: *A*ttention, *R*elevance, *C*onfidence, and *S*atisfaction (ARCS). These conditions are illustrated in Figure 9.3.

Critical Thinking: What conditions have to exist for students to be motivated to achieve academically?

Attention. The term *attention* has been examined as part of the discussion of information-processing and social cognitive theories. In those discussions, *attention* referred to a process. In the ARCS model, *attention* is a state or condition of the learner. A student in the classroom is either attending or not attending to the achievement-related stimuli. In the ARCS model attention is a necessary condition for motivation.

Connection: How do information-processing theory (Chapter 7) and social cognitive theory (Chapter 8) relate to this discussion of attention?

One of the things that new teachers worry most about is their ability to gain students' attention so they can learn. It's possible to study many different attention-getting devices by observing teachers in the field. Some teachers will clap their hands or make some sudden noise that will automatically get the attention of students. Other teachers will engage in a particular routine that signals to students that it's time for them to pay attention.

ARCS model A model teachers can use to identify and solve motivational problems in their classrooms. The ARCS model defines four categories of motivation that must exist for students to be motivated to learn: attention, relevance, confidence, and satisfaction.

If we want students to learn the pronunciation of a single word, we need to attract their attention only for a moment. However, in the context of student motivation, attention must be sustained over long periods of time. Maintaining attention is even more important than attracting it.

Consider the children's program, *Sesame Street,* which is designed not only to capture but also to sustain attention. The program's attention-sustaining ability appears to stem from the use of humor, incongruity, and encouragement of viewer anticipation (Lesser, 1974). This anticipation comes in the form of known characters, such as Big Bird, Oscar the Grouch, Grover, Bert and Ernie, and the Count. Viewers come to know these characters' personalities and anticipate their actions. When they see Oscar the Grouch emerge from his residence, a garbage

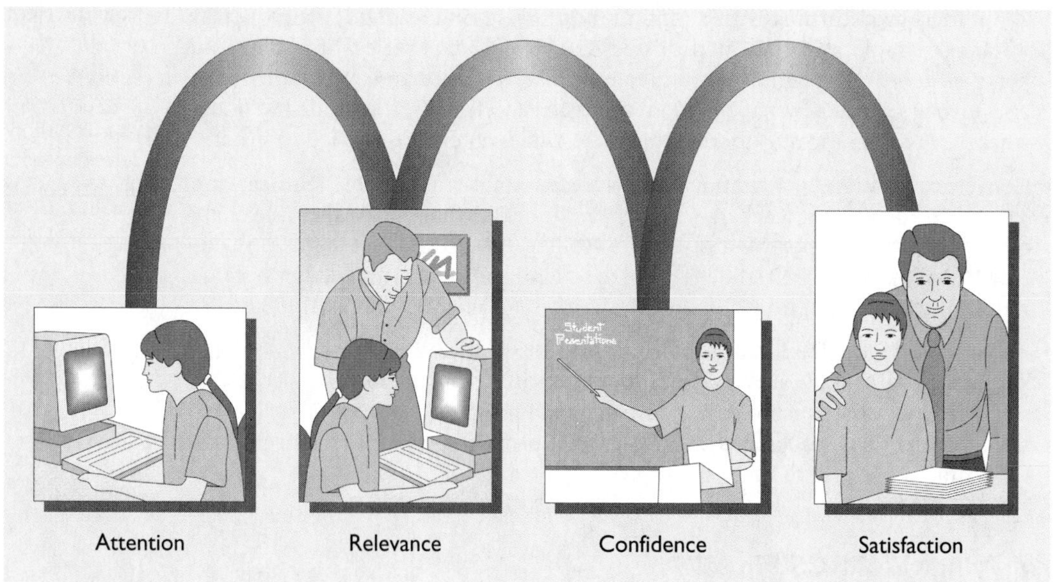

FIGURE 9.3

The ARCS Model: Conditions Needed for Motivation to Learn

can, viewers anticipate the kinds of comments Oscar will make. To satisfy their curiosity and to determine whether their anticipations are correct, viewers listen to Oscar the Grouch to see what he has to say.

Reflection: How do educational programs on television maintain viewers' attention?

Perhaps you are a fan of a particular soap opera on television. If so, you know the personality characteristics of the soap opera characters quite well. You can, therefore, predict the types of behaviors they are likely to display. Your attention to their activities is sustained because you are curious to see how their personalities will influence events.

The attention condition in the ARCS model appeals to a particular kind of learner interest. It is the interest that people have in events that makes them curious.

Relevance. Relevance, the second condition in the ARCS model, requires the engagement of learner interest; that is, learners must perceive that the content of the material presented is important to them.

Critical Thinking: What makes lessons relevant to students?

Beginning teachers are often advised to make their lessons relevant to students' lives by relating the lesson to the experiences of students. One way to demonstrate the relevance of material is to convince students that the material will enable them to achieve an instructional goal. For example, in the Teacher Chronicle at the beginning of this chapter, Marita might have demonstrated how brainstorming makes story writing easier. Demonstrating relevance is an effective approach for students who view instructional goals or learning outcomes as important, for either intrinsic or extrinsic reasons.

For some students, lessons can be made relevant by the use of humor or by the use of the unexpected. Recall the teacher who told the story about a truckload of canaries. The story itself is relevant for some students, not because it illustrates the principle of air support but because it is funny. They can take the story home and entertain their parents with it. The entertainment value of the story makes it relevant for students who fancy themselves storytellers. For a student with storytelling goals, the story establishes a condition of motivation. Other students may find the information relevant because it provides a unique example of a scientific principle.

Example: Making a connection with prior knowledge by means of concrete imagery makes that information *relevant* and enhances retention of the information in memory.

Suppose that you were going to teach a lesson about the solar system. Part of your job is to teach the students about the dimension and properties of the Sun. The size of the Sun, for example, could be communicated in any number of ways. It could simply be communicated by numbers. The Sun's diameter is 864,000 miles; it weighs 330,000 times as much as Earth, and its mean distance from Earth is 92.9 million miles. Each square centimeter of the Sun's surface radiates 1,500 calories of energy per second. Unless your students are studying for an imminent appearance on a television game show, these numbers may hold little relevance for them. Suppose, however, that after providing the appropriate numbers you then describe the size of the Sun in the following terms:

> The Sun could be hollowed out so that half of it were hollow. We could place Earth with the Moon still orbiting around it in the hollow half. At the turn of the century, Sir James Genes calculated that if he could remove matter the size of a pinhead from the core of the Sun, and place that bit of matter on Earth, the heat from that pinhead of matter would kill a human being ninety-four miles away.

Describing the dimensions of the Sun in these terms rather than only in terms of statistics might, for some students, prove relevant to their interests and, therefore, motivate them to attend to the rest of the lesson.

The notion of relevance takes us back to the importance of goals in considering the motivation of students. If you understand what goals students bring with them to your classroom, then you are better able to present information in a way that will be relevant to them.

Connection: How does confidence relate to self-efficacy, described earlier in the chapter?

Confidence. Confidence refers to students' beliefs that they can perform competently in a particular learning situation. Learners are motivated when they believe that they can be successful in learning new material and performing new tasks. Confidence relates to self-efficacy and contributes to achievement. Studies have shown that confident learners are better able to attain goals than learners who do not have confidence in their own abilities (Bandura, 1977; Jones, 1977). When students have successful learning experiences, they infer that they can perform effectively. Such success builds confidence and enhances expectations of efficacy.

How can you build confidence in your students? Besides providing learning opportunities during which students can experience success, you can help them to expect success by making your own expectations clear. This means clearly communicating both the behaviors necessary for goal achievement and your beliefs that students are capable of performing these behaviors. You can also build confidence in students with challenging but not overwhelming tasks, during which you provide decreasing amounts of assistance as learners become capable of independently achieving the task.

Finally, consistent with attribution theory, you can help students to become more confident in their abilities by encouraging them to see learning as a consequence of their own efforts and effective study strategies. When you give detailed feedback explicitly showing students what they did wrong and why, they are able to attribute poor performance to specific problems that can be corrected.

Satisfaction. Satisfaction occurs when expectations about learning are met. For example, a student who has successfully completed all required tasks in a course may expect to receive some sort of extrinsic reward, such as a good grade, teacher praise, or parental encouragement. However, the satisfaction of learning expectancies may lead also to self-reinforcement, as in the case of a student who achieves competence in a skill that he or she wanted to learn. Finally, the condition of satisfaction is met when a student fulfills his or her need to achieve.

How can you assure that students' expectations about learning will be satisfied? For students who are intrinsically motivated, it is important that they be able to use their newly acquired knowledge or skills in a meaningful way. In math, for example, students could solve problems from situations in their lives, such as how many squares on their block, how many worms in their yard, or how many RBIs their favorite baseball player has this season. Marita, in the Teacher Chronicle, helps to assure Bronson's satisfaction in learning to write by allowing him to write about something of personal interest.

When students are extrinsically motivated, they will be satisfied when their learning results in the anticipated reward. When you have done well on all course assignments and exams, you expect to receive an A in the course and are satisfied when you do. Imagine your feelings, however, in a situation where you believe you have done well on a course project, successfully meeting all of the instructor's preset criteria, but you receive a grade of B without so much as an explanation for why the grade wasn't an A. It is likely that you would feel very unsatisfied with the learning experience and probably unmotivated to work hard on the next assignment. This aspect of satisfaction concerns equity, or how consistently standards and consequences for achievement are applied. Students must perceive that they are being fairly and equitably treated to derive satisfaction from a learning experience.

The ARCS model identifies four conditions that must be met if students are to be motivated to learn. Although these conditions should exist within the learning situation in your classroom, it is important to keep in mind that many of these conditions may arise from earlier events in your students' experiences. How do you determine, then, if there are motivational problems in your class and what motivational strategies you should incorporate into your instruction?

Here's How to Identify and Solve Motivational Problems in the Classroom

- Develop a profile of your students' motivation in terms of the categories of ARCS—attention, relevance, confidence, and satisfaction.
- Based on the student profile, define motivational objectives.
- For each motivational objective, select corresponding motivational strategies to incorporate into your lessons.
- Try out the strategies you selected and observe the results. If student motivation does not improve, revise your analysis of the problem(s) and your selection of motivational strategies.

Try This: For a class you teach or plan to teach, try out the ARCS model to identify motivational problems you may face and to plan ways you could avoid or overcome those problems.

In the first step, you should think about your students in terms of the ARCS model and develop a profile of their motivation. Who are your learners? Are they likely to experience problems paying attention or finding relevance in the subject matter of the lesson? Do they have little confidence in their abilities? If the answer to any of these questions is yes, then satisfaction in learning could also be a problem. From your knowledge of the students in your class, you can identify the variables that are likely to be potential sources of motivational problems.

From the student profile, you can determine the likely motivational needs that exist in your class, providing the basis for defining specific motivational objectives (the second step). For example, suppose you are teaching a class of students who have tested below average in reading. The self-efficacy of these students as readers is likely to be low, which means that their confidence in their ability to read will be low. With this knowledge in mind, you may define a motivational objective: Students will gain confidence in reading. In defining a motivational objective, you should also give some thought to how you will know when it has been achieved. What is an indicator of increased confidence in reading, for example? In the Teacher Chronicle Conclusion, Bronson demonstrates reading confidence by his willingness to read aloud in class.

The third step is to select corresponding motivational strategies to integrate into your instruction that will help meet the identified motivational objectives. For instance, Marita's setting up Bronson to read his story about getting rid of broccoli is a strategy designed to build his confidence. She knew the other students would enjoy Bronson's story and give him positive attention as a result.

The final step is to try out the strategies you selected, observe the results, and revise if necessary. For example, Marita learned that allowing a student to complete a writing assignment by using a topic of personal interest is an effective means of establishing relevance and sustaining attention for this task. She recognized Bronson's need, tried the strategy, and found that it worked. She is now likely to add this strategy to her repertoire and use it again with students who exhibit similar needs.

The ARCS model provides a systematic means of improving the motivational appeal of instruction. It is one of the tools teachers can use to help their students become and stay motivated.

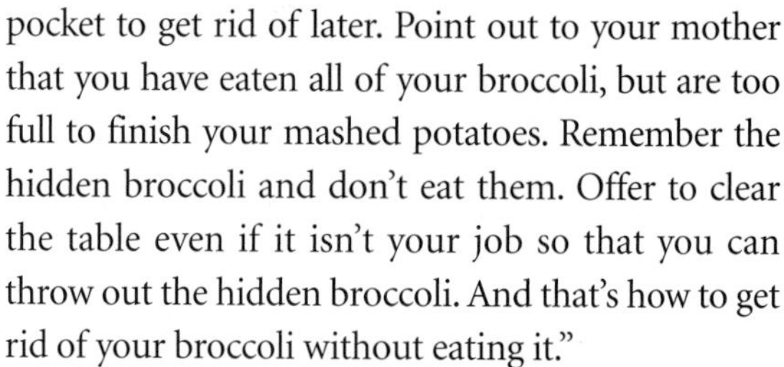

TEACHER Chronicle Conclusion

GOLDEN OPPORTUNITIES

Marita Vasquez stands in front of her class, ready to hand back the writing assignments.

"I want to tell you how pleased I was with how you completed the assignment. Most of you put a lot of thought into your writing. I suggested changes on your papers, and we will get to those in a minute. But first I want to ask you a question." She pauses, looking at Bronson. "What would happen if you were served something you didn't like and you wanted to get rid of it before your mother found out? For example, what if Bronson didn't like broccoli?" Everyone shifts to look at Bronson, who is grinning like a jack-o-lantern.

Normally he doesn't like to be the center of attention, but Marita has made a connection with him by allowing him the freedom to do the assignment differently from the others. "Bronson, would you be willing to read your story?" Marita asks.

Bronson hesitates momentarily and then begins in a clear voice. "What To Do When Your Mother Serves You Broccoli. First you look at it and say, 'Yuck, broccoli again.' This is to trick her into thinking you hate broccoli like you always have so she suspects nothing. Then, you cut up the broccoli into ten small pieces and spread them around on your plate. You hide two of the pieces under the mashed potatoes. You chew up three pieces and then spit them into your napkin. Make sure you have a paper napkin. Now, you spill two pieces on the floor and clean them up with your napkin. Throw the napkin away immediately and get a clean one. This time chew three pieces and spit them into your napkin and put this in your pocket to get rid of later. Point out to your mother that you have eaten all of your broccoli, but are too full to finish your mashed potatoes. Remember the hidden broccoli and don't eat them. Offer to clear the table even if it isn't your job so that you can throw out the hidden broccoli. And that's how to get rid of your broccoli without eating it."

By the time Bronson finishes everyone is laughing, not at him but with him. They have understood every word.

"It's just about lunchtime," Marita says. "When we come back this afternoon, we will talk more and you can write your stories."

APPLICATION QUESTIONS

1. In terms of the concepts and theories presented in this chapter, what motivational factors influenced the behavior of Bronson and his classmates? What are the sources of those factors?
2. What might Marita have done if Bronson did not want to read his story?
3. How is Bronson's self-efficacy for writing likely to be influenced by this experience?
4. If Bronson gained more confidence with his speech, how might this affect his motivation?
5. How might learned helplessness come into play with Bronson? What other techniques could Marita or Bronson's other teachers use to help him overcome learned helplessness?
6. Is Marita high or low in teaching efficacy? Why? What can you do to develop your own teaching efficacy?
7. Analyze the events in this Teacher Chronicle in terms of the ARCS model. How did Marita design instruction to enhance students' motivation for accomplishing her instructional goals? Using the ARCS model, analyze a lesson you plan to teach and develop motivational strategies that you could incorporate.

CHAPTER SUMMARY

WHAT IS MOTIVATION TO LEARN?

All students are motivated, but not all students may be motivated to do the things that teachers ask of them or for the reasons that teachers expect. When students develop a motivation to learn, they initiate learning activities, they stay involved in a learning task, and they exhibit a long-term commitment to learning. Understanding the internal and external sources of student motivation enables you to provide a learning environment that is motivating and to assist students in developing adaptive motivational patterns.

HOW DO STUDENTS' NEEDS AND WANTS AFFECT THEIR MOTIVATION TO LEARN?

Some students work toward a goal because they wish to satisfy some personal need or interest. Others pursue a goal in order to obtain rewards from the environment or people in that environment. The needs and wants of students affect their choice of goals and their willingness to engage in certain types of activities.

HOW DO STUDENTS' BELIEFS AFFECT THEIR MOTIVATION TO LEARN?

Students are likely to persist in learning goals that are challenging but still within their perceived competence to attain. They are also likely to remain motivated when they attribute their successes and failures to their own effort and study strategies, rather than to ability or luck. These attributions are associated with beliefs that ability is malleable, that knowledge is complex and multifaceted, and that learning takes time and effort.

HOW DO TEACHERS' BELIEFS AFFECT STUDENT MOTIVATION?

When teachers communicate differential expectations to their students, they can adversely affect student behavior and motivation. You can avoid negative effects of teacher expectations by becoming aware of your own beliefs and monitoring your behavior in the classroom to ensure that you treat all students fairly. Moreover, the more you believe that you can influence learning and motivation, the more likely you are to use effective strategies for motivating your students.

HOW CAN YOU ENHANCE YOUR STUDENTS' MOTIVATION TO LEARN?

By arousing your students' curiosity, using reinforcement strategies prudently, and organizing your classroom to support cooperation, you can enhance students' motivation to learn. Motivational training—that is, teaching students how to set realistic goals, plan for goal attainment, and make appropriate attributions about their successes and failures—is a means for helping them develop self-regulation and intrinsic motivation. Finally, using the ARCS model, you can identify potential motivational problems in your classes, select appropriate motivational strategies, and implement these strategies in your instruction.

KEY CONCEPTS

achievement motivation
ARCS model
attribution theory
attribution training
classroom goal structure
competitive goal structure
cooperative goal structure
curiosity
deficiency needs
extrinsic motivation
goal structure
growth needs
hierarchy of needs
individualistic goal structure
intrinsic motivation
learned helplessness
learning goal
motivation to learn
need for autonomy
performance goal
Pygmalion effect
self-actualization
self-efficacy
self-regulation
teaching efficacy
undermining effect

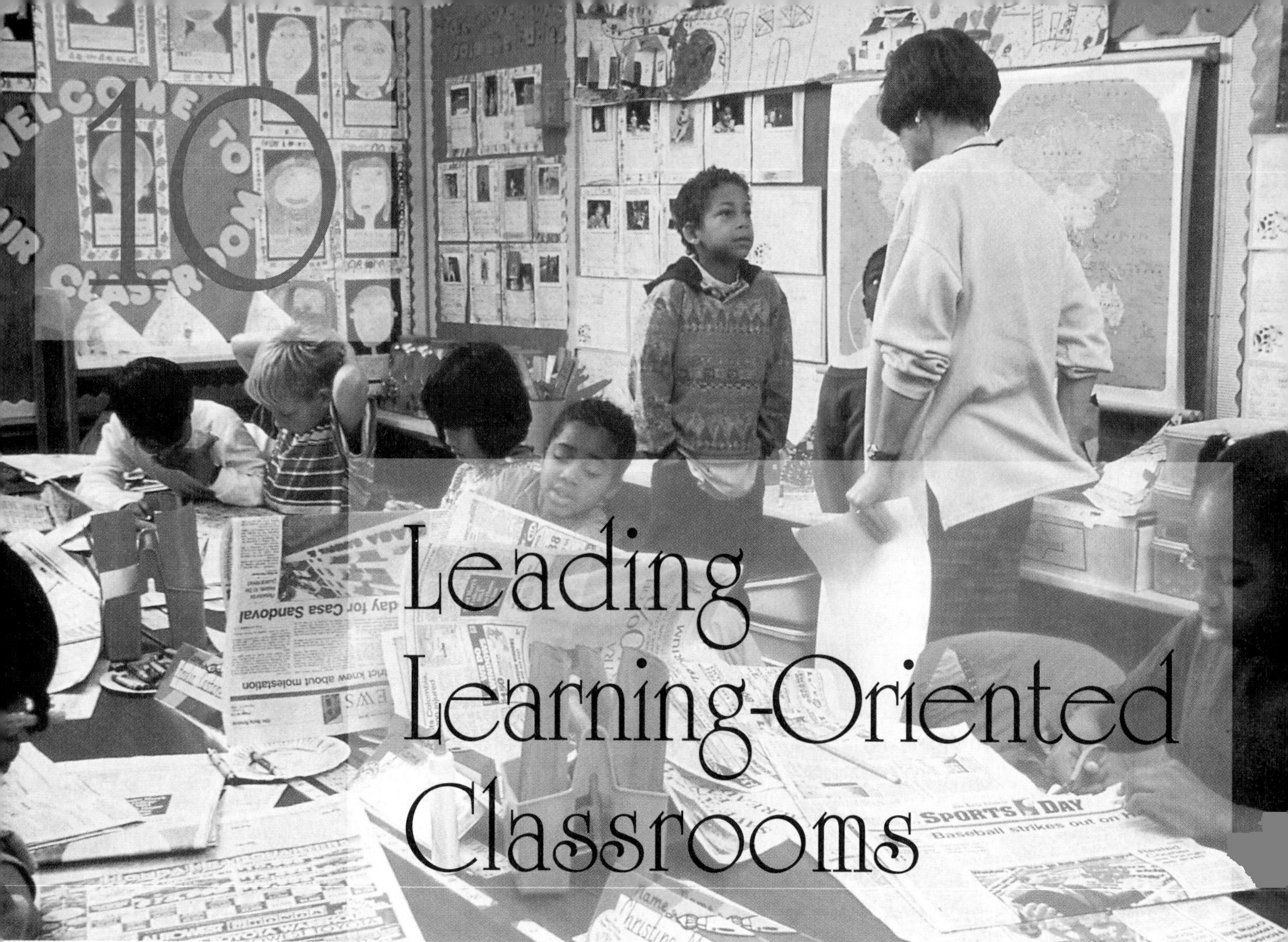

10 Leading Learning-Oriented Classrooms

CHAPTER OUTLINE

TEACHER

Chronicle

REFLECTING ON RANDY

Jean Oxford sits at her desk after school, looking over the empty desks. It is so quiet and peaceful now that the busy buzz of the day has ended. Overall, her room arrangement seems fine. The desks can be moved easily to accommodate various activities. Her second graders are learning their roles in the cooperative groupings she has established. The rules that her students created, with her guidance, are working, especially the individualized reinforcers. Everything is going smoothly; everyone seems to have settled into a good working pattern . . . well, almost everyone. There's Randy.

"Randy, sit down. Randy, stop interrupting. Randy, finish your work. Randy, you don't need to wash your hands again. Randy, Randy, Randy . . . that's all I seem to say all day long," Ms. Oxford thinks. "If I say 'Randy'one more time, I am going to explode. And this is only the first month of school!"

She thinks, "I have to find ways to help him experience success, to protect him from the distractions that seem to get him off track, to help him focus all of that wonderful energy toward learning and away from disruption. But how?" Ms. Oxford picks up a pencil and starts to list Randy's positive and negative behaviors:

POSITIVE	*NEGATIVE*
Reads (and enjoys it!)	Interrupts
Helps during clean-up	Aggressive on playground
Helps when line leader	Always asking to wash hands
Accepts praise well	Often out of his seat
	Complains about group members and vice versa
	Disrupts cooperative work and bothers people by wandering around the room

Next, Ms. Oxford thinks about how she has responded to Randy's misbehavior. She makes another list.

RANDY'S MISBEHAVIOR	*MY RESPONSE*
Interrupting	Reprimand; loss of recess
Playground aggression	Reprimand; loss of recess
Hand washing	Reprimand; restricted to washing at lunch and recess
Wandering	Reprimand; loss of free time
Complaints about and from neighbors	Reprimand; seated alone
Bothering others	Reprimand; restricted to desk

She sees a pattern in her approach with Randy: first a reprimand and then punishment. If this is her pattern of responses to Randy's misbehavior and if Randy has not shown any improvement in the first month of school, then it is clear that she needs to find other ways of responding.

As she ponders her lists, Ms. Oxford notices how few positive items she has written. Shouldn't the positives at least equal the negatives? She decides to try to create situations for Randy in which the positives would begin to exceed the negatives. But what situations can she create that will capitalize on his strengths?

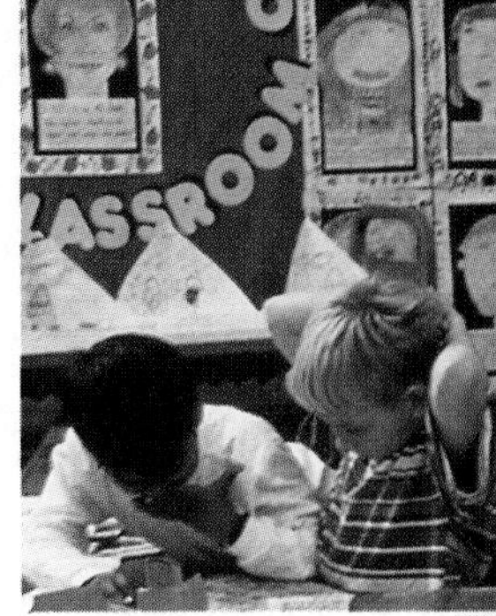

FOCUS QUESTIONS

1. How would you characterize Ms. Oxford's approach to managing her classroom? Do you get the impression that she is more of a leader or a manager? How would you distinguish a classroom leader from a classroom manager?

2. What do Ms. Oxford's reflections reveal about how she conceptualizes the relationship between management, discipline, and learning? Are these concepts products or processes?
3. Using the lists that Ms. Oxford made to help her think about Randy's behavior, state four classroom rules that she has posted. What evidence do you have to support your inferences? How do classroom rules contribute to student learning?
4. During the first month of school, Ms. Oxford has apparently reprimanded Randy numerous times. Why have the reprimands been ineffective? Are there techniques that would have been more effective in eliminating his misbehavior?
5. Aside from Randy, Ms. Oxford's class seems to have started the school year well. What preparations do you think Ms. Oxford made before the school year began? What do you think happened in the classroom on the first day of school? Why is the beginning of the school year so important in establishing classroom routines?
6. Ms. Oxford is looking for ideas to help Randy. List three ideas she might try. Which idea is most likely to work? Why? If the first idea fails, are the other two worth trying? Why or why not? What questions would you ask of Randy's parent or caregiver that might help you develop some strategies to help Randy learn?

WHAT IS CLASSROOM MANAGEMENT AND LEADERSHIP?

The way a teacher manages his or her classroom says a great deal about what that teacher values. Consider the case of Ms. Oxford in the Teacher Chronicle, for example. Although you do not see her interacting with her students, you can infer that she takes her responsibility for managing her class quite seriously. But why does she go to the trouble to ponder the problems of one child? Is it because she values a quiet classroom and Randy is noisy, or does she value learning and is seeking ways to help Randy learn? The way one teaches reveals what one considers to be important, and classroom management is central to teaching.

Try This: Interview a retired teacher who had a long career in the classroom. Ask the teacher to describe ideas and practices concerning classroom management that have changed over the course of his or her career.

Classroom management has long been recognized as one of the primary responsibilities of teaching (e.g., Bagley, 1907). It is critical because it influences students' behaviors, feelings, and learning. Your knowledge of and skill in classroom management will, to a great extent, determine the success with which you facilitate student learning. Therefore, your management skills will also influence how others perceive you as a teacher. Students who find themselves in a poorly managed classroom must fight an uphill battle to learn and will judge the teacher in that classroom as ineffective. Students may not submit a formal evaluation, but their views of teachers are shared and teachers' reputations are quickly established. A parent whose child is in a poorly managed classroom will—at the very least—fail to become the teacher's ally. An administrator who observes a poorly managed classroom will submit negative evaluations of the teacher. The converse is also true. Well-managed classrooms provide an environment for student learning, make good impressions on parents, and are positively evaluated by administrators.

Teachers who work in well-managed classrooms enjoy their work, enjoy their students, and feel a sense of accomplishment (cf. Cangelosi, 1993). Teachers who enjoy their work are likely to be more enthusiastic about their teaching and the students whom they teach. The knowledge and skills discussed in this chapter can make a difference in your self-esteem as a teacher, your sense of self-efficacy as a teacher, and ultimately, the degree to which you are satisfied with a career in teaching. Classroom management is one of the keys to effective teaching because it affects all who have a stake in education, but especially learners.

Given the importance of classroom management to educational stakeholders, it is not surprising that serious efforts to reform education are beginning to focus on the way classrooms and, by extension, schools are managed (McCaslin & Good, 1992). Classroom management will continue to be the focus of efforts to improve education because it is central to the work of schools, the work accomplished through the teaching–learning process. Understanding classroom management requires understanding how management is related conceptually to discipline, instruction, and ultimately learning. Becoming an effective classroom manager also requires that you identify the outcomes you value for your students.

Critical Thinking: How will classroom activities and teacher responsibilities change if curricula become integrated across subject areas? If bell schedules in junior high and high schools are eliminated?

Whether a teacher values obedience or learning, solitary effort or social interaction, is revealed not only in classroom practice but also in the metaphors he or she uses to conceptualize how classrooms should operate. Our management metaphors are frameworks that define what we view as possible in our classrooms (Randolph & Evertson, 1994). In turn, our views of what is possible influence how well our students learn. Ms. Oxford, in the Teacher Chronicle, tried for a month to improve Randy's behavior so that he could learn. Her efforts failed, but as we leave Ms. Oxford in her reflections, it is clear that she thinks it is possible to find ways of helping Randy learn.

Metaphors for Managing Classrooms

Research has shown clearly that one of the most perplexing challenges faced by novice teachers is managing student behavior (Lashley, 1994; Veenman, 1984). Furthermore, some of these difficulties can be traced to the metaphors beginning teachers use to think about classroom management (Weinstein, Woolfolk, Dittmeier, & Shanker, 1994).

Reflection: Review the metaphors of teaching discussed in Chapter 1. How do the metaphors relate to those mentioned in this section? How does your own metaphor of classroom management compare to those mentioned in the book?

Researchers have identified metaphors ranging, for example, from *prison guard* to *boss* to *negotiator* to *facilitator* (Lashley, 1994; Randolph & Evertson, 1994; Weinstein et al., 1994). The first two metaphors conjure images of the teacher as overseeing students, initiating student activity through orders, and holding those in his or her charge accountable for getting their work done. The last two metaphors suggest something different about the nature of the interaction between teacher and students and the outcomes of that interaction. Negotiation and facilitation suggest that teachers work with students to help them learn. Teachers, especially beginning teachers, who see themselves as overseers of students' work rather than as facilitators of students' learning are more likely to experience difficulties in managing student behavior (cf. Good & Brophy, 1994; Marshall, 1990).

The research on metaphors used by teachers to conceptualize classroom management and the effects associated with those metaphors have led to a useful distinction between classrooms that are work oriented and those that are

Point: The distinction between work-oriented and learning-oriented classrooms reflect one of the assumptions of this book: *Teachers coordinate the context for learning.*

learning oriented (Evertson & Randolph, 1995). **Work-oriented classrooms** are those in which students tend to be directed by a teacher who values production. Students are expected to follow directions closely because, by doing so, they will complete the work efficiently. **Learning-oriented classrooms** are those in which students are encouraged, rather than directed, by a teacher who values learning. Following directions in learning-oriented classrooms is important as well, but students are encouraged to question directions and explore possibilities. An effectively managed work-oriented classroom is likely to be orderly and quiet, a well-oiled machine. An effectively managed learning-oriented classroom is likely to be noisy, a beehive of activity. Students in work-oriented classrooms are more likely to reconstruct information, whereas students in learning-oriented classrooms are more likely to construct knowledge (Evertson & Randolph, 1995). Obedience is valued in work-oriented classrooms; taking responsibility for one's learning is valued in learning-oriented classrooms (cf. Curwin & Mendler, 1988; McLaughlin, 1994).

Thomas Good & Jere Brophy (1994) describe a system of critical attitudes that exists in well-managed, learning-oriented classrooms. They call it a system because each of the three attitudes supports the others and because all attitudes are supported by a value of learning. A depiction of the system is given in Figure 10.1.

work-oriented classrooms Classrooms in which the teacher values production and is directive of student activity.

learning-oriented classrooms Classrooms in which the teacher values learning and facilitates, rather than directs, student activity.

The most important aspect of this system is the value context. Effective classroom managers value learning and communicate that value through their actions. Imagine a teacher who promises that, "If you all behave yourselves until the end of the period, I will not assign homework tonight." What sort of message does this send to students? By establishing this contingency, the teacher ignores the learning that homework might foster and treats what could be a legitimate learning activity as something to be avoided or used as a bargaining chip. Teachers who devalue learning often use a *factory* metaphor to think about classroom management (Randolph & Evertson, 1994). In a factory metaphor, students are laborers who complete work in exchange for

FIGURE 10.1

A System of Attitudes that Supports Learning-Oriented Classroom Management

Source: Based on the discussion of essential teacher attitudes in *Looking in Classrooms* (6th ed., pp. 133–134), 1994, by Thomas Good and Jere Brophy, New York: Harper Collins.

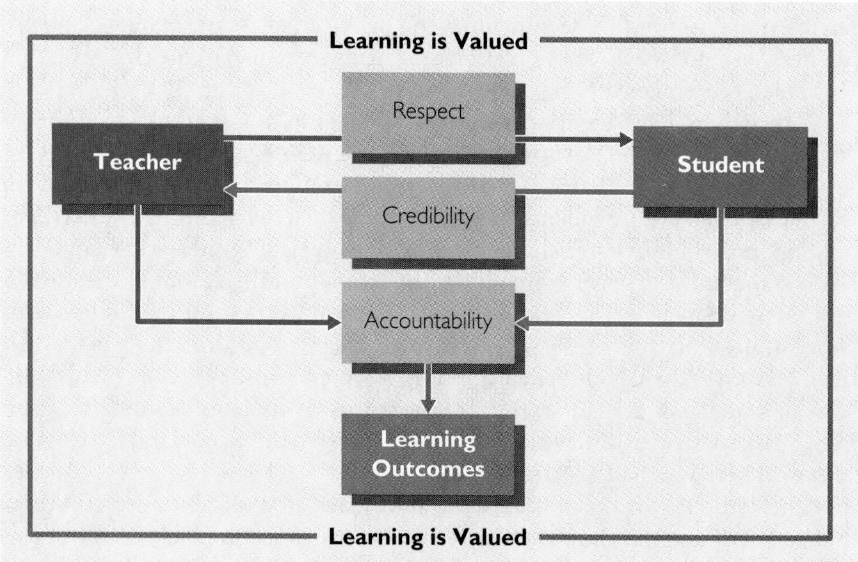

grades, privileges, or other incentives. Teachers are bosses or paymasters who focus on the work and not on what might be learned by doing the work. Good & Brophy (1994) describe teachers who devalue learning as those who "think of school-related tasks as unrewarding drudgery and do not expect students to enjoy them. Their students soon learn to wince, sigh, or protest at the mention of assignments" (p. 134). However, a teacher who values learning views the classroom in terms of the learning, not just the work, that takes place there. The essential ingredient of learning-oriented classrooms and the foundation of Good & Brophy's system of critical attitudes is a teacher who values learning (Marshall, 1990, 1992).

Try This: Ask friends and colleagues to identify the best classroom they were ever in and the worst. How was each of those classrooms managed? What sorts of learning activities were used? What were the rules and procedures in those classrooms? How was misbehavior managed? Characterize your data in terms of contrasting metaphors.

Building on a foundation of the value of learning, the first critical attitude is respect for students. Good & Brophy's observations of classrooms suggest that teachers who successfully manage classrooms like and respect their students. It seems unlikely that a person who does not enjoy working with children or adolescents would be likely to earn their respect in return. In their discussion about teachers' attitudes toward students, Good & Brophy emphasize the importance of a teacher's concern for students as individuals. Consider Ms. Oxford in the Teacher Chronicle at the beginning of the chapter. Although the class as a whole demonstrated a level of discipline that was resulting in positive growth, she was spending time carefully reflecting on the behavior and accomplishments of one student. Her efforts indicate her concern not just for the class as a whole but for each individual in the class and, therefore, an attitude of respect.

The second critical attitude is credibility. Students perceive teachers who manage effectively as credible, as people who do what they say they will do. Credibility requires that teachers practice what they preach and that they practice and preach consistently. According to Good & Brophy (1994), unless a teacher is willing to say to students, "I intend to treat each of you fairly and if I do not, I want to know about it immediately," credibility will be difficult to establish. Unless a teacher is willing to follow through on such claims, credibility will be difficult to maintain.

Reflection: Which of your teachers did you find most credible? How did they establish that credibility with you? What are some of the ways in which your credible teachers were similar? How will you establish yourself as credible in the eyes of your students?

The teachers and students of well-managed classrooms jointly maintain the third critical attitude: Teachers who manage effectively hold themselves and their students accountable for learning. Furthermore, in a learning-oriented classroom, teachers encourage students to develop an attitude of self-accountability. Teachers who take an interest in their students and who deal with them credibly must adopt the attitude that the important outcome is what students learn. This may require some tough-mindedness from time to time. It may be easy to overlook a lack of achievement in a student who has shown considerable improvement in his or her effort. While a teacher, in this case, would certainly want to encourage the student to continue his or her effort, the teacher must help the student keep in mind that effort without learning is not good enough.

Connection: You have already encountered the concept of active learning in Chapter 7 and will encounter it again in Chapter 12. Active learning relates to the idea that effort and activity are necessary for, but do not guarantee, learning.

Processes and Products of Classroom Management

A summary of research on effective schools and classrooms, published by the Association for Supervision and Curriculum Development (ASCD), found a relationship between high achievement in students and the skills possessed by teachers. Students who achieve consistently had teachers who demonstrated skill in managing, in preparing and organizing classroom activities as well as establishing and maintaining learning environments. Teachers whose students achieved well were also found to be skilled at guiding student learning (Squires, Huitt, & Segars, 1983).

If these are the teaching skills that are associated with student learning, how are they related to each other and how do they affect learning? One way to conceptualize these important relationships is to view managing and instructing as processes. This chapter first examines the relationship between the process of management and its product, discipline. Then instruction and learning are added to the conceptual mix.

Try This: Before reading further, jot down your ideas about the terms *classroom management* and *discipline*. As you read this section, compare your prior knowledge of these terms with any new ideas or information you encounter.

Managing for Discipline. The terms *classroom management* and *discipline* are often used interchangeably (Bellon, Bellon, & Blank, 1992). This is true of people both outside and inside the world of education. Even those who are preparing to teach often use the terms synonymously. We asked aspiring teachers and veteran teachers identified as effective classroom managers to reflect on what classroom management meant to them. The vast majority of aspiring teachers seemed to assume that classroom management means dealing with discipline problems. They wrote of the disciplinarian role of a teacher, handling disruptive students, making students listen, keeping students under control, and making sure students know who's the boss. Two themes emerged from the written comments of aspiring teachers. One was that classroom management required control. The other was that classroom management is strictly reactive. Although reacting to problem behaviors is a part of classroom management, prevention is at least as important. This proactive aspect of classroom management, involving cooperation and collaboration, was reflected in the comments of veteran teachers.

Veteran teachers, in reflecting on the meaning of classroom management, rarely used the word *discipline* in their descriptions. For the veteran teachers, classroom management meant establishing rules, involving students in decision making, organizing for instruction, finding and preparing materials for lessons, and creating active learning experiences that maintain interest and keep students focused on the material being taught. Essentially, veterans' answers revolved around planning and organization. The best way to establish discipline in the classroom, say the veterans, is to be organized. This advice from expert practitioners is supported by a considerable body of research findings (Brophy, 1988; Doyle, 1986; Emmer & Ausiker, 1990; Evertson & Harris, 1992; Gettinger, 1988; Jones & Jones, 1995; McCaslin & Good, 1992). One review of this research, for example, concluded that teachers who view "classroom management as a process of establishing and maintaining effective learning environments tend to be more successful than teachers who place more emphasis on their roles as authority figures or disciplinarians" (Good & Brophy, 1994, p. 129).

Critical Thinking: Some educators use the term *discipline* to refer to actions taken by teachers to deal with problem behavior. In this chapter, the term is used to refer to student behavior because it helps in thinking about how management and discipline are related to learning. Why should this product view of discipline make it easier to think about the relationship of discipline to learning?

Classroom management and discipline are related but are not synonymous. According to Emmer (1987), **classroom management** refers to the actions taken by teachers to encourage student learning, while **discipline** is the extent to which students act appropriately and are involved in learning activities. Discipline, therefore, is a function of sound classroom management. Poor classroom management yields a lack of discipline. Thus, classroom management is viewed as a process and discipline as a product of that process (Figure 10.2). The next section examines another process and product that are based on the management–discipline relationship. As you move to the discussion of instruction and learning, keep in mind that both management and discipline are defined with reference to learning.

classroom management Actions taken by a teacher to facilitate student learning.

discipline The extent to which students are engaged in learning or other classroom-appropriate activities.

Instructing for Learning. Classroom management is central to teaching, but the instructional process is at least as important as management. While management is critical to success as a teacher, it is important that instruction does not become subordinate to management (e.g., Allington, 1983; Brophy, 1982; Duffy & McIntyre, 1982). Instruction is of such importance that we will revisit it in a later section in this chapter and in the chapters that follow. Planning for instruction is the focus of Chapter 11. Instructional techniques are discussed in Chapter 12. Chapter 13, on classroom assessment, also has an instructional focus; indeed, it argues that assessing student learning is a form of instruction. The focus of this section, however, is on defining the process of instruction, identifying the product of that process, and determining how it is related to management and discipline. How is classroom management related to the teaching-learning process?

Driscoll (1994) defines **instruction** as "the deliberate arrangement of learning conditions to promote the attainment of some intended goal" (p. 332). One obvious commonality between the definition of teaching and instruction is that of intent. Teaching is undertaken with the intent to facilitate learning. Instruction, however, is defined more specifically. The intent that underlies the process of instruction focuses on a particular learning goal. Intent is further implied in the definition of instruction through the phrase "deliberate arrangement of learning conditions." What are the conditions of learning for a particular goal? Consider the following example, taken from Driscoll (1994).

> Suppose we are interested in students learning how to calculate averages of groups of numbers. From our knowledge of motivation, we know that for students to acquire this skill, they must have some confidence in their ability to learn it, and they must see some value in learning it. Information processing theory suggests additional conditions required for learning. Students must already know how to add, multiply, and divide, because these skills are components of the rule for calculating averages. Furthermore, the new information (i.e., the rule itself) should be presented to learners in a way that facilitates encoding. (p. 332)

Thus far, the example identifies the conditions of learning that need to be met in order for the particular learning goal to be attained. How might a teacher establish those conditions and motivate their students to assume responsibility for their own learning? He or she might choose to demonstrate the rule and to follow the demonstration with meaningful problems for students to solve. These problems might be presented in a worksheet constructed by the teacher, assigned from a textbook, or embedded in a long-term project—such as tracking the performance of stocks in an investment portfolio—that

Reflection: To this point in your preparation to teach, how have you thought about the terms *management* and *instruction*. Are they separate in your mind? Are they related? If so, how? If not, why not?

Point: Instruction is central to teaching. Recall the definition of teaching in Chapter 1 as "action taken with the intent to facilitate learning."

instruction According to Driscoll, the deliberate arrangement of learning conditions to promote the attainment of some intended goal.

FIGURE 10.2

The Process-Product View of Classroom Management and Discipline

Insights ON SUCCESSFUL PRACTICE

In your experience, what role does teacher planning play in successful classroom management?

Planning is critical to successful lessons and to positive classroom management. Planning each lesson with an objective and a map for how students will accomplish that objective enables teachers to teach and students to learn and eliminates many disciplinary problems from developing. Although lessons may change, evolve, and diverge from original expectations, a core plan is the first step to gaining student cooperation and success.

For example, in my unit on fossils, my eighth-grade earth science students were having difficulty understanding the difference between external molds (impression of the outside of an organism) and casts (exact copy of an organism). I realized this as I was instructing and therefore decided the next lesson needed to be making plaster casts and plaster external molds. Through this hand-ons experience, I thought students would be able to understand the difference between a cast and an external mold.

After making this decision, I collected all the materials required for this project: plaster, shells, water, stir sticks, plastic bowls, Vaseline, paper towels for cleanup. I carefully thought through each step in this activity as I prepared the lesson in order to anticipate the challenges of the next day.

During the mold making, despite simple, clear, concise instructions and all the necessary materials, I was bombarded with questions and comments: "Is this thick enough?" "My plaster is already hard and I can't push my shell into it!" "Why isn't mine drying yet?" Students spilled plaster, overflowed wastebaskets with wet paper toweling, and got their shells permanently buried into plaster (future fossils!). However, even though the room looked like a disaster area, all students were on task. Everyone was learning. Even my most challenging students were motivated to make their personal casts and external molds. I had no discipline problems.

Imagine this classroom activity without careful planning and established classroom management. What if students do not have enough plaster of Paris, or there aren't enough bowls or plaster stirring sticks? What if students are not certain what they are supposed to do? What if the noise is not the buzz of constructive classroom exploration but just loud talking and jeers? Without careful planning, a lesson such as this would become chaos with little or no learning taking place.

Clear goals and well-planned activities excite, involve, and educate students and allow you to manage all students in a productive way.

CONNIE B. ROOP, North High School, Appleton, Wisconsin

Insights

What aspects of instructional planning does this teacher make it a point to consider? What role does goal setting play? How might planning or the lack of it affect classroom management?

requires students to identify and solve problems involving the calculation of averages. Thus, by determining ways of establishing the learning conditions necessary for students to attain the intended goal, the teacher has devised a certain plan for instruction tied to a particular learning goal.

If the conditions of learning are established properly and if instruction is effectively implemented, then the outcome of instruction is student learning. In a sense, the process of instruction builds on discipline. If the management process is successful, then students are prepared to learn—the conditions of learning identified by Driscoll are in place. The teacher can then instruct with greater probability of success (Evertson, Emmer, Clements, & Worsham, 1994). The relationship between management and discipline, depicted in Figure 10.2, can now be expanded to include the process of instruction and the outcome of that process, learning (Figure 10.3).

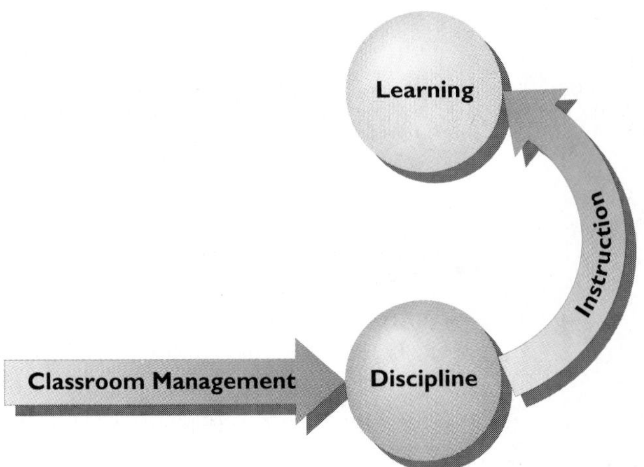

FIGURE 10.3

The Process-Product View of Classroom Management and Discipline Expanded to Include Instruction and Learning

Classroom Leadership and Authority

Teachers are leaders of learning and learners. In order to establish discipline, teachers must essentially gain the cooperation of their students (cf. Good & Brophy, 1991). In order to bring about learning, teachers must engage students in the instructional tasks that are designed to lead to the attainment of learning goals. Leading students means engaging students' minds, finding ways of eliciting their active participation in the teaching–learning process, and keeping students focused on the goal of learning. As Goodlad (1983) stated: "Being a spectator not only deprives one of participation, but also leaves one's mind free for unrelated activity. If academic learning does not engage students, something else will" (p. 554). If discipline is not established through effective management techniques and if instruction fails to engage students, problem behaviors will develop.

Try This: Interview a practicing teacher to discover his or her views on how to arrange the conditions of learning. Ask for examples or give the teacher Driscoll's example from page 317 and ask him or her to analyze it for you.

Leadership is a difficult concept to define, as evidenced by the number of definitions that have been supplied by scholars who study it (Hoy & Miskel, 1991). Even so, there are some elements in definitions of *leadership* that occur with considerable frequency. One of those elements is the concept of *goals*. Fiedler and Garcia (1987) suggest that a leader is someone who directs or coordinates a group's efforts to attain a particular goal. A leader is also someone who can shape or articulate the goals. In classrooms, one of the responsibilities of a teacher is to lead students toward the attainment of learning goals. How should a teacher direct students toward learning goals? In what manner should a teacher lead?

Connection: Go back to the earlier reflection in this chapter in which you anticipated the relationship between management, discipline, and learning. Compare it to Figure 10.3.

The answer is that it depends on the kind of classroom atmosphere you wish to create. Do you expect your students to *comply* with your requests or demands? Do you want them to *identify* with you and to emulate you? Do you want them to *internalize* attitudes and behaviors and thus demonstrate autonomy and independence (see Kelman 1958; 1961; see also McCaslin & Good, 1992)? At one level, complete compliance with classroom rules and procedures is desirable. Suppose that, for instance, in the case of a fire drill, students are to line up in alphabetical order (in order to account for everyone in the class). A lack of compliance in this case could be a threat to safety. At another level, however, students need to act of their own accord, use their own judgment, or take the initiative in formulating and pursuing their own goals. In such instances, there may be little or no guidance available from outside sources; that is, there may be no external guidelines with which to comply.

Example: Consider persons you regard as great leaders in history. What were the goals they pursued? Consider how their ability to articulate goals and vision contributed to their ability to lead others.

Management styles can be likened to a classic model of parenting styles

What roles does instruction play in classroom management? What metaphors other than "manager" describe how teachers create and maintain learning-oriented environments?

(McCaslin & Good, 1992). The model formulates a continuum from little or no control (permissive) to a great deal of control (authoritarian) (Baumrind, 1971, 1991). Authoritarian parents control decision making and issue orders to their children with little effort to discuss or explain their orders. Their purpose is to gain obedience.

Critical Thinking: Why are guidelines for a child's behavior important? Would it be better to allow children to discover their own guidelines of behavior? Why or why not?

In the middle of this continuum is the authoritative style, in which parents provide firm guidelines for the behavior of their children but are flexible in the interpretation of those guidelines. Authoritative parents communicate their standards through discussion and explanation and value self-realization in their children's behavior. Children from authoritative homes tend to have greater confidence and independence and healthier self-concepts than do children of authoritarian or permissive parents, and they enjoy higher academic achievement (Steinberg, Elman, & Mounts, 1989). The work of Diana Baumrind and others suggests that, with some qualifications, effective classroom management might be viewed as **authoritative leadership** (McCaslin & Good, 1992).

Try This: Ask a teacher to characterize his or her leadership style. Then, with the teacher's permission, ask students to characterize the teacher's leadership style. The teacher may be very interested in discussing your findings with you.

Reflect for a moment on the metaphors that were suggested at the beginning of the chapter. Most of the approaches to classroom management would be considered either authoritarian or authoritative. For instance, work-oriented classrooms are more authoritarian while learning-oriented classrooms are more authoritative (see Evertson & Randolph, 1995). The outcomes of authoritative leadership in the classroom are more consistent with learning goals such as critical thinking, self-understanding, self-evaluation, and other higher level thinking skills. "We cannot expect that students will profit from the incongruous messages we send when we manage for obedience and teach for exploration and risk taking" (McCaslin & Good, 1992, p. 12).

Point: Your metaphors of teaching are frameworks for what is possible in your classrooms. The importance of this type of reflection is signified in one of the basic assumptions of this book: *Your view of the teaching–learning process affects one's classroom practice.*

How can teachers lead authoritatively? How can you display the values and attitudes that are characteristic of classrooms that are authoritatively led and learning centered? Generating a classroom management plan that respects students and values learning is an important first step in establishing the classroom discipline on which instruction and learning can be built.

authoritative leadership Authority established through the flexible implementation of standards and characterized by discussion with and explanation to followers.

HOW CAN YOU CREATE A LEARNING-ORIENTED ENVIRONMENT?

Even before we examine the elements of a sound classroom management plan, it is important to note that planning is associated with the development of positive learning environments (Evertson & Emmer, 1982). Planning enables a teacher to avoid inappropriate student behavior by organizing the classroom and materials so that the physical environment is conducive to learning. Advanced planning also allows a teacher to establish classroom rules and procedures that will help prevent problem behavior (Brophy & Evertson, 1976; cf. Jones & Jones, 1995; Kounin, 1970). In this section, we will examine the research and the recommendations for organizing a classroom, establishing rules, and developing classroom procedures. These research-based recommendations can be used as the foundation of a plan for effective classroom management.

Try This: Ask teachers to share with you their classroom management plans. Also call school districts to see if there are classroom management requirements or recommendations that teachers in the district follow. How do the plans compare to the recommendations in this book?

Arranging the Classroom

A good place to begin developing a plan for classroom management is with the physical environment. Teacher Peter Roop begins preparing for each school year by spending time in his classroom a few days before students return from summer break. He describes his thoughts and feelings in the following brief passage, called "Room for Improvement."

> My room seems so empty when I walk in at the beginning of the school year—nothing on the walls, the bookcases covered with paper to keep off the summer dust, the desks in a jumble in one corner, my desk in another. I am reminded of Ichabod Crane's one-room schoolhouse after Brom Bones plays his Halloween prank and changes everything around.
>
> My first inclination is to begin arranging the desks. This is a ritual for me. I know, however, that over the next three days I will move everything at least three more times before the kids come to class. Nonetheless, I move the desks, thinking how much easier it would be to sketch a floor plan on paper or on the board. I could sketch where my desk will be, which board I will be using most often and where I want their attention directed, where my activity table will be placed, where my big armchair for reading aloud will be. But there is something about physically moving furniture that helps me reenter the world of the classroom, so I keep shoving things around.
>
> I am satisfied with my first arrangement. For now. I sit down and think about the room. It really is a world. There is the immediate physicalness—the space, the desks, the shelves—that part of the environment that must be accepted but can also be improved. There are other, less tangible aspects of our world that become apparent only when the students arrive: their needs, my goals and expectations, interactions between the students and myself, and how I will lead.
>
> Picking up a class roster I read down through the names: Ernesto, Paula, Raeanne, Todd, James, Meghan, Karl, Matt, Daniel. How well will this world meet their social needs? Will my management style match their learning needs? Patrick, Jonathan, Clint, Melissa, Halley, Lida, Adam, Pam, Scott, Nick, Brad. Who will find this environment stimulating, engaging, demanding, and intriguing? Who will prefer another environment, less open, more controlled, less demanding?
>
> It takes sunlight about eight minutes to reach Earth, I thought. How long will it take me to reach some students? I wonder. And I only have three days to get ready for this world of human emotions, ideas, thoughts, problems, interests, feelings, and growth.
>
> Enough daydreaming. Hopping off my desk, I wonder, wouldn't a circular arrangement encourage more peer interaction?

Reflection: What are your favorite types of physical spaces for learning? Which of your classrooms was most physically appealing to you? Most comfortable? Draw a floor plan of your favorite classroom from memory. What other memories of your experiences in that classroom are brought to life as you draw the physical layout?

The physical arrangement of your classroom will not, by itself, guarantee effective management. However, a thoughtful arrangement can contribute to the learning outcomes you seek. Emmer, Everston, Clements, & Worsham (1994) specify several aspects of good classroom arrangement.

The most important aspect is to select a room arrangement that is consistent with your learning goals and instructional activities. If your instruction will consist primarily of presentations, demonstrations, and teacher-led discussions with the whole class, you will want to be sure that all students have a clear view of the main instructional area, including the chalkboard and overhead or computer-generated projections (Figure 10.4). If your instructional approach calls primarily for small group work, however, an arrangement like that depicted in Figure 10.5 might be more appropriate.

Critical Thinking: What are the advantages and disadvantages of the classroom layouts in Figures 10.4 and 10.5?

Although the classroom arrangements in Figures 10.4 and 10.5 are quite different, they are similar in one important aspect. They both afford the teacher proximity to students (Wolfgang, 1995). In either of these arrangements, a teacher can move easily around the room and bring himself or herself into fairly close proximity to any student. By using such arrangements teachers are less likely to attend to one group of students at the expense of others.

action zones The areas in a classroom where a teacher directs most of his or her attention.

In a classroom that is arranged in traditional rows, there is a tendency for teachers to spend most of their time in the front of the classroom and to direct most of their attention to students seated there. The front of the room becomes what is called an action zone. **Action zones** are those areas in a seating arrangement where teachers direct most of their attention. Students who

FIGURE 10.4

A Possible Classroom Arrangement
Source: From *Solving Discipline Problems* (3rd ed., p. 216) by C. H. Wolfgang, 1995, Needham Heights, MA: Allyn & Bacon. Reprinted by permission.

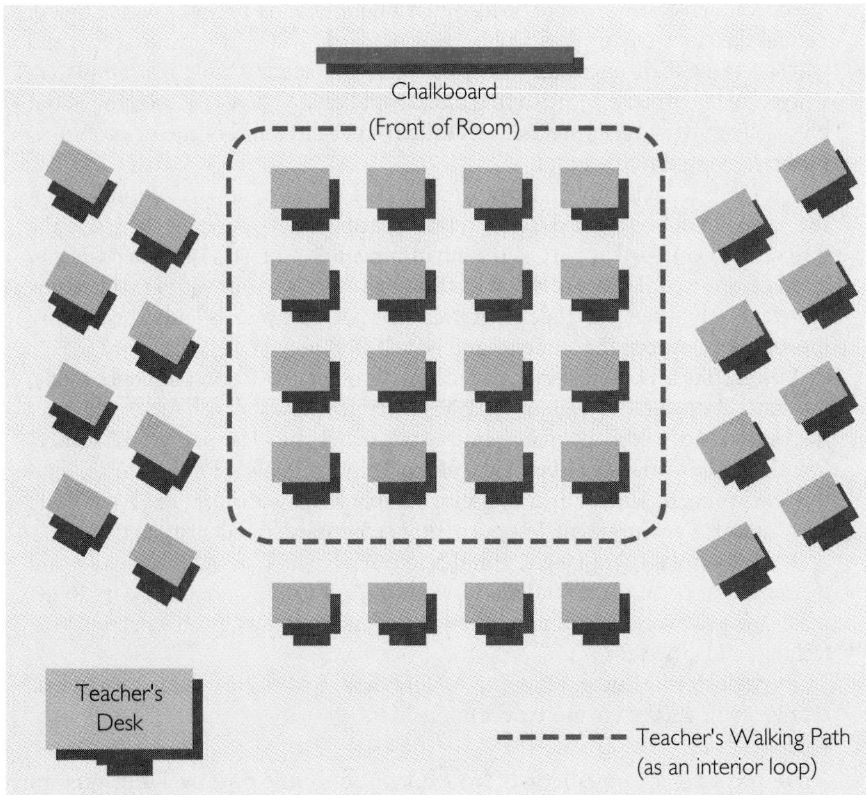

are not in the front of the classroom tend to contribute less to class discussions, are judged to be less attentive, and achieve at lower levels than students who are in the front (Adams & Biddle, 1970; Daum, 1972; Delefes & Jackson, 1972; Schwebel & Cherlin, 1972). Daum (1972) demonstrated that low-ability students who are moved to an action zone improve their level of achievement. Coincidentally, high-achieving students who were placed farther from the teacher in the classroom did not suffer a decrease in achievement. As a way of maintaining the attention of all students, the seating arrangement is not simply a matter of arranging the desks but also arranging the students who sit at those desks.

Connection: Student groupings are discussed in greater detail in Chapter 12.

Another key to good room arrangement is keeping high-traffic areas—such as frequently used bookcases, supply areas, the pencil sharpener, and the waste basket—clear of furniture. It is also a good idea to arrange the room so that high traffic areas are dispersed throughout the space. Other keys to good room arrangement include maintaining clear sightlines—between the teacher and students and, for classrooms in which peer interaction is valued, sightlines among students—and keeping frequently used materials easily accessible (Emmer et al., 1994).

Try This: Go to a local teachers' store and browse through the materials available for bulletin boards or borrow materials catalogs from a teacher. How might you use such material? How might your students construct their own bulletin boards?

Imagine that because you value peer interaction and wish to establish a learning-oriented classroom, you have selected the arrangement shown in Figure 10.5. Now imagine that when your students enter the room on the first day of class, the walls, bulletin boards, and chalkboard are empty. If you want your room to become a "beehive of activity," that should be part of your students' first impression. But how can you establish that expectation? Here's How lists some ideas (cf. Emmer et al., 1994).

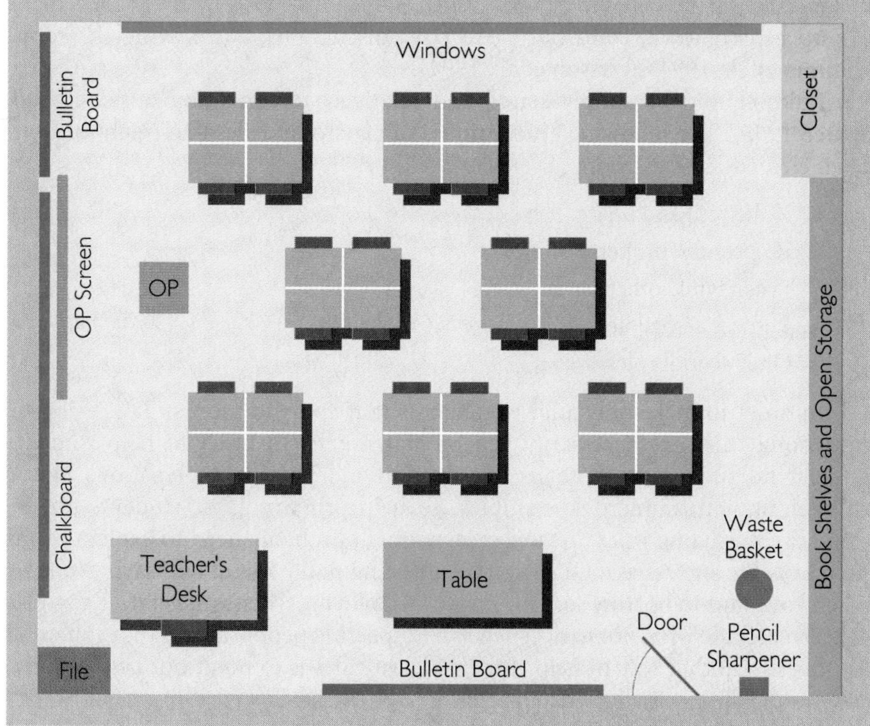

FIGURE 10.5

A More Interactive Classroom Arrangement

Source: From *Classroom Management for Secondary Teachers* (3rd ed., p. 13) by Emmer, Evertson, Clements, and Worsham, 1994, Needham Heights, MA: Allyn & Bacon. Reprinted by permission.

here's how

Here's How to Use Walls and Bulletin Boards

- At the beginning of the school year, you should have, at the very least, a display area that can be used to list daily assignments and a decorative display that welcomes students to the room.
- You should have a wall or bulletin board display of classroom rules. If you plan to establish classroom rules in collaboration with your students, the display can be labeled Classroom Rules—To Be Decided Jointly.
- You should have instructionally relevant displays, such as an example of proper paper heading and a display depicting a topic that will be covered in the class.
- If you run out of ideas, visit other classrooms to see what other teachers do to make their rooms feel welcoming and alive. There are also books on bulletin board design at school supply stores.
- If you are stuck for time as you prepare for the beginning of the school year—a likely possibility for any new teacher—simply cover the bulletin boards with colored paper and invite students to construct their own displays.

Establishing Rules and Procedures

Rules and procedures both refer to expectations of student behavior. **Rules** are general statements of standards of behavior that are meant to apply across all classroom situations. An example of a rule is: Be helpful and polite to others. **Procedures** also identify standards of behavior but apply to specific activities. For instance, you will probably establish procedures for collecting homework, making up missed work, contributing to class discussions, and leaving the room (Emmer et al., 1994; Evertson et al., 1994).

Example: One of the classroom rules is: Respect other people's property. When a student picks up a pencil from another student's desk, the teacher asks, "Lisa, I am wondering if you remembered our rule about respecting other people's property and asked Sam's permission to use his pencil."

Rules should be simply stated and relatively few in number (Charles & Senter, 1995). The following are examples of classroom rules that might be used in an elementary classroom (Evertson et al., 1994).

1. Be helpful and polite.
2. Respect the property of others.
3. Listen while others speak.
4. Respect all people.
5. Obey school rules.

In order to make only a few statements that apply to most situations in the classroom, rules are necessarily general statements. In order to help students understand such general statements, you should provide explanations of the rules along with numerous examples. To help primary grade students understand the preceding rules, for instance, you will probably need to explain terms such as *polite* and *respect*. One example of being polite might be, "saying 'please' when you want to borrow something and 'thank you' when you get it." Examples can also include what not to do, such as, "Respecting people means that you don't hit them." Another way to help students learn rules is to point out events in the classroom when rules have been and have not been followed.

rules General standards of behavior that are meant to apply across all classroom situations.

procedures Standards of behavior that are specific to a particular classroom task or set of related tasks.

Classroom rules for older students should address points similar to rules for elementary students and may include additional, task-oriented statements, such as: Be ready to begin work when the bell rings (cf. Emmer et al., 1994). Even though students in junior high and high school can be expected to comprehend rule statements more easily than their younger peers, it is still advisable to provide secondary students with illustrations.

Although examples or illustrations of these rules might include inappropriate behavior, note that the rules are stated positively. In general, stating rules positively is preferable to negative statements. Positively stated rules make it easier for teachers to focus on and reinforce student behavior (Burke, 1992). Consider the rule: Respect all people. A negatively stated version of that rule might be something like: Do not call people names. Suppose that students have worked very well together to complete a group brainstorming task. The message to students is much clearer if a teacher praises the students for respecting each others' opinions rather than congratulating them for getting through the session without calling anyone a name. If positively stated rules are more easily reinforced, students who follow the rules and receive reinforcement are more likely to serve as models for classmates. In terms of Bandura's social learning theory, discussed in Chapter 8, reinforcing a student for appropriate behavior provides other students with an opportunity to learn those behaviors vicariously.

Critical Thinking: From an operant-conditioning point of view, why would positively stated rules work better than negatively stated ones?

Procedures are methods for completing all sorts of routine activities in a classroom (Emmer, 1987). Another way of thinking about procedures is that they provide a how-to plan for routine activities in a classroom. In formulating the procedures that will be part of your classroom management plan, you will need to account for academic work routines. These routines should answer the how-to questions that students might ask about academic work in your classroom. The procedures you establish for academic work should answer the following questions for students (Emmer, 1987).

1. How do I find out what my assignments are?
2. How do I complete work missed when I am absent?
3. How do I get help if I need it?
4. How do I find out how well I am progressing in this class?
5. How do I earn grades in this class?

Reflection: Think about your own questions when you entered this class on the first day. Compared to your concerns, how complete is Emmer's list? What else might students want to know?

In addition to academic activities, there are other routine tasks that require procedural planning (Evertson, 1987; Weinstein & Mignano, 1993). These nonacademic procedures include use of equipment and learning centers, using the rest room and drinking fountain, leaving and returning to the room (as, e.g., during a fire drill), housekeeping chores (such as watering plants or changing bulletin board notices), beginning and ending the school day. Procedures for both academic and nonacademic classroom routines need to be explained to students just as rules are explained. Having a management plan that meticulously addresses every possible classroom procedure is of little use if students are unaware of or do not understand procedures (Good & Brophy, 1994.)

Try This: Interview a practicing teacher about making preparations for the school year. What specific goals does the teacher have for the first week of school? The first month? Ask for recommendations for how you should prepare for your very first teaching assignment.

Building a Positive Atmosphere

Some of the most influential classroom management research of the past 15 years is the beginning-of-the-school-year studies conducted by educational psychologists at the University of Texas (e.g., Emmer, Evertson, & Anderson, 1980; Emmer et al., 1994; Evertson, 1987; Evertson et al., 1994). In these studies, the

What makes this classroom a learning-oriented environment? What rules and procedures might be part of the classroom management plan? What roles can students play in establishing a learning-oriented environment?

researchers made frequent observations of a large number of classrooms during the first few weeks of the school year. They continued making observations as the year progressed, although the frequency of the observations decreased. During some of the later visits, the researchers discovered that some classrooms were operating very well and some were not. Furthermore, the well-managed classrooms, where discipline had been attained, were producing a considerably higher level of student achievement than the poorly managed classrooms.

After determining which teachers were the effective classroom managers and which were less effective, the researchers went back to their observations made at the beginning of the school year. They discovered differences in how the good managers and poor managers started the year. Thus, their observations suggested that establishing a positive classroom atmosphere—one in which students display disciplined behavior and achieve well—is influenced by early student–teacher interactions. To further test the validity of their conclusions, the researchers developed principles of classroom management from their observations of effective teachers. These principles were then taught to other teachers who used them in their own classrooms. The results attained by the new teachers supported the conclusion that there are techniques that can be used at the beginning of the school year to establish a positive learning environment. What are those techniques? How can you start the year in a way that will increase discipline and learning? Here's How presents two lists, one for elementary students and one for secondary students.

Reflection: From your experience as a student, identify examples of classes in which discipline and learning did not occur. Try to recall how those classes began. Do you think the first class meetings made a difference?

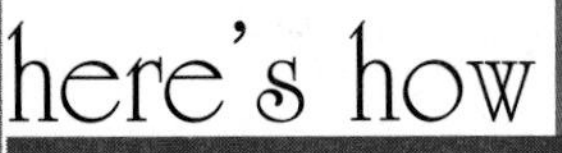

Here's How to Begin the School Year in an Elementary Classroom

- Greet the students. A warm greeting of each student as he or she enters the room helps students feel welcome in their new learning environment. Have name tags prepared ahead of time, with some extras for unexpected students, so that you can give students a name tag when they enter the room. Have an independent activity for students to work on at their desks as you greet other arriving students.
- Conduct introductions. Once students have arrived, introduce yourself and tell them something about yourself. A long autobiographical presentation would be inappropriate, but take a moment to share some of your interests. Have students introduce themselves to the class as well.

- Describe the room. Begin acquainting your students with the various areas of the room. Make sure to point out any areas or materials that they will be using on the first day.
- Present and discuss rules and procedures. First present any major school rules—for example, "No running in the halls." Ask students to think about why that rule is necessary or provide the explanation yourself. Next present and discuss the classroom rules, which you have already posted before the students arrived. As you present rules and procedures, also discuss the consequences of not following them.
- Communicate with parents. If not the first day, then certainly during the first week of school, send a letter home to parents. Include information about materials their child will need for school, how parents may contact you, and special events such as parent–teacher conferences and open house. Take time to craft a letter that presents yourself well. Use the letter to establish your professionalism. Have a colleague read a draft to ensure clarity, correct grammar, and correct spelling. You may include a list of the school and class rules with the letter. Have parents sign and return the list. This allows you to check that all parents have received the letter and informs parents that you are serious about managing your classroom (see Evertson et al., 1994).

---

here's how

Here's How to Begin the School Year in a Secondary Classroom

- On the first day of class, stand near the door to help students find the correct room. Greet students as they enter your class, but avoid long conversations. Tell students that they may choose their seats for this first class meeting. When most students have arrived, enter the room, stay in prominent view, and monitor student behavior. You can do this while engaging students in pleasantries.
- When the bell rings, state your name and the course number—which should already be written on the chalkboard—so that students can check their schedules to ensure they are in the correct room.
- Check attendance. Get to this administrative task quickly. As you call the names on the roster, have students raise their hand, rather than call out, to indicate their presence. Calling the roster gives you a chance to start associating names and faces. Using the hand-raising technique communicates the idea that being recognized is more desirable than calling out. If you intend to establish hand raising as a procedure for speaking in class, this technique helps to establish that norm early.
- Conduct introductions. Tell students something about yourself: your interests, hobbies, and why you enjoy teaching the course they have just started. If students do not know each other, a brief, get-acquainted activity would be in order. You might administer a brief interest survey. After introductions, give students an overview of the course, and describe some of the more interesting activities that they can anticipate in the course.
- Present and discuss rules and procedures. Some secondary school teachers prefer to call these "guidelines." In any case, design your presentation of rules and procedures to eliminate student uncertainty. As you present each rule, provide examples and a rationale. Invite students to contribute examples and reasons for a particular rule. If you anticipate that one of the class rules or procedures will be difficult to follow, you should acknowledge that possibility and assure students that you will help them develop appropriate behaviors (see Emmer et al., 1994).

HOW CAN INSTRUCTION BE MANAGED TO SUPPORT A LEARNING-ORIENTED ENVIRONMENT?

Connection: This chapter focuses on managing learning activities. In Chapter 12, the focus will be on the activities themselves. Both here and in Chapter 12, it is important to realize that management and instruction occur interdependently.

A good start to the school year is critical to the atmosphere that will develop in your classroom. A good start is just that, however—a start. Building and maintaining a positive, learning-oriented environment requires attention to the procedures for managing the instructional activities you employ to facilitate student learning (Good & Brophy, 1994).

One of the best ways to maintain discipline and thus to prevent misbehavior is to engage students in interesting activities that, when completed, yield a feeling of accomplishment. But finding an interesting activity does not ensure that the activity will prove a success. The activity must be managed well if it is to produce learning. Students must become involved with the activity; the activity must engage their cognitive efforts. Vernon Jones and Louise Jones (1995) describe instructional management skills that facilitate the active engagement of learners in the instructional task (cf. Rosenshine, 1983). Some of the instructional management skills examined in this section were first addressed by Kounin (1970). These skills, to be discussed in turn, are (1) giving clear instructions, (2) gaining attention, (3) maintaining attention, (4) pacing, (5) summarizing, and (6) making smooth transitions.

Connection: This discussion relates to instructional goals and their influence on motivation discussed in Chapter 9.

Giving Clear Instructions

A healthy proportion of disruptive behavior in classrooms occurs when students are unsure of what to do when assigned a particular task (Brophy, 1988). Students who are unsure of how to ask for assistance or move to a new activity when a task is completed are more likely to display disruptive behavior than students who know what procedures to follow and what actions to take after the task is completed (cf. Brophy & Evertson, 1976; Jones and Jones, 1990; Kounin, 1970). Giving clear instructions is one of the skills Jones and Jones identify as increasing the time students spend engaged with academic tasks, referred to as **on-task behavior.** By increasing on-task behavior, teachers reduce the amount of disruptive behavior in their classrooms.

Precise Directions. Teachers can take several steps to make sure their instructions are clear. First, you should make sure that directions to students are precise. These directions should include information about what students will be doing, the reason for doing it, how students can find help if it is needed, and what they should do when their work is completed. Students express their uncertainty about tasks in a number of disruptive ways. As an example, they might ask questions repeatedly about the task they have been assigned. Other forms of disruption might occur as expressions of boredom or acting out.

Providing precise directions tells students *what* they are to do. Expectations can be made clearer by also describing *how well* students should perform. Jones and Jones report that one teacher uses three labels to inform students of the desired quality of their work. The first label, *throwaway,* is for practice material, material that will not be handed in. The second label, *everyday learning,* is applied to work that will be turned in and graded. This work, therefore, should be neatly

on-task behavior Any time a student is engaged with an academic task.

Insights ON SUCCESSFUL PRACTICE

In your experience, what role does teacher communication play in successful classroom management?

Presenting a clear and consistent message to everyone in the school and parent community is vital for the success of my classroom management. I firmly believe that both parents and teachers want to see children develop as happy, well-adjusted students who are successful and confident. Because we have the same goal in mind, it is imperative to work side by side and continue a consistent and clear line of communication between home and school. Parents need to feel that they are a vital link in the success of their child's educational experience, which encompasses their academic, emotional, and social success in the classroom, school, and larger community. As the teacher it is my responsibility to foster and reinforce the concept of a three-way partnership. It is a chain that connects parents to teachers with the most important link in the middle—the student. When the students understand that the significant adults are working together with the goal of helping them succeed, they are motivated to do their best and strive to reach the high expectations we have of them for becoming all that they can be.

The first week of school I make personal contact with each family by phone and invite them to attend Back-to-School Night, at which time I go over the program for their child and how they can help at home. I am always amazed at the reaction I get, for there are always those who express surprise and appreciation for this small professional courtesy. Many have the perception that a phone call from the teacher is an indication of a problem! It's nice to break that pattern and show them that I am fostering the three-way partnership.

Students call home if a reoccurring problem arises that prevents others from getting the most out of the day and focusing on their responsibilities. Oftentimes a few minutes on the phone with the parent helps the student get refocused through reinforcement from that critical link in the chain. But parents also receive calls that validate their child's efforts and successes in school, and success in itself is a powerful motivator. Parents sign newsletters attached to their child's homework. When students return their homework completed on time I give them a ticket that enters them into a monthly drawing for breakfast with the teacher. I am communicating that their efforts and responsibility carry rewards, and it is my way of supporting and reinforcing that behavior.

I ask that parents communicate with me as well so that I gain a better understanding and appreciation of the unique dynamics of each family. I have seen so many changes happen in a child's life at home, and for some the classroom structure provides consistency in an otherwise chaotic home environment. Communication must travel two ways to be the most effective. I expect students to be active participants at their parent– teacher conferences. It is an opportunity for students to share openly with their parents and teacher their concerns, surprises, and future goals, and then we brainstorm together as a team on strategies toward successfully meeting those goals and how each person in this three-way partnership has a role. Through this spirit of mutual support and cooperation I see children thrive and become empowered as they are validated as being capable individuals.

JENLANE GEE MATT, Sipherd Elementary School, Modesto, California

What three-way communication link does this teacher nurture? Why is this link important to student success, and what pragmatics of classroom life are served by it? What guidelines for effective communication can you infer from this essay?

done. The presentation does not have to be perfect, however; the main purpose of everyday learning work is to check the student's understanding of the material. The final label, *keeper*, refers to work that the students may want to retain permanently or work that may be displayed.

Student Involvement. One way to check if students understand your instructions is to ask them to paraphrase the directions they have received. Checking students' understanding of instructional content is an important part of active instruction. It is helpful to check students' understanding of the instructions to make sure they are engaged correctly in a task.

Try This: Observe a primary grade classroom and a secondary classroom. In particular, observe the way in which directions are presented. What are the similarities? Do the guidelines in this chapter apply to both classrooms?

Write instructions on a chalkboard or bulletin board so that students may refer to them, or ask students to write out the instructions before beginning the activity to ensure that they have understood them correctly. If students are experiencing some difficulty in following a complex set of instructions, you can break down the instructions into smaller units. Directions should always be given immediately prior to presenting the activity that the students are being asked to do.

No matter how clearly teachers present instructions to their students, and no matter how well students listen to those instructions, there will be times when students must ask questions about what they are to do. Applying Maslow's hierarchy of needs (Chapter 9) suggests that student questions should be accepted in a positive manner. If you accept students' questions in a positive way, that acceptance contributes to the classroom atmosphere in which students work. If they find the teacher to be a willing helper, who will support their efforts, the atmosphere in the classroom will seem safe. A safe atmosphere encourages risk taking by students who will now attempt to meet higher-level needs because the lower-level need of safety has been satisfied.

Example: Another example of a theoretical justification for responding to students' questions is Lickona's model of character education, discussed in Chapter 3.

Gaining Attention

The best time to engage students in a learning activity is when it begins. A lesson that fails to capture attention at the beginning is not likely to turn into an exciting learning experience (see Kounin, 1970). Experienced teachers have developed a number of strategies for gaining attention at the start of a lesson (Jones & Jones, 1995).

One strategy is to select or teach a cue that signals to the students that a lesson is about to begin. Using phrases such as "OK, we're just about ready to get started here, so everyone pay attention" or "OK, let's get ready to start" are so common that they tend to be ineffective in capturing students' attention. Jones and Jones report a method they have used successfully to gain attention. Their method is to invent a phrase that will, for some period of time, serve as a cue for the entire class. Students are invited to generate the catch phrase. One year, students chose the catch phrases "boo" for October, "gobble gobble" for November, and "ho ho ho" for December.

Point: Inviting students and parents to participate in the management of learning activities is consistent with a basic assumption of this book: *Classroom management is a shared concern.*

Some signals can serve additional purposes, such as communicating the teacher's interest or enthusiasm to the students. For example, one teacher always wears a sport coat to class but never wears it while teaching. The sport coat is merely a prop. When the administrative details at the beginning of a period are complete, the instructor always removes his coat. On those occasions when he is wearing long sleeves, he rolls them up to indicate that he is ready to get to work.

The use of a verbal or visual cue must be followed by a waiting period. If the catch phrase or signal succeeds in directing students' attention to the teacher, then the delay will be short. It is important for the teacher not to begin until everyone in the classroom is paying attention, however long the delay. The effectiveness of the signal is diminished if the teacher begins the lesson before all students are paying attention.

Many students are easily distracted. Before beginning a lesson, you should look around your classroom and remove any potential distractions. For instance, if there is noise coming from the hallway, close the door. Such preparations can serve as additional signals that the lesson is about to begin.

Maintaining Attention

The time that students spend directly engaged in learning activities relates positively to their level of achievement (Fisher, Berliner, Filby, Marliave, Cahen, & Dishaw, 1980; Fisher, Filby, Marliave, Cahen, Dishaw, Moore, & Berliner, 1978). If students are to be engaged in instructional tasks, the teacher must develop strategies to help them maintain their attention during a lesson. Fisher et al. (1978) report that the amount of time students spend working directly on instructional tasks varies from less than 50 percent for some teachers to more than 90 percent for others. Earlier in this chapter, you learned about seating arrangements and how an effective arrangement can enhance student attention. Other attention management skills include recognizing students and encouraging student interaction.

Critical Thinking: One of the criticisms of time-on-task studies is that knowing the time a student spends working on a task does not tell you what is going on cognitively. What kind of study could be done to investigate the quality of on-task behavior rather than the quantity?

Recognizing Students. One way to keep students alert during a lesson is to avoid establishing a predictable pattern when calling on students to respond in class. Achieving unpredictability is not as complicated as it may sound. *Random* calling means that each student has an equal probability of being selected to answer a particular question. You can, with a bit of practice, approximate random selection. One helpful tip is to monitor the extent to which you call on low-achieving students. The tendency, for many teachers, is to call on high-achieving students disproportionately more often (Brophy & Good, 1974; Cooper & Good, 1983). Another tip is to return occasionally to a student who has recently responded to a question. Such practices keep students alert because they are unable to predict accurately who the teacher will call on next.

A more systematic approach, suggested by Jones and Jones (1995), is to keep a tally sheet and mark it each time a student is called on. You can also inform students—as you present classroom procedures on the first day of class—that you intend to call on each of them. If students understand your intentions, it is less likely that students who volunteer frequently will experience frustration if you do not call on them as often as they would like.

You will enhance attention if you ask the question before calling on a particular student. When you ask the question prior to calling on a student and use an unpredictable pattern of selection, all students tend to listen more carefully to the question. When a teacher selects a student before asking a question, the other students in the classroom are relieved from responsibility. Consider the reaction of students in a class where the teacher says, "Ronald, what do we call a word that modifies a verb?" In this case, Ronald is on the spot, and the other students in the classroom are more likely to respond to the fact that they were not called on than to the question being asked. Questioning can have powerful effects on students' attention. We will examine this skill in more detail in our discussion of active learning in Chapter 12.

Try This: Observe several lessons, focusing on the questioning techniques of the teacher. Note the nature and length of students' responses as well as the class's overall level of attention. What are your observations about the effectiveness of the questioning techniques?

Encouraging Student Interaction. Another way to maintain attention is to encourage students to interact with their classmates. One way to do this is to ask students if they agree with the answers that other students have provided. Keep in mind that it is helpful to avoid repeating the answers that students give to questions. Jones and Jones (1995) have observed that many teachers parrot nearly every answer that students give, which teaches the students that they do not have to speak clearly or loudly when answering. Students learn that the teacher is the only one who is required to hear the answer. They pay less attention to peers because they have learned that the teacher will provide the answer. Finally, students learn that the teacher is the source of all information in the classroom. These effects, taken together, decrease the attention that students pay.

Example: Teacher modeling of active learning is an excellent way to encourage that behavior in other students. Another way to encourage active listening is to ask a student to paraphrase another student's answer.

Students will listen carefully to their classmates' answers when they are encouraged to do so by the example of their teacher. If teachers pay close attention to what students say, they are modeling good listening behavior for students. A teacher can demonstrate careful listening by asking students to repeat, clarify, or elaborate what they have said. This practice indicates that you not only are interested in what the student has to say but also want to understand clearly the student's point of view.

Maintaining attention can be facilitated by a teacher who is animated. The animation in the teacher's voice and facial expression is indicative of a high level of energy for the topic being discussed. This demonstrated enthusiasm can be further enhanced by using more positive than negative verbal statements. Verbal reinforcement should be sincere. If the teacher follows every student response by saying, "Oh, what an insightful answer!" students will learn that any response will receive verbal reinforcement, and that will diminish the reinforcing effect of verbal praise.

Connection: Chapter 12 presents a discussion of wait-time, which refers to the interval between asking a question and calling on a student to respond as well as to the interval between the student's response and the teacher's reaction.

It is important to keep in mind that the silences between utterances also communicate information to the students. The research on wait-time (discussed in Chapter 12) indicates that silence can give students an opportunity to think more clearly about the question at hand. Silence can also gain attention. Silences serve to separate verbally related thoughts from each other. When writing we can separate thoughts by using periods, paragraphs, and sections. Silences in the classroom are the auditory equivalent to that separation and can signal to students when an idea is important.

Pacing

Pacing refers to the tempo a teacher establishes while teaching and, therefore, can be affected by other instructional management skills. The tempo with which you present your lessons is partially dictated by your teaching style. Some people speak faster than others. Some are more likely to digress, telling a story or providing other examples. Some prefer rapid-fire drill and practice to a more leisurely seat-work assignment. But pacing is determined by more than just personal style. It is determined by the way you organize your material and by your ability to observe students' responses. As you reflect on your performances in the classroom, you will become more skilled at judging the appropriateness of our pacing. As you gain field experience or as you videotape lessons in your teacher education program, ask others and yourself questions such as, Did I speak too quickly? Did I exhibit enthusiasm? Did I pace the lesson by modulating my voice? Did I use silences effectively? Did I repeat myself too often?

Insights ON SUCCESSFUL PRACTICE

What advice can you give novice teachers about preventing discipline problems?

Good discipline is dependent on a dynamic learning environment, mutual respect, clear rules, and consistent enforcement of rules. The teacher needs to establish discipline guidelines early in the school year. Students need to understand that the guidelines set have the sole purpose of ensuring that each student will have an opportunity to be successful in the classroom. The teacher must model the expected behaviors.

An important ingredient for good discipline is a daily learning plan that engages all of the students in the classroom. Students who are encouraged to be active learners will not have an opportunity to be disruptive. Students who are motivated to learn will work at minimizing or totally eradicating discipline problems. Using peer pressure to create a well-disciplined class is a skill that successful teachers must acquire.

Teachers must constantly demonstrate respect for a student's opinions. Teachers should not make false assumptions. Teachers should attempt to gather information from students when warranted. Many times discipline problems can be eliminated by simply asking a student why a certain behavior is present. Discretion must be used when addressing minor discipline problems. I usually address these problems with notes attached to a student's assignment. If the problem is creating a distraction in class, I address it immediately. All attempts are made to make in-class disciplinary moves nonconfrontational. Students should not be placed in a situation where they feel threatened or where they feel that they must fight back.

Clear rules and consequences for not following the established rules are very important. These rules should be consistently enforced. Time should be taken to justify the rules. Students should be encouraged to comment on these rules. Providing written class rules is suggested. Convey to students that the respect they want for themselves is the same respect they should give to their teachers and peers. Do not allow a student to belittle another student's contributions to the class. Thank students for being risk takers. Do not allow ridiculing of students. Show students that you are human; thus mistakes are a part of the learning process.

Bruce Lee, martial artist and actor, defined a master teacher as one who had the ability to produce students that exceeded the teacher's accomplishments. Students who are given an opportunity to view you as this type of teacher will make a genuine effort to contribute to a well-disciplined classroom environment. A teacher's ability to think like a student will provide the needed insight to perform with a student's interests at heart. Never forget what *you* expected of teachers. Stress the importance of communication. When necessary, explain the importance of voicing concerns. Accept responsibility for your actions as a teacher, and communicate the same expectations for your students. Respect your worth as an individual and that of your students.

LEO ARMANDO RAMIREZ, SR., McAllen High School, McAllen, Texas

According to this teacher, what are the most important elements in the relationship between teacher and students? How do you think these relational elements fit in with other aspects of classroom leadership?

Point: Informal surveys of students are helpful not only in improving a teacher's instructional delivery but also in showing the students that the teacher is serious about teaching well, thus enhancing credibility.

Connection: This chapter also examines approaches for handling disruptive behavior. One of those approaches assumes that misbehavior always represents a problem that the student is experiencing and is, therefore, an opportunity to help the student identify and solve the problem.

Asking these questions of your students can yield useful information about pacing. You may also ask students whether you are accurately picking up their cues when they do not understand or if you provide sufficient time for them to complete seatwork. You can obtain this feedback after a lesson, in either an informal question-and-answer period, or through written evaluations. One high school teacher reported that he wanted to improve his pacing without interrupting the class and without spending time after the lesson reviewing the form of the lesson rather than its substance. The teacher taught his students several hand signals that they could use during a lesson to inform him of the appropriateness of his pacing—whether he was talking too much or repeating himself, talking too fast, or presenting material that they did not understand (Jones & Jones, 1995).

Kounin (1970) found that teachers who were able to scan their rooms and to respond to problems effectively before they became serious had fewer discipline problems. For example, if a student appears restless—shifting in his or her seat, playing with materials on the desk—the teacher can avoid disruptive behavior by simply recognizing the student's restlessness and asking the student for an explanation. There are two reasons for asking a student why he or she is having difficulty paying attention. First, the student's answer provides you with direct feedback on your pacing. Second, this approach encourages students to share their feelings because the teacher is taking their observations and opinions seriously.

Summarizing

Providing students with summaries of what has been taught during a particular lesson or, in the case of primary grades, over the course of a day is a way of helping them organize information. By stepping back at the end of an instructional unit and putting the material into perspective, you facilitate the development of organized knowledge structures or schemata.

There are several ways in which students can become actively involved in summarizing activities. One way is to have them write, perhaps in a daily journal, something that they have learned in the lesson or during the instructional day. Such an activity also provides the teacher with an opportunity to diagnose problems (e.g., if a student has difficulty writing down something he or she has learned).

Role playing can also be used as a summary-generating technique. Students might play the role of a reporter and provide a news summary of the learning events that occurred during the lesson. A teacher might say something like, "We go now to our classroom correspondent, Christopher Michael, who will report on the vandalism that destroyed a considerable amount of English tea in the Boston Harbor. Come in, Christopher." Summaries can also be facilitated by asking students to create learning displays or to develop newspaper articles or schematic drawings indicating the key points in the lesson.

If student-centered summarizing is not possible, the teacher can provide the summary. In that case, frequent reviews should be provided in order to increase the chances that the information will be retained and to reinforce the concept that learning builds on previous learning. Frequent reviews also encourage students to synthesize the concepts from one lesson with information from another lesson.

Finally, tests can be used as summarizing tools. Going over a test after it has been completed provides students with feedback about the correctness or incorrectness of their responses. Such a review provides students who have made errors with an opportunity to correct those errors. It also acts as an additional presentation of important information from the unit.

Too often, our students perceive the academic tasks we present to them as a set of unrelated hoops to jump through. By summarizing material we can show them how what they are doing relates to what they have been doing in past lessons and what we hope to accomplish in upcoming class sessions.

Making Smooth Transitions

A great deal of classroom time is spent in transitions—that is, moving from one activity to the next. Consider a junior high or high school, where students change classes approximately every forty to fifty minutes. Packing up from one class, moving into the hall, meeting friends, talking, stopping at the locker, and moving into the next class where materials are retrieved, notebooks are opened, and pencils are readied are major transitions in themselves. Add to this any change of focus or topic that may occur during a period. In elementary schools, nearly 15 percent of classroom time is taken up with approximately thirty major transitions each day (Gump, 1967; Rosenshine, 1980). A major difference between master teachers and less-skilled classroom managers is the way in which they handle transitions (Arlin 1979; Doyle, 1984). Because students are not engaged in an academic task during transitions, the time is ripe for disruptive behavior.

Try This: Ask teachers who are recognized for their classroom management expertise to describe their techniques for moving the whole class from one activity to the next. How do they handle small group transitions? Transitions in individualized instruction? Transitions to labs or library sessions?

The physical arrangement of the classroom should enable students who need to retrieve or turn in materials at different times to do so without disturbing other students. In addition, a daily schedule can be posted for easy reference by the students, and any changes in the schedule can be discussed each morning (Evertson et al., 1994; Charles & Senter, 1995; Weinstein & Mignano, 1993). Scheduling is especially important in elementary classrooms. Having materials prepared in advance—including possibly an outline of the lesson for the next period or a videotape or software package loaded and ready to switch on—decreases the time that students spend in transition. A teacher who must spend time preparing materials during class is inviting the students in the classroom to move off task.

Connection: Look at Figures 10.4 and 10.5. Do those classroom arrangements facilitate the efficient retrieval and distribution of materials? In which of those two arrangements would you expect that the teacher would have to play a more prominent role in distribution and collection of materials?

When you end one lesson, do not relinquish the students' attention until you have introduced or provided instructions for the following activity. The "packing-up syndrome" is common at all instructional levels. It is important to keep students focused through the end of one lesson and to give them on-task directions before packing up is permitted.

Another way of shortening transitions is to ask students to do certain management tasks. For example, if you can have a student take attendance, hand out papers, or collect materials, you will have more time to engage in other tasks in preparation for a lesson, thus reducing the transition time. If students perform administrative and logistical tasks, you will also have more time to monitor the classroom and attend to individual needs.

HOW CAN MISBEHAVIOR BE ADDRESSED AND THE LEARNING ORIENTATION RESTORED?

misbehavior According to Doyle, any behavior, by one or more students, that competes with or threatens learning activities.

The instructional management skills discussed in this chapter are meant to keep students engaged in learning. If students are actively involved in learning activities, they are unlikely to disrupt learning by misbehaving. **Misbehavior** is any

Try This: Discuss with your classmates the distinction between prevention and reaction with regard to classroom management. How did you think about classroom management before you read this chapter and how do you think about it now?

behavior, by one or more students, that competes with or threatens learning activity in the classroom (Doyle, 1986, 1990). If a sound management plan is implemented and if instructional management is done well, then misbehavior will be minimized. Even in the best managed classrooms, however, not all misbehavior is prevented. How will you manage misbehavior? The management techniques examined in this section are ways to respond to misbehavior.

Jacob Kounin identified two skills that are key to the effective management of misbehavior: *withitness* and *overlapping* (Kounin, 1970). Kounin coined the term *withitness* when the phrase "being with-it," meaning being alert or aware, was popular. "**Withitness** is knowing what is going on in every part of the classroom at every moment, in a way that is evident to students" (Charles & Senter, 1995, p. 135). Teachers who possess withitness skills have the ability to identify misbehavior quickly and accurately. **Overlapping** is the ability to attend to two issues simultaneously. For example, suppose that two students in the back of the room are working together while the teacher is consulting with a group in the front of the room. Student A grabs a pencil from Student B's desk. Student B shouts out, "Hey, give me that back." A teacher who possesses overlapping skills might address the disruption with a quick glance at both students, making eye contact that sends the message, "That is inappropriate behavior; get back on task." At the same time, the teacher continues addressing the question from the group with whom she is consulting.

Withitness and overlapping skills come with experience and are most likely to evolve in the classroom of a teacher who projects an image of being in charge (Charles & Senter, 1995). Reflect for a moment on the earlier discussion of classroom management as authoritative leadership. A teacher who has not established a learning-oriented environment, has not communicated respect for students, and is not perceived as credible by students will have a more difficult time resolving disruptions. As you consider the approaches to managing misbehavior presented in the following sections, consider how a learning-oriented environment and being perceived as an authoritative leader contribute to the efficacy of these approaches.

A Self-Correctional Approach to Student Misbehavior

Point: The idea that teachers' use of power determines the amount of control that students can exercise supports the basic assumption that: *Classroom management is a shared concern.*

Minimum uses of teacher power leave the student in control of rectifying behavior. As the use of teacher power in handling misbehavior escalates, the student has fewer options and, as we shall see, so does the teacher. The self-correctional approach described here uses minimum teacher power. The idea is to help students view their misbehavior as a problem and to help students solve that problem for themselves.

This approach to handling misbehavior was first developed by Thomas Gordon and is sometimes called the Teacher Effectiveness Training (TET) Model, after the title of the book Gordon wrote in which he presented his ideas (Gordon, 1974; see also Gordon, 1988). There are two essential assumptions of the approach. First, student misbehavior can be self-corrected, and second, misbehavior is remedied best though authentic communication between teacher and student (Wolfgang, 1995). *Authentic communication* means that the teacher does not simply hear an utterance but also understands the message behind the utterance. Authentic communication can take several forms.

withitness According to Kounin, the teacher's ability to observe all situations in the classroom and to deal effectively with misbehavior.

overlapping A teacher's ability to deal with more than one issue at the same time.

Imagine that a student has just screamed an obscenity in the middle of an exam. One way to deal with the misbehavior is simply to look at the student.

What management and leadership models are available to the teacher for responding to this student misbehavior? What might be the most effective way to restore this classroom to a learning-oriented environment?

With the right kind of look, a teacher can communicate the message, "I am aware of what you said, but I trust that you can correct yourself. If you need some help, I'm here for you." That is a lot of meaning to put into a look, but if an authentic relationship has been established between the teacher and the student, looks can be very effective. If a look does not lead to a remedy, the student can be encouraged to verbalize his or her discomfort through gestures or a nondirective statement such as, "You must be having difficulty with this exam." The statement acknowledges that some emotion underlies the misbehavior and invites the student to talk about those feelings. The next step is to issue a direct invitation to discuss the misbehavior. According to Gordon, if the student accepts an invitation to discuss the misbehavior, you must take care to avoid offering advice or a solution for the student. Actively listening to the student in order to paraphrase and help the student pinpoint his or her feelings and to understand the reasons underlying the misbehavior is key. The urge to take control of the problem and solve it for the student may be great, but if students are to learn how to correct their own behavior problems, they must be given opportunities to do so.

Try This: Observe classroom activities that require the teacher to move about the room to monitor small groups or individual work. Take particular note of the nonverbal communication that occurs. What happens when the teacher is in close proximity? How does the teacher make eye contact? Does the teacher use a special look?

Communicating with students goes beyond active listening. Teachers must be clear about why they perceive a student's action as misbehavior. One way of achieving this clarity is to use I-messages. An **I-message** addresses the problem behavior and its effects, expresses the teacher's feelings, but does not attack the self-concept of the misbehaving student (Ginott, 1972; Gordon, 1988). Consider an example from Wolfgang (1995): "When students run down the stairs (behavior), I am fearful (feelings) that people will fall and get injured (effect), and my job is to keep people safe" (p. 27). I-messages can be used to express feelings about situations that provoke strong emotions such as anger or frustration in a teacher. For example, a teacher may become angry with a student who talks during sustained silent reading, particularly at the end of a long, hard teaching day. Rather than directing this anger at the student personally, the teacher might say, "The class has established the rule that talking is forbidden during sustained silent reading (behavior). We have another rule in this class that if you have something to say, at any time, you should raise your hand. Because talking during sustained silent reading interrupts important work (effect), and because it breaks the rules that we all worked on (effect), I get angry (feelings)."

The self-correcting approach recognizes that there are times in all classrooms when serious conflicts between student and teacher arise. One way to resolve conflicts is for the teacher to impose a resolution. This may be necessary in extreme instances where a student may be in danger of hurting someone or being hurt. In most situations, this is not the best way to approach conflict resolution. If the teacher uses his or her power to take control over the student's

I-message A clear statement by a teacher that tells how he or she feels about misbehavior but that does not lay blame on a student.

behavior, the teacher is not demonstrating respect for the student's ability to self-correct and the student is seen as the loser in the conflict. A second way to resolve conflicts is for the teacher to give in to the student and abandon his or her view of the conflict. There may be times when a student argues so compellingly that the teacher should concede the argument and withdraw from further discussion. This should not become a pattern, however. If a teacher continually loses conflicts, students will have difficulty perceiving the teacher as credible. So, how can a teacher resolve a conflict with a student and at the same time maintain the attitudes of respect and credibility that support learning-oriented classrooms? This question is addressed by the "no-lose method" (Gordon, 1974, 1988).

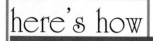

Critical Thinking: Think back to some of the characteristics of effective models discussed in Chapter 8. How might losing a conflict undermine a teacher's effectiveness?

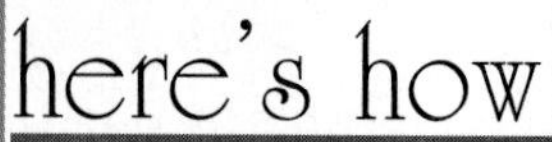

Here's How to Resolve Conflicts without Creating Losers

- Define the problem together. Identify the misbehavior clearly, and then have each person explain what he or she wants out of the situation. Listening carefully to the other person is critical here.
- Brainstorm resolutions. Together, the participants generate as many resolutions to the conflict as possible. It is critical that ideas not be evaluated at this point. The purpose of this step is to collaborate on generating ideas—both good and bad.
- Evaluate each possible resolution. At this stage in the process, evaluate ideas for resolving the conflict. An important rule here is that any participant may veto any idea. If participants veto all ideas, the process reverts to brainstorming.
- Reach a decision. The participants choose one possible resolution by means of consensus. No votes are allowed. Everyone must be able to live with the decision reached.
- Plan and implement the decision. Reaching a decision is not the end of the process. In order to carry out the decision ask questions such as what will we need to resolve the conflict as we have decided? Who will be responsible for what? What is our time frame for implementing our decision?
- Evaluate the implementation. After following the plan for a period of time, reconvene the participants to find out if everyone is satisfied. Ask whether changes should be made in order to improve matters for everyone.

The Control Theory Approach to Misbehavior

The basic assumption of the **control theory** approach is that students behave or misbehave in an attempt to control for themselves the satisfaction of their own basic needs: survival, belonging, power, fun, and freedom (Glasser, 1986). There are three additional assumptions underlying control theory.

- Students feel pleasure when their needs are met and frustration when they are not met.
- Because schools rarely empower students to meet their needs, students rarely work to their potential.
- Schools must create conditions that meet student needs. Teachers should provide encouragement, support, and help. This assumption implies that teachers do not blame, punish, or use coercive management strategies.

control theory The view that students need to be empowered to control to meet their own needs and thus experience success in school.

Glasser has described these assumptions and their implications in greater detail using the labels *quality schools* and *quality teachers* (1990, 1993). Glasser advocates control theory as a way of creating quality learning environments that allow students to meet their needs and thus experience the pleasure of success. If students can satisfy their needs in a classroom, they experience no frustration and do not misbehave. Even so, he recognizes that his approach will not eliminate all misbehavior. From Glasser's point of view, misbehavior occurs when one of two essential rules is broken. Those rules are: Be kind to others, and, Do your best work (Glasser, 1990; see also Charles & Senter, 1995). If one of these rules is broken, then a problem exists and the teacher's responsibility is to collaborate with students to solve that problem.

Example: There is a growing consortium of schools and educators who are using Glasser's ideas to restructure classrooms through the control theory approach to management. For more information, you can write to the Institute for Reality Therapy, 7301 Medical Center Drive, Suite 104, Canoga Park, CA 91307.

Suppose that two students are caught pushing each other in the hall. Following Glasser's approach, the teacher intervenes in a calm, unemotional manner. It is important to avoid fueling what is already an emotionally charged situation with comments that would put students on the defensive. The teacher might say, "I see there is a problem here. How can I help?" The students will likely start blaming one another, at which point the teacher might say, "I want both of you to go calm down. I'm not interested in punishing either of you, I want to help work out whatever the problem is. When you have had a chance to calm down, we will try to solve the problem." Later, after the students are less emotional, the teacher calls them together and says, "What you two were doing is against our rules. Now, what can we do to ensure that this doesn't happen again?" The teacher keeps the focus on a problem that caused the misbehavior, not on determining who is at fault. Once students are engaged with the teacher in a discussion of the problem that caused the misbehavior, the no-lose method of conflict resolution discussed in the previous section might be profitably employed.

Critical Thinking: How would implementing the no-lose method in the context of control theory differ from its use as part of the self-correcting approach? Why is control theory viewed as utilizing more teacher power than the self-correcting approach?

The Applied Behavior Analysis Approach to Misbehavior

Applied behavior analysis is the analysis of behavior problems and the prescription of remedies based on behavioral learning principles, sometimes called behavior modification (Alberto & Troutman, 1990; Madsen & Madsen, 1981). The approach is based on operant-conditioning principles examined in Chapter 6. From an applied behavior analysis perspective, misbehavior is behavior that the teacher finds undesirable. The natural tendency is to respond to misbehavior by simply telling the student to stop, which is not always effective. In the Teacher Chronicle at the beginning of the chapter, Ms. Oxford learns that reprimands and other punishments do nothing to correct Randy's misbehavior. What else can she do?

The Role of Rules. Rules play an important role in applied behavior analysis approaches to misbehavior. One technique, called rules-ignore-praise (RIP), works as follows: rules are established, misbehavior is ignored, students who follow the rules are praised. No consequence for misbehavior occurs, following Skinner's principle that positive reinforcement is the best way to bring about change in behavior. The RIP technique has been found to work fairly well at the elementary school level but not at the secondary school level (Charles, 1992).

Critical Thinking: Why has the RIP technique been found to be more effective at the elementary level than at the secondary level?

applied behavior analysis The analysis of behavior problems and the prescription of remedies.

A variation on the theme is called rules-reward-punishment (RRP). This technique introduces limits and aversive consequences absent from RIP. As in the case of the RIP, RRP starts with the establishment of rules and emphasizes posi-

Insights ON SUCCESSFUL PRACTICE

What approaches to dealing with discipline problems have worked best for you and your students?

In general, disciplining students is not something that warrants a great deal of my time. I really can't define or describe a specific method or process I use to prevent chaos in my classes. However, I believe that my philosophy could be summarized in two short phrases: "Catch them being good," and "Have fun."

Problems with my sixth graders are limited because I practice "preventive discipline"—being organized but flexible enough to capitalize on student interest and questions, keeping students actively involved in their learning by allowing them to make choices and accepting the consequences that follow, and having a sense of humor through it all. Acknowledging appropriate behaviors when they occur sends an extremely powerful message; others will often imitate those actions that gain your attention. Accentuate the positive!

Cooperative learning is not only a way of helping students develop skills for working with others, but it is an effective structure for managing my classroom. During the first two to three weeks of school, time is spent "teaching" my expectations for classroom procedures and behaviors while reviewing some basic geography skills and modeling appropriate social skills. Daily activities then occur smoothly and efficiently throughout the year.

If students are interested and active participants in their education, they won't have time to get in trouble. In my classroom students are often presented with several alternatives to accomplish the desired outcomes, which in turn provides them with opportunities to make many decisions; this ownership in their education alleviates much of the power struggle that can arise when teachers design/dictate all that students are to do.

I enjoy learning about our world right along with my students, and I think this kind of enthusiasm is contagious. Students never know what I might do next to get their attention. It could be the props I use or the costumes I wear, but I will do anything I can to keep the students from becoming passive. I think students can sense whether a teacher is in the profession for a paycheck or because its something she or he truly loves doing. Teaching is my hobby as well as my source of income.

LINDA K. HILLESTAD, Brookings Middle School, Brookings, South Dakota

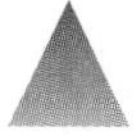 Insights

What strategies does this teacher use to prevent discipline problems in her classroom? What is the "catch 'em being good" philosophy? What teaching style does this teacher describe as a common source of avoidable power struggles between teachers and students?

tive reinforcement for students who follow the rules. However, RRP does not ignore misbehavior. The rules that are established under the RRP approach include not only a statement of the rules but also a statement of the consequences for breaking those rules. Students are informed that they have a choice to make. They can choose to abide by the established rules or they can choose to receive the prescribed punishment. Presenting the contingency in this way means that the teacher does not punish misbehavior, rather the students choose to punish themselves. Charles (1992) argues that the RRP approach is very effective with older students, especially if they have had a hand in establishing both the rules and the consequences of breaking the rules.

Token Economies. Because Skinner argued that positive reinforcement is a more powerful behavior change technique than using aversive consequences, one way to deal with misbehavior is to encourage desirable behavior. Recall the discussion of token economy techniques in Chapter 6, which proposes rewarding students with tokens for exhibiting desirable behaviors. The value of various desirable behaviors is determined in advance so that students know what the positive consequences of their appropriate behavior will be. In addition to earning tokens, students are given access to tangible goods that they may buy with their tokens. Prizes might include stickers, pencils, some forms of food, a book, magazine, drawing paper, crayons, or other objects that students in the class find desirable. It is important for teachers who use token economies to take care in keeping records so that tokens are distributed fairly and consistently. Using this approach also means that class time must be set aside for shopping (Martin & Pear, 1992).

Try This: Visit a classroom in which a token economy is operating. Based on your observations, address the following questions: Does the token economy work well? What criteria would you develop to judge the effectiveness of token economies? Do these criteria focus on learning outcomes?

Tokens can also be used to purchase activities. A student who earns a sufficient number of tokens may purchase, for example, free time on the computer to play games. During shopping time, the teacher can issue a voucher for such activities. In essence, a token economy that sells activities is an application of the Premack principle described in Chapter 6. Students engage in task behaviors (presumably of low probability) that will eventually be rewarded with an opportunity to engage in purchased behaviors (presumably of higher probability).

Charles (1992) suggests that any teacher who chooses to implement a token economy explain clearly and completely to the principal, to parents, and to students how the token economy will work before implementing it. It is necessary to use this approach to minimize misbehavior. Nothing is quite so disruptive as a token economy gone awry. Token economies have been used successfully in a variety of classroom situations at all grade levels, including classrooms that have students with disabilities.

Token economies delay the delivery of primary reinforcement following a desirable student behavior by using secondary reinforcement (tokens) as an immediate consequence of behavior. The effect is to lengthen, sometimes considerably, the time between the appropriate behavioral response and primary reinforcement. If we can instill in our students an ability to delay gratification for their efforts, we are providing them with an opportunity to learn that sustained effort can bring rewards.

Contingency Contracting. Contingency contracting, which involves drawing up a contract between the teacher and the student, is an applied behavior analysis technique that can be used to encourage desirable behavior and discourage misbehavior. A contract should include terms or conditions under which appropriate behaviors will be displayed or will define the limits on misbehavior. For example, a teacher might use a contract to increase the amount of seat work the student completes and, simultaneously, decrease the student's out-of-seat behavior. In this case, the contract should specify how much out-of-seat behavior the teacher will tolerate and under what conditions he or she will allow it, as well as the amount of seat work students must complete. Contracts have been quite successful across grade levels; they can also be helpful with younger children. Many teachers who employ this technique use the contract itself to introduce variety into the learning situation. Figures 10.6 and 10.7 provide examples of contingency contracts.

Reflection: Imagine a class in which you sign a contract. How might signing the contract make you feel? How might it influence your motivation? How might you feel about not fulfilling your contract?

The Assertive Discipline Approach to Misbehavior

The approach to discipline called **assertive discipline**, developed by Lee Canter and Marlene Canter, makes use of several of the principles of applied behavior analysis, including the establishment of rules and consequences prior to the

assertive discipline An approach to misbehavior based on principles of applied behavior analysis.

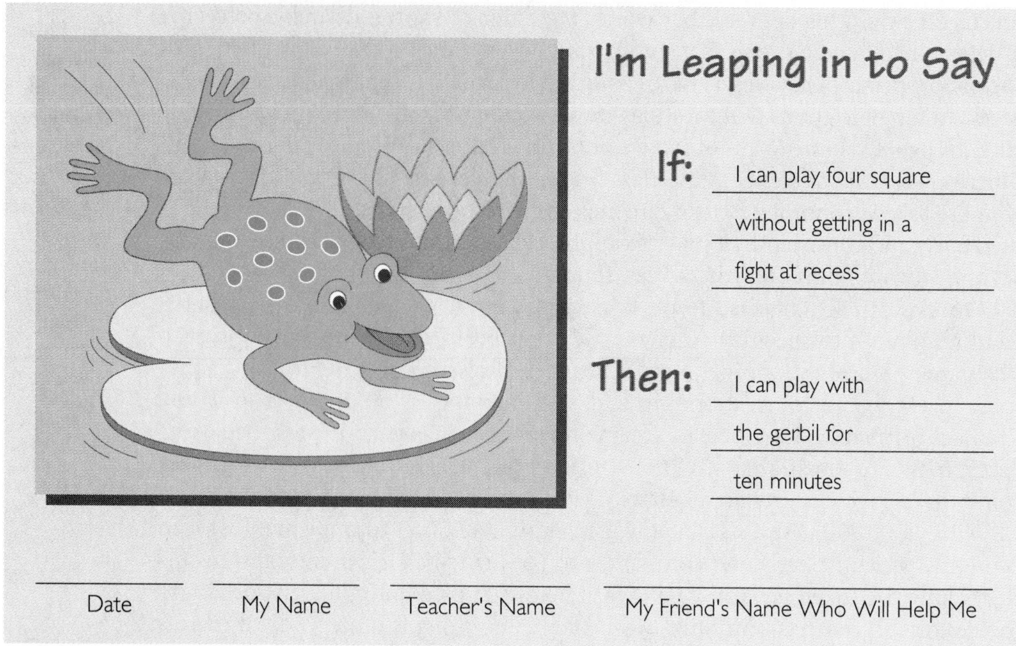

FIGURE 10.6

A Behavior Contract for an Elementary Student
Source: *Comprehensive Classroom Management* (3rd ed., p. 369) by V. F. Jones and L. S. Jones, 1990, Needham Heights, MA: Allyn & Bacon. Copyright 1990 by Allyn & Bacon. Reprinted by permission.

implementation of disciplinary actions (Canter & Canter, 1976, 1992, 1993). In addition to the establishment of rules, assertive discipline emphasizes that teachers follow through with consequences and that the consequences be delivered fairly and consistently.

A communication that is characteristic of assertive discipline is a clear and succinct statement that identifies the problem and suggests a way of remedying it. Charles (1981) provides three examples of responses to fighting in the classroom. Of the three, the last is characteristic of the assertive approach.

- Nonassertive: "Please try your very best to stop fighting."
- Hostile: "You are acting like a disgusting savage again!"
- Assertive: "We do not fight. Sit down until you cool off so we can talk about it."

Example: The assertive discipline approach enjoys considerable popularity in certain parts of the country. It does, however, have its critics. This approach is an example of a package solution to problems. There are useful ideas in this package, but one should always be wary of assuming that any one technique will work with all students or in all situations.

Examining the three responses, you can see that the first expresses some dissatisfaction on the part of the teacher, but the response does not help assert the authority of the teacher or suggest a remedy to the situation. Nor is it delivered in terms that are likely to influence the behavior of students who are engaged in fighting. The hostile response is aggressive but not assertive; it crosses the boundary of the situation and attacks personality. The third response, an example of assertive discipline, provides a clear message about what the problem is and a clear message about how the problem will be solved.

Imagine that a student talks out during sustained silent reading. Let's see how an assertive discipline approach might be used to respond verbally to the disruption.

Name of Student: Suzy Jones Grade: 9th Date: ______
School: Middle School Contract Monitor*: Mrs Smith
Reason for Contract: Demonstrates difficulty controlling anger with regard to peer interaction

---

Student Expectations for Responsible Behavior

1. Follow all classroom and school rules.
2. Expectations requiring additional instructions and clarification:
   A. When angry, Suzy is expected to remain in control by making responsible choices to handle her anger. This applies in the classroom so students can continue working and applies to unstructured time outside the classroom.

Student Choices

Responsible choices
(ways to meet expectations)

A. Ignore situation
B. Remove self from situation
C. Ask for five minutes time out at desk
D. Do deep breathing or relaxation exercises at desk
E. Write down feelings until I can talk the situation over with teacher or counselor

Irresponsible choices
(choosing negative consequences)

A. Not doing work
B. Refusing to continue working
C. Distracting classmates from work
D. Yelling at peers or teachers
E. Running away
F. Fighting

Student Consequences

Consequences for Responsible Behavior at School

A. Stay in class
B. Be with friends
C. Learn new things
D. Have a boyfriend
E. Feel good about my ability to control my anger

At Home:

If Suzy chooses to control her anger all week at school, she will earn an extra half-hour on the weekend to have private time with mother.

Consequences for Irresponsible Behavior

A. If the behavior occurs, Suzy will go to the office and fill out a Problem-Solving Worksheet; she must be able to control herself prior to returning to class.
B. If the behavior occurs during unstructured time, she will be expected to sit on the curb until end of free time and then will be expected to go to the office to fill out Problem-Solving Sheet.

Contract Monitor Agrees to:

1. Consistently apply stated consequences for both responsible and irresponsible behavior.
2. Regularly review contract with student every three weeks.
3. Review contract at staffings as appropriate.

Contract Termination Criteria:

Contract will be terminated when student consistently makes responsible choices to deal with her anger for a three-week period.

Student Signature: ______ Date: ______
Contract Monitor Signature: ______ Date: ______
Parent Signature: ______ Date: ______

*Staff member responsible for contract development, application, and review.

FIGURE 10.7

A Behavior Contract that Emphasizes Student Responsibility

Source: From *Comprehensive Classroom Management: Motivating and Managing Students* (3rd ed., pp. 381–382) by V. F. Jones and L. S. Jones, 1990, Needham Heights, MA: Allyn & Bacon. Copyright 1990 by Allyn & Bacon. Reprinted by permission.

The teacher, on hearing the talking out, says, "Marsha, our rules do not tolerate talking out during sustained silent reading. You must not talk out again."

Marsha says, "But I need something."

The teacher responds, "That may be the case, but talking out during sustained silent reading is against the rules. If you have something to say, raise your hand and I will come to you."

"But, but, George is bothering me."

"If it happens again, raise your hand and I will come over. I'll keep an eye on things, but you may not talk out during sustained silent reading."

In this exchange, the teacher asserts the rule that is being broken and follows through by continuing to assert the rule. By reminding the student that she may speak to the teacher after raising her hand, the teacher also provides a remedy to the problem. To summarize, using the assertive discipline approach means that teachers make promises, not threats.

HOW CAN YOUR KNOWLEDGE OF CLASSROOM MANAGEMENT HELP YOU BECOME AN EFFECTIVE TEACHER?

Point: Recall the point discussed in Chapter 1: *Teaching and learning are aspects of the same process.*

Perhaps the most important lesson to learn from the theories and research on classroom management is that it is a process inextricably connected to student learning. The problems that arise from poor classroom management and the benefits that accrue from sound management cannot be isolated from learning. If a teacher manages a classroom poorly, student learning will suffer. Conversely, teachers who do not value learning will experience management problems. Learning is not only an effect of sound management but also a cause. If learning is truly occurring for every student in a classroom, that classroom will be easy to manage.

A second lesson teachers can take from what educational psychologists have learned about classroom management is that communication is a key element in learning-oriented classrooms. Our actions as teachers, and not just our words, send messages to our students. Our actions tell our students that we do or do not value learning and their input or are or are not concerned about their problems. Without saying a word about it, we tell our students whether we see them as subordinates or partners. Our students send messages to us as well. Their behaviors and misbehaviors are signals that they are learning successfully or that they are not. If we can understand them as individuals, their behavior can reveal their needs to us and we can then respond to those needs.

A final lesson to learn is that classroom management teaches our students a great deal about themselves. The way we interact with our students allows them to infer how capable they are of making decisions, of taking responsibility, and of contributing to the community of the classroom. Although sound management serves as a foundation for instruction in math, reading, science, and other academic areas, it also instructs directly. And what it teaches directly is important.

In this last section of the chapter we focus on what our classroom management practices teach our students and on what we, as teachers, can learn through our practices.

Teaching Self-Responsibility

One of the clear findings from the research examined in this chapter is that management practices contribute significantly to the nature of the learning environment. Depending on a teacher's approach—and the underlying values reflected by that approach—a classroom can afford students a variety of opportunities. Recent work in the general area of motivation and, more specifically, volition, suggests that a critical ingredient in realizing personal goals is environmental affordance. **Affordances** are the opportunities offered a person by his or her environment (Corno, 1995; Snow, Corno, & Jackson, 1995). In some classroom environments, students are afforded opportunities to take responsibility for their own behavior and learning.

Reflection: How many opportunities were you afforded in your classrooms to take responsibility for your own learning and behavior? How might such opportunities have been structured in those classrooms? How do you think you would have responded to those opportunities?

A sense of self-responsibility means establishing goals for oneself and then finding ways to achieve those goals. A sense of self-responsibility is arguably one of the most important learning outcomes that we can help our students attain. And motivation and volition play a significant role in its development. Motivation is connected to volition by means of a "commitment pathway" (Heckhausen & Kuhl, 1985). Corno (1995) explains that pathway as follows:

> Motivation establishes goals, while volition implements them. Motivation promotes goals, while volition protects them. Motivation involves individual thinking about goals; while volition involves the initiation of processes for accomplishing goals. Motivation embraces foresight, while volition embraces follow-through. . . . Both motivation and volition are important psychological components involved in getting . . . "what you want." (p. 3)

This theoretical account of motivation and volition suggests that if we want our students to develop self-responsibility, we need to afford them opportunities to establish their goals and then follow through on them. But how do we afford them appropriate opportunities? Part of the answer is to establish learning-oriented as opposed to work-oriented classroom environments. Here's How suggests ways to facilitate the development of self-responsibility within learning-oriented environments.

here's how

Here's How to Develop a Sense of Self-Responsibility in Your Students

- Ask students what they would like to accomplish. With regard to academic goals, you will be constrained by the curricular requirements of your school district. Even if you were not so constrained, it would not be wise to allow students absolute freedom in determining learning outcomes. Nevertheless, you can ask students to identify those skill areas in which they would most like to improve. You may wish to give them a menu of goals similar to a Premack principle menu of possible reinforcements.
- Confer with your students to clarify their goals. Once students have identified their

affordances Opportunities offered a person by his or her environment.

goals, it is important that you confer with them to determine how clear the goals are. If a student has only a vague notion of a goal, it is not likely that the student will accomplish that goal. In order to arrive at a destination, you have to know where you are going. Ask questions that will help students clarify and focus their goals, starting with, "What will you be able to do when you have reached your goal?"

- Help students formulate an action plan to meet their goal. During the same conference in which you meet with them to clarify their goal, discuss an action plan for attaining that goal. Your role in these conferences is to encourage the student to develop his or her own plan. As much as you may be tempted to develop a prescription for the student, you should allow the student to develop his or her own ideas. Keep in mind that not all of the student's learning activities will be determined in this way, only those activities that pertain to his or her selected goals.
- Encourage students to monitor progress toward their goals. Ask for weekly reports from students regarding goal-related activities. Ask them to judge how much progress they made and to think about what they might do differently next week to get them closer to their goals.
- Do not let students give up on their goals. Some students will undoubtedly experience difficulties and frustration. Assure them that frustration is a natural part of the process and that it is often the case that scientists, artists, and teachers have to try several different approaches before they accomplish what they set out to do. By sharing your own experiences in this regard, you will serve as a coping model for your students.

Managing Cultural Diversity

The values that teachers have are reflected in the ways they manage instruction and the ways they respond to misbehavior. As you learned in Chapter 4, the values students bring to the classroom are at least partially determined by their cultural backgrounds. You also learned that conflicts between value systems can cause problems for both students and teachers. This is especially true when the expectations for classroom behavior are based on cultural norms that are not shared by teacher and students. Consider, for example, two differences between European American culture and Native American culture. First, European American youth often demonstrate that they are listening by making direct eye contact; many Native American and Hispanic American youth avoid making direct eye contact (Baruth & Manning, 1992). Second, European Americans are accustomed to having rules for almost every possible situation; most Native Americans expect few rules (Baruth & Manning, 1992). Now suppose that a teacher has established a classroom rule that says, "Listen while others are speaking." Suppose also that the teacher, because he or she has internalized European American cultural norms, expects students to follow the rule and to demonstrate their compliance by making eye contact. If a Native American student follows his or her own cultural norms, the teacher is likely to interpret the student's behavior as breaking a rule.

Connection: Mismatches of expectations because of differences in cultural norms are discussed in Chapter 4 and throughout this book.

Consider another rule that is commonly used in classrooms, "Respect other people." One's interpretation of what it means is likely to be influenced by one's cultural background. Most African American youth have encountered either overt or implied racism. European American youth are much less likely to have faced such attitudes. If African American students have been sensitized by their experience to comments that, by tone or inference, are insulting, then they may feel disrespected by comments thought by others to be perfectly innocent. Given the importance of clear communication in effective classroom management, teachers and students must take care to learn about one another's cultural norms and the behavioral expectations they carry.

Cultural diversity among students is most prevalent in urban schools. How should teachers approach the demands of managing an urban classroom? Curwin & Mendler (1988) have some suggestions.

here's how

Here's How to Manage an Urban Classroom

- Get to know your students and let them know you. Many teachers, especially young teachers, who start their careers in an urban school, are fearful. While it is only prudent to be on your guard in any environment that has the potential for hostile behavior, doing so with your students will only succeed in perpetuating your stereotypes about them and theirs about you. Share some of your interests and hobbies, and invite them to return the favor.
- Provide ways for students to appropriately express feelings. Many urban youth have developed a persona or front that they show to the world. They often try to appear detached and indifferent because their experience has taught them such characteristics are signs of strength and maturity. But urban students have feelings like anyone else. One way to provide an outlet for feelings is to schedule a regular but optional sharing time each day. Another is to set up a so-called gripe box into which students may anonymously place complaints.
- Capitalize on the resources of the city. Visit businesses, police and fire stations, and hospitals. Many businesses are adopting schools and help provide many resources that would not otherwise be available. Some of these adoptions include scholarships for students through programs such as the "I Have a Dream Foundation." Visit museums and historical landmarks often taken for granted by the residents of a city. A city can be a remarkable learning laboratory. This is also an excellent opportunity for you to work with other teaching colleagues in planning and coordinating visits.
- Enlist community leaders. There are many organizations that are interested in contributing to the education of urban children and youth. Contact the local chapter of the NAACP, the Urban League, YMCA, YWCA, YMHA, YWHA, and neighborhood improvement groups, and invite their leaders to spend time with your students. Find out if there are any projects or programs in which your class might participate. Let your students see and talk to adults who are actively working to improve their city and the prospects of its youth.

Teaching Ourselves to Share the Power

The approaches to managing misbehavior, discussed earlier in the chapter, were presented in a sequence that represents movement along a continuum. The continuum ranges from minimum use of teacher power, such as self-correctional approaches, to maximum use of teacher power, such as assertive discipline. **Teacher power** can be thought of as the extent to which students are given autonomy and control to change their behavior. There is an inverse relationship between teacher power and student control. If a teacher exerts very little power, students are enabled to exert a great deal of control. If, however, a teacher decides that he or she will exercise maximum power to bring about a change in student

teacher power The authority that teachers have available to them to manage student behavior; inversely, the extent to which students control their own behavior.

Try This: Interview teachers to investigate the extent to which they exercise their power to control student behavior. Ask them to describe the techniques they use to address misbehavior. How does the information you gather relate to information in this chapter?

behavior, the student has very little control. The continuum also represents a framework for organizing approaches to managing misbehavior called three faces of discipline (Wolfgang, 1995; Wolfgang & Wolfgang, 1995). The three faces are

- Relationship–Listening
- Confronting–Contracting
- Rules and Consequences

The relationship–listening face represents those approaches to managing misbehavior that employ minimum teacher power. The focus of such approaches is on establishing a positive relationship with students and listening actively in an attempt to understand the problem that caused the misbehavior. The techniques employed by teachers using a relationship–listening approach are typically eye contact and nondirective statements. The self-correcting approach to misbehavior examined earlier is an exemplar of the relationship–listening face.

The confronting–contracting face represents those approaches to misbehavior that require a teacher to exert a moderate amount of power. Moving from a relationship–listening approach to a confronting–contracting approach can be viewed as escalating teacher intervention. According to Wolfgang, the teacher who uses a confronting–contracting approach is saying, in effect, "I am the adult. I know misbehavior when I see it and will confront the student to stop the behavior. I will grant the student the power to decide how he or she will change, and encourage and contract with the student to live up to a mutual agreement for behavioral change" (Wolfgang, 1995, p. 6). Questioning is a typical form of intervention in confronting–contracting approaches. Glasser's control theory is an exemplar of this face.

The applied behavior analysis and the assertive discipline approaches examined earlier represent another escalation of teacher power into the category of rules and consequences. A teacher who uses these types of approaches to misbehavior leaves the student very little control over changing his or her behavior. The teacher's position here is that, "There are rules and behaviors that I desire to see exhibited by students. I will assert my authority and control contingencies in order to bring those behaviors about." Typical interventions in this category include directive statements, altering the environment (as in the case of delivering reinforcements), and demonstrating desired behaviors.

If we use this continuum of teacher power to place (1) the metaphors of management, (2) learning styles, and (3) value orientation in that order, we arrive at a consistent and powerful conclusion. Figure 10.8 shows this continuum.

Recalling the research examined in this chapter, teachers who personify the facilitator metaphor have been found to be more effective classroom managers than teachers who view themselves as boss. Authoritative leaders are better classroom managers than authoritarian leaders. Learning-oriented classrooms are better managed than work-oriented classrooms. And the bottom line is that better managed classrooms produce more student learning.

Perhaps Rick Curwin and Allen Mendler were right in quoting the old adage, "If you want true power, you must give some of it away" (1988, p. 25).

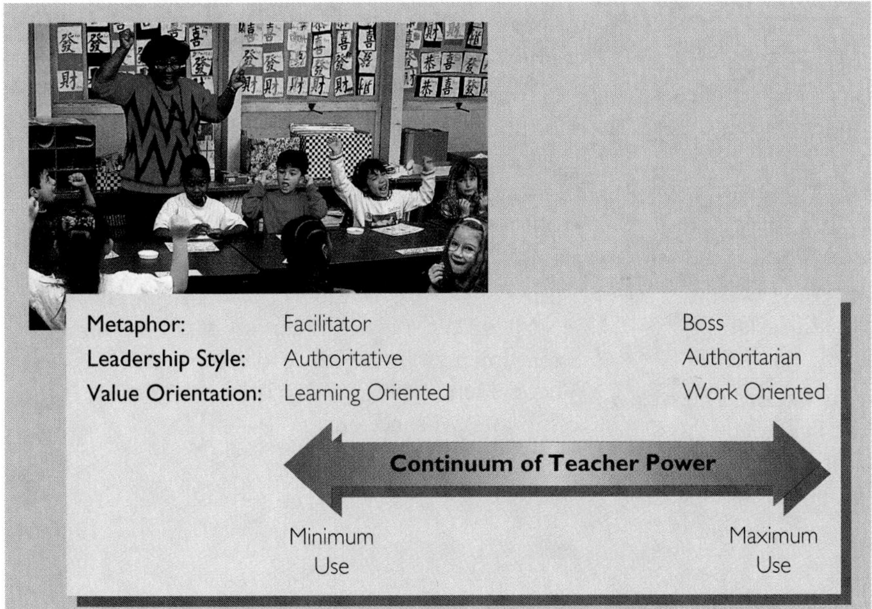

FIGURE 10.8

Metaphors of Management, Leadership Styles, and Value Orientations Placed on a Continuum of Use of Teacher Power

TEACHER Chronicle Conclusion

REFLECTING ON RANDY

Jean Oxford doesn't come up with a solution for working with Randy until the following weekend. Looking at the list again she links his love of reading, his orderliness (the appeal of cleaning up), and his interest in being in charge of things. She has been planning on setting up a class library with all of the books she has collected over the summer. Why not make Randy the class librarian?

Ms. Oxford and Randy discuss the library and his responsibilities. He takes to being librarian like a bear to honey. He gets up whenever his work is finished and checks in returned books. He has a valid context for washing his hands. He is "in charge" in a positive way, making sure that books are checked out properly. He straightens the books and organizes them by title.

Over time, Randy's behaviors change; the frequency of his interruptions decreases, his interaction with his peers improves, and although his confrontations with Ms. Oxford do not disappear entirely, they do diminish significantly. The overall atmosphere of the room improves. And Ms. Oxford no longer feels like a broken record repeating "Randy" over and over again.

APPLICATION QUESTIONS:

1. Why did Ms. Oxford's idea to make Randy the class librarian work? Would such an approach work with a middle school student? High school? Why or why not?
2. Write a pre-librarian conversation between Ms. Oxford and Randy. Write a post-librarian conversation. In what ways do the conversations differ? What about conversations with peers before and after the librarian assignment? How might they be different?
3. Imagine that the students in Ms. Oxford's class kept interactive journals. Write five brief entries for Randy. Write five entries for a fellow student. Write Ms. Oxford's responses to both.
4. Draw a map of Ms. Oxford's second-grade room as you imagine it to be. Draw a map of a middle school classroom. A high school classroom. How do your maps differ? Why?
5. How might an art teacher manage Randy's behavior? A lab-based science teacher? A gym teacher? Assume that all three teachers possess withitness skills.
6. Where would you place Ms. Oxford on the continuum of use of teacher power? What are her values? What is her metaphor of classroom management? What is her leadership style? What evidence and characteristics can you cite to support your inferences?

CHAPTER SUMMARY

WHAT IS CLASSROOM MANAGEMENT AND LEADERSHIP?

Research has shown that the way teachers think about classroom management influences their management practices. Various metaphors of management are discussed along with their implications. Management is viewed as a process whose product is discipline. Management and discipline are related to another product–process pair, instruction and learning. Effective classroom managers are authoritative leaders.

HOW CAN YOU CREATE A LEARNING-ORIENTED ENVIRONMENT?

A learning-oriented classroom is one in which assignments and other instructional activities are viewed as a means to learning outcomes, not outcomes in their own right. The contributions of the physical arrangement of the classroom and classroom rules and procedures to a positive, learning-oriented environment are described.

HOW CAN INSTRUCTION BE MANAGED TO SUPPORT A LEARNING-ORIENTED ENVIRONMENT?

Instructional management skills enable a teacher to keep students focused and actively involved in learning tasks. These skills include giving clear instructions, gaining attention, maintaining attention, pacing, summarizing, and making smooth transitions.

HOW CAN MISBEHAVIOR BE ADDRESSED AND THE LEARNING ORIENTATION RESTORED?

Misbehavior is behavior by one or more students that disrupts or competes with the primary activity of learning. Several approaches for addressing misbehavior are presented. The approaches differ in terms of the amount of teacher intervention or the use of teacher power required by each approach. Self-correctional and control approaches use less teacher power than applied behavior analysis approaches.

HOW CAN YOUR KNOWLEDGE OF CLASSROOM MANAGEMENT HELP YOU BECOME AN EFFECTIVE TEACHER?

The theories and research on classroom management are interpreted in light of teaching students self-responsibility. The cultural norms of various groups influence the nature of communication and interaction. These potential differences need to be accounted for so that rules and consequences will be understood clearly and applied fairly. Ideas for managing an urban classroom are discussed. The chapter ends by analyzing the continuum of teacher power in relation to management metaphors, value orientations, and leadership style.

KEY CONCEPTS

action zones
affordances
applied behavior analysis
assertive discipline
authoritative leadership
classroom management
control theory
discipline
I-message
instruction
learning-oriented classrooms
misbehavior
on-task behavior
overlapping
procedures
rules
teacher power
withitness
work-oriented classrooms

PART V

Teachers and students are both learners

Teaching and learning are part of the same process, and both involve the same principles of educational psychology. In using the knowledge base and classroom practice to develop a theory of teaching and to build teaching expertise, you are a learner. Planning, orchestrating, and delivering curriculum and instruction are among the key skills teachers learn.

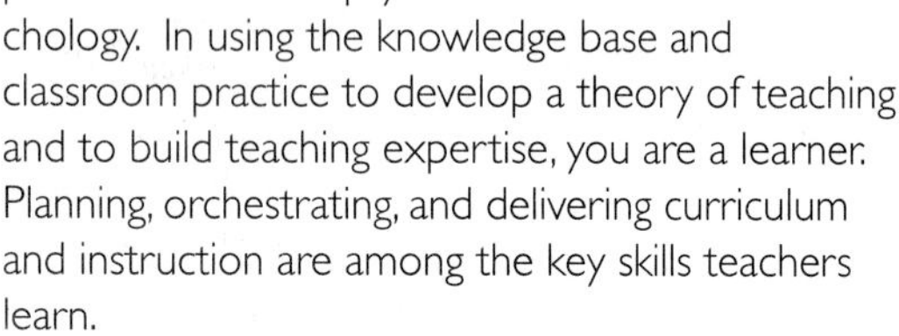

Overview of Chapter 11

A significant part of a teacher's role is planning instruction. In this chapter, we examine how teachers plan—from the decisions they make about what students should learn to the activities they include in an instructional lesson.

We begin the chapter with a look at the learning outcomes teachers desire for their students. Outcomes are considered across the cognitive, affective, and psychomotor domains and in terms of Gagné's learned capabilities. We examine next how general instructional goals can be further specified as performance objectives to facilitate planning the instructional events that will best support students' learning. Discovery and reception learning are discussed, along with how lessons can be structured to promote transfer of learning. The chapter concludes with a systematic model of effective instruction that you can use to plan instruction.

Overview of Chapter 12

Active learning occurs when students are interested in what they are learning and in how they are learning it. As you will see, there are a variety of instructional approaches that can facilitate active learning by your students. Some of those approaches center on you, the teacher. Other approaches give you the role of "guide on the side" rather than "sage on the stage." The instructional techniques presented in Teaching for Active Learning will not require you to make a choice but will allow you to build a repertoire of teaching behaviors suitable for a variety of learning situations.

Effective Instruction

Teachers coordinate the context for learning

Learning is active and situated; that is, students learn by acting, reflecting, and interacting in specific situations. By coordinating a variety of grouping strategies, learning tasks or opportunities, and instructional models, teachers create the contexts in which learning can take place through active construction.

Instructional technologies support teaching and learning

In this Information Age, computer, telecommunications, and multimedia technologies have transformed the modern way of life. These technologies have become vital tools in education at all grade levels for instruction as well as for record keeping and planning. Communications networks link the classroom to the home, community, university, government, mass media, and the world, transforming the teaching–learning process.

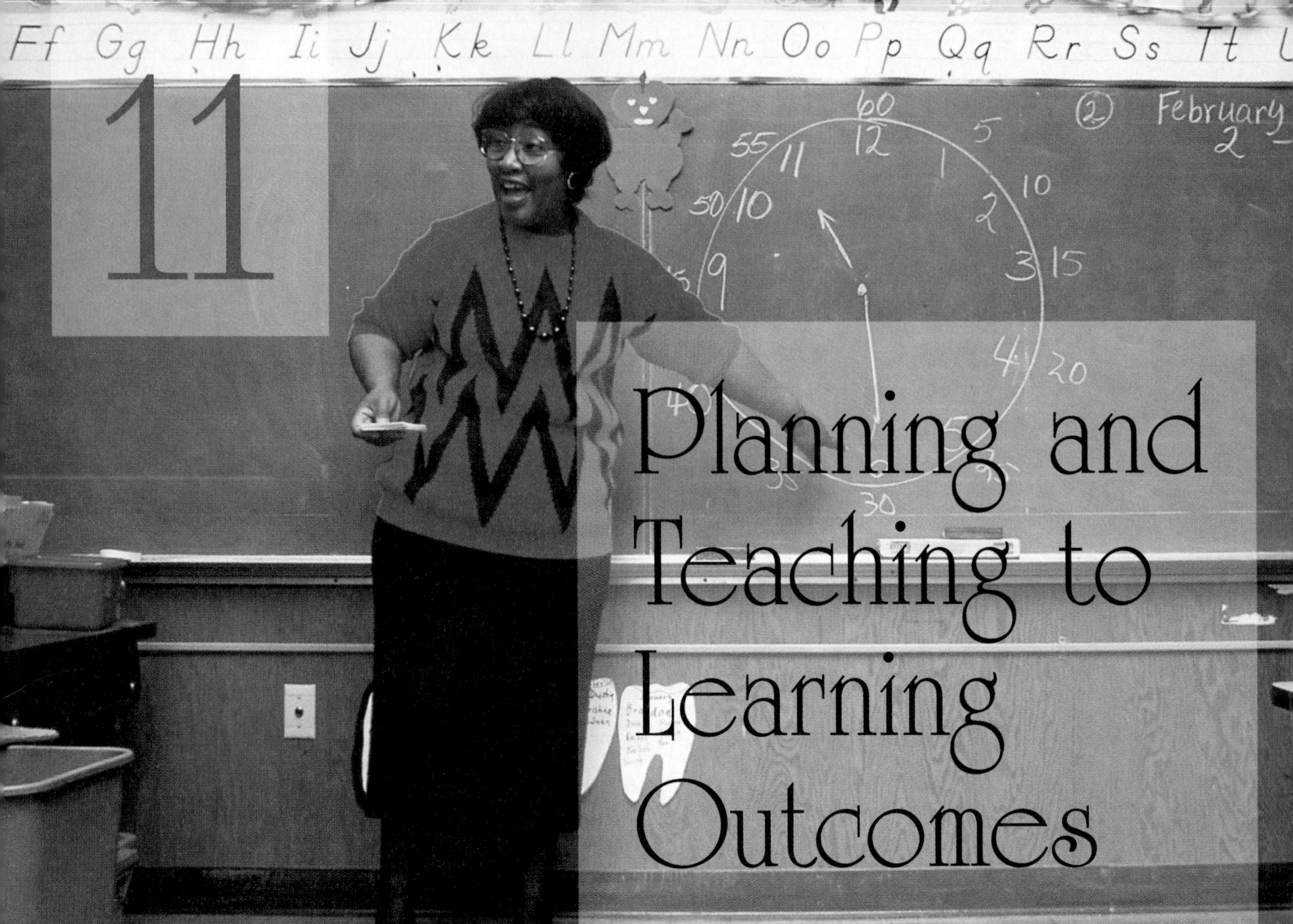

11 Planning and Teaching to Learning Outcomes

CHAPTER OUTLINE

TEACHER Chronicle

WORD POWER

Antoine Azzi is a mentor teacher at P.S. 195. One of his responsibilities (besides teaching his twelfth-grade English classes) is to help beginning teachers and student teachers. This afternoon he is reading Irving Barne's student teaching journal. Irving is pursuing his secondary certification. Antoine opens Irving's journal to a page entitled "Classroom Observations."

"My first observation was in Mr. Blandworth's class, Word Power," Irving wrote. "The class is in its fourth week. I was immediately puzzled by how the students took their seats, filling them from the back right corner toward the front left center. By the end of the class it became clear why the students sat the way they did. I will describe only one class because, although the characters changed, the scenario remained the same, day in and day out.

"The first thing Mr. Blandworth did was to arrange his teaching materials as the students opened their workbooks (all to the same page). He began the class the same way every day, saying, 'Yesterday, we completed the words on page 36. Your homework for today was page 37.' He turned to the student seated at the first desk in the far left corner of the room and said, 'Tania, please begin.'

"Tania began reciting. She pronounced the first word on the workbook page, gave its definition, and described its etymology. When she had finished, Mr. Blandworth said, 'OK, very good. Any questions? No? Carlos, you're next. Carlos repeated the same drill. As Carlos recited, I watched the other students. Most of them were counting those seated in front of them. After completing their counting, they worked furiously in their dictionaries and workbooks.

"The recitations proceeded in order down the first row and through the second and third rows. After a student completed his or her recitation, Mr. Blandworth asked if there were any questions. There never were, as the students were all too busy writing in their workbooks. Mr. Blandworth sat behind his desk, his eyes glued to his materials. As a student recited, other students completed the blank entries in their workbooks by writing down what their fellow students recited. I suddenly realized that most of the students had come to class without doing their homework. 'Next,' repeated Mr. Blandworth.

"A student closed her dictionary and announced her word, *Impropriety*. The student next to her began desperately counting the words on her page and flipping through her dictionary.

"Mr. Blandworth said, 'OK, any questions? Good. Next.' Several seconds went by before Mr. Blandworth looked up and said, 'Who's next?'

"The panicked student raised her hand and said, 'I am.' 'OK, Karen. Let's keep going,' Mr. Blandworth said. 'We have to get through the rest of this list by the end of the period.' Karen cleared her throat and said, 'Creepy dee chine.' Mr. Blandworth looked hard at her and said, 'You obviously didn't complete your homework, did you?'

"'Not all of it,' Karen replied. 'I did everything except for numbers 26 through 33.'

"'That's not good enough, Karen,' Mr. Blandworth said. 'I'll record that as an F for the day unless you turn in a thousand-word essay using every word on the list by next Tuesday. Next.'

"The routine repeated itself until all the words were done. Mr. Blandworth's wristwatch alarm rang. He said, 'It's important for you to do your work every day. That's how you build a vocabulary. Tomorrow we'll do page 38. That will be all for today.' Seconds later the bell rang and the students filed out.

"The next class was a repeat of the first and so on all week. There is not much else to write down about this boring class. The students have figured out the pattern and it is only when they miscount that anything happens. I am glad I have finished observing Mr. Blandworth and can go on to another class. I sure hope Ms. Estefan's class will be better. It certainly can't be any worse. I hope I'll never be a Blandworth!" Antoine picks up a pencil and writes in Irving's journal, "Irving, I don't think you will be!"

FOCUS QUESTIONS

1. What outcomes are being achieved in Mr. Blandworth's class? What outcomes may he have intended for students to achieve?
2. How do the conditions of instruction influence the outcomes of learning?
3. What are important variables in effective teaching practice?
4. What are different ways of organizing a lesson to facilitate different kinds of learning outcomes?
5. How can one instance of learning help or hinder another instance of learning?
6. How effective is Mr. Blandworth's instruction likely to be?

WHAT ARE POSSIBLE OUTCOMES OF LEARNING?

What are students supposed to learn in school? What *can* they learn? How do teachers determine and specify what their students ought to learn in their classes? These questions concern learning outcomes that teachers use as a basis for planning their instruction. In making decisions about what students should learn, teachers consider the knowledge, skills, and attitudes that can be acquired in a given subject area.

Think about some of the things you've learned in your career as a student. You probably know certain facts, such as the names of U.S. presidents or the capital cities of countries around the world. You probably know how to calculate your grade point average and how to write a research paper. You may be aware that you learn best by visualizing information or viewing diagrams of concept relationships. You may drive a car competently but prefer to ride your bicycle to school. These are all capabilities you have acquired over the years.

Instructional theorists have found it useful to distinguish among the variety of things people can learn (Driscoll, 1994). In doing this, they make a fundamental assumption that learning proceeds differently depending on what outcome or capability students are acquiring. For example, learning how to throw a softball underhand requires very different instruction than learning how to spell.

Likewise, learning to appreciate jazz requires different learning conditions from learning to recite one's part in a school play.

There are different ways to characterize what students can learn, but the result is usually a *taxonomy*, or classification system, of learning outcomes.

Gagné's Taxonomy of Learning Outcomes

Try This: Examine textbooks and accompanying teachers' materials in the content areas you plan to teach, and identify prescribed learning outcomes. Which categories of Gagné's taxonomy do they exemplify?

Robert M. Gagné viewed learning as accounting for all of the attitudes, values, skills, and knowledge acquired by human beings. When people learn, they become capable of a variety of performances (Gagné, 1977, 1985; Gagné & Driscoll, 1988; Driscoll, 1994). According to Gagné, there are five types of learned capabilities, or **learning outcomes**:

1. Verbal information
2. Intellectual skills
3. Cognitive strategies
4. Attitudes
5. Motor skills

Although we examine each type of learning outcome separately, it is important to keep in mind that most instructional goals include several types of outcomes.

Verbal Information. Verbal information is one capability that makes communication possible. When a student states that Herman Melville wrote *Moby Dick*, he or she is declaring some knowledge. The declaration provides evidence that the student has acquired some verbal information. Being able to make declarations about the environment enables us to communicate. For example, a young child begins asking questions about his or her environment in order to communicate about the environment. The endless chain of questions that parents often hear is the child's search for verbal information.

Critical Thinking: What are examples of verbal information outcomes in the content area you expect to teach?

"What's that, Daddy?"
"A tree."
"Mommy, what's that?"
"A car."
"What's that?"
"An airplane."
"What's that?"
"A giraffe."

Acquiring verbal information enables the child to communicate. Gagné and Driscoll (1988) identified names, facts, principles, and generalizations as units of verbal information. A child may be able to state that the name of the household cat is Meatball. A student may be able to state that the capital of Missouri is Jefferson City, that chefs prepare food in restaurants, or that the Pythagorean theorem is *a* squared plus *b* squared equals *c* squared. Mr. Blandworth's students in the Teacher Chronicle may be able to state the definitions of vocabulary words. But, just because a student is able to make a particular statement of fact does not mean that he or she fully understands the implications of the statement. For example, because students can state the Pythagorean theorem does not mean they can use it to solve problems involving right triangles.

learning outcomes According to Gagné, capabilities acquired by students resulting from the interaction of internal and external conditions of learning.

verbal information A learning outcome that enables learners to communicate about objects, events, or relations; declarative knowledge.

By its nature the learning outcome that we call verbal information allows us to make statements. The acquisition of verbal information serves other functions for the learner as well. One function of verbal information is that it provides labels that allow us to operate in everyday situations. Preschool students are often quizzed on their home addresses and on emergency phone numbers. Children might be taught that they should wait by an elevator if they become lost while shopping with their parents. In Great Britain, a child would be advised to wait next to the lift. The terms are different but they both serve the function of labels.

Verbal information also serves as a basis for thinking or as a vehicle for thought (Gagné & Driscoll, 1988). For example, because a mechanic possesses verbal information about car engines, he or she is able to hypothesize about the causes of various engine problems. The ability to hypothesize is evidence of another kind of learning outcome, intellectual skill.

Connection: How does Gagné's distinction between verbal information and intellectual skills relate to declarative versus procedural knowledge as discussed in Chapter 7?

Intellectual Skills. Whereas verbal information refers to knowing "what," intellectual skill refers to knowing "how." **Intellectual skills** include making discriminations, identifying and classifying concepts, and applying and generating rules. When we state that "*a* squared plus *b* squared equals *c* squared," we express verbal information. If we can use the formula to derive the length of one side of a right triangle when the length of two sides are given, we show intellectual skill.

Connection: Relate the concept of discrimination to the discussion of relevance in modeling (Chapter 8) and in using the ARCS model (Chapter 9).

Intellectual skills are not necessarily more complex than verbal information, just different. Table 11.1 shows how intellectual skills can be ordered in terms of complexity, from simpler to more complex skills.

The simplest kind of intellectual skill is the knowledge of how to make discriminations. **Discrimination** is the ability to distinguish between two or more environmental stimuli. Detecting a difference in shapes, for example, enables a preschool child to put the round block in the round hole and the triangle block in the triangular hole. Similarly, an inability to detect differences in color would make it difficult for a student to tell whether the litmus paper had changed color in testing for acids and bases.

Critical Thinking: Explain the difference between verbal information and intellectual skills in terms of the possibility of discriminating between types of rocks without knowing their geologic labels.

The capability to discriminate requires experience. A baby may learn that the red object rolls and the yellow object rattles. The baby may also learn that the white cylindrical object yields milk but the blue cylindrical object, mother's

Table 11.1 Categories of Intellectual Skills

Intellectual Skill	Example of Performance Based on the Capability
Discrimination	Distinguishing printed *p*'s from *q*'s
Concrete concept	Identifying the spatial relation *below*
Defined concept	Classifying a city by using a definition
Rule	Applying the rule for finding the area of a triangle to specific examples
Higher-order rule	Generating a rule for predicting rainfall in a particular location

Source: From *Essentials of Learning for Instruction* (p. 61) by R. M. Gagné and M. P. Driscoll, 1988, Englewood Cliffs, NJ: Prentice-Hall. Copyright ©1988 by Allyn & Bacon. Reprinted by permission.

intellectual skills According to Gagné, learned capabilities that enable learners to make discriminations, identify and classify concepts, and apply and generate rules; procedural knowledge.

discrimination Distinguishing between and responding differently to two or more stimuli.

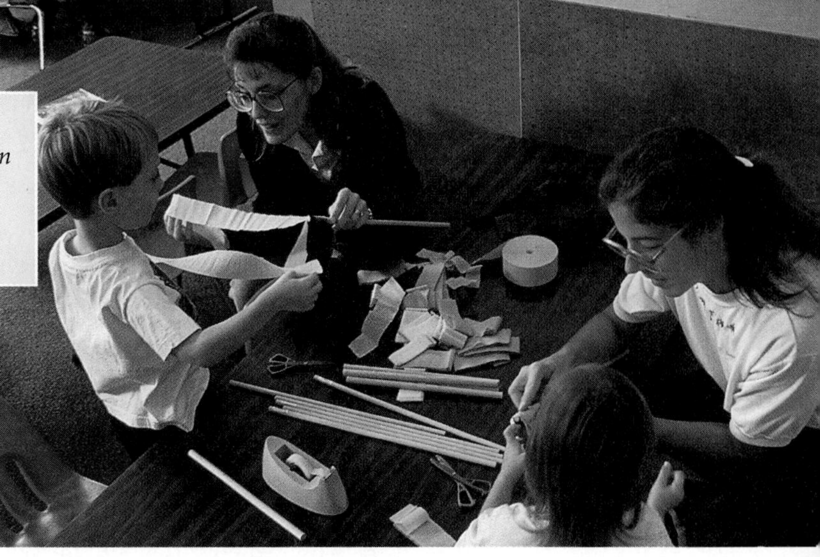

According to Gagné's theory, what types of capabilities might these children be learning in this situation? What other learning outcomes do children achieve as they become more capable of more complex thinking?

antique vase, is not to be touched. As children enter school, they are still acquiring the ability to discriminate. In school, a great deal of their discrimination learning revolves around symbols. Children must learn to discriminate between the letter *T* and the letter *F*, and between the numeral 5 and the numeral 3. As children proceed through school, the discriminations they are required to make become finer and finer. Consider the junior high school student who learns the difference between the pronunciation of the French *R* and the English *R*.

Connection: How does Gagné's theory resemble Piaget's theory of cognitive development in Chapter 2?

After the child has developed the skill to determine that horses, cows, sheep, and dogs are all different from one another, the child is ready then to learn what these animals are. **Concrete concepts** refer to objects, events, and relations that can be observed or experienced.

Dog is a concrete concept. It is an object, something that can be pointed to in the environment. Humans acquire concrete concepts by making appropriate discriminations in a number of instances—in this case, acquiring knowledge of the critical features that make an animal a dog but not a horse. If you consider the wide range of features included in the concept *dog*, you can see that although the concept may be concrete, it is not necessarily simple. For example, a Chihuahua and the Newfoundland are both instances of the concept *dog*.

Concrete concepts are not only objects or classes of object features; they can also be events. A student may learn, for example, that one sound is produced by a violin and a different quality of sound is produced by a piano. A child will also learn the critical features that distinguish parades from the lines of people entering a ride at Disney World.

Critical Thinking: What is the importance of defined concepts in generating plans or theories? How might defined concepts contribute to your theory of teaching?

Concrete concepts include the spatial relations among objects. Take, for example, the concepts of above and below. A child will learn through experience that the red light is above the green light on a traffic signal. Other relational concrete concepts include the concepts of up, down, higher, lower, near, and far. The successful acquisition of concrete concepts allows students to identify entire classes of objects, events, or relations and point them out in the environment. Keep in mind the difference between the outcome of verbal information and that of intellectual skill. Just because a student can point out an example of a concept in his or her environment does not mean he or she is able to name the concept. In order to communicate about the concept, some verbal information is necessary.

concrete concepts Abstractions based on objects, events, people, and relations that can be observed.

defined concepts Abstractions that cannot be observed in the environment but must be defined (e.g., liberty).

Among the many concepts that we expect our students to acquire or construct are **defined concepts**—concepts that cannot be pointed out in the environment the way that concrete concepts can and, thus, must be defined. Take as an example the concept *information*. There are many instances of information in our environment and many sources of information as well, but information itself is not a concrete object, event, or relation.

Students who understand defined concepts are able to use them in an abstract fashion. The student cannot point to liberty in the environment. However, the student can learn to use the notion of liberty to discuss the Constitution.

Concrete concepts can acquire the properties of defined concepts. A child who first learns the concept *dog* by seeing concrete instances in the environment may later become capable of defining the concept in abstract terms. The student who can classify a dog as a quadrupedal mammal with a carnivorous diet has provided a kind of definition for the concept *dog*. Once a student understands a defined concept, it is not necessarily the case that the student no longer uses his or her concrete concept. In many instances, learners store in memory both a concrete and a defined concept.

Next in order of complexity is an intellectual skill called **rules**. Normally, we think of a rule as a verbal statement such as "*i* before *e* except after *c*." As a learned capability, this rule allows us to spell correctly the word *receive*. Rules allow learners to use symbols. Typically, the symbols used in school are linguistic and mathematical. There are other symbols that operate in a classroom, however. For example, consider the signals that a teacher's body language or facial expressions provide. Students learn these symbols because they have acquired or constructed rules.

Reflection: Think of examples from your own experience of each type of intellectual skill.

Students learn the rules of grammar, the rules of decoding words, the rules of algebraic manipulation, and the rules of verb conjugation. A learner who understands rules is able to interact with his or her environment in generalized ways. In a classroom, for example, a student may be told that his or her name should appear always in the upper right-hand corner of the paper. As a type of intellectual skill, the rule-governed behavior is the student's ability to remember to put his or her name in the upper right-hand corner of all papers.

Connection: In the information-processing model (Chapter 7), cognitive strategies are represented by the executive control function. As students acquire the various capabilities discussed in this chapter, they become more adept at regulating the cognitive processes by which they attend, encode, and retrieve information, and solve problems.

Students with an understanding of concrete and defined concepts can, as a result, acquire or construct rules, allowing them to respond to a class of events. Thus, knowing Strunk and White's (1979) rule that "a participial phrase at the beginning of a sentence must refer to the grammatical subject" saves us from writing an incorrect sentence such as: "Being in a dilapidated condition, I was able to buy the house very cheap" (p. 14). Knowing the rule also helps us to respond to sentences that we read and that we have never seen before.

The most complex type of intellectual skill is called higher-order rules. **Higher-order rules** are formed by combining two or more rules, which allows a student to solve problems. In the case of mathematics, the application of higher-order rules is easily seen. For example, in order to calculate an average of a set of numbers, students must use rules of addition (add the set of numbers to find their sum), counting (count the numbers to determine how many there are), and simple division (divide the sum by the count). After practicing on many such problems, students apply the individual rules in an algorithmic fashion as part of a single, higher-order rule (add the numbers to find the sum, count how many numbers there are, and divide the sum by the count). Through this process, they have generated a higher-order rule. Students solve problems in other content areas as well by generating higher-order rules (Gagné & Driscoll, 1988). When a student attempts to apply the economic principle of supply and demand, he or she is generating a higher-order rule.

rules The ways phenomena work. As a learned capability, rules enable learners to use symbols.

higher-order rules Rules formed by combining two or more rules, thus allowing students to solve problems.

cognitive strategies A learned capability that enables learners to organize and regulate their own internal processes.

In summary, intellectual skills vary in complexity and can be ordered according to that complexity. Learning simple intellectual skills, such as discrimination, allows the learner to acquire more complex capabilities, such as concepts.

Cognitive Strategies. Another type of learning outcome, other than verbal information and intellectual skills, is cognitive strategies. Gagné uses the term **cognitive strategies** to identify the capability to internally organize skills that regulate and monitor the use of concepts and rules (Gagné, 1985). Gagné (1985, p. 138) stated that

> [I]n other words, they learn *how* to learn, *how* to remember, and *how* to carry out the reflective and analytic thought that leads to more learning. It is apparent as individuals continue to learn that they become increasingly capable of *self-instruction* or even what may be called *independent learning*. This is because learners acquire increasingly effective strategies to regulate their own internal processes. This new function of control over internal cognitive processes is what distinguishes [cognitive strategies] from the intellectual skills. [emphasis in original]

Cognitive strategies serve a metacognitive function; they enable students to organize and monitor their cognitive processes, such as perception, encoding, and retrieval. For example, a high school student who is facing a unit test on John Steinbeck's work may develop a cognitive strategy in order to study effectively for the exam. The student determines as precisely as possible what is expected and then adopts the following approach:

1. Review the vocabulary list handed out at the beginning of the unit.
2. Reread the synopsis written as one of the assignments in the unit.
3. Answer the textbook discussion questions at the end of each of Steinbeck's stories.
4. Reread part or all of a particular Steinbeck story to find or develop answers as needed.

There is a distinction between *problem solving* and *problem finding* (Bruner, 1971). The student who is preparing for the unit exam on John Steinbeck may be presented with several problems. One problem may be to compare and contrast the symbolism in *The Red Pony* with the symbolism in *Cannery Row*. While looking for similarities and differences between the use of symbols in the two stories, the student may discover something about Steinbeck's use of dialogue that opens up a new line of analysis. In this way, the student has found a new problem; that is, the problem was not assigned by the teacher but was generated by the learner using cognitive processes.

Pressley, Borkowski, and O'Sullivan (1984) recommend that more attention be given to metacognition or the learner's awareness of his or her thinking process. Metacognitive awareness seems to play a critical role in the learner's ability to develop self-instruction skills and skillfully transfer learning strategies. According to Derry and Murphy (1986), educators should take a two-part approach to teaching learning strategies. First, they should devote the beginning of each school year to training learning skills. Second, they should embed cognitive strategies in the curriculum and apply them across the content areas.

Brown (1988) investigated whether preschool children can learn a principle on the basis of one or two examples, and, if so, whether or not the ability to abstract a principle was affected by the ability to explain why a concept is an instance of a rule. The results indicated that preschool children are able to form mind-sets that aid them in looking for analogous solutions to problems. The effect was both rapid and quite dramatic. The results indicated that the effect was facilitated by the elaborations and explanations the students were asked to make. The conclusion is that reflection about one's cognitive activity is important. Metacognition plays a role.

Attitudes. An **attitude** is a personal feeling or belief that influences a student's tendency to act in a particular way (Gagné, 1985; Gagné & Driscoll,

Reflection: Identify a unit or lesson you expect to teach. What intellectual skills will students need to acquire in order to master the topic? What cognitive strategies do you think are important for the students to learn? How would you facilitate the development of cognitive strategies while teaching this unit?

Connection: Metacognition is discussed in detail in Chapter 7.

Critical Thinking: Would asking students to describe how they read help them develop cognitive strategies?

attitude According to Gagné, a learned capability that influences a person's choice of personal action.

1988; Dick & Reiser, 1989; Driscoll, 1994). We acquire attitudes toward any number of things. For example, a student may acquire an attitude toward teachers that influences his or her behavior toward them.

Connetion: Cultural beliefs and values of students are discussed in Chapter 4. How these affect motivation is discussed in Chapter 9.

Students acquire attitudes that influence other social behavior. Often such attitudes are instilled at an early age, and, in many cases, they are learned at home. For example, a student may have acquired an attitude toward people of a different religion or race. This attitude influences the student's behavior toward people who are perceived as different.

Try This: Interview teachers regarding how they determine student attitudes. What attitudes do they hope to facilitate in their instruction?

In general, attitudes affect the choices that a learner makes. The learner who comes to class on time with the materials needed for the day's lesson is exhibiting an attitude. The simple observation of one action, however, does not provide sufficient information to judge whether a student has acquired a particular attitude. Teachers look for consistent actions over time as evidence that a student has a positive attitude toward school, for example. Examples of attitudes teachers often hope to instill in students include courtesy toward other students and a desire to do one's best. Attitudes related to social issues, such as making a decision to recycle waste, are also targeted as desirable goals by teachers.

Motor Skills. The final type of learning outcome that Gagné discusses is motor skills. **Motor skills** are physical capabilities that require muscle control and hand-eye coordination, such as the ability to ride a bike or use a computer keyboard. Motor skills, such as riding a bike, also involve cognitive and affective outcomes. You have a cognitive representation of riding a bicycle and feelings or attitudes about bike riding. Similarly, executing a pas de deux in *Swan Lake* involves motor, cognitive, and affective capabilities.

Try This: Examine a curriculum guide for your district or state. What learning outcomes in the cognitive, affective, and psychomotor domains do they prescribe?

Bloom's Taxonomy for the Cognitive Domain

Benjamin Bloom, a contemporary of Gagné, conceived of learning outcomes in a somewhat different way. Instead of considering cognitive, affective, and psychomotor domains of learning within the same taxonomy, Bloom developed a taxonomy for the **cognitive domain** alone that has been widely applied in curriculum guides (Bloom, Englehart, Furst, Hill, & Krathwohl, 1956).

Bloom's taxonomy consists of six levels, progressing from simple to complex. The examples given at each level specify a behavior a student might be asked to perform.

Level 1: Knowledge—the recall of specific facts, methods and processes, patterns and structures. The focus of these outcomes is remembering. For example, being able to list the four basic food groups is a knowledge outcome.

Level 2: Comprehension—the first level of understanding. At this level, the learner can know what is being communicated and make use of the idea appropriately. For example, a student may be able to distinguish between nouns, verbs, and other parts of speech.

Level 3: Application—ability to use information in new situations. The information can be general ideas, rules, methods, principles, or theories that must be remembered and then applied. For example, students demonstrate application when they use the appropriate formula to solve an equation.

Level 4: Analysis—ability to identify elements embedded in a whole and recognize relations among elements. For example, students might analyze elements of a character, setting, and plot in a story.

motor skills According to Gagné, learned capabilities relating to movement or to muscles that induce movement, such as the ability to ride a bicycle or to operate a computer.

cognitive domain Learning outcomes that relate to memory, understanding, and reasoning.

Bloom's taxonomy Bloom's classification of behavior in the cognitive domain. From simplest to complex, it consists of knowledge, comprehension, application, analysis, synthesis, and evaluation.

Level 5: Synthesis—ability to put elements together to form a new whole. For example, when students design a scientific experiment, draft an essay, or choreograph a dance, they are performing synthesis.

Level 6: Evaluation—judgments based on criteria of value or worth. For example, a student might use the four principles of music appreciation to evaluate Beethoven's Fifth Symphony or use criteria for judging the effectiveness of an argument.

The level of the cognitive taxonomy identifies the level of complexity. The higher the taxonomic level, the more complex the learning involved.

Bloom's taxonomy can be used to plan instruction based on learning outcomes. For example, in the cognitive domain, the teacher decides whether students should know, comprehend, apply, synthesize, or evaluate. The teacher states these decisions as performance objectives—what students will know and be able to do. Table 11.2 shows the words teachers use to identify what students might be expected to do for each level of the cognitive domain (Tuckman, 1988). As the following sections illustrate, we can also specify performance objectives for the affective and psychomotor domains of learning. Later sections discuss how to construct performance objectives.

Try This: Using Bloom's taxonomy, set goals for the intellectual skills and cognitive strategies for a lesson or unit you plan to teach. Using the affective and, if appropriate, the psychomotor taxonomy, specify other goals you would like to see students attain during instruction.

Krathwohl's Taxonomy for the Affective Domain

The five levels in Krathwohl's affective taxonomy represent a progression of capabilities leading to learning outcomes in the **affective domain**—changes in attitudes and emotional responses (Krathwohl, Bloom, & Masia, 1964).

Level 1: Receiving or Attending—Receiving or attending involve the learner's becoming sensitive to or aware of certain stimuli. These outcomes include a willingness to receive or selectively respond to experiences. An example would be a willingness to listen to a guest speaker.

Level 2: Responding—Responding refers to the learner's motivation to learn. The category includes a willingness to respond and the ability to find satisfaction in responding. For example, students in a computer lab willingly adhere to posted rules for using equipment.

Level 3: Valuing—Valuing is evident when the learner expresses a value or shows that a behavior has worth. The category includes acceptance of a value, preference for a value, and commitment to a value. An example is a student who,

Table 11.2 A Selected List of Verbs for Writing Cognitive Objectives

Knowledge	define/ describe/ identify/ label/ list
Comprehension	convert/ defend/ distinguish/ estimate/ explain
Application	change/ compute/ demonstrate/ discover/ manipulate
Analysis	diagram/ differentiate/ discriminate/ distinguish/ identify
Synthesis	categorize/ combine/ compile/ compose/ create
Evaluation	appraise/ compare/ conclude/ criticize/ describe

Source: From *Testing for Teachers* (2nd ed., p. 17) by B. W. Tuckman, 1988, Orlando, FL: Harcourt Brace Jovanovich. Copyright @1988 by Harcourt Brace Jovanovich. Reprinted by permission.

affective domain Learning outcomes that relate to emotions, values, and attitudes, as classified by Krathwohl's taxonomy.

because of a committed belief, chooses to participate in an environmental conservation project.

Level 4: Organizing—Through organization individuals develop a value system. As ideas, opinions, and beliefs become internalized, the learner gives some of them priority over others and in the process conceptualizes values and organizes a value system.

Level 5: Characterization—At the level of characterization, an individual's behavior consistently reflects the values that he or she has organized into some kind of system. Learners at this level practice what they preach and believe deeply in these values.

Reflection: From personal experience, list one example for each level in each of the three domains of learning.

Harrow's Taxonomy for the Psychomotor Domain

Harrow (1972) proposed a taxonomy of outcomes for the **psychomotor domain**. This taxonomy, which includes six levels of performance, can be used to specify psychomotor outcomes in areas of physical education, dance, art, theater, and motor development therapies for students with disabilities (Table 11.3). Psychomotor outcomes are also evident in many other subjects. In science, for example, well-developed hand and eye coordination is required to operate laboratory equipment. Positioning a mouse on a microcomputer to insert the cursor at a particular point on the screen is another example of a psychomotor outcome.

psychomotor domain Learning outcomes that relate to skilled physical movements, as classified by Harrow's taxonomy.

Thinking in the Content Areas

Acquiring various learning outcomes as they are defined in taxonomies does not guarantee that students will use these skills and knowledge. In fact, criticism of education often centers on the fact that students do *not* routinely use the knowledge and skills they learn in school (Brown, Collins, & Duguid, 1989). According to some researchers, one reason for the problem of inert knowledge is that most instruction occurs at the content level and rarely focuses on the cultural level (Tishman, Perkins, & Jay, 1995). Thus, students learn facts, principles, and basic problem-solving skills within a discipline but do not learn what it means to participate in the culture of a discipline—that is, to do what historians do or to think like a mathematician. This participation requires thinking skills and dispositions that are situated and acquired within the cultural context of a subject matter discipline.

How might you plan for this learning outcome and the events leading up to it using the taxonomies for the cognitive, affective, and psychomotor domains?

Table 11.3 Harrow's Taxonomy for the Psychomotor Domain

Level 1:	Reflex movements—involuntary movements present at birth or developed during maturation *Example:* grasping reflex in infants
Level 2:	Basic movements—fundamental movements as components of more complex actions *Example:* movement of the hand to hold a pencil
Level 3:	Perceptual abilities—the brain's ability to receive sensory stimuli and transmit motor messages to appropriate muscle groups *Example:* perception of properties of a writing surface
Level 4:	Physical abilities—characteristics of a person that, depending on development, permit efficient movement *Example:* ability to write persistently
Level 5:	Skilled movements—simple and complex that are learned *Examples:* forming cursive letters; learning to use a word processor
Level 6:	Nondiscursive communication—nonverbal communication *Examples:* expression through gestures, facial expressions, mime, or dance

According to Tishman et al. (1995, pp. 2–3), there are six **dimensions of good thinking**:

1. *A language of thinking*—the language used by teachers and students in the classroom to talk about thinking and to encourage high-level thinking. For example, students in social studies might use such thinking words as *claim*, *evidence*, *research*, and *justify* in discussing the issue of park rules in the national park system.
2. *Thinking dispositions*—habits of mind regarding thinking, such as the disposition to look beyond what's given, to explore alternative points of view, and to remain alert to possible error. Students demonstrate a thinking disposition when they ask a lot of questions about a story they have read, questions that lead them to explore new concepts.
3. *Mental management*—thinking about and controlling one's thinking processes. Science students exhibit mental management when they plan a strategy for conducting an experiment that builds on their individual strengths and assures completion of the investigation in the time allotted.
4. *The strategic spirit*—the attitude of responding to learning challenges with appropriate thinking strategies. For example, given the assignment to select a topic for an independent project, a student plans how to search for a good idea by stating a goal, brainstorming ideas, and thinking about the pros and cons of a few of the most interesting ideas.
5. *Higher-order knowledge*—the ways of solving problems, using evidence, and making inquiries that are specific to a subject area. For example, students in English class explore possible interpretations of a poem by considering the evidence supporting each interpretation.
6. *Transfer*—the application of knowledge and strategies from one context to another and the exploration of how different areas of knowledge connect to one another. For example, students learning about important historical developments come to understand the significance of literary characters' decisions in historical contexts.

Connection: How does the notion of the cultural level of instruction relate to Vygotsky's theory (Chapter 2) and situated learning (Chapter 7)?

Connection: How does the concept of mental management relate to metacognition discussed in Chapter 7? To Gagné's cognitive strategies?

Critical Thinking: Are the six dimensions of good thinking reflected in Gagné's learning outcomes or Bloom's taxonomy? How are they alike or different?

dimensions of good thinking Six aspects that characterize skill in thinking critically, which include a language of thinking, thinking dispositions, mental management, a strategic spirit, higher-order knowledge, and transfer.

ON SUCCESSFUL PRACTICE

In your experience, what are the most important aspects of planning and providing effective instruction?

I devoted energy to planning and creating activities for learning. I tried to invite student participation rather than mandate it, preferring to say, "I invite you to try. . . ," or "Would you please join me in. . . ?" rather than, "What I want you to do is. . . ." I usually had more than one activity prepared so students were free to choose ones they would enjoy. Alternative activities had the effect of decreasing my ownership in the product and increasing the students' ownership. Planning should also include varying formats and making certain each student has an opportunity to actively contribute to a lesson or discussion.

I tried anything to make the material more personal for students and to reduce tension and anxiety about participating in class. It is important that students recognize and point out connections and relationships in what they are learning. I also took risks in minimizing classroom stress. I offered prearranged late work and test retakes within reason. I talked to them about my own academic struggles and occasional failures with time management and human relations.

I worked to keep classroom life vital and the goals high. Backward and forward. . . that's how I wanted to know my subject matter. But no teacher can be fully prepared. "Fully prepared" is some sort of distant destination that no real teacher ever reaches because of the demands of teaching assignments. Real teachers learn to prioritize and improvise. If I wasn't secure in my preparation, I would say, "I haven't tried this yet. Let's see what we can do."

DOROTHY SAWYER, Retired high school teacher, Gladstone, Oregon

Planning is crucial, according to this teacher, but teachers can't ever be "fully prepared." Why not? In what ways can flexibility in planning pay off?

Regardless of the subject matter or grade level, teachers must make decisions about what learning outcomes they want students to achieve. How do they do this in a way that will help them plan the daily, weekly, and yearly activities that make up their instruction?

HOW DO TEACHERS DETERMINE AND SPECIFY INSTRUCTIONAL OUTCOMES?

The business of determining and specifying the learning outcomes that will guide instruction is an important part of the classroom teacher's job. While blue-ribbon panels, state departments of education, or school districts largely determine curricular goals, the classroom teacher must translate these goals into specific objectives for instruction.

Decisions about what to teach in schools are shared by local school boards, educational administrators and teachers, taxpayers, parents, and students. Sometimes curriculum committees adopt plans developed outside the community and marketed for wide use. In most cases, local educators are free to exercise their professional judgment regarding site-specific curriculum decisions.

Teachers are given the responsibility to lead students through a curricular maze. By the end of the year, a student should be able to use certain skills, know certain facts, apply certain concepts, and evaluate certain materials. A good number of the learning outcomes that students are to attain have been prescribed for the teacher by external sources.

Information provided by those who put together lists of educational objectives, such as the National Assessment of Educational Progress, objectives based on the taxonomies presented earlier, and curricular objectives set by state education departments and local school districts, define what students should be able to do. The task of determining outcomes for a particular course, units within that course, and lessons within those units must be determined by the teacher. Using the prescriptions for content coverage, the teacher's job becomes one of planning the trip through the content of a course. A first-grade teacher, for example, is given the assignment to teach first graders in several content areas. Along with that assignment come sets of print and nonprint curricular materials. These materials will define to some extent the learning outcomes students will attain in that class, but the teacher must still make decisions about what students should do with these materials.

Deciding on Instructional Goals

Once teachers have decided generally what they want students to learn, they can specify these outcomes in ways to better guide instructional planning and assessment. Outcomes are first defined generally as goals and then analyzed into component objectives. **Instructional goals** are broad statements of desired learning outcomes that often encompass an array of specific performances to be attained. For example, the goal, "communicate effectively in writing," involves such subordinate performances as "generate a topic sentence" and "provide supporting details," as well as such grammatical prerequisites as "use appropriate punctuation" and "spell correctly."

Following are examples of instructional goals.

A. Use a recipe to bake a cake from scratch.

B. Demonstrate courteous behavior in the halls.

C. Perform numeric operations.

D. Employ an efficient strategy for carrying out a class assignment.

Reflection: Imagine that you are going to a school as a substitute teacher tomorrow. In what form do you hope to find the instructional objectives (as general goals, specific behaviors, or both)? Why?

Notice that these examples differ in specificity and the degree to which enabling or subordinate objectives are implied. For students to attain the goal in example A, they would have to demonstrate such skills as adjusting the amount of ingredients (intellectual skill) and breaking the eggs and stirring the batter (motor skill). The goal in example B requires that students know what kinds of behaviors are considered courteous. For the goal in example C to be useful to a teacher, the teacher must make it specific to the context in which it is to be performed. The teacher might expect students to perform numeric operations in counting objects, solving a geometry problem, setting up the budget for a school project, or determining the amount of fertilizer needed for a particular size field. Example D is a thinking goal with enabling objectives that would be specific to a particular content area or grade level.

instructional goals General statements of what students should be able to do as a consequence of instruction.

Specifying Performance Objectives

Performance objectives, then, are statements of specific performances to be demonstrated by students as evidence of their goal attainment. Usually, objectives are stated in behavioral terms, because behaviors can be directly observed and measured.

Robert Mager's model of **behavioral objectives** has influenced the way in which generations of teachers have gone about preparing performance objectives (Mager, 1962). Behavioral objectives are based on the operant-conditioning view of learning. Operant conditioning's emphasis on observable behavior gave educators a way of specifying what outcomes to expect of their students. Behavioral objectives also provided a way to monitor teacher accountability with regard to the outcomes of their instruction. Skinner (1968) said, "The first step in designing instruction is to define the terminal behavior. What is the student to do as the result of having been taught?" A behavioral objective states what students should be able to do as a result of instruction.

Try This: Interview a teacher regarding the use of Mager's model for defining objectives and why he or she uses it.

According to Mager (1962), behavioral objectives should contain three elements: (1) a statement of the observable behavior students are to perform as a consequence of instruction, (2) the conditions under which the behavior will be demonstrated or exhibited, and (3) the criteria by which attainment of the objective will be judged. Consider the following examples, and identify in each the three elements of a behavioral objective.

A. Using a ruler, students will correctly identify centimeters and millimeters.

B. Given an unlabeled sky chart, students will correctly identify at least seven constellations.

C. In an essay, students will contrast the postwar economies that developed in Japan and in the United States.

D. From examples, students will compose a formally correct haiku and limerick.

Mager's model for defining objectives set the standard. Clearly there are other ways to specify objectives that appear in textbooks, curriculum guides, and state regulations. Many curriculum guides, for example, provide objectives in a format that presents a general goal followed by statements that specify subject matter and behavioral outcomes. This approach is based on the work of N. E. Gronlund. Following Gronlund's (1991) model, a curriculum guide for chemistry might include the following entry:

1. General objective: Demonstrate knowledge of acids and bases. The student will

1.01. Define the term *ions*.

1.02. Identify common acidic solutions.

1.03. Distinguish between an acid and a base.

1.04. Demonstrate a litmus test.

behavioral objectives Specific statements of goals, which include the behavior students should be able to perform as a result of instruction, the conditions of their performance, and the criteria used to judge attainment of the goals.

As a result of recent reform efforts in education, some curriculum guides produced by state departments of education include goals and objectives that call for higher-order thinking skills. For example:

2. General objective: Use numeric operations to describe, analyze, disaggregate, communicate, and synthesize numeric data and to identify and solve problems.

2.01. Accurately identify and perform appropriate numeric procedures with problems found in numeric, symbolic, or word form.

2.02. Estimate approximate numeric solutions to problems without using calculating devices.

2.03. Accurately analyze, synthesize, and evaluate numeric ideas, concepts, and information through appropriate formulae, symbols, theorems, equations, graphs, diagrams, and charts.

These objectives drive the development of appropriate assessments. Classroom tests and performance assessments should reflect the instructional goals, the conditions under which the performance is to be demonstrated, and the criteria for determining if the goals have been attained.

Reflection: In your experience as a student, what are some advantages and disadvantages of teaching to behavioral objectives?

Behavioral objectives have been criticized for limiting the teacher's focus of instruction and choice of instructional methods. Research results have also been equivocal concerning their effective use by learners (e.g., Klauer, 1984). However, objectives do help teachers remain oriented to desired learning outcomes (Dick & Reiser, 1989).

Outcomes-Based Education

In the current climate of school reform, a movement has surfaced called **outcomes-based education (OBE)**. In OBE, the focus is on the learning outcomes students are expected to achieve by the end of their twelve years in school. Also called competency-based education, OBE is associated with the development of national and statewide standards in education. General goals are identified that individual school districts are expected to address in so-called school improvement plans. These are plans specifying how the school or district will ensure that its students achieve the state or national goals. In Florida, for example, Blueprint 2000 is a state-initiated program describing goals not only for student achievement but also for improving the safety of schools and increasing parent involvement in schools. Each school has a school advisory council or school improvement team that is charged with targeting specific areas for improvement and generating a plan for how to accomplish these improvements. The school improvement plan must also include the indicators by which the school will judge the success of its plan.

Part of the reasoning behind OBE stems from a belief that reform efforts are best handled at the local level. For change to occur, administrators, teachers, parents, students, and others in the community must all be involved. What could this mean for you as a teacher? You may become involved with the school improvement planning efforts in your school or district. At the very least, however, you will be responsible for translating the goals for student achievement in your school's plan to specific objectives that you can use for instructional planning.

HOW DO INSTRUCTIONAL EVENTS FACILITATE LEARNING OUTCOMES?

Distinguishing among types of outcomes helps us understand the cognitive processes involved in achieving learning outcomes. Knowledge of outcomes does not ensure, however, that students will achieve them. Teachers must determine the instructional events (the outward conditions of learning) that will support the cognitive processes involved.

outcomes-based education (OBE) A movement in school reform associated with the development of national and statewide standards in education that become the focus of local school improvement.

Critical Thinking: How do instructional events influence a student's cognitive processes?

Teaching and learning are two sides of the same coin. A teacher who claims to have taught when students do not learn is like a salesperson who claims to have made a sale even though the customer did not buy anything. The teacher's actions and instructional decisions should engage the learner and support the cognitive processes required for learning.

Gagné's Events of Instruction

Figure 11.1 identifies the learning processes that occur in classroom learning situations in relation to the instructional events that support those processes. The processes represent phases of learning (Bell-Gredler, 1986; Gagné, 1977).

Connection: Gagné's model is based on information-processing theory and combines principles of behavioral and cognitive learning theories (see Chapters 6 and 7).

The nine events in **Gagné's events of instruction** follow the typical sequence of a direct instruction lesson, and effective lessons are assumed to include all nine events in one form or another. The order of events and who provides them may change, however, depending on the method of instruction. In cooperative learning, for example, students may search out information relevant to a project on which they are working rather than wait for the teacher to provide them with needed materials. In addition, they may depend on each other, instead of the teacher, for feedback. Likewise, students conducting independent study would provide some of the events of instruction for themselves.

Connection: How does the instructional event, gaining attention, relate to the ARCS model (Chapter 9)?

Preparation Phase. The first three events of instruction—gaining attention, informing the student of the objective, and stimulating prior knowledge—comprise the preparation phase of learning (Bell-Gredler, 1986). When the teacher is successful in gaining the student's attention, the student apprehends or becomes aware of relevant stimuli pertaining to the lesson. Teachers use a variety of verbal signals, such as "Listen up!" or "Open to page twenty-seven in your book" or "Take a look at this picture" to accomplish this event. Visual and auditory signals (e.g., turning on the overhead projector, shaking a rattle) can also be very effective at gaining and directing students' attention.

The second event of instruction is informing the student of the goals or objectives of the lesson. If students know what they are expected to do, they can make appropriate decisions throughout the lesson. When you orient students toward the goal of the lesson, you activate their motivation. For example, if students know that they will be expected to write a summary at the end of a lecture, they will study differently than if they expect to have to define terms introduced during the lesson. A student who has a clear sense of what he or she is supposed to do is less likely to procrastinate on a task or fail to meet the goal. Building expectancies for students activates their motivation.

Connection: See the sections on prior knowledge and selective attention in Chapter 7.

Stimulating recall of prior knowledge is the third event of instruction. By encouraging students to retrieve prior knowledge appropriate to the goals of the lesson, you will enhance their acquisition, construction, and retention of material to be learned. Recall can be stimulated through formal means, such as pretests, or through informal means, such as reviewing with students what they learned previously or inviting reports of relevant personal experiences.

Gagné's events of instruction According to Gagné, the external conditions required to support and facilitate the cognitive processes that occur during learning.

Acquisition and Performance Phase. After students are prepared for learning, the acquisition and performance phase begins (events 4–7 in Figure 11.1). This phase is the essence of classroom instruction (Bell-Gredler, 1986). The fourth instructional event in a typical lesson is the presentation of stimulus material. Teachers or students present material in lectures, discussions, and live demonstrations. Textbooks and overhead transparencies present material in

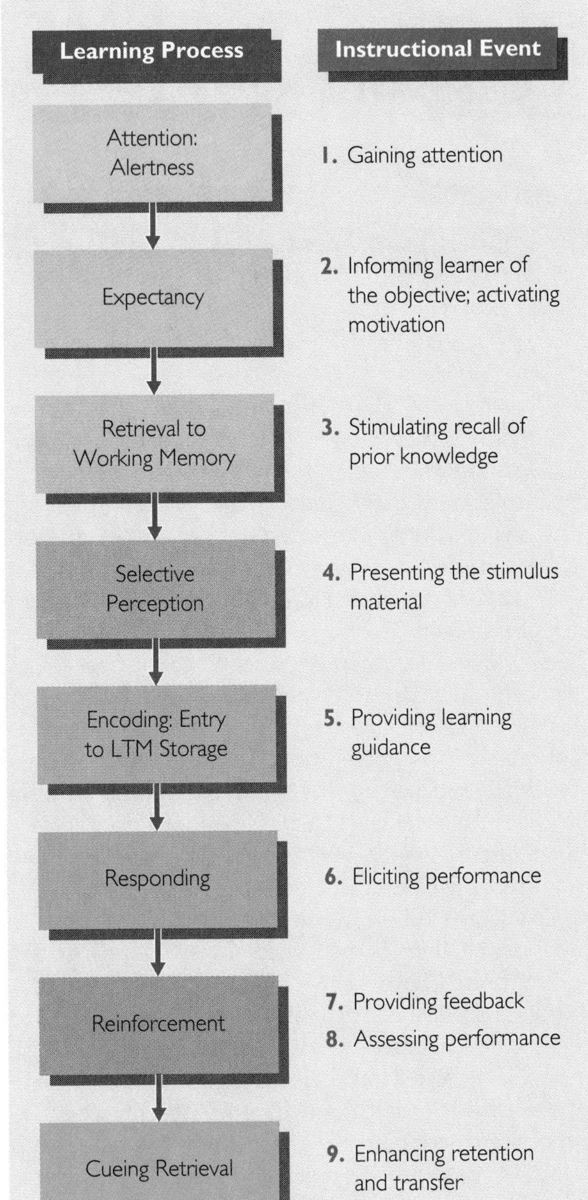

FIGURE 11.1

Gagné's Instructional Events and Learning Processes
Source: From *Essentials of Learning for Instruction* (2nd ed., p. 128) by R. M. Gagné and M. P. Driscoll, 1988, Englewood Cliffs, NJ: Prentice-Hall. Copyright 1988 by Allyn & Bacon. Reprinted by permission.

print, diagrams, and pictures. Computers present material in many forms (print, diagrams, video, and audio) that are often sequenced on the basis of the student's responses. In whatever form material is presented, however, it should help students to selectively perceive the important stimuli in the situation. By focusing on just the important elements, the student is better able to store the elements in short-term memory.

The form in which material is presented should also be appropriate to the desired learning outcome. To support a learning outcome such as "serve a tennis ball," information is more effectively presented via a live demonstration or a slow

Insights ON SUCCESSFUL PRACTICE

What has been your experience with outcomes-based education (OBE)?

The idea that decisions about instruction should be built around what the learner should be able to do is not foreign to most teachers I know. Curricula and assessment were too heavily based on simple acquisition of knowledge, at the expense of understanding and creating that knowledge. I've always felt that an instructional environment built around learner engagement and authentic learning provides the richest learning—learning far from that inert stuff that we forget 30 percent of! The emergence of outcomes-based education (OBE) allows me to be faithful to my own educational philosophy.

OBE has contributed to making my classroom environment truly an active one. More monies have been allocated locally for the purchase of and training in technologies and related materials. With those technologies and materials, it becomes possible to give students real responsibilities as learners to do and create, not just watch and reproduce! Students explore, apply, and communicate mathematics using graphics calculators, computers, and presentation devices. In a supportive and cooperative environment that emphasizes questioning and creating understanding, students themselves often formulate problems and design their solutions.

Teaching is no longer just telling students; it is learning with them and about them. I get to model "doing" mathematics with my students so they see that those final solutions often presented are not always so easily arrived at! And it is now OK that I use class time for implementing activities that do not have me as the center of attraction.

OBE has validated my use of cooperative techniques in its many and varied forms in my classroom. Unlike some traditional settings where many students are often left disengaged, not able to participate in even the most rudimentary way, it is through cooperative activities that ALL my students get opportunities to generate responses, communicate, question, make decisions, and create what each could probably not do alone.

OBE has driven me to implement some different and varying kinds of assessment other than paper and pencil tests. I have begun to use portfolios, projects, writing assignments, observation, class presentations, and holistic evaluations to assess students' learning of mathematics. Here, differing student cognitive styles shine in their varied splendor. I've discovered students who have magnificent understanding of complex mathematics who are stifled by paper and pencil "show all the steps" assessments.

OBE has allowed me to offer to my students the thrill and joy of learning as I have experienced it. It has put a thrill back into teaching for me as well. I am growing with my students each year as I am actively engaged in learning with them. What better way to model the fun and excitement of learning?

GREGORY HOLDAN, Mt. Lebanon High School, Pittsburgh, Pennsylvania

What is outcomes-based education? What role do active learning and cooperative learning play? How does OBE affect the assessment of student learning? What clear advantages has OBE had for this teacher and his students?

motion video than a verbal description in a textbook. Similarly, for an outcome such as "determine the altitude of a rocket launched straight up," information could be presented by the teacher or textbook as a series of steps to follow.

The teacher's actions during the next event of instruction, providing learning guidance, support the student's creation of a mental representation of the stimulus information that can be stored in long-term memory. In terms of the information-processing model examined in Chapter 7, the student makes meaningful sense of the stimulus information. Meaningful information is more easily stored and is retained longer.

The sixth event of instruction is referred to as eliciting performance. This is practice. Students learning to play tennis must have the opportunity to practice serving. Likewise, students learning to determine altitude using an inclinometer to measure the angle of incidence could practice by determining the height of trees or school buildings in addition to determining the altitude of rockets.

Feedback follows practice and is the basis for both reinforcement and response correction. Feedback functions to confirm the student's expectations about the goal of the lesson. Performance that results in goal attainment is reinforced. Feedback also serves to correct inaccurate performances. Students who compute an entirely different number than the rest of the class for the altitude of a particular rocket launch obtain feedback indicating that they made a mistake.

Transfer Phase. The final two events of instruction, called the *transfer phase*, support the cognitive processes necessary for the **transfer of learning**. This occurs when knowledge or skills learned in one situation are used in another. Assessing performance requires that the teacher give students opportunities to use or demonstrate what they have learned. If students are truly capable of making a discrimination or applying a rule, they should be able to use the new capability in a variety of situations. Assessment allows students to test their wings and allows teachers to determine that the knowledge is not limited to the specific circumstances in which the initial learning took place. For example, the student who has learned to serve a tennis ball should be able to do so competently in a variety of settings and situations.

Actions that enhance retention and transfer encourage the student to retrieve the learned information in new situations. A student who can generalize beyond the instructional context in which information was learned has developed an elaborate encoding of the information and more retrieval cues for using the information in the future.

Integrating Multiple Instructional Goals. Most lessons are intended to support more than one instructional goal, which means that teachers must ensure that the events of instruction they plan are appropriate for all goals contained in the lesson. One way for teachers to do this is through an enterprise schema. The **enterprise schema** provides an overall learning context that integrates multiple instructional goals and communicates the purpose for learning these goals (Gagné & Merrill, 1990).

Thematic lessons provide an example. A fifth-grade teacher decides to teach a social studies lesson on maps. The overall goals of the lesson are for students to (1) locate specific destinations on a map in relation to their school, (2) determine distances between specified locations using the map's scale, and (3) plan the best route to a particular location, considering factors such as necessary stops along the way

transfer of learning The application of knowledge acquired in one situation to other situations.

enterprise schema An overall learning context that integrates multiple instructional goals and communicates the purpose for learning these goals.

What multiple instructional goals might this learning enterprise serve? What instructional methods might best serve these goals? In what ways might students transfer this learning to other situations?

and types of roads travelled. To attain these goals, students must acquire intellectual skills (solving distance problems, estimating travel times), motor skills (measuring distances along a route), and cognitive strategies (finding an efficient solution). The enterprise of planning a class field trip provides the context and purpose for acquiring these learning outcomes. It also provides the context for determining and selecting specific events of instruction to be used during the course of the lesson.

Try This: Develop a thematic lesson for a class you expect to teach. What is the enterprise schema in your lesson? What instructional goals does the lesson integrate?

Teaching methods also need to be integrated with multiple instructional goals. Consider again the core phases of instruction. How should material be presented? Guidance given? Performance elicited? Feedback provided? The answers to these questions depend on whether a teacher decides to facilitate learning through discovery or through reception. These methods of instruction are often complementary. Teachers may use both at different times within a lesson in order to support particular goals.

Point: *Teachers coordinate the context for learning.* They do this by implementing the events of instruction and by organizing discovery and reception learning.

Bruner's Discovery Learning

Discovery learning occurs when students are presented with problem situations that require them to discover the essential concepts of the subject matter (Bruner, 1960). Bruner advocates learning through discovery because it supports active learning. A teacher who uses a discovery learning approach to instruction presents examples or problems and then asks students to examine and think about them inductively with a goal of formulating a general principle. For example, a teacher might give students equal amounts of fresh water and salt water and ask them to experiment with samples to find out the differences between the two—differences in appearance, taste, weight, and other properties. Students could be encouraged to find out how well various objects float in the two containers. By experimenting, the students would discover and articulate the essential properties rather than being told what they are. Discovery learning encourages students to actively use their intuition, imagination, and creativity. Because the approach starts with the specific and then moves to the general, it also facilitates inductive reasoning.

What conditions promote effective discovery learning? To begin with, "discovery, like surprise, favors the well-prepared mind" (Bruner, 1961, p. 22). When students have little or no prior knowledge related to principles they are asked to discover, they can experience frustration and failure. Asking them to make connections to related ideas as they enter a discovery learning environment can help students begin to determine what information is relevant and what steps they should take to solve a problem.

discovery learning
Bruner's approach to teaching, in which students are presented with specific examples and use these examples to form general principles. Discovery learning is inductive.

Providing models to guide discovery is another important condition for discovery learning. "The constant provision of a model, the constant response to the

Insights ON SUCCESSFUL PRACTICE

As a teacher, how do you model learner characteristics and learning performances for your students?

In adopting performance criteria for our students, our district and community agreed that all students should become self-directed learners and resourceful, innovative problem solvers. In the process of providing training for the staff in the usual instructional strategies associated with cooperative learning, mastery learning, and responsibility training, our district also adapted Dr. Margaret Wang's Adaptive Learning Environment Model to our needs and goals. Our model, Continuous Progress Instruction (CPI), gives us a way to assess student progress, make prescriptives, and guide students toward these performance criteria.

A CPI unit is designed to allow students to make choices about what material they will cover, how they will use the time allotted to them, and what types of products they will produce. CPI also allows me to prescribe certain types of work for the students based on how I assess their needs at any given point.

In our last unit, the English 9 team looked at the objectives we wanted to cover, the works we had available, and the time we had in which to do all this work. We divided the readings into three major groupings and asked students to select their first and second choices from these groupings. For each grouping we developed a series of learning centers, which were designed to allow students a full range of exploratory possibilities. Some were group oriented while others were individual oriented. Drawing on Howard Gardner's work with both multiple intelligences and project-based education, we designed the learning centers so that students also had a choice of products they could produce, including poems and artistic creations. The products had to demonstrate the student's understanding and comprehension of the concepts and works in the unit.

After all these choices were made, each team had to set a work schedule that would allow them to complete all group work while still allowing individuals time to complete their own work..

In essence, then, students were responsible for their own lessons, for assigning work to be done in and out of school, for scheduling work time and due dates, and for solving problems associated with the learning centers, time management, and group activities.

On a follow-up self-evaluation, one of the questions we asked was: "What do you feel you have gained from this unit?" Representative samplings of student responses include the following statements.

> From the group activities, I have gained the skills of working with people, cooperating in a group, compromising, and making decisions. In the independent unit, I've gained the knowledge of how to map out an independent schedule of goals for myself.

> I learned how to decipher different types of writing. I had to read many poems that were written in different styles. I had to read law books in order to answer my research question.

> I learned to link dissimilar stories together and work independently to find out my learning speed and style.

From the smaller CPI units we run throughout the year in English 9 to the final nine-week unit, I feel that students come to be self-directed learners and creative, innovative problem solvers.

MICHAEL A. BENEDICT, Fort Chapel Area High School, Pittsburgh, Pennsylvania

What is continuous progress instruction? What role do responsibility training and cooperative learning play? How does CPI affect the assessemnt of student learning? What clear advantages has CPI had for this teacher and his students?

Example: A kindergarten teacher has each of her children pick an object from a box each day and describe it. In the box, she has gathered everything from old records to nuts and bolts. After each child has described the object, the teacher asks him or her how the object might be used. At first, the children's guesses range far afield from the actual use of the object. But as they become more skilled in describing, they also begin to realize the functional attributes of the objects. Why do you think the teacher takes the time to do this exercise, and what value might it have for the children?

individual's response after response, back and forth between two people, constitute 'invention' learning guided by an accessible model" (Bruner, 1973, p. 70). In teaching the concept of alliteration, for instance, a teacher could provide both examples and nonexamples and systematically guide students through an exploration of their similarities and differences. By asking certain kinds of questions and prompting students to generate hypotheses, the teacher also models the inquiry process. What students can learn by discovery, then, includes not just content-specific concepts and information but also critical thinking skills and a disposition toward critical thinking.

A third condition that promotes discovery learning is the use of contrasts to stimulate cognitive conflicts. In science, for example, a teacher could begin a lesson on air and air pressure with a demonstration that shows water flowing uphill. This is a surprising event because we are accustomed to the force of gravity causing water to flow downhill. In trying to resolve the discrepancy, students discover how air exerts pressure that can overcome the force of gravity.

Discovery learning is an effective approach for facilitating students' acquisition of information, concepts, and problem-solving skills. It is also highly motivational. Most teachers who use discovery learning in their classrooms report that students want to find out the answers to problems and will engage in purposeful activities to do so (Friedl, 1991). Moreover, if students are not successful in finding all the answers, they benefit more from a teacher's explanations than when such explanations are given without the students having first engaged in inquiry.

There are drawbacks to discovery learning. Teachers can find it time consuming, costly, and complex to implement. There is also a risk that process will begin to outweigh content. Many science programs implemented in the 1970s that were based on the concepts of discovery failed because content was ignored, and teachers found that "process without content did not produce results" (Friedl, 1991, p. 2). It is important, therefore, to keep desired learning outcomes in full view when designing and implementing discovery learning programs.

Ausubel's Reception Learning

Meaningful learning occurs when students actively process the information they are asked to learn. Whereas Bruner advocated a discovery approach to meaningful learning, Ausubel believed that knowledge is best acquired through reception rather than discovery. **Reception learning** occurs when students receive the essential principles or concepts, think about them deductively, and are then shown how to apply them in specific instances (Ausubel, Novak, & Hanesian, 1978).

reception learning
Ausubel's approach to teaching, in which students are presented with material in a complete, organized form and are shown how to move from broad ideas to more specific instances. Reception learning is deductive.

advance organizer
Information presented prior to instruction that assists in understanding new information by relating it to existing knowledge.

For Ausubel, active processing of information occurs when the ideas presented are well organized and clearly focused. In order to present effectively, teachers must carefully organize, sequence, and explain the material so that students can process it efficiently. The kind of instruction that leads to reception learning is called expository teaching. (Exposition means explanation.) An essential element of expository teaching is the advance organizer.

An **advance organizer** is information presented prior to learning that assists in understanding new information (Ausubel, Novak, & Hanesian, 1978). Suppose that a teacher is lecturing about Buddhism. For an advance organizer, the teacher could ask students to read and discuss a passage about the relationship between Christianity and Buddhism (see Ausubel & Youssef, 1963). Advance organizers are thought to provide a context for unfamiliar information by activating prior knowledge. An advance organizer for a lesson on occupational roles might be to ask children what they want to be when they grow up or what jobs family members hold.

Continuing research on advance organizers led Ausubel et al. (1978) to conclude that organizers can enhance learning if two conditions are met. The first condition is that the target information must be a unitary topic or a set of related ideas. Topics that are too broad would require an organizer too general to be meaningful. The second condition for effective use of advance organizers is that the organizing statement or activity must activate the prior knowledge of the learner. If it is unrelated to a learner's prior knowledge, the advance organizer becomes an additional piece of information to be learned rather than an aid to understanding the lesson.

Connection: What is the process by which advance organizers might activate preexisting schemas (see Chapters 2 and 7)?

here's how

Here's How to Construct and Use Advance Organizers

- Examine the new lesson or unit to discover necessary prerequisite knowledge and skills. List.
- Reteach if necessary.
- Find out if students know this prerequisite material.
- List or summarize the major general principles or ideas in the new lesson or unit (this could be done first).
- Write a paragraph or plan an activity (the advance organizer) emphasizing the major general principles and similarities to previous learning.
- Provide verbal or visual information prior to learning of new material that does not contain specific content from the new material.
- Provide a means of generating the logical relationships between old and new topics and elements in the information to be learned.
- Cover the main subtopics of the unit or lesson in the same sequence as they are presented in the advance organizer. (Mayer, 1979, p. 392; West, Farmer, & Wolff, 1991, p. 125)

Try This: Observe several classrooms to discover the variety of advance organizers teachers use. Develop an advance organizer for a lesson or unit you might teach.

In expository teaching, advance organizers enable learners to integrate new information and prior knowledge. Whether material is learned through reception or through discovery, students must be able to use what they learn, not only in the circumstances in which learning occurs but in new situations as well.

Reflection: How can one instance of learning help or hinder another instance of learning? Think of examples from your own learning experiences.

Transfer of Learning

As defined previously, transfer of learning refers to the influence of learning something in one situation on learning in other situations. We hope, for example, that the problems students learn to solve on Monday will help them solve new problems on Tuesday, on Friday, and next year. How does transfer occur?

Vertical and Lateral Transfer. Gagné (1985) defined two types of transfers, vertical and lateral (see also Royer, 1979). When complex skills are more easily learned because of simple skills that were acquired earlier, *vertical transfer* has occurred. A good example is the acquisition of intellectual skills—learning discriminations facilitates learning concepts. Therefore, one outcome of acquiring the discrimination capability is to facilitate the acquisition of concepts. Likewise, the acquisition of concepts results in easier acquisition of rules.

Connection: How does lateral transfer relate to Gagné's ninth event of instruction? To the transfer dimension of thinking?

Lateral transfer is the generalization of knowledge or skill to a new situation—one that is different from the original situation in which the knowledge or skill was acquired but is not more complex. Lateral transfer is promoted when students are given novel tasks that require they use what they learned previously. For example, a student who has finished studying a spelling list might work on a word game activity containing the spelling words.

Vertical and lateral transfer can be near or far. *Near transfer* refers to situations in which acquired skills are applied in new ways that are very similar to the original learning situation. *Far transfer* occurs when the skill is applied in situations that are quite far removed from the original learning situation. For example, learning to type on a manual typewriter facilitates using a computer keyboard. The situations are quite similar and would be referred to as near transfer. Learning to type might also facilitate the use of a stenographic machine. However, the situations are quite different and would be an example of far transfer.

Connection: How does high-road transfer relate to the transfer dimension of thinking? How does low-road transfer relate to automaticity (Chapter 7)?

Low-Road and High-Road Transfer. Salomon and Perkins (1989) suggested another way of looking at transfer. *Low-road transfer* is the "spontaneous automatic transfer of highly practiced skills with little need for reflective thinking" (p. 118). Low-road transfer involves a great deal of practice to attain the automaticity of skills required. Salomon and Perkins use the example of driving a truck after one has learned to drive a car. Low-road transfer would also occur when students begin to read expository prose after learning to read narrative prose.

Critical Thinking: How can lessons support the transfer of learning? Why should they?

High-road transfer involves "the explicit conscious formulation of abstraction in one situation that allows making a connection to another" (p. 118). An example is applying math procedures in designing a poster. High-road transfer can occur in a forward-reaching sense when a general principle is so well learned that it suggests itself spontaneously in a new situation. It can occur in a backward-reaching sense when a need arises in a new situation that causes the learner to look back at past experiences for a potential solution. In either case, high-road transfer depends on mindful abstraction. The learner must deliberately use a principle acquired in one context in a new context.

Generating the abstraction and making a decision to use that abstraction in a new way requires the learner to think about his or her own thinking—metacognition.

A Cultural Approach to Teaching Thinking

As we saw earlier in the chapter, transfer of learning can be considered one of the six dimensions of thinking, which also includes aspects of metacognition in mental management. Because thinking is enculturated within subject matter disciplines, Tishman, Perkins, & Jay (1995) advocate "culture-based teaching" as a means for students to acquire good thinking skills. Specifically, they recommend that teachers provide these four **cultural forces**:

cultural forces Four teaching strategies used to help students acquire thinking skills: (1) providing models of the culture, (2) explaining important cultural knowledge, (3) providing interaction among students and other members of the cultural community, and (4) providing feedback on students' use of thinking skills.

1. *Models* of the culture, which are examples or illustrations of good thinking practices. This means that teachers themselves should use the language of thinking in their disciplines and model thinking strategies in solving problems.
2. *Explanation* of culturally important knowledge, such as explaining how a thinking strategy works and why it is important. In discussing a particular interpretation of a poem, for example, an English teacher might describe why it is valuable to identify metaphors in writings.
3. *Interaction* between students and members of the cultural community.

Cooperative problem solving, either as a class or in small groups, provides a structure for thinking along with others.

4. *Feedback* on students' thinking processes. Teachers can provide direct feedback on whether students have justified their decisions, for example, or they can provide feedback that redirects student effort instead of criticizing it. Questions such as, "Have you considered all the options?" help students to correct impulsive actions that interfere with good thinking.

Connection: How do these cultural forces relate to Vygotsky's theory (Chapter 2) and situated learning (Chapter 7)?

Although these recommendations can be implemented by individual teachers in their classrooms, Tishman et al. (1995) argue that entire schools should become cultures of thinking. As an example, they offer a vision of what a thinking-centered school might look like. At the entrance, a chalkboard greets visitors with the heading, "Things I Wonder about Today," under which both teachers and students write questions. In one classroom, a teacher has posted "Thinking Goals: Be organized, Be curious, Be neat when you make your weather chart, Be patient, and Don't be afraid to ask questions." In another classroom, students are experimenting with what happens to a graph when changes are made to the mathematical equation that it represents. In the gym, the PE teacher has students making up their own calisthenics.

here's how

Here's How to Create a Culture of Thinking in the Classroom

- Identify the things you already do in the classroom that touch on any or all of the six dimensions of thinking and build on them, making use of the four cultural forces.
- Learn as you go. Start experimenting with one thinking dimension at a time, and be alert to how it naturally draws in others.
- Start small. Think big. Think about multiunit, interdisciplinary projects that might span weeks or months, and start with a pilot project that lasts several days.
- Be explicit with students about what you are trying to do: Make cultural change a joint effort.
- Whenever possible, work with colleagues.
- Try to use the thinking dimensions as bridges across different content areas.
- Be bold: Don't be afraid to plunge in and experiment with thinking-centered activities, even if you feel unsure about exactly what to do. (Tishman et al. 1995, pp. 197–199)

HOW CAN YOU MAKE INSTRUCTIONAL DECISIONS THAT WILL HELP ALL STUDENTS LEARN?

Teachers spend most of their instructional planning time in the following ways: allocating time to various learning activities; studying and reviewing content to be taught; organizing daily, weekly, and term schedules; attending to administrative requirements; and assisting substitute teachers (Clark & Peterson, 1986; McCutcheon, 1980). Much of this planning is done to implement the plans and wishes of educational administrators, school boards, and state departments of education. As the agent of implementation, however, you will determine how much time is allotted to the various prescribed outcomes, how the outcomes are interpreted, what supplemental materials to use, and how those materials are used. How can you plan instruction to assure effective learning for all your students?

A Systematic Approach to Planning Effective Instruction

Dick & Reiser (1989) define effective instruction as "instruction that enables students to acquire specified skills, knowledge, and attitudes" and "instruction that students enjoy" (p. 2). They offer a systematic planning process that can provide you with an outline for delivering effective instruction. This process consists of interrelated steps as shown in Figure 11.2. Although the figure presents the steps as a linear process, the planning of expert teachers is dynamic, with many of these steps occurring nearly simultaneously (Moallem & Driscoll, 1994). The important thing is, for instruction to be effective, your planning must in some way accommodate these steps. Let's examine each step in turn.

Set Goals. This step involves examining and reflecting upon all the various sources of instructional goals that are available to you: state or district curriculum guides, textbooks adopted by your school or district, plans developed by school committees or parent/teacher organizations, and your professional judgment. Consider the types of learning outcomes you want students to acquire and within what time framework—during the school year, within a multilesson unit of instruction, in a single lesson. Think about how the goals relate to one another.

Select or Write Objectives. With this step, you must determine more specifically what you expect students to do as a result of instruction that demonstrates their attainment of instructional goals. It requires you to translate general goals into specific objectives that you can use both to plan instruction and to assess student performance. Thinking about assessment is often a very effective way of generating objectives. This is because writing test items or performance assessments requires you to be very specific about what you mean by goals such as "write effectively" or "employ an efficient strategy." It also requires you to be very specific about the conditions under which you expect students to perform as well as the standards you will use to judge their performance.

Point: *Teachers and students are both learners.* An important part of your planning will be learning about the needs of your students, as well as about instructional models and methods and about yourself as a teacher.

Analyze Student Characteristics. While it is important to keep desired outcomes firmly in mind while planning instruction, you also know that learners are diverse in the characteristics they bring to the classroom. This means that you may modify your objectives in order to plan instruction that is appropriate for your particular students. For example, a middle school teacher wants students to manage their own learning to a large extent but knows that they have great difficulty keeping track of time during class assignments. Therefore, while keeping self-regulation of learning as a general goal, the teacher selects time management as a more immediate and achievable objective.

Select or Develop Assessments of Student Performance. Assessment of student performance is the means by which you will determine how well students have attained the instructional goals. Although most curriculum series come with

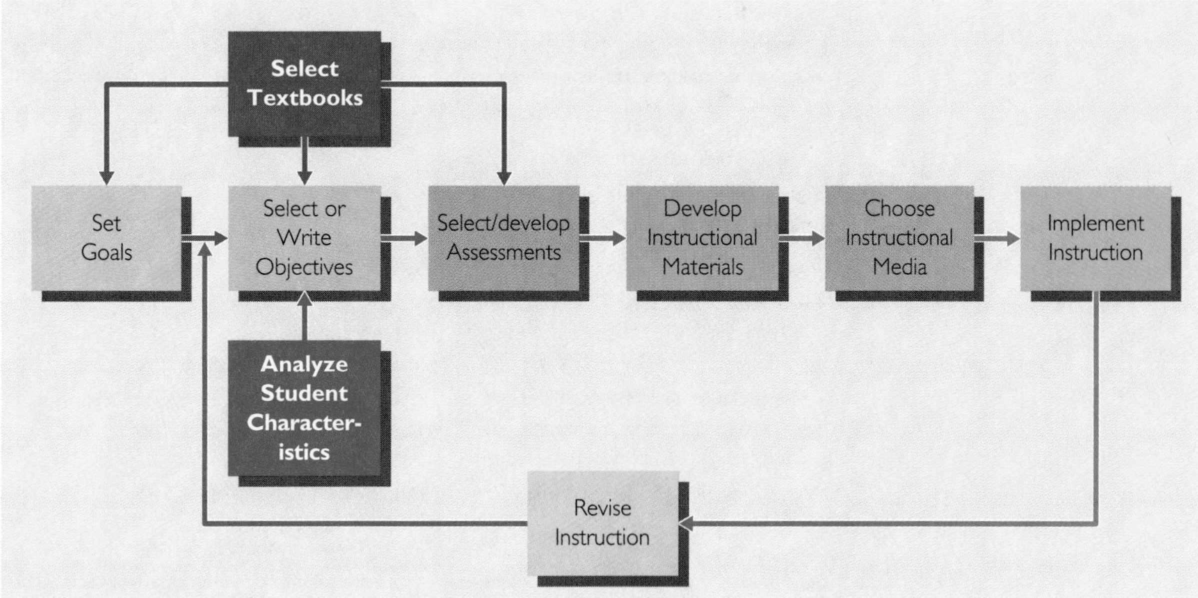

FIGURE 11.2

Dick & Reiser's Model for Developing Effetive Instruction
Source: From *Planning Effective Instruction* by W. Dick and R. A. Reiser, 1989, Englewood Cliffs, NJ: Prentice-Hall, Inc. Copyright ©1989 by Allyn & Bacon. Reprinted by permission.

tests keyed to objectives listed in the textbook, it is a good idea to examine those tests for what they actually measure. In a recent study, for example, objectives provided in each chapter of a science textbook reflected the higher levels of Bloom's taxonomy (application, analysis, evaluation). The accompanying tests, however, assessed primarily fact and vocabulary learning (Driscoll, Moallem, Dick, & Kirby, 1994). How you assess student performance should depend on what you want students to learn (and what you have actually taught them).

Select Textbooks and Other Materials. Determining the instructional resources you will use to present information or provide learning guidance is a decision ideally made when you plan specific instructional activities related to your objectives. In most schools, however, textbooks remain the mainstay of instruction, and they are generally adopted without much regard for the instructional goals of individual teachers. Whether or not you are involved in the adoption process, you face the choice of using the textbook (or not) in your own instruction.

Dick and Reiser (1989) provide a set of criteria to help teachers in selecting textbooks and other print materials. The criteria pertain to content, presentation, instructional design, and classroom use and are summarized in Figure 11.3.

Point: *Instructional technologies support teaching and learning.* Depending on your objectives, you may select various kinds of media as well as textbooks and other print materials.

Develop Instructional Activities and Choose Instructional Media. Instructional activities are what you do in the classroom to help students meet the instructional goals. Both what you do and how you do it should be explicitly oriented to the type of learning outcome you expect students to achieve. Using the recommendations discussed in this chapter, you can devise an instructional plan that identifies your goals of instruction, specific objectives, possible assessment

Content	Instructional Design
Is the content accurate? • Is information factually stated? **Is the content up to date?** • Is the copyright date within the last five years? **Is the content comprehensive?** • Is the content congruent with district and/or state curriculum guidelines? **Are social issues treated fairly?** • Are ethnic groups, males, and females shown in nonstereotyped roles through words and pictures?	**Are the instructional components congruent?** • Does the content match the objectives and assessments? **Do the instructional characteristics facilitate learning?** • Are summaries included in each unit or chapter? • Are practice activities included in the text or teacher's edition? • Do practice activities match the content and skills? • Do practice activities match the test items? • Are motivational activities included?

Presentation	Classroom Use
Does the text format make learning easy? • Do the chapters address a single, main theme? • Do print size and type ensure legibility for the grade level of students? • Do the illustrations reinforce the text? **Is the content presented at the appropriate grade level for the intended learners?** • Do vocabulary and symbols match grade level of students? **Does the writing style help make learning easy?** • Is the tone appropriate for the intended learners? • Are the directions and explanations clearly stated?	**Are the materials effective with students?** • Are there data indicating that students learn from the materials? • Are there data indicating that students like the materials? **Is use of the instructional materials compatible with the teaching conditions?** • Are preferred settings for conducting instructional activities available in user schools? • Are staff development services available from the publisher? **Do the supplementary print materials help make learning easier?** • Does the teacher's edition match the content of the student text? • Are workbook activities congruent with the content of the text? • Do users state their satisfaction with the materials?

FIGURE 11.3

Criteria for Selecting Textbooks and Supplementary Print Materials
Source: From *Planning Effective Instruction* by W. Dick and R. A. Reiser, 1989, Englewood Cliffs, NJ: Prentice-Hall, Inc. Copyright ©1989 by Allyn & Bacon. Reprinted by permission.

strategies, specific instructional strategies (including events of instruction), and the means or methods you intend to use for implementing those activities. Beginning teachers often find it useful to write detailed plans, so that they have something concrete to keep them on track during the day. With experience, you will probably find that your written instructional plans will become briefer and more of your planning will take place mentally. A sample format for writing an instructional plan is shown in Figure 11.4

Try This: Interview teachers regarding their instructional plans. How much of each plan is written and how much is mental? Do they follow a particular format in constructing lesson plans? Why?

Implement Instruction and Revise as Necessary. You have now reached the point of trying out your instructional plan in the classroom. You may have decided to implement a discovery approach or to have students work in cooperative groups. You may be using computers to supplement your teaching or to provide tutorial instruction to students on specific skills or knowledge. You will be using presentation, management, and communication skills as you implement your plan, and you will need to reflect on how well your plan is working.

Sometimes you will get immediate feedback from your students that a particular strategy is ineffective. Perhaps you did not allow enough time for students to complete an assignment, for example. Or perhaps they do not understand the directions for how to complete a task. You can easily remedy problems of this nature during the lesson by allowing additional time or explaining a task

Goal:
Objective(s):
Sample Assessment:

Instructional Activity	Content of Activity	Means of Presenting Activity
1. Motivation		
2. Objectives		
3. Prerequisites		
4. Information and Examples		
5. Practice and Feedback		
6. Assessment		
7. Enrichment and Remediation		

FIGURE 11.4

Format for an Instructional Plan
Source: Adapted from *Planning Effective Instruction* by W. Dick and R. A. Reiser, 1989, Englewood Cliffs, NJ: Prentice-Hall.

ON SUCCESSFUL PRACTICE

As you match teaching methods with learning objectives, how do you incorporate affective outcomes into your lesson plans?

Teaching for me is a means of creative self-expression. I consider myself a teacher/artist, and as such, I am engaged with my students in the appreciation and love of learning, literature, and writing. As a writer, I am able to model for my students, to share my own work, to write with them, and to learn from them. They are as much a part of my creations as I am of theirs. I share with them the evolution of a poem, for example, and ask for their criticisms. They, in turn, seek and respect my comments.

My classroom is a laboratory of experimentation. I continually test new ideas and strategies. The students are my partners in what I view as a joyous journey. After a lesson, I ask the students to evaluate the strategy to see if it worked. I engage their imaginations to help make the next lesson better. I teach my writing classes using a workshop format. I favor hands-on lessons, individual and group participation, shared writings, and peer editing and critiquing. I rarely lecture, but rather, I teach inductively by modeling or demonstrating activities so learning can be self-discovery.

I strive for an exciting and inspiring educational environment. Too often learning is segmented. Isolated skills are developed with little satisfaction to the students. My lessons are all planned around the synthesis of the critical and affective domains. When reading a literary work, students take objective tests and write critical evaluative essays, but they also have a creative project that allows them to respond through their feelings and imaginations.

NANCY GORRELL, Morristown High School, Morristown, New Jersey

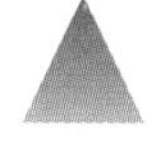 Insights

How does this teacher match teaching methods with instructional goals? How does she incorporate affective objectives and use student feedback to improve instruction? What range of methods will you employ when planning your lessons?

in another way. At other times, reflection after action can reveal problems with your instruction. Perhaps a large number of students performed poorly on a unit test, and you realize that additional instruction on prerequisite skills was probably needed. Or perhaps a group of students is having difficulty with a lesson because of a particular thinking disposition or cultural difference. These problems can be overcome by revising the instruction in some way to better meet the needs of the students.

Information that can help you determine what revisions are necessary includes student performance on tests or other assessment measures during and after instruction, student attitudes toward instruction, and observation of student behavior during instruction. Considering this information in light of your goals, objectives, assessments, and instructional strategies will help you to systematically pinpoint deficiencies in your plan that can be revised for more effective instruction.

A Flexible Approach to Delivering Instruction: Accommodating Student Diversity

As Figure 11.4 suggests, instructional plans are like blueprints. A blueprint provides a plan for that which will be built. Although the blueprint identifies what elements will be built and how those elements will relate to each other, it does not specify the techniques that will be used to construct the various elements of the building. Instructional plans provide us with the elements of a lesson and suggest the sequence in which those elements should occur. But no plan can be so prescriptive as to eliminate the professional judgments of teachers and remain an effective model for instruction.

Plans may provide the structure for your teaching efforts, but you and your students provide the context. Teaching is a highly personal activity. How you teach depends very much on who you are. Regardless of which techniques you choose, you will adapt them to better suit your own characteristics as a teacher and your students' characteristics as learners.

Each student will respond differently to your instructional actions. Assuming your job is to facilitate the achievement of your students, you must make decisions about instructing them while keeping their individual characteristics in mind. There is no one best way to teach, and effective teachers respond to their personal strengths or weaknesses, the characteristics of their students, and the desired instructional outcomes.

Reflecting in action can help you respond during class to individual students' needs. You might discover, for example, that one group of students requires more time to complete an activity than you had planned or than other groups require. Having to adjust the timing of activities during a lesson is a common occurrence, especially for beginning teachers. Reflecting after action is a way to consider changes in your plan that you might make based on events you observed in class. In the Teacher Chronicle, Irving is reflecting after action when he records his thoughts and reactions to his classroom observations.

At the same time, reflecting before action can help you prepare for unexpected occurrences—either things that go wrong or teachable moments that arise during a lesson. For example, things can sometimes go wrong with even the best laid plans. Equipment to conduct an experiment might fail, or a demonstration might not turn out as expected. If you have considered the variety of possible things that could go wrong with your lessons, then you are in a good position to react appropriately when something does go wrong. Likewise, when you expect the unexpected, you can exploit teachable moments in a positive way to support desirable, if unintended, outcomes.

How do you develop the flexibility with which to respond to the ever-changing needs of your students and yourself? One way is through regular reflection on your teaching and its effects on your students. We have stressed throughout this book that teaching is a continual process of learning—about yourself as a teacher, about instructional models and methods, and about students.

Point: *Reflective construction is necessary for the development of teaching expertise.* Improving your teaching practices depends on your reflection of how they work.

TEACHER Chronicle Conclusion

WORD POWER

Antoine Azzi opens Irving's journal. He is looking forward to seeing how Irving responded to Ms. Estefan's American literature class. "I feel like I'm in heaven after suffering through hell last week. These are the same students I observed in Mr. Blandworth's class, but boy are they different! It is hard to describe all that goes in this class. There is so much variety, the kids are really engaged. Ms. Estefan has a special relationship with each class. She does many of the same things with them, but each class has its own distinctive feel to it. For starters, she lets them chat among themselves for five minutes before class starts. When I asked her about this she said, 'Other teachers might think it is a waste of teaching time. I've found my students concentrate better once they talked for a while and gotten some of it out of their systems.'

"When she is ready to begin class she writes a saying on the board. The one for Monday was 'Most of the basic material a writer works with is acquired before the age of fifteen. Willa Cather.' 'Today we will be discussing how a writer's life influences his or her writing. This is in preparation for a discussion at the end of next week about how real life experiences influenced American writers. Take a few minutes now to think about what Willa Cather said and what it means. Then we'll brainstorm which authors we'd like to discuss in terms of Willa Cather's statement.'

"Some students stared at the board while others opened their notebooks and began jotting down their thoughts. Glancing around I saw that everyone was concentrating. The brainstorming session was a lively exchange of names and points of view. Again, almost everyone participated. I especially noticed how animated Karen was, pressing her point of view, using an extensive vocabulary to do so. Remember, she's the student who got an F from Mr. Blandworth. She has an incredible amount of Word Power already! After 30 minutes the students narrowed the list of authors to discuss to five—Mark Twain, Willa Cather, Sinclair Lewis, Ernest Hemingway, and O. Henry, from which they were to pick one book to read in and out of class in preparation for the discussion the following week.

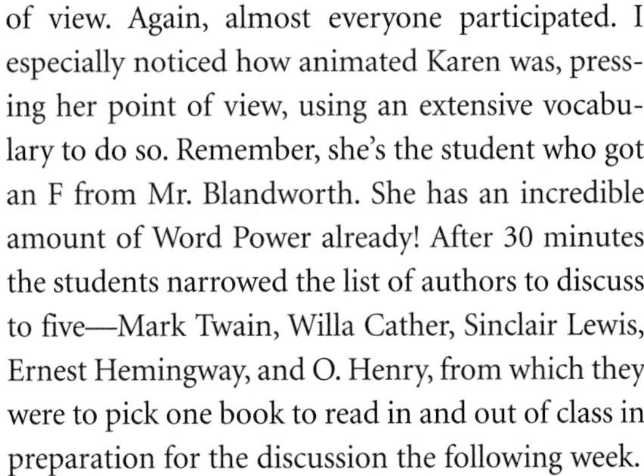

"I hated to see this first class end. The time flew by." Antoine put down Irving's journal and smiled. No, Irving would never be a Mr. Blandworth.

APPLICATION QUESTIONS

1. Using Bloom's taxonomy, analyze Mr. Blandworth's and Ms. Estefan's lessons for the kinds of learning goals they seem to support.
2. Apply Gagné's taxonomy to both classes. How are the results similar or different from those using Bloom's taxonomy?
3. Use Gagné's events of instruction to critique Mr. Blandworth's instruction. What events are missing from his current plan? How might he improve his instruction?
4. Analyze Ms. Estefan's lesson in terms of discovery versus reception learning. What elements in the lesson might lead to transfer of learning?
5. How might metacognitive skills help the students in Mr. Blandworth's class? Ms. Estefan's?
6. Plan a lesson with activities that support the six dimensions of good thinking. What other learning outcomes might be facilitated by this lesson?
7. Use Dick and Reiser's model of effective instruction to develop an instructional plan for a subject you plan to teach.

CHAPTER SUMMARY

WHAT ARE POSSIBLE OUTCOMES OF LEARNING?

Students learn many different things in school, from specific facts and critical thinking in subject matter disciplines to attitudes and motor skills. By categorizing these different types of learning outcomes, teachers assume that different learning conditions are necessary for students to acquire the various outcomes.

HOW DO TEACHERS DETERMINE AND SPECIFY INSTRUCTIONAL OUTCOMES?

Teachers rely on state requirements, curriculum guides, district and school guidelines, as well as their own professional knowledge to determine what their students should learn in a school year and within a particular lesson. To help them plan instruction and assessment, teachers can generate specific objectives—which in-clude desired student performance, conditions of performance, and criteria by which to judge performance—from more general goals.

HOW DO INSTRUCTIONAL EVENTS FACILITATE LEARNING OUTCOMES?

Gagné's nine events of instruction provide guidelines as to what external conditions should be provided during instruction to facilitate internal processes of learning. These are implemented differently depending on a teacher's decision to use discovery or reception learning in the classroom. To facilitate transfer of learning and other dimensions of thinking, teachers can employ four cultural forces in their instruction—models, explanation, interaction, and feedback.

HOW CAN YOU MAKE INSTRUCTIONAL DECISIONS THAT WILL HELP ALL STUDENTS LEARN?

By employing Dick and Reiser's (1989) model of effective instruction, you can systematically plan instruction to meet students' individual needs and to facilitate learning of particular outcomes. No matter how thoroughly you plan, however, situations are bound to arise in the classroom that call for a flexible and reasoned response. Cultivating a reflective attitude is one way to be prepared for all eventualities.

KEY CONCEPTS

advance organizer
affective domain
attitude
behavioral objectives
Bloom's taxonomy
cognitive domain
cognitive strategies
concrete concepts
cultural forces
defined concepts
dimensions of good thinking
discovery learning
discrimination
enterprise schema
Gagné's events of instruction
higher-order rules
instructional goals
intellectual skills
learning outcomes
motor skills
outcomes-based education
psychomotor domain
reception learning
rules
transfer of learning
verbal information

12 Teaching for Active Learning

CHAPTER OUTLINE

TEACHER Chronicle

ELECTRICITY

Mick Kowal is beginning a unit on electricity and wants to assess his students' knowledge of electrical concepts. He already has many activities in mind for these eighth-grade science students, but by learning what they know, he hopes to better match his lessons to their learning.

Mr. Kowal writes twenty electrical concepts on the board and says, "Look over this list. Think about the concepts you already understand. If you don't know a word, write it down in your notebooks. I want to match the experiments we will be doing with what you already know."

The students, accustomed to this format whenever beginning a new unit, write for fifteen minutes.

"Now," Mr. Kowal says. "I'd like you to break into your cooperative groups for thirty minutes to talk about the concepts. Have your recorder write down your five best known concepts and five least known. Then we'll share these as a whole class."

As the students settle into their groups, Mr. Kowal walks around listening to the discussions. He stops by one group.

"I already know all of the words," Karl says.

"Well, I can't even pronounce the third one," admits Lisa.

"That's 'rheostat,' " Lena tells her.

"What does 'series' mean?" asks Paul.

"Let's go down the list and discuss each word. With Karl's expertise, we should be able to come to some understanding," Wa Meng suggests. Karl nods in agreement, remembering how much Wa Meng contributed during the unit on the moon when he knew so little.

"I'll be recorder," offers Lena.

"I'll start with 'positive' and 'negative,'" Paul says.

Mr. Kowal turns to another group.

During the whole-class sharing at the end of the period, it becomes clear to Mr. Kowal that some students have very little understanding of electricity, some have a moderate understanding, and some are electrical wizards. This is what he had expected. As he listens to their sharing, he jots down notes about what lab stations he wants to set up for the following day's experiments. He repeats this introductory lesson with his other four classes that day. When school ends, he knows just which labs he'll set tomorrow and how he will group the students for lab work.

FOCUS QUESTIONS

1. How does Mr. Kowal actively engage students in their own learning? How can you tell that Mr. Kowal's students are actively engaged?
2. How does problem solving support active learning?
3. Does Mr. Kowal use small group and whole-class discussion well? How might he use the techniques to better advantage?
4. Under what conditions is it advantageous for students to receive direct instruction?
5. How does cooperative learning work? What are some of the benefits of using cooperative learning approaches?
6. How does instructional technology support active learning?
7. What decisions are made when teaching exceptional learners? How can instruction be modified to meet their needs?

WHAT IS ACTIVE LEARNING?

Active learning is a general term for learning that occurs when the learner is mentally involved in a task. The notion of active learning has been around for a long time, but its meaning has evolved considerably over the last four decades. The term was first used by researchers in psychology and education in the late 1950s and early 1960s as they sought to move our understanding of learning away from the behavioristic explanations that had dominated American psychological thought for four decades and toward cognitive explanations. Behaviorism, reflected in the theory of operant conditioning, assumed that learning is reflected in behavior and that nonobservable mental activity does not have to be considered to understand how human beings learn. As cognitive views of learning developed, the mental activity of learners became the focus of theoreticians and researchers. Thus, active learning was learning in which cognitive activity played a major role.

Connection: See the assumptions of operant conditioning in Chapter 6.

As cognitive views gained greater currency in the psychological and educational research literature, the meaning of the term *active learning* continued to evolve. By the mid 1970s, for example, Merlin Wittrock had proposed his *generative model of learning* (Wittrock, 1974; Wittrock, Marks, & Doctorow, 1975). The basic premise of the model is that learners comprehend and understand what they are learning in ways that are consistent with their prior knowledge. The implications of this and other models of cognitive activity have fostered research that continues to illuminate the nature of active learning (Kourilsky & Wittrock, 1992; Wittrock, 1990, 1991).

Today, the term *active learning* has a connotation of constructivism that is consistent with one of the working assumptions of this book: Learning is actively constructed in social contexts. The basic idea is that learners construct meaning through their interactions with their environment. As you read this paragraph, you are the one constructing its meaning. And because your prior knowledge and experiences are different from those of other readers, the meanings you construct may differ—slightly or more significantly—from theirs. This view of knowledge construction as building bridges from the known to the unknown underlies many of the teaching techniques that are described in this chapter (Haring-Smith, 1994a, 1994b, 1993). The common thread in all uses of *active learning* is that learners are involved in constructing their own knowledge.

Point: Several chapters in this book have discussed constructivist views. The constructivist view underlies one of the basic assumptions of this book: *Learning is active construction in social contexts.*

New approaches to the teaching–learning process seek to make students active participants in knowledge construction rather than passive recipients of didactic presentations. The teaching approaches examined in this chapter emphasize active learning but include direct instruction. Good teaching—new *and* traditional—has always produced active learning. A lesson or lecture that provokes a student to consider a topic from a new perspective has involved the student in constructing knowledge.

Before proceeding to an examination of teaching strategies that produce active learning and problem solving, there is one qualification that must be kept firmly in mind. Active learning is not simply a matter of activity. Teachers structure the learning environment and many of the learning tasks that students undertake, and it is possible for a teacher to plan a lesson that keeps students engaged and active. However, it is also possible for that same lesson to produce little or no learning. Activity does not guarantee active learning.

active learning Learning that occurs when the learner is mentally engaged in a task.

Starko (1995) describes a lesson in which students were taken outside where they worked together to manipulate a parachute. The object of the lesson was to facilitate creative thinking. The teacher carefully described how students were to grip their portions of the parachute and how to move in relation to each other. The result of this "choreography with parachute" was the creation of intriguing forms. The students were enthusiastic manipulators of the parachute. There was lots of shouting. Students enjoyed the activity very much—as did others who were watching the performance—but Starko questions the value of the activity. The teacher demonstrated creativity in using the parachute as a prop for a cooperative activity, but how did the activity facilitate creative thinking in the students? What did students learn in this lesson? What did they think about?

One way to consider the kinds of teaching that yield active learning is to focus on student thinking. What kind of thinking helps students acquire basic skills? Find and solve problems? Think critically? When we answer these questions we will be prepared to discover the kinds of teaching that yield active learning.

Student Thinking

We have addressed the ways students think, directly or indirectly, a number of times in this book. In Chapter 5, we discussed thinking dispositions as a source of variability among individual learners. Thinking dispositions, you will recall, are mental habits, inclinations, or tendencies in a person's thinking that occur over time and across thinking and learning situations (Tishman, Perkins, & Jay, 1995). Shari Tishman and her colleagues suggest that good learners are disposed toward curiosity, flexibility, precision, organization, and patience in their thinking.

Critical Thinking: Thinking dispositions were discussed in Chapter 5 as a source of variability among learners. What role do you predict thinking dispositions will play in this chapter on instructional approaches and techniques?

In Chapter 7, we examined the way students remember information, how they construct mental representations, how they identify and solve problems. The steps involved in teaching problem-solving skills include identifying, defining, and representing the problem; predicting candidate solutions; trying out and evaluating solutions; and reflecting on the problem-solving process. We also examined the metacognitive skills that allow students to monitor their thinking and problem solving.

In the context of active learning, thinking dispositions and problem-solving skills are equally important. Most efforts to teach higher-level thinking, such as problem solving, however, have focused on skills and have failed to account for the dispositional differences among students. Yet those who do not have good thinking dispositions are not as likely to use the skills they have been taught. One way to improve the teaching and learning of thinking is to focus on the development of dispositions to use sound thinking. But how do you teach dispositions? How can you facilitate the development of thinking dispositions that contribute to learning? You can incorporate thinking dispositions into your classroom culture. Some specific ways of enhancing thinking dispositions (based on suggestions from Tishman et al., 1995; Woditsch & Schmittroth, 1991) are presented in Here's How. As you examine the instructional approaches in this chapter that facilitate active learning, consider how the thinking dispositions might be encouraged.

here's how

Here's How to Cultivate Good Thinking Dispositions

- Model good thinking dispositions: Show students how you think. Share the questions you ask when learning, demonstrate persistence in the face of difficult problems, and show how you consult additional sources of information. Critically analyze with students the thinking of historical figures. What was Kennedy's thinking during the Cuban Missile Crisis, for example? Encourage students to model good thinking dispositions for each other.
- Build an awareness of good thinking dispositions: Encourage and prompt students to take advantage of opportunities to display good thinking dispositions. One teacher kept a poster in plain view and referred to it often during class discussions. The poster addressed the five thinking dispositions with these simple pieces of advice:

  Don't give up.
  Ask lots of questions.
  Generate multiple ideas and explanations.
  Be critical.
  Don't stop too soon. (Tishman et al., 1995, p. 47)
- Use "thinking alarms": In addition to encouraging the use of good thinking dispositions, you should also point out instances in which poor thinking dispositions are used by sounding thinking alarms. Here's another poster example that lists both the impetus for the alarm and the good thinking disposition that the alarm should encourage.

THINKING ALARM	THINKING DISPOSITION
Lazy thinking	Be curious and questioning.
Narrow thinking	Be broad and adventurous.
Messy thinking	Be clear and careful.
Scattered thinking	Be organized.
Hasty thinking	Give thinking time. (Tishman et al., 1995, p. 53)

- Encourage your students to interact: Provide opportunities for student-to-student interaction in your classes. Encourage students to listen for poor thinking and to sound alarms. Likewise encourage students to identify and praise instances of good thinking.

Reflection: What were the learning activities that caused you to think at the highest levels? Were they solitary activities or did you interact with others? What role does social interaction play in critical thinking?

Critical Thinking

Cognitive taxonomies such as the one described in Chapter 11 postulate different levels of thinking. Lower levels of thinking like recall of knowledge and basic comprehension require less complex cognitive activity than higher levels like synthesis and evaluation, the key ingredients in **critical thinking**. Critical thinking can be defined as cognitive activity that allows a learner to analyze or synthesize information in order to make a judgment. The outcomes that we seek for our students involve the ability to think critically. We want students to leave the classroom not only capable of synthesizing and evaluating but also with a desire to apply their critical thinking abilities to problems. We want them to persist when the problem is difficult and to generate creative solutions to those problems. Knowledge is the result of doing, predicting, testing, talking; it is actively constructed in a social context.

critical thinking Higher-level thinking used to analyze, synthesize, and evaluate.

Applying critical thinking skills in the classroom can be encouraged whenever students are required to solve problems. For example, as students are attempting to define or clarify a problem, they judge what information is relevant or irrelevant, determine if additional information is necessary, and formulate appropriate questions. Often problems require the student to distinguish fact from opinion, to recognize value judgments and unsupported assumptions, and analyze multiple sources of data to determine if they are adequate for use in formulating a solution (Kneedler, 1985). By encouraging students to analyze, synthesize, and evaluate whenever they have an opportunity to solve problems, we will help them acquire good thinking dispositions as well.

Teaching that Yields Active Learning

There are many ways to facilitate active learning. This chapter examines traditional teaching techniques that have been around for hundreds of years as well as more recent techniques. One of the major distinctions made in this chapter is between teacher-centered instruction and student-centered instruction. This distinction refers to the locus of learning activity. For example, teachers who present the key concepts of a unit through lecture are at the center of learning activity in their classrooms. If students have a question or are in need of clarification, they go to the source of the information, the teacher. This is **teacher-centered instruction**. In **student-centered instruction**, a teacher may organize students into learning groups, provide them with the necessary resources and materials, and then expect the students to teach each other the key concepts. In this case, if clarification is needed, students would consult each other before going to the instructor.

Try This: Observe a variety of classroom teachers. Which ones would you classify as characterizing teacher-centered instruction? Why? Which teachers characterize student-centered approaches to instruction? Why?

Teacher-centered techniques concentrate the responsibility for guiding the teaching-learning process in the teacher; student-centered techniques spread the responsibility between teacher and students. Both sets of techniques can be used to foster active learning in students.

Reflection: Think back to a dynamic teacher you had in elementary school who epitomized direct instruction. What behaviors did the teacher display during instruction? Was the teacher effective? Why or why not?

HOW CAN TEACHER-CENTERED INSTRUCTION SUPPORT ACTIVE LEARNING?

Teacher-centered instruction occurs when the teacher exerts a high degree of control over the teaching–learning process. A form of teacher-centered instruction that captures the essence of such approaches is called direct or explicit instruction, terms coined by Barak Rosenshine (1979, 1986).

> **Direct instruction** refers to academically focused, teacher-directed classrooms using sequenced and structured materials. It refers to teaching activities where goals are clear to students, time allocated for instruction is sufficient and continuous, coverage of content is extensive, performance of students is monitored, . . . and feedback to students is immediate and academically oriented. In direct instruction, the teacher controls instructional goals, chooses materials appropriate for the student's ability, and paces the instructional episode. (p. 38, boldface added)

Direct instruction may be teacher centered, but that does not mean that students are not actively involved. Gagne's events of instruction, which was discussed in Chapter 7, represent a model of direct instruction that encourages active learning. Another example of a teacher-centered approach to instruction is **mastery teaching**. Madeline Hunter's Mastery Teaching Program, for example

teacher-centered instruction Instruction in which the teacher is the focus of learning activity.

student-centered instruction Instruction in which the student is the focus of learning activity.

direct instruction A form of teacher-centered instruction in which goals are clear and the teacher controls the material and the pace.

mastery teaching Refers to Madeline Hunter's seven-step lesson model.

(1982, 1984, 1991), is one of the most widely recognized models of teacher-centered instruction among practicing teachers. Hunter identifies seven elements that constitute an effective lesson. As you examine the elements, picture where the action is in the classroom. Whom do you envision doing most of the talking? Who controls the pace of the lesson? Who identifies the key questions to be answered or the key issues to be resolved?

1. ***Anticipatory set*** refers to a mind-set that leaves students curious about the remainder of the lesson. Their curiosity leads them to speculate about or anticipate what is to come. This is the part of a lesson through which the teacher captures the attention of the student.
2. *Objective and purpose*, the second element in Hunter's model, provides students with the explicit objectives or purpose of the lesson. By informing the students of what you expect them to be able to do, you are building on the anticipatory set.
3. *Input* is the presentation of new material. Input, as an element of an effective lesson, requires that information be well organized and presented in a logical sequence. Hunter suggests that presenting information in a verbal and a visual manner can make input effective.
4. Modeling means that you should use frequent examples in the lesson to clarify meanings. Hunter refers to the modeling phase of a lesson as "modeling what you mean." When the objective of the lesson is to attain a skill, modeling serves the same purpose as Bandura's observational learning. If the objective of the lesson is to attain a concept or acquire verbal information, modeling calls for the use of examples or analogies or metaphors.
5. *Checking for understanding* is the evaluation of students' comprehension and understanding by asking questions orally or on a written quiz. The teacher may also ask the students to provide an example of the material on their own.
6. ***Guided practice*** begins the process of transfer by presenting students with a few problems or questions to answer on their own. Immediate feedback guides their practice in answering such questions in the classroom and gives students a way to check their own understanding and to receive help on any aspect of the lesson that they may have misunderstood.
7. *Independent practice* encourages students to answer questions or work problems on their own. Providing immediate feedback after independent practice is particularly helpful. However, feedback may occur after students have completed a homework assignment, another form of independent practice.

Critical Thinking: With reference to Bandura's theory of social learning, in what respects is Hunter's use of the term *modeling* similar and different? What are the outcomes of Hunter's modeling? How do they compare with the outcomes of Bandura's modeling?

Studies of the effectiveness of Hunter's method have generally concluded that training teachers in the method does not significantly increase student learning (e.g., Mandeville & Rivers, 1991; Stallings & Krasavage, 1986). In one study, teachers were taught the Hunter method as part of an in-service project that included two years of supervised program implementation and a one-year maintenance follow-up period, during which teachers and administrators were to continue the project on their own. During the two implementation years, teachers increased their use of Hunter's principles; however, they decreased their use during the last year. The amount of time students spent engaged in tasks and achievement of those tasks increased during the two years of implementation. These too decreased during the last year. The research indicates that close monitoring of classroom practice may be required in order for the Hunter method to be as effective as possible (Stallings & Krasavage, 1986) .

anticipatory set The first step in Hunter's approach to lesson delivery. This step establishes expectancies or a mind-set in students that anticipates the material to be covered.

guided practice The sixth step in Hunter's approach to lesson delivery. This step begins the process of transfer.

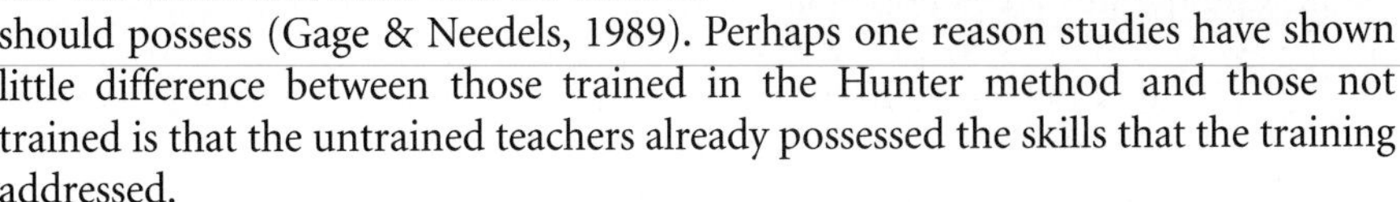

What thinking dispositions on the part of learners should teachers encourage for active learning? How can this teacher provide direct instruction that is effective and that supports active learning?

Although training in the Hunter method and in other forms of direct instruction does not seem to enhance student learning in a consistently significant way, many educators see value in Hunter's method for aspiring teachers. The value is that Hunter's method identifies the minimum skills that all teachers should possess (Gage & Needels, 1989). Perhaps one reason studies have shown little difference between those trained in the Hunter method and those not trained is that the untrained teachers already possessed the skills that the training addressed.

When the teacher is the hub around which learning activities turn, it is likely that the information flow in the classroom is from teacher to student. More important than the direction of the information flow, however, is what happens to the information when it reaches the student. Are students actively processing the information that reaches them? In the next several sections we examine teaching behaviors or techniques that are common in teacher-centered classrooms. For each type of teaching behavior, we seek to discover how that behavior can facilitate active learning in students.

Lecturing

Lecturing, that is, presenting information to a group, is the most common teaching behavior in elementary and secondary schools, colleges and universities, and training programs within business and industry (Johnson & Johnson, 1994). Your own experience probably reflects the prevalence of lecturing. Despite its status as the method of choice among teachers at all levels, lecturing has come under criticism (Good & Brophy, 1994; Henson, 1988). One criticism is that the lecture format assumes that all students need the same information presented in the same way at the same pace. Another criticism is that lectures provide little opportunity for learners to interact either with each other or with the presenter and therefore discourage the social construction of knowledge and skills. A third criticism is that lectures often outlast student attention and are boring, poorly organized, irrelevant, or redundant. You have no doubt experienced lectures that did not meet your needs, did not allow you to talk about your reactions to ideas, or failed to capture and maintain your interest. Such complaints are more properly directed at the lecturer rather than the technique itself, however. Overuse and inappropriate use are to blame for much of the criticism heaped on lectures (Good & Brophy, 1994).

Lecturing is a mainstay in the collective repertoire of teaching behaviors, and there are good reasons why that is so. Lecturing is practical and efficient because one teacher can present material to many students at one time. Lecturing is flexible and adaptable because teachers can exercise a high degree of control and can change the

lecturing A discourse given in class for the purpose of instruction.

content as circumstances in the classroom require. For example, a lecturer can "read" his or her audience directly. If a point is unclear to students, the lecturer can detect the difficulty and offer immediate clarification or remediation. The flexibility of the technique, as you will soon see, also allows an effective teacher to overcome the drawbacks of lecturing without abandoning it entirely.

Try This: Observe teachers using the lecture technique. Which lecturers seem to be most effective? Which lecturers evidence signs of "reading" the class? What behaviors indicate that they are reading student reactions? Are the more effective lecturers the better readers?

Lecturing is appropriate and effective in some situations and not in others. A number of researchers have identified the conditions under which lecturing is an appropriate instructional technique (e.g., Bligh, 1972; Good & Brophy, 1994; Henson, 1988; McKeachie, 1986; McLeish, 1976; Verner & Dickinson, 1967). The optimal conditions include:

- When information presented in the lecture is not readily available from another source
- When material needs to be organized in a special way for a particular group
- When a new topic of study or a task needs to be introduced
- When the information to be presented is a unique integration of multiple sources
- When it is important to present points of view that differ from assigned materials
- When information needs to be summarized or synthesized

Equally important is lecture preparation and delivery. The following guidelines for effective lectures (Chilcoat, 1989; Duffy et al., 1986) reflect an emphasis on the cognitive processes involved in active learning:

- Start with an advanced organizer or an anticipatory set that allows students to create a context for what is to be presented.
- Present the behavioral objectives, instructional goals, or expected learning outcomes of the presentation. This will orient students to expectations and alert them to new material and key concepts.
- Present new material with reference to students' prior knowledge.
- Elicit student responses from time to time to check for comprehension and to ensure learning is active.
- Review the main points of the lecture.
- Follow the lecture with an assignment or questions that require students to paraphrase key concepts and apply them in novel ways.

Example: Another example of a learning task that requires relatively long periods of attention is reading. Adults are usually capable of sustaining attention for longer periods. Why should this be the case?

The guidelines for delivering an effective lecture are designed to help you overcome some of the shortcomings of the technique. In particular, the idea of periodically eliciting student responses during the lecture is designed to combat the problem of maintaining student attention, a fundamental prerequisite for active learning. Even highly motivated learners have difficulty attending actively for extended periods. Research suggests that adults are capable of active attention for only ten to fifteen minutes (e.g., Johnson, Johnson, & Smith, 1991; Penner, 1984; Stuart & Rutherford, 1978).

If motivated adults have attention difficulties, how can teachers of children and adolescents maintain the attention necessary for active learning? One solution, which is consistent with the guidelines presented here, is to use lectures with *book ends* and *pair shares* (Johnson & Johnson, 1994). Book ends refer to focused discussions that occur just before and just after a lecture. The prelecture discussion serves as an advanced organizer for the lecture. Instead of the teacher presenting the advanced organizer, however, students work on a task that allows them to access

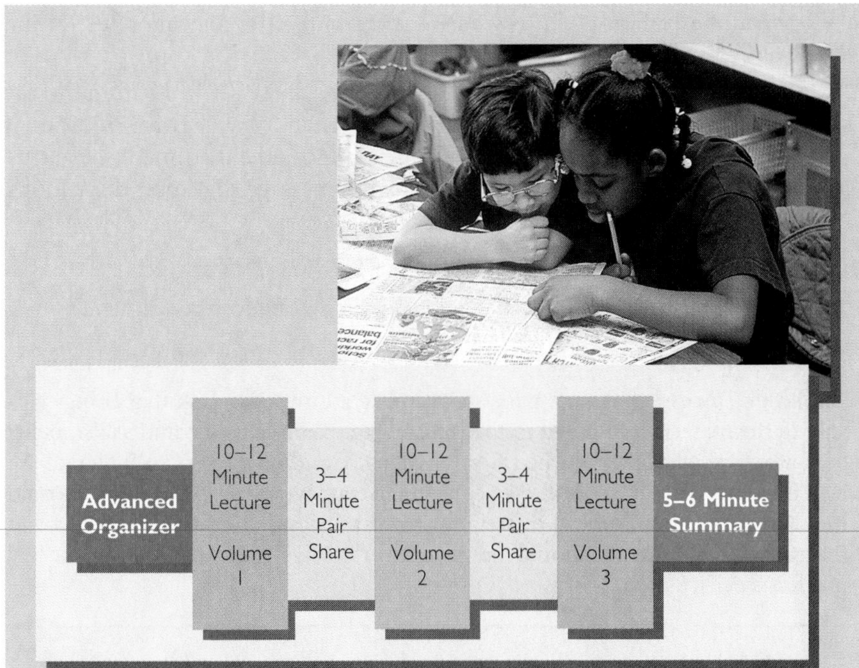

FIGURE 12.1

Lecturing with Books Ends and Pair Shares
Source: Adapted from *Learning Together and Alone* (4th ed., p. 130) by D. W. Johnson & R. T. Johnson, Needham Heights, MA: Allyn & Bacon.

pertinent prior knowledge. The postlecture discussion serves to bring closure on the topics presented in the lecture. **Pair shares** refer to short discussions between pairs of students, interspersed with periods of lecture (Figure 12.1). The technique of lecturing with book end and pair share discussions allows students to interact with each other in order to actively construct their understanding of new concepts.

Critical Thinking: From an information-processing point of view, why should book ends and pair shares solve the attention problem that accompanies the use of lecture?

Here's How to Deliver a Lecture that Encourages Active Learning

- *Prelecture Focused Discussion.* Have students pair with the person seated next to them. You may wish to have students change seats from time to time so that subsequent pairings will vary. Assign the advance organizing task.
- *First Lecture Segment.* Deliver the first part of your lecture. Make sure that the segment lasts no longer than ten minutes.
- *First Pair Share.* Give students a task that addresses the material you covered in the first segment of the lecture. Allow three or four minutes for the pair to complete the task. Announce the time allotted and then stick to the deadline. The task may be to answer a question that you pose, to react to a theory or position that you have presented, or to relate the lecture material to past learning. The pairs use the following process to complete the task:
  - Individuals *formulate* their own answers.
  - Students *share* their formulations with their partners.
  - Students *listen* intently to their partners' answers.

pair shares Short discussions between student dyads. Such discussions are usually interspersed with periods of lecture.

• Together, the pair *creates* a new answer that synthesizes and improves on the answers of both individuals.

Randomly select two or three students to give thirty-second summaries of each pair's answer. Make sure that students understand that they are not speaking for themselves, but for the pair. It is important to take the time to have students make summary statements. This sends the message that their discussions are to be taken seriously.

- *Second Lecture Segment.* Deliver the second part of your lecture.
- *Second Pair Share.* Assign a task that addresses the second lecture segment.
- *Repeat the lecture* segment–pair share steps until the lecture is complete.
- *Postlecture Discussion.* Assign pairs to complete a discussion task that brings closure to the material presented in the lecture. For example, you could ask students to summarize what they learned from the lecture and how they can integrate the new information into some extant conceptual framework. The closure task could lead students into a homework assignment or preview concepts to be covered at the next class. Students should be given four to five minutes to complete the postlecture discussion.

Try This: How many of your friends are good at explaining? Interview those who are. Ask why they explain well. Ask them a question that requires an explanation. Write down their responses and then analyze the responses to see if you can identify elements that make the explanations effective.

Explaining

Another form of instructional interaction that, in this case, focuses on teacher–student interaction is explanation. Successful explanations reward teachers with the "lightbulbs" of understanding above their students' heads. Explanations are more focused than lectures. The purpose of **explanation** is to define, clarify, or provide an account of concepts, events, and relationships (cf. Gage & Berliner, 1988). Although lectures often include explanations, explanations are not always presented in the context of a lecture. For instance, an explanation could be triggered by a student's question about a concept from the previous night's reading assignment.

The teacher who presents explanations effectively tends to be more responsive to the specific needs of the student and has a clearer idea of the student's misunderstanding. The explanation that such a teacher offers provides information that goes to the heart of the student's problem. Effective teachers also tend to provide a context or framework for the answers that their explanations provide (Duffy, Roehler, Meloth, & Vavrus, 1986). For example, suppose a student, after reading the assigned chapter, asks the economics teacher for help in understanding the concept of supply. One way of responding to the student's request would be to provide a formal definition of the term such as, "Supply is the amount of goods and services available in the marketplace." A second way of responding would be to provide the definition and then go on to describe how supply and demand operate to influence price. The first response by the teacher, the definition, might help the student memorize the definition by repeating the term and its meaning. But the definition by itself does not help the student put the term into a larger context or framework. The second response in this example does help the student connect the concept of supply to other concepts such as demand, price, and market. Useful explanations can also include the use of nonexamples as well as examples. For instance, the economics teacher might have pointed out, "An example of supply might be the

explanation A clarification that provides a context or framework for a concept, event, or relationship.

Insights ON SUCCESSFUL PRACTICE

What advice can you give novice teachers about grouping students for instruction?

Instead of having a classroom filled with students listening passively and doing seat work, I encourage a high level of stimulating interaction between teacher and students. Use fewer worksheets and implement a wider range of teaching practices. Try more individualization of lessons, allowing students to take control of their learning. Also try more peer teaching. A student's classmates are an important resource in any classroom.

Teachers should shift from large-group instruction to small-group teaching and back again in different subject areas to give children opportunities to experience and function in both types of learning situations. I eliminate all achievement and ability groupings because I feel they limit the chance for children in lower groups to keep pace with their peers. Periodic regrouping should take place; once children get labeled in a group, they tend to become stuck there.

Studies show that teachers use better teaching methods with high-achieving groups than with low-achieving groups. High achievers are expected to be the independent thinkers, the leaders, and the problem solvers, while low achievers are too often expected to be only followers. Also, educators often teach high-achieving groups a different content, which creates a communication gap among the students. For these reasons I would like to see all groups of children kept heterogeneous, with more cooperative learning among mixed-ability groupings, and with more positive feedback given to all children regardless of their level of ability.

NANCI MAES, Riverview Elementary School, Wautoma, Wisconsin

number of tickets available for a rock concert, but not the number of people who wanted those tickets. The number of people would be demand." Such explanations help students build cognitive structures or schemata in terms of which they make sense of experience. Thus, teachers should attempt to focus clearly on the student's request but should also help the student connect the information being sought with his or her prior knowledge. Explanations are also occasions for instructing students on how to use the information in other learning situations, thus contributing to metacognitive awareness and transfer of learning.

Insights

According to this teacher, how should small-group and whole-group instruction be arranged? What are some disadvantages of grouping students by ability? What role should forms of peer-mediated instruction play?

Questioning

Questions are basic to teaching and learning. Teachers and learners both ask and answer questions. This section focuses on the questions that teachers ask of students as a way of facilitating learning. **Questioning** refers to anticipating, soliciting, and reacting to student responses as a means of instruction. But what types of questions should be asked and under what conditions?

Questioning is an instructional technique that reaches back to antiquity and is used in classrooms from preschool to graduate school. Moreover, it is used quite frequently. Research has shown that primary grade teachers ask approxi-

questioning The act of asking questions as a tactic of instruction.

Point: Asking questions seems like a very straightforward idea. Yet there has been considerable study of the questioning techniques of teachers. The questions a teacher asks of his or her students provide a context for learning, which is one of the underlying assumptions in this book: *Teachers coordinate the context for learning.*

mately 150 questions per hour. University professors in undergraduate education classes ask approximately 25 questions per class hour (Duell, Lynch, Ellsworth, & Moore, 1992).

Socrates taught by asking questions that challenged students' conceptions and led them to higher and higher levels of thought. A well-known modern teacher, Jaime Escalante, successfully taught calculus to students from East Los Angeles using questions for drill and practice. He asked questions to help students learn the basic math facts they needed to master in order to understand and use more advanced concepts.

In terms of Bloom's taxonomy of cognitive objectives (see Chapter 11), questions such as those Socrates asked can be used to teach objectives at the higher levels of analysis, synthesis, and evaluation. The drill and practice questions used by Escalante address objectives at the taxonomic levels of knowledge, comprehension, and application. In both cases, the teacher's questions require the student not only to attend to the teacher but also to formulate and deliver responses. The interactive nature of the questioning tactic leads to active rather than passive learning. The nature of the questions, the manner in which teachers elicit responses, and the type of feedback or reaction to the students' answers determine the outcomes questioning will produce in a particular classroom situation.

A useful way for teachers to think about questioning includes three stages: *structure*, setting the stage for the questions that follow; *solicitation*, asking the questions; and *reaction*, responding to the students' answers (Clark, Gage, Marx, Peterson, Staybrook, & Winnie, 1979; see also Good, 1988; Tobin, 1987).

Connection: Consider how Mr. Kowal's actions constitute the use of an advance organizer as described in Chapter 6.

Structure. Structure is established through lecture, explanation, assigned reading, or other activities and anticipates students' responses to questions. This stage sets up students, providing them with the appropriate background information and format to use when answering questions. Recall how Mr. Kowal in the Teacher Chronicle prepared his students to answer questions about concepts as they began the unit on electricity. He wrote the concepts of electricity on the board and told the students to think about those they already knew and to write down the ones they didn't know. He also explained why he wanted students to work on the concepts. When it was time for questions, the students understood the context in which they were being asked. Teachers can establish structure by providing rules that govern the answers students give. For example, a teacher might prepare a class for a review session by saying, "I am going to ask you some practice questions similar to the ones that will be on the test Friday. As you know, Friday's test will require short essay answers. For today's review, I want you to give a brief answer followed by supporting evidence. Let's try the first review question." Providing students with a context allows them to access the prior knowledge they will need to respond appropriately.

From an information-processing perspective, answering questions requires students to retrieve information from long-term store (Duell, 1994; Gagné, Yekovich, & Yekovich, 1993). First, consider a question that requires simple recall of the definition of a key term, a case of drill and practice on basic factual information. An example might be "What is a rheostat?" The student must locate the definition of *rheostat* in long-term store, transfer the definition into short-term or working memory, check to make sure the definition matches the key term, and then generate the answer. Now consider a question that requires a student to apply a concept in a new situation, a higher level of thinking. An example here might be, "How might a rheostat be used to control the temperature of an oven?" In this instance, the student begins as before, retrieving pertinent information from long-term store into working memory. In working memory, the student integrates the retrieved information (not only what a rheostat is but also how it works) with information about the new situation (ovens, temperature) to determine if the prior knowledge is applicable to the new situation. If additional information is necessary—which is often the case when higher-level thinking is required—the student must locate and retrieve the additional information. This process of retrieval from long-term store and evaluation of the resulting integration in working memory is repeated until an answer is generated. The point here is that the level of the question influences the cognitive activity that occurs as students respond to a teacher's questions.

It is important to note that the level of the question can be influenced by the structure provided by the teacher. Suppose, for example, that a teacher sets up the question "What is a rheostat?" as follows. "I am going to ask you to identify some key terms from the unit on electricity. Now, when I ask you about a key concept, your job is to give not only the definition, but to identify a real-life example in which that concept is used and to explain how the concept works." By structuring the question in this way, the teacher is demanding more complex cognitive activity than would be required had the teacher simply solicited definitions. Thus, active learning can be enhanced by asking higher-level questions or by structuring questions so that higher-level responses are required.

Try This: Observe questioning in a classroom. Using Bloom's taxonomy, identify the taxonomic level of each question.

Solicitation. If questioning in ways that increase thinking is advantageous, it would be foolish to ask high-level questions without providing students the necessary time to think. We have already seen from the research that wait-time increases the quality of learning. By reacting or calling on students only after some time has elapsed, we give students the time to engage in higher-level thinking. Time to think, however, is also a function of solicitation. To illustrate, think back to a class in which your teacher was asking students, in a large group, to answer questions. Maybe it was a review of a homework assignment. The teacher structured the questioning session in such a way that you knew the teacher was checking to see who had and had not done the assignment. Suppose that the teacher solicitation routine was to call on a student and then ask the question. What was your reaction each time another student was chosen? Orpha Duell (1994) provides the following analysis of such a situation.

> If the teacher names a student before asking a question, although all students could engage in the processing sequence required to respond, it is likely that at least some will not because it is clear they are not expected to answer the question. If the teacher asks questions, pauses, and then names a student to respond, it is more likely that all students will do the processing sequence in an attempt to be ready should they be called upon. (p. 398)

Reflection: Which of your teachers used the technique described here? Was your attention in the class affected? If so, how? If not, why not?

Although asking questions is a critical teaching function, it is useful to keep in mind that professionals who elicit information from others—such as psychiatrists, lawyers, pollsters, and teachers—gain more information from their clients when they ask fewer questions and give their clients more time to think and talk (Dillon, 1988, 1990; Kloss, 1993). The research described previously suggests that the keys to facilitating active learning by means of questioning are encouraging students to think at higher levels and providing them with the time to do that thinking.

Try This: If you have the opportunity to tutor children or adolescents, take a stop watch to your next session. Each time you ask a question, do not let the student answer for at least three seconds. At the end of the session, review the quality of your students' answers.

wait-time I The length of time between the teacher's question and the student's response.

wait-time II The length of time between the student's response and the teacher's reaction to that response.

Reaction. Between solicitation (asking the question) and reaction (responding to the student's answer), there is the period of time, called **wait-time I,** when the student formulates his or her answer and delivers it. The period of time between the student's answer and the teacher's reaction to that answer is called **wait-time II** (Rowe, 1986) (Figure 12.2).

The routine a teacher uses to acknowledge or call on students affects the length of wait-time I. For example, if students in a classroom are allowed to respond spontaneously, without first being acknowledged by the teacher, wait-time I will be decreased. If students are required to raise their hands and be acknowledged before responding, the teacher can control the length of wait-time I, which has its advantages. Research has shown that lengthening wait-time to three seconds is accompanied by increases in the attainment of higher-level outcomes (Rowe, 1986; Tobin, 1987). Other benefits that accrue by extending wait-time include greater student attention, more complex student answers (Fagan, Hassler, & Szabo, 1981; Tobin & Capie, 1982), more relevant student questions, and fewer disciplinary comments from teachers (Rowe, 1986).

Although longer wait-times are generally related to higher-level thinking, the decisions you make about solicitation and reaction must take into account the outcomes you are trying to help your students achieve. "There are many classroom contexts in which shorter pauses between speakers can be justified. For example, when rote memorization or recall of facts is required, drill and practice activities might be conducted at a brisk pace using shorter wait-time" (Tobin, 1987, p. 91).

FIGURE 12.2

Wait-Times Associated with Questioning

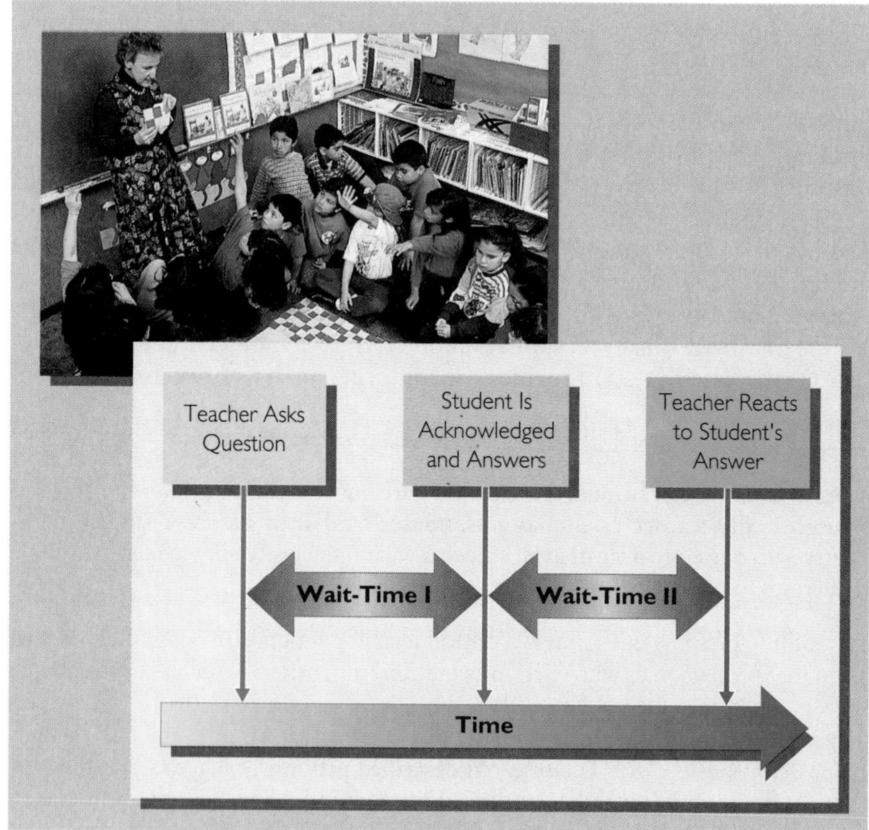

Reciprocal Questioning. The techniques associated with wait-time are commonly used in teacher-centered instruction. One student-centered approach to questioning is called **reciprocal questioning**. Reciprocal questioning is a technique that encourages students to develop and answer their own high-level questions (King, 1990). Typically, reciprocal questioning occurs at the conclusion of a lecture or other presentation of new material. The teacher organizes students into pairs or triads and gives them the beginnings of questions, called *stems*, that they must complete and then answer. Students complete the stems with reference to the material that the teacher presented in the lecture. Some examples of the question stems are:

- How might you use . . . to . . . ?
- How are . . . and . . . similar? How are they different?
- What might happen if . . . ?
- Another example of . . . is . . . ?
- Why is it important to understand . . . ?
- What are the advantages and disadvantages of . . . ?

Try This: As you study this chapter or any other reading assignment, keep this list of stems close at hand. Stop periodically in your reading, and use these stems to develop your questions.

Students who have been trained to use the stems in response to a lecture process the information more deeply than students who merely discuss their reactions to a presentation. The explanation of the technique's effectiveness lies in the reflection, critical thinking, and active learning facilitated by the question stems. Are there some other ways of encouraging the reflective thinking that is characteristic of active learning?

here's how

Here's How to Increase Active Learning through Response

- Make declarative statements that encourage elaboration. Example: "The protagonist seems to be in a dilemma at this point of the story." (In the context of a class discussion, this comment invites your students to speculate on the nature of the dilemma.)
- Make a reflective paraphrase of a student's comment. Example: "So, Jocelyn, you think the best way to approach this problem is to start by finding out the country's average family income." (This shows you are attending to the student and invites the student to confirm or deny.)
- Describe your own views. Example: "I'm feeling a little lost. I thought you were arguing against that position a few minutes ago." (This expresses your interest and invites the student to clarify his or her position.)
- Invite student elaboration. Example: "I need to be convinced that your group's solution is the most efficient way of estimating load factors." (This probes for additional evidence or comparisons.)
- Maintain silence. (Silence gives students a chance to reflect on what has come before, to formulate their questions, and to think critically.)

Independent Practice

Independent practice refers to tasks a student completes independently while in the classroom or at home. In many classrooms, seat work constitutes a large proportion of the student's day. This is especially true in elementary school class-

reciprocal questioning A technique that uses question stems that students complete. The technique encourages critical thinking.

independent practice Tasks that students complete independently either in the classroom or at home.

rooms. Rosenshine (1980) estimates that elementary students spend between 50 percent and 70 percent of their time doing seat work (see also Stigler, Lee, & Stevenson, 1987). One reason seat work is so common in elementary classrooms is that elementary teachers tend to work with their students in groups. While the teacher is working with one group, the other students need to fill the time with a task that does not require the teacher's constant attention. In many instances, the most practical solution to this problem is seat work.

Connection: See the discussion of self-efficacy in Chapter 8.

Evertson, Emmer, and Brophy (1980) documented the amount of time seventh- and eighth-grade math teachers devoted to lecture versus seat work. The most effective math teachers divided class time between lecture and seat work almost equally. Students of those teachers who were the least effective spent more than three times as long doing seat work as they did learning from lectures or demonstrations. Heavy reliance on seat work can compound the problem of low-achieving students (Anderson, Brubaker, Alleman-Brooks, & Duffy, 1985). Many low-achieving students lack the adequate motivation and confidence necessary for effective independent work. Some of these students lack reading and other basic skills and have not developed the kinds of self-monitoring and organizational skills that would allow them to benefit from seat work. For many of these students, simple completion of the assignments is the goal that guides their efforts on seat work.

According to principles of direct instruction, examined earlier, independent practice should be preceded by guided practice. If a student enters into independent practice without a clear notion of what the task is, or with a mistaken idea of how a skill is to be applied, the student will practice making errors (Gunter, Estes, & Hasbrouck Schwab, 1990). Thus, in order to use seat work effectively, students must know what to do and how to do it.

Because seat work does offer practical value, it is likely to stay in the repertoire of many teachers. When you find it necessary or desirable to use seat work in your own classroom, there are several guidelines that can enhance its effectiveness.

If you will use seat work as a regular feature in your classroom, spend time early in the year establishing rules and procedures that will enable students to

How can teachers structure learning situations using questioning? What are the best ways to solicit and react to students' answers? How can this teacher use the technique of questioning to facilitate students' active learning and higher-level thinking?

work independently. Make students aware of rules for talking among themselves during seat work, how to obtain help, under what conditions they can get out of their seats, and what to do when they have completed their seat work (cf. Emmer, Evertson, Clements, & Worsham, 1994). Formulating general rules and procedures will eliminate many nonacademic, procedural questions that might distract you while you are helping other students.

Establishing seat work procedures will allow you to be as available as possible to students during their practice sessions. If students are clear as to how they should work, you are free to walk around the room and spot-check the progress of students so that you can readily intervene when a student is working poorly or incorrectly. Moving about the room while monitoring seat work also sends a message to students that you are aware of their behavior and that you place some importance on the task at hand (Fisher, Berliner, Filby, Marliave, Cahen, & Dishaw, 1980).

A number of studies have found a strong correlation between the amount of homework assigned and higher grades (e.g., Keith, 1982; Marshall, P.M. 1982; Wolf, R.M. 1979). The guidelines that apply to seat work also apply to homework (Good & Brophy, 1994). The obvious difference between homework and seat work is the teacher's ability to monitor the performance of students. Although the teacher can suggest procedures and routines that will help students to complete homework more efficiently, the teacher is not available to answer students' questions as they arise. Preparing students in class for their homework assignments is, therefore, a critical element of the tactic. If students are confused or unclear about what they are to accomplish at home or how they are to accomplish it, they are less likely to derive benefits from homework.

Critical Thinking: How is preparation for homework related to the structure stage of questioning? How is it different?

Finally, evaluating seat work and homework is likely to increase student engagement in the tasks they are given. If students, especially less motivated students, perceive seat work and homework as just practice, they will be less likely to put forth their best efforts. Thus, evaluating independent work and incorporating student performance into any grades you assign is a good way of emphasizing the importance of independent work. In the case of homework, you should check the work and give feedback in the form of comments to your students. Using written commentary in evaluating homework enhances achievement (Elawar & Corno, 1985).

HOW CAN STUDENT-CENTERED INSTRUCTION SUPPORT ACTIVE LEARNING?

This part of the chapter focuses on teaching behaviors that move the locus of learning activity away from the teacher and toward the students. Student-centered approaches define the teacher as a *facilitator,* not an *orator*; a *coworker,* not a *boss*; a *guide on the side*, rather than a *sage on the stage* (Johnson & Johnson, 1994). Many student-centered teaching approaches are therefore consistent with constructivist views of learning (Prawat, 1992). Before examining student-centered approaches, let's consider some of the key characteristics of the constructivist view of the teaching–learning process. One constructivist benchmark is that learning is best done in real-life environments, complete with the ill-defined problems characteristic of everyday situations. Another benchmark, consistent with Vygotsky's view of intellectual growth, is that social negotiation is essential to learning. A third constructivist benchmark is that ideas and concepts should be learned in diverse ways (Driscoll, 1994; Marshall, 1992). Consider these benchmarks in relation to a learning activity designed by James Ellington, a fourth-grade teacher in Moorehead, Minnesota (Adams Johnson, 1992).

On a bright spring day, Mr. Ellington takes his class outside to a large, carefully outlined rectangle of grass. He is talking with his students about the concept protective coloration in nature. He sprinkles three hundred colored toothpicks throughout the rectangle of grass, sixty red ones, sixty blue, sixty yellow, sixty natural, and sixty green. As he does, he asks his students to imagine that the toothpicks are worms and that on such a nice day robins will be hunting for them. He then poses a question, "What color worm do you want to be?" The students make predictions, such as "I sure don't want to be yellow against the green grass." They get down on their hands and knees and collect as many of the toothpicks as they can find and then analyze the results. The students found fifty-six of the sixty yellow toothpicks and only seven of the green toothpicks. They discuss fractions and draw a graph to indicate their findings.

Notice how this lesson addresses the constructivist benchmarks presented earlier. Learning about protective coloration in this way is more authentic than hearing a lecture. The social interaction that is facilitated by being outdoors on hands and knees is more natural than that found in the classroom, and the lesson adds variety to the learning activities of the students.

The reason to use constructivist benchmarks in evaluating teaching behaviors is that those benchmarks are the best standards we have for determining the extent to which learning is both active and student centered. For as Pamela Adams Johnson, Iowa Teacher of the Year and the chronicler of James Ellingson's worm lesson, says, "Schooling should not be viewed as a spectator sport for students, where adults perform while students watch" (Adams Johnson, 1992, p. 67).

Student-centered instruction can be provided in the form of small group discussions, peer teaching, cooperative learning, and interactive instructional technology.

Small Group Discussions

Small group discussions allow students to exchange information and opinions. The groups that worked on the electricity concepts in the Teacher Chronicle would be considered discussion groups. Small group discussion is helpful in fostering a student's ability to think critically because students must express, support, and modify their assumptions, conclusions, and opinions (Gage & Berliner, 1988). A student's reasoning then becomes part of the content of the group's discussion.

Try This: Ask a number of your friends if they prefer to discuss their reading assignments in their classes or not. For those who voice a preference for discussion, ask them to explain why they think discussion helps.

If students are to learn effectively in a discussion group, they must develop communication, interaction, and social skills. For example, students need to listen and respond to what they hear. The ability to listen for the purpose of responding to group discussion is different from the ability to listen effectively to a lecturer. Thus, students learn to think through problems as part of a group process.

small group discussion Exchange of information and opinion among a small number of students.

Students faced with the challenge of marshaling arguments in small group discussions must also learn to reason and think critically about questions, issues, or problems. Evidence suggests that small group discussions can also stimulate changes in attitudes and behavior. Students who take a position in a group discussion are making a public statement that implies a course of action on their part.

In choosing small group discussion as a means of instruction, teachers are well advised to consider the learning objectives students are to attain. General objectives in low-consensus content areas are most appropriate for discussion formats. Low consensus describes the lack of a high degree of agreement as to what is and is not true or important. Topics in social studies or literature, for example, are more suitable for discussion than formulas and equations. Areas of low consensus that are emotionally charged, such as a discussion of legislation and court decisions involving civil liberties, will elicit a variety of opposing views. Many teachers try to avoid controversial topics, but Johnson and Johnson (1994) suggest that they should address controversial topics. A discussion that requires one to take and defend a position against the positions of others forces students to find new information, to organize their thinking, and to negotiate conflicts. In addition, such discussions encourage students to construct logical arguments that can withstand or account for new information and other perspectives. Finally, discussions of controversial topics contribute to the development of self-knowledge.

Reflection: In which classes do you find discussion more productive? Is there a connection with the general level of consensus of the material discussed? If you will teach math, how will you structure small group discussions?

The teacher's role in small group discussions is to avoid interfering while at the same time facilitating effective group dynamics. Some teachers have a natural tendency to respond to any difficulty students are having and to suggest solutions before the group has had a chance to develop its own ideas. Other teachers might watch helplessly as discussion groups break into quarrels or lapse into silence. Here's How presents some strategies for facilitating discussions (Good & Brophy, 1994; Johnson & Johnson, 1994; Gage & Berliner, 1988).

here's how

Here's How to Intervene in Small Group Discussions

- If several small groups are discussing a topic, briefly monitor all of the groups on a rotating basis.
- If discussion is flagging, ask a leading question.
- If digressions are occurring, remind the group of the task at hand or ask a question that refocuses attention.
- If one student is monopolizing the discussion, ask other members of the group to comment on the group's progress—or lack of it.
- If lengthy pauses occur between contributions to the discussion, intervene. Long pauses may be a sign that students are becoming confused or have forgotten the task at hand.
- If students are having difficulties distinguishing values or opinions from facts, intervene. If you doubt the group's ability to discern the difference, ask a question such as "Is Rodney's statement an opinion or a fact?"
- If logical fallacies stated by one member of the group go undetected by other members, the validity of the discussion is damaged. Logical fallacies may include overgeneralization or reasoning based on unsound premises. Questions such as "Is that true?" or "Does that make sense?" can help focus students' attention on issues of logic as they pertain to the discussion.
- Provide closure to discussions by asking each group to report results or write brief summaries.

Peer Teaching and Learning

Peer teaching and learning can take several forms. In some cases, you can assign one student to tutor another student. In such cases, you can easily infer that the student who is being tutored needs help. In other cases, students learn together on a more equal footing by teaching each other. Teachers can also work with students in an effort to transfer gradually the responsibilities for teaching from teacher to students working together.

One form of peer teaching is peer tutoring, which occurs when one student is assigned to help another learn assigned material (see the discussion of peer modeling in Chapter 8). According to research, peer tutoring improves the academic performances and attitudes of both the student who tutors and the student who is tutored (Cohen, Kulik, & Kulik, 1982). The two basic types of peer tutoring are cross-age tutoring and same-age tutoring. There is little research to suggest what specific characteristics of the tutor and the tutored teachers should consider in forming groups. Establishing pairs of students of the same age can be difficult, because when a teacher appoints one classmate to tutor another, it implies a relationship based on ability, and both students are likely to perceive the tutor as superior. One solution is to have study pairs—study buddies—alternate in the roles of tutor and tutee in a way that maximizes each student's strengths. Peer tutoring, in which the responsibility for tutoring alternates between students, is a basic element in cooperative learning techniques (Johnson, Johnson, & Holubec, 1993).

Critical Thinking: How might you overcome the so-called social perception problem associated with same-age peer tutoring? What steps could you take in a classroom to prevent the problem?

Similarly, teachers can also pair peers so they can learn together without implying teaching responsibilities in the relationship. For example, middle school students who were assigned to learn together outperformed students who worked individually on a cognitive reasoning task (Kutnick & Thomas, 1990). The students who were paired did not necessarily share similar achievement histories. Furthermore, the scores on the reasoning task indicated enhancement in the performance of each partner, not merely an average enhancement for the pair. Not all studies of peer learning have shown such gains, however. In a study of mathematical problem solving, high school students who were paired randomly—with a few students working in triads—performed less well than students working alone (Stacey, 1992). One explanation of the results, however, was that the students working in groups tended to choose simpler, often incorrect, solutions to the math problems. The groups seemed to adopt a norm of minimal brainstorming in considering possible solutions. Perhaps the students were unfamiliar with peer learning or simply perceived this particular task as inconsequential.

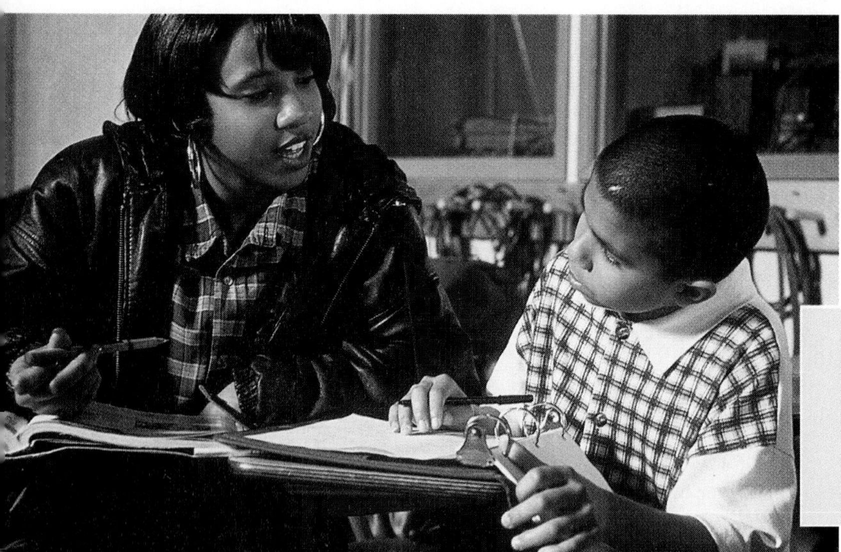

In what form of peer teaching are these students engaged? What are some other ways students can instruct each other effectively and share greater responsibility for their learning? What makes peer teaching approaches so successful?

Reciprocal teaching is a specialized form of peer teaching designed initially to help poor readers develop and apply metacognitive skills (Palincsar, 1986; Palincsar & Brown, 1984). The instructional arrangement involves the teacher working with small groups of students. The instructional task is to acquire four reading strategies that facilitate reading comprehension and understanding. Those strategies are: summarizing the content of a passage, formulating a question about the key point, clarifying unclear portions of the reading material, and predicting what will be addressed later in the the passage.

The teacher begins by explaining and modeling these strategies for students. Gradually, the teacher encourages students to take over the teacher's role by modeling the strategies for peers. Students eventually learn to ask themselves strategic questions about the material they are reading. For example, students may ask themselves the following in response to a passage about the circus:

- What part of the circus did this paragraph address?
- How did the circus start?
- Why was the fire at the P. T. Barnum Museum important? Is that the section I should reread?
- Is the next section about clowns?

Research on reciprocal teaching has shown it to be an effective method of improving reading achievement in poor readers (Palincsar, 1987; Palincsar & Brown, 1984; Rosenshine & Meister, 1991). These and other studies have also suggested that the technique is most effective when (1) the shift of responsibility from teacher to student occurs gradually, (2) when the difficulty of the task and the teaching responsibilities are matched to the student's ability, and (3) when teachers observe students carefully as they teach in order to determine how the student is thinking about the reading material.

Try This: Find a teacher who uses reciprocal teaching as a technique. Ask the teacher to describe cases in which the shift from teacher to student occurred too quickly. Ask the teacher to explain how one should gauge the shift.

Cooperative Learning

Cooperative learning is an instructional technique that calls for students to be teamed together to attain certain goals (Kagan, 1989; Slavin, 1991). Johnson and Johnson (1994) identify five basic ingredients of cooperative learning (Figure 12.3). *Face-to-face promotive interaction* refers to students talking with each other in order to share insights and ideas. *Individual responsibility* refers to the necessity for teachers to hold students accountable for themselves to prevent freeloading in a learning group. *Collaborative skills* include the skills necessary for effective group functioning, such as leadership, team building, and conflict resolution. *Group processing* refers to how well the group is functioning aside from the academic products or performances on which they are working. Addressing the quality of working relationships gives the group opportunities to improve the way it works.

Successful cooperative learning groups also show *positive interdependence* among participants. Positive interdependence exists when students perceive that their individual fates are linked to the fates of others in the group. A belief that "we sink or swim together" fuels the group to interact in positive ways, to hold themselves accountable to others, to collaborate, and to reflect on the quality of group functioning.

Cooperative learning techniques require teachers to place themselves in an entirely different role than do teacher-centered techniques such as lecturing. To

Reflection: Recall learning groups in which you have participated that worked well and not so well. Were there any freeloaders in the group that did not work well? What can a teacher do to ensure that each individual feels responsible to the other members of the group?

reciprocal teaching A technique that begins with the teacher's questions designed to enhance metacognitive skills and that progresses to a gradual transfer of the control of questioning to the students, who work cooperatively.

cooperative learning Students working together to attain common learning goals.

FIGURE 12.3

Elements of Cooperative Learning
Source: Adapted from *Learning Together and Alone* (4th ed.), 1994, by D. W. Johnson & R. T. Johnson, Needham Heights, MA: Allyn & Bacon.

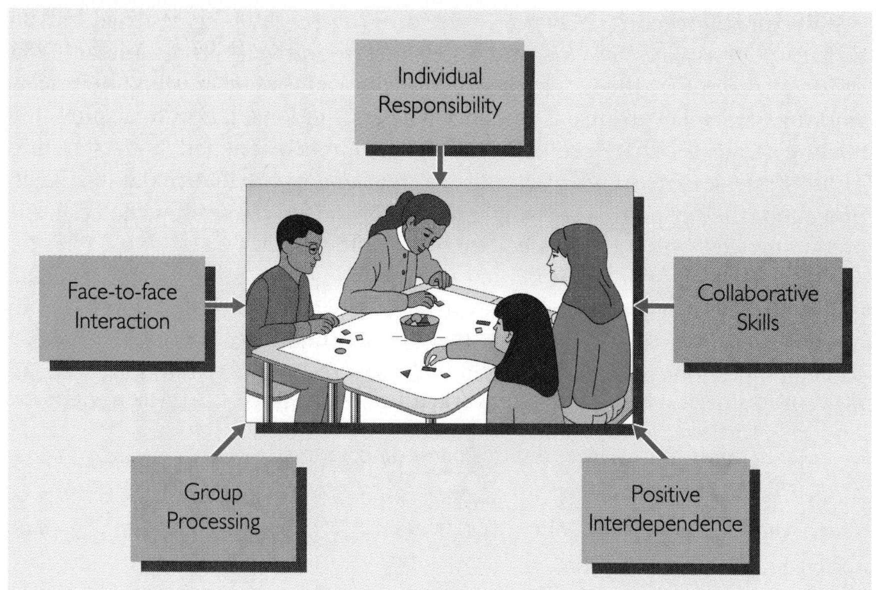

some degree teachers share authority with students over the knowledge students gain. As students become more responsible for their own learning, teachers and students become collaborators, sharing responsibility for determining what is to be learned (Bruffee, 1993). The issue of who determines what is to be learned has been used to distinguish cooperative learning from collaborative learning (Haring-Smith, 1993, 1994a, 1994b).

One approach to collaborative learning is called teaching for understanding (Talbert & McLaughlin, 1993). This approach is based on three principles: that knowledge is constructed; that the teacher is a guide, a collaborator in the construction of student knowledge; and that the classroom is a learning community that supports its members. Translated into classroom practice, these principles mean that sometimes topics are generated by students rather than presented by the teacher (Perkins, 1993).

Informal cooperative learning groups are formed on a temporary, ad hoc basis. While the group has a goal to attain, the nature of the work needed to attain that goal is usually short lived, and therefore the group may last for only a few minutes or perhaps a full class period. The purpose of informal learning groups is to focus student attention on the content to be learned and to help students actively process that content. The groups formed in the Teacher Chronicle to review the concepts of electricity are an example.

Formal cooperative learning groups, in contrast, are more structured and may last up to several weeks or months. Members of formal learning groups have two major responsibilities. They are responsible for maximizing not only their own learning but also the learning of all other members of the group. Formal learning groups work to complete a specific task, usually resulting in some performance or product. The outcomes—the performances or products generated by the group—can range from acquiring information to problem solving to cooperative composition. The following sections describe formal cooperative learning programs that were extensively researched and developed during the 1980s and 1990s.

Student Teams–Achievement Divisions. One type of team that can be formed is referred to as **Student Teams–Achievement Divisions (STAD)**, a cooperative learning method that employs a cycle of teaching tactics, consisting of lecture, cooperative study in small groups, and quiz (Slavin, 1987). Rewards are given to teams whose members show the greatest improvement over their own past performances, the real-world equivalent of increased productivity. STAD teams work best when each comprises four or five students.

A lesson using the STAD procedure begins with a lecture presentation of material, usually conducted over one or two class periods. During the cooperative study phase, which lasts for one or two class periods, the teacher provides each team with worksheets or other materials pertaining to the topic covered in the lecture. Each team is to make sure that all of its members master the material. In order to encourage real teamwork, a teacher can insist that team members work together on just one or two copies of the worksheets.

The team score is the total amount of improvement of each individual over his or her past performances on assessments. Teachers compute a team score by adding together the number of improvement points earned by the team and dividing that number by the number of team members assessed.

After calculating team scores, the teacher delivers some reward or recognition to any team that averaged two or more improvement points. Rewards are based not on the performance of the team compared with other teams, but with its own past performance.

Critical Thinking: Explain how the STAD procedure enhances positive interdependence.

Consider the following STAD procedure for teaching math. After you have lectured on the objectives of a math lesson and teams have convened for team study, you might distribute worksheets containing math problems based on the lecture just presented. In this case, each student on the team should work each problem. Each student should compare his or her answer with those of the other teammates. If any member of the team has missed a problem, it is the responsibility of the other teammates to provide remediation. The STAD procedure emphasizes that team study is not complete until all members of the team have mastered the material. Students should address questions that arise during team study to teammates before consulting the teacher. After students complete team study, the teacher gives a test to the entire class and calculates team scores. The teacher assigns students to new STAD teams every five or six weeks, and students who were on low-scoring teams have a chance to try again or achieve greater success. This recommendation is similar to the idea of changing the membership of teams on a playground when one team has won a number of games in a row.

student teams–achievement divisions (STAD) A cooperative learning method that uses heterogeneous groups of four to five students. Rewards are given to teams whose members show the greatest improvement over their own past performance.

teams-games-tournaments (TGT) A cooperative learning method that uses heterogeneous groups of four to five students. Team members leave their teams to compete as individuals in homogeneous weekly tournaments. An individual's performance in the weekly tournament contributes to his or her team's score.

Teams-Games-Tournaments. Another form of team learning is **Teams-Games-Tournaments (TGT)** (Slavin, 1987, 1991). As in the STAD procedure, the team is responsible for preparing each team member for competition. In TGT, a team comprises four or five members of varying ability levels. Once the teacher forms the mixed-ability teams, the prepared members leave their teams to compete as individuals in homogenous three-person competition groups. Each team member competes against members of other teams in weekly tournaments. The competitive groups change each week, but the level of ability within groups remains constant. An individual's performance in the weekly tournament contributes to his or her team's score.

In each competition group, players take turns serving one of three functions: Reader, Challenger I, or Challenger II. The Reader on a particular turn reads the problem or question to the two challengers. The Reader attempts to solve the problem or answer the question. Challenger I can then choose to challenge the reader's answer by giving a different answer, or Challenger I may pass. Challenger II may challenge or pass. Challenger II then checks the correct answer to the problem or question using an answer sheet provided by the teacher. Students exchange roles so that each student plays each role within a tournament. The score received by each player is his or her contribution to the team's total score for a particular tournament.

Try This: Interview a teacher who uses either STAD or TGT. Ask how the teacher establishes the procedures for record keeping. Is this a group responsibility? Individual responsibility? A teacher responsibility?

The three players who compete against each other in a group change each week. The winners in each group are moved to a higher-ability group for the next week's tournament. The low scorer in each group is moved to a lower-level group for the next week's tournament. In this way, each team member has an increased chance of contributing points to the team's overall performance.

Team-Assisted Individualization. The **Team-Assisted Individualization (TAI)** approach prescribes that students work individually at their own pace with programmed materials. However, students also study and practice together in mixed-ability groups as in STAD. Although the assigned content provided to each student is in the form of programmed instruction—usually, but not necessarily presented via computer—the teammates are available to check work and to encourage and remediate. Because the team as a whole is rewarded for the work of individual players, it is to each individual's advantage to assist others on the team. The TAI approach allows teammates to become a source of motivation for individual students. Another advantage of TAI is that teammates can perform some of the clerical work that otherwise the teacher would perform. This variation of cooperative learning has proved very effective in elementary-school mathematics (Slavin & Karweit, 1985). In studies of math classes, classes taught via TAI compared favorably to classes taught in a more traditional way (Good et al., 1983; Slavin, 1985, 1991).

team-assisted individualization(TAI) A teaching tactic in which students work on programmed materials as members of a heterogeneous group. Rewards for completing the work accurately and quickly are given to the team as a whole.

cooperative integrated reading and composition (CIRC) Pairs of students from one homogeneous reading group join another pair from a different reading group to work cooperatively on comprehension and writing skills.

Cooperative Integrated Reading and Composition. In most classrooms where reading groups are used, the groups tend to be homogeneous. This allows the teacher to work with groups using materials that are similar in difficulty and to proceed at a pace that is appropriate for each group rather than at one pace for the entire class. One of the consequences of using homogeneous reading groups is that while the teacher is working with one group, other students must work independently. Typically, the time spent working independently is not used very effectively. Another disadvantage of using homogeneous reading groups is that the achievement benefits of heterogeneous cooperative learning groups are lost (Johnson & Johnson, 1991; 1992; Slavin, 1990).

One solution to both of these difficulties is an approach called **cooperative integrated reading and composition (CIRC)**. CIRC combines a pair of students from one reading group and a pair of students from another into a mixed-ability cooperative learning group. While the teacher is busy leading one of the reading groups, CIRC groups—formed from the students in the remaining reading groups—are engaged in a variety of tasks. The four members of a CIRC group take turns reading to each other and answering questions about what they have read. The group practices new vocabulary, spelling, and reading comprehension skills. The group also writes about what they read. Research on the

Insights ON SUCCESSFUL PRACTICE

How have you and your students benefited from the use of cooperative learning groups?

As a seventh-grade physical science teacher, I have always recognized the potential of science classes to motivate students who might otherwise have little or no interest in academic achievement. This is because science classes usually involve active, hands-on experiences where students conduct investigations and experiments, and because students generally work in groups so they can share materials and interact with each other. I have discovered that group work can be a powerful teaching strategy that allows for a wide range of academic abilities.

A major portion of the seventh-grade physical science curriculum is the study of motion, forces, and energy. In the past, I taught these concepts during the second semester, allowing time for the many prerequisite math skills to be taught during the first. But this year, because I intended to cover most of the physics curriculum through a thematic unit on rockets, it was necessary to select cooperative learning groups such that each group had at least one high math student. Also, because rockets may be more interesting to some groups of students than others, I was careful to mix the groups by gender and race as well as academic ability.

The cooperative learning groups, consisting of three or four members per group, worked together for fifteen weeks. To promote interdependence and accountability among group members, each student was assigned a specific role or job to perform, but all group members were required to learn the concepts and skills covered throughout the unit. These skills were extensive. In order to study the physics of rockets, it was necessary to build them, fly them, observe them, measure them, redesign them, make predictions, identify variables and constants, and design controlled experiments. The math skills involved precise measurements of length, mass, and volume (using metric units), an understanding of geometry and simple trigonometry, expressing recorded data in terms of ratios and percents, solving equations and rounding numbers to given place values, using calculators and computers, analyzing data, and constructing graphs.

I am thoroughly convinced that group work is an effective technique for achieving many kinds of intellectual and social learning goals. I believe that if students are able to use each other as resources, everyone can be exposed to the grade-level curriculum and even more challenging material. If cooperative groups are carefully selected so that they are truly heterogeneous, the combined skills and knowledge can be shared among group members and individual learning is enhanced. Finally, I think that successes experienced in group work help promote a sense of individual achievement for each student.

MICHAEL DU BOIS, Wakulla Middle School, Crawfordville, Florida

According to this teacher, what kinds of student groups are optimal for cooperative learning? What makes cooperative learning experiences successful in this teacher's classroom? What will you do to promote effective cooperative learning in your classroom?

Critical Thinking: How does CIRC avoid the problems that sometimes occur when same-age pairs are brought into a tutoring arrangement? Does having four students in each group contribute to success? Why or why not?

Try This: Interview a teacher who has embraced technology in the classroom. Ask the teacher to explain the advantages of technology in terms of student learning.

Reflection: Recall a computer simulation that you found particularly intriguing. If you have not had that experience, try to find someone who has. Why did the simulation hold your attention? Did you feel you had control over the environment created by the computer program? Did your ability to try repeatedly to succeed influence your learning?

computer-assisted instruction (CAI) Instruction delivered by a computer including tutorial, simulation, drill, and practice.

CIRC approach indicates that it has a positive effect on students' reading skills and on standardized scores from reading and language achievement tests (Stevens, Madden, Slavin, & Farnish, 1987; Slavin, 1987).

Interactive Instructional Technology

A survey of schools in the United States conducted during 1992 and 1993 reports that microcomputers are used in 98 percent of U.S. schools. On average, U.S. schools provide one computer for every sixteen students (Quality Education Data, 1993). Clearly, computers are part of the learning environment you will encounter, and they are capable of supporting the teaching–learning process in a number of ways. Computer technology, including data storage systems such as videodiscs, is capable of multimedia presentations of information to learners that include text, graphics, video, sound, and animation. The technology allows learners to enter simulated environments that are remarkably realistic. Computers can help students be understood in their own classrooms or to communicate with a stranger on another continent.

Computers and Instruction. Educational technology found its foothold in the classroom by means of **computer-assisted instruction (CAI)**. Computer-assisted instruction approaches employ the computer as a tutor to present information, provide drill and practice, simulate problems, assess a learner's level of knowledge, and provide remediation. For example, a student might learn about deforestation through a tutorial program that presents basic facts, maps, and a video clip of a speech made by a legislator in favor of banning the import of lumber from the Brazilian rain forest. After taking a test to determine if the student acquired the background information, the program assesses the student's responses and, if needed, presents a remedial lesson. When the student is ready to move on, the technological environment changes from a tutorial mode into a simulation mode. Simulation programs approximate activities that cannot be done in the classroom because they are too expensive, dangerous, time consuming, or otherwise not feasible. In the simulation mode, the student can learn about the importance of rain forests and the effects of deforestation by using computer models. Students can cut down trees with key strokes and examine the effects of deforestation on the global climate. Programs such as *ScienceVision* and *Science 2000* are simulation programs that allow students to conduct realistic experiments and work on realistic problems at relatively small cost and without dangerous risks (Coburn, 1993; Tobin & Dawson, 1992). Microworlds offer more realistic environments than simulations and are consistent with constructivist notions of learning (Rieber, 1991a, 1991b). They are designed to encourage students to explore and discover (Papert, 1993). *TinkerTools,* for example, is software that allows students to explore a series of environments or microworlds while discovering the basic principles of physics (White, 1993).

Computers and Thinking. Computer technology supports the development of higher-level thinking in at least two ways. First, the technology can provide students with opportunities to develop their problem-solving skills. Second, the technology can serve as a tool for thinking and problem solving.

The first function is illustrated by an imaginative use of technology that allows students to develop their problem identification as well as their problem-solving skills. The Cognition and Technology Group at Vanderbilt (CTGV) developed a video-based environment for mathematical problem solving called the *Jasper Woodbury Problem Solving Series* (1990, 1991, 1992, 1993). In each pair of lessons, a complex problem is presented via video with both relevant and irrelevant information embedded in the context of an adventure story. Students must decide what problems must be solved in order to reach a resolution to the story. To help them in solving these subproblems, they can access any part of the videodisc using a bar code reader to replay segments that may contain relevant information. In most of the lessons, students can find three or four possible solutions, depending on the approach students take to the problem. The video adventures capture the students' attention and imagination and motivate them to engage in problem solving for extended periods of time.

Example: Perhaps you recall the build-your-own-story books in which you, the reader, had to answer questions at various points in the book. Depending on your answer, you were directed to a particular page to finish the story.

As a tool for problem solving, computers can extend not only our ability to retrieve information—through networked databases and videodisc encyclopedias—but also our ability to think. We refer to computer programs that are designed to help learners brainstorm, analyze, and organize ideas as cognitive tools.

Well-designed computer programs can facilitate learning by extending a student's ability to think. In other words, they become mind-extension cognitive tools (Derry & Lajoie, 1993).

Critical Thinking: Do you think that the evolution of computer technology has contributed to the emergence of constructivist approaches to teaching and learning? Why or why not?

> Good computer-based cognitive tools can support such social problem solving processes by providing physical representations of abstract strategies and concepts, making them tangible for inspection, manipulation, and discussion, thereby encouraging generalized metacognitive awareness and self-regulatory ability. (p. 6)

One such program called *Inspiration* helps students brainstorm, diagram information, and develop meaningful links among concepts. The program allows students to identify and define concepts, to write and store comments, to establish links between concepts and to define the nature of those links. The program is especially useful for members of a cooperative learning group. By using both the graphic and text capabilities of *Inspiration*, cooperative groups can develop a concept map of their consensual understandings. The map as a product is not so important as the process group members must go through in negotiating meaning as they construct the map.

Computers, Cultures, and Communication. Perhaps the most exciting instructional prospect to arise from recent enhancements in educational technology is in the areas of telecommunications and telecomputing. *Telecomputing* is a term that has recently gained currency to distinguish computer access at a distance from the more general term *telecommunications.* Telecommunications refers to satellite-based information delivery systems such as telephone links and instructional television (Kearsley, Hunter, & Furlong, 1992).

Try This: Interview students who have had the experience of working on a joint project with other students at a distance.

Telecomputing provides access to World Wide Web, Gophers, and the Internet, global networks that can link a student sitting at a computer to vast storehouses of information and to other learners around the world. Access to people who live in different countries or who live differently in our own cities provides enormous learning opportunities. Telecomputing not only allows students to learn about people from other cultures but to learn with them as well. A geography class in Hull, Quebec, and a class in Bologna, Italy, are comparing the environmental concerns of their respective communities. High school students

Insights ON SUCCESSFUL PRACTICE

How do you use computers in your classroom, and what do you and your students gain from instructional software?

Computers have had a significant impact on the Technology Education curriculum at Elm Street Junior High. Our Technology Education Department is arranged in the clusters of Communication Technology; Construction Technology; Manufacturing Technology; and Power, Energy, and Transportation Technology. Students use a variety of computer hardware and software applications to complete assignments. Following each cluster we have listed the topics for which students select and operate Macintosh or IBM-compatible computers to complete their assignments.

Communication: word processing, desktop publishing, graphic design, computer-aided drafting (CAD), multimedia.

Construction: engineering technology, bridge building, stress forces and testing, career assessment.

Power, Energy, and Transportation: design analysis of an automobile. Model car time trial and race analysis are also recorded by a computer application.

Manufacturing: Lego Logo (currently an Apple II-E programming application that uses motors and sensors in the management of their multiple task control).

Our application of computers is student centered, and the applications are a firsthand experience for most students. Computers are also used for teacher classroom management. Record keeping and learning activity packets are computer generated. We do not teach students software expertise; rather, we use the computer as another tool to help in the completion and enhancement of an assignment. Students who have completed one or more courses recognize the ability of the computer to enhance their work in other areas and often return to apply their knowledge to totally different course assignments. The computer allows activities that were not practical before. The computer has allowed digitized photography where we would not have chosen the expense of a darkroom and placed students in that high chemical environment.

The curriculum is not designed around the computer, but the computer measurably improves the outcome and increases the pace of that outcome. The computer is to our courses what a portable cordless tool is to a traditional contractor. Speed, accuracy, flexibility, and improved quality are the sum of the attributes of computer access while providing the students with valued technical literacy.

PETER OLESEN LUND and DAVID W. PURINGTON,
Elm Street Junior High, Nashua, New Hampshire

In this essay, how are computers used for both instruction and classroom management? Which of these uses do you plan for your classroom? What proposal for curriculum integration might you make to link a technology course with a course you teach?

in Seattle received eyewitness reports of the destruction of the Berlin Wall from their colleagues at the Marie-Curie-Oberschule in Berlin. Students in Juneau, Alaska, and Moscow, Russia, are collaborating on a vision statement about global health in the year 2000 (Kearsley, Hunter, & Furlong, 1992).

In addition to allowing students to communicate across cultures, computer-based technology can also enable students who have special needs. Adaptive hardware is available, for example, to allow students who are physically disabled to both input information into the computer or receive information from it. Devices that attach to the head or foot can be used by students who have manual disabilities that prevent them from keyboarding. Computers can be operated solely through voice commands or even eye blinks. Once a student is given access to the computer, the computer can serve as a medium of communication with a classmate or as a gateway to information and people throughout the world (Geisert & Futrell, 1995).

HOW WILL YOUR KNOWLEDGE OF ACTIVE LEARNING TECHNIQUES HELP YOU BECOME A MORE EFFECTIVE TEACHER?

As you have seen, teaching for active learning requires a focus on what students do and how they think when they learn. As you use teacher-centered instructional approaches you are thinking about how your behaviors as a teacher influence the cognitive activity of your students. And, as you use student-centered instructional approaches, you are thinking about how your students' behaviors influence their cognitive activity and that of their peers. Knowing active learning techniques therefore helps you to fulfill your role in the teaching–learning process.

Connection: Think back to the discussion in Chapter 1 in which the basic assumption that *Teaching and learning are aspects of the same process* was made.

Knowing active learning techniques also helps you advance your own construction of the teaching–learning process as you learn to teach effectively in a variety of ways with a variety of instructional aids. Expert teachers have developed a teaching repertoire–a variety of instructional approaches, strategies, and formats. Using a variety of techniques increases your ability to engage student interest, to respond to situations flexibly, and to match curriculum and instruction to the thinking dispositions and learning characteristics of your students. Research suggests that the effective use of broad-based teaching repertoires fosters higher student achievement (Brown & McIntyre, 1993; Hiebert, 1991).

Here's How to Develop Your Teaching Repertoire

- Discover and analyze the metaphors for teaching and learning that form the basis of your theory of teaching.
- Through personal investigation, professional collaboration, and classroom practice, expand your knowledge base about instructional approaches, techniques, and formats and about the instructional goals and learning outcomes they serve.
- Remain open to trying new ideas and new teaching behaviors. Test those ideas and behaviors, and evaluate the results. What works? When? How? What is appropriate for students? Effective for active learning? Satisfying for you? Also explore and test instructional materials, including educational technologies.
- Continually integrate your expanding knowledge base with your theory of teaching through reflective construction.

TEACHER Chronicle Conclusion

ELECTRICITY

The following morning, Mr. Kowal sets up eight lab stations, including one using his three computers. There is a buzz of excitement when the students come in, and Mr. Kowal allows them some time to look around before taking attendance. "As you can see, I've set up eight stations. I am going to pass out a map of the stations. On the back is a list of each station and what you will need to complete at that station. For the next ten minutes, meet in your cooperative groups and decide at which five stations you will work. Remember, your grade for this unit will depend in part on how you cooperate as well as what you accomplish. Tomorrow, after you've had a day to get involved with a station, we'll discuss my expectations for the unit test at the end. Any questions?"

"What if two groups want to work at the same thing at the same time?" Gordon asks.

"Your two groups will have to meet and work out a solution."

Amid a buzz of excitement, the students break into groups. At the end of ten minutes, he calls for attention and lets each group select their first station. As the students experiment, Mr. Kowal roams the room questioning, prompting, and demonstrating. About halfway through the period, he steps back to observe the dynamics of the class. At the various stations, bells ring sporadically, lights flicker, motors whirr, the computer printer clatters, and conversations spin one into another. It looks like they're getting a "charge" out of this lesson, Mr. Kowal thinks, a smile crossing his face.

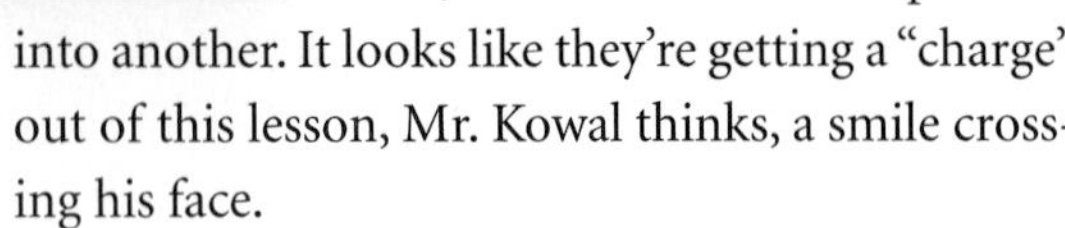

APPLICATION QUESTIONS

1. In what ways is Mr. Kowal's instruction teacher centered?
2. What specific techniques of effective instruction can you identify in the Teacher Chronicle? In what ways do those techniques support active learning on the part of Mr. Kowal's students?
3. In what ways is his instruction student centered?
4. What specific instructional choices reflect a constructivist approach to teaching? In what ways do those choices support active learning on the part of Mr. Kowal's students?
5. Create a dialogue among a group of students at one of Mr. Kowal's lab stations that reveals the benchmarks in thinking or cognitive processing that students can attain when they are engaged in active learning in a social context.
6. What opportunities for peer teaching are implicit in Mr. Kowal's lesson plan? What forms of peer teaching might be most appropriate in relation to his instructional goals and the needs of his students?
7. How might the lesson in the Teacher Chronicle be accomplished through formal cooperative learning groups? Which program or technique described in this chapter might you choose for this purpose, and why?
8. What is required to make cooperative learning work? In what ways can cooperative learning approaches benefit students? In what ways can they benefit teachers?
9. What instructional technologies might Mr. Kowal use to support student learning? What specific purposes might those technologies serve in his class?
10. Create a revised lesson plan for Mr. Kowal and his students that integrates multiple uses of instructional technology in the classroom.

CHAPTER SUMMARY

WHAT IS ACTIVE LEARNING?

Active learning refers to student engagement in the process of learning. Thinking is an important aspect of active learning. Good thinking dispositions can support active learning and we examined ways to encourage the development of good thinking dispositions. Critical thinking refers to higher levels of the cognitive taxonomy; critical thinking requires learners to be actively engaged with the learning material. Teaching that facilitates active learning can be either teacher centered or student centered.

HOW CAN TEACHER-CENTERED INSTRUCTION SUPPORT ACTIVE LEARNING?

There are a variety of instructional techniques in which the teacher's behavior is central to learning. In teacher-centered learning, much of the responsibility for learning rests with the teacher; the teacher must engage the student's attention and thinking. Teacher-centered techniques include lecturing, explaining, questioning, and independent practice.

HOW CAN STUDENT-CENTERED INSTRUCTION SUPPORT ACTIVE LEARNING?

Student-centered approaches to instruction take the teacher out of the hub of instructional interaction in the classroom. Students are more responsible for learning outcomes than when teacher-centered approaches are used. Student-centered approaches are theoretically consistent with constructivist views of the teaching–learning process. These approaches to instruction include small group discussion, peer teaching and learning, cooperative learning, and the use of technology.

HOW WILL YOUR KNOWLEDGE OF ACTIVE LEARNING TECHNIQUES HELP YOU BECOME A MORE EFFECTIVE TEACHER?

Whether teacher-centered or student-centered approaches to instruction are employed, the teacher must always focus on the effects of instructional activity on the learner's thinking. It is important to build a repertoire of teaching behaviors by considering new metaphors and ideas for teaching and testing new techniques in the classroom. Reflecting on the results of these efforts will help you build your theory of teaching.

KEY CONCEPTS

active learning
anticipatory set
Computer-Assisted Instruction (CAI)
Cooperative Integrated Reading and Composition (CIRC)
cooperative learning
critical thinking
direct instruction
explanation
guided practice
independent practice
lecturing
mastery teaching
pair shares
questioning
reciprocal questioning
reciprocal teaching
small group discussions
student-centered instruction
Student Teams-Achievement Divisions (STAD)
teacher-centered instruction
Team-Assisted Individualization (TAI)
Teams-Games-Tournaments (TGT)
wait-time I
wait-time II

PART VI

Assessment serves multiple purposes

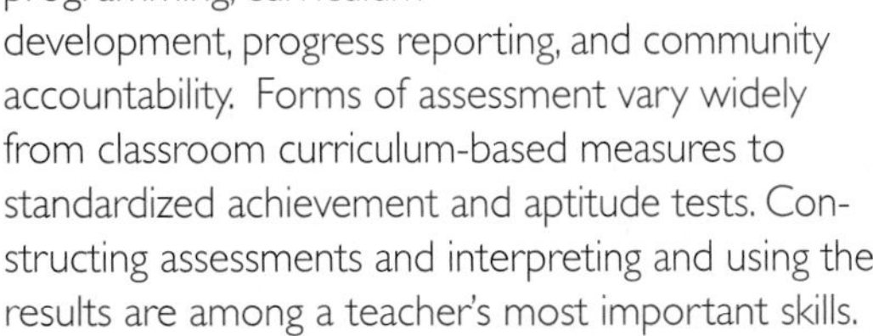

Assessment of students' capabilities and learning are used for diagnosis, placement, promotion, programming, curriculum development, progress reporting, and community accountability. Forms of assessment vary widely from classroom curriculum-based measures to standardized achievement and aptitude tests. Constructing assessments and interpreting and using the results are among a teacher's most important skills.

Overview of Chapter 13

To this point, we have considered how students learn, the sources of differences that affect their learning, how teachers plan, and various instructional methods that will support the learning of desired outcomes. The final section of the book is devoted to evaluation—the methods used to determine what and how well students have learned.

Assessing Student Performance focuses on the methods teachers use to evaluate student learning. These include paper-and-pencil tests and alternative assessments, such as portfolios and performance assessment. Advantages and disadvantages of assessment types are discussed to help you make decisions about the type of assessment that will best meet your purposes of evaluation. Guidelines are also provided to help you construct appropriate assessments for your purposes and to help you improve the quality of your assessments. The chapter concludes with a discussion of ways you can involve students in assessment and create a positive assessment environment in the classroom.

Overview of Chapter 14

One of the most important tasks you will undertake as a teacher is to evaluate student progress, but of equal importance will be communicating your judgments and those of other education professionals to your students and their parents or caregivers. Evaluation is based on comparison, and as you will see in this chapter, Communicating Student Progress, there are two primary benchmarks that are used as the basis for evaluative judgments. One type of benchmark is the performance criterion or goal that serves as the standard of measure. The other type of

Evaluation

benchmark is the performance of a group of people. Judgments about student progress are made both ways. Sometimes your job will be to translate or interpret information about the progress of your students. At other times, your job will be to make the judgments.

Assessment improves teaching and learning

Assessments provide feedback to both teachers and students. Among the most important uses of assessment are improving instruction and giving students a greater stake in their learning. Teachers therefore need to understand the links between lesson planning, teaching objectives and learning outcomes, instructional delivery models, and the assessment of student learning.

Authentic activity provides a basis for assessment

Authentic learning activities include real-life, student-centered questions, problems, or challenges that actively involve students. Evaluation is based on students' achievement of learning outcomes as demonstrated not through paper-and-pencil tests but through actual performance or through presentations of evidence of progress in knowledge or skills. Authentic assessment, such as performance-based assessments and portfolios, is appropriate for all grade levels.

13 Assessing Student Performance

CHAPTER OUTLINE

TEACHER Chronicle

TESTING TRIALS

Louisa Mendoza, a first-year teacher, plops down in a chair in the lounge and lets out a long sigh. Amy Pearson-Wood, a friend and fellow science teacher, joins her.

"You look bushed," she says. "Good thing it's Friday."

Ms. Mendoza smiles at her concern. "Yes, it has been a long week. But it's not that so much as the disaster my kids made of a unit test I just gave them. I don't know if it's them, my teaching, or the test that's the problem."

She looks at Mrs. Pearson-Wood, a veteran teacher, and asks, "Amy, how do you make up your tests? Your kids always complain about how hard your tests are, but they never complain that they aren't fair."

Amy laughs. "I really enjoy creating tests. Creating might seem a funny way to think of what one does in putting a test together, but test making is a creative thinking and writing process for me. When I create a test for my science classes, I want it to be a fair representation of the material we have covered since the previous test. So I give multiple-choice questions related to class lectures and lab experiments. And I include some open-ended questions that can be answered correctly in a number of ways."

Mrs. Pearson-Wood continues. "I also give them practice tests to familiarize them with my formats. One way to make a test reliable is to eliminate the possibility that someone could miss an item he or she really knows. The test score is only an estimate of a student's knowledge, but it should be the best estimate that I can make it. So I encourage students to read the test questions carefully and consider their responses. I want them to read through every possible answer first before deciding on a solution. My students have difficulty with this at the beginning of the year, but most get to be quite adept at it by the end of the first quarter."

"Are your tests mostly multiple-choice then?" Ms. Mendoza asks.

"No, I ask at least one essay question covering the material presented in the labs. My labs are set up as small-group activities. In order to ensure that each student participates to the best of his or her ability, I make the essay question one that links together things they should have learned."

Mrs. Pearson-Wood pauses before continuing. "In the essays, I give points for details covered in class or discovered in a close reading of the textbook. As a vocabulary extension, I also include jokes and riddles based on the terminology covered in the unit. The students enjoy these jokes, and over the years I have found that such wordplay actually improves their scientific vocabulary."

Ms. Mendoza shakes her head. "There's a lot more that goes into a good test than I ever thought."

"Yes, Louisa, and you don't always need paper-and-pencil tests either. Sometimes I use performance assessments to test skills. There's a great deal that can be learned from assessments and not just who knows what. I use tests as a check on my teaching and on the instructional materials we're using. It took me a few years to learn to develop good tests. You'll get there sooner, I'm sure."

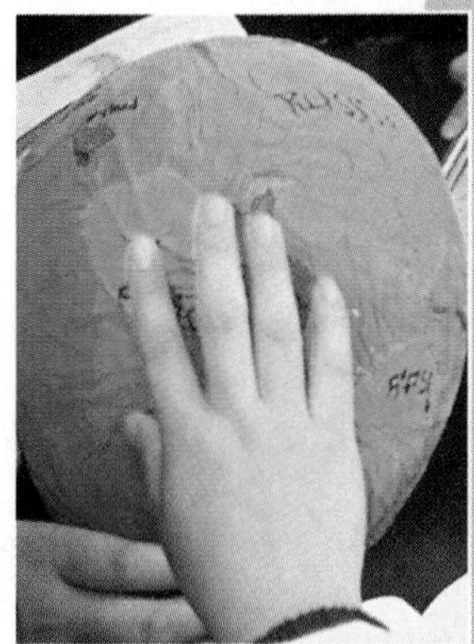

FOCUS QUESTIONS

1. What purposes could assessments serve Ms. Mendoza?
2. What kinds of assessments does Ms. Pearson-Wood use, and what are some advantages and disadvantages of each?
3. What is authentic assessment?
4. How should Ms. Mendoza construct her test items?
5. What is involved in designing alternative assessments?
6. What makes an assessment valid and reliable?
7. How can you best prepare students for assessments?
8. How can assessments be used to improve teaching and learning?

WHAT IS ASSESSMENT AND HOW ARE ASSESSMENT PRACTICES CHANGING?

In the Teacher Chronicle, Louisa Mendoza faces a typical problem of beginning teachers: how to construct and administer an assessment that will accurately measure what the students have learned. When people talk about classroom assessment, they use a variety of terms interchangeably: evaluation, assessment, measurement, test. Although the terms are related, their distinctions are important for the decisions teachers must make about student progress and student achievement. In order to understand these distinctions, consider this example: Leland and Darlene correctly answer 90 percent of the questions on a geography test. Now let's examine what this example means in relation to assessment, evaluation, measurement, and test.

Defining Assessment

Assessment is the process of gathering, analyzing, and interpreting information about students and their progress in school. It is a comprehensive and multifaceted analysis of performance (Wiggins, 1993). As you will see in this chapter, teachers conduct a great deal of assessment, from administering tests to observing student performance on tasks in class. They gather information about student characteristics (thinking dispositions and cultural backgrounds), achievement (skills and knowledge in geography), and attitudes (enjoyment of place names, anxiety about map reading). Teachers assess student characteristics and entry levels of skill and knowledge so that they may better plan more effective instruction. They assess student performance in order to facilitate learning. Successful learning depends upon accurate and informative feedback following assessment of progress toward a goal. And teachers conduct assessments to communicate student progress to a variety of audiences, including students, parents, and the community.

assessment The process of gathering, analyzing, and interpreting information about students and their progress in school.

Assessment is the most general of the four terms and describes all of the activities that yield various sorts of information about students. The geography test, then, is one form of assessment. It provides one kind of information about a student's knowledge of geography. The different kinds of tests given by Ms. Mendoza and Mrs. Pearson-Wood in the Teacher Chronicle are also forms of assessment.

Assessment provides the context for **measurement**, which is the process of describing a student's particular characteristics. Measurement answers the question, "How much?" (Gronlund, 1993). The geography test is a measurement because it shows how much of the information on the test Leland and Darlene knew. In this case, it is also a *quantitative* description because it answers the question of how much knowledge the student has of geography in numerical terms. How else might teachers judge a student's knowledge of geography? Perhaps the student can locate cities or countries on a map and trace the shortest route between them. Describing students' knowledge in terms of qualities they possess or performances they can demonstrate, rather than in terms of numerical scores on tests, provides a *qualitative* measure of their individual achievement. In the assessment of writing skills, for example, the teacher might say that Leland scored a 5 out of a possible 7 on the essay test (a quantitative description). Or the teacher could say that Leland applied the basic mechanics of writing, used language appropriate to the topic and reader, but failed to fully develop and support ideas introduced in the opening paragraph (a qualitative description). Quantitative and qualitative measurements both provide teachers with valuable information about student progress, but the nature of the information they provide is different and generally complementary.

Point: *Assessment serves multiple purposes.* A score on a test can be used to judge how well students have achieved and how effective was the instruction.

A **test** is a formal procedure or an instrument used for measuring a sample of student performance. Tests can be constructed in a variety of formats, from objective pencil- and paper-items (e.g., multiple-choice, true/false, fill-in-the-blanks) to performance assessments (e.g., constructed response tests based on realistic tasks). The geography test mentioned earlier is probably made up of objective items, whereas asking students to locate cities on a map and trace routes between them is a form of performance assessment. All tests provide some kind of information about students, but depending on their format, the information may be quantitative or qualitative in nature. As you will see, there are advantages and disadvantages to using any particular test format.

Critical Thinking: Why is the purpose for which evaluation is used so critical?

Finally, **evaluation** is the process by which teachers make specific judgments about their students using information gained from formal and informal assessment. Evaluation enables a teacher to answer the question, "How good?" or "How well?" (Gronlund, 1993). For example, Ms. Stein might judge how good Leland and Darlene are in geography or how well Leland writes by the students' test scores. Likewise, Ms. Stein might judge how good the geography lessons were by how many students in the class achieved scores of 90 percent on the test. Evaluation judgments lead to such decisions as what the students' activities will be for the next several minutes and which students should be placed in a particular reading group or special education program. In the first case, teachers are likely to have conducted an informal evaluation that told them the class needed an extra few minutes to complete a class activity. In the second, it is more likely that the teacher formally evaluated performance to determine how well students were reading.

measurement The process of describing a student's particular characteristics. Measurement answers the question, "How much?"

test A formal procedure or an instrument used for measuring a sample of student performance.

evaluation The process by which teachers make specific judgments by answering the questions "How good?" or "How well?" (e.g., How well have students understood this concept? How good is this instruction?).

Assessment is an integral part of teaching and learning, not just a means of monitoring or auditing student performance (although it does serve this purpose as well). Assessment is a way to improve learning, because teachers and students alike can use assessment information to adjust the learning experience. And because learning gives rise to a diversity of understandings, teachers, administrators, and policy makers should all have expertise in a variety of assessment methods. They should be able to construct sound assessments and use them effectively in gathering desired information about students.

Teachers today are experiencing some fundamental changes in the way they view and conduct assessment in American schools (Stiggins, 1991; Wiggins, 1993). At a societal level, assessment reform is calling into question standardized testing practices that have been developed over the last sixty years. At the classroom level, teachers are calling for better ways to determine what their students are learning. It is worthwhile to review some of the changes that are occurring as an introduction to specific assessment methods.

Changing Views of Assessment

Connection: Standardized testing and how teachers can interpret the results of standardized tests are discussed in detail in Chapter 14.

Critical Thinking: Debate continues over what standardized tests should be designed to measure. How are the results of this debate likely to affect teachers' decisions in the classroom?

Connection: How would the assumptions that constructivists make about learning (discussed in Chapter 7) affect their views of assessment?

In the last sixty years there has been an explosion of standardized testing programs and the refinement of the most dominant assessment format: the objective paper-and-pencil test. As Stiggins (1991) summarized it, standardized tests were first used in the 1930s to select high school students for college, a practice that became a standard part of college admission in the 1940s and beyond. In the 1950s and 1960s, standardized tests became accountability tools, used to determine whether students achieved basic skills required for graduation and whether teachers had basic skills required for certification. Statewide testing gained prominence in the 1970s, national and international assessment in the 1980s. In the 1990s came the development of national standards in the content areas, such as science and mathematics. During this time, the assessment enterprise became so technically complex that educators abdicated any role in the process. They assumed that teachers should teach while evaluators assess. As a result, teachers often left it to test and textbook publishers to produce so-called scientifically accurate measurement instruments (Stiggins, 1991).

The effects of this wide-scale, standardized assessment are quite visible in today's schools. Policy makers have relied on these tests to measure school outcomes, so that schools are evaluated on the basis of how well their students perform on the standardized exams. Teachers are held accountable for making sure their students learn what's covered by the tests, so they must orient at least some of their curriculum and instruction toward the tests (cf. Popham, 1993). The question of concern to assessment reformers is, what do the tests actually measure? If they are to be used as an indicator of school effectiveness, then they should be measuring the goals of present-day schools.

Authentic Assessment

objective tests Paper-and-pencil tests made up of items, such as true/false and multiple-choice, that can be objectively scored (i.e., scored in exactly the same way no matter who or what is doing the scoring).

authentic assessment Assessment of higher-order skills such as problem solving and critical thinking in real-life contexts through the use of projects, exhibitions, demonstrations, portfolios, observations, science fairs, peer- and self-assessments.

Because "assessment can legitimately be viewed as the manifestation of a system's educational values" (Baron, 1991, p. 307), the move toward new educational values has brought a similar move toward new assessment strategies. Scholars and teachers alike are seeking ways other than **objective tests** of assessing student performance, ways that comprise a reform movement known as authentic assessment. Also called alternative assessment, performance assessment, holistic assessment, and observation-based assessment, **authentic assessment** concerns the measurement of complex performances and higher-order thinking skills in real-life contexts. Often, these higher-order thinking skills are conceived as the standard practices of experts in a subject matter discipline.

As a concept, authentic assessment is not especially new. Examples such as writing assessments, Red Cross swimming tests, and driving tests have existed for years (Hambleton & Murphy, 1992). The goal of authentic assessment is to make tests more integral to learning tasks so that skills such as problem solving and critical thinking can be measured. Venues for conducting authentic assessment include activities such as projects, exhibitions, demonstrations, observations, science fairs, and peer- and self-assessment (Hart, 1994).

Proponents of authentic assessment have argued that it provides a more direct measure of higher-order learning goals than do more traditional measures such as paper-and-pencil tests (Frederiksen & Collins, 1989; Wiggins, 1989). For example, scores on an objective test may indicate that students know the components of a well-written essay, but can they write one? The only way to know for sure is to ask them to perform the task. Authentic assessment is also thought to reflect a more constructivist orientation to learning because it requires students to demonstrate complex tasks rather than small, discrete skills practiced in isolation (Shepard, 1991). Finally, the insertion of authentic tasks into standardized achievement tests is expected to bring an increase in instructional attention to those tasks, just as standardized writing assessments led to an increase in instructional time devoted to composition (Popham, 1993).

Point: *Authentic activity provides a basis for assessment.* Authentic activity is exemplified in tasks such as driving, but it can also be a part of paper-and-pencil tests. Using a protractor to measure an angle is an authentic activity.

So what does this all mean for assessment practices in classrooms? For assessment to improve learning, it should provide a multidimensional picture of what students know and can do. It should respect students' diversity in ways of understanding. It should suggest actions teachers can take to improve the educational development of their students and the quality of their educational programs. To accomplish these goals, teachers have available to them a broader array of assessment techniques than ever before. Taking advantage of them, however, requires understanding of assessment goals, procedures for constructing assessments, and criteria for judging and improving the quality of assessments. It is to these issues that we now turn.

Types of Assessment Goals

Look back for a moment to Mrs. Pearson-Wood's test in the Teacher Chronicle. What might the essay question measure that is different from what is measured by the multiple-choice questions? What kind of learning outcome is implicit in the teacher's statement that she wants to encourage students to "read the test questions carefully and consider their responses"?

Teachers must decide, in any subject area they teach, what to assess. As you have seen from Chapter 11, assessment goals should coincide with instructional goals. It is a useful practice for teachers to consider what to assess and how they wish to assess student progress at the same time

Connection: How would Bloom's or Gagné's taxonomies (discussed in Chapter 11) be used to specify knowledge and skill goals for assessment?

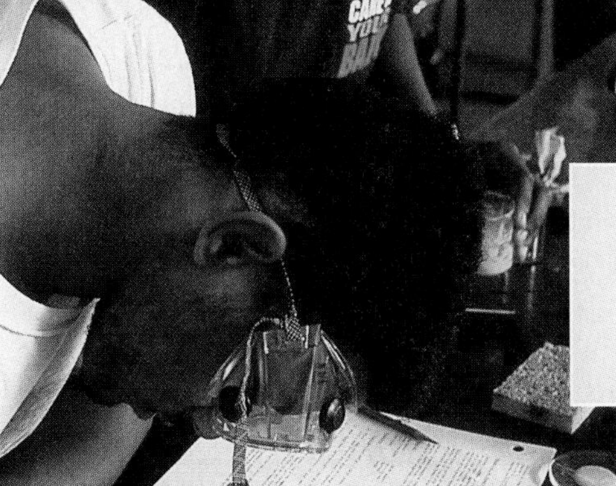

How can paper-and-pencil tests be constructed to assess students' higher-order thinking skills? What are all the factors that teachers must take into consideration when planning and constructing assessments?

Insights ON SUCCESSFUL PRACTICE

In developing assessments, how do you include measures of students' higher-level thinking?

As a science teacher, I always have realized how important writing and critical thinking skills are to the understanding and learning of science. I have tried several times in the past to encourage students to write about science content in an essay format. However, after years of hearing, "I don't know what to write!" and "How long does this have to be?" I finally found a formula for writing success that has been very useful in teaching writing skills to my science students.

I decided that I wanted my students' writing to demonstrate their knowledge of the subject. The material had to be written in an orderly fashion, emphasizing logic and critical thinking skills as well as the students' opinions, viewpoints, and English skills. To accomplish this goal, I devised a lesson with specific outcomes for each of these objectives. I do not teach English skills to students but do emphasize the importance of subject–verb agreement, complete sentences, and correct punctuation in their science writing.

Because many students seem unsure of what to write about, I started this writing program by having all students write an essay on the same topic. I gave the writing assignments after we had covered a particular unit of content. This provided each student with a similar background in the subject; the essays would serve as a good review of the material. I have found that sentence statements or topic statements are successful with beginning writers. Instead of telling students to write something about forests, cells, molecules, or the treatment of waste water, I use statements such as "Forests are more than trees" (that year's theme of National Wildlife Week), "The pathway of a drop of water through a treatment facility is an important journey," or "A cell is an organism."

I use the sentence topic to accomplish my first science teaching objective—students should be able to demonstrate their knowledge. I write the topic on the board and then ask for student ideas about the topic. Students usually come away from this brainstorming activity and the resultant discussion with lots of ideas about what to write.

I then focus the students' attention on the fact that they can group many of their ideas into categories. Often several different groupings are possible. Students then complete an outline on their topic. The outline helps to accomplish my second objective—student writing should be orderly and stimulate logic and critical thinking skills. Students use thinking skills—analysis, synthesis, comparison. and contrast—when preparing categories of information.

I focus my comments and criticism on the students' outlines, and after I return the outlines to the students, they write their essay. I emphasize the importance of using correct grammar, punctuation, and spelling in their essays. On the day students turn in their essays, either the students or I read them in class. This allows students to get immediate feedback on their work.

A writing activity of this type helps students to realize that English skills do play an important part in science. This activity helps them strengthen their knowledge of a particular content area and use some critical thinking skills. It also gives students an opportunity to express their own viewpoints on a topic and deepens my appreciation of the English teacher across the hall.

LINDA VYGODA, Houston High School,
Lake Charles, Louisiana

What is higher-level thinking? How does this science teacher use writing assignments to encourage critical thinking and problem solving? In the subject area you plan to teach, how will you stimulate higher-level thinking on the part of students?

they determine instructional goals. Unfortunately, many a teacher has experienced writing a "really good test item" only to discover that he or she hadn't really taught what the item assessed. Therefore, thinking about assessment first often clarifies instructional goals and keeps one congruent with the other.

What types of things do teachers want to assess? The most obvious, perhaps, are the knowledge and skills teachers hope students will acquire. Knowledge and skills are often quite specific and can be defined using any of the taxonomies described in Chapter 11. Examples include tracing the historical development of cultural diversity in Western civilization (knowledge), making observations of leaves and communicating these observations through written or verbal descriptions (skills), and writing a simple declarative sentence (skill).

Sometimes teachers are interested in assessing more complex goals such as critical thinking and problem solving. These higher-order thinking skills may consist of any number of prerequisite knowledge and skills, but knowing the prerequisites does not guarantee that students can successfully synthesize them in the context of a larger problem-solving activity. Therefore, assessments are sought that provide complex problems and require students to integrate previously learned skills and knowledge.

Critical Thinking: What outcomes of active learning, discussed in Chapter 12, might become targets of assessment?

Achievement-related behaviors and achievement-related products can also be goals of assessment that teachers target. *Achievement-related behaviors* are behaviors that students exhibit during activities or assignments that facilitate their achievement. Cooperating in a group to reach a common goal is an example. Communicating results of an investigation, perhaps in graphical or prose formats, is another. A third example is performing certain motor tasks, such as a floor exercise in gymnastics. Achievement-related products, by contrast, refer to the artifacts students produce that illustrate what they have learned. Project reports, essays, and artwork are all examples of achievement-related products.

Critical Thinking: Think about some of the goals you might want to assess. On what knowledge and skills would you assess student progress? What achievement-related behaviors and achievement-related products would you target for assessment? What attitudes or dispositions do you think are important to assess?

Finally, teachers are often interested in assessing the status of student affect. In other words, what achievement-related attitudes do students exhibit toward what they are learning? Are they motivated to learn the material? How confident are they of their ability to succeed? How do they attribute the errors they make in learning? Assessing student affect helps teachers to understand what other conditions affect student performance besides their mastery of the curriculum. The variety of goals that teachers can choose to assess is represented in Figure 13.1.

HOW DO YOU PLAN AND CONSTRUCT CLASSROOM TESTS?

Teachers must find or design assessment methods that will succeed in gathering desired information for making sound judgments about their students. In doing this, teachers are wise to consider the effect of different types of test formats and tasks on different students. Students' test scores depend to some degree on the particular methods used to assess their performance, because each method provides a different view of what students know and can do (Shavelson, Baxter, & Pine, 1992).

Example: One school district uses only the results of an IQ test to place students in its gifted program, while a neighboring school district places students using peer recommendations, teacher observations, and parental evaluations in addition to IQ test results. Which approach is better suited to the purpose of evaluation and why?

Some tasks used on tests may even be so inherently interesting as to affect positively students' attitudes toward testing. In a study comparing two approaches to testing student understanding of volume, for example, Wiggins (1993) reported that the performance test so engaged students that some of the worst students were among the best performers on the test. Some also pleaded with

FIGURE 13.1

What Do Teachers Assess?

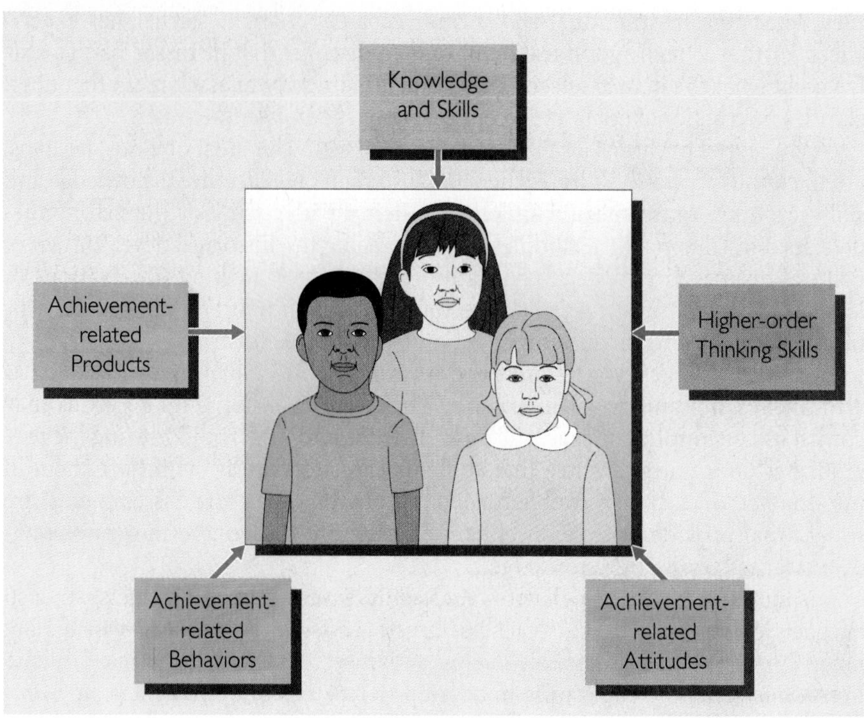

their teacher to continue working on the problem after school! It seems advisable, then, for teachers to consider using a variety of different assessment methods within any unit of instruction in order to gain a more complete picture of each student's achievements.

This section discusses paper-and-pencil tests that teachers can administer in class during a single class period. These tests include item formats ranging from multiple-choice to essay. The next section presents alternative assessment methods that are more commonly associated with authentic assessment. For each method, we discuss advantages and disadvantages that should help you in selecting those most appropriate for your assessment purposes.

readiness A goal of assessment that shows whether students have the necessary prerequisite skills and knowledge to begin a unit of instruction.

placement A goal of assessment that determines what level of difficulty a student is capable of handling in instruction.

formative assessment An assessment used to diagnose learning difficulties and to provide feedback to students to improve their learning.

summative assessment An assessment administered at the end of an instructional unit for the purpose of assigning a grade.

Planning Objective Tests

Teachers use objective tests to help them make a variety of decisions. A test that is given *prior* to the instruction can help teachers determine students' **readiness** for instruction—that is, whether they have the necessary prerequisite skills and knowledge. Testing prior to instruction also helps teachers assign students' placement at particular levels of instruction. **Placement** tests are commonly used in reading instruction, for example, to determine what level of reading difficulty a student is capable of handling.

Tests that are given *during* the learning process to monitor student progress are called **formative assessments**. Teachers might use these tests to diagnose learning difficulties, to improve instruction, or to provide feedback to students to improve their learning. Daily or weekly quizzes are an example. **Summative assessments** are given at the *end* of an instructional unit for evaluation, for example, to assign a grade (Gronlund, 1993).

When teachers construct a test, they must decide in advance on its purpose, because the purpose will influence the types of items constructed, the length of the test, and the scope and depth of content covered. The purpose of a test can also influence its administration. If its purpose is formative, for example, the teacher may consider allowing students to answer the questions using their textbooks or to work in cooperative groups. Tests used for placement purposes, however, must provide information about each individual's capabilities to ensure that appropriate instruction is provided. Therefore, these would be given to individuals to answer without benefit of outside resources.

To plan a test, teachers must be sure that the items they write or choose (from existing item banks or unit tests accompanying published curricula series, e.g.) actually measure their goals and objectives. This is most easily done by constructing a **table of specifications**, a framework or matrix that shows the content areas or objectives to be assessed along with the desired level of skill for each outcome (Table 13.1). Here's How lists the steps to produce a table of specifications (Gronlund, 1993; Kubiszyn & Borich, 1987).

Try This: Discuss with a teacher how he or she uses tests for formative and summative purposes. How are these uses different?

here's how

Here's How to Produce a Table of Specifications for Test Writing

- Identify the learning outcomes and content areas to be measured by the test. Table 13.1, for example, identifies five objectives that relate to the goal of subtracting without regrouping.
- Determine the category of outcome to which each instructional objective belongs. Table 13.1 assigns objectives to the categories of knowledge (K), comprehension, (C) and application(A) from Bloom's taxonomy.

Try This: Develop a table of specifications to construct a test for a unit in a subject area you plan to teach.

TABLE 13.1 A Table of Specifications for a Test on Subtraction without Borrowing

Content Outline	K	C	A	Percentage
1. Distinguishes addition and subtraction signs	1			4
2. Distinguishes addition problems from subtraction problems	2			8
3. Identifies correctly and incorrectly solved subtraction problems		4		16
4. Correctly solves single-digit subtraction problems			6	24
5. Correctly solves double-digit minus single-digit subtraction problems			6	24
6. Correctly solves double-digit problems that do not require borrowing			6	24
Total	3	4	18	25 items
Percentage	12	16	72	100

Source: From *Educational Testing and Measurement: Classroom Application and Practice* (2nd ed., p. 65) by T. Kubiszyn and G. Borich, 1987, Glenview, Il: Scott, Foresman. Copyright 1987 by Scott, Foresman, and Company. Adapted by permission of HarperCollins Publishers.
Key: K = Knowledge; C = Comprehension; and A = Application.

Critical Thinking: How could you use a table of specifications as a tool for planning instruction?

table of specifications Used for planning a test, a two-way chart or matrix that shows the content areas or objectives to be assessed along with the desired level of skill for each outcome.

- Determine the number of test items that need to be constructed for each objective. This should reflect how much weight to give each outcome on the test. In other words, measure objectives that are most important or that were given the most attention in the instruction by more test items. Table 13.1, for example, assigns objective 1 only one item and objectives 4, 5, and 6 six items each.
- Add the number of items in each column.
- Determine what percent of the test measures each objective and each category of learning. Check to be sure that these percentages match the relative importance of the objectives and desired outcomes.

Look at Table 13.1 again. What does it suggest about the importance this teacher placed on application? On solving specific kinds of subtraction problems?

Because the table of specifications shows the types of learning outcomes to be assessed on the test, it also provides guidance to the teacher in selecting or generating types of items that are appropriate for each outcome (Popham, 1981). Items in which students select an answer from possible alternatives are called **selection-type items**, whereas items that ask students to generate an answer are called **supply-type items**. The characteristics of different item types present both advantages and disadvantages in constructing classroom tests that meet teachers' needs (Table 13.2).

Constructing Selection-Type Items

Connection: How might the process of recognition (discussed in Chapter 7) relate to student performance on selection-type items? How might the process of recall relate to performance on supply-type items?

Selection-type items include multiple-choice; binary-choice items, such as true/false; matching; and interpretive formats (an interpretive item is often a lengthy case followed by several multiple-choice questions, e.g.). These formats typically require a process of recognition and are especially useful for assessing knowledge of facts, understanding of concepts, and, with interpretive items, problem solving (see Table 13.2). Let's examine how selection-type items are

Try This: Generate several instructional objectives and write test items to measure them using the item formats described in this section. Try to write at least one item of each format. What are the advantages of each type of item for your purposes? What are the disadvantages?

selection-type items A test item format in which students select an answer from possible alternatives.

supply-type items A test item format in which items ask students to generate an answer.

TABLE 13.2 Summary of the Relative Merits of Selection-Type Items and Supply-Type Items

Characteristic	Selection-Type Items	Supply-Type Items	
		Short Answer	Essay
Measures factual information	Yes	Yes	Yes
Measures understanding	Yes	No	Yes
Measures synthesis	No	No	Yes
Easy to construct	No	Yes	Yes
Samples broadly	Yes	Yes	No
Eliminates bluffing	Yes	No	No
Eliminates writing skill	Yes	No	No
Eliminates blind guessing	No	Yes	Yes
Easy to score	Yes	No	No
Scoring is objective	Yes	No	No
Pinpoints learning errors	Yes	Yes	No
Encourages originality	No	No	Yes

Source: From *How to Make Achievement Tests and Assessments,* 29 by N. E. Gronlund, 1993, Needham Heights, MA: Allyn and Bacon. Reprinted by permission.

constructed (guidelines are derived from Carey, 1988; Cunningham, 1986; Ebel & Frisbie, 1986; Gronlund, 1993; Hopkins & Antes, 1985; Hopkins & Stanley, 1981; Nitko, 1983; Popham, 1981).

Binary-Choice Items. **Binary choice items** include any selected response item that offers two optional answers from which to select. Examples include true/false items, yes/no items, and items that require the student to classify a statement as fact or opinion, or as cause or effect. Other kinds of classifications may also be assessed with binary items, such as when a teacher directs students to identify words in a list as nouns or verbs.

Binary-choice items offer a number of advantages. They are efficient in covering a great deal of material, and they are useful in covering content topics that can be placed into two categories. Binary-choice items are also easy to score. It takes very little of the teacher's time to correct a binary-choice item test.

One disadvantage of binary-choice items, however, is that the items are subject to guessing. With only two choices, students have a 50 percent chance of answering an item correctly simply by guessing. Constructing longer tests can help to solve this problem, because a longer test will provide a better sample of the item population. In this sense, it is more difficult to guess the correct answers to forty binary-choice items than to guess correctly on twenty items. Another disadvantage of binary-choice items is that poorly written items tend to encourage rote memorization rather than a higher level of cognitive processing.

here's how

Here's How to Construct Binary-Choice Test Items

- Write items about substantive content (not trivialities), but avoid broad general statements if students must judge them true or false.
- Avoid the use of negative statements, especially double negatives. Do not add the word *not* to make a statement false. Negative statements are more difficult for students to comprehend than positive statements and so become a test of language skills rather than of content knowledge.
- Avoid long, complex sentences that include two ideas in one statement unless the item measures cause and effect or if/then relations.
- If opinion is used, attribute it to some source unless the ability to identify the opinion is what is being measured specifically.
- Make sure that true statements and false statements are approximately equal in length and number.
- Avoid specific determiners that give unintended cues, such as *always*, *never*, *all*, or *none*.
- Paraphrase statements from instructional material, rather than lifting them verbatim, thus requiring students to understand.
- Make false statements plausible to someone who does not know the correct answer.
- Make sure the item is definitely either true or false to avoid ambiguity.
- Avoid constructing a predictable pattern of correct answers. For example, true true, false false, true true, false false.

binary-choice items Any selected response item that offers two optional answers from which to select.

- Do not create trick statements using petty wording.
- Include directions that specify the type of judgment to be made and how students are to record their answers. This helps to ensure that students who know the material will correctly interpret the questions.

Good binary-choice items should be conceptualized in pairs. Write true and false statements about the same information, but use only one item from the pair on the test.

Matching Items. **Matching items** usually consist of two columns of words or phrases to be matched. Items on the left are called *premises*. Items on the right are called *responses*. Matching items are compact in form and are efficient for measuring associations. They are also easy to score.

The disadvantage of matching items is that they are restricted to material that students can associate based on simple relations. Because classroom learning often requires multiple associations among ideas and concepts, the *double matching* format may prove more useful (Carlson, 1985; Figure 13.2). Matching items are difficult to write because they require homogeneous material throughout the unit to be tested. Matching items are also susceptible to unintended clues and tend to focus on lower-level outcomes. In short, matching items work well when they are appropriate for the learning outcome and when they are well constructed.

FIGURE 13.2

Example of a Double Matching Test Item

Source: From *Creative Classroom Testing* (p. 133), by S. B. Carlson, 1985, Princeton, NJ: Educational Testing Service. Reprinted by permission.

Topic: Biology — The Circulatory System
Objective: Knowledge of Specific Facts

For each of the parts of the circulatory system listed below, determine the direction of blood flow and oxygen content. Place the letter for oxygen content (A or B) and blood flow (A–C) in the appropriate space.

Oxygen Content	Blood Flow
A. Blood with oxygen	**A.** Toward heart
B. Blood without oxygen	**B.** Away from heart
	C. Not applicable

Oxygen Content	Parts of Circulatory System	Blood Flow
______	Left Ventricle	______
______	Right Ventricle	______
______	Right Atrium	______
______	Aorta	______
______	Pulmonary Artery	______
______	Pulmonary Vein	______
______	Arteries	______
______	Veins	______
______	Capillaries	______

matching items Any test item consisting of two columns of words or phrases to be matched.

here's how

Here's How to Construct Matching and Double Matching Items

- Use homogeneous material in a given exercise. A set of matching items must deal with the same material. It is difficult to write matching items across topics.
- Use more responses than premises, providing directions that responses may be used once, more than once, or not at all, to avoid giving away answers.
- Keep the list of premises and responses brief, especially the responses that students have to scan for the correct one.
- List responses in a logical order. This means that if students were to read only the response column, the responses, as a group, make sense.
- Indicate in the test directions the basis to be used for matching premises to responses.
- Place all items for one matching exercise on the same page.
- Label the premises with numbers and the responses with letters.

A variation of matching items, *tabular* or *matrix* items can be used to distinguish among ideas in a more comprehensive fashion than by matching or double matching (Carlson, 1985). The matrix can present very complex interrelations among elements to be associated in the instruction. In Figure 13.3, for example, students are asked to make a variety of judgments about sentence structure by indicating on the matrix what structures are present in a set of test sentences. A matrix item can be scored by counting the number of misplaced entries, or by counting only the correct answers and ignoring the errors.

Multiple-Choice Items. **Multiple-choice items** consist of questions or incomplete sentences that are accompanied by three or more alternative responses, one of which is to be selected as the correct or best answer. The question or statement in the multiple-choice items is called the *stem*. The responses are called *alternatives*. Incorrect alternatives are called *foils* or *distractors*.

Reflection: What have been your experiences with multiple-choice tests? What strategies have you used in responding to multiple-choice questions? How are these strategies related to the guidelines for writing good multiple-choice items? What test-taking skills might you teach your students?

An important advantage of multiple-choice items is that they can measure a wide variety of learning outcomes, including higher-level outcomes, if they are properly constructed. The flexibility of multiple-choice items also overcomes some of the shortcomings of other objective items. For example, multiple-choice items eliminate some of the guessing that can take place with binary-choice items. They can cover a wider array of material than matching items, and there is no need for the material covered on the test to be homogeneous. If alternatives are well written, multiple-choice items can facilitate diagnosis of learning errors and misconceptions. Multiple-choice items are easy to score and they are relatively unaffected by response patterns.

multiple-choice items Test items consisting of questions or incomplete sentences that are accompanied by three or more alternative responses, one of which is to be selected as the correct or best answer.

The primary disadvantage of multiple-choice items is that it is often difficult to write plausible foils that do not provide clues to the correct or best answer. Sometimes foils can also cause unintended interpretations of the item, which could be correct depending on the frame of reference used by the student in answering the question. One way of overcoming this problem is to ask students to explain or justify their answer choices to multiple-choice items, but the best solution is to make sure that foils are unambiguously wrong.

Topic: English Grammer
Objective: Comprehension of Sentence Structure

For each of the following sentences, place an X in the appropriate box(es) of the table:

1. Bill and Joe went to the store and bought candy.
2. The soldiers not only surrounded the enemy base, but they also successfully attacked it.
3. The girls who entered the contest were photographed for the newspaper and a local magazine.
4. If it rains tomorrow, the picnic and the parade will be postponed until next week.
5. Anyone who chooses may go to the movies with us or may stay at home.
6. The teacher assigned math and English homework over the weekend.
7. Ducks and geese are related, but are different species.

	Simple Sentence	Compound Sentence	Complex Sentence	Simple Subject	Compound Subject	Compound Verb	Contains Prepositional Phrase(s)	Contains Direct Object(s)	
1									1
2									2
3									3
4									4
5									5
6									6
7									7

FIGURE 13.3

Example of a Tabular or Matrix Test Item
Source: From *Creative Classroom Learning* (p. 114), by S. B. Carlson, 1985, Princeton, NJ: Educational Testing Service. Reprinted by permission.

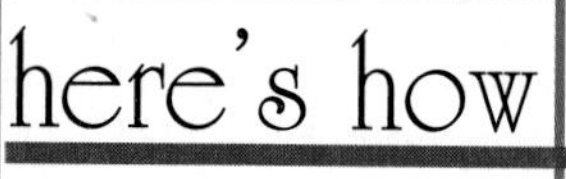

Here's How to Construct Multiple-Choice Items

- Write the stem of the item so that it is meaningful and presents a clear problem without the student's having to look at the alternatives. See the example in Figure 13.4, and refer to it as you read the guidelines.
- Include as much of the item as possible in the stem without providing irrelevant material.
- Use negatively stated items rarely and only if absolutely necessary. If used, emphasize the negative using boldface type or capital letters.
- Make the alternatives grammatically consistent with the stem to avoid providing inadvertent clues to the correct answer.
- Make sure there is only one correct or clearly best answer.
- Provide plausible foils to avoid giving away the answer. Use foils that represent likely mistakes of students to help diagnose misconceptions or errors in reasoning.
- Avoid verbal associations between the stem and the answer that give unintended clues.
- Make sure the length of the correct alternative does not provide clues by being either significantly longer or shorter than the foils.

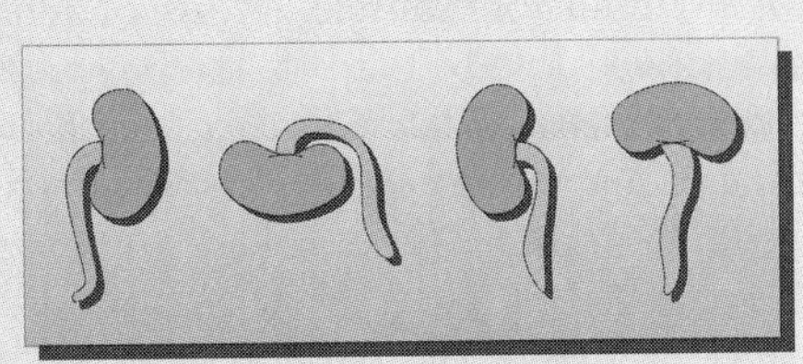

Lupe decided to sprout his bean seeds before planting them in the school garden. The picture above shows several bean seeds that have started to grow. The direction of the growth of the root is a response of the root to

a. light
b. heat
c. oxygen
d. gravity

FIGURE 13.4

Example of a Multiple-Choice Item in Fifth-Grade Science

Source: From "Authentic Assessment: A Systemic Approach in California," by K. B. Comfort, in *Science and Children*, October 1994, 42–43, 65. Reprinted by permission.

- Make each alternative position (A, B, C, or D) the correct answer approximately an equal number of times. The correct answer position should be arranged randomly. (This can be achieved most of the time by arranging the foils in alphabetical order.)
- Avoid using "all of the above" and "none of the above" unless there are specific reasons for doing so. These add to the difficulty of interpreting the item without necessarily being better measures of students' knowledge.
- Avoid requiring personal opinion, which will lead to the possibility of more than one correct answer.
- Avoid wording that is taken verbatim from the textbook or other instructional materials, as this encourages memorization rather than understanding.
- Avoid linking two or more items together, except when writing interpretive exercises. Items should be independent and not provide clues to other items.

Interpretive items might be a paragraph or two describing a problem or case followed by several multiple-choice or open-ended questions asking students about the case or problem. Teachers can also use graphs, charts, and math problems in interpretive items. Teachers often assess reading comprehension with interpretive exercises in which they give a reading selection followed by comprehension questions asking about the meaning of events in the story. Similarly, interpretive exercises can be useful in science when they provide an experiment and ask students to make predictions or synthesize interpretations about the results.

Constructing Supply-Type Items

When students generate answers to supply-type items, they must recall information from memory rather than recognize an alternative presented. This often makes supply-type items more difficult to answer. In contrast, these items, which include short answer and essay formats, are useful in assessing reasoning and synthesis. Let's examine how supply-type items are constructed.

short answer items Supply-type items that include incomplete statements, such as fill-in-the-blanks or direct questions requiring a brief response.

Short Answer Items. **Short answer items** are supply-type items that include incomplete statements, such as fill-in-the-blanks (completion items) or direct questions requiring a brief response. Short answer items can be answered with a word, a number, a phrase, or a symbol, for example. A form of a short answer item called a statement and comment item can be used to require students to interpret information, predict outcomes, evaluate evidence, and explain their understanding of concepts or their reasoning in solving problems. Consider the following example of a statement and comment item (also called an open-ended item):

> Neesha put snails and plants together in a jar of pond water. She sealed the jar and placed it in a spot where it would receive some light. After several days, Neesha checked the jar and found that the snails and plants were alive and healthy. Explain why the snails and plants stayed alive. (Comfort, 1994, p. 42).

An advantage of open-ended items like this one is that they ask for students to demonstrate higher-order thinking. Another advantage is that they reduce guessing to a minimum. A disadvantage of short answer items is that they can be difficult to score, arising from the unanticipated answers that must be considered, poor handwriting, and interpretation of phrases used by students.

Guidelines for writing and scoring short answer items are:

1. Make sure the required answer is brief and specific. Too broad a question makes it difficult for students to figure out what information is being solicited.
2. Avoid verbatim statements from the textbook that encourage memorization.
3. Word the item as a direct question, if possible.
4. For completion items, provide the numerical unit desired where appropriate (e.g., feet, pounds, kilometers).
5. If fill-in-the-blank items are used, use only one blank per statement and place it toward the end of the statement. The use of more blanks that occur early in the statement can leave out too much information and create ambiguous questions.
6. Omit the most important, not trivial, words in completion items in order to assess understanding of relevant concepts.
7. Avoid unintended grammatical cues.
8. Prepare a scoring key with anticipated acceptable answers or model answers.
9. Provide sufficient answer space, making all blanks the same length to avoid providing clues to the correct answer.

Essay Items. **Essay items** require students to construct written responses of varying lengths. *Restricted-response essays* strictly limit the desired response in terms of content and length. *Extended-response essays* allow more latitude in the content of the responses and usually require longer answers. This format is particularly useful when synthesis of content is desired. Following are examples of both types of essay items:

Restricted-response essay question	Three theories have been proposed about the nature of light energy. Briefly describe each theory and the evidence that supports it.
Extended-response essay item	For a course that you are teaching or expect to teach, prepare an assessment plan for evaluating student achievement. Be sure to include the procedures you would follow, the assessment strategies you would use, and the reasons for your choice.

essay items Test items that require students to construct written responses of varying lengths.

Teachers can use essay items to measure very complex and high-level outcomes, such as analysis or synthesis. These items also assess students' differing abilities to express their thoughts in writing.

The primary disadvantage to the use of essay items, however, lies in the difficulty of scoring them fairly. Scoring the answers to essays entails some subjectivity on the part of teachers, who can be influenced by their general impressions of the students whose papers they are grading. A halo effect can occur when the teacher, knowing the student by reputation or because other items on the test have been answered well, assumes that the essay answers will be equally as good. Likewise, a teacher may assume that a student who has scored poorly on the rest of the test will also answer poorly on essay items. Scoring essays also consumes a great deal of the teacher's time. Finally, it may take students considerable time to answer each essay question, which means that teachers can ask only a limited number of such questions, and thus can cover only a limited sample of the material from the unit on the test.

Despite these problems, essay tests can be a very useful form of assessment, when conducted following these guidelines.

Here's How to Construct Essay Items

- Use essay questions only for high-level outcomes not satisfactorily measured by objective formats.
- Phrase the question to clearly define the task.
- Provide approximate length expectations, point values, and time limits for each question. This alerts students to the relative importance of the item and helps them to gauge their time appropriately during the test.
- Avoid optional questions or extra credit items unless there is a specific reason—for example, individualized instruction.
- Ask a colleague to critique the questions. This helps to keep questions clear and focused and prevents unintended interpretations by students.
- For the most part, ask several short items rather than one or two very long items. Longer items put more emphasis on the writing style and capability of the students rather than on their knowledge of the material.
- Verify the question by writing a trial response.

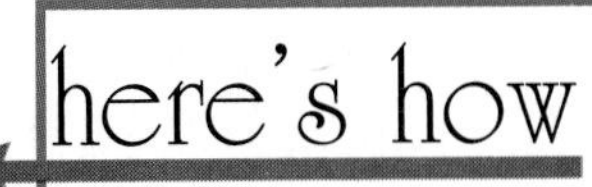

Here's How to Score Answers to Essay Items

- To obtain an idea of the quality of answers you expect on the essays, review all materials in the text and instructional activities regarding the topic of the essay before scoring. Also read a sample of the answers. Then, prepare an outline of the answer or write a model answer that can be used as a scoring guide.
- Decide how to handle factors that are irrelevant to the learning outcomes you wish to assess, such as spelling and grammar. You may wish to provide corrective feedback on spelling and grammar even though mistakes do not contribute to the student's overall essay score.

- Score all answers to one question before going on to the next question in order to avoid a halo effect.
- Score answers anonymously in order to avoid a halo effect.
- If the results are very important to the student, as in borderline cases where the score makes a difference between the students passing or failing, obtain a second opinion or reread the papers.
- Provide feedback to students on their answers. Later sections of the chapter discuss specific ways to provide constructive feedback in detail.

Reflection: How do the guidelines for writing and scoring essay items match your current view of the value of essay items?

HOW CAN YOU CONSTRUCT ALTERNATIVE ASSESSMENTS?

When teachers set instructional goals that involve the use of higher-order thinking skills and the coordination of a broad range of knowledge, they sometimes experience frustration in developing objective tests that will adequately measure these goals. Conventional test items and procedures function well in assessing unitary skills and discrete aspects of knowledge, but they are less effective in assessing achievement-related behaviors, dispositions, and products (Stiggins, 1991). When these constitute assessment goals, then teachers are likely to find that alternative, authentic assessments provide a more holistic picture of students' learning.

Assessments are authentic when they meet the following criteria (adapted from Wiggins, 1993, p. 229, and Hart, 1994, p. 10):

- Assessments are engaging and worthy problems or questions of importance.
- They represent real-life, interdisciplinary challenges.
- They present students with complex, ambiguous, open-ended problems and tasks that integrate knowledge and skills.
- They require students to produce a *quality* product and/or performance.
- They require students to justify or defend their products or choices.
- They provide criteria and standards that may be modified through discussion.
- They recognize and value students' multiple abilities, varied learning styles, and diverse backgrounds.

These criteria stem from the belief that any task worth learning is worth assessing, so that learning and assessment become hard to distinguish as separate activities. Tasks worth learning are also those worth repeating and practicing. They may require students to work together in order to complete, and they most certainly require varying amounts of time for different students or groups of students to complete. Finally, authentic assessments often allow for a significant degree of student choice in what product or performance is attempted and how it is completed (Hart, 1994).

Authentic assessments differ from classroom tests not only in format but also in the roles played by teacher and student. Most classroom tests are developed or selected by teachers, so that the student is a passive recipient of assessment. With authentic assessment, however, the student becomes an active partner in the assessment enterprise. Although the teacher serves as the more expert partner in providing appropriate feedback, students involved in authentic assessment activities learn to judge their own work and adopt goals for self-improvement.

Insights ON SUCCESSFUL PRACTICE

How have you used authentic assessments of students' academic performances and with what results?

One method I have used In the classroom as a way to assess whether my students have learned something—a math problem, science concept, or other lesson—is to have them demonstrate it or teach it to someone else or even to a group. This type of assessment is based on the idea that in order to teach somebody else, the student must have learned and understood the material him- or herself.

The "teaching" can be done through a number of different ways—lecture or demonstration (such as role playing), illustrations (designing posters or charts), or writing (producing books or other publications). Class discussion periods are one way I have used to give the student a chance to teach and help each other and give me the opportunity to assess their progress. The following is an example of how student teaching went far beyond our classroom.

The most valuable lesson my students with learning disabilities can learn is how to become their own advocates—how to help themselves, how to teach others about their problems, and how they best can be helped. This requires the students to learn and understand as much as possible about their own particular problems, their strengths and weaknesses, and what helps them the most. In addition, they must learn to deal with parents, teachers, and classmates who do not understand about learning disabilities.

Numerous class discussions dealing with issues relating to learning disabilities led to the decision by the students to write a book about them. The entire class was involved in the production—writing, typing, Illustrating, assembling, mailing, publicity, and bookkeeping. The lessons and skills learned through the publication of the book were invaluable—but the greatest outcome was the increased self-confidence and self-esteem of the authors as they learned how to deal with their learning disabilities by teaching and helping others. The book, now in its third edition, is being used around the world and has been translated into several languages.

The students also developed and presented workshops on learning disabilities for parents, teachers, and children. By teaching others about their problems, they learned about themselves and it was easy to accurately assess their competence.

PAMELA MANIET-BELLERMANN, Maniet-Bellermann
Foundation for the Learning Disabled,
South Orange, New Jersey

The advantages of authentic assessments are numerous. They work well in responding to student diversity, including varying abilities, learning styles and cultural backgrounds. They tend to be motivational in providing students with tasks that they perceive as worthwhile, interesting, and relevant. Authentic assessments provide teachers with a multidimensional view of student performance, which illustrates not just achievement but also affective characteristics such as motivation to learn. Authentic assessments help students to learn how to monitor their own performance and provide a means of communication among students, parents, and teachers. Finally, authentic assessments have **systemic validity**, which means that they can serve as an impetus for curriculum change (Frederiksen & Collins, 1989). When teachers adopt authentic tasks as a way to assess learning, they tend as well to adjust their instruction to provide more practice with the same kinds of tasks.

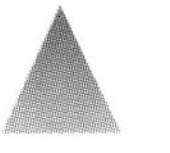 Insights

In this example, how is peer teaching used for authentic assessment? What are the benefits of peer teaching and student-directed curricula? In this teacher's experience, what role does self-advocacy play in her student's learning?

systemic validity A property of assessment in which assessment serves as an impetus for curriculum change.

Try This: Observe in classrooms where teachers are using various forms of alternative assessment. What goals are being assessed? What are students' reactions to these assessments?

Authentic assessments also have their disadvantages, however. Chief among them is the amount of time required to conduct authentic assessment. Whereas objective tests take up a class period or less, authentic assessments are likely to span several class periods and can continue for as long as a grading period or semester. Authentic assessments may also require more resources and considerable effort on the part of the teacher to plan. Careful planning is necessary, though, to ensure that tasks are effective, criteria for completion are clear, and students have access to the resources they will need. Finally, evaluating student performance on authentic assessments is a more complicated matter than counting correct answers on an objective test. In many cases, teachers must rely on their professional judgments without much external guidance for setting performance standards and criteria.

Just as there are different forms of classroom tests and procedures for developing them, so there are different types of authentic assessments and appropriate means of constructing them. Like classroom tests, teachers can also construct authentic assessments to serve different purposes. For finding out about students' needs and characteristics, serving the purpose of diagnosis and placement, observation-based assessment is a useful strategy. For keeping track and monitoring student development over a period of time, portfolio assessment is appropriate. For checking up on individual student performance and assigning grades, performance assessment is common (cf. Chittendon, 1991). Let's examine each in turn.

Try This: Interview teachers regarding their use of observation-based assessments. What methods do they use to conduct and record observations? For what purposes do they use observation-based assessment?

Observation-Based Assessments

Teachers observe students in class all the time. Almost without thinking about it, teachers become familiar with various aspects of their students' intellectual, physical, social, and emotional development. They know which students prefer listening to reading as a mode of learning. They know which students work well in groups and which work better alone. To be a useful part of any assessment program, however, observations should be systematic, objective, selective, unobtrusive, and carefully recorded.

To make their observations systematic, teachers should follow these guidelines (Hart, 1994):

1. Observe all students.
2. Observe often and regularly.
3. Record observations in writing.
4. Note the typical as well as the atypical. Observations of the routine are just as valuable as observations of the extraordinary.
5. Aggregate multiple observations in order to discern patterns of behavior.
6. Synthesize evidence from different contexts for a holistic picture of each student.

As for what to observe and how to record it, most teachers find checklists of various sorts to be useful. A checklist is composed of a listing of the behaviors or traits that the observer should be assessing. Checklists are best used for making yes/no, present/absent decisions about behaviors. Is a student on task? Does a student participate in small group discussion? Does the group divide labor on a cooperative project? Have students completed all steps in a procedure? Does a student use punctuation correctly when writing an essay? Each of these questions can be answered with a yes or no. The behavior is either observed or not. When it is desirable to rate the behavior on a continuum of excellent to poor or some other scale, then a rating scale should be used instead of, or in conjunction with, the checklist. Checklists also serve their function best when they include specific, well-defined behaviors or characteristics to be observed.

Try This: Develop a checklist for assessing student performance on a unit in a content area you plan to teach.

Other useful tools for focusing and documenting observations include rating scales and interview sheets. **Rating scales** are measurement instruments used to make judgments about some continuing behavior or performance. Rating scales allow the teacher to judge the frequency of occurrence of some behavior or the quality of some performance. Rating scales that use numbers typically consist of a list of attributes that can be rated numerically from "excellent" to "poor" or from "satisfactory" to "unsatisfactory." The following item is an example from a rating scale on student characteristics:

Student turns in homework assignments on time.

1	2	3	4
Always	Usually	Seldom	Never

Interview sheets are useful for recording a teacher's observations during a conference with the student. They generally consist of a list of questions to be asked of each student together with space for recording the student's responses (Hart, 1994). The questions reflect what the teacher wants to observe. In the sample language arts interview sheet shown in Figure 13.5, for instance, the questions can provide insight to the teacher regarding how students reacted to a story they had read.

rating scale A measurement instrument used in observation-based assessment to make judgments about some continuing behavior or performance.

interview sheet A means of recording a teacher's observations during a conference with the student, which generally consists of a list of questions to be asked of each student together with space for recording the student's responses.

Literature Review Sheet

Reader's Name ______________________ Date ________

Interviewer's Name ______________________

Book Title ______________________

Author ______________________

1. Whom did you like most in the story?
2. Whom did you like least?
3. Where does the story take place?
4. When does the story take place?
5. Why did the story keep your interest?
6. Did the author do anything that surprised you?
7. What was the saddest part of the story?
8. What was the happiest part of the story?
9. Did any part of the story make you laugh or cry?
10. What do you wish you could ask the author?
11. What type of person do you think would most enjoy reading this book?

FIGURE 13.5

Example of an Interview Sheet

Source: From *Assessment and Evaluation in Whole Language Programs,* Bill Harp, ed. Copyright 1991 Christopher–Gordon Publishers, Inc. Reprinted by permission.

These students are having their geography presentation videotaped. What artifacts, reproductions, attestations, and productions might be included in their cooperative learning assessment portfolio?

Recording observations does not have to be burdensome or time consuming to the teacher. The key to minimizing record keeping is developing systems for taking notes, such as checklists and rating scales, that require little writing and recording time. With the increase in computer technologies, electronic performance support tools are available to help teachers record observations in the classroom.

Portfolio Assessments

"A **portfolio** is a container of collected evidence with a purpose" (Collins, 1992, pp. 452-453). Artists and photographers, for example, develop portfolios of their best work for submitting to galleries or potential employers. Financiers develop portfolios containing all of their financial holdings and transactions in stocks, bonds, real property, and other assets. In education, students can develop portfolios for several different purposes that determine what types of evidence are collected and assembled in the portfolio. To show achievement in writing, for example, students might collect samples of their best work—best poem, best short story, best expository piece. To show development or progress in their understanding of how science is integrated with their daily lives, students would collect evidence of improved observational skills and changes in reasoning.

Reflection: Portfolio assessment is becoming more common in classes taken by prospective and returning teachers. What has been your experience in putting together a portfolio? What evidence of your progress did you include? How well do you think the portfolio reflected your achievement during the course?

Assessment portfolios have the potential of enabling teachers to assess student progress; parents, teachers, and students to communicate about a student's work; teachers and administrators to evaluate instructional programs; and students to evaluate and showcase their own achievements (Hart, 1994). For example, in the Middle School Science and Technology project, Powell (1993) used portfolios to document student progress toward particular goals in science. Likewise, portfolios serve several purposes in the Arts PROPEL project in the Pittsburgh public schools, from showing students' best work to documenting their development in writing skill (Wolf, 1989). Teachers must be clear about which purpose they are designing a portfolio assessment to serve, because the purpose will influence what types of evidence they should require in the portfolio.

Collins (1990, 1991, 1992; Collins & Dana, 1993) has distinguished four types of evidence that are routinely collected for inclusion in portfolios. *Artifacts* are documents produced by students during normal instruction, such as a project report, paper-and pencil-test, or drawings to accompany stories they have written. *Reproductions* are documents that display events in which students have participated. These include, for example, photographs of a student's entry in the school science fair or a videotape of a student group presenting two sides of a controversial social issue. *Attestations* are documents prepared by other people that provide external evidence of the student's performance or progress. A letter

portfolio A collection of evidence pertaining to students' developing knowledge and expertise, serving a particular assessment purpose.

from the school principal praising a student's plan to recycle waste from the cafeteria is an attestation, as is a music critic's glowing review of a student's flute recital. Finally, *productions* are documents prepared especially for the portfolio, such as reflections on the learning process, captions for other submitted work, and explanations for the inclusion of certain pieces of evidence in the portfolio.

here's how

Here's How to Design and Use Portfolio Assessments

- Determine the purpose(s) of the portfolio.
- Decide what will count as evidence (artifacts, reproductions, attestations, productions).
- Specify how much evidence should be included, based on the *value-added principle*; that is, for each piece of evidence to be required, ask, "What will be added to the portfolio if this piece of evidence is included?" Including too few items makes it difficult for the teacher to judge achievement or progress in a valid way; including too many items can result in duplication of evidence and confusion.
- Indicate how the evidence should be organized (i.e., chronologically, thematically, or by classes of evidence). (Adapted from Collins, 1992, and Hart, 1994)

When it comes to evaluating portfolios, there are no hard and fast rules for teachers to follow. You can define criteria based on the types of evidence included in the portfolio, the degree to which the evidence shows progress and achievement, and your expectations of what students should have achieved. Once you define specific criteria, you can assemble them in a checklist and scoring rubric. A **rubric** is a "scaled set of criteria that clearly defines for the student and teacher what a range of acceptable and unacceptable performance looks like" (Pate, Homestead, & McGinnis, 1993, p. 25). A general scoring rubric could include the following categories:

Poor: The student did not do the task, did not complete the assignment, or shows no comprehension of the activity.

Inadequate: The product or assessment does not satisfy a significant number of the criteria, does not accomplish what was asked, contains errors, or is of poor quality.

Fair: The product or assessment meets some of the criteria and does not contain gross errors or crucial omissions.

Good: The product or assessment completely or substantially meets the criteria.

Outstanding: All the criteria are met, and the product or assessment exceeds the assigned task and contains additional, unexpected, or outstanding features. (Price & Hein, 1994, p. 29)

One purpose of using portfolios is to develop students' abilities in self-assessment. Therefore, teachers may ask students to set their own evaluation criteria (Hart, 1994). Alternatively, expert judgment is a promising means of evaluating portfolios. "Expert judgment implies that the person doing the scoring recognizes the value of the performance as a whole" (Collins, 1992, p. 461), as music or art critics judge an orchestral performance or painting on its entire composition rather than its individual parts. The point to remember is that whatever procedures you use for scoring, they should be consistent with the purpose for which the students developed the portfolios.

Try This: Interview teachers who use portfolio assessment in their classes. For what purpose(s) do they use portfolios? How do they determine what types of evidence should be included? How do they help students learn to assemble a good portfolio? How do they score student portfolios?

rubric A scaled set of criteria clearly defining for the student and teacher the range of acceptable and unacceptable performance on a performance assessment.

Insights ON SUCCESSFUL PRACTICE

In your experience, what is the best way to develop and use a system of portfolio assessment?

At Metro High School, we have been working on establishing a system of school-wide portfolios since the fall of 1990. As I reflect on our progress, four key areas seem to surface.

The first is that it is important to develop a small, solid core of individuals who are committed to the use of portfolios. This group becomes the "champions for change." The committee accepts responsibility for developing and synthesizing the theoretical and practical research basis. This group also develops formal and informal methods to explain the proposed program to the entire staff. A further purpose of the committee is to address and alleviate questions and concerns as they arise.

Second, attention must be given to the personal concerns of staff members. During the first year, the majority of our discussions centered on personal considerations rather than educational issues. These concerns centered on procedural, mechanical, and time issues. Until these concerns are addressed, it is difficult, if not impossible, to implement educational reform.

The third area relates to the implementation process. We found that trying to delineate graduation expectations, develop authentic assessments, and implement portfolios as a unified package was too much for some of our staff members. We chose to use what Michael Fullan refers to as the Ready-Fire-Aim approach. We developed the rationale for portfolios (got ready), encouraged teacher participation (fired), and are now attempting to connect graduation expectations, demonstrations, and portfolios (aiming). An alternate method, which may have been more effective, would have been to focus initially on the graduation expectations. Once consensus is reached regarding the expectations, it seems that authentic assessments become a natural consequence. Student portfolios become the obvious method to collect, document, and assess progress toward meeting the expectations.

Finally, it must be recognized that portfolio implementation is a slow and evolutionary process. It has been over four years since we began the process, and there are still several faculty members who either do not understand or do not accept portfolios as a viable system. The portfolio response sheets and other materials have gone through several revisions. In addition, we are continuing to develop methods that provide the time for the effective and efficient use of portfolios by students and staff. Most important, we are just beginning to formally link our graduation expectations, demonstrations, and portfolios.

These key areas are not unique to the implementation of portfolios. They apply to most examples of reform efforts. I would suggest that anyone contemplating the implementation of portfolios first become familiar with the research relating to the change process.

DON DAVIS, Metro High School,
Cedar Rapids, Iowa

According to this teacher, what are the four key elements of an effective system of portfolio assessment? What are some drawbacks, and why can implementing school-wide portfolios take time? How might you use portfolios in the subject area you plan to teach?

Performance Assessments

Performance assessments are a demonstration of learning, an exhibition of curriculum mastery (Monson & Monson, 1993). They involve tasks that focus on students' use of knowledge and skills in a variety of realistic situations and contexts (Hart, 1994). Tasks that work well in performance assessments are integrative, permit multiple solutions or solution paths, and require sustained effort (Baron, 1991). They can be loosely or ill structured, so that students must not only figure out how to solve the problem but also decide what the problem is to solve. Performance assessment tasks can also be complex enough to require students to work together in small groups.

Critical Thinking: For what kinds of instructional objectives are performance assessments particularly appropriate?

When deciding whether and how to use performance assessments, teachers should consider, as they do with all forms of assessments, what purpose the performance assessment is to serve. Some kinds of skills can be measured *only* through performance testing. To determine whether a prospective medical lab technician knows how to properly draw a blood sample, for instance, one must observe the person actually doing it. Likewise, the language arts teacher knows whether students can use proper punctuation in a composition only by having students produce a writing sample. However, other targets of performance assessment are not always so clearly identified.

Point: *Authentic activity provides a basis for assessment.* In performance assessment, the activities are usually complex, problem-oriented tasks that often cross subject matter disciplines.

Whether students understand the concept of volume in order to be able to solve problems, for example, can be assessed using the items shown in Figure 13.6(A). If teachers are interested in students' reasoning processes as they answer questions like these, then the test items could be modified to require students to "show all work" or "explain and justify your answer." But when teachers want to know the extent to which students can use their understanding of volume in actual situations where such knowledge is required, then a performance task is preferred, such as that shown in Figure 13.6(B).

Try This: Interview teachers on their use of performance assessments. What are some of the advantages and disadvantages they see?

Performance assessments are appropriate for measuring metacognitive as well as cognitive development. How well students plan, whether they are proficient at monitoring and evaluating their own work, and how skilled they are at reflection are all possible metacognitive targets of performance assessment. Finally, dispositions are often a target of performance assessment, such as perseverance or flexibility (Quellmalz, 1991). In short, performance assessments are most useful when "essential tasks, achievements, habits of mind, or other valued 'masteries' are falling through the cracks of conventional tests" (Hart, 1994, p. 42).

performance assessment A demonstration of learning, or an exhibition of curriculum mastery that typically involves tasks focusing on students' use of knowledge and skills in a variety of realistic situations and contexts.

Once teachers have decided to use performance assessments, how should they go about designing them? Guidelines have been derived from a variety of sources (Baron, 1991; Hambleton & Murphy, 1992; Hart, 1994; Quellmalz, 1991; Wiggins, 1993).

here's how

Here's How to Design and Use Performance Assessments

- Select or design tasks that are meaningful and interesting to students and require integration of knowledge, skills, and dispositions. The volume problem shown in Figure 13.6(B) is an example of this and the following guidelines.
- Select or design tasks that are complex, well structured, and/or permit multiple solutions.
- Situate tasks in real-world contexts that are developmentally appropriate for students.

- Ensure that students have access to needed resources and sufficient time to develop assignments and projects.
- Impose authentic constraints on task completion, such as whether students may seek help from others or work in teams.
- Clearly state what performance is expected of students and how this performance will be judged. If self-assessment or peer-assessment are used, indicate what procedures will be followed to develop performance criteria.

Like other forms of authentic assessment, performance tasks require careful and systematic planning by the teacher, and they take longer to administer and score. Scoring itself represents a special problem with performance assessment, because there are so many different variables that a teacher may want to measure. When different solutions to a problem are possible, the quality of the solution must be judged, and judging quality depends upon criteria that the teacher has determined are important. When multiple goals are being assessed with a single, multifaceted performance, then criteria must be established for each goal.

FIGURE 13.6

Two Approaches to Testing Student Understanding of Volume

Source: From *Assessing Student Performance* (p. 114), by G. P. Wiggins, 1993, San Francisco, CA: Jossey-Bass Publishers. Reprinted by permission.

1. Objective Test Questions

1. What is the volume of a cone that has a base area of 78 square centimeters and a height of 12 centimeters?
   a. 30 cm^3
   b. 312 cm^3
   c. 936 cm^3
   d. 2808 cm^3
2. A round and a square cylinder share the same height. Which has the greater volume?

2. A Multiday Performance Assessment on Volume

Background: Manufacturers naturally want to spend as little as possible, not only on the product, but on packing and shipping it to stores. They want to *minimize* the cost of production of their packaging, and they want to *maximize* the amount of what is packaged inside (to keep handling and postage costs down: the more individual packages you ship, the more it costs).

Setting: Imagine that your group of two or three people is one of many in the packing department responsible for M&M's candies. The manager of the shipping department has found that the cheapest material for shipping comes as a flat piece of rectangular paperboard (the piece of posterboard you will be given). She is asking each work group in the packing department to help solve this problem: *What completely closed container, built out of the given piece of posterboard, will hold the* largest volume *of M&M's for safe shipping?*

1. Prove, in a *convincing* written report to company executives, that both the *shape* and the *dimensions* of your group's container maximize the volume. In making your case, supply all important data and formulas. Your group will be asked to make a three-minute oral report at the next staff meeting. Both reports will be judged for *accuracy*, *thoroughness*, and *persuasiveness*.
2. Build a model (or multiple models) out of the posterboard of the container shape and size that you think solves the problem. The models are *not* proof; they will *illustrate* the claims you offer in your report.

Checklists and rubrics, as described earlier, can be useful in scoring performance tasks. Rubrics are especially useful because they can be used to score almost any dimension of performance, including how much assistance the student required to complete a task or the nature of that assistance (Quellmalz, 1991). To develop a rubric for use in scoring performance assessments, teachers should:

- Make a list of important parts of the performance task, such as content, process, mechanics, presentation, source variety, number of cues needed to complete the task.
- Develop a scale for each section showing expected criteria.
- Weight the rubric sections. (Pate et al., 1993)

An example of a rubric teachers might use to score student presentations is shown in Figure 13.7. You can see that the teacher has identified six components of the performance to be separately scored. Performance on each component is judged on the

	Criterion 1	Criterion 2	Criterion 3	Score x Weight	Total
Section One Eye Contact with Audience	Rarely	Not often	Often	______ x 6 =	______ points
Section Two Posture	Often slouches, sways, turns back on audience, fidgets	Sometimes slouches, sways, fidgets, turns back on audience	Stands straight, faces audience, movements appropriate to presentation	______ x 6 =	______ points
Section Three Voice Projection	Words not pronounced clearly and volume too low	Words not pronounced clearly or volume too low	Words pronounced and heard clearly	______ x 6 =	______ points
Section Four Organization	Information not presented in a logical, interesting sequence; the audience could not follow	Information was interesting, but not presented in a logical order	Information presented in a logical, interesting sequence which the audience could follow	______ x 7 =	______ points
Section Five Visual Aides	Two different types of media; information not relevant to outcomes/content; messy; minimal artistic effort	Two different types of media; information relevant to outcomes/content; adequate artistic effort	More than two different types of media; information relevant to outcomes/content; very neat; excellent artistic effort	______ x 5 =	______ points
Section Six Time	Less than 10 minutes	10 to 14 minutes	15 minutes or more	______ x 3 =	______ points
				Bonus Points	______ points

FIGURE 13.7

Example of a Rubric for Scoring Performance Assessments

Source: From Designing rubrics for authentic assessment, by P. E. Pate, E. Homestead, & K. McGinnis, in *Middle School Journal,* 1993, 25(2), 25–27. Reprinted by permission.

basis of criteria defined at three levels. Then an overall score is calculated by multiplying each component score by a weighting factor and adding the results.

HOW CAN YOU ENSURE SOUND ASSESSMENT PRACTICES?

This chapter has examined various types of assessments and guidelines for constructing them. By following these guidelines, you will increase the likelihood that your assessments will be sound. What does this mean? Sound assessment practices yield evaluative information about student performance that is accurate and consistent. With accurate information, teachers can be confident in their diagnoses of student learning problems, their decisions about student placement, and their selection of instructional activities to best meet student needs. For assessment practices to be sound, however, they must have the properties of validity and reliability.

Validity

Validity is the most important property of sound assessments and therefore the most important quality for teachers to consider as they construct either classroom tests or authentic assessments. **Validity** concerns the extent to which interpretations of assessment results will be appropriate, meaningful, and useful (Gronlund, 1993).

Example: Think of content-related evidence of validity in terms of the following question: Does the assessment measure what it purports to measure?

To be sure that the results of a test or authentic assessment are valid, teachers can draw on various sources of evidence. To begin with, assessments typically measure only a sample of the tasks students can perform in the content domain being assessed. For example, a teacher who wants to know how well students use a dictionary cannot construct an assessment that contains all the possible tasks in which a dictionary is appropriately used. Instead, the teacher must depend on a representative sample of tasks that will enable him or her to infer students' competence in dictionary use. *Content-related evidence* of validity, then, refers to how representative the assessment tasks are of those in the overall content domain.

To improve the validity of their assessments, teachers should carefully identify desired learning outcomes. When constructing tests, they should use a test plan (table of specifications) and be sure there are sufficient items to measure each learning outcome. When constructing authentic assessments, they should select tasks that best represent the content domain and types of learning outcomes they want students to acquire.

Criterion-related evidence of validity is important when the purpose of a test or alternative assessment is to accurately predict performance, either at the present time or in the future. An assessment may be administered, for example, in order to predict whether a student should be moved into a higher-ability grouping for mathematics class. The test is used to predict the student's achievement in the new class. Tests such as the Scholastic Aptitude Test (SAT) are used to predict how well the test takers will perform in the future—in this case, how well they are likely to perform in college.

validity A property of assessment concerning the extent to which interpretations of assessment results will be appropriate, meaningful, and useful.

An assessment is valid when the students it predicts will perform well in a new situation actually do so. So, for example, if a student is moved to a higher-ability group in mathematics based on assessment scores and continues to perform well, we can infer that the results of the assessment must be valid.

A third type of evidence used to judge the validity of assessments is called *construct-related evidence.* This type of evidence is important if the purpose of an assessment is to measure some psychological trait or construct. Take, for example, the IQ tests discussed in Chapter 5. Intelligence is a construct. It is a concept that theorists literally constructed as an explanation of certain observations. IQ tests are designed to measure the psychological characteristics that make up a kind of intelligence. IQ scores are interpreted to mean that people either possess or do not possess these characteristics. A test of IQ is considered valid on the basis of how well its scores correlate with the characteristics theoretically associated with intelligence.

Connection: Intelligence tests are discussed further in Chapters 5 and 14.

Reliability

Although validity is the most important quality of sound assessment, it is not the only quality necessary. Reliability of assessment is also crucial, and **reliability** concerns the degree to which assessments are free of measurement errors. The results teachers observe of student performance on tests or other forms of assessments are actually estimates of students' true levels of achievement. As such, they always contain a certain amount of error. Errors creep into student performance due to problems in conducting assessments as well as problems internal to the students. For example, perhaps a fire drill interrupted an essay test and students didn't have adequate time to finish writing. Or perhaps a student was recovering from a severe head cold at the time a music recital was scheduled. Measurement errors can be caused by student carelessness, variations in motivation, luck in guessing, and temporary fluctuations in memory. Errors can also be caused by variations in assessment conditions and inconsistent scoring of results.

Example: Think of reliability in terms of the following question: Would the results obtained on a particular test be the same if the test were given at a different time or if the same questions were asked in a different way?

Assessments are reliable, then, when they give a consistent picture of student performance over time and between one type of measurement and another. What is also important for teachers, however, is whether assessments are reliable in classifying masters from nonmasters. The student who has mastered the material should perform consistently well on measures designed to assess mastery, whereas the student who has not mastered the subject should consistently perform below the established mastery criterion. Remember that Mrs. Pearson-Wood in the Teacher Chronicle is concerned about writing tests that eliminate the possibility students will miss an item that they really know. She wants her assessments to distinguish consistently between students who have mastered instructional content and met performance criteria from those who have not. When teachers use multiple means of assessment to determine what their students know and can do, they increase the reliability with which they will make sound assessment decisions.

Try This: Interview teachers to discover ways they try to ensure the validity and reliability of assessment results. In what ways do they deal with potential bias in assessment?

Teachers can also improve the reliability and validity of their assessment decisions by evaluating their assessment practices. Test or assessment **bias** occurs when procedures or items discriminate unfairly among students. For example, when test items draw on the experiences and backgrounds of upper-middle-class or European American students to the exclusion of poor or minority group students, then the latter are not likely to perform as well even when they are equally competent in the subject matter. Bias can also occur when some students are given more time and resources than other students to complete tasks. Teachers should check for possible bias before administering an assessment, but they can check the quality of test items after administration as well.

reliability A property of assessment that concerns the degree to which assessments are free of measurement errors.

bias The result of procedures or items used in assessment that unfairly discriminate among students.

Conducting Item Analysis

Teachers who regularly use objective tests for evaluating their students begin to accumulate test items of different types, some of which work better than others for measuring student performance. Evaluating items after tests are administered serves an important instructional function. **Item analysis** allows the teacher to determine whether an item functions in the way the teacher intends it to. By reviewing an item and your students' responses to it, you can determine whether the item is testing the intended objective, whether it measures at the appropriate level of difficulty, and whether it distinguishes those who know the content from those who don't.

For multiple-choice tests, item analysis also allows the teacher to determine how well different foils work within an item. Analyzing items in class—perhaps reviewing the items on the test after grading them—is a way to provide students with feedback at the same time you acquire valuable information that may be used for improving items. Item analysis by means of in-class review also helps the teacher determine common student errors and difficulties. Item analysis can suggest ways to revise curriculum and improve your test-writing skills (Nitko, 1983). Once suitable tests have been developed, their validity and reliability can be improved by using item analysis procedures.

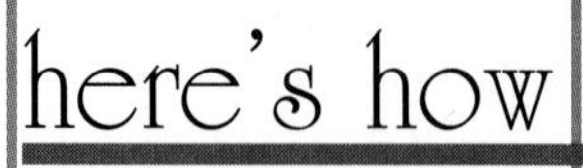

Here's How to Perform an Item Analysis

- **Step 1.** Arrange the test scores in order from the highest score to the lowest. See Figure 13.8 for an illustration of this item analysis procedure.
- **Step 2.** Identify an upper and a lower group. The upper group is the highest scoring 25 percent of the entire class; the lower group is the lowest scoring 25 percent.
- **Step 3.** For each item, count the number of upper-group students who chose each alternative. Repeat the count for the lower group.
- **Step 4.** Record the counts for each item on a copy of the test.
- **Step 5.** Add the two numbers (from the upper and lower groups) for the keyed response (i.e., correct answer). Divide this sum by the number of students in both the upper and lower groups. Multiply this decimal value by 100 to form a percentage. This percentage is an estimate of the *index of item difficulty*.
- **Step 6.** For the keyed response, subtract the count of the lower group from that of the upper group, and divide this number by the number of examinees in one of the groups. You can use the number in either group because both groups are the same size. The result is a decimal that is the *index of discrimination*. (Ebel & Frisbie, 1991)

The *index of item difficulty*, the result of Step 5, estimates the proportion of students who answered the item correctly. This is because the procedure does not include all of the students who took the test, only the upper and lower groups. The difficulty index is a measure of how hard students found each item to be. An index of 50 percent, for example, means that approximately half of the students answered that item correctly. If fewer than half the students correctly answered an item, it is probably too hard and should be modified in some way.

item analysis A procedure used to evaluate test items for the purpose of determining whether the item functions in the way the teacher intends it to.

Suppose, conversely, that the index of item difficulty for a particular item turns out to be 95 percent, which means that nearly all the students got it right.

Test Item: Students in a religion class draw concept maps as a means of learning differences among the many religions they are studying. This tactic is most likely to influence which process?

a. long-term storage
b. performance
c. search and retrieval
d. semantic encoding

Suppose that 150 students took the test. The upper 25 percent consists of the highest 37 scorers, whereas the lower 25 percent consists of the lowest 37 scorers. Their scoring patterns on this item are shown below.

Item Alternatives	A	B	C	D*
Upper 37	5	0	0	32
Lower 37	8	4	5	20

*correct answer

$$\text{Index of Difficulty} = \frac{\text{Upper Correct} + \text{Lower Correct}}{\text{Total Upper and Lower}} = \frac{32 + 20}{74} = .70 \times 100 = 70\%$$

$$\text{Index of Discrimination} = \frac{\text{Upper Correct} - \text{Lower Correct}}{(1/2)\ \text{Total}} = \frac{32 - 20}{37} = .32$$

FIGURE 13.8

An Illustration of Item Analysis

Does this mean that the item is too easy? Perhaps, but remember that a test should be measuring what students have learned from instruction. If instruction is effective, then most of the students should be correctly answering many of the items. A test that contains too many hard items will simply be discouraging to students and may indicate problems with the instruction or the test.

Critical Thinking: Under what condition would a low or high index of item difficulty be desirable?

The *index of discrimination*, the result of Step 6, is a measure of the extent to which an item differentiates students who do well on the entire test from those students who perform poorly overall. The discrimination index can vary between .00 and 1.00. The closer to 1.00, the better the item discriminates between those who did well and those who did poorly on the test, because a discrimination value of 1.00 means that all of the upper group got the item right whereas none of the lower group did. If the same number of students in each group answered an item correctly, then the index of discrimination will be .00.

Unless the index of discrimination is exactly .00, then it will be either positive or negative. It will be positive when a greater number of students in the upper group answered correctly than students in the lower group. When more students in the lower group answered correctly, the index of discrimination will be negative. Good test items should discriminate between well-performing and poorly performing students, so they should have discrimination indices that are positive. A negative index is a signal that the item is bad, either because it is poorly worded or ambiguous or because it assessed content that was not taught.

Critical Thinking: How would the results of an item analysis on a multiple-choice test help you determine how students are understanding a particular concept?

By examining the pattern of students' choices of foils in a multiple-choice question, teachers can find clues to what might be wrong with any given item. Suppose, for example, that half of the upper group and most of the lower group chose a particular foil. This could be an indication of more than one correct answer to the question or a strong misconception held by students. A good item is one answered correctly by most of the students in the upper group, with some students in the lower group selecting each of the foils. Reflecting on Ms. Mendoza's problem in the Teacher Chronicle, what might she have learned by conducting an item analysis on the test on which students performed so poorly?

Try This: Generate an item analysis that demonstrates a good multiple-choice item.

Avoiding Pitfalls in Assessment

With practice at using the guidelines in this chapter and experience in your classroom, you will become accomplished at devising valid and reliable assessments and learn to avoid many of the problems commonly experienced by practicing teachers (Ebel & Frisbie, 1991). One problem is that teachers tend to rely too heavily on subjective judgments that stem from informal observations rather than on reliable and valid measurements.

Observations yield necessary and highly useful data, but it is important that they be considered along with other sources of evidence about student achievement, such as formal assessment. Any time two sources of evidence converge toward the same conclusion, you can be more confident that the conclusion is correct. Similarly, if the inferences you draw from observations diverge from assessment results, you have found a problem worthy of additional thought and investigation.

Too many teachers cause themselves problems by putting off assessment planning and preparation until the last minute. One consequence is that paper-and-pencil tests, rather than performance assessments, must be used to save time. Teachers also construct tests sometimes that are heavily weighted toward the material at the end of the unit while ignoring material from the beginning of the unit. Planning ahead will help you make better decisions about what assessment methods you should use in your classes, and using a table of specifications will help you to ensure a more valid and reliable test.

When it comes to objective tests, many teachers construct and administer tests that are simply too short. A test that is too short increases the likelihood that the items on the test will not be representative of the content domain to be measured and thus run the risk of being unreliable. Writing tests that are too short, putting off test preparation until the last minute, and relying on subjective judgments rather than specifying objectives and the cognitive level at which items ought to be written all yield an overemphasis on trivial details to the exclusion of some of the more important principles or applications in the unit.

Failure to use test construction guidelines tends to yield items that are ambiguous and that tend to answer each other by providing unintentional clues. Many teachers, once they have the test results in hand, forget that all measurement, no matter how carefully designed, is prone to error and imprecision. Frequent assessment and the use of multiple modes of assessment are ways to avoid this problem. The item analysis procedure is another means of overcoming problems with test items. Failure to use item analysis yields tests that, over time, do not improve in quality.

HOW CAN YOU USE ASSESSMENT TO IMPROVE TEACHING AND LEARNING?

Although you will use assessment to communicate student progress to parents, other teachers, and the community and to measure the effectiveness of your instruction, you are likely to find its greatest benefit is improving the learning of your students. Besides making sure that assessment results are valid and reliable, you can improve learning by providing effective feedback, involving students in assessment, using assessment results to improve instruction, and creating a positive assessment environment in your classroom.

Point: *Assessment improves teaching and learning.* Results of assessments provide information to learners about their achievement and information to teachers about their instruction.

Providing Effective Feedback

Objective tests have been a predominant form of assessment for so long that many people have come to equate test scores with feedback. After all, test scores provide an indication of how well a student performed in comparison to other students or to some external standard. But consider how much information is conveyed to the learner by a test score. Not much. There is nothing in a score that tells a learner how to improve his or her performance if it did not come up to standard. Feedback is "information that provides the performer with direct, usable insights into current performance, based on tangible differences between current performance and hoped-for performance" (Wiggins, 1993, p. 182). Feedback enables learners to self-correct, to adjust and improve their performances.

Try This: Observe teachers to discover ways they provide effective feedback. What feedback do they give students on written work or other achievement-related products?

What is effective feedback? Many teachers believe they are providing helpful feedback when they assign a grade or write comments on student work that either praise or point out mistakes. Knowing that they have made a mistake, however, is not enough to help students correct their errors. They need to know why the mistake is a mistake and why an alternative answer would be better. For example, a student who has miscalculated in an arithmetic problem can be shown how to solve the problem correctly and encouraged to try again. Effective feedback is descriptive in nature ("you should try to include specific details to support your initial assertion"), not evaluative ("your writing is below average") or judgmental ("you're a poor student").

Depending on how confident students are of their test answers, they will attend to feedback differently (Kulhavy & Stock, 1989). Students who are very sure of an answer they get wrong will likely spend

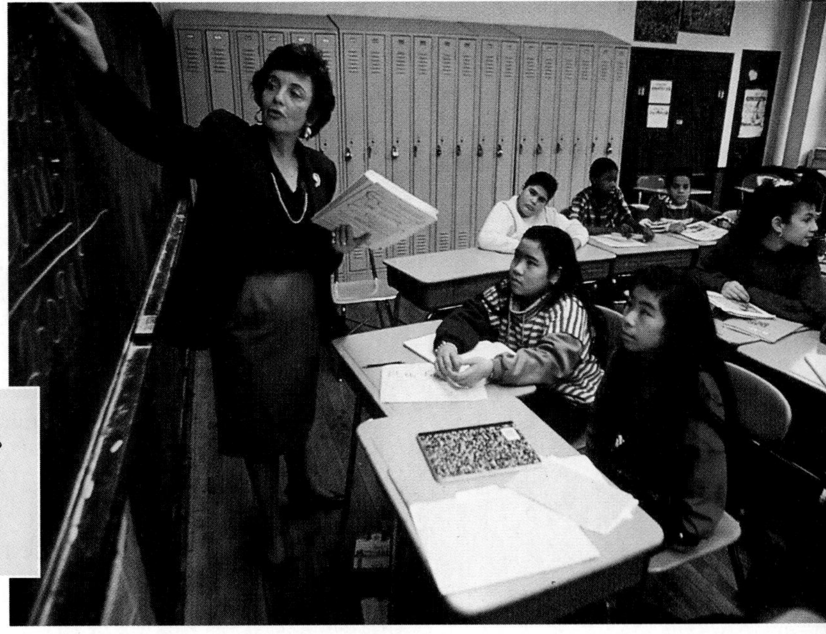

What will determine the effectiveness of the assessment feedback this teacher is providing? How might the teacher involve students more in evaluating their own achievement of learning outcomes?

more time trying to understand why they erred than students who are very unsure of their answers. Lack of confidence in their responses can signal that these students lack fundamental understandings that might require additional instruction. Effective feedback helps students to confirm their right answers, debug their mistakes, and reveal their lack of understanding. Effective feedback also provides students with standards and criteria they can use in self-assessment. Table 13.3 displays a comparison of effective and ineffective feedback that can help you in providing constructive feedback to your students to improve their learning.

Involving Students in Assessment

One of the hallmarks of the current assessment reform is that students should be just as involved in the assessment process as their teachers (Hart, 1994). "If we want people to gain control of important habits of standards and habits of mind, then they have to know . . . how to accurately view those things and to apply criteria to their own work" (Wiggins, 1993, p. 54). When students learn to self-assess, they not only begin to internalize performance standards but also increase their sense of ownership over their learning.

TABLE 13.3 A Comparison of Effective versus Ineffective Feedback

Effective Feedback	Ineffective Feedback
Provides guidance and confirming (or disconfirming) evidence.	Provides praise or blame, and non-situation-specific advice or exhortations.
Compares current performance and trends against successful result.	Naively assumes that instructions and hard work will bring people to their goal.
Is timely and immediately useful.	Is not timely; suffers from excessive delay in usability or arrives too late to use at all.
Measures in terms of absolute progress; assesses the accomplishment; specifies degree of conformance with the exemplar, goal, or standard.	Measures in terms of relative change or growth, relative to the self or norms; tells students how far they have come (not how far they have left to go).
Is characterized by descriptive language.	Is characterized by evaluative or comparative language.
Is useful to a novice; offers specific, salient diagnoses and prescriptions for each mistake.	Is not useful for a novice; offers a general summary of strengths and weaknesses.
Allows the performer to perceive a specific, tangible effect of his or her efforts.	Obscures any tangible effect so that none (beyond a score) is visible to the performer.
Measures essential traits.	Measures easy-to-score variables.
Derives the result sought from analysis of exit-level or adult accomplishment.	Derives the result sought from an arbitrarily mandated or simplistic goal statement.

Source: Compiled from Wiggins (1993), *Assessing Student Performance.* San Francisco: Jossey-Bass.

In a kindergarten class in Florida, for example, the teacher found that students could accurately judge their writing development on a scale she posted in the classroom (Lamme & Hysmith, 1991). Once they began to view their work in these terms, they also took more risks with their writing.

Peer assessment occurs when students evaluate each other's work. This happens informally all the time when students look to see what their neighbors are doing in comparison to their own efforts. But when you provide assessment forms or checklists or conduct discussion about individual student products, then you have elevated peer assessment to a more formal process. Peer assessment works especially well in situations where students collaborate on the performance criteria or standards to be used in judging their work. In a sense, setting the criteria also means that students have set goals that they expect their performance to meet. Setting their own goals makes it likely that students will work hard to achieve them and may rely on each other in doing so.

Try This: Interview teachers regarding whether and how they involve students in the assessment process. What are some advantages and disadvantages in doing this?

Collaborative or group assessment is a third way in which students can become involved in the assessment process. In some cases, an entire class may set common performance goals, such as "understanding the mathematics that we do," or "being open to new ideas and new approaches" (Hart, 1994). Then, on a regular basis, they examine their common progress toward goal attainment. Asking evaluative and reflective questions helps students to do this, such as "What did you learn doing this assignment?" "Is there another way this problem could be solved?" "What new questions did this activity raise for you?" Having students keep a journal or learning log in which they list goals, keep assignments, draw conclusions, and evaluate their own learning is another means to reflect on individual or class progress and process.

Finally, assessment questionnaires are a useful way of having cooperative groups assess their teamwork and individual contributions to a project or assignment. You can direct questions not only toward the performance criteria to be used in judging the learning product but also toward the process used in completing the project or assignment. Figure 13.9 shows a sample of questions that might be useful for groups in assessing their performance.

Modifying and Improving Instruction

In the Teacher Chronicle, Ms. Mendoza wonders whether the poor performance of the students on her test is a problem with them, her teaching, or the test. By conducting an item analysis, she could discover whether problems existed on the test, and her prior knowledge of the students would give her insight as to whether their performance on this test was consistent with their performance on other measures. Suppose Ms. Mendoza decided that the test was fair but that students' performance on it was simply not representative of what she knew they could achieve. How could the test results help her to pinpoint possible problems in the lesson itself?

Reflection: Recall an episode from your schooling in which a teacher changed the activities of a class based on the results of a test or quiz. How effective were these changes?

Assessment data of all sorts are useful to teachers in determining what went right and what went wrong with their instruction. By finding out what went wrong, they can modify and improve their instructional strategies. What kind of information might you collect to help you in revising instruction? Dick and Reiser (1989) recommend that essential sources of information include student performance on unit tests and their attitudes after instruction. Additional useful information may include what students knew and how they felt about the

FIGURE 13.9

Portion of an Assessment Questionnaire for Self- and Group Assessment

Directions: Circle the number that best reflects your opinion or assessment.

1. How would you rate your understanding of the material covered in Unit 4?

Limited	1	2	3	4	5	Full

2. How helpful was your group in discussing the concepts in Unit 4?

Not very	1	2	3	4	5	Very

3. What was your own level of engagement in your group's discussion?

Low	1	2	3	4	5	High

4. How would you rate the engagement of each member of your group in the discussion? (*Write in the first name of each person in the space provided.*)

________	Low	1	2	3	4	5	High
________	Low	1	2	3	4	5	High
________	Low	1	2	3	4	5	High

subject matter before instruction, their performance on activities and exercises during instruction, and your observations of students during instruction.

Example: One of the purposes of diagnostic evaluation is to determine whether students belong in gifted or special education programs or need modifications of curriculum, instruction, or environment in inclusive classrooms. Assessment of motor and cognitive skills may be accomplished by using written, oral, and physical tests.

Once you have collected assessment data, the task is to organize and analyze it. You could begin by summarizing data according to the objectives dealt with in the lesson. For example, following the table of specifications for the unit test (review Table 13.1), you could list average student performance on each objective and each type of outcome. This would tell you whether students had difficulty with a particular objective (solving double-digit problems that do not require regrouping) or whether they had trouble with a type of outcome (application of concepts they could otherwise define). Depending on the problem you identify, you could provide additional practice, teach the concepts in an alternate way, or find new examples that might be a better fit to your students' backgrounds.

Just as test scores help you to identify possible areas for revising instruction, so does information about student attitudes, both during and after instruction. During instruction, looks of confusion or boredom on the faces of students are potent indicators of a lesson gone awry. Even after instruction, finding out how students reacted to specific aspects of a lesson can help you decide whether to retain an activity you tried out for the first time or to revise it because it didn't keep students' interest. In any event, you can continuously improve your teaching by heeding the things you learn from student assessments.

Creating a Positive Assessment Environment in the Classroom

Assessment improves learning and performance when it is respectful of students and in the students' interest (Wiggins, 1993). As Figure 13.10 suggests,

FIGURE 13.10

Assessment Bill of Rights for Students

Source: From *Assessing Student Performance* (p. 28) by G. P. Wiggins, 1993, San Francisco, CA: Jossey-Bass. Reprinted by permission.

1. Worthwhile (engaging, educative, and authentic) intellectual problems that are validated against worthy real-world intellectual problems, roles, and situations.
2. Clear, apt, published, and consistently applied teacher criteria in grading work and published models of excellent work that exemplify standards.
3. Minimal secrecy in testing and grading.
4. Ample opportunities to produce work that students can be proud of, thus, ample opportunity in the curriculum and instruction to monitor, self-assess, and self-correct their work.
5. Assessment, not just tests: Multiple and varied opportunities to display and document achievement, and options in tests that allow the students to play to their strengths.
6. The freedom, climate, and oversight policies necessary to question grades and test practices without fear of retribution.
7. Forms of testing that allow timely opportunites for students to explain or justify answers marked as wrong but that they believe to be apt or correct.
8. Genuine feedback: Usable information on their strengths and weaknesses and an accurate assessment of their long-term progress toward a set of exit-level standards framed in terms of essential tasks.
9. Scoring/grading policies that provide incentives and opportunities for improving performance and seeing progress against exit-level and real-world standards.

teachers should be flexible in their use of assessment and responsive to individual student needs. More than this, however, teachers can set standards of excellence in their classes and then adopt classroom policies that support student progress toward attaining those standards.

It is important to point out that *standards* of performance are not the same thing as *expectations* of performance. As Wiggins (1993) put it, standards are ideals, always out of reach but eminently desirable nevertheless. He gives the example in industry of "zero defects per million," a standard commonly set by manufacturers. Although this standard is virtually impossible to achieve, and manufacturers don't really *expect* to achieve it, the standard provides a benchmark toward which they can strive. What is *expected* is that everyone will work continuously toward narrowing the gap between present performance and ideal performance.

Try This: Teachers have implicit views about assessment that reflect their views of students and learning. Visit several different teachers' classrooms and try to determine the extent to which they adhere to the Assessment Bill of Rights for Students.

Ideal performance, it is also important to point out, does not have to be a singular measure of excellence. Standards and criteria depend upon the context and purpose of the assessment (Wiggins, 1993). Writing a letter to the editor, for example, must meet different criteria than writing a report of a scientific investigation. Moreover, while the standards of performance for writing a scientific article might include ability to pass a peer review for publication, you would not expect an eighth-grade student to achieve that standard.

How might teachers achieve a positive assessment environment in the classroom, then? To begin with, they must define standards of performance that are:

- concrete exemplars or specifications, not general goals
- benchmarks, not norms
- the quality of acceptable performance demanded, not the scoring criteria used to distinguish acceptable from unacceptable performance
- the quality of the performance, not the difficulty level of the task
- ultimate and milestone standards, not age-cohort expectations
- indicators and valid descriptors of acceptable performance, not arbitrary cut scores
- demanding quality work from everyone, not arbitrary quotas (Wiggins, 1993, pp. 287-288)

Once this is done, assessment serves the functions of determining what you can reasonably expect of students and of helping students continually adjust their performance so that it comes nearer to the standards. The following tips from teachers who have made assessment a positive and integral part of their instruction may help you to get started:

1. *Establish your own personal evaluation plan.* Choose assessment strategies that are most likely to provide you with the information you need to help students learn.
2. *Share your plan with students.* Make your standards and expectations clear. Involve students in determining some of these expectations.
3. *Make assessment part of your daily class routine.* Integrate assessment strategies into your instruction. Have students evaluate their own and each other's work, and discuss the results as a class.
4. *Use volunteer assessment aides.* Solicit the help of parents or other volunteers to collect assessment data or evaluate student work against standards of excellence.
5. *Set up an easy and efficient record-keeping system.* Consider file folders and computer-based systems for compiling and recording student progress. Consider ways of having students keep their own records. (adapted from Hart, 1994, pp. 87-88)

A system of continuous progress often depends on regular and open communication among teachers, students, parents, and the community at large. Sound assessment practices can provide you with a solid foundation for communicating your instructional goals and your students' progress toward goal attainment. How to do this effectively is the focus of Chapter 14.

TEACHER Chronicle Conclusion

TESTING TRIALS

During the weekend after her conversation with Mrs. Pearson-Wood, Louisa Mendoza redesigns the test on which her students did so poorly. Reflecting on her colleague's remarks, she rewrites her multiple-choice questions and includes an essay question. She also adds some authentic problems for students to solve using what they have learned. On Monday she announces the new test.

APPLICATION QUESTIONS

1. What should Ms. Mendoza do to prepare her students for the new test?
2. Construct a sample of test items for the new test, based on a unit or lesson in a content area you plan to teach.
3. Analyze your sample test. How do the items reflect learning outcomes and instructional goals?
4. How can you be sure the test and its results will be valid? reliable?
5. In what ways could you use the test results and for what reasons?

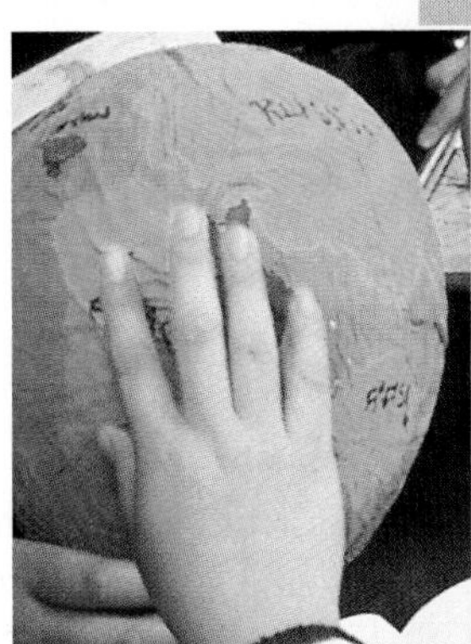

CHAPTER SUMMARY

WHAT IS ASSESSMENT AND HOW ARE ASSESSMENT PRACTICES CHANGING?

Assessment is a process of gathering, analyzing, and interpreting data in order to make judgments about student learning. Classroom tests provide one form of assessment commonly used by teachers, but authentic assessment provides an alternative and sometimes more useful means of assessing complex thinking and problem-solving skills.

Teachers assess many different knowledge and skill competencies acquired by their students. They also evaluate student dispositions toward learning, as well as achievement-related products and processes. Teachers specify assessment goals based on their professional knowledge, curriculum guides, and input from the community.

HOW CAN YOU PLAN AND CONSTRUCT CLASSROOM TESTS?

To construct classroom tests that best match the content and learning outcomes they want to assess, teachers should use a table of specifications for planning their tests. Depending on their goals, teachers have available a variety of item formats, such as binary-choice, matching, multiple-choice, short answer, and essay items.

HOW CAN YOU CONSTRUCT ALTERNATIVE ASSESSMENTS?

Authentic assessments, including observation-based assessment, portfolios, and performance tasks, provide teachers with the means to assess the development of student knowledge and skill over time and the application of these skills in realistic contexts and situations.

HOW CAN YOU ENSURE SOUND ASSESSMENT PRACTICES?

For assessment practices to be sound, they must first be valid, which means that interpretations of assessment results must be appropriate, meaningful, and useful. Assessments must also be reliable, or as free from measurement errors as possible. Teachers can improve the soundness of their assessment practices by evaluating items, planning ahead, using assessment construction guidelines, and using multiple means of judging student learning.

HOW CAN YOU USE ASSESSMENT TO IMPROVE TEACHING AND LEARNING?

In addition to following the other suggestions offered in the chapter, you can use assessment to improve learning by providing effective feedback to your students, involving them in the assessment process, revising and improving instruction, and creating a positive assessment environment in your classroom.

KEY CONCEPTS

assessment
authentic assessment
bias
binary-choice items
essay items
evaluation
formative assessment
interview sheet
item analysis
matching items
measurement
multiple-choice items
objective tests
performance assessment
placement
portfolio
rating scale
readiness
reliability
rubric
selection-type items
short answer items
summative assessment
supply-type items
systemic validity
table of specifications
test
validity

CHAPTER OUTLINE

TEACHER

Chronicle

BENEFIT OF THE DOUBT

Roy Clark, a middle school math teacher, reaches into his mailbox and takes out a note from Louise Geiger, his principal. The note says, "Could I please see you at your break to discuss math placements for next year?"

Mr. Clark jots a quick response, puts it in Mrs. Geiger's mailbox, and goes to get his math record book. He reviews it during his study hall assignment in the fourth period. He already knows that Mrs. Geiger has decided to make next year's math placements based on the most recent achievement test scores. Anyone with a 7 stanine or higher would automatically be slotted for algebra.

Mr. Clark makes a note beside Heidi Rogers' name. She is a good average student who works really hard in math, which does not come easy for her. She had done extremely well on the standardized math test to get a 6 stanine. After the test, Mr. Clark had been pleasantly surprised that Heidi's stanine was 6 because he had expected it to be a 5.

Heidi's study habits, motivation, and support from home indicate to Roy that, even though algebra would be a challenge, Heidi should be placed there. Knowing that the standardized tests are only one measurement tool, he takes a firm grip on his record book and heads for the principal's office, determined to convince Mrs. Geiger.

"Let's sit at the table while we look at the test scores," Mrs. Geiger suggests.

"Fine," Mr. Clark replies, pulling out a chair and opening his grade book.

"Most of your students have done very well," Mrs. Geiger begins. "With 7 as the standard for entering algebra, your class fits the curve." She paused before asking, "Are there any students about whom you have particular concerns?"

"Yes," Mr. Clark answers. "Heidi Rogers. I realize that she scored in the 6th stanine on this test, but I feel it would be a disservice to her not to place her in algebra next year."

"Why?" his principal asks, scanning the grade book for Heidi's name. Finding it, Mrs. Geiger spends a moment looking at her grades. "She has only a B average in your class."

"For two major reasons," Mr. Clark answers. "Look at her test scores again. Heidi was in the 7th stanine for computation, but only in the 5th for math reasoning. Her daily work reflects this split, too, but to a greater degree. Heidi is an extremely hard worker in class. She is attentive in every lesson, but she has difficulty grasping new concepts without a lot of extra work. For example, Heidi's mother told me at the last conference that she spends an hour every night working on math problems. When the class begins a new unit, she sometimes spends two or three hours trying to understand the new material. I have seen too many girls drop out of harder math because we expect them to fail."

Mrs. Geiger nods her head. "What's the second reason?"

"The 5th stanine reflects the difficulty she has in math reasoning. I see it in class and on her homework. She has a hard time figuring out word problems. She often guesses which operation to use. When she does the computation, she is usually correct. However, more often than not, she uses the wrong operation to answer the problem."

"How can she do the work in algebra then?"

"I was planning on coaching her in math reasoning. With her determination, I think she can master it."

"But won't she get discouraged when she finds out how difficult algebra can be?"

Roy laughs. "Not Heidi. Where others see a hurdle too high to jump over, she sees an opportunity. She'll stick with it until she succeeds."

"Well, Roy. You have me convinced. After you've met with Heidi and her mom, let me know what they think."

"Thanks, Louise. I appreciate the opportunity to discuss Heidi with you. This is a good decision for her."

"I appreciate discussing this with you, Roy. It helps me remember that our students are not just numbers on a printout."

FOCUS QUESTIONS

1. How do educators use standardized test scores to make decisions about student placement?
2. What does the Teacher Chronicle suggest about the role of classroom teachers in interpreting standardized test scores?
3. What other assessment tools might Mr. Clark include in evaluating Heidi's progress and predicting her success in algebra?
4. What is the relationship between Heidi's stanine score of 6 and her grade of B in the course?
5. How should Mr. Clark explain the situation to Heidi and her mother?

WHAT ARE THE BENCHMARKS OF STUDENT PROGRESS?

As you saw in Chapter 13, teachers use assessments of various kinds for various reasons. One important use is to make evaluative judgments about the achievement and the capabilities of students. Some types of assessments are based on the classroom performances of our students. We use such assessments to assign grades. Grades represent evaluative judgments, and the grades we assign to our students stay with them throughout their academic careers.

Another category of assessments, called standardized tests, can also exert considerable influence on a student's future. In many instances, the results on standardized tests can override in importance students' cumulative grades. In other cases, the scores on standardized tests can reinforce the judgments reflected by cumulative grades. In the Teacher Chronicle, the principal was prepared to make a judgment about Heidi based only on standardized test scores; Mr. Clark argued that his classroom assessments should be considered as well. Teachers do not design standardized tests, but they adminster them, receive the results, and are asked to make instructional judgments based on those results. As you enter the teaching profession, you too will assess classroom performance and receive the results of standardized tests. Using the information from both types of assessments, you will be expected to interpret them for your students and for their parents, to make professional judgments, and to justify those judgments.

So, what are the bases of professional judgments? How can we justify the inclusion of a student in a program for gifted and talented students, the assignment of a particular letter grade, or the referral of a student for diagnostic testing by the school psychologist? Professionals make judgments on the basis of benchmarks. **Benchmarks** are standards or criteria against which evidence is compared in order to make an evaluative judgment. Lawyers compare a set of events against a particular law—which serves as the benchmark—to see if that law is applicable to the set of events. Physicians compare blood samples against particular criteria—a minimum red blood cell count, for example—in order to render a judgment or diagnosis of the patient's malady. Teachers also use benchmarks as a basis for professional judgments. Those benchmarks are of one of two types: criterion referenced and norm referenced.

Criterion-Referenced Benchmarks

In Chapter 13, we examined various techniques by which teachers assess their students' classroom performances. We also examined how those assessments can be interpreted. Rubrics to score performance assessments and item analysis in multiple-choice tests are examples. The measurements obtained from classroom assessment techniques must then be compared with a standard of performance in order to judge the quality of that performance. Suppose you were informed that a student received a score of 37 on a quiz. How would you judge the student's performance? Does a score of 37 represent mastery of some content? Does it represent failure to collaborate with others? Is it the highest score in the class? The lowest? Evidence must be compared against some benchmark so that a teacher, school psychologist, curriculum supervisor, or principal can determine and then communicate a student's progress. The score of 37 on the quiz might be compared against the number of points possible on the test, say 40. Perhaps the score is compared against the performance of other students who took that same test. A score of 37 might mean that the student has outperformed 80 percent of his or her classmates. If the basis of comparison or benchmark is some external criterion—for example, "the student will score at least 90 percent correct to receive an A"—then the score is being used to make what are called **criterion-referenced judgments**. If the basis of comparison is the performance of other students in the class, then the score is being used to make **norm-referenced judgments** (see Carey, 1994; Hanna, 1993; Popham, 1990). As we will see, the type of benchmark used as the basis for comparison restricts the kinds of judgments that should be made.

Connection: See the discussion of scoring rubrics in Chapter 13.

Connection: See the discussion of learning outcomes and their specifications in Chapter 11.

benchmarks Standards against which evaluative judgments are made.

criterion-referenced judgments Assessment scores are compared to a set performance standard.

norm-referenced judgments The performance of one student is compared against the performances of others.

Criterion-referenced evaluation is undertaken to answer the basic question: What can students do? Criterion-referenced evaluation uses measures of specific domains of competency; it has sometimes been called domain-referenced evaluation. These domains have been conceptualized in a variety of ways since the 1960s, including "mastery criteria," "behavioral objectives," "minimum competencies", and more recently, "performances" and "outcomes" in reference to outcomes-based education. Although there are significant differences between, for example, minimum competencies and outcomes, the underlying concept of criterion-referenced evaluation is that performance is judged against achievement goals (Stiggins, 1994).

The emphasis on student performance and criterion-referenced evaluation grew from the "accountability movement" that began in the 1960s. The fundamental idea of accountability is that educators be held responsible for student learning and performance. In response to this call for greater accountability, Robert Glaser (1963) argued for the use of criterion-referenced evaluation in classrooms in order to assess student attainment of specific learning objectives. Glaser remains committed to the idea that classroom assessment should focus on specific domains of student performance. More recently, he—and many other educational researchers—have advocated for innovations that integrate assessment activity and learning activity (e.g., Herman, Aschbacher, & Winters, 1992; Glaser & Silver, 1994).

The following vignette illustrates the innovative assessment approach. Notice how the teacher, Ms. Inouye, emphasizes active student performance in her assessment and, in turn, how that activity enhances the quality of the learning.

We encounter Ms. Inouye sitting at her kitchen table shortly after returning from a summer trip to Plymouth, Massachusetts. Ms. Inouye has decided to use the idea of a living history as a performance assessment for the unit on the Colonial period that she teaches in her U.S. history course at North High School. Ms. Inouye was impressed by the interpreters who played the roles of various members of the original Plymouth settlement, the Native Americans of the Wampanoag nation who greeted the Pilgrims, and crew members of the *Mayflower*. Each interpreter had carefully studied the historical records surrounding the events that led to the meeting of two cultures at Plymouth in 1623. Further, each interpreter had studied the particular historical person whom he or she portrayed in and around the settlement or on board ship. Visitors, including Ms. Inouye, toured the Pilgrim settlement; the homesite of Hobbamock, the Wampanoag who lived near the settlement; and the ship. During the tour, the interpreters, who spoke in historically accurate dialect and who always stayed in character, encouraged visitors to converse with them in order to learn about the history of the Plymouth settlement. Ms. Inouye came away from the experience having enjoyed both what and how she learned, wanting to know more, and convinced that the interpreters—as accomplished as they were—were still learning about the history they portrayed.

Ms. Inouye planned that her Colonial period unit would include the traditional criterion-referenced tests and quizzes she had always used to ensure that students had acquired basic knowledge of the events of the Colonial period. This time, however, the goal would be to use what they had learned of the events to support further study of the specific people involved in those events in order to become interpreters. The final assessment would come during the living history that her students would present and to which she would invite junior high students, adults from the local historical society, and perhaps school and district administrators. As we leave Ms. Inouye, she is drafting a list of questions that she might encourage the junior high students to ask, a scoring rubric to document the performances of her students as historical interpreters, and forms that the adults from the historical society will use to provide feedback to her students.

Teachers could use the idea of a living history to assess performance for any period of history. They might also adapt the technique for the study of literature, science, or math. Students could perform as interpreters of characters in a novel, authors, scientific or mathematical theorists, or those engineers, architects, and others who have applied scientific theories or mathematical principles. The point of the vignette is that assessment enhances learning because the assessment requires active performance.

Try This: Share the living history idea with a practicing teacher. Ask the teacher for ideas on how you might implement this in your classroom.

Insights ON SUCCESSFUL PRACTICE

What alternatives to conventional criterion-referenced self-made teacher tests have you tried with your students and with what results?

Once a year I had students in all my classes write their own individual exams and respond to their own questions. I used this process with all my students regardless of ability level, and it seemed effective with every group.

The process began with keeping organized notebooks during the term, because on exam day all materials used during the term were available for taking one's test. Everything was open notes, open book. It is my experience that the open-book procedure encourages note taking and research skills. As students worked on their questions, I referred them to indexes, glossaries, dictionaries, and encyclopedias to locate details for planning their responses. Some discovered the resource features of their texts for the first time.

Students had ample time to prepare and discuss their test items, which they had to write according to certain specifications. They were to construct twelve task instructions or essay questions at four different learning levels: knowledge, comprehension, application, and analysis. My activity sheet gave them a list of action verbs for each of the four levels to use in constructing test items.

With self-made tests in hand, students completed their responses in class during a two-hour open-notes exam block. They also filled out a self-assessment form in which they compared self-testing to teacher tests and noted new knowledge and skills they had gained from the experience. In a class discussion students reported the processes they used in their work and the triumphs and trials they experienced.

Students always reported that creating their own tests was much more time consuming than reviewing for a teacher-made test. Many also expressed a feeling of pride and accomplishment never experienced in conventional tests. I was always impressed with the depth and detail of the test product and the effort students expended to include creativity and artistry. The detail was such that I usually asked students to mark their four best responses, and those were the ones used for a grade.

DOROTHY SAWYER, retired high school teacher,
Gladstone, Oregon

What are some advantages and potential disadvantages of using student-made tests as a basis for evaluation? What forms of alternative assessments might you use with your students?

The criteria by which teachers judge performances (including tests or quizzes) and portfolios (collections of performances) tell us what students can do. Teachers account for and communicate student progress by documenting demonstrations of performance, mastered objectives, and the products of learning. As Richard Stiggins (1994) put it, accountability has pressured schools to become "performance-driven institutions." In terms of classroom assessment, this means that "schools are working effectively only when they articulate clear and specific achievement targets for their students and build instruction around the principle that all students attain those standards" (p.29).

Norm-Referenced Benchmarks

The benchmark for criterion-referenced evaluation is the achievement goal that a student seeks to attain. The benchmark for norm-referenced evaluation is the performance of other people; that is, norm-referenced judgments about a student are made by comparing that student's performance to the performances of other students. The standardized achievement test that the principal used for math placements in the Teacher Chronicle is an example of an assessment that is used to make norm-referenced judgments. The other students who took the achievement test with Heidi are known collectively as the norm group. Norm-referenced evaluation usually uses assessments that are designed to be broader and more general in scope than tests used in criterion-referenced evaluation and are typically more comprehensive.

The famous bell-shaped curve is also called the **normal curve** (Figure 14.1). The practice of grading on the curve is based on the assumption that any group of students represents a range of achievement or ability: There would be very few people in the class who would excel and there would be very few people in the class who would fail. Most of the people in the class would perform somewhere in the middle. Looking at the distribution of grades along the bell-shaped curve in Figure 14.1, we can see how the assumption of variable performance or ability led to the assignment of grades according to the normal curve.

Imagine that you are a high school student who walks into the first class and hears the teacher announce that you will be graded on the curve. As a high school student, you may be unaware of the practice of norm-referenced measurement and what it means technically, but you have an intuitive notion of what it means to be graded on the curve. Your intuition tells you that only a few people will receive A's. It also means that you will compete for those A's, so you begin looking around to identify the students whom you think will do well in the class. You compare your-

Reflection: Think back to your reactions to the various grading systems your teachers used. Does the grading system influence the atmosphere of the class? The nature of the interactions between teacher and students? Among students?

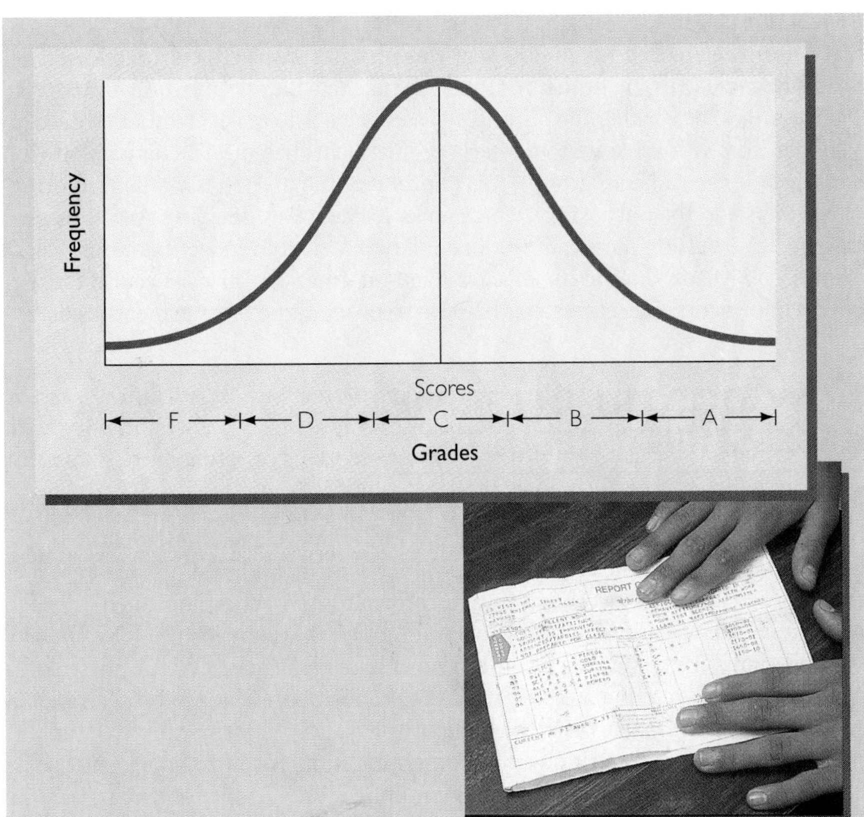

FIGURE 14.1

Grades Based on the Normal Curve

normal curve A mathematically defined function that approximates many educational phenomena.

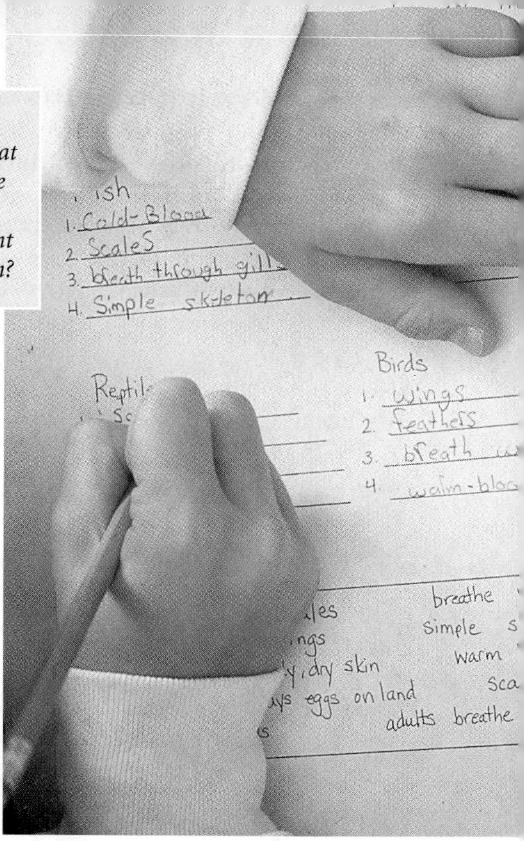

How would you determine if this test is criterion-referenced or norm-referenced? What difference would this make in interpreting the results? What quantitative and qualitative information about student performance might you derive from this instrument of evaluation?

self with the top students in order to determine the possibility that you might receive an A in the course. Some of your classmates look around to see which of the other students will likely receive failing grades. They are hoping that a sufficient number of failures occur so that they will be excluded from that category.

The use of norm-referenced evaluation as a way of assigning grades is no longer the predominant practice in schools. As we saw in the last chapter, grades are determined primarily on the basis of criterion-referenced assessments. This is not to say, however, that norm-referenced evaluation is of no value. Norm-referenced evaluation yields legitimately useful information for educators. The scores from standardized tests can be used to make norm-referenced judgments that can improve instructional practices, diagnose individual learning difficulties, and provide benchmarks of student progress.

Regardless of whether the purpose of assessment is to make judgments based on a comparison with achievement criteria or judgments based on a comparison with other people (i.e., a norm group), it is critical that the user of assessment information understand the purpose for which an assessment was designed. An assessment designed to measure inferential reading ability but used to judge decoding skills is being used invalidly. Invalid use of assessment information can also occur if the user of that information inaccurately or inappropriately interprets assessment results.

Example: Think about writing a paragraph for a chapter that you have been assigned as an example of summarizing qualitative information.

HOW DO YOU INTERPRET ASSESSMENT RESULTS?

Accurate interpretation of assessment results is necessary for valid judgments. In order to accurately interpret results, it is necessary to understand the nature of the information produced by the assessment. Assessment information can be either qualitative or quantitative. **Qualitative information** is communicated through words; **quantitative information** is communicated through numbers (Krathwohl, 1993; Wiersma, 1995). Even when the performance being assessed is not based on a paper-and-pencil test, the assessment of that performance tends to be described in either words or numbers. The assessment of a dance performance, for example, could be either a written critique or a numerical rating. For most people, interpreting assessment results means interpreting numbers, and for the most part, they are right because educational assessments generally yield numbers. This is one reason why we will focus in this section on the interpretation of quantitative assessment

qualitative information Information communicated through words.

quantitative information Information communicated through numbers.

information. The second reason is that qualitative assessment information tends to be verbal descriptions. Of course, verbal descriptions can be either written or oral, but both describe with words. Interpreting verbal descriptions is a task with which most of us are quite familiar. The interpretation of quantitative information—especially from standardized tests—is relatively unfamiliar to most aspiring teachers.

Qualitative and Quantitative Information

First, let's consider examples of how qualitative information might be used to make judgments about students. In the Teacher Chronicle, Mr. Clark, the teacher, orally describes the quality of Heidi's work habits and parental support to the principal during the meeting to decide math placements. The description was a succinct summary of the teacher's observations of Heidi in the classroom and of his conference with Heidi's mother, and it was relevant to the placement judgment to be made. Further summarization and interpretation of the description is unneccessary. As another example, assume that a teacher sends home a written report to parents in which the teacher assesses a student's attitude. The teacher does not assign a number to the student's attitude but communicates an appraisal of the student's attitude with words only. The comments represent the teacher's judgment based on observing, among other things, the student's behavior, general demeanor, and the quality of interaction with classmates. Again, the written description is a summary of student behavior. In most cases, written assessments are not further summarized because they address directly the criteria used to make evaluative judgments.

Now consider examples of how quantitative information is used in making judgments. Returning to the Teacher Chronicle, the principal bases her initial judgment about Heidi's placement on stanine scores. Stanine scores are numerical categories that result from standardized tests; these and other types of scores from standardized tests will be examined later in the chapter. Teachers collect, and subsequently interpret, a great deal of quantitative information. The scores on a quiz or test are clearly quantitative. Some information that may seem on the surface to be qualitative is quantified. Consider, for example, the use of a simple survey used to assess the quality of a student presentation. The teacher may circle "strongly disagree" to "strongly agree" for several statements such as those on the checklist in Table 14.1.

TABLE 14.1 An Example Checklist that Demonstrates How Judgments of Quality Can Be Quantified

Student presenter: ______________________________

Note to the Teacher: In response to the student's presentation, circle a number from 1 to 5 for each statement below.

The scale is defined as follows:
1 = strongly agree
2 = agree
3 = neutral
4 = disagree
5 = strongly disagree

1. The student began with a sound premise.	1	2	3	4	5
2. The student cited outside sources.	1	2	3	4	5
3. The student spoke clearly.	1	2	3	4	5
4. The student summarized well.	1	2	3	4	5

Try This: Contact a local school district or check the curriculum library for performance assessments and their scoring rubrics. Notice how many times the assessments are converted to numbers.

The interpretation of quantitative information usually requires summarization. One way of summarizing the scores from the checklist in Table 14.1 would be to add the ratings of the four statements. Each student would then receive one score for his or her presentation. (The minimum score would be 4, the maximum 20.) If, instead of using the checklist to assess the presentations, the teacher had written comments, the comments would have been the summary. Thus, the quantitative summary would be one number, whereas the qualitative summary would have been written statements of perhaps a paragraph in length. Because quantitative information is more economical, numbers are used frequently to communicate student progress. In most cases, for example, scoring rubrics convert performances into quantitative summaries (California Assessment Collaborative, 1993; Herman et al., 1992; Marzano, Pickering, & McTighe, 1993; Virginia Education Association & Appalachia Educational Laboratory, 1992).

Summarizing Quantitative Information

Suppose, for example, you were to give a test to your class. Suppose, furthermore, that you were asked by your principal to describe your class's performance on that test. You might provide your principal with a statistic: a number that summarizes all of the scores in the distribution.

Every distribution of scores has two properties. One is called the central tendency. The **central tendency** of a distribution is a description of where the middle of the distribution is. For example, in describing the performance of your class to your principal, you might tell him or her what the average score for the class was. If there were 50 possible points on the test and the average performance of your students was 38, you might say to your principal, "The average was 38 out of a possible 50 points." The number 38 is a statistic used to describe the other numbers in the distribution.

A second property of distributions is called **dispersion,** which is an indication of how similar or different the scores in the distribution are from one another. Your principal, having learned the average or central tendency of the distribution, might inquire further about the performance of the class. If the principal were to ask you what was the lowest score and the highest score on the test, he or she would be inquiring about the dispersion of scores.

Measures of central tendency are numerical descriptions of the average, or typical, value in a distribution. There are three different ways to describe the property of central tendency: mode, median, and mean. Each method of describing the central tendency yields a statistic. The **mode** of a distribution is the most frequently occurring score, as illustrated in Figure 14.2. Ten students took the test. The distribution of scores is called a frequency distribution because it shows the frequency with which each score occurs in the distribution. (The score of 84, for example, occurs twice in Figure 14.2.) The mode of this distribution of scores is 78 because the score of 78 was attained by more students than any other score.

The **median** of the distribution is that point along the distribution of scores that divides the set of scores into two equal halves. Half of the scores will be above the median; half of the scores, below. In Figure 14.2, the median of the distribution is 80.

The third way to describe the central tendency of a distribution is the mean. The **mean** of a distribution is its arithmetic average. If your notion of taking an

central tendency A score that is typical of a distribution of scores. Mode, median, and mean are three measures of central tendency.

dispersion An indication of how similar or different the scores in a distribution are from one another.

mode The most frequently occurring score in a set of scores; one of the three measures of central tendency.

median: The central score of a set of scores; the score that divides the set of scores into two equal halves; one of the three measures of central tendency.

mean The arithmetic average of a set of scores; one of the three measures of central tendency.

Student Name	Score
Sara M.	79
George B.	84
Lyndon J.	78
Brenda W.	78
Lupe E.	85
Sean W.	81
Ruth V.	85
Denora T.	78
Samuel C.	84
Oscar H.	78

FIGURE 14.2

A Hypothetical Distribution of Students' Scores

average is to add scores and divide the sum by the total number of scores in the distribution, then you have the correct notion of a mean. By adding the ten scores in the distribution in Figure 14.2 and dividing the total sum by 10, we arrive at the index of central tendency called the *mean,* which in this case is 81.

The mean, median, and mode are three statistics, three numbers that describe the central tendency of a distribution of other numbers. The mean is the preferred index of central tendency because it is takes extreme scores into account, which the median and mode do not. To illustrate this point, suppose that the distribution of quiz scores in Figure 14.2 was changed by adding the score of a student who did very poorly on the exam. Perhaps the student felt ill or fell asleep during the quiz. Whatever the reason for the performance, his or her score is now part of the distribution in Figure 14.3.

Adding this extreme score to the distribution does not change the mode at all, the most frequent score is still 78. The median of the new distribution is 79, not much change from the previous median of 80. The mean of the new distribution, however, is changed considerably. The mean of the new distribution is 74.09 compared to the previous mean of 81. Thus, the mean is the index of central tendency that is most sensitive to extreme scores. If it is important to consider all members of the group—as it is for most evaluative purposes—then the mean is the preferred measure of central tendency.

Dispersion refers to the extent to which scores in a distribution are similar to one another. One way to describe dispersion is to report the **range** by subtracting the lowest score from the highest score. The range is a relatively crude

Connection: See the discussion of reliability and validity in Chapter 13.

range The difference between the highest and lowest scores in a set of scores.

FIGURE 14.3

A Hypothetical Distribution of Students' Scores

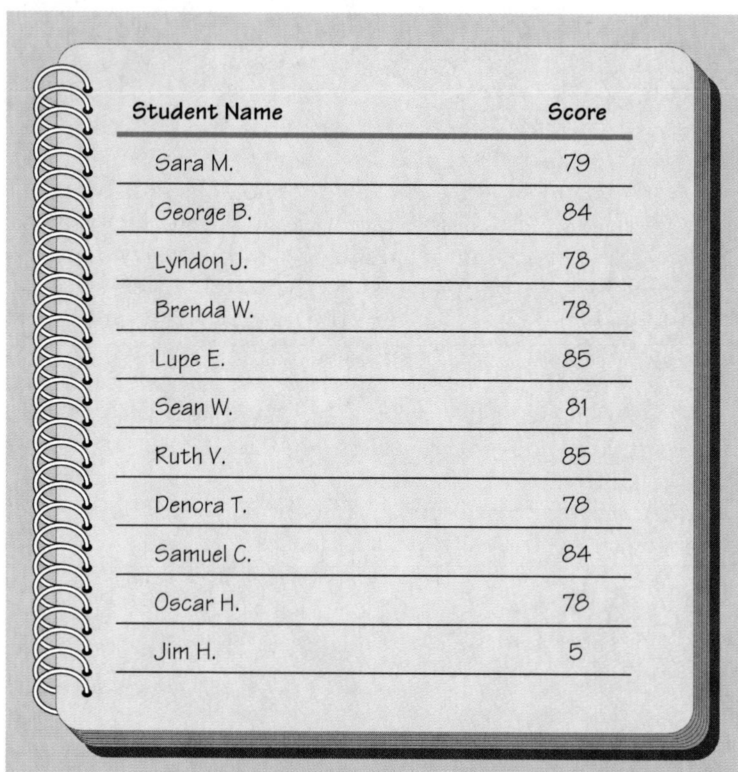

Student Name	Score
Sara M.	79
George B.	84
Lyndon J.	78
Brenda W.	78
Lupe E.	85
Sean W.	81
Ruth V.	85
Denora T.	78
Samuel C.	84
Oscar H.	78
Jim H.	5

measure of dispersion that, although it provides a quick estimate of the dispersion of scores, can be influenced considerably by extreme scores. Consider, for instance, how the ranges of the distributions in Figures 14.2 and 14.3 change because of the extreme score. The range, then, tells us only about the difference between the two most extreme scores. If we want an index of dispersion that tells us something about all of the scores in a distribution, we need to use a statistic called the standard deviation.

The **standard deviation** describes the average distance between each score in the distribution and the mean of the distribution. Similar scores in a distribution yield a small standard deviation. A distribution in which scores are highly dissimilar yields a large standard deviation.

standard deviation A statistic that expresses the variability in a distribution of scores.

As an example, let's consider the following distribution of scores: 20, 22, 24, 26. The mean of this distribution is 23. The first and last scores in the distribution are three units away from the mean. Thus, the score of 20 in this distribution can be said to deviate by a distance of 3 units. The score of 26 also deviates by 3. The middle scores in the distribution (22 and 24) each deviate by 1. By adding the deviations (which equal 8 in this example) and dividing by the number of scores (4 in this example) we get an estimate of standard deviation (in this example, the standard deviation is 4). Conceptually, a standard deviation is the average deviation in a distribution. Although the formulas that are actually used to calculate standard deviations are more complicated than indicated here, what is important is that you understand the essential concept. The concepts of mean and standard deviation underlie the interpretation of standardized tests.

HOW DO YOU INTERPRET STANDARDIZED TEST RESULTS?

Try This: Ask practicing teachers to recount their first parent–teacher conferences. Ask them what they have learned about preparing for them.

Imagine that you are now nine weeks into your first teaching job. You feel that you are beginning to get a handle on the administrative routine in the school. You are starting to understand and communicate with your colleagues. The students in your classroom have settled into a good working rhythm. As you walk into the office to pick up your mail, you find yourself thinking about the progress you have made during those first nine weeks. You notice in your mailbox that there is an official looking memo from the superintendent of the school district (Figure 14.4).

You finish reading the memo on the way to the teachers' lounge to grab a cup of coffee and to look over your lesson plans. Although the prospect of parent–teacher conferences is a bit daunting, you feel prepared to discuss and justify the grades you have assigned your students during the first grading period. The idea of discussing the results of standardized tests that you did not design and score, however, is a bit worrisome. You start to wonder, what exactly did those tests measure?

INTEROFFICE MEMO

Date: October 10, 1995
To: All School Personnel
From: M. Jones, Superintendent
Re: Parent-Teacher Conference

A reminder to all school personnel, especially principals and classroom teachers:

Parent-teacher conferences will be scheduled in your school during the second week of November. In addition to discussing the grade reports that parents of your students will receive next week, parents have also been advised that they may discuss with you the results of the standardized achievement tests that were administered during the first week of school. The achievement tests provide us with important data concerning the academic levels of our students. It is important for parents to understand and appreciate the results of those tests. They have been advised that they may bring any questions they may have about the results of the tests to the conference. Therefore, you should be familiar not only with the classroom work of your students, but with their performances on the achievement tests.

FIGURE 14.4

A Memo Regarding Standardized Test Scores

Types of Standardized Tests

Standardized tests are used to make norm-referenced judgments; they are designed to enable the evaluator to make comparisons between one person who took that test and other members of the norm group. Standardized tests can be used to measure achievement and aptitude or to make diagnoses (see Gronlund, 1990; also Kubiszyn & Borich, 1993).

Achievement tests measure students' knowledge in various content areas. According to Gronlund (1990), standardized achievement tests are useful in five ways:

1. To evaluate general educational development in basic skill areas
2. To evaluate progress during the year or over years
3. To group students for instruction
4. To determine broad areas of strength and weakness
5. To compare achievement with aptitude

A recent trend among companies who design achievement tests is to provide, in addition to the norm-referenced data, criterion-referenced data. Criterion-referenced information is provided through the reporting of results by instructional objective or by specific skill area. Standardized test results may include criterion-referenced information, but they have been designed for other purposes. The number of items used to measure each skill area is usually quite small.

Aptitude tests measure learned abilities based on a broader spectrum of in-school and out-of-school experiences. An example of an aptitude test is the Scholastic Aptitude Test—recently renamed the Scholastic Assessment Test—(SAT) or ACT (American College Testing Program) that you probably took as a junior in high school. A common distinction between achievement and aptitude tests is that achievement tests measure what has been learned and aptitude tests measure learning potential. Gronlund suggests that it is too simplistic to make distinctions in this way. A better way to think about the distinction is that achievement tests measure what is learned from school activities and experiences.

Aptitude tests are usually shorter than achievement tests. They are less likely to be biased with respect to students of differing backgrounds. We will return to this issue later under the label cultural bias. Aptitude tests can be used before training because they are not designed to measure achievement. Aptitude tests are used to identify underachievers in combination with achievement tests.

Critical Thinking: How do the different aspects of validity discussed in Chapter 13 apply to each of the three types of standardized tests described in the text?

Diagnostic tests can be used to identify learning difficulties by pinpointing student errors. Such tests do not identify the causes of such difficulties. They do, however, identify specific strengths and weaknesses. Having identified strengths and weaknesses by means of a diagnostic test, a teacher can then engage in careful observation and seek other information in search of the source of a student's learning problem. Diagnostic tests also confirm or disconfirm the judgments made on the basis of other tests. You must always keep the purpose of the test in mind as you interpret results (Worthen & Spandel, 1991). Likewise, you must always remember that norm groups serve as the basis for comparison in norm-referenced tests. In order to compare a second grader with an eighth grader, both students must have taken the same exam.

standardized tests Tests that are prepared to provide accurate and meaningful data on students' performances compared to others at their age or grade levels.

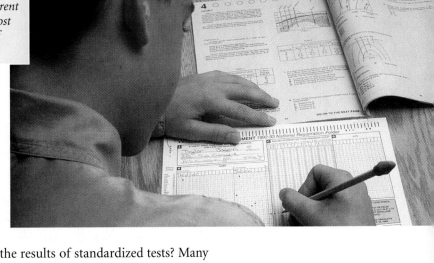

How is this standardized aptitude test different from an achievement test? What are the most appropriate uses of these and other types of standardized tests?

The Normal Distribution

Earlier in the chapter, we encountered five statistics that teachers use to describe the score distributions. Three of those statistics serve as indices of central tendency: mean, median, and mode. Two statistics serve as indices of dispersion in a distribution: range and standard deviation. The question that remains is, How do these indices serve as the basis for understanding and then communicating the results of standardized tests? Many such scores conform to the bell-shaped or normal curve mentioned earlier in the chapter. Understanding the properties of the normal curve is critical for communicating where a student stands in relation to other students.

The standard deviation is a ruler applied to the normal distribution. (The normal distribution discussed earlier is given in Figure 14.5.)

Looking at Figure 14.5, we see that the normal distribution is symmetrical and that most of the scores in a normal distribution are located near the center. Because the highest point in the distribution is in the exact center of the symmetrical curve, the mean, median, and mode coincide.

The normal distribution is a theoretical distribution. It is derived from mathematical formulas. Even though the normal distribution is theoretical, it describes many naturally occurring distributions. Consider the height of

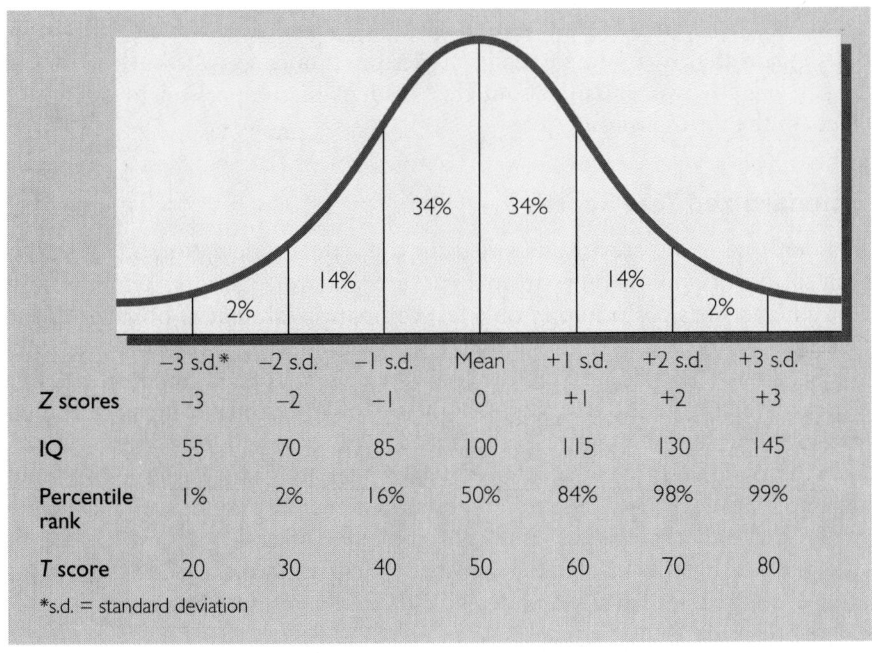

FIGURE 14.5

Standardized Test Scores in Relation to the Normal Curve

Source: From *Essentials of Educational Measurement* (5th ed., p. 69) by R. L. Ebel and D. A. Frisbie, 1991, Englewood Eliffs, NJ: Prentice Hall. Copyright 1991 by Allyn and Bacon. Reprinted by permission.

human beings. If we were to measure the height of all human beings over eighteen years of age and construct a frequency polygon of that distribution, the distribution would be normal in shape. Most people would be of average height. As we move to the extremes of the distribution—people who are very tall or people who are very short—we should find fewer and fewer people. The normal distribution matches many actual distributions of psychological characteristics as well.

As mentioned, the mean of a normal distribution resides at the center of the distribution along with the median and the mode. Properties of the normal distribution include the relations of various points on the curve to the standard deviation. Suppose, for example, characteristic *X* is normally distributed. By adding all of the *X* scores in the distribution and dividing by the number of *X* scores in that distribution, we can calculate the average score of the *X* distribution.

Having calculated the mean of that distribution, we can then determine how far each score in the distribution deviates from the mean by calculating the statistic called standard deviation. The properties of the normal distribution are such that one standard deviation (the average distance of all scores from the mean of the distribution) accounts for certain percentages of the area defined by the normal distribution.

Looking once more at Figure 14.5, we can see that the normal distribution has been divided into areas defined by standard deviation units. If we move in either direction from the mean of the distribution to a distance that is equal to one standard deviation unit, we find that each unit above and below the mean accounts for roughly 34 percent of the entire distribution. Taken together, the two standard deviation units on either side of the mean account for a total of 68 percent of all of the scores in the *X* distribution. The area of the normal curve defined by the area between one and two standard deviation units above or below the mean accounts for approximately 14 percent of all of the scores in the distribution. Figure 14.5 also includes the percentages accounted for between two and three standard deviation units. Once we are beyond three standard deviation units above or below the mean, we have accounted for approximately 99 percent of all of the scores in a distribution. This means that by finding a single student in a normal distribution, we can make evaluative statements about that student in comparison to other students in the norm group.

Standardized Test Scores

Standardized scores are assigned by using the standard deviation of a distribution to identify points on a normal curve. Standardized scores tell educators how one person's performance on a test compares with that of other people in the same norm group. Although there are a number of different types of standardized test scores used in educational assessment, all are ways of identifying where a student stands in relation to the others in his or her norm group. As you examine several common standardized scores in the following sections, keep in mind that the type of score reported does not change a student's standing in the norm group. Using different scores merely communicates that standing in different terms. The same idea applies to temperature, which can be measured using either a Centigrade or a Fahrenheit scale. Depending on the scale used, the number used to describe the temperature will change, but not the temperature itself.

Z Scores and Percentile Ranks. One form of standardized score is called a *Z* score (shown in Figure 14.5). A ***Z* score** is a score given in standard deviation units. The mean of any normal distribution is assigned a *Z* score of zero. Standard deviation units define *Z* scores above and below the mean. A score on the normal distribution that is one standard deviation unit above the mean is assigned a *Z* score of +1. A score that resides two standard deviation units above the mean is assigned a *Z* score of +2. Scores that reside below the mean are given minus or negative *Z* scores. Note that we can assign *Z* scores to any normal distribution regardless of the mean and the standard deviation of that distribution. Once *Z* scores are assigned, we can determine the percent of people in the distribution who are above or below a particular *Z* score. **Percentile rank,** another standardized score, defines the percentage of people in the norm group above whom an individual scores. For example, the percentile rank of a person who is at the mean of the distribution is 50. The percentile rank of the individual with a *Z* score of +1 is 84 (see Figure 14.5).

IQ Scores. A more familiar standardized score is provided by the intelligence quotient (IQ). IQ is based on standard deviation units as well. Once we have assigned the standard deviation ruler to a normal curve, it is possible to compute any of the standardized scores such as *Z* scores, IQ scores, percentile ranks, or *T* scores.

Connection: See the discussion of the construct of intelligence in Chapter 5.

Before describing some of the other standardized scores, let's look at an example of where IQ scores come from and how they are interpreted in relation to the normal curve. (IQ scores are given in Figure 14.5.) Suppose an intelligence test has a mean of 100 and a standard deviation of 15. Interpreted in terms of these standardized scores, if you had an IQ of 115, you would have an IQ that is higher than 84 percent of the general population. We can calculate that percentage by examining the areas under the normal curve defined by standard deviation units. Note also that an IQ score of 115 is equivalent to a *Z* score of +1.

***T* Scores.** Another standardized score that has been developed is called the ***T* score.** The distribution of a *T* score has a mean of 50 and a standard deviation of 10. An IQ score of 115 converts to a *T* score of 60. Any number of standardized scores could be derived in this way. Normal curve equivalents (NCE scores), for example, are defined as having a mean of 50 and a standard deviation of 21.06. An NCE of 71.06 is equivalent to a *Z* score of +1. (The NCE is a score used by the U.S. Office of Education in its evaluations of programs that receive federal funding.)

Consider the scores we have examined to this point. They have all been defined in terms of standard deviation units applied to the normal curve. IQ scores, which we use most often and tend to think of as having certain numeric properties, are defined scores. Suppose you invented an IQ test. Your IQ test has sixty-three items on it. You can assign a score to any one person's performance, ranging from 0 to 63. Let's assume that you administer your IQ test to a large number of people, perhaps 5,000. After collecting 5,000 scores on your IQ test, you could then calculate the mean score. Let's assume that the mean score on your IQ test is thirty-eight items correct. With the distribution of your IQ scores in hand, you can then calculate the standard deviation of the distribution. Let's assume that the average deviation from the mean of all the 5,000 scores is 4. This is another way of saying that the standard deviation is equal to 4.

A mean equal to 38 and a standard deviation equal to 4 are based on the obtained scores on your IQ test. Obtained scores are often called raw scores.

Z score A score given in standard deviation units. The mean of any normal distribution is assigned a Z score of 0. Scores above the mean are plus scores; scores below the mean are minus scores.

percentile rank A standardized score that gives the test taker the percentage of people in the norm group above whom he or she has scored.

T score A standardized score that converts raw scores to a distribution with a mean of 50 and a standard deviation of 10.

Because of the size of your sample and the nature of the characteristics being measured, we can assume that the distribution of scores is normal around a mean of 38, with a standard deviation of 4. When the time comes for you to report the results of your IQ test, you could report the raw scores.

For example, a person who scored one standard deviation above the mean would have a raw IQ score of 42. Instead of reporting the raw score, you could also report derived scores. One such score would be the Z score. Instead of reporting the raw score of 42, you could inform the person who received the raw score of 42 that his or her score is a +1 in Z-score terms. Alteratively, you could report a T score of 60, or a percentile rank of 84.

Example: Stephen Jay Gould's book, *The Mismeasure of Man,* has an interesting history of intellectual tests.

You could, however, follow the more common pattern of reporting IQ scores by converting the raw score mean into a defined IQ score of 100. You could also define the standard deviation of your IQ distribution to be equal to fifteen IQ-point units. Thus, instead of the person receiving an IQ score of 42 in raw score terms, you could report that person's defined IQ score as 115.

Stanine Scores. Another common standardized score is a **stanine**. You will recall from the Teacher Chronicle that Mrs. Geiger used stanine scores to make math placements. Stanine scores are standardized scores that range from 1 to 9, each of which represents a range or band of percentages under the normal distribution. The stanine bands are depicted in Figure 14.6. A stanine score of 5 represents the middle 20 percent of the distribution and includes those students who

stanine A standardized score from 1 to 9, each of which represents a range or band of raw scores.

FIGURE 14.6

Stanine Scores in Relation to the Normal Curve

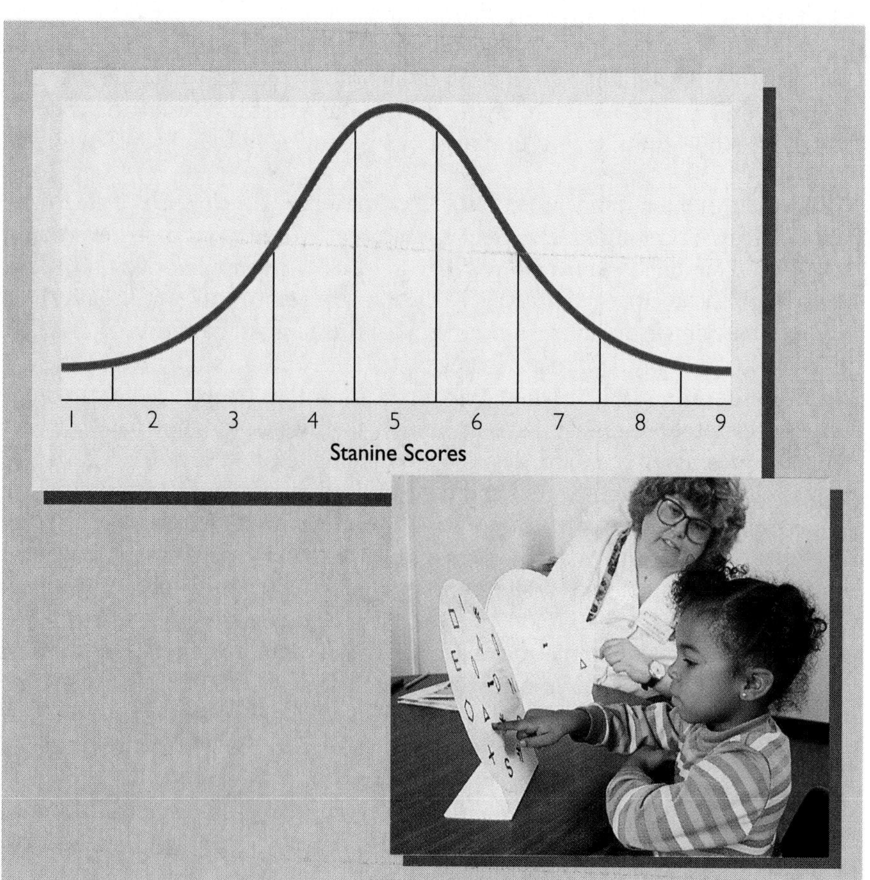

scored at the mean of the distribution. Stanine scores greater than 5 indicate performances that are above average. Stanine scores below 5 indicate performances below the average. One advantage of reporting stanine scores is that small differences between scores are less likely to be interpreted as real differences. It is important that we keep in mind that all standardized tests, as indeed all educational measurement, contain error.

Grade Equivalent Scores. Along with stanines and percentile ranks, perhaps the most popular form of reporting standardized test results is the use of grade equivalents (see Carey, 1994; Kubiszyn & Borich, 1993). Recall the imaginary situation early in this chapter: You learned of parent–teacher conferences and your responsibility to report and interpret the standardized scores of your students. Suppose that one of your second graders has a reading score that is equivalent to that of a fourth grader. On a superficial level, it seems obvious that a student in the second grade who scores at a fourth-grade reading level is capable of reading as well as the average fourth grader. As obvious as that may seem, it is not the case and is the reason why grade equivalents are so often misinterpreted.

Try This: Ask several teachers to explain grade equivalent scores to you; ask them how they use those and other standardized test scores.

Typically, **grade equivalent scores** are generated by using a test to measure the performance of the target grade, and grades one level below and one level above the target grade. Thus, the norm group and the tables of scores used for that second grader's norm group come from the performances of first, second, and third graders. Fourth graders, with whom the second grader is being compared, are not part of the group who took the second grader's test. In this example, second graders and fourth graders are not members of the same norm group. Remembering the caveat about norm groups, that only members of the norm group are eligible for comparison, we can see the mistake that a parent or teacher makes who assumes that the second grader is performing at the same level as the average fourth grader.

The reason our second grader earned a grade equivalent score of fourth grade is that scores beyond one grade level above and below the target are extrapolated, or estimated, from the obtained scores of the three grades. Grade equivalent scores that are much higher or much lower than the student's actual grade level merely indicate that the student differs considerably from the average performance of his or her own norm group. Extreme grade equivalent scores say nothing about the specific skills that a student may possess.

In addition to this common problem of misinterpretation, there are additional problems related to the use of grade equivalent scores. Kubiszyn and Borich (1993) list four problems.

1. Equal differences among grade equivalent scores do not necessarily reflect equal differences in achievement. For example, the difference between Student A who performs at a grade equivalent of 2.6 (sixth month of the second grade) and Student B who scores at a grade equivalent level of 3.6 is not the same as the difference between Student C who scores a grade equivalent of 5.6 and Student D who scores at a grade equivalent of 6.6.
2. Grade equivalents are not useful unless a subject is taught across all of the grades that are represented in the grade equivalent scores. For example, to report that a student's achievement in geometry is at the grade equivalent level of 5.4 is meaningless, since fifth graders do not take geometry. If this is the case, what does it mean to achieve in geometry at the level of the average fifth grader in the fourth month of that grade?

grade equivalent score A standardized test score that uses grade-level performances to place individuals.

3. Grade equivalents are often interpreted as standards rather than norms. Grade equivalents are averages; a grade equivalent of 9.3, for example, represents the median point in a distribution of scores obtained by students in the third month of the ninth grade. Grade equivalents, then, are based on a comparison with other students; that is, they are norm-referenced, not criterion-referenced, evaluations.
4. It is difficult to compare grade equivalents across various school subjects. A student who is a full grade level behind in math may be further behind in math than the same student who is one full grade level behind in reading. Students progress at different rates in different subjects; therefore, the norms for reading and for math are not comparable.

Critical Thinking: What might account for the variety of standardized test scores? Why do you think grade equivalent scores were invented?

Despite all of these problems, it is very likely that you will receive grade equivalent scores for your students. It is also very likely that at some point you will have to interpret those scores in order to make instructional or placement decisions about your students. You will also be asked to explain the results of standardized tests to curious parents.

Confidence and Test Scores

Use the preceding descriptions of standardized test scores to interpret the report provided in Figure 14.7. This is the type of report that you will use, in combination with criterion-referenced assessments, to discuss student progress at parent–teacher conferences, instructional placement conferences, and other judgments that affect the teaching–learning process.

Reflection: Try to recall an occasion when you first learned of your score from a standardized test. How did you interpret it? How did you feel when you learned what the scores meant?

An important aspect of the report in Figure 14.7 are the bands of scores indicated in the graph of national percentile. ("National" in this report means that the norm group includes students from the entire nation.) The bands represent what are called confidence bands or confidence intervals. **Confidence bands** identify a range of scores that are probable limits of a student's true score. Confidence bands are used because assessments are not perfectly reliable. There is always some error that distorts the true score. The more reliable the assessment, however, the less the distortion. (If this does not sound familiar, you may want to review the discussion of reliability, true score, and error score in Chapter 13.) How should a teacher interpret the confidence bands and other scores on a report of standardized test results? For purposes of illustration, the following list refers specifically to the reading vocabulary scores in Figure 14.7.

here's how

Here's How to Read a Standardized Test Report

- The Comprehensive Test of Basic Skills is not just one test but a series of subtests. The collection of subtests is called a battery. The first column indicates the various subtests in the entire battery. Focusing on the first row, reading vocabulary, and moving across from left to right, the first score is the national stanine (NS). This student's performance compared with the national norm group placed him or her in the 7th stanine, clearly above average.
- The second score reported is grade equivalent (GE). This student's grade equivalent on reading comprehension is 8.5. This is a fifth-grade student, and although reading vocabulary is probably taught across grades five through grades eight and nine, the safest interpretation from the grade equivalent is that the student is clearly

confidence bands An interval around a particular score in which the true score probably lies.

CTBS/4 Comprehensive Tests of Basic Skills, Fourth Edition

STUDENT INTERPRETIVE REPORT
STUDENT: STEVENS RAINA GRADE: 5.7
BIRTH DATE: 8/27/78
CODES: ....

B C D

	A	NS	GE	NCE	SS	NP	RANGE
READ VOCABULARY		7	8.5	73	760	87	79-93
READ COMPREHENSION		7	9.5	73	766	86	77-92
• TOTAL READING		7	9.1	73	763	87	81-91
LANGUAGE MECHANICS		4	4.4	59	736	67	56-76
LANGUAGE EXPRESSION		5	5.5	48	728	46	36-57
• TOTAL LANGUAGE		5	4.3	54	732	58	50-64
MATH COMPUTATION		4	5.0	30	706	28	21-37
MATH CONCEPTS & APPL		5	5.6	48	721	46	37-56
• TOTAL MATHEMATICS		4	5.3	43	714	38	31-45
• TOTAL BATTERY		6	6.5	57	736	63	59-68
SPELLING		6	6.6	59	738	66	54-77
STUDY SKILLS		6	6.5	56	735	61	51-71
SCIENCE		6	6.9	57	746	63	52-75
SOCIAL STUDIES		5	5.5	47	728	43	34-54

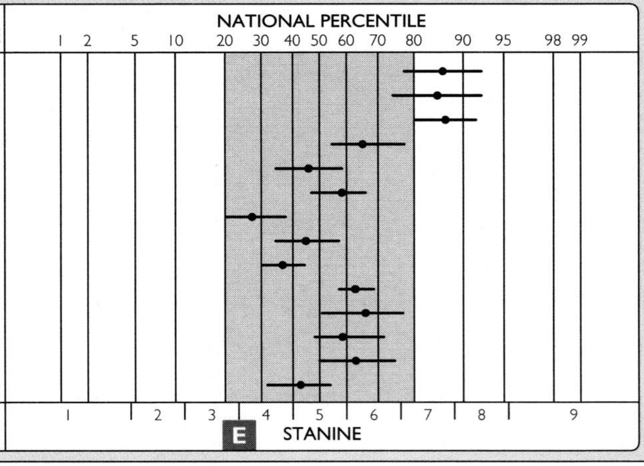

NATIONAL PERCENTILE
1 2 5 10 20 30 40 50 60 70 80 90 95 98 99
1 2 3 4 5 6 7 8 9
E STANINE

NS: NATIONAL STANINE
GE: GRADE EQUIVALENT
NCE: NORMAL CURVE EQUIVALENT
SS: SCALE SCORE
NP: NATIONAL PERCENTILE

F

INTERPRETATION OF SCORES

NORMS This student's test performance may be compared with that of the National Norm Group by referring to the National Percentile column (NP) above. Achievement in the basic skills is best summarized by the "Total" scores. The student's Total Battery score is above the national average (the 50th percentile). In Total Reading, the student's achievement was better than approximately 87 percent of the nation's 5th graders; in Total Language, better than approximately 58 percent; in Total Mathematics, better than approximately 38 percent.

OBJECTIVES Content areas included in CTBS/4 are indicatied as follows: Reading (R), Language (L), Mathematics (M), Spelling (SP), Study Skills (ST), Science (SC), Social Studies (SS).

The student is strong in skills related to:

G

APPLYING CONCEPTS OF GEOMETRY (M), RECOGNIZING CORRECT NOUN AND PRONOUN USE (L), APPLYING CONCEPTS OF NUMBER THEORY(M), RECOGNIZING CORRECT ADJECTIVE AND ADVERB USE (L), RECALLING DETAILS STATED IN PASSAGES (R).

The student may need futher instruction to develop skills related to:

PERFORMING COMPUTATIONS INVOLVING FRACTIONS (M), APPLYING CONCEPTS RELATED TO ALGEBRA (M), RECOGNIZING ELEMENTS OF PARAGRAPH COHERENCE (L), APPLYING CONCEPTS OF SOCIOLOGY, ANTHROPOLOGY (SS), ASSESSING, APPLYING SOCIAL STUDIES CONCEPTS (SS).

FORM-LEVEL: A-15 **SCORING:** PATTERN (IRT) **CITY:** MT VERNON **CLASS:** POLK
NORMS FROM: 1988 **QUARTER MONTH:** 31 **STATE:** NY **SCHOOL:** TAFT
TEST DATE: 4/24/89 **DISTRICT:** WINFIELD

FIGURE 14.7

A Sample Student Intepretive Report

Source: Reprinted with permission from a 1992 catalog of materials for the Comprehensive Tests of Basic Skills, (4th ed., p. 155), Monterey, CA: Macmillian/McGraw-Hill School Publishing Company.

Insights ON SUCCESSFUL PRACTICE

What advice can you give novice teachers about interpreting scores from standardized tests?

Standardized assessment is an integral part of every school's evaluation process. It is intended to provide the teacher with data pertinent to the student's performance when compared with that of the norm population. This process of evaluation has its beneficial advantages in assessment when used prudently.

There are several aspects of standardized testing of which teachers should be cognizant. Teachers should realize that the scores of such tests should be interpreted critically and cautiously. As teachers, we sometimes make the mistake of interpreting the results of a student's standardized score as an indication of his or her instructional level.

Standardized tests are designed to evaluate achievement over broad curriculum areas while simultaneously comparing the performance of groups. Often scores are used to compare one school group with another. Because standardized tests are named with a specific population, it is imperative to keep in mind that the group of students being evaluated may or may not be very similar to the norm population. To make an accurate comparison of students' performance with that of the norm group, the teacher should examine the objectives of the test to ensure that the test items are congruent with those of the class and curriculum objectives.

Individual factors may affect a student's performance on a standardized test, and these are often not considered when interpreting the student's performance. Although students are often given advance notice of when a test will be administered, they may still enter the testing situation with test anxiety. Specific circumstances that may affect a student's performance may include an unusual situation preceding the test, illness during the test, or the child's unfamiliarity with the format of the test.

Using standardized test performance to place students in homogeneous or heterogeneous groups is not recommended. There may be a wide disparity between one subtest score and another.

When employed as an integral part of an evaluation procedure, standardized tests may furnish valuable clues about the nature of a student's strengths and weaknesses.

LELLA THERESA GANTT BONDS,
Marvin Pittman Laboratory School,
Georga Southern University, Statesboro, GA

According to this teacher, what are the factors you should keep in mind when interpreting, reporting, and using standardized test results? What list of do's and dont's might you derive from this brief essay?

above average in comparison with his or her norm group. Before making additional interpretations, the test manual should be consulted to determine how the test was normed. One question to ask, for example, is did eighth graders take this form of the reading vocabulary test?

- The next score is the normal curve equivalent (NCE). This student's NCE score is 73. This places the student approximately one standard deviation above the mean. This is no surprise. The other standardized scores, if converted to Z scores, would also be approximately $Z = +1$. Remember that all standardized test scores supply essentially the same information because all are based on the application of the standard deviation ruler to the normal curve.
- The scale score (SS) refers to the score obtained on the reading vocabulary test before being converted into the other standardized scores reported. The illustration of developing your own IQ test and defining a standardized score pertains here. Keep in mind that all of the other reading vocabulary scores in this report are based on the scale score.

- The percentile rank (again, the norm group is fifth graders from across the nation) is 87. This means that the student performed better than 87 percent of the norm group. Note that the narrative section of the report refers to percentile ranks, but with reference only to total reading, total language, and total math subtests. The reading vocabulary subtest is combined with reading comprehension to form total reading.
- The range is the confidence band around the percentile rank. Although standardized tests are quite reliable, there is some error associated with the student's percentile rank. The interpretation of the range is that it is highly probable that the student's true percentile rank—compared to fifth graders nationwide—is between 79 and 93. (The exact probability associated with this range is most likely 95 percent, meaning that you can be 95 percent sure that the student's national percentile rank is between 79 and 93. To determine the exact probability used to construct confidence bands on this or any standardized test, you could consult the test manual or the guide to interpretation that often comes to teachers with the test results.)
- The graphic results, with national percentile on the top and stanine on the bottom, are redundant. These scores have already been presented in the columns discussed earlier. Nevertheless, the graph can be very helpful in explaining results to students and to parents. (To help you relate the graph to this discussion of standardized scores, imagine that the normal curve in Figure 14.5 or 14.6 is superimposed on the graph. The reading vocabulary score would be slightly to the right of the first standard deviation unit above the mean and within the 7th stanine. Notice the lower limit of the confidence band is in the 6th stanine and the upper limit is in the 8th stanine.)
- The Interpretation of Scores section of the report in Figure 14.7, mentioned in step 5, provides not only a narrative interpretation in the subsection labeled "Norms" but also a qualitative description of the student's strengths and weaknesses in the subsection labeled "Objectives."

Issues in Standardized Testing

The use of standardized tests provides a basis for comparing students with each other, for making norm-referenced judgments. In Chapter 13, we looked at classroom assessments that teachers used primarily to make criterion-referenced judgments. In recent years, there has been a greater emphasis on criterion-referenced tests in schools in order to more carefully track the progress of students across objectives. This recent trend—to track carefully the instructional progress of students—has led to another trend: providing criterion-referenced information with norm-referenced test results. The information comes in the form of scores on content or skill clusters. Such information can take the form of an individual profile, the profile of a school, or the profile of an entire district.

Although standardized testing practice continues to evolve in light of changing views of assessment, it is still the target of much criticism. Among the complaints are that tests are biased against some kinds of students, they reduce teaching to preparing students for the tests, and they focus time on lower-order thinking skills (Haney and Madaus, 1989).

Test Bias. In order to communicate student progress based on standardized test results, a teacher must account for or explain why particular results were obtained. One alternative explanation of standardized test results is that they are biased toward certain types of students. Popham (1990) provides a general definition of test bias. **Test bias** occurs whenever an aspect of a test, the way a test is administered, or the way the result is interpreted, unfairly penalize or benefit individuals who are members of some subgroup. There are a number of ways in which test bias could manifest itself (Flaugher, 1978). For example, a test might be considered biased if the scores of one group of students are lower, on average, than those of other groups. Several recent publications raising the possible relationship between intelligence, social class, gender, and race have once again brought this issue into the limelight (e.g., Herrnstein & Murray, 1994).

Some researchers have argued that a test is biased if the following assumption is made: Tests measure the same characteristics for all examinees. Suppose, for example, that if all examinees taking a math achievement test can read the instructions equally well, then we would attribute any differences in their scores to math ability. However, if students of equal math ability are unequal in their ability to read and follow instructions on the test, differences in reading ability and not math ability would account for differences on the test.

Critical Thinking: How does the use of a test influence its fairness? Does use of the test influence its reliability or validity? Why or why not?

Other critics have argued that the sexist or racist content of a test is a form of bias. When the language and pictures used on a test do not represent the gender and racial balance of the examinees, or when they perpetuate undesirable role stereotypes, the test is culturally biased. A test can also be biased if it predicts performance more accurately for one group than for another group. If, for example, the SAT did a better job of predicting success in higher education for students from urban high schools than for students from rural high schools, the test would be considered biased. However, some recent research on this issue indicates that most standardizd tests predict school achievement equally well across groups of students (Sattler, 1992).

Reflection: How important was the SAT to you and your friends in high school? How much of your thoughts did it occupy during your junior year? How will you prepare your students for this or a similar test?

A test can be biased if it is used in the wrong way. Suppose a company tested its prospective employees using an examination that measured skills and aptitudes that were irrelevant for the job but that systematically excluded one group or another. If the test results did not accurately predict success on the job, the use of that test would result in bias.

Tests can be biased if they are administered under conditions that unfairly affect certain groups. For example, a test might be administered that prevented someone with a physical disability from demonstrating the appropriate knowledge or skills needed to answer a question or questions.

Bias and Anxiety. Bias can occur because of the anxiety that tests foster. Students come to learn very quickly how much importance is placed on standardized achievement tests. Standardized aptitude tests, especially those given later in a child's academic career, are even more critical to their futures. For example, tests such as the SAT are used to make decisions about college admission (Smith, 1991). Hill (1984) suggests that test anxiety affects as many as ten million elementary school students in the United States, the most serious cases occurring in formal testing situations. They know the material but cannot demonstrate their knowledge in a formal testing situation. For such students, the tests provide low and invalid estimates of their abilities.

test bias An unfair disadvantage (less frequently an unfair advantage) that affects members of some subgroups because of some aspects of the test, the way the test is administered, or the way the result is interpreted.

Hill's review of the research indicates that there are three characteristics of standardized testing that contribute most heavily to test anxiety. The first is the time limits and pressures of a standardized test. The second is test difficulty. Standardized tests are norm referenced; the goal of the test is to discriminate between students. Such tests are bound to contain difficult items. The final characteristic that contributes to test anxiety is the mechanics of the test, such as the instructions and the question formats. Hill recommends that teachers can help alleviate test anxiety by teaching test-taking skills to students who suffer from this anxiety in standardized test situations.

Here's How to Help Students Overcome Test Anxiety

- Familiarize your students with various item types, have them read test instructions carefully, and give them feedback on their interpretations of those instructions prior to taking the tests. Such feedback can alleviate some of the student's anxiety, and help the learner gain confidence in his or her ability to take such tests.
- If the test is a criterion-referenced classroom assessment, consider giving anxious students additional time to complete the exam. This is often a necessary accommodation for students with learning disabilities. If the test is a formal, standardized assessment, coordinate with school administrators to provide students with learning disabilities a special administration of the exam that extends the time limit (this is a common practice in most school districts).
- For anxious students who do not qualify for extended-time administrations, pass along guidelines that will help them use the time available to their best advantage. Advise your students to do the following:

  a. Start immediately and work quickly before you get tired.

  b. Keep moving through the items. Answer the easy items; if you get stuck, mark the item so that you can come back later, and then move on!

  c. If you have a doubt about an item, go ahead and answer it but mark it so that you can return later, and then move on!

  d. If you are working on an essay test, do not leave an item unanswered. If you are running out of time, at least write an outline to communicate to the examinee that you knew something about the question, but were unable to finish.
- Review problem-identifiying and problem-solving skills. Remind your students also to monitor their own thinking and to use the metacognitive strategies you have taught them: considering all the alternatives, questioning the degree to which they are certain or uncertain of an answer, and checking their work to avoid careless mistakes.

Minimum Competency Testing. An important trend in standardized testing is the use of so-called minimum competency tests. Minimum competency testing came about as a response to the public's perception that our educational system was not teaching our students basic skills (O'Neil, 1991). Most states created laws requiring minimum competency testing, and many are advocating national standards of student competency (O'Neil, 1993). The most common type of minimum competency testing requires students to pass comprehensive exams before being awarded high school diplomas. Minimum competency tests have also been used as a basis for promotion at various grade levels.

Try This: Interview teachers and students who are in a school that uses a graduation exam.

The purpose of minimum competency testing, as first designed, was twofold. First, these tests were to ensure that students graduating with a high school diploma had achieved minimum skills. Second, they were to provide schools with an incentive to better educate students in basic skills. As minimum competency testing became more common, legal issues were raised, including the fairness of such tests when administered to special education students and minorities. Again, this is the issue of test bias. A major related problem that remains unsolved is the lack of a preceise definition of *minimum competency*. What should be the benchmarks of competency? You will likely find yourself working with colleagues to answer this and other questions of assessment. Many school districts are responding to the trend toward authentic assessment by forming task forces of teachers to investigate and formulate plans that include the assessment of minimum competency (see Cunningham, 1986).

Critical Thinking: Is assessment-driven instruction something to be avoided or embraced? Explain your answer with reference to reliability and validity.

One result of minimum competency testing has been referred to as assessment-driven instruction, which "occurs when a high-stakes test of educational achievement, because of the important contingencies associated with a student's performance, influences the instructional program that prepares students for the test" (Popham, 1987, p. 680). A high-stakes test is one that qualifies students for promotion or graduation or one that is used to evaluate instructional quality and acts, therefore, as a curricular magnet.

Popham (1987) argues that measurement-driven instruction can improve the quality of education if it meets five criteria:

1. Clearly described criterion-referenced tests must be used so that teachers can target their instruction.
2. Tests must measure worthwhile content and skills.
3. Tests should each be limited to a reasonable number of essential skills. (Popham suggests five to ten.)
4. Tests should be constructed so that they lead to effective instructional sequences.
5. Instructional support must be provided.

The general idea is that in those cases where measurement drives instruction, teachers must construct the instruments used for measurement with that effect in mind.

Tests by their very nature have the capability of driving instruction. Take, for example, a large urban school district whose students were given a state-mandated test, as were students in all of that city's districts. The test was originally designed to measure basic skills and was administered to determine which schools within the districts had an unacceptably high percentage of students who had not achieved basic skills. The state's Department of Education would use the test results as the basis for its allocation of monies for remedial instruction. Thus, the purpose of the test was to formulate a plan for the allocation of instructional monies.

After the first administration of this test, a local newspaper printed the results of the test by rank, ordering the performance of the schools within the district. The publicity led some schools in the district to encourage their teachers to focus their instructional efforts on the skills represented on the test. Because of the economic ramifications, the test became a matter of very high stakes for a number of schools, and the original purpose of the test was subverted. The assessment began to drive instructional programs. Again, a caveat comes into play: When using tests, we must be aware of the purpose for which they are designed. Bracey (1987) argues that assessment-driven instruction leads to a fragmented and narrow curriculum, to trivialism, and to stagnation of the curriculum and instruction. This threat is one of the reasons for the trend toward the assessment of authentic performances.

Computerized Adaptive Testing. Another trend in standardized testing is computerized adaptive testing (Eller, Kaufman, & McLean, 1986–1987; Geisert & Futrell, 1995). Computerized adaptive testing uses computer programs that gather information about a student's ability and then provides test questions based on that information. The most sophisticated software systems evaluate ability after each question. Computerized adaptive testing is one way in which technology may contribute to alternatives in testing, expanding the range of information obtained from testing. Although the widespread use of computerized adaptive testing has not yet occurred, clearly we will continue to see growth of this technique for obtaining evaluative information.

Connection: See the discussion of instructional technology in Chapter 12.

Some problems with this technology as a basis for assessment have become evident as the use of computer-based testing continues to grow (Sarvela & Noonan, 1988). Given the rapidity with which the technology changes, it is likely that the problems educational researchers will address in the future are not clearly definable in the present (Callister, 1994). The problems of human factors or how humans interact with computers are some of the computer-based testing issues researchers are exploring. Such questions include the degree of feedback provided by computer programs and the timing of that feedback; the nature of the assessment is being addressed as well as the question of motivation. The effect of negative consequences, in particular, is being investigated and also questions about differential motivation effects for high and low achievers.

Using computer-based assessments requires the analysis of many different items that address similar skill areas. This is a problem of nonequivalence of groups. Very often, students will see different numbers of items and items that are different. The order in which the items are presented will change and items will be administered at different times in a course. All of these problems result in nonequivalent comparison groups, and as you have learned, in order to make norm-referenced judgments, norm groups must consist of people who have been tested under identical conditions.

HOW CAN CRITERION-REFERENCED JUDGMENTS HELP YOU ASSIGN GRADES?

We use assessments and observations of various sorts to collect evidence, which will be the basis of our evaluative judgments. One of the most important judgments we make as teachers are the grades that we assign to students. Although some schools or districts are experimenting with nongraded instruction, aspiring teachers should anticipate the need to develop and use a grading system. A teacher's grading system is the method by which information generated through the assessment techniques discussed in Chapter 13 is interpreted.

Try This: Survey a number of practicing teachers to see which side of this issue they take. If possible, sample across grades levels to see if elementary and secondary teachers differ. What would you predict?

Grading is an important part of teaching for several reasons. Grades provide students with a means by which to evaluate themselves. Grades are important for reporting progress to parents, to future teachers, and to potential employers. Grades also provide a basis for future educational decisions. Grades serve to motivate and reward some students as well (Ebel & Frisbie, 1991; Frisbie & Waltman, 1992).

Those who criticize grades argue that they provide extrinsic but not intrinsic motivation. They also argue that grades become more important than what students learn. The counter-argument is that rather than placing less importance on grades, educators should improve the way in which grades are assigned, making sure that they are accurate, valid, meaningful, and correctly interpreted (Ebel & Frisbie, 1991).

The lack of a clear definition of what a grade means is a major problem in grading. As a result, there is a good deal of variability in grading practices and procedures among teachers, courses, and schools. Another major problem is that grades are often awarded on the basis of insufficient evidence or irrelevant criteria. Unsound evidence results in grades that are, from an evaluation standpoint, unreliable. We must establish the criteria that are used to assign grades in conjunction with a plan for evaluating students before the construction of tests occurs. If we follow the guidelines we develop for generating well-constructed tests, we lessen the impact that less-than-reliable grading has.

Grading Systems

One of the decisions educators must make about grading systems is what the standard of comparison will be. Remember, educators make all evaluative statements on a comparative basis. They judge student's performance against some standard. That standard may be absolute or relative. An **absolute standard** is based on the amount of course content the student has learned; its criterion is the content. Students' grades are therefore independent of one another. What they are subject to is called a criterion-referenced evaluation. The basis for the comparison is some external criterion of performance.

A **relative standard** is based on the student's performance vis-a-vis other students; it is referred to as norm-referenced grading. Teachers decide relative or norm-referenced grading not only on the basis of a student's performance but also on how well that student performed compared with all other students.

Teachers can report either type of grading, absolute or relative, with traditional letter grades. Table 14.2 provides some descriptors of what the traditional letter grades mean using either an absolute or relative standard (Frisbie & Waltman, 1992).

Achievement or Effort?

Among the questions that teachers must answer for themselves are, Should grading be done on the basis of achievement? On the basis of effort? On the basis of the two in combination? There is a general agreement among measurement specialists that grades should simply reflect achievement. Effort, behavior, and other factors should be kept separate. But because they are kept separate does not mean that they are precluded from evaluation. Based on attribution research and research on classroom goal structures, many educational psychologists recommend focusing on effort as part of a teacher's general evaluation (e.g., Johnson & Johnson, 1994; Weiner, 1986). In any case, the teacher and anyone who has been assigned a grade by the teacher should understand what the grade reflects.

Some educators respond to the intuitive appeal of grading simply on the basis of achievement as opposed to judging a person's potential or aptitude. Grading on the basis of aptitude takes into account the individual differences that exist among students. Some educators reason that because there are differences in the aptitude of their students, they should take those differences into account. As a result, they try to grade each student on a separate set of criteria

absolute standard A grading system in which scores are compared to a set performance standard.

relative standard A grading system in which the performance of one student is compared against the performance of others.

TABLE 14.2 Descriptors of Grade-level Performances Using Absolute or Relative Standards

Absolute Scale, Criterion-Referenced	Relative Scale, Norm-Referenced
• Firm command of knowledge domain • High level of skill development • Exceptional preparation for later learning	Far above class average
• Command of knowledge beyond the minimum • Advanced development of most skills • Has prerequisites for later learning	Above class average
• Command of only the basic concepts of knowledge • Demonstrated ability to use basic skills • Lacks a few prerequisites for later learning	At the class average
• Lacks knowledge of some fundamental ideas • Some important skills not attained • Deficient in many of the prerequisites for later learning	Below class average
• Most of the basic concepts and principles not learned • Most essential skills cannot be demonstrated • Lacks most prerequisites needed for later learning	Far below class average

Source: From *Developing a Personal Grading Plan, Educational Measurement: Issues and Practice*, Fall 1992, p. 37, by D. A. Frisbie and K. K. Waltman. Reprinted by permission.

designed with that student's aptitude in mind. The basic argument, however, is that this is not a good practice, simply because there is not a valid enough case for measuring aptitude.

A similar problem arises when we consider the advisability of grading on the basis of improvement. In order to grade on the basis of aptitude or improvement, it is necessary to have a valid starting point. Grading on the basis of improvement can be done as long as the teacher has available valid pre- and post-measures of achievement. Even if measurements are taken before and after instruction, however, the scores reported for each student are problematic. The scores reported in a pre- and posttest design are called gain scores. One problem is that part of the difference between the pretest and posttest might be explained not by what was learned after the pretest, but by the fact that merely taking a pretest improves scores on the posttest. This is referred to as the practice effect. If the practice effect were identical for all students, then the problem would not be serious. But if one student's aptitude allows him or her to benefit more from a pretest than another student's, then it becomes more difficult to use gain scores as an index of achievement. Gain scores are unreliable for several reasons, not the least of which is that students can quickly catch on to the idea that they are being graded on improvement and make sure that they score low on a pretest.

Reflection: Would (or did) receiving grades based on your effort influence your motivation to learn? Consider this issue in light of the discussion in Chapter 9 on self-efficacy.

Try This: Interview a sample of college students. Try to discover the extent to which these students are aware of working the system in some way to give them an edge in terms of grades.

Pass/Fail Grading

One approach to grading has been to assign grades of passing or failing to student performance rather than traditional letter grades. Hopkins and Antes (1990) have identified the advantages and disadvantages of using a pass/fail grading system.

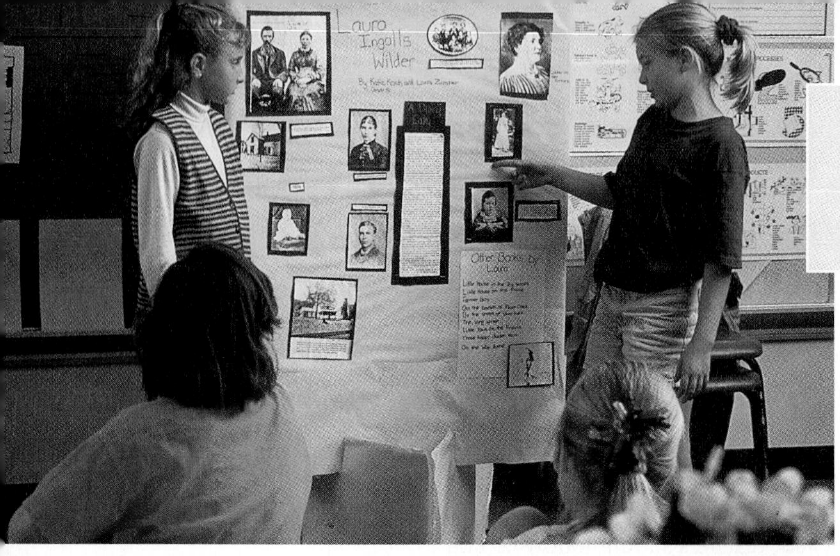

What criteria and scoring rubric might you use to evaluate these students' performance? What system might you use for reporting a grade? What are some of the other alternatives for evaluating student progress?

One advantage of pass/fail grading is that students may experience less anxiety by eliminating some of the competition. The use of pass/fail grading may create an atmosphere that encourages more intellectual risk taking. Suppose, for example, you give your students the following assignment: "Show me that you understand the concepts of time, speed, and distance and how they are related. You are free to demonstrate your knowledge in any way you wish, with one exception: you may not write or speak." Deliberate attempts to encourage creative problem solving require a classroom environment that supports risk taking and that allows students to try again if they fail. A pass/fail grading system seems to fit the bill, especially if students are given more than one opportunity to succeed. An advantage to this type of system is that students may work toward fulfilling requirements with less pressure. And finally, the teacher and the student may work together to determine the criteria for a pass grade.

Critical Thinking: Would Pass/Fail grading be more or less fair if all assessment information were qualitative? Would the nature of the information—qualitative or quantitative—make a difference? If so, why? If not, why not?

One disadvantage of using pass/fail grading is that the grades themselves provide less information for future teachers, for parents, and for the students. Another disadvantage is that students may do less work without the graduated criteria of letter grades. The students' efforts may fall to the lowest acceptable or pass level. Students who fail in a pass/fail course may experience even greater pressure from such failure than students who fail in traditionally graded courses. Pass/fail grading does not provide information on the specific strengths and weaknesses of a student's work. As with other forms of grading, what constitutes a pass grade varies from instructor to instructor. Although this is true of traditional letter grades, the range of variation within the grade "pass" is, by definition, greater.

In some cases, a pass/fail system has been combined with the traditional letter grade system. In such cases, whether a student passes or fails depends on whether or not he or she is doing enough work to earn a traditional grade of D. The basis for the combined grading system leans heavily on the traditional grading system.

Contract Grading

One of the conclusions that has been drawn from the literature on grading is that students like **contract grading** (see Taylor, 1980). Contract grading is a system in which the performances that are necessary for each letter grade are specified in advance. Further, students decide which grade they intend to pursue and sign a contract that says they understand that in order to earn the grade they have targeted, they will do the work specified. Teachers who used contracts assigned more high grades than those who used conventional methods. In terms of stu-

contract grading Using an agreement that states what performances are required for a particular grade.

dent achievement, however, contract grading was no better than conventional grading. Contract grading appears to be best suited to very small classes or to independent studies. Written agreements should be used in order to avoid misunderstandings of the criteria by which students will be judged. As in all grading systems, but especially those that employ contracts, the achievement targets must be clearly understood by students and teacher. The targets must specifiy what is to be done by the student as well as what is an acceptable level of performance.

Although the term *contract grading* refers specifically to the practice described here, all grading systems are, in a sense, contracts. Students earn grades by fulfilling the requirements established by the teacher. If the student meets the requirements, then the teacher is expected to hold up his or her end of the bargain. Furthermore, once grades have been assigned, they continue to be a medium of exchange. Parents may reward or punish students for certain grades. Students use grades to gain entrance into programs and colleges (Brookhart, 1991). No matter what form of grading they use, teachers should follow certain guidelines to ensure a sound system (Hopkins and Antes, 1990).

here's how

Here's How to Ensure a Sound Grading System

- Collect information from a variety of sources, a number of tests, a number of different types of tests, and a number of evaluative procedures other than tests, including observation.
- Good grading requires that data be recorded in a systematic fashion. Maintenance of an up-to-date grade book qualifies here.
- Quantify the collected information in some way, that is, give it a numerical value. Although value judgments are important, save them until the final evaluation. Parent–teacher conferences are an ideal place to communicate such judgments.
- Weight the final evaluation more heavily on information collected near the end of a grading period so that the focus of the grade is on terminal performance.
- Base grades only on achievement data. Do reports on other traits separately.

Research on Grading

Researchers have examined the impact that evaluation processes have on students. Natriello (1987) suggests that higher evaluative standards lead to more effort and to higher performance, but only if students view those standards as obtainable. The research also suggests that there is a relationship between evaluative standards and effort in performance such that students should be challenged but not frustrated in their efforts. Figure 14.8 describes the relationship as curvilinear. As evaluative standards increase, so do effort and performance, but only up to a point. As standards continue to increase beyond a certain point, effort and performance decrease.

The effects of absolute versus relative grading on achievement have yielded mixed results, although studies seem to favor absolute standards for assigning grades. Focusing on the individual and using an absolute basis for comparison in deriving grades may be most beneficial to students whose initial performance is poor, who have low self-esteem, and who have an external locus of control. Self-referenced standards (comparison against self rather than against

FIGURE 14.8

The Effects of Standards on Effort or Performance

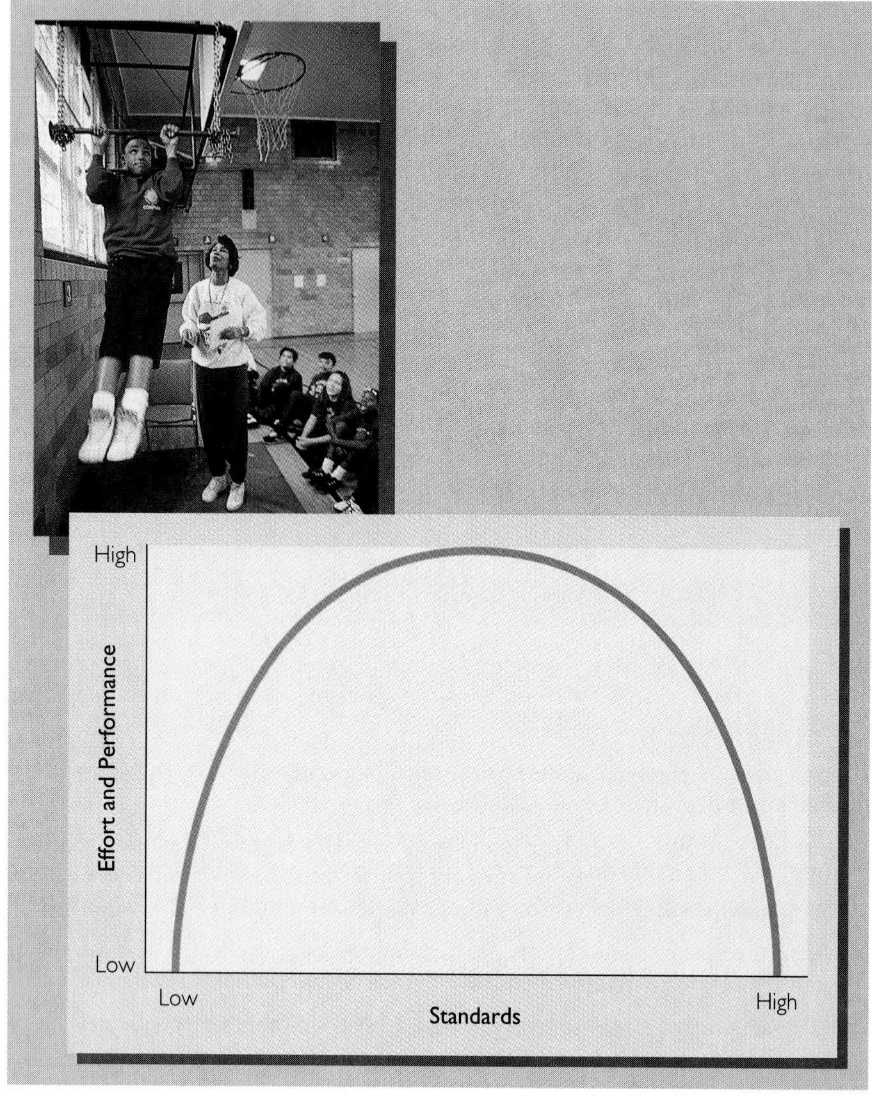

an absolute, and therefore an external, criterion) seem to work best for students with low self-esteem and an internal locus of control. Norm-referenced standards—the type used to generate percentile ranks, stanines, and other standardized test scores—work best for students with high esteem. The results of the research suggest that teachers need to consider individual differences in grading (Natriello, 1987).

Reflection: Did grades have a "social" use for you or your parents or caregivers? Did your grades influence relationships or interactions with family and friends? Does the way grades are used define what a grade means?

In an important study of teachers' grading practices, Brookhart (1993) asked practicing teachers questions about the meaning and use of grades. Although measurement experts have for years recommended that grades reflect only achievement and not effort, Brookhart's data suggest that teachers do not follow that recommendation (see also Stiggins, Frisbie, & Griswold, 1989). Teachers think about both the meaning of grades and the consequences of grades as they implement their grading systems. Teachers do not follow the recommendation to consider only achievement as the basis for assigning grades because they are concerned for the use to which grades are put (Brookhart, 1991, 1993).

Teachers function in two roles: They are both judges of the students and advocates. As advocates, teachers concern themselves with more than just judging the achievement level of a student. Teachers are concerned with the development of student self-esteem, a sense of self-efficacy, and their motivational consequences (cf. Brookhart & Freeman, 1992). If teachers must function as both judges and advocates, then it will be a difficult matter for them to ignore the effort of students. Stiggins (1994) suggests that effort can be included in a grading system only if the teacher defines effort clearly, treats all students consistently, and meets the standards of sound assessment discussed in Chapter 13. Even so, Stiggins warns that using effort as a source of data for grading is "a mine field." His recommendation, if teachers are to report effort at all, is to report achievement and effort outcomes separately.

Because classroom evaluation affects students in so many ways, teachers should plan their assessment and evaluation procedures very carefully. Teachers who want to plan carefully must devote a sufficient amount of time to generating achievement goals. They also need time to consider the cognitive level of each objective in order to provide coverage representative of the material that students have studied in the unit (Crooks, 1988).

Classroom evaluation should encourage the development of understanding, transfer of learning, and higher-level thinking skills. The active learning techniques described in Chapter 12 and the authentic assessment practices described in Chapter 13 support a basic assumption of this book: Assessment improves teaching and learning. Instructional techniques that support active learning are useful in enhancing both content goals and thinking skills; assessment procedures can also serve those functions. Think of the logic in terms of Bloom's taxonomy of cognitive learning outcomes. If teachers tie assessments to the learning objectives and if students realize that they must engage in application, synthesis, or evaluation to attain those objectives, the teacher increases the likelihood of higher-level thinking.

As was discussed in Chapter 13, classroom assessment should assist learning. One way in which assessment supports the teaching–learning process is through feedback. Guidelines for providing useful feedback from assessments were part of that discussion. But what of the feedback that students' grades communicate? Some researchers argue that grades, as a form of feedback, should be deemphasized. By themselves, grades provide the student with little useful information. A letter grade does not identify the specific areas in which the student needs to improve (Jones & Jones, 1995). This information is provided best during teacher–student conferences that outline the effort the student will have to make to improve specific skills. In addition to grades, teachers should provide some detailed comments that honestly identify weaknesses and provide suggestions for improvement in the content area. Teachers who provides students with some possible courses of actions are more likely to motivate those students to pursue content goals than those who do not. As Covington and Beery (1976) state, "Grades tend to motivate those students who least need it; that is, those who are already successful; while, perversely the very students who need motivating the most (poor students) are most put off and threatened by grades" (p. 116).

Connection: See the discussion of feedback in Chapter 13.

Insights ON SUCCESSFUL PRACTICE

What system have you developed for assigning grades and why do you use it?

"How can I better motivate my students?" is a perennial question teachers ask themselves. The ways in which students respond to their teachers' efforts vary according to student age and content material. Shaping student commitment and attitudes plays a role in motivating students. Teachers must be particularly concerned with the critical problem of student motivation. Embodied in motivation are factors such as commitment, attitude, and interest.

As a chemistry teacher, I instituted the use of a contract grading system to encourage commitment, elevate level of interest, and enhance positive attitudes among advanced placement chemistry students. Contracts encouraged students to make a deeper commitment to their responsibility for learning.

Students actively participated in setting standards for grading. They did this in an informal setting through discussions of standards and expectations as one of several preliminaries to beginning the formal course work. In addition to standards, discussion focused on specific course requirements. The students negotiated with each other and with me for certain stipulations that eventually became a formalized, written grading agreement. The one requirement in the process and its outcome(s) was that the agreement, or any portion thereof, could not violate district or school policies, mandates, or guidelines for student evaluation.

Following the development of the written agreement, each student made a commitment to a set of goals while working within the framework of the established standards for each of four grading periods. Once a contract had been finalized, it usually contained such things as alternatives to certain kinds of work as well as opportunities for make-up work, extra credit, and the like. The contract might stipulate that different kinds of written work be graded in different manners, such as assigned point values, letter grades, and "satisfactory" versus "unsatisfactory." Each student signed the agreement with the understanding that the class and I could mutually renegotiate the agreement, or portions of it, at the beginning of each new grading period if undesirable consequences, impractical items, or unrealistic stipulations surfaced along the way.

The concept of a grading agreement, or contract, lends itself to the achievement of higher levels of competency with an emphasis on quality rather than quantity. It aids students in realizing the importance of long-range planning and established priorities. It encourages student participation in setting standards. It may also be constructed in such a way that it allows alternatives for the student to work at a pace more suited to his or her needs.

GERALD E. WALKER, Vice Principal for Instructional Services,
Livingston High School, Livingston, New Jersey

Insights

What were the outcomes of this teacher's experiment with contractual grading agreements? To what extent do you think grading contracts might benefit all students? Why might you use or not use this approach with your students?

HOW WILL YOUR KNOWLEDGE OF STUDENT PROGRESS HELP YOU BECOME A MORE EFFECTIVE TEACHER?

As you read in Chapter 13, the landscape of classroom assessment is changing. Not only are the techniques for assessing student performance changing, but so are the methods for communicating student achievement. Collectively, these methods are referred to as *student-centered communication* (Stiggins, 1994).

Critical Thinking: Are the standards discussed in this section a cause or effect of the student-centered instructional approaches described in Chapter 12?

Reporting Student Progress

Student-centered communication of achievement outcomes goes beyond the traditional practice of providing parents with report cards; student-centered communication supports the teaching–learning process. Table 14.3 summarizes various aspects of assessment communication systems. By contrasting how a traditional system and a student-centered system would address the various aspects, we can see how student-centered communication would change communication practices.

As suggested by Table 14.3, student-centered communication means that what is being assessed is described in richer detail than in traditional communication. For example, instead of defining an achievement goal as simply "Reading," as is often the case on traditional report cards, this form provides more precise information. A student-centered communication about reading might address whether a student can use context to infer meaning or whether he or she evidences metacognitive awareness through self-monitoring (Stiggins, 1994). Another important change from the traditional paradigm is that students, parents, and teachers contribute to both the assessments and the communications about the results of those assessments.

If student-centered communication is to provide more information about progress toward achievement targets, then forms of communication other than or in addition to traditional report cards are needed. Some of those forms were

TABLE 14.3 Traditional and Student-Centered Communication Compared

Facet of communication	Traditional	Student-centered
Definition of Goals	Simple labels for grades, subject names	Detail regarding components of academic success
Manager of Communication	Teacher	Teacher, student, or parent; varies with context
Keeper of vision	Teacher	All parties share
Assessor/interpreter of results	Teacher	All parties share
Direction of communication	One-way	Bidirectional for all parties
Primary language used	Grades, test scores	Scores, ratings, examples; oral and written reports
Communication methods	Report cards; conference	Narrative reports; conferences; portfolios

Source: From *Student-centered Classroom Assessment* (1994, p. 400) by R. J. Stiggins, New York: Merrill. Adapted by permission.

Try This: Interview teachers about the ways—other than report cards—that they communicate student progress to students, parents, and administrators.

described in Chapter 13. Rating forms, anecdotal or narrative reports, and self- and peer evaluations could supplement the summative evaluations provided by report cards.

Consider the *checklist* as an alternative or supplement to grades. The checklist provides statements and the teacher checks the statement that corresponds to the degree to which the student has achieved a target or objective. Checklists are advantageous because they provide detailed information, are easy to understand, and can include information on behavior, effort, or other nonacademic characteristics. However, teachers need many statements and judgments for each student if the checklist is to provide an accurate profile. If teachers use checklists or narrative reports during the assessment of performance, however, then the only change required is to communicate those data to parents and students rather than just the grade that represents those data.

Involving Students and Parents

Students are the most important users of the information gained through assessments (Stiggins, 1994). If we are to encourage students to continuously progress toward achievement targets, then we must provide them with information that allows them to see their progress and to reflect on the learning activity that has brought them to their current achievement status.

Peer feedback, as discussed in Chapter 12 in the section on cooperative learning, is a source of information for the student that is sometimes ignored in traditional communication systems. Peer assessment in this context would be very useful to teachers, parents, and students in judging the students' progress toward healthy interpersonal relations or team building. For example, a teacher might ask a cooperative learning group to brainstorm periodically on how well the group is learning. The brainstorm session might be initiated with the following question: "What have we done as a group to help each other learn?" Depending on the age of the students and the kind of assessment information sought, the teacher might also ask each member of the the group to

Critical Thinking: What sorts of norms around group processing (as discussed with reference to cooperative learning in Chapter 12) should be in place before encouraging peer assessment? What should peers assess?

- Name one thing the group could do improve everyone's learning.
- Name at least one thing that each member of the group has done to help others learn.

If a teacher uses such items, he or she might need to take care that some students do not become targets of criticism. One way to avoid this is to stress that the task is to identify what individuals have done to help the group; the task is not to identify ways the group has been harmed. Students could also be reminded that listening is an important way to help others learn. By allowing students to talk to each other about their learning, students not only become more aware of the group's purpose and how their peers view their contributions but the teacher also acquires information about how well students are working with their peers.

Try This: Observe cooperative learning groups in classrooms and, with the teacher's permission, interview some group members to find out how they tell each other that some improvement is needed in the group.

An additional source of student feedback, in addition to peer feedback, is self-evaluation. Students can be encouraged to make comments about how well they feel they are learning. For very young students, a checklist with pictures and very simple word categories that indicate how the student feels about his or her own learning might be used as the basis for self-evaluation. In a recent evaluation of instructional practice, for instance, first graders demonstrated that they are capable of completing such a checklist to indicate how they felt about their effort on a particular assignment, whether they would like more assignments of that nature, and how difficult they found the assignment for each piece of work collected in their portfolios (McCown, Casile, & Brookhart, 1994). Furthermore, after a week or two of training and practice, most first graders were capable of completing the checklists independently. Older students could be required to keep a journal in which they record their assessments of their own performances. Students can also be encouraged to share their self-appraisals with their peers.

Whether students record their self-assessments on a checklist or in a journal, it is important for the teacher to confer with students about their work and about the students' appraisals of their work. These conferences do not have to be major commitments of time; they can be done informally during seat work, or if students work regularly in cooperative learning groups, the teacher can confer with students a group at a time. Some teachers regularly collect and write brief comments about their students' self-assessments. If teachers give students an active role in monitoring their own progress toward achievement goals and respond to those reports, the student will feel empowered. The opportunity to assess one's own progress and then compare that with the assessment of others includes the student in the communication system. Compare such a system to a situation in which the student generates data for someone else—the teacher—and must await the teacher's judgment.

Report cards are not the only means of communicating with parents or caregivers. You can bring parents into the assessment communication loop by sending home narrative reports, sharing portfolios, and initiating contact (Hopkins, Stanley, & Hopkins, 1990). A narrative report, in the form of a letter to a student's caregiver, allows the teacher to address the unique strengths and weaknesses of the students. Teachers can suggest specific ways that parents can help their children academically. Letters also open a line of communication between parents and teachers. Although it takes more time, Hopkins, Stanley, and Hopkins consider the use of a letter an advantage to the teacher because it forces the teacher to think about the individual student's achievements. Some schools, especially elementary schools, have replaced report cards with narrative reports (Stiggins, 1994). Letters sent to parents could also invite parent feedback and questions.

Try This: Try to locate a district or school that relies solely on narrative reports. Ask the teachers and administrators at the school how parents respond to such reports.

Another way to involve parents—one used in most cases in addition to grade reports—is the parent–teacher conference. These conferences offer the parents and the teacher a chance to discuss each student's progress and the instructional plan most suited to that student. Parents can provide pertinent information that will help the teacher to understand the student in his or her classroom. Experienced teachers view these conferences as important. The first round of conferences for a new teacher usually arouses a considerable amount of anxiety. There are several factors to keep in mind in preparing for and conducting parent–teacher conferences (Carey, 1994; Hopkins, Stanley, & Hopkins, 1990). How should you conduct a parent–teacher conference?

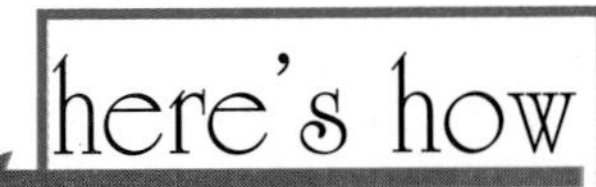

Here's How to Conduct Parent–Teacher Conferences

- Review the student's cumulative records and the student's portfolio prior to the conference. If portfolios are not used in your classroom, assemble samples of the student's work.

- Use a structured outline to guide the conference. List questions to ask parents and try to anticipate parents' questions.
- Be professional and maintain a positive attitude. Be willing to listen, be understanding, and encourage two-way communication. Be honest. Begin by describing the pupil's strengths. Accept some of the responsibility for any problems.
- Conclude the conference with an overall summary. Keep a succinct written record of the conference. List problems and suggestions with a copy for the parents.
- Avoid blaming parents or putting them on the defensive. Avoid making derogatory comments about other teachers, other students, or the school. Never argue. A parent who leaves a conference with negative feelings about the school, your classroom, or you will not be an ally.
- Avoid discussing conferences with other parents or caregivers. The only other adults that may need to discuss a parent–teacher conference are other school personnel directly involved with the student.

Involving Parents from Culturally and Socially Diverse Backgrounds

Assessment of a student's progress is, in most cases, the primary focus of the communications between the school and the home. Such communications—in the form of report cards, narrative reports, or parent–teacher conferences—reflect what has been called the school's institutional perspective (Finders & Lewis, 1994). The prevailing institutional perspective is that students who are less successful in school come from homes in which the parents do not become involved in school activities or do not support the goals of the school. This perspective includes a perception that families of less successful students require training in order to support the goals of the school (Mansbach, 1993). The perspective of the school is based on the cultural majority. It is a view that sometimes conflicts with the perspectives of parents from cultural backgrounds that represent minority values. For example, in Hispanic culture, as in others to a greater or lesser degree, parents and children are not viewed as having equal status. A parent who is not fluent in English might have to rely on his or her child to translate at a parent–teacher conference. This situation places the child and the parent in a social situation that violates a cultural norm and, thus, decreases the likelihood that the parent will participate in the conference at school (Finders & Lewis, 1994). There are, of course, ways to avoid this situation by using another adult to interpret, but the situation illustrates that the school's perspective does not always accommodate a parent's cultural background. Becoming sensitive to the cultural norms of your students' parents and accommodating those norms is one way to enhance parent involvement.

Connection: The notion of institutional perspective relates to the values discussion in Chapter 4.

Differences between the school's institutional perspective and the cultural backgrounds of parents are not the only dynamics that prevent parents or caregivers from participating in school activities and supporting school goals. Parents have diverse school histories. The institutional perspective held by most educators does not take into account the parents' experiential histories in school. "For many parents, their own personal school experiences create obstacles to involvment. Parents who have dropped out of school do not feel confident in school settings" (Finders & Lewis, 1994, p. 51). Parents who have had unpleasant experiences with the assessment systems of schools are not likely to anticipate happily a parent–teacher conference.

Parents also have diverse time and other constraints that can prevent participation in the school–home communication loop. Many parents carry work loads or schedules that do not afford them the flexibility to attend meetings or conferences during the school day. Parents who work at night cannot attend an evening open house. Often, financial concerns create an obstacle to participation in or support of school activities. For instance, one mother who was placed in the difficult position of denying her child eight dollars to purchase the school yearbook questioned the school's understanding of her situation. The economic constraints of her home in combination with the economic demands of the school prevented her child from participating fully in the life of the school. This woman's perception of the school is that it cares little for her problems and that perception will likely prevent her from communicating with school officals, including her child's teacher (Finders & Lewis, 1994).

If the institutional perspective of schools prevents some parents from communicating with the school about their children's progress, how can those obstacles be overcome? One way to discover an answer is to ask the parents. What follows are suggestions from parents whose cultural, social, or economic background does not match the institutional perspective (Finders & Lewis, 1994).

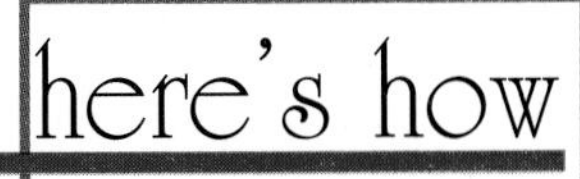

Here's How to Involve Parents from Culturally and Socially Different Backgrounds

- Clarify how parents can interact with school officials, especially you. Many parents who do not share the institutional perspective do not know what channels of communication with you or other school officials are considered appropriate. Parents want to know: Is it okay to call? If so, when is the best time? May I call you at home? Should I send a note with my child? How should I, who do not share your language(s), communicate with you? Is there someone besides my child who could translate? Successfully answering these questions for parents may prove difficult because you must first establish a communication link. But if the parents who asked for clarification are an indication, your efforts will be worth it.
- Encourage parents to assert their concerns and frustrations. If parents feel they cannot communicate because of misunderstandings, then part of your professional responsibilities should be first to discover the sources of misunderstanding in order to remedy them.
- Establish trust through a personal relationship. Parents feel that this is a critical element in establishing the home–school communication link. One way to encourage this kind of relationship is to assure parents that they are welcome to drop by anytime they can. When parents do appear, make sure you welcome them warmly.
- Build on, do not denigrate, the home environment. The institutional perspective often carries an assumption that children from economically constrained homes do not have "good living environments." If you communicate this message to your students and their parents, you can destroy the link you are trying to create.
- Use parent experience and expertise. Just because some parents did not experience a great deal of success in school does not mean they have no experience or expertise to share. Find out what the parents of your students do, and then build on their experience. One teacher whose students came from a community in which many of the parents worked in construction built a unit around the field of construction. The parents became enthusiastic guest experts and, subsequently, attended parent–teacher conferences in record numbers.

Standards of Assessment Quality that Support the Teaching–Learning Process

Assessment is an integral part of the teaching–learning process. As such, classroom assessment should support the efforts of the teacher who is attempting to encourage learning and the student who is attempting to learn. One of the problems that face teachers, however, is the expectation that they play the dual roles of judge and advocate (Brookhart, 1993). Some observers have argued that the roles are incompatible and that teachers should serve the role of advocate and leave the role of judge to external assessment (Bishop, 1992). Exclusive use of external assessment procedures would mean a significant change in the way classroom performance is currently assessed and evaluated. One problem would be to find external assessors who were adequately trained in assessment techniques to ensure reliable and valid judgments. Although this is an intriguing idea that should attract serious discussion among those advocating school reform, the idea will probably be impractical for most teachers in the foreseeable future.

Try This: Interview one or two teachers and ask them to respond specifically to their feelings about playing the dual roles discussed in this chapter.

Assessment improves learning and instruction if it is built on a system that clearly defines learning outcomes, accurately assesses those outcomes, and fairly evaluates the results. Clarity, accuracy, and fairness are also the characteristics that must be in place for a teacher to serve as both an advocate for and a judge of student learning. The person who is primarily responsible for building and initiating the assessment system is the teacher. It is imperative, therefore, that teachers understand the standards of assessment quality (Stiggins, 1994) in order to create an assessment environment that supports the teaching–learning process.

The most important standard of assessment quality is *clear and appropriate goals.* If the teacher and student are certain of both the goal and the criteria for its attainment, then the teacher can direct the student's learning efforts and, at the same time, serve as an impartial judge of the student's performance. When students and teachers do not share an understanding of the goal, misunderstandings occur and the teaching–learning process suffers. Suppose, for example, that a goal is to plan and prepare a well-balanced meal but that no scoring rubric has been established to assess the performance. If the teacher and the student are not clear about what constitutes a well-balanced meal, the student may, in the course of instructional activity, develop criteria for planning and preparing the meal that do not match the teacher's subjective criteria. If this happens, the teacher is likely to judge the performance inadequate. The student, unaware of the teacher's criteria, will feel that the assessment was unfair. This is especially true if the student has made a sincere effort to meet what he or she perceived as the goal.

Critical Thinking: How does the standard of clear and appropriate goals influence the reliability and validity of performance assessments as presented in Chapter 13?

Misunderstandings between the learner, whose performance is assessed, and the teacher, who is responsible for assessing, are at the heart of any breakdown in the teaching–learning process. The lack of clear and appropriate goals is one source of misunderstanding. The other standards of quality assessment can also be viewed as potential sources of misundertandings and, therefore, threats to the teaching–learning process. Another standard, for example, is that the *purpose of assessment is clear.* Imagine that a student takes a quiz, believing that the score will not affect his or her grade, only to discover later that the quiz counts. How will this affect the teacher–student relationship? How will that relationship influence the teaching–learning process? There is a standard that the *method of assessment matches the goal.* If a teacher uses an essay to assess an outcome that requires a performance, the student who tries to write the essay is likely to feel that the assessment is unfair.

Another standard of assessment quality is that there is a *sufficient and representative sample* of items that measure what students have to learn. Imagine students who worked and studied very hard to learn a mathematical principle. Now imagine that when tested, the exam prevented the students from demonstrating the extent of their learning because only one question addressed that principle. Students who have worked very hard to achieve a goal and then are denied the opportunity to demonstrate their achievements are not likely to feel supported by their teacher.

Try This: Paraphrase this standard using the terms *true score* and *error score*.

The final standard of assessment quality is that *sources of extraneous interference are controlled.* This standard is met by following the guidelines for constructing reliable and valid assessments that were the focus of Chapter 13. If the teacher assesses a student by methods that do not reflect what a student has actually learned or if the teacher misuses the results of the assessment, the student again becomes confused about the connection between what is being learned and what is being assessed.

The standards of quality assessment are standards that you will not attain merely by reading this book, but they are worthy of your pursuit because they support the teaching–learning process. And your major responsibility as a teacher is to facilitate student learning. Attainment of these standards will require experience and reflective construction of your theory of teaching based on that experience and the knowledge base of educational psychology. The challenge is left to you and should you accept it, we hope that what you have learned from this book will help you help your students learn.

Connection: See the discussion on building your theory of teaching in Chapter 1.

TEACHER Chronicle Conclusion

BENEFIT OF THE DOUBT

Mr. Clark welcomes Heidi and her mother to a conference to discuss Heidi's math placement.

"Mrs. Rogers, Heidi, have a seat." Mr. Clark opens a folder with samples of Heidi's math work along with an index card showing her grades and standardized test scores.

"Do you have any questions about Heidi's work so far?"

"Yes," Mrs. Rogers says. "What exactly is a stanine? We were concerned about placement in algebra next year. Heidi really wants to take it, but she says her grades aren't good enough."

"Well," Mr. Clark begins. "In some cases that might be true, but not in Heidi's case. With the extra work she has done this semester in math reasoning and her hard work and determination, I feel certain she should take algebra."

Heidi bursts into a smile. "Really?" she asks.

"Yes. I have no doubts. It might not be easy and you'll have to work over the summer to keep your math skills fine-tuned, but I know you can do it."

Mrs. Rogers looks at her daughter. "With track and soccer and your other classes?"

"Sure, Mom. I know I can pass algebra if I work hard enough. I just have to want to and I do."

APPLICATION QUESTIONS

1. How did qualitative and quantitative information influence the final decision about Heidi's placement in algebra? How confident are you that Heidi will succeed in algebra?
2. Assume that the principal's guideline that a stanine score of 7 is required for algebra placement is based on evidence and is not just an arbitrary cut-off score. What kind of norm-referenced evidence would be necessary? Criterion-referenced evidence?
3. What does Mr. Clark's grade book look like? What are the entries in the grade book? How many assessments do you think Mr. Clark would have made on Heidi during the last six weeks preceding the placement meeting? How did his grade book support his position in the meeting with the principal?
4. Why are confidence bands important in interpreting standardized test scores? Could Mr. Clark have used confidence bands in building his argument for Heidi's placement? Are confidence bands really necessary in interpreting stanines when each stanine represents a range of scores?
5. Heidi's mother sounds a bit apprehensive about Heidi's ability to succeed in algebra. Is this something Mr. Clark should try to address before the end of the conference? If so, how? If not, why not?
6. Assume that Mr. Clark always writes a letter to the math teacher that each of his students will have next year. Write what you think would be his letter about Heidi.

CHAPTER SUMMARY

WHAT ARE THE BENCHMARKS OF STUDENT PROGRESS?

Evaluation requires judgments and all judgments require some benchmark or standard that serves as a basis for comparison. There are two kinds of benchmarks used in educational evaluation. The first is criterion-referenced benchmarks. A student's performance is compared against some set of external criteria. The second type is norm-referenced benchmarks that use the other constituents of the norm group as the basis for comparison.

HOW DO YOU INTERPRET ASSESSMENT RESULTS?

A distinction is made between two types of assessment information: qualitative and quantitative. Qualitative information is communicated with words. Quantitative information is communicated with numbers. Many times information that seems to be qualitative is easily transformed into quantitative because the latter is more easily summarized and more economically described.

HOW DO YOU INTERPRET STANDARDIZED TESTS?

Standardized test scores are based on the application of the standard deviation rule to the normal curve. The various kinds of standardized test scores (Z scores, T scores, percentile ranks, stanines) are different forms of the same information. Essentially, all standardized test scores provide information about where one student stands in relation to the other students who took the same test, the norm group.

HOW CAN CRITERION-REFERENCED JUDGMENTS HELP YOU ASSIGN GRADES?

Grading systems can be based on absolute standards of quality of performance or can be based on student performance relative to that of other students. Many teachers assign grades based on evaluation of both achievement and effort. Guidelines suggest that grades be based on achievement only. This does not mean a teacher cannot evaluate effort separately. Evaluations of classroom work do not have to take the traditional form of grades; they can be presented qualitatively as well as quantitatively. In addition, students can contract for grades, thus participating in the establishment of criteria used to assign grades.

HOW WILL YOUR KNOWLEDGE OF STUDENT PROGRESS HELP YOU BECOME A MORE EFFECTIVE TEACHER?

Student-centered communication focuses evaluative information on specific achievement goals. Communicating student progress requires open lines of communication, especially between home and school. Some parents are uncomfortable or anxious about participating in school acitivities, including parent–teacher conferences. Teachers who understand the barriers that are created when parents' perspectives do not match the institutional perspective can help overcome those barriers. Clear communication of goals is key to quality assessment and communication of assessment information.

KEY CONCEPTS

absolute standard
benchmarks
central tendency
confidence bands
contract grading
criterion-referenced judgments
dispersion
grade equivalent score
mean
median
mode
norm-referenced judgments
normal curve
percentile rank
qualitative information
quantitative information
range
relative standard
standard deviation
standardized tests
stanine
***T* score**
test bias
***Z* score**

REFERENCES

AAMR Ad Hoc Committee on Terminology and Classification. (1992.) *Mental retardation: definition, classification, and systems of support* (9th edition). Washington, D.C.: American Association on Mental Retardation.

Achenbach, T. M. (1985). *Assessment and taxonomy of child and adolescent psychopathology.* Beverly Hills, CA: Sage Publications.

Adams, R. S., & Biddle, B. J. (1970). *Realities of teaching: Explanations with videotape.* New York: Holt, Rinehart & Winston.

Adams Johnson, P. (1992). Hunting for worms. In D. Seymour, T. Seymour, (Eds.), *America's best classrooms: How award-winning teachers are shaping our children's future.* Princeton, NJ: Peterson's Guides.

Alberto, P. A., & Troutman, A. C. (1990). *Applied behavior analysis for teachers* (3d ed.). New York: Merrill-Macmillan.

Allington, R. L. (1983). The reading instruction provided readers of differing reading abilities. *Elementary School Journal, 83* (5), 548–559.

Allison, M. (1992). The effects of neurologic injury on the maturing brain. *Headlines, 3* (5), 2–10.

Alschuler, A. S. (1973). *Developing achievement motivation in adolescents.* Englewood Cliffs, NJ: Educational Technology Publications.

American Association of University Women. (1992). *How schools shortchange women.* Annapolis Junction, MD: AAUW.

American Speech-Language-Hearing Association. (1982). Definitions: Communicative disorders and variations. *ASHA, 24,* 942–950.

Ames, C., & Ames, R. (1984). Goal structures and motivation. *The Elementary School Journal, 85,* 39–52.

Ames, C. A. (1990). Motivation: What teachers need to know. *Teachers College Record, 91,* 409–421.

— (1992). Classrooms: Goals, structures, and student motivation. *Journal of Educational Psychology, 84,* 261-271.

Anderson, C. M. B., & Craik, F. I. M. (1974). The effect of a concurrent task on recall from primary memory. *Journal of Verbal Learning and Verbal Behavior, 13,* 107-113.

Anderson, J. R. (1983). *The architecture of cognition.* Cambridge, MA: Harvard University Press.

— (1990). *The adaptive character of thought.* Hillsdale, NJ: Erlbaum.

Anderson, J. R. (1993) Problem solving and learning. *American Psychologist, 48,* 35–44.

Anderson, L., Brubaker, N., Alleman-Brooks, J., & Duffy, G (1985). A qualitative study of seatwork in first-grade classrooms. *Elementary School Journal, 86,* 123–140.

Anderson, R. C. (1977). Schema-directed processes in language comprehension. In A. Lesgold, J. Pelligreno, S. Fokkema, & R. Glaser (Eds.), *Cognitive psychology and instruction.* New York: Plenum Press.

— (1984). Some reflections on the acquisition of knowledge. *Educational Researcher, 13* (10), 5–10.

Anderson, R. C., & Ortony, A. (1975). On putting apples into bottles: A problem of polysemy. *Cognitive Psychology, 7,* 167–180.

Anderson, R. C., Pichert, J. W., Goetz, E. T., Schallert, D. L., Stevens, K. V., & Trollip, S. R. (1976). Instantiation of general terms. *Journal of Verbal Learning and Behavior, 15,* 667–679.

Arlin, M. (1979). Teacher transitions can disrupt time flow in classrooms. *American Educational Research Journal, 16,* 42–56.

Armbruster, B. B. (1986). Schema theory and the design of content-area textbooks. *Educational Psychologist, 21,* 253–267.

Armstrong, T. (1994). *Multiple intelligences in the classroom.* Alexandria, VA: Association for Supervision and Curriculum Development.

Aronson, E. (1972). *The social animal.* San Francisco: W. H. Freeman.

Ashton, P.T. & Webb, R.B. (1986). *Making a difference: Teachers' sense of efficacy and student achievement.* New York: Longman.

Asian and Pacific Islander data: 80 census goldmine (1988). *Census and You, 23,* 3.

Assante, M.K. (1991). The Afrocentric idea in education. *The Journal of Negro Education, 60,* 170–180.

Atkinson, J. W. (1964). *An introduction to motivation.* Princeton, NJ: Van Nostrand.

Atkinson, R. C. (1975). Mnemotechnics in second-language learning. *American Psychologist, 30,* 821–828.

Atkinson, R. C., & Raugh, M. R. (1975). An application of the mnemonic keyword method to the acquisition of a Russian vocabulary. *Journal of Experimental Psychology: Human Learning and Memory, 104,* 126–133.

Atkinson, R. C., & Shiffrin, R. M. (1968). Human memory: A proposed system and its control processes. In K. Spence & J. Spence (Eds.), *The psychology of learning and motivation* (Vol. 2). New York: Academic Press.

— (1971, August). The control of short-term memory. *Scientific American,* pp. 82-90.

Ausubel, D. P., Novak, J. D., & Hanesian, H. (1978). *Educational psychology: A cognitive view* (2d ed.). New York: Holt, Rinehart & Winston.

Ausubel, D. P. & Youssef, M. (1963). Role of discriminability in meaningful parallel learning. *Journal of Educational Psychology, 54,* 331–336.

Ayllon, T., & Azrin, N. H. (1968). *The token economy.* New York: Appleton-Century-Crofts.

Azrin, N. H., & Holz, W. C. (1966). Punishment. (pp. 380–447). In W. K. Konig (Ed.), *Operant behavior: Areas of research and application.* New York: Appleton-Century-Crofts.

Bagley, W. C. (1970). *Classroom management: Its principles and technique.* New York: Macmillan.

Bailey, S. M. (1993). The current status of gender equity research in American schools. *Educational Psychologist, 28* (4), 321–339.

Bandura, A. (1962). Social learning through imitation. In N. R. Jones (Ed.), *Nebraska Symposium in Motivation.* Lincoln: University of Nebraska Press.

— (1965). Influence of models' reinforcement contingencies on the acquisition of imitative response. *Journal of Personality and Social Psychology, 1,* 589–595.

— (1969). *Principles of behavior modification.* New York: Holt, Rinehart & Winston.

— (1971a). *Psychological modeling: Conflicting theories.* Chicago, IL: Aldine-Atherton.

— (1971b). Vicarious and self-reinforcement processes (pp. 228–278). In R. Glaser (Ed.), *The nature of reinforcement.* New York: Academic Press.

— (1977). *Social learning theory.* Englewood Cliffs, NJ: Prentice Hall.

— (1982). Self-efficacy mechanism in human agency. *American Psychologist, 37,* 122–147.

— (1982). Self-efficacy mechanisms in human agency. *American Psychologist, 37,* 122–147.

— (1986). *Social foundations of thought and action.* Englewood Cliffs, NJ: Prentice Hall.

Bandura, A., Ross, D., & Ross, S. A. (1963). Vicarious reinforcement and imitative learning. *Journal of Abnormal and Social Psychology, 67,* 601–607.

Bandura, A., & Walters, R. (1963). *Social learning and personality development.* New York: Holt, Rinehart & Winston.

Banis, H. T., Varni, J. W., Wallander, J. L., Korsch, B. M., Jay, S. M., Adler, R., Garcia-Temple, E., & Negrete, V. (1988). Psychological and social adjustment of obese children and their families. *Child: Care, Health and Development, 14,* 157–173.

Banks, J.A. (1987). *Teaching Strategies for Ethnic Studies* (4th ed.) Boston, MA: Allyn & Bacon.

Banks, J. A. (1994a). *An introduction to multicultural education.* Needham Heights, MA: Allyn & Bacon.

— (1994b). Multicultural education: Characteristics and goals. In J. A. Banks and C. A. McGee Banks (Eds.), *Multicultural education: Issues and perspectives.* Needham Heights, MA: Allyn & Bacon.

— (1994c). *Multiethnic education.* Needham Heights, MA: Allyn & Bacon.

Banks, J. A., & Banks, C. A. M. (1993). *Multicultural education: Issues and perspectives* (2d. ed.). Needham Heights, MA: Allyn & Bacon.

Barenboim, C. (1977). Developmental changes in the interpersonal cognitive system from middle childhood to adolescence. *Child Development, 48,* 1467–1474.

Baron, J. B. (1991). Strategies for the development of effective performance exercises. *Applied Measurement in Education, 4* (4), 305–318.

Baruth, L. G., & Manning, M. L. (1992). *Multicultural education of children and adolescents.* Needham Heights, MA: Allyn & Bacon.

Bates, E., O'Connell, B. & Shore, C. (1987). Language and communication in infancy. In J. D. Osofsky (Ed.), *Handbook of infant development.* (2d. ed.). New York: Wiley.

Baumrind, D. (1967). Childcare practices anteceding three patterns of preschool behavior. *Genetic Psychology Monographs,* 75, 43–88

Baumrind, D. (1973). The development of instrument competence through socialization. Dr. A. Pick (Ed.) *Minnesota Symposium on Child Psychology* (vol. 7). Minneapolis, MN: University of Minnesota Press.

Baumrind, D. (1971). Current patterns of parental authority. *Developmental Psychology Monograph, 4* (Number 1, Part 2).

— (1991). The influence of parenting style on adolescent competence and substance abuse. *Journal of Early Adolescence, 11,* 56–95.

Beane, J. A., and Lipka, R. P. (1980). Self-concept and self-esteem: A construct differentiation. *Child Study Journal, 10,* 1–6.

— (1986). *Self-concept, self-esteem, and the curriculum.* New York: Teachers College Press.

Becker, J. M. (Ed.). (1979). *Schooling for a global age.* New York: McGraw-Hill.

Bell, R. (1980). *Changing bodies, changing lives: A book for teens on sex and relationships.* New York: Random House.

Bell-Gredler, M. E. (1986). *Learning and instruction: Theory into practice.* New York: Macmillan.

Bellon, J. J., Bellon, E. C., & Blank, M. A. (1992). *Teaching from a research knowledge base: A development and renewal process.* New York: Macmillan.

Bempechat, J. (1990). *The role of parent involvement in children's academic achievement: A review of the literature trends and issues, No. 14.* New York: ERIC Clearinghouse on Urban Education, Institute for Urban and Minority Education.

Bennet, C. I. (1995). *Comprehensive multicultural education: Theory and practice* (3d ed.). Needham Heights, MA: Allyn & Bacon.

Berger, K. S. (1986). *The developing person through childhood and adolescence.* (2d ed.). New York: Worth.

Berk, L. E. (1992). Children's private speech: An overview of theory and the status of research. In R. M. Diaz & L. E. Berk (Eds.), *Private speech: From social interaction to self-regulation.* Hillsdale, NJ: Erlbaum.

— (1994). *Child development* (3rd ed.). Needham Heights, MA: Allyn and Bacon.

Berliner, D. C. (1986). In pursuit of the expert pedagogue. *Educational Researcher, 15* (7), 5–13.

— (1987). Ways of thinking about students and classrooms by more and less experienced teachers. In J. Calderhead (Ed.), *Exploring teacher's thinking.* London: Cassell Educational Limited.

— (1988). The development of expertise in pedagogy. Charles W. Hunt Memorial Lecture presented at the Annual Meeting of the American Association of Colleges for Teacher Education, New Orleans.

— (1992). Redesigning classroom activities for the future. *Educational Technology, 32* (10), 7–13.

Berlyne, D. E. (1965). Curiosity and education. In J. D. Krumbolz (Ed.), *Learning and the educational process.* Chicago: Rand McNally.

Bernstein, B.B (1971). *Class, codes and control.* London: Routledge and K. Paul.

Berrueta-Clement, J. R., Schweinhart, L. J., Barnett, W. S., Epstein, A. S., & Weikart, D. P. (1984). *Changed lives.* Ypsilanti, MI: High Scope.

Bialystok, E. and Ryan, E. (1985). Toward a definition of metalinguistic skill. *McRill Palmer Quarterly, 31,* 235–252

Birman, B. F., Oraland, M. E., Jung, R. K., Anson, R. J., Garcia, G. N., Moore, M. T., Funkhouser, J. E., Morrison, D. R., Turnbull, B. J., & Reisner, E. R. (1987). *The current operation of the Chapter 1 program.* Washington, D.C.: Office of Educational Research and Improvement, U.S. Department of Education.

Bishop, J. H. (1992). Why U.S. students need incentives to learn. *Educational Leadership, 49* (6), 15–18.

Bivens, J. A., & Berk, L. E. (1990). A longitudinal study of the development of elementary school children's private speech. *Merrill-Palmer Quarterly, 36,* 443–463.

Bligh, D. A. (1972). *What's the use of lectures?* (2d ed.) Harmondsworth, England: Penguin.

Block, J. (1983). Differential premises arising from differential socialization of the sexes: Some conjectures. *Child Development, 54,* 1335–1354.

Bloom, B. S. (1986, February). "The hands and feet of genius." Automaticity. *Educational Leadership,* 70–77.

Bloom, B. S., Englehart, M. D., Furst, E. J., Hill, W. H., and Krathwohl, D. R. (1956). *Taxonomy of educational objectives, Handbook I: Cognitive domain.* New York: McKay.

Book, C. L., & Freeman, D. J. (1986). Differences in entry characteristics of elementary and secondary teacher candidates. *Journal of Teacher Education, 37* (2), 47–51.

Borko, H., & Shavelson, R. J. (1990). Teacher's decision making. In B. Jones & L. Idols (Eds.), *Dimensions of thinking and cognitive instruction.* Hillsdale, NJ: Erlbaum.

Bower, G. H. (1972). Mental imagery and associative learning. In L. W. Gregg (Ed.), *Cognition in learning and memory.* New York: Wiley.

Bower, G. H., & Hilgard, E. R. (1981). *Theories of learning* (5th ed.). Englewood Cliffs, NJ: Prentice Hall.

Bowman, B. T. (1989). Educating language-minority children: Challenges and opportunities. *Phi Delta Kappan, 71,* 118–120.

Boykin, A.W. (1986). The triple quandary and the schooling of Afro-American children. In U. Neizser (Ed.) *The school achievement of minority children.* Hillsdale, NJ: Erlbaum.

Brabeck, M. (1986). Moral orientation: Alternative perspectives of men and women. In R. T. Knowles & G. F. McLean (Eds.), *Psychological foundations of moral education and character development: An integrated theory of moral development.* Lanham, MD: University Press of America.

Bracey, G. W. (1987). Measurement-driven instruction: Catchy phrase, dangerous practice. *Phi Delta Kappan, 68,* 683–686.

Brainerd, C. S. (1978). *Piaget's theory of intelligence.* Englewood Cliffs, NJ: Prentice Hall.

Bransford, J. D. (1979). *Human cognition: Learning, understanding, and remembering.* Belmont, CA: Wadsworth.

Bransford, J.D., Goldman, S.R., & Vye, N.J. (1991). Making a difference in people's abilities to think: Reflections of a decade of work and some hopes for the future. In L. Okagaki and R.J. Sternberg (eds.), *Directors of development: Influences on children.* Hillsdale, NJ: Erlbaum.

Bransford, J. D., & McCarrell, N. S. (1974). A sketch of a cognitive approach to comprehension: Some thoughts about understanding what it means to comprehend. In W. B. Weiner & D. S. Palermo (Eds.), *Cognition and the symbolic processes.* Hillsdale, NJ: Erlbaum.

Brodkin, A. M. & Coleman, M. F. (1994). Reaching out to a dislocated child. *Instructor, March,* 18-21.

Bray, G. (1976). *The obese patient: Major problems in internal medicine* (Vol. 9). Philadelphia: Saunders.

Brenner, D., & Hinsdale, G. (1978). Body build stereotypes and self-identification in three age groups of females. *Adolescence, 13,* 551–561.

Brody, J., & Fox, L. H. (1980). An accelerative intervention program for mathematically gifted girls. In L. H. Fox, L. Brody, & D. Tobin (Eds.), *Women and the mathematical mystique.* Baltimore, MD: Johns Hopkins University Press.

Brookhart, S. M. (1991). Grading practices and validity. *Educational Measurement: Issues and Practices,* Spring, 35–36.

— (1993). Teachers' grading practices: Meaning and values. *Journal of Educational Measurement, 30,* 123–142.

Brookhart, S. M., & Freeman, D. J. (1992). Characteristics of entering teacher candidates. *Review of Educational Research, 62* (1), 37–60.

Brookhart, S. M., Miller, T. E., Loadman, W. E., & Whordley, D. (1990, October). *Profiles of entering teacher candidates: Gathering baseline data for teacher education program evaluation.* Paper presented at the Annual Meeting of the American Evaluation Association, Washington, D.C.

Brophy, J. E., & Evertson, C. (1976). *Learning from teaching: A developmental perspective.* Needham Heights, MA: Allyn & Bacon.

Brophy, J. E., & Good, T. L. (1974). *Teacher–student relationships: Causes and consequences.* New York: Holt, Rinehart & Winston.

Brophy, J. E. (1982). How teachers influence what is taught and learned in classrooms. *Elementary School Journal, 83,* 1–13.

— (1988). Educating teachers about managing classrooms and students. *Teaching and Teacher Education, 4,* 1–18.

Brown, A. L. (1988). Motivation to learn and understand: On taking charge of one's own learning. *Cognition and Instruction, 5,* 311–321.

Brown, A. L., & Campione, J. C. (1990). Communities of learning and thinking, or a context by any other name. In

D. Kuhn (Ed.), *Developmental perspectives on teaching and learning thinking skills: Contributions to human development* (vol. 21), 108–126.

Brown, J. S., Collins, A., & Duguid, P. (1989). Situated cognition and the culture of learning. *Educational Researcher, 18* (1), 32–42.

Brown, S., & McIntyre, D. (1993). *Making sense of teaching.* Philadelphia: Open University Press.

Bruffee, K. A. (1993). *Collaborative learning: Higher education, interdependence, and the authority of knowledge.* Baltimore, MD: Johns Hopkins University Press.

Bruner, J. S. (1960a). *The process of education.* New York: Vintage Books.

— (1960b). Readiness for learning. In Bruner (Ed.), *The process of education.* Cambridge, MA: Harvard University Press.

— (1961). The act of discovery. *Harvard Educational Review, 31* (1), 21–32.

— (1973a). Culture and cognitive growth. In Bruner (Ed.), *The relevance of education.* New York: Norton.

— (1973b). Some elements of discovery. In Bruner (Ed.), *The relevance of education.* New York: Norton.

Brutsaert, H. (1990). Changing sources of self-esteem among girls and boys in secondary school. *Urban Education, 24* (40), 432–439.

Burke, J. C. (1992). *Decreasing classroom behavior problems: Practical guidelines for teachers.* San Diego, CA: Singular.

Bushell, D., Wrobel, P., & Michaelis, M. (1968). Applying "group" contingencies to the classroom study behavior of pre-school children. *Journal of Applied Behavior Analysis, 1,* 55-61.

Butterfield, F. (1982). *China: Alive on the bitter sea.* New York: Bantam Books

Cain, K. M., & Dweck, C. S. (1989). The development of children's conception of intelligence: A theoretical framework. In R. J. Sternberg (Ed.), *Advances in the psychology of human intelligence.* Hillsdale, NJ: Erlbaum.

California Assessment Collaborative. (1993). *Charting the course: Toward instructionally sound assessment.* San Francisco: California Assessment Collaborative.

Callister, T. A. (1994). Educational computing's new direction: Cautiously approaching an unpredictable future. *Educational Theory, 44 (2),* 239–256.

Cangelosi, J. S. (1993). *Classroom management strategies: Gaining and maintaining students' cooperation* (2d ed.). White Plains, NY: Longman.

Canter, L., & Canter, M. (1976). *Assertive discipline: A take-charge approach for today's educator.* Los Angeles: Lee Canter and Associates.

— (1992). *Assertive discipline: Positive behavior management for today's classroom.* Santa Monica, CA: Lee Canter & Associates.

Caplan, N., Choy, M., & Whitmore, J. (1992). Indochinese refugee families and academic achievement. *Scientific American, 266* (2), 36–42.

Carey, L. M. (1994). *Measuring and evaluating school learning* (2d ed.). Needham Heights, MA: Allyn & Bacon.

Carey S. (1977). The child as ward learner. In M. Halle, J. Bresnan, & G. A. Miller (Eds.), *Linguistic theory and psychological reality.* Cambridge, MA: MIT Press.

Carlson, S. B. (1985). *Creative classroom testing.* Princeton, NJ: Educational Testing Service.

Carter, K. (1987). Cooperating teachers' conceptions of teaching. Unpublished paper prepared for the University of Arizona Cooperating Teachers Project, funded by OERI, U.S. Department of Education.

— (1990). Teacher's knowledge and learning to teach. In W. R. Houston (Ed.), *Handbook of research on teacher education.* New York: Macmillan.

Carter, K., Cushing, K., Sabers, D., Stein, P., & Berliner, D. (1988, May–June). Expert-novice differences in perceiving and processing visual classroom information. *Journal of Teacher Education,* 25–32.

Carter, K., Sabers, D., Cushing, K., Pinnegar, S., & Berliner, D. (1987). Processing and using information about students: A study of expert, novice, and postulant teachers. *Teaching and Teacher Education, 3* (2), 147–157.

Case, R. (1984). The process of stage transition: A neo-Piagetian view. In R. J. Sternberg (Ed.), *Mechanisms of cognitive development.* New York: W. H. Freeman.

— (1985). *Intellectual development: Birth to adulthood.* New York: Academic Press.

— (1993). Theories of learning and theories of development. *Educational Psychologist, 28* (3), 219–234.

Chadwick, D. (1989). Protecting abused kids. *NEA Today, 8* (5), 23.

Chance, P. (1993). Sticking up for rewards. *Phi Delta Kappan, 74,* 787–790.

Charles, C. M. (1992). *Building classroom discipline: From models to practice* (2d ed.). New York: Longman.

Charles, C. M. & Senter, G. W. (1995). *Elementary classroom management* (2d ed.). White Plains, NY: Longman.

Chi, M., Feltovich, P., & Glaser, R. (1981). Categorization and representation of physics problems by experts and novices. *Cognitive Science,* 5, 121–152.

Chilcoat, G. (1989). Instructional behaviors for clearer presentations in the classroom. *Instructional Science, 18,* 289–314.

Chittendon, E. (1991). Authentic assessment, evaluation, and documentation of student performance (pp. 22–31). In V. Perrone (Ed.), *Expanding student assessment.* Alexandria, VA: Association for Supervision and Curriculum Development.

Chiu, L-H. (1992-1993). Self-esteem in American and Chinese (Taiwanese) children. *Current Psychology: Research and Reviews, 11,* 309–313.

Church, J. A., Allen, J. R., & Stiehm, E. R. (1986). New scarlet letter(s), pediatric AIDS. *Pediatrics, 77,* 423–427.

Clark, R.E. (1983). Reconsidering research on learning from media. *Review at Educational Research, 53,* 445–459.

Clark, C., & Peterson, P. L. (1986). Teachers' thought processes. In M. Wittrock (Ed.), *Handbook of research on teaching* (3d ed.). New York: Macmillan.

Clark, C. M., Gage, N. L., Marx, R. W., Peterson, P. L., Staybrook, N. G., & Winne, P. H. (1979). A factorial experiment on teacher structuring, soliciting, and reacting. *Journal of Educational Psychology, 71,* 534–552.

Clark, H. H., & Clark, E. V. (1977). *Psychology and language.* New York: Harcourt Brace Jovanovich.

Clark, J., & Tollefson, N. (1991). Differences in beliefs and attitudes toward the improvability of writing of gifted students who exhibit mastery-oriented and helpless behavior. *Journal of Education of the Gifted, 14* (2), 119–133.

Clark-Johnson, G. (1988). Black children. *Teaching Exceptional Children, 20,* 46–47.

Clay, M. M. (1993). *Reading recovery: A guidebook for teachers in training.* Auckland, New Zealand: Heinemann.

— (1994). *An observation survey of early literacy achievement.* Auckland, New Zealand: Heinemann.

Cobb, P. (1994). Where is the mind: Constructivist and sociocultural perspectives on mathematical development. *Educational Researcher,* 23 (7), 13–20.

Coburn, J. (1993). Opening new technological horizons for middle and high school. *Technology & Learning* (special supplement).

Cochrane-Smith, M., & Lytle, S. L. (1990). Research on teaching and teacher research: The issues that divide. *Education Researchers, 19* (2) 2-10

Cochrane-Smith, M. (1991). Reinventing student teaching. *Journal of Teacher Education, 42* (2), 104–118.

Cognition & Technology Group at Vanderbilt. (1991). Technology and the design of generative learning environments. *Educational Technology, 31*(5), 34–40.

— (1990). Anchored instruction and its relationship to situated cognition. *Educational Researcher, 19* (4), 2–10.

— (1992). The Jasper experiment: An exploration of issues in learning and instructional design. *Educational Technology Research and Development, 40* (1), 65–80.

— (1993). Anchored instruction and situated cognition revisited. *Educational Technology, 33* (3), 52–70.

Cohen, E. G. (1986). *Designing groupwork.* New York: Teachers College Press.

Cohen, P. A., Kulik, J. A., & Kulik, C. C. (1982). Educational outcomes of tutoring: A meta-analysis of findings. *American Educational Research Journal, 19,* 237–248.

Coladarci, T. (1992). Teachers' sense of efficacy and commitment to teaching. *Journal of Experimental Education, 60* (4), 323–337.

Colburn, D., & Melillo, W. (1987, June 16). Hispanics: A forgotten health population. *Washington Post,* p. 16.

Colby, C., & Kohlberg, L. (1984). Invariant sequence and internal inconsistency in moral judgment stages. In W. Kurtines & J. Gewirtz (Eds.), *Morality, moral behavior, and moral development.* New York: Wiley-Interscience.

Cole, M., & Engestrom, Y. (1993). A cultural-historical approach to distributed cognition. In G. Salomon (Ed.), *Distributed cognitions: Psychological and educational considerations.* Cambridge, MA: Harvard University Press.

Collins, A. (1990). Portfolios for assessing student learning in science: A new name for a familiar idea. In A. B. Champagne, B. E. Lovitts, & B. J. Calinger (Eds.), *Assessment in the service of instruction.* Washington, D.C.: American Association for the Advancement of Science.

— (1991). Portfolios for assessing student learning in science. In G. Kulm & S. Malcom (Eds.), *Science assessment in the service of reform.* Washington, D.C.: American Association for the Advancement of Science.

— (1992). Portfolios for science education: Issues in purpose, structure, and authenticity. *Science Education, 76* (4), 451–463.

Collins, A., & Dana, T. M. (1993). Using portfolios with middle school students. *Middle School Journal, 25* (2), 14–19.

Comer, J. P. (1988). Educating poor minority children. *Scientific American, 259,* 42–48.

Comfort, K. B. (1994, October). Authentic assessment: A systemic approach in California. *Science and Children,* 42–43, 65.

Conway, M. A., Cohen, G., & Stanhope, N. (1991). On the very long-term memory of knowledge acquired through formal education: Twelve years of cognitive psychology. *Journal of Experimental Psychology: General, 120,* 395–409.

— (1992). Very long-term memory of knowledge acquired at school and university. *Applied Cognitive Psychology,* 6, 467–482.

Cooper, G., & Sweller, J. (1987). The effects of schema acquisition and rule automation in mathematical problem-solving transfer. *Journal of Educational Psychology,* 79, 347–362.

Cooper, H. M., & Good, T. L. (1983). *Pygmalion grows up: Studies in the expectation communication process.* White Plains, NY: Longman.

Corbett, A. T. (1977). Retrieval dynamics for rote and visual image mnemonics. *Journal of Verbal Learning and Verbal Behavior, 16,* 233–246.

Corbin, C. (1972). Mental practice (pp. 93–118). In W. Morgan (Ed.), *Ergogenic aids and muscular performance.* New York: Academic Press.

Corno, L. (1995). Working toward foresight and follow-through. *Mid-Western Educational Researcher, 8* (1), 2–10.

Covington, M., & Beery, R. (1976). *Self-worth and school learning.* New York: Holt, Rinehart & Winston.

Crooks, T. J. (1988). The impact of classroom evaluation practices on students. *Review of Educational Research, 58,* 438–481.

Cunningham, G. K. (1986). *Educational and psychological measurement.* New York: Macmillan.

Curwin, R. L., & Mendler, A. N. (1988). *Discipline with dignity.* Alexandria, VA: Association for Supervision and Curriculum Development.

Cushner, K., McClelland, A., & Safford, P. (1992). *Human diversity in education.* New York: McGraw-Hill.

Damon, W. (1991). Putting substance into self-esteem: A focus on academic and moral values. *Educational Horizons, 70,* 12–18.

Damon, W., & Hart, D. (1982). The development of self-understanding from infancy through adolescence. *Child Development, 53,* 841–864.

— (1988). *Self-understanding in childhood and adolescence.* New York: Cambridge University Press.

Daum, J. (1972). Proxemics in the classroom: Speaker-subject distance and educational performance. Paper presented at the 18th Annual Meeting of the Southeastern Psychological Association, April 6–8, Atlanta, GA.

DeCharms, R. (1976). *Enhancing motivation.* New York: Irvington.

— (1980). The origins of competence and achievement motivation in personal causation. In L. J. Fyans, Jr. (Ed.), *Achievement motivation.* New York: Plenum.

Deci, E. L. (1971). Effects of externally mediated rewards on intrinsic motivation. *Journal of Personality and Social Psychology, 18,* 105-115.

— (1975). *Intrinsic motivation.* New York: Plenum.

Deci, E. L., & Ryan, R. M. (1985). *Intrinsic motivation and self-determination in human behavior.* New York: Plenum.

Deci, E. L., Vallerand, R. J., Pelletier, L. G., & Ryan, R. M. (1991). Motivation and education: The self-determination perspective. *Educational Psychologist, 26,* 325-346.

DeCorte, E., Verschaffel, L., & DeWin, L. (1985). Influence of rewording verbal problems in children's problem representations and solutions. *Journal of Educational Psychology,* 77, 460-470.

DeFord, D. E., Lyons, C. A., & Pinnell, G. S. (1991). *Bridges to literacy: Learning from reading recovery.* Portsmouth, NH: Heinemann.

Delefes, P., & Jackson, B. (1972). Teacher-pupil interaction as a function of location in the classroom. *Psychology in the Schools, 9,* 119–123.

Delisle, J. (1982). Learning to underachieve. *Roeper Review, 4,* 16-18.

Derry, S. J., & Lajoie, S. P. (1993). A middle camp for (un)-intelligent instructional computing: An introduction. In S. P. Lajoie & S. J. Derry (Eds.), *Computers as cognitive tools.* Hillsdale, NJ: Erlbaum.

Derry, S. J., & Murphy, D. A. (1986). Designing systems that train learning ability: From theory to practice. *Review of Educational Research, 56,* 1-39.

Dick, W., & Reiser, R. A. (1989). *Planning effective instruction.* Englewood Cliffs, NJ: Prentice Hall.

Dillon, J. (Ed.) (1988). *Questioning and teaching: A manual of pratice.* London: Croom Helm.

— (1990). *The practice of questioning.* New York: Routledge.

Divoky, D. (1988). The model minority goes to school. *Phi Delta Kappan, 70,* 219–222.

Dorris, M. A. (1981). The grass still grows, the rivers still flow: Contemporary Native-Americans. *Daedalus, 110* (2), 43–69.

Douvan, E., & Adelson, J. (1966). *The adolescent experience.* New York: Wiley.

Douvan, E., & Gold, H. (1966). Modal patterns in American adolescence. In M. L. Hoffman & L. W. Hoffman (Eds.), *Review of developmental research* (Vol. 2). New York: Russell Sage.

Doyle, W. (1984). How order is achieved in classrooms: An interim report. *Journal of Curriculum Studies, 16,* 259-277.

— (1986). Classroom organization and management. In M. C. Wittrock (Ed.), *Handbook of research on teaching* (3d ed.). New York: Macmillan.

— (1988). Work in mathematics classes: The context of students' thinking during instruction. *Educational Psychologist, 23,* 167–180.

— (1990). Classroom management techniques. In O. C. Moles (Ed.), *Student discipline strategies: Research and practice.* Albany: State University of New York Press.

Driscoll, M.P., Klein, J. D., and Sherman, G. P. (1994, March). Perspectives on instructional planning: How do teachers and instructional designers conceive of ISD planning practices? *Educational Technology,* 34–42.

Driscoll, M. P., & Rowley, K. (in press). Semiotics: Toward learning-centered instructional design. In C. Dills & A. Romiszowski (Eds.), *Instructional development: The state of the art, Vol. III. The paradigms, models, metaphors, and viewpoints.* Englewood Cliffs, NJ: Educational Technology Publications.

Driscoll, M. P. (1994). *Psychology of learning for instruction.* Needham Heights, MA: Allyn & Bacon.

Driscoll, M. P., Moallem, M., Dick, W., & Kirby, E. (1994). How does the textbook contribute to learning in a middle school science class? *Contemporary Educational Psychology, 19,* 79–100.

Duell, O. K. (1994). Extended wait time and university student achievement. *American Educational Research Journal, 31* (2), 397–414.

Duell, O. K., Lynch, D. J., Ellsworth, R., & Moore, C. A. (1992). Wait-time in college classes taken by education majors. *Research in Higher Education, 33,* 483-495.

Duffy, G. G., & McIntyre, L. D. (1982). A naturalistic study of instructional assistance in primary-grade reading. *Elementary School Journal, 83* (1), 15–23.

Duffy, G. G., Roehler, L. R., Meloth, M. S., & Vavrus, L. G. (1986). Conceptualizing instructional explanation. *Teaching and Teacher Education, 2,* 197–214.

Dunn, R., Beaudry, J. S., & Klavas, A. (1989). Survey of research on learning styles. *Educational Leadership, 47* (7), 50–58.

Dunphy, D. C. (1963). The social structure of urban adolescent peer groups. *Sociometry, 26,* 230–246.

Dusek, J. B. (1987). *Adolescent development and behavior.* Englewood Cliffs, NJ: Prentice Hall.

Dweck, C. S. (1975). The role of expectations and attributions in the alleviation of learned helplessness. *Journal of Personality and Social Psychology, 31*, 674–685.

— (1986). Motivational processes affecting learning. *American Psychologist, 41*, 1040–1048.

— (1989). Motivation. In A. Lesgold & R. Glaser (Eds.), *Foundations for a psychology of education*. Hillsdale, NJ: Erlbaum.

Dweck, C. S., & Leggett, E. L. (1988). A social-cognitive approach to motivation and personality. *Psychological Review, 95*, 256–273.

Eagly, A. H. (1987). *Sex differences in social behavior: A social-role interpretation*. Hillsdale, NJ: Erlbaum.

Ebel, R. L., & Frisbie, D. A. (1986). *Essentials of educational measurement* (4th ed.). Englewood Cliffs, NJ: Prentice Hall.

— (1991). *Essentials of educational measurement* (5th ed.). Englewood Cliffs, NJ: Prentice Hall.

Eder, R. A. (1989). The emergent personologist: The structure and content of 3 1/2-, 5 1/2-, and 7 1/2-year-olds' concepts of themselves and other persons. *Child Development, 60*, 1218–1228.

— (1990). Uncovering young children's psychological selves: Individual and developmental differences. *Child Development, 61*, 849-863.

Edwards, J. R. (1979). *Language and disadvantage.* London: Wauld.

Eggen, P., & Kauchak, D. (1994). *Educational psychology: Classroom connections*. New York: Merrill Publishing Co.

Elam, S. M., Rose, L. C., & Gallup, A. M. (1992). The 24th annual Gallup/Phi Delta Kappa Poll of the public's attitudes toward the public schools. *Phi Delta Kappan, 74* (1), 41-53.

Elawar, M. C., & Corno, L. (1985). A factorial experiment in teachers' written feedback on student homework: Changing teacher behavior a little rather than a lot. *Journal of Educational Psychology, 77*, 162-173.

Eller, B. F., Kaufman, A. S., & McLean, J. E. (1986–1987). Computer-based assessment of cognitive abilities: Current status/future directions. *Journal of Educational Technology Systems, 15*, 137–147.

Ellerod, F. E., & McLean, G. F. (Eds.). (1986). *Act and agent: Philosophical foundations for moral education and character development.* Washington, D.C.: University Press of America.

Elliott, E. S., & Dweck, C. S. (1988). Goals: An approach to motivation and achievement. *Journal of Personality and Social Psychology, 54* (1), 5–12.

Emmer, E. T. (1987). Classroom management and discipline. In V. Richardson-Koehler (Ed.), *Educator's handbook: A research perspective*. White Plains, NY: Longman.

Emmer, E. T., & Ausiker, A. (1990). School and classroom discipline programs: How well do they work? In O. C. Moles (Ed.), *Student discipline strategies: Research and practice*. Albany: State University of New York Press.

Emmer, E. T., Evertson, C. M., & Anderson, L. M. (1980). Effective classroom management at the beginning of the school year. *Elementary School Journal, 80*, 219–231.

Emmer, E. T., Evertson, C. M., Clements, B. S., & Worsham, M. E. (1994). *Classroom management for secondary teachers* (3d ed.). Needham Heights, MA: Allyn & Bacon.

Epstein, C. (1980). Brain growth and cognitive functioning. In *The emerging adolescent: Characteristics and implications.* Columbus, OH: NMSA.

Epstein, M. H., Polloway, E. A., Patton, J. R., & Foley, R. (1989). Mild retardation: Student characteristics and services. *Education and Training in Mental Retardation, 24* (1), 7-16.

Erickson, F., & Schultz, J. (1982). *The counselor as gate keeper: Social interaction in interviews*. New York: Academic Press.

Erikson, E. (1963). *Childhood and society* (2d ed.). New York: Norton.

— (1968). *Identity, youth and crisis.* New York: Norton.

Evertson, C.M. (1987). Managing classrooms: A framework for teachers. In D. Berliner & B. Rosenshine (eds.), *Talks to teachers*. New York: Random House.

Evertson, C.M., & Emmer, E.T. (1982). Effective management at the beginning of the school year in junior high classes. *Journal of Educational Psychology, 74*, 485–498.

Evertson, C. M., Emmer, E., & Brophy, J. (1980). Predictors of effective teaching in junior high mathematics classrooms. *Journal of Research on Mathematics Education, II*, 167–178.

Evertson, C. M., Emmer, E. T., Clements, B. S., & Worsham, M. E. (1994). Classroom management for elementary teachers (3d ed.) Needham Heights, MA: Allyn & Bacon.

Evertson, C. M., & Harris, A. (1992). What we know about managing classrooms. *Educational Leadership, 49*, 74–79.

Evertson, C. M., & Randolph, C. H. (1995). Classroom management in the learning-centered classroom. In A. Ornstein (Ed.), *Teaching: Theory and practice.* Needham Heights, MA: Allyn & Bacon.

Fagan, E. R., Hassler, D. M., & Szabo, M. (1981). Evaluation of questioning strategies in language arts instruction. *Research in the Teaching of English, 15*, 267–273.

Fagot, B. I. (1977). Consequences of moderate cross-gender behavior in preschool children. *Child Development, 48*, 902–907.

— (1985). Changes in thinking about early sex-role development. *Developmental Review, 5*, 83–98.

Federal Register (1977, August). Washington, D.C.: U.S. Government Printing Office.

Feiman-Nemser, S. (1983). *Learning to teach*. East Lansing, MI: Institute for Research on Teaching.

Feldman, R. D. (1982). *Whatever happened to the Quiz Kids?* Chicago: Review Press.

Feltz, D. L., & Landers, D. M. (1983). Effects of mental practice on motor skill learning and performance: A meta-analysis. *Journal of Sport Psychology, 5*, 25–57.

Fenstermacher, G. (1990). Moral consideration on teaching as a profession. In J. Goodlad, R. Soder, & K. Sirotnik (Eds.), *The moral dimensions of teaching.* San Francisco: Jossey-Bass.

Ferster, C. B., & Skinner, B. F. (1957). *Schedules of reinforcement.* New York: Appleton-Century-Crofts.

Fiedler, F. F., & Garcia, J. E. (1987). *New approaches to effective leadership: Cognitive resources and organizational performance.* New York: Wiley.

Finders, M., & Lewis, C. (1994). Why some parents don't come to school. *Educational Leadership, 51* (8), 50–54.

Fisher, C. W., Berliner, D. C., Filby, N. N., Marliave, R., Cahen, L. S., & Dishaw, M. M. (1980). Teaching behaviors, academic learning time, and student achievement: An overview. In C. Denham & A. Lieberman (Eds.), *Time to learn.* Washington, D.C.: National Institute of Education.

Fisher, C. W., Filby, N. N., Marliave, R., Cahen, L. S., Dishaw, M. M., Moore, J. E., & Berliner, D. C. (1978). *Teaching behaviors, academic learning time, and student achievement: Final report of phase III-B, Beginning Teacher Evaluation Study* (Tech. Report V-1). San Francisco: Far West Laboratory for Educational Research and Development.

Fisher, C., Berliner, D., Filby, N., Marliave, R., Cahen, L., & Dishaw, M. (1980). Teaching behaviors, academic learning time, and student achievement: An overview. In C. Denham & A. Lieberman (Eds.), *Time to learn.* Washington, DC: National Institute of Education.

Fishkin, J., Keniston, K., & MacKinnon, C. (1973). Moral reasoning and political ideology. *Journal of Personality and Social Psychology, 27,* 109–119.

Flaugher, R. L. (1978). The many definitions of test bias. *American Psychologist, 33,* 671-679.

Flavell, J. H. (1985). *Cognitive development* (2d ed.). Englewood Cliffs, NJ: Prentice Hall.

Fleming, M., & Chambers, B. (1983). Teacher-made tests: Windows on the classroom. In W. E. Hathaway (Ed.), *Testing in the schools: New directions for testing and measurement,* No. 19. San Francisco: Jossey-Bass.

Ford, B. A., & Jones, C. (1990). An ethnic feelings book: Created by students with developmental handicaps. *Teaching Exceptional Children, 22* (4), 36–39.

Forrest-Pressley, D. L., MacKinnon, E., & Waller, T. G. (Eds.). (1985). *Metacognition, cognition, and human performance.* New York: Academic Press.

Frederiksen, J. R., & Collins, A. (1989). A systems approach to educational testing. *Educational Researcher, 18* (9), 27–32.

Frederiksen, N. (1984). The real test bias. *American Psychologist, 39,* 193–202.

Frey, G. (1983, Summer). The Middle Ages: The social studies core of the fifth grade. *Moral Education Forum,* 30–34.

Friedl, A. E. (1991). *Teaching science to children: An integrated approach.* (2d ed.). New York: McGraw-Hill, Inc.

Frieze, I., & Weiner, B. (1971). Cue utilization and attributional judgments for success and failure. *Journal of Personality, 39,* 91–109.

Frisbie, D. A., & Waltman, K. K. (1992). Developing a personal grading plan. *Educational Measurement: Issues and Practices,* Fall, 35–42.

Fuson, K. C., & Willis, G. B. (1989). Second graders' use of schematic drawings in solving addition and subtraction problems. *Journal of Educational Psychology, 81,* 514–520.

Gage, N. L., & Berliner, D. C. (1988). *Educational psychology.* Boston: Houghton Mifflin.

— (1992). *Educational psychology.* Boston: Houghton Mifflin.

Gage, N.L., & Needels, M. C. (1989). Process-product research on teaching: A review of criticism. *Elementary School Journal, 89,* 253–300.

Gagné, E. D., Yekovich, C. W., & Yekovich, F. R. (1993). *The cognitive psychology of school learning* (2d ed.). New York: HarperCollins.

Gagné, R. M. (1977). *The conditions of learning* (3d ed.). New York: Holt, Rinehart, & Winston.

— (1985). *The conditions of learning* (4th ed.). New York: Holt, Rinehart & Winston.

Gagné, R.M., & Driscoll, M.P. (1988). *Essentials of learning for instruction* (2d ed.). Englewood Cliffs, NJ: Prentice Hall.

Gagné, R. M., & Glaser, R. (1987). Foundations in learning research. In R. M. Gagné (Ed.), *Instructional technology: Foundations.* Hillsdale, NJ: Erlbaum.

Gagné, R. M., & Merrill, M. D. (1990). Integrative goals for instructional design. *Educational Technology Research & Development, 38,* 23–30.

Gallimore, R., & Tharp, R. (1990). Teaching mind in society: Teaching, schooling, and literate discourse. In L. C. Moll (Ed.), *Vygotsky and education.* New York: Cambridge University Press.

Garcia, E. E. (1992). Hispanic children: Theoretical, empirical, and related policy issues. *Educational Psychology Review, 4,* 69-94.

Gardner, H. (1975). *The shattered mind.* New York: Knopf.

— (1979). Developmental psychology after Piaget: An approach in terms of symbolization. *Human Development, 15,* 570–580.

— (1982). *Art, mind and brain.* New York: Basic Books.

— (1993). *Creating minds: An anatomy of creativity seen through the lives of Freud, Einstein, Picasso, Stravinsky, Eliot, Graham, and Gandhi.* New York: BasicBooks.

Gardner, H., & Hatch T. (1989). Multiple intelligences go to school: Educational implications of the theory of multiple intelligences. *Educational Researcher, 18* (8), 4–10.

Gardner, H., Howard, V., and Perkins, D. (1974). Symbol systems: A philosophical, psychological and educational investigation. In D. Olson (Ed.), *Media and symbols.* Chicago: University of Chicago Press.

Gardner, H., & Wolf, D. (1983). Waves and streams of symbolization. In D. R. Rogers & J. A. Sloboda (Eds.), *The acquisition of symbolic skills.* London: Plenum.

Garlett, M. W. (1993). Making parents into partners. *Teachers in Focus,* 2 (3), 7–8.

Geisert, P. G., & Futrell, M. K. (1995). *Teachers, computers, and curriculum: Microcomputers in the classroom* (2d ed.). Needham Heights, MA: Allyn & Bacon.

Genesee, F. (1985). Second language learning through immersion: A review of U. S. programs. *Review of Educational Research, 55,* 541–561.

Gettinger, M. (1988). Methods of proactive classroom management. *School Psychology Review, 17,* 227–242.

Gilligan, C. (1977). In a different voice: Women's conceptions of self and of morality. *Harvard Educational Review, 47,* 481–517.

— (1982). *In a different voice.* Cambridge: Harvard University Press.

Ginott, H. (1972). *Teacher and child.* New York: Macmillan.

Glaser, R. (1963). Instructional technology and the measurement of learning outcomes: Some questions. *American Psychologist, 18,* 519–521.

Glaser, R., & Silver, E. (1994). Assessment, testing, and instruction: Retrospect and prospect. In Darling-Hammond (ed.), *Review of Research in Education,* Vol. 20. Washington, D.C.: American Educational Research Association.

Glass, G. V., & Smith, M. L. (1977). *Pull out in compensatory education.* Washington, D.C.: Department of Health, Education, and Welfare.

Glasser, W. (1986). *Control theory in the classroom.* New York: HarperCollins.

— (1990). *The quality school.* New York: HarperCollins.

— (1993). *The quality school teacher.* New York: HarperCollins.

Goin, M. T., Peters, E. E., & Levin, J. R. (1986, March-April). *Effects of pictorial mnemonic strategies on the reading performance of students classified as learning disabled.* Paper presented at the Annual Meeting of the Council for Exceptional Children, New Orleans.

Goldenberg, C. N. (1992). The limits of expectations: A case for case knowledge about teacher expectancy effects. *American Educational Research Journal, 29,* 517-544.

Gollnick, D. M., & Chinn, P. C. (1990). *Multicultural education in a pluralistic society* (3d ed.). Columbus, OH: Merrill.

Good, T. L. (1988). Teacher expectations. In D. Berliner & B. Rosenshine (Eds.), *Talks to teachers.* New York: Random House.

Good, T. L., & Brophy, J. E. (1994). *Looking in classrooms* (6th ed.). New York: HarperCollins.

Good, T. L., Grouws, D., & Ebmeier, H. (1983). *Active mathematics teaching.* New York: Longman.

Goodlad, J. (1983). A study of schooling: Some implications for school improvement. *Phi Delta Kappan, 64,* 465-470.

Goodlad, J. I,. & Lovitt, T. C. (Eds.). (1993). *Integrating general and special education.* Columbus, OH: Merrill/Macmillan.

Gordon, E. W. (1991). Human diversity and pluralism. *Educational Psychologist, 26,* 99-108.

Gordon, T. (1974). *T.E.T.: Teacher effectiveness training.* New York: Peter H. Wyden.

— (1988). *Teaching children self-discipline: At home and at school.* New York: Times Books.

Gould, S. J. (1981). *The mismeasure of man.* New York: W. W. Norton.

Grabe, M. (1986). Attentional processes in education. In G. D. Phye & T. Andre (Eds.), *Cognitive classroom learning: Understanding, thinking and problem solving.* New York: Academic Press.

Graham, S. (1994). Motivation in African Americans. *Review of Educational Research, 64* (1), 55–117.

Graham, S., & Barker, G. P. (1990). The down side of help: An attributional-developmental analysis of helping behavior as a low-ability cue. *Journal of Educational Psychology, 82,* 7–14.

Greer, J. G., & Withered, C. E. (1987). Learned helplessness and the elementary student: Implications for counselors. *Elementary School Guidance and Counseling, 22* (2), 157–164.

Gresham, F. (1981). Social skills training with handicapped children: A review. *Review of Educational Research, 51,* 139–176.

Gronlund, N. E. (1990). *Measurement and evaluation in teaching* (6th ed.). New York: Macmillan.

— (1991). *How I write and use instructional objectives* (4th ed.). New York: Macmillan.

— (1993). *How to make achievement tests and assessments* (5th ed.). Needham Heights, MA: Allyn & Bacon.

Grossman, H. (1983). *Classification in mental retardation.* Washington, D.C.: American Association on Mental Deficiency.

Grossman, H., & Grossman, S. H. (1994). *Gender issues in education.* Needham Heights, MA: Allyn & Bacon.

Gruber, H. E., & Voneche, J. J. (1977). *The essential Piaget.* New York: Basic Books.

Guilford, J. P. (1967). *The nature of human intelligence.* New York: McGraw-Hill.

— (1980). Fluid and crystallized intelligences: Two fanciful concepts. *Psychological Bulletin, 88,* 406–412.

— (1985). The structure-of-intellect model. In B. B. Wolman (Ed.), *Handbook of intelligence.* New York: Wiley.

Gump, P. (1967). *The classroom behavior setting: Its nature and relation to student behavior* (Report No. BR-5-0334). Washington, D.C.: Office of Education, Bureau of Research.

Gunter, M. A., Estes, T. H., & Hasbrouck Schwab, J. (1990). *Instruction: A models approach.* Needham Heights, MA: Allyn & Bacon.

Haertel, G. D., Walberg, H. J., Junker, L., & Pascarella, E. T. (1981). Early adolescent sex differences in science learning: Evidence from the National Assessment of Educational Progress. *American Educational Research Journal, 18* (3), 329-341.

Hale-Benson, J. E. (1986). *Black children: Their roots and their culture* (rev. ed.). Baltimore, MD: Johns Hopkins University Press.

Hallahan, D. P., & Kauffman, J. M. (1991). *Exceptional children: Introduction to special education* (5th ed.). Needham Heights, MA: Allyn & Bacon.

Hallahan, D. P., & Kauffman, J. M. (1994). *Exceptional children: Introduction to special education* (6th ed.). Needham Heights, MA: Allyn & Bacon.

Hambleton, R. K., & Murphy, E. (1992). A psychometric perspective on authentic measurement. *Applied Measurement in Education, 5* (1), 1-16.

Hammill, D. D. (1990). On defining learning disabilities: An emerging consensus. *Journal of Learning Disabilities, 23,* 74-85.

Haney, W., & Madaus, G. (1989). Searching for alternatives to standardized tests: Why, whats, and whithers. *Phi Delta Kappan, 70,* 683-687.

Hanna, G. S. (1993). *Better teaching through better measurement.* Orlando, FL: Harcourt Brace Jovanovich.

Harel & Papert, S. (1992). Software design as a learning environment. Dr. I. Harel & S. Papent (Eds.) *Constructionism,* Norwood, NJ: Ablox.

Haring-Smith, T. (1993). *Learning together: An introduction to collaborative learning.* New York: HarperCollins.

— (1994a). *Writing together: Collaborative learning in the writing classroom.* New York: HarperCollins.

— (1994b, June). *Why collaborative learning backfires.* Paper presented at the conference What Works: Building Effective Collaborative Learning Experiences, sponsored by the National Center on Postsecondary Teaching, Learning, and Assessment, Pennsylvania State University, State College, PA.

Harris, F. R., Wolf, M. M., & Baer, D. M. (1967). Effects of adult social reinforcement in child behavior. In S. W. Bijou & D. M. Baer (Eds.), *Child development: Readings in experimental analysis.* New York: Appleton-Century-Crofts.

Harrow, A. J. (1972). *A taxonomy of the psychomotor domain: A guide for developing behavioral objectives.* New York: David McKay.

Hart, D. (1994). *Authentic assessment: A handbook for educators.* Menlo Park, CA: Addison-Wesley Publishing Co.

Harter, S. (1982). The perceived competence scale for children. *Child Development, 53,* 87-97.

— (1986). Processes underlying the construction, maintenance, and enhancement of self-concept in children. In S. Suhls & A. Greenwald (Eds.), *Psychological perspectives of the self* (Vol. 3). Hillsdale, NJ: Erlbaum.

— (1990). Issues in the assessment of the self-concept in children and adolescents. In A. LaGreca (ed.), *Through the eyes of a child.* Needham Heights, MA: Allyn & Bacon.

Harter, S., & Pike, R. (1984). The pictorial scale of perceived competence and social acceptance for young children. *Child Development, 55,* 1969-1982.

Hartman, J. S., & Askounis, A. C. (1989). Asian-American students: Are they really a "model minority"? *The School Counselor, 37,* 109–111.

Hartshorne, H., & May, M. A. (1930). *Studies in deceit.* New York: Macmillan.

Heckhausen, H., & Kuhl, J. (1985). From wishes to action: The dead ends and short cuts on the long way to action. In M. Frese & J. Sabini (Eds.), *Goal-directed behavior: The concept of action in psychology.* Hillsdale, NJ: Erlbaum.

Henson, K. (1988). *Methods and strategies for teaching in secondary and middle schools.* New York: Longman.

Herman, J. L., Aschbacher, P. R., & Winters, L. (1992). *A practical guide to alternative assessment.* Alexandria, VA: Association for Supervision and Curriculum Development.

Herrnstein, R. J., & Murray, C. A. (1994). *The bell curve: Intelligence and class structure in American life.* New York: Free Press. Chih–Mei, C., & Mc Devitt, T. M.

Hess, R., Chih-Mei, C., & McDevitt, T. M. (1987), Cultural vaniation in family beliefs about children's performance in mathematics: Comparisons among People's Republic of China, Chinese-American, and Caucasian-American families. *Journal of Educational Psychology, 79,* 179–188

Hetherington, E. M., & Parke, R. D. (1993). *Child psychology: A contemporary viewpoint.* New York: McGraw-Hill.

Heward, W. L., & Orlansky, M. D. (1992). *Exceptional children* (4th ed.). New York: Merrill.

Heyman, G. D., Dweck, C. S., & Cain, K. M. (1992). Young children's vulnerability to self-blame and helplessness: Relationship to beliefs about goodness. *Child Development, 63,* 401–415.

Hiebert, F. (Ed.). (1991). *Literacy for a diverse society.* New York: Teachers College Press.

Hill, K. T. (1984). Debilitating motivation and testing: A major educational problem—Possible solutions and policy applications. In R. E. Ames & C. Ames (Eds.), *Research on motivation in education: Vol. 1, Student motivation.* New York: Academic Press.

Hoge, R. D., and Renzulli, J. S. (1993). Exploring the link between giftedness and self-concept. *Review of Educational Research, 63* (4), 449–465.

Hohn, R. L. (1995). *Classroom learning and teaching.* White Plains, NY: Longman.

Holstein, B. (1976). Irreversible, stepwise sequence in the development of moral judgment: A longitudinal study of males and females. *Child Development, 47,* 51-61.

Honebein, P. C., Duffy, T. M., & Fishman, B. J. (1994). Constructivism and the design of authentic learning environments: Context and authentic activities for learning. In T. M. Duffy, J. Lowyck, & D. Jonassen (Eds.), *Designing environments for constructive learning.* Hillsdale, NJ: Erlbaum.

Hopkins, K. D., & Antes, R. L. (1990). *Classroom measurement and evaluation* (3rd ed.). Itasca, IL: F. E. Peacock.

Hopkins, K. D., Stanley, J. C, & Hopkins, B. R. (1981). *Educational and psychological measurement and evaluation* 3rd ed.). Englewood Cliffs, NJ: Prentice Hall.

Hopkins, K. D., Stanley, J. C, & Hopkins, B. R. (1990). *Educational and psychological measurement and evaluation* (7th ed.). Englewood Cliffs, NJ: Prentice Hall.

Houser, N. (1987). Toward a Peircean semiotic theory of learning. *American Journal of Semiotics, 5* (2), 251–274.

Houston, J. P. (1986). *Fundamentals of learning and memory* (3d ed.). New York: Harcourt Brace Jovanovich.

Hoy, W., & Woolfolk, A. E. (1993). Teachers' sense of efficacy and the organizational health of schools. *Elementary School Journal, 93* (4), 355–372.

Hoy, W. K., & Miskel, C. G. (1991). *Educational administration: Theory, research, and practice* (4th ed.). New York: McGraw-Hill.

Huck, C. S., & Pinnell, G. S. (1991). Literacy in the classroom. In D. E. DeFord, C. A. Lyons, & G. S. Pinnell (Eds.), *Bridges to literacy: Learning from reading recovery.* Portsmouth, NH: Heinemann.

Huling-Austin, L. (1994) *Becoming a teacher: What research tells us (booklet).* West Lafayette, IN: Kappa Delta Pi.

Hunt, E. B. (1971). What kind of computer is man? *Cognitive Psychology, 2,* 57–98.

Hunter, M. (1982). *Mastery teaching.* El Segundo, CA: TIP Publications.

— (1984). Knowing, teaching, and supervising. In P. Hosford (Ed.), *Using what we know about teaching.* Alexandria, VA: Association for Supervision and Curriculum Development.

— (1991). Hunter lesson design helps achieve the goals of science instruction. *Educational Leadership, 48* (4), 79-81.

Hwang, K. (1986). A psychological perspective of Chinese inter-personal morality. In M. H. Bond (Ed.), *The psychology of the Chinese people.* New York: Oxford University Press.

Hyde, J. S., Fennema, E., & Lamon, S. J. (1990). Gender differences in mathematics performance. *Psychological Bulletin, 107,* 139–155.

Inhelder, B., & Piaget, J. (1958). *The growth of logical thinking from childhood to adolescence* (A. Parsons and S. Seagrin, Trans.). New York: Basic Books.

Iran-Nejad, A., Marsh, G. E., & Clements, A. C. (1992). The figure and ground of constructive brain functioning: Beyond explicit memory processes. *Educational Psychologist, 47,* 473–492.

Iran-Nejad, A., Wittrock, M., & Hidi, S. (Eds.). (1992). Special Issue: Brain and Education. *Educational Psychologist, 27* (4). Washington, D.C.: American Psychological Association.

Jacoby, L. L., & Bartz, W. H. (1972). Rehearsal and transfer to LTS. *Journal of Verbal Learning and Verbal Behavior, 11,* 561–565.

Johnson, D. W., & Johnson, R. T. (1987). *Learning together and alone: Cooperative, competitive, and individualistic learning* (2d ed.). Englewood Cliffs, NJ: Prentice Hall.

— (1989). *Cooperation and competition: Theory and research.* Edina, MN: Interaction Book Company.

— (1990). Cooperative learning and achievement. In S. Sharan (Ed.), *Cooperative learning theory and research.* New York: Praeger Publishers.

— (1991). *Teaching students to be peacemakers.* Edina, MN: Interaction Book Company.

— (1992a). *Creative controversy: Intellectual challenge in the classroom.* Edina, MN: Interaction Book Company.

— (1992b). *Positive interdependence: The heart of cooperative learning.* Edina, MN: Interaction Book Company.

— (1994). *Learning together and alone: Cooperative, competitive and individualistic learning* (4th ed.). Needham Heights, MA: Allyn & Bacon.

Johnson, D. W., Johnson, R. T., & Holubec, E. (1993). *Cooperation in the classroom* (6th ed.). Edina, MN: Interaction Book Company.

Johnson, D. W., Johnson, R. T., & Smith, K. (1991). *Active learning: Cooperation in the college classroom.* Edina, MN: Interaction Book Company.

Johnston, P., Allington, R., & Afflerbach, P. (1985). The congruence of classroom and remedial instruction. *Elementary School Journal, 85,* 465–477.

Jones, R. A. (1977). *Self-fulfilling prophesies: Social psychological and psychological effects of expectancies.* New York: Halsted Press.

Jones, V. F., & Jones, L. S. (1990). *Comprehensive classroom management: Motivating and managing students* (3d ed.). Needham Heights, MA: Allyn & Bacon.

— (1995). *Comprehensive classroom management: Creating positive learning environments for all students.* Needham Heights, MA: Allyn & Bacon.

Jussim, L. (1986). Self-fulfilling prophecies: A theoretical and integrative review. *Psychological Review, 93,* 429–445.

Kagan, S., Zahn, G. L., Widamin, K. F., Schwartz Wald, J., and Tyrrell, G. (1985). Classroom structural bias: Impact of cooperative and competitive structures on cooperative and competitive individuals and groups. In. R. E. Slavin et al. (Eds.) Learning to cooperate, cooperating to learn, New York: Plenam Press.

Kagan, J. (1964a). *Developmental studies of reflection and analysis.* Cambridge, MA: Harvard University Press.

— (1964b). Impulsive and reflective children. In J. D. Krumbolz (Ed.), *Learning and the educational process.* Chicago: Rand McNally.

Kagan, S. (1989). *Cooperative learning: Resources for teaching.* Laguna Beach, CA: Resources for Teachers.

Kahle, J. B., & Meece, J. L. (1994). Research on girls in science: Lessons and applications. In D. Gabel (Ed.), *Handbook of research in science teaching & learning.* Washington, D.C.: National Science Teachers Association.

Kalaian, H. A., & Freeman, D. J. (1990, April). *Is self-confidence in teaching a multidimensional or unidimensional trait?* Paper presented at the Annual Meeting of the American Educational Research Association, Boston.

Katz, P., & Zalk, S. R. (1978). Modification of children's racial attitudes. *Developmental Psychology, 14,* 447-461.

Kearsley, G., Hunter, B., & Furlong, M. (1992). *We teach with technology: New visions for education.* Wilsonville, OR: Franklin, Beedle, & Associates.

Keith, T. Z. (1982). Time spent on homework and high school grades. A large-sample path analysis. *Journal of Education Psychology, 74,* 248–253.

Keller, A., Ford, L., & Meacham, J. A. (1978). Dimensions of self-concept in preschool children. *Developmental Psychology, 14,* 483–489.

Keller, J. M. (1983). Motivational design of instruction. In C.

M. Reigeluth (Ed.), *Instructional-design theories and models: An overview of their current status.* Hillsdale, NJ: Erlbaum.

— (1984). The use of the ARCS model of motivation in teacher training. In K. Shaw (Ed.), *Aspects of educational technology: XVII. Staff development and career updating.* New York: Nichols.

— (1987a, October). Strategies for stimulating motivation to learn. *Performance and Instruction Journal,* 1–7.

— (1987b, November/December). The systematic process of motivational design. *Performance and Instruction Journal,* 1–8.

Kelman, H. C. (1958). Compliance, identification, and internalization: The processes of opinion change. *Journal of Conflict Resolution, 2,* 51–60.

— (1961). Processes of attitude change. *Public Opinion Quarterly, 25,* 57-78.

Kennedy, M., Jung, R., & Orland, M. (1986). *Poverty, achievement, and the distribution of compensatory education services.* Washington, D.C.: U.S. Department of Education.

Kesner, R. P. (1991). Neurobiological views of memory. In J.L. Martinez, Jr. & R. P. Kesner (Eds.), *Learning and memory: A biological view* (2d ed.). San Diego: Academic Press.

King, A. (1990). Enhancing peer interaction and learning in the classroom through reciprocal questioning. *American Educational Research Journal, 27,* 664–687.

Kirk, S., & Chalfant, J. (1984). *Developmental and academic learning disabilities.* Denver: Love Publishing Co.

Kirshnit, C. E., Richards, M. H., & Ham, M. (1988, August). *Athletic participation and body image during early adolescence.* Paper presented at the 96th Annual Convention of the American Psychological Association, Atlanta, GA.

Klauer, K. J. (1984). Intentional and incidental learning with instructional texts: A meta-analysis for 1970-1980. *American Educational Research Journal, 21,* 323–340.

Klein, J. P. (1985). Separation of church and state: The endless struggle. *Contemporary Education, 54* (3), 166–170.

Kloss, R. J. (1993). Stay in touch, won't you?: Using the one minute paper. *College Teaching, 41* (2), 60–63.

Kneedler, P. (1985). California assesses critical thinking. In A. Costa (Ed.), *Developing minds: A resource book for teaching thinking.* Alexandria, VA: Association for Supervision and Curriculum Development.

Knight, R. S., Duke, C. R., & Palcic, R. (1988). *A statistical profile of secondary education teachers at Utah State University at the completion of their teacher education program.* Logan: Utah State University (ERIC Document Reproduction Service No. ED 292 773).

Knowles, R. T., & McLean, G. F. (Eds.). (1992). *Psychological foundations of moral education and character development: An integrated theory of moral development* (2d ed.). Washington, D.C.: The Council for Research in Values and Philosophy.

Koffler, S. L. (1987). Assessing the impact of a state's decision to move from minimum competency testing toward higher level testing for graduation. *Educational Evaluation and Policy Analysis, 9,* 325–336.

Kohlberg, L. (1969). Stage and sequence: The cognitive-developmental approach to socialization. In D. A. Goslin (Ed.), *Handbook of socialization theory and research.* Chicago: Rand McNally.

— (1971). From is to ought: How to commit the naturalistic fallacy and get away with it in the study of moral development (pp. 151–235). In T. Mischel (Ed.), *Cognitive psychology and epistemologies.* New York: Academic Press.

— (1978). Revisions in the theory and practice of moral development. *Moral Development: New Directions for Child Development, 10* (2), 83–88.

Kohn, A. (1993). Rewards vs. learning: A response to Paul Chance. *Phi Delta Kappan, 74,* 783–787.

Kounin, J. (1970). *Discipline and group management in classrooms.* New York: Holt, Rinehart & Winston.

Kourilsky, M., & Wittrock, M. C. (1992). Generative teaching: An enhancement strategy for the learning of economics in cooperative groups. *American Educational Research Journal, 29* (4), 861–876.

Krathwohl, D. R. (1993). *Methods of educational and social science research: An integrated approach.* New York: Longman.

Krathwohl, D. R., Bloom, B. S., and Masia, B. B. (1964). *Taxonomy of educational objectives, Handbook II: Affective domain.* New York: McKay.

Krechevsky, M. (1991). Project Spectrum: An innovative assessment alternative. *Educational Leadership, 48* (5), 43–48.

Kubiszyn, T., & Borich, G. D. (1987). *Educational testing and measurement.* Glenview, IL: Scott, Foresman.

— (1993). *Educational testing and measurement: Classroom application and practice* (4th ed.). New York: Harper-Collins.

Kukla, A. (1972). Foundations of an attributional theory of performance. *Psychological Review, 79,* 454–470.

Kulhavy, R. W. (1977). Feedback in written instruction. *Review of Educational Research, 47,* 211–232.

Kulhavy, R. W., Schwartz, N. H., & Peterson, S. (1986). Working memory: The encoding process. In G. D. Phye & T. Andre (Eds.), *Cognitive classroom learning.* New York: Academic Press.

Kulhavy, R. W., & Stock, W. A. (1989). Feedback in written instruction: The place of response certitude. *Educational Psychology Review, 1,* 279–308.

Kutnick, P., & Thomas, M. (1990). Dyadic pairings for the enhancement of cognitive development in the school curriculum: Some preliminary results on science tasks. *British Educational Research Journal, 16* (4), 399–406.

LaBerge, D., & Samuels, S. J. (1974). Toward a theory of automatic information processing in reading. *Cognitive Psychology, 6,* 293–323.

Lakoff, G., & Johnson, M. (1980). *Metaphors we live by.* Chicago: University of Chicago Press.

Lamme, L. L., & Hysmith, C. (1991, December). One school's adventure into portfolio assessment. *Language Arts,* p. 632.

Landman, G. B. (1987). An evaluation of the effects of being regarded as "unmotivated": Developmental and behavioral disorders; *Clinical Pediatrics* (Special issue), *26* (5), 271–274.

Landry, R. (1987). Reading comprehension in first and second languages of immersion and Francophone students. *Canadian Journal of Exceptional Children, 3* , 103–108.

Langlois, J. H., & Downs, A. C. (1980). Mothers, fathers, and peers as socialization agents of sex-typed play behaviors in young children. *Child Development, 51,* 1237–1247.

Lashley, T. J. (1994). Teacher technicians: A "new" metaphor for new teachers. *Action in Teacher Education, 16* (1), 11–19.

Laski, F. J. (1991). Achieving integration during the second revolution. In L. H. Meyer, C. A. Peck, & L. Brown (Eds.), *Critical issues in the lives of people with severe disabilities.* Baltimore: P. H. Brookes.

Lave, J. (1988). *Cognition in practice: Mind, mathematics and culture in everyday life.* New York: Cambridge University Press.

Lebow, D. (1993). Constructivist values for instructional systems design: Five principles toward a new mindset. *Educational Technology Research and Development, 41* (3), 4–16.

Leder, G. C. (1987). Student achievement: A factor in classroom dynamics? *Exceptional Child, 34* (2), 133-141.

LeFrancois, G. R. (1991). *Psychology for teaching* (7th ed.). Belmont, CA: Wadsworth.

Lefton, L. A. (1991). *Psychology* (4th ed.). Needham Heights, MA: Allyn & Bacon.

Leinhardt, G. (1992, April). What research on learning tells us about teaching. *Educational Leadership,* 20–25.

Leinhardt, G., & Greeno, J. G. (1986). The cognitive skill of teaching. *Journal of Educational Psychology, 78,* 75–95.

Lemke, J. L. (1988). Genres, semantics, and classroom teaching. *Linguistics and Education, 1* (1), 81–99.

Lenneberg, E. H. (1967). *Biological foundations of language.* New York: John Wiley.

Leont'ev, A.N. (1978). The development of writing in the child. In M. Cole (Ed.), *The selected writings of A. R. Luria.* White Plains, NY: Sharpe. (Originally published 1929).

— (1981). *Language and cognition.* Washington, D.C.: Winston.

Lepper, M. R., Greene, D., & Nisbett, R. E. (1973). Undermining children's intrinsic interest with extrinsic rewards: A test of the overjustification hypothesis. *Journal of Personality and Social Psychology, 28,* 129–137.

Lerner, J. W. (1993). *Learning disabilities: Theories, diagnosis, and teaching strategies.* Boston: Houghton Mifflin.

Lerner, R. M., & Schroeder, C. (1971). Physique identification, preference, and aversion in kindergarten children. *Developmental Psychology, 5,* 538.

Lesser, G. S. (1974). *Children and television.* New York: Random House.

Levin, H. M. (1993). Editor's introduction. *Review of Educational Research, 63* (3), 245–247.

Levin, J. R. (1985). Educational applications of mnemonic pictures: Possibilities beyond your wildest imagination. In A. A. Sheikh (Ed.), *Imagery in the educational process.* Farmingdale, NY: Baywood.

Levin, J. R., Dretzke, B. J., McCormick, C. B., Scruggs, T. E., McGivern, S., & Mastropieri, M. (1983). Learning via mnemonic pictures: Analysis of the presidential process. *Educational Communication and Technology Journal, 31,* 161–173.

Lewis, A. B. (1989). Training students to represent arithmetic word problems. *Journal of Educational Psychology, 81,* 521–531.

Lickona, T. (Ed.). (1976). *Moral development and behavior: Theory, research and social issues.* New York: Holt, Rinehart & Winston.

Lickona, T. (1987). Character development in the elementary school classroom. In K. Ryan & G. F. McLean (Eds.), *Character development in schools and beyond.* New York: Praeger.

Lindsay, P. H., & Norman, D. A. (1977). *Human information processing: An introduction to psychology* (2d ed.). New York: Academic Press.

Linn, M. (1991). Gender differences in educational achievement (pp. 11–50). In *Proceedings of the 1991 ETS Invitational Conference: Sex equity in educational opportunity, achievement, and testing* . Princeton, NJ: Educational Testing Service.

Little, A. (1987). Attributions in a cross-cultural context. *Genetic, Social, and General Psychology Monographs, 113* (1), 61–79.

Livingston, C., & Borko, H. (1989, July-August). Expert-novice differences in teaching: A cognitive analysis and implications for teacher education. *Journal of Teacher Education,* 36–42.

Locke, E. A., Shaw, K. N., Saari, L. M., & Latham, G. P. (1981). Goal setting and task performance: 1969-1980. *Psychology Bulletin, 90,* 125–152.

Lopez, J. (1994). Personal communication.

Lockwood, A. (1978). The effects of value clarification and moral development curriculum on school age subjects: A critical review of recent research. *Review of Educational Research, 48,* 325–364.

Lum, D. (1986). *Social work practice and people of color: A process-stage approach.* Monterey, CA: Brooks/Cole.

Lytton, H., & Romney, D. M. (1991). Parents' sex-related differential socialization of boys and girls: A meta-analysis. *Psychological Bulletin, 109,* 267-296.

Macionis, J. J. (1994). *Sociology* (4th ed.). Englewood Cliffs, NJ: Prentice Hall.

MacKenzie, A. A. & White, R. T. (1982). Fieldwork in geography and long-term memory. *American Educational Research Journal, 19,* 623–632.

Madden, N. A., Slavin, R. E., Karweit, N. L., Dolan, L. J., & Wasik, B. A. (1993). Success for all: Longitudinal effects of a restructuring program for inner-city elementary schools. *American Educational Research Journal, 30,* 123–148.

Madsen, C. H., & Madsen, C. K. (1981). *Teaching/discipline: A positive approach for educational development.* Raleigh, NC: Contemporary Publishing.

Maehr, M. L., & Anderman, E. M. (1993). Reinventing schools for early adolescents: Emphasizing task goals. *The Elementary School Journal, 93,* 593–610.

Magee, L. J., & Price, K. R. (1992). Propel: Visual arts in Pittsburgh. *School Arts Magazine, 91,* (8), 42–45.

Mager, R. (1962). *Preparing instructional objectives* (2d ed.). Palo Alto, CA: Fearon.

Malkus, U., Feldman, D. H., & Gardner, H. (1988). Dimensions of mind in early childhood. In A. D. Pellegrini (Ed.), *Psychological bases of early childhood.* New York: Wiley.

Mandeville, G. K., & Rivers, J. L. (1991). The South Carolina PET study: Teachers' perceptions and student achievement. *Elementary School Journal, 91,* 377–407.

Maniet-Bellerman, P. (with others). (1994). *L.D. Does NOT Mean Learning Dumd!,* South Orange, NJ: Maniet-Bellermann Foundation, Inc.

Mansbach, S. C. (1993, February/March). We must put family literacy on the national agenda. *Reading Today,* 37.

Marcia, J. E. (1967). Ego identity status: Relationship to change in self-esteem, "general adjustment," and authoritarianism *Journal of Personality, 35* (1), 119–133.

— (1980). Ego identity development. In J. Adelson (Ed.), *The handbook of adolescent psychology.* New York: Wiley.

Marsh, H. W. (1984). Relations among dimensions of self-attributions, dimensions of self-concept and academic achievement. *Journal of Educational Psychology, 76,* 1291–1308.

Marsh, H. W., Craven, R. G., & Debus, R. (1991). Self-concepts of young children 5 to 8 years of age: Measurement and multidimensional structure. *Journal of Educational Psychology, 83,* 377–392.

Marsh, H. W., Smith, I. D., & Barnes, J. (1985). Multi-dimensional self-concepts: Relations with sex and academic achievement. *Journal of Educational Psychology, 77,* 581–596.

Marshall, H. H. (1989). The development of self-concept. *Young Children, 44* (5), 44–51.

— (1990). Beyond the workplace metaphor: Toward conceptualizing the classroom as a learning setting. *Theory into Practice, 29* (2), 94–101.

— (Ed.). (1992). *Redefining student learning: Roots of educational change.* Norwood, NJ: Ablex.

Marshall, P. M. (1982). *Homework and social facilitation theory in teaching elementary school mathematics.* Unpublished doctoral dissertation, Stanford University, Stanford, CA.

Martin, G., & Pear, J. (1992). *Behavior modification: What it is and how to do it* (4th ed.). Englewood Cliffs, NJ: Prentice Hall.

Marzano, R. J., Pickering, D., & McTighe, J. (1993). *Assessing student outcomes: Performance assessment using the dimensions of learning model.* Alexandria, VA: Association for Supervision and Curriculum Development.

Maslow, A. H. (1943). A theory of human motivation. *Psychological Review, 50,* 370–396.

— (1954). *Motivation and personality.* New York: Harper & Row.

Mayer, R. E. (1979). Can advance organizers influence meaningful learning? *Review of Educational Research, 49,* 371–383.

McCaslin, M., & Good, T. (1992, April). Compliant cognition: The misalliance of management and instructional goals in current school reform. *Educational Researcher,* 4-17.

McClelland, D. C. (1958). Risk taking in children with high and low need for achievement. In J. W. Atkinson (Ed.), *Motives in fantasy, action, and society.* Princeton, NJ: Van Nostrand.

McClelland, D. C., & Pilon, D. (1983). Sources of adult motives in patterns of parent behavior in early childhood. *Journal of Personality and Social Psychology, 44,* 564–574.

— (1965). Toward a theory of motive acquisition. *American Psychologist, 20,* 321–333.

McClelland, J. L. (1988). Connectionist models and psychological evidence. *Journal of Memory and Language,* 27, 107–123.

McClelland, J. L., Rumelhart, D. E., & the PDP Research Group. (1986). *Parallel distributed processing: Explorations in the microstructure of cognition* (Vol. II). Cambridge, MA: Bradford Books.

McCombs, B.L. (1984). Processes and skills underlying continuing intrinsic motivation to learn: Toward a definition of motivational skills training interventions. *Educational Psychologist, 19,* 199–218.

— (1988). Motivational skills training: Combining metacognitive, cognitive, and affective learning strategies. In C. E. Weinstein, E. T. Goetz, & P. A. Alexander (Eds.), *Learning and study strategies: Issues in assessment, instruction, and evaluation.* New York: Academic Press.

McCombs, B. L., & Marzano, R. J. (1990). Putting the self in self-regulated learning: The self as agent in integrating will and skill. *Educational Psychologist, 25,* 51–70.

McCormick, C. B., & Levin, J. R. (1987). Mnemonic prose-learning strategies. In M. Pressely & M. McDaniel (Eds.), *Imaginary and related mnemonic processes.* New York: Springer-Verlag.

McCown, R. R., Casile, W. J., & Brookhart, S. M. (1994). *Continuous progress instruction: Evaluation report.* Pittsburgh, PA: Fox Chapel Area School District.

McCutcheon, G. (1980). How do elementary school teachers plan? The nature of planning and influences on it. *The Elementary School Journal, 81* (1), 4–23.

McDaniel, E. A., & McCarthy, H. D. (1989). Enhancing teacher efficacy in special education. *Teaching Exceptional Children, 21* (4), 34-38.

McKeachie, W. J. (1986). *Teaching tips: A guide book for the beginning college teacher.* Lexington, MA: D. C. Heath.

McLaughlin, B. (1984). Second language acquisition in childhood: Vol. 1. Preschool children (2d ed.) Hillsdale, NJ. Erlbaum.

McLaughlin, H. J. (1994). From negation to negotiation:

Moving away from the management metaphor. *Action in Teacher Education, 16* (1), 75–84.

McLaughlin, M. W., & Talbert, J. E. (1993). Introduction: New visions of teaching. In D. K. Cohen, M. W. McLaughlin, & J. E. Talbert (Eds.), *Teaching for understanding: Challenges for policy and practice.* San Francisco: Jossey-Bass.

McLeish, J. (1976). The lecture method. In N. L. Gage (Ed.), *The psychology of teaching methods: Seventy-fifth yearbook of the National Society for the Study of Education.* Chicago, IL: University of Chicago Press.

McLellan, H. (1993, March). Situated learning in focus: Introduction to special issue. *Educational Technology, 33,* 5–9.

Meichenbaum, D. (1977). *Cognitive behavior modification: An integrative approach.* New York: Plenum.

— (1985). *Stress inoculation training.* New York: Pergamon.

Meyer, R. G., & Salmon, P. (1988). *Abnormal psychology* (2d ed.). Needham Heights, MA: Allyn & Bacon.

Meyers, J., Gelzheiser, L., Yelich, G., & Gallagher, M. (1990). Classroom, remedial and resource teachers' views of pull-out programs. *Elementary School Journal, 90* (5), 531–545.

Miller, G. A. (1956). The magical number seven, plus or minus two: Some limits on our capacity for processing information. *Psychological Review, 63,* 81–97.

Millsap, M., Turnbull, B. J., Moss, M., Brigham, N., Gamse, B., & Marks, E. M. (1992). *The Chapter 1 implementation study: Interim study.* Washington, D.C.: U.S. Department of Education.

Mira, M. P., & Tyler, J. S. (1991). Students with traumatic brain injury: Making the transition from hospital to school. *Focus on Exceptional Children, 23* (5), 1–12.

Mitchell, T. (1990). Project 2000 gateway to success for some black males. *Black Issues in Higher Education, 7* (18), 49–50.

Moallem, M., & Driscoll, M. P. (1994, April). *An experienced teacher's model of thinking and teaching.* Paper presented at the Annual Meeting of the American Educational Research Association, New Orleans, LA.

Moll, L. C., Tapia, J., & Whitmore, K. F. (1993). Living knowledge: The social distribution of cultural resources for thinking. In G. Salomon (Ed.), *Distributed cognitions: Psychological and educational considerations.* Cambridge: Cambridge University Press.

Monson, M. P., & Monson, R. J. (1993). Exploring alternatives in student assessment: Shifting the focus to student learning in the middle school. *Middle School Journal, 25* (2), 46–50.

Morgan, M. (1984). Reward-induced decrements and increments in intrinsic motivation. *Review of Educational Research, 54,* 5–30.

Munby, H. (1987). Metaphor and teachers' knowledge. *Research in the Teaching of English, 21,* 377–397.

Murphy, J. M., Jellinek, M., Quinn, D., Smith, G., Poitrast, F. G., and Goshko, M. (1991). Substance abuse and serious child mistreatment: Prevalence, risk, and outcome in a court sample. *Child Abuse and Neglect, 15,* 197–211.

Natriello, G. (1987). The impact of evaluation processes on students. *Educational Psychologist, 22,* 155–175.

Newman, D., Griffin, P., & Cole, M. (1989). *The construction zone: Working for cognitive change in school.* New York: Cambridge University Press.

Newman, P. (1982). The peer group. In B. Wolman (Ed.), *Handbook of developmental psychology.* Englewood Cliffs, NJ: Prentice Hall.

Nitko, A. J. (1983). *Educational tests and measurement: An introduction.* New York: Harcourt Brace Jovanovich.

Norman, D. A. (1968). Toward a theory of memory and attention. *Psychological Review, 75,* 522–536.

— (1983). Some observations on mental models. In D. Gentner & A.L. Stevens (Eds.), *Mental models.* Hillsdale, NJ: Erlbaum.

Nye, R. D. (1979). *What is B. F. Skinner really saying?* Englewood Cliffs, NJ: Prentice Hall.

Nystul, M. S. (1984). Positive parenting leads to self-actualizing children. *Individual Psychology Journal of Adlerian Theory, Research and Practice, 40,* 177–183.

O'Brien, M., & Huston, A. C. (1985). Development and sex-typed play behavior in toddlers. *Developmental Psychology, 21* (5), 866–871.

Office of Educational Research and Improvement. (1990). *Grant announcement: National educational research and development center program.* Washington, D.C.: U.S. Department of Education.

Okagaki, L., & Sternberg, R. J. (1991). Cultural and parental influences on cognitive development. In L. Okagaki & R. J. Sternberg (Eds.), *Directors of development: Influences on the development of children's thinking.* Hillsdale, NJ: Erlbaum.

Okagaki, L., Sternberg, R. J., & Divecha, D. J. (1990, April). *Parental beliefs and children's early school performance.* Paper presented at the annual meeting of the American Educational Research Association, Boston.

O'Loughlin, M. (1992). Rethinking science education: Beyond Piagetian constructivism toward a sociocultural model of teaching and learning. *Journal of Research in Science Teaching, 29,* 791–820.

Olson, L. (1988). Children flourish here: 8 children and a theory changed a school world. *Education Week, 18* (1), 18–19.

O'Neil, J. (1991). Drive for national standards picking up steam. *Educational Leadership, 48* (5), 4–8.

— (1993). Can national standards make a difference? *Educational Leadership, 50* (5), 4–8.

Ormrod, J. E. (1990). *Human learning: Theories, principles, and educational applications.* New York: Macmillan.

Oser, F. K. (1994). Moral perspectives on teaching. In L. Darling-Hammond (Ed.), *Review of Research in Education* (volume 20). Washington, D.C.: American Educational Research Association.

Paivio, A. (1971). *Imagery and verbal processes.* New York: Holt, Rinehart & Winston.

— (1975). Coding distinctions and repetition effects in

memory. In G. H. Bower (Ed.), *The psychology of learning and motivation* (Vol. 9). New York: Academic Press.

— (1978). Dual coding: Theoretical issues and empirical evidence. In J. M. Scandura & C. J. Brainard (Eds.), *Structural/process models of complex human behavior*. Leyden, The Netherlands: Sijthoff & Nordhoff.

Palincsar, A. S. (1986). The role of dialogue in providing scaffolded instruction. *Educational Psychologist* (Special Issue on learning strategies), *21*, 73–98.

— (1987, April). *Reciprocal teaching: Field observations in remedial and content-area reading*. Paper presented at the annual meeting of the American Educational Research Association, Washington, D.C.

Palincsar, A. S., & Brown, A. L. (1984). Reciprocal teaching of comprehension-fostering and monitoring strategies. *Cognition and Instruction, 1*, 117–175.

Pallas, A. M., Natriello, G., & McDill, E.L. (1989). The changing nature of the disadvantaged population: Current dimensions and future trends. *Educational Researcher, 18* (5), 16–22.

Papalia, D. E., & Olds, S. W. (1992). *Human development* (5th ed.). New York: McGraw-Hill.

Papert, S. (1993). *The children's machine: Rethinking school in the age of the computer*. New York: Basic Books.

Parten, M. B. (1932). Social participation among preschool children. *Journal of Abnormal and Social Psychology, 27*, 243–269.

Pate, P. E., Homestead, E., & McGinnis, K. (1993). Designing rubrics for authentic assessment. *Middle School Journal, 25*(2), 25–27.

Patton, J. M. (1992). Assessment and identification of African-American learners with gifts and talents. *Exceptional Children, 59*, 150–159.

Pelletier, L. G., & Vallerand, R. J. (1989). Behavioral confirmation in social interaction: Effects of teachers' expectancies on students' intrinsic motivation. *Canadian Psychology, 30* (2a), 404.

Penner, J. (1984). *Why many college teachers cannot lecture*. Springfield, IL: Charles C. Thomas.

Pepitone, 1985

Pepitone, E. A. (1985) Children in cooperation and competitions: Antecedents and consequences of self-orientation. In R. E. Slavin et al (Eds.) *Learning to cooperate, cooperating to learn*. New York: Plenum Press.

Perkins, D. N. (1993). Teaching for understanding. *American Educator: The Professional Journal of the American Federation of Teachers, 17* (3) 8, 28–35.

Peters, E. E., & Levin, J. R. (1986). Effects of a mnemonic imagery strategy on good and poor reader's prose recall. *Reading Research Quarterly, 21*, 179–192.

Peters, R. (1977, August 19–26). *The place of Kohlberg's theory in moral education*. Paper presented at the First International Conference on Moral Development and Moral Education, Leicester, England.

Peterson, L. R., & Peterson, M. J. (1959). Short-term retention of individual verbal items. *Journal of Experimental Psychology, 58*, 193–198.

Peterson, P. L., & Comeaux, M. A. (1987). Teachers' schemata for classroom events: The mental scaffolding of teachers' thinking during classroom instruction. *Teaching and Teacher Education, 3*, 319–331.

Phye, G. D., & Andre, T. (Eds.). (1986). *Cognitive classroom learning*. Orlando, FL: Academic Press.

Piaget, J. (1932/1948). *The moral judgment of the child* (M. Cabain, Trans.). Glencoe, IL: Free Press.

— (1952). *The origins of intelligence in children* (M. Cook, Trans.). New York: International Universities Press.

— (1965). *The moral judgment of the child*. New York: Free Press. (Original work published 1932.)

— (1969). *Science of education and the psychology of the child*. New York: Viking.

— (1970). *Genetic epistemology*. New York: Columbia University Press.

Piaget, J., & Inhelder, B. (1969). *The psychology of the child*. New York: Basic Books.

Pinnell, G. S. (1989). Reading recovery: Helping at-risk children to read. *Elementary School Journal, 90*, 161–182.

Popham, W. J. (1981). *Modern educational measurement*. Englewood Cliffs, NJ: Prentice Hall.

— (1987, May). The merits of measurement-driven instruction. *Phi Delta Kappan, 68*, 679–682.

— (1990). *Modern educational measurement* (2d ed.). Englewood Cliffs, NJ: Prentice Hall.

— (1993). Educational testing in America: What's right, what's wrong? *Educational Measurement: Issues and Practice, 12* (1), 11–14.

Postman, N., & Weingartner, C. (1969). *Teaching as a subversive activity*. New York: Delacorte Press.

Powell, J. C. (1993). What does it mean to have authentic assessment? *Middle School Journal, 25* (2), 36–42.

Prawatt, R. S. (1989). Promoting access to knowledge strategy and disposition in students. *Review of Educational Research*, 59, 1–41.

(1992). Teacher beliefs about teaching and learning: A constructivist perspective. *American Journal of Education, 100*, 354–395.

Premack, D. (1959). Toward empirical behavior laws: I. Positive reinforcement. *Psychological Review, 66*, 219–233.

— (1965). Reinforcement theory (pp. 123–180). In D. Levine (Ed.), *Nebraska Symposium on Motivation* (Vol. 13). Lincoln: University of Nebraska Press.

Pressley, M., Borkowski, J. G., & O'Sullivan, J. T. (1984). Memory strategy instruction is made of this: Metamemory and durable strategy use. *Educational Psychologist, 9* (2), 94–107.

Price, S., & Hein, G. E. (1994, October). Scoring active assessments. *Science and Children*, 26–29.

Quality Education Data. (1993). *Educational technology trends, public schools, 1992–93*. Denver, CO: Quality Education Data.

Quay, H. C. (1986). Classification. In Quay & J. S. Werry

(Eds.), *Psychopathological disorders of childhood* (3d ed.). New York: Wiley.

Quay, H. C., & Peterson, D. R. (1987). *Manual for the Revised Behavior Problem Checklist.* Unpublished manuscript.

Quellmalz, E. S. (1991). Developing criteria for performance assessments: The missing link. *Applied Measurement in Education, 4* (4), 319–331.

Rachlin, H. (1991). *Introduction to modern behaviorism* (3d ed.). New York: W. H. Freeman.

Ramos-Ford, V., & Gardner, H. (1990). Giftedness from a multiple intelligences perspective. In N. Colangelo & G. Davis (Eds.), *The handbook of gifted education.* Needham Heights, MA: Allyn & Bacon.

Randolph, C. H., & Evertson, C. M. (1994). Images of management for learner-centered classrooms. *Action in Teacher Education, 16* (1), 55–63.

Rathus, S. A. (1988). *Understanding child development.* New York: Holt, Rinehart & Winston.

Ravitch, D. (1990). Multiculturalism: E Pluribus Plures. *The American Scholar, 54,* 337–354.

Reese, H. W. (1977). Imagery and associative memory. In R. V. Kail & J. W. Hagen (Eds.), *Perspectives on the development of memory and cognition.* Hillsdale, NJ: Erlbaum.

Reglin, G. L., & Adams, D. R. (1990). Why Asian-American high school students have higher grade point averages and SAT scores than other high school students. *The High School Journal, 73,* 143–149.

Reimer, R. H., Paolitto, D. P., & Hersh, R. H. (1983). *Promoting moral growth: From Piaget to Kohlberg* (2d ed.). New York: Longman.

Renzulli, J. (1982). Dear Mr. and Mrs. Copernicus: We regret to inform you . . . . *Gifted Child Quarterly, 26,* 11–14.

Renzulli, J. S., & Reis, S. M. (1991). The schoolwide enrichment model: A comprehensive plan for the development of creative productivity. In N. Colangelo & G. Davis (Eds.), *Handbook of gifted education.* Needham Heights, MA: Allyn & Bacon.

Resichauer, E. O. (1981). *The Japanese.* Cambridge, MA: Harvard University Press.

Reynolds, G. S. (1968). *A primer of operant conditioning.* Glenview, IL: Scott, Foresman.

Ribich, F., Barone, W., & Agostino, V. R. (1991, February). *A semantic differential: Perspectives on underachieving gifted students.* Paper presented at the Eastern Educational Research Association, Boston.

Richardson, E. H. (1981). Cultural and historical perspectives in counseling American Indians. In D. W. Sue (Ed.), *Counseling the culturally different.* New York: John Wiley.

Rieber, L. (1991a). Animation, incidental learning, and continuing motivation. *Journal of Educational Psychology, 83,* 318–328.

— (1991b, February). *Computer-based microworlds: A bridge between constructivism and direct instruction.* Paper presented at the Annual Meeting of the Association of Educational Communications and Technology, Orlando, FL.

Rogoff, B. (1990). *Apprenticeship in thinking.* New York: Oxford University Press.

Rosenberg, M. (1979). *Conceiving the self.* New York: Basic Books.

Rosenkrans, M. A. (1967). Imitation in children as a function of perceived similarity to a social model and vicarious reinforcement. *Journal of Personality and Social Psychology, 7,* 301–315.

Rosenshine, B. V. (1979). Content, time, and direct instruction. In P. Peterson & H. Walberg (Eds.), *Research on teaching: Concepts, findings, and implications.* Berkeley, CA: McCutchan.

— (1980). How time is spent in elementary classrooms. In C. Denham & A. Lieberman (Eds.), *Time to learn.* Washington, D.C.: National Institute of Education.

— (1983). Teaching functions in instructional programs. *Elementary School Journal, 83,* 335–351.

— (1986). Synthesis of research on explicit teaching. *Educational Leadership, 43* (7), 60–69.

Rosenshine, B., & Meister, C. (1991, April). *Reciprocal teaching: A review of nineteen experimental studies.* Paper presented at the Annual Meeting of the American Educational Research Association, Chicago.

Rosenthal, R., & Jacobson, L. (1968). *Pygmalion in the classroom: Teacher expectations and pupils' intellectual development.* New York: Holt, Rinehart & Winston.

Rosenthal, T. L., & Bandura, A. (1978). Psychological modeling: Theory and practice. In S. L. Garfield & A. E. Bergin (Eds.), *Handbook of psychotherapy and behavior change: An empirical analysis* (2d ed.). New York: Wiley.

Rotter, J. (1954). *Social learning and clinical psychology.* Englewood Cliffs, NJ: Prentice Hall.

Rowe, M. B. (1986). Wait time: Slowing down may be a way of speeding up! *Journal of Teacher Education, 37* (1), 43–50.

Rowland, G. (1994). Designing and evaluating: Creating futures and appreciating error. *Educational Technology, 34* (1), 10–22.

Royer, J. M. (1979). Theories of the transfer of learning. *Educational Psychologist, 14,* 53–69.

Royer, J. M., & Cable, G. W. (1976). Illustrations, analogies, and facilitative transfer in prose learning. *Journal of Educational Psychology, 68,* 205–209.

Royer, J. M., & Feldman, R. S. (1984). *Educational psychology: Applications and theory.* New York: Alfred A. Knopf.

Ruben, K., Maioni, T., & Hornung, M. (1976). Free play behaviors in middle and lower class preschools: Parten and Piaget revisited. *Child Development, 47,* 414–419.

Ruben, K., Watson, K., & Jambor, T. (1978). Free play behaviors in preschool and kindergarten children. *Child Development, 49,* 534–536.

Rubin, L. J. (1985). *Artistry in teaching.* New York: Random House.

Ruble, D. N., Boggiano, A. K., Feldman, N. S., & Loebl, J. H. (1980). Developmental analysis of the role of social comparison in self-evaluation. *Developmental Psychology, 16,* 105–115.

Rumelhart, D. E. (1980). Schemata: The building blocks of cognition. In R. Spiro, B. C. Bruce, & W. F. Brewer (Eds.), *Theoretical issues in reading comprehension*. Hillsdale, NJ: Erlbaum.

Rutter, M. (1980). *Changing youth in a changing society: Patterns of adolescent development and disorder.* Cambridge, MA: Harvard University Press.

Ryan, K., & McLean, G. F. (Eds.). (1987). *Character development in schools and beyond.* New York: Praeger.

Sacks, O. W. (1989). *Seeing voices: A journey into the world of the deaf.* Berkeley: University of California Press.

Sadker, M., Sadker, D., & Klein, S. (1991). The issue of gender in elementary and secondary education. In G. Grant (Ed.), *Review of Research in Education*, Vol. 17. Washington, D.C.: American Educational Research Association.

Salend, S. J. (1994). *Effective mainstreaming: Creating inclusive classrooms* (2d ed.). New York: Macmillan.

Salomon,G., & Perkins, D. N. (1989). Rocky roads to transfer: Rethinking mechanisms of a neglected phenomenon. *Educational Psychologist, 24* (2), 113–142.

Sanders, D. (1987). Cultural conflicts: An important factor in the academic failures of American Indian students. *Journal of Multicultural Counseling and Development, 15,* 81–90.

Sappington, T. E. (1984). Creating learning environments conducive to change: The role of fear/safety in the adult learning process. *Innovative Higher Education, 9* (1), 19–29.

Sarafino, E. (1984). Intrinsic motivation and delay of gratification in preschoolers: The variables of reward salience and length of expected delay. *British Journal of Developmental Psychology, 2* (2), 149–156.

Sarvela, P. D., & Noonan, J. V. (1988). Testing and computer-based instruction: Psychometric considerations. *Educational Technology, 28* (5), 17–20.

Sattler, J. (1992). *Assessment of children* (3d ed., rev.). San Diego: Jerome M. Sattler.

Saxe, G. B. (1990). *Culture and cognitive development: Studies in mathematical understanding.* Hillsdale, NJ: Erlbaum.

Schoenfeld, A. H. (1988). When good teaching leads to bad results: The disasters of "well-taught" mathematics classes. *Educational Psychologist, 23,* 145–166.

Schommer, M. (1990). Effects of beliefs about the nature of knowledge on comprehension. *Journal of Educational Psychology, 82,* 498–504.

— (1993). Epistemological development and academic performance among secondary school students. *Journal of Educational Psychology, 85,* 406–411.

Schunk, D. H. (1983). Developing children's self-efficacy and skills: The roles of social comparative information and goal setting. *Contemporary Educational Psychology, 8,* 76–86.

— (1987). Peer models and children's behavioral change. *Review of Educational Research, 57,* 149–174.

— (1991). *Learning theories: An educational perspective.* New York: Macmillan.

Schunk, D. H., & Gaa, J. P. (1981). Goal-setting influence on learning and self-evaluation. *Journal of Classroom Interaction, 16* (2), 38–44.

Schunk, D. H., Hanson, A. R., & Cox, P. D. (1987). Peer-model attributes and children's achievement behaviors. *Journal of Educational Psychology, 79,* 54–61.

Schunk, D. H., & Zimmerman, B. J. (Eds.) (1994). *Self-regulation of learning and performance: Issues and educational applications.* Hillsdale, NJ: Erlbaum.

Schwebel, A. I., & Cherlin, D. L. (1972). Physical and social distancing in teacher-pupil relationships. *Journal of Educational Psychology, 63,* 543–550.

Scott, K. P., Dwyer, C. A., & Lieb-Brilhart, B. (1985). Sex equity in reading and communication. In S. S. Klein (Ed.), *Handbook for achieving sex equity through education.* Baltimore, MD: Johns Hopkins University Press.

Scott, L. (December, 1994). Personal communication.

Seifert, K. L., & Hoffnung, R. J. (1987). *Child and adolescent development.* Boston: Houghton Mifflin.

Seligman, M. E. P. (1975). *Helplessness: On depression, development, and death.* San Francisco: W. H. Freeman.

Seligman, M. E. P., & Meier, S. F. (1967). Failure to escape traumatic shock. *Journal of Experimental Psychology, 74,* 1–9.

Semb, G. B., & Ellis, J. A. (1994). Knowledge taught in school: What is remembered? *Review of Educational Research, 64,* 253–286.

Shank, G. (1995). Personal communication.

Sharan, S. (1985). Cooperative learning and the multiethnic classroom (pp. 255–276). In R. Slavin, S. Sharan, S. Kagan, R. Lazarowitz, C. Webb, & R. Schmuck (Eds.), *Learning to cooperate, cooperating to learn.* New York: Plenum.

Sharan, S. (Ed.) (1990). *Cooperative learning: Theory and research.* New York: Praeger.

Shavelson, R. J., Baxter, G. P., & Pine, J. (1992). Performance assessments: Political rhetoric and measurement reality. *Educational Researcher, 21* (4), 22–27.

Shepard, L. A. (1991). Psychometricians' beliefs about learning. *Educational Researcher, 29* (7), 2–16.

Shepherd-Look, D. (1982). Sex differentiation and the development of sex roles. In B. Wolman (Ed.), *Handbook of developmental psychology.* Englewood Cliffs, NJ: Prentice Hall.

Shiffrin, R. M., & Schneider, W. (1977). Controlled and automatic human information processing: Perceptual learning, automatic attending, and a general theory. *Psychological Review, 84,* 127–190.

Sidorowicz, L. S., & Lunney, G. S. (1980). Baby X revisited. *Sex Roles, 6,* 67–73.

Siegler, R. S. (1983). Five generalizations about cognitive development. *American Psychologist, 38,* 263–277.

— (1984). Mechanisms of cognitive growth: Variation and selection. In R. J. Sternberg (Ed.), *Mechanisms of cognitive development.* New York: Freeman.

— (1986). *Children's thinking.* Englewood Cliffs, NJ: Prentice Hall.

Simon, H. A. (1974). How big is a chunk? *Science, 183,* 482–488.

Simon, S., Ditricks, R., & Speckhart, L. (1975). Students in observational paired-associate learning: Informational, social, and individual difference variables. *Journal of Experimental Child Psychology, 20,* 81–104.

Simpson, G. E., & Yinger, J. M. (1985). *Racial and cultural minorities.* New York: Harper & Row.

Simpson, R. L. (1980). Modifying the attitudes of regular class students toward the handicapped. *Focus on Exceptional Children, 13* (3), 1–11.

Skinner, B. F. (1938). *The behavior of organisms: An experimental analysis.* New York: Appleton-Century-Crofts.

— (1953). *Science and human behavior.* New York: Macmillan.

— (1954). The science of learning and the art of teaching. *Harvard Educational Review, 24,* 86–97.

— (1958). Teaching machines. *Science, 128,* 969–977.

— (1963). Operant behavior. *American Psychologist, 18,* 503–515.

— (1968). *The technology of teaching.* New York: Appleton-Century-Crofts.

— (1969). *Contingencies of reinforcement.* Englewood Cliffs, NJ: Prentice Hall.

— (1987a). What ever happened to psychology as the science of behavior? *American Psychologist, 42,* 780–786.

— (1987b). *Upon further reflection.* Englewood Cliffs, NJ: Prentice Hall.

— (1989). The origins of cognitive thought. *American Psychologist, 44,* 13–18.

Slavin, R. E. (1988). Cooperative learning: A best evidence synthesis, Dr. R. E. Slavin (Ed.). *School and Classroom Organization.* Hillsdale, N.J.: Erlbaum.

Slavin, R. E. (1987). Grouping for instruction: Equity and effectiveness. *Equity and Excellence, 23,* 31–36.

— (1990). *Cooperative learning: Theory, research, and practice.* Englewood Cliffs, NJ: Prentice Hall.

— (1991). Synthesis of research on cooperative learning. *Educational Leadership, 48* (5), 71–82.

— (1995). *Cooperative learning* (2d ed.). Needham Heights, MA: Allyn & Bacon.

Slavin, R. E., & Karweit, N. (1985). Effects of whole class, ability grouped, and individualized instruction on mathematics achievement. *American Educational Reseach Journal, 22,* 351–368.

Slavin, R. E., Karweit, N. L., & Wasik, B. A. (1994). *Preventing early school failure: Research on effective strategies.* Needham Heights, MA: Allyn & Bacon.

Sleeter, C. E., & Grant, C. A. (1987). An analysis of multicultural education in the United States. *Harvard Educational Review, 57,* 421–444.

— (1988). *Making choices for multicultural education: Five approaches to race, class, and gender.* Columbus, OH: Merrill.

Smith, G. B. (1986). Self-concept and the learning disabled child. *Journal of Reading, Writing, and Learning Disabilities International, 2* (3), 237–241.

Smith, J. (1991). What will the new SAT look like? An interview with Lawrence Hecht. *d'News: The Newsletter of Division D of the American Educational Research Association, 1* (2), 1–4.

Snider, V. E. (1990). What we know about learning styles from research in special education. *Educational Leadership, 48* (2), 53.

Snow, R. E., Corno, L., & Jackson, D. (1995). Individual differences in affective and conative functions. In D. C. Berliner (Ed.), *Handbook of educational psychology.* New York: Macmillan.

Snyder, L., Bates, E., & Bretherton, I. (1981). Content and context in early lexical development. *Journal of Child Language, 8,* 565–582.

Soodak, L. C., & Podell, D. M. (1993). Teacher efficacy and student problems as factors in special education referral. *Journal of Special Education, 27* (1), 66–81.

Spence, J. T. (1984). Gender identity and its implications for concepts of masculinity and femininity. In T. B. Sonderegger (Ed.), *Nebraska Symposium on Motivation* (Vol. 32). Lincoln: University of Nebraska Press.

Spiro, R. J., Feltovich, P. J., Jacobson, M. J., & Coulson, R. L. (1991, May). Cognitive flexibility, constructivism, and hypertext: Random access instruction for advanced knowledge acquisition in ill-structured domains. *Educational Technology, 31,* 24–33.

Squires, D. A., Huitt, W. G., & Segars, J. K. (1983). *Effective schools and classrooms: A research-based perspective.* Alexandria, VA: Association for Supervision and Curriculum Development.

Stacy, K. (1992). Mathematical problem solving in groups: Are two heads better than one? *Journal of Mathematical Behavior, 11* (3), 261–275.

Stallings, J., & Krasavage, E. M. (1986). Program implementation and student achievement in a four-year Madeline Hunter follow-through project. *Elementary School Journal, 87* (2), 117–138.

Starko, A. J. (1995). *Creativity in the classroom: Schools of curious delight.* White Plains, NY: Longman.

Starrat, R. J. (1987). Moral education in the high school classroom. In K. Ryan & G. McLean (Eds.), *Character development in schools and beyond.* New York: Praeger.

Steinberg, L., Elman, J. D., & Mounts, N. S. (1989). Authoritative parenting, psychosocial maturity, and academic success among adolescents. *Child Development, 60,* 1424–1436.

Stephan, W. G. (1985). Intergroup relations. In G. Lindzey & E. Aronson (Eds.). *The handbook of social psychology, Vol. 2.* (3d ed.). New York: Random House.

Sternberg, R. J. (1986). *Intelligence applied: Understanding and increasing your own intellectual skills.* New York: Harcourt Brace Jovanovich.

— (1989). *The triarchic mind: A new theory of human intelligence.* New York: Penguin Books.

Stevens, R. J., Madden, N. A., Slavin, R. E., & Farnish, A. M. (1987). Cooperative integrated reading and composition: Two field experiments. *Reading Research Quarterly, 22,* 433–454.

Stevenson, H. W., & Lee, S. (1990). Contexts of achievement. *Monographs of the Society for Research in Child Development, 55* (1-2, Serial No. 221).

Stewart, M. J., & Corbin, C. B. (1988). Feedback dependence among low confidence preadolescent boys and girls. *Research Quarterly for Exercise and Sport, 59,* (2), 160–164.

Stiggins, R. J. (1991). Facing the challenges of a new era of educational assessment. *Applied Measurement in Education, 4* (4), 263–273.

— (1994). *Student-centered classroom assessment.* New York: Merrill-Macmillan.

Stiggins, R. J., Frisbie, D. A., & Griswold, P. A. (1989). Inside high school grading practices: Building a research agenda. *Educational Measurement: Issues and Practices, 8* (2), 5–14.

Stigler, J. W., Lee, S., & Stevenson, H. W. (1987). Mathematics classrooms in Japan, Taiwan, and the United States. *Child Development, 58,* 1272–1285.

Stipek, D. J. (1993). *Motivation to learn: From theory to practice* (2d ed.). Needham Heights, MA: Allyn & Bacon.

Stipek, D. J., & McIver, D. (1989). Developmental change in children's assessment of intellectual competence. *Child Development, 60,* 531–538.

Stipek, D. J., Recchia, S., and McClintic, S. (1992). Self-evaluation in young children. *Monographs of the Society for Research in Child Development, 57* (1, Serial No. 226).

Strauss, C. C., Smith, K., Frame, C., & Forchand, R. (1985). Personal and interpersonal characteristics associated with childhood obesity. *Journal of Pediatric Psychology, 10,* 337–343.

Strauss, S. (1993). Theories of learning and development for academics and educators. *Educational Psychologist, 28* (3), 191–204.

Strunk, W., Jr., & White, E.B. (1979). *The elements of style* (3d ed.). New York: Macmillan.

Stuart, J., & Rutherford, R. (1978). Medical student concentration during lectures. *Lancet, 2,* 514–516.

Sulzer, B., & Mayer, G. R. (1972). *Behavior modification procedures for school personnel.* New York: Holt, Rinehart & Winston.

Sulzer-Azaroff, B., & Mayer, G. R. (1986). *Achieving educational excellence through behavioral strategies.* New York: Holt, Rinehart & Winston.

Suzuki, B. H. (1983). The education of Asian and Pacific Americans: An introductory overview. In D. Nakanishi & M. Hirano-Nakanishi (Eds.), *The education of Asian and Pacific Americans: Historical perspectives and prescriptions for the future.* Phoenix: Oryx Press.

Swanson, H. L., O'Connor, J. E., & Cooney, J. B. (1990). An information processing analysis of expert and novice teachers' problem-solving. *American Educational Research Journal , 27,* (3), 533–556.

Talbert, J.E., & McLaughlin, M.W. (1993). Understanding teaching in context. In D. K. Cohen. M. W. Mclaughlin, & J. E. Talbert (Eds.), *Teaching for understanding: Challenges for policy and practice.* San Francisco: Jossey-Bass.

Tanner, J. (1978a). *Education and physical growth* (2d ed.). London: Hadder & Stoughton.

— (1978b). *Fetus into man: Physical growth from conception to maturity.* Cambridge, MA: Harvard University Press.

Taylor, R. P. (Ed.). (1980). *The computer in the school: Tutor, tool, tutee.* New York: Teachers College Press.

Templin, M. C. (1957). Certain language skills in children: Their development and interrelationships. *University of Minnesota Institute of Child Welfare Monograph,* 26.

Terrace, H. (1963a). Discrimination learning with and without errors. *Journal of Experimental Analysis of Behavior, 6,* 1–27.

— (1963b). Errorless transfer of a discrimination across two continua. *Journal of Experimental Analysis of Behavior, 6,* 223–232.

Thorndike, E. L. (1913). *Educational psychology. Vol. II. The psychology of learning.* New York: Teachers College, Columbia University.

Tishman, S., Perkins, D., & Jay, E. (1995). *A thinking classroom: Learning and teaching in a culture of thinking.* Needham Heights, MA: Allyn & Bacon.

Tobias, S. (1982). When do instructional methods make a difference? *Educational Researcher, 11* (4), 4–10.

Tobin, K. (1990). Changing metaphors and beliefs: A master switch for learning? *Theory into Practice, 29* (2) 122–127

Tobin, K. G. (1987). The role of wait-time in higher cognitive level learning. *Review of Educational Research, 57,* 69–95.

Tobin, K. G., & Capie, W. (1982). Relationships between classroom process variables and middle-school science achievement. *Journal of Educational Psychology, 74,* 441–454.

Tobin, K. G., & Dawson, G. (1992). Constraints to curriculum reform: Teachers and the myth of schooling. *Educational Technology Research and Development, 40* (1), 81–92.

Triandis, H. C. (1986). Toward pluralism in education. G. K. Verma, K. Mallick, & C. Modgil (Eds.) In S. Modgil, *Multicultural education: The interminable debate,* London: Falmer.

Tucker, J. A. (1985). Curriculum-based assessment: An introduction. *Exceptional Children, 52,* 199–204.

Tuckman, B. W. (1988). *Testing for teachers* (2d ed.). Orlando, FL: Harcourt Brace Jovanovich.

Tudge, J., & Rogoff, B. (1989). Peer influences on cognitive development: Piagetian and Vygotskian perspectives. In M. H. Bornstein & J. S. Bruner (Eds.), *Interaction in human development.* Hillsdale, NJ: Erlbaum.

Tulving, E. (1972). Episodic and semantic memory. In E. Tulving & W. Donaldson (Eds.), *Organization of memory.* New York: Academic Press.

Turnbull, H. R., III. (1993). *Free appropriate public education: The law and children with disabilities.* Denver: Love Publishing.

Tyler, R. W. (1989). Educating children from minority families. *Educational Horizons, 67* (4), 114–118.

Unger, R. K., Draper, R. D., & Pendergrass, M. L. (1986). Personal epistimology and personal experience. *Journal of Social Issues, 42* (2), 67–79.

U.S. Department of Education. (1989). *Eleventh annual report to Congress of the implementation of the Education of the Handicapped Act.* Washington, D.C.: U.S. Government Printing Office.

— (1992). *Fourteenth annual report to Congress on the Individuals with Disabilities Act.* Washington, D.C.: U.S. Department of Education.

Valero-Figueira, E. (1988). Hispanic children. *Teaching Exceptional Children, 20,* 47–49.

Vasquez, J. A. (1990). Teaching to the distinctive traits of minority students. *The Clearing House, 63,* 299–304.

Vasudev, J., & Hummel, R. C. (1987). Moral stage sequence and principled reasoning in an Indian sample. *Human Development, 30,* 105–118.

Veenman, S. (1984). Perceived problems of beginning teachers. *Review of Educational Research, 54* (2), 143–178.

Verner, C., & Dickinson, G. (1967). The lecture: An analysis and review of research. *Adult Education, 17* (2), 85–100.

Villegas, A. (1991). *Culturally responsive pedagogy for the 1990s and beyond.* Princeton, NJ: Educational Testing Service.

Virgina Education Association & Appalachia Educational Laboratory (1992). *Alternative assessments in math and science: Moving toward a moving target.* Charleston, WV: Appalachian Educational Laboratory.

von Glasersfeld, E. (1988). *The construction of knowledge.* Salinas, CA: Intersystems Publications.

Vosniadou, S. (1988, April). *Knowledge restructuring and science instruction.* Paper presented at the Annual Meeting of the American Educational Research Association, New Orleans.

Vygotsky, L. S. (1962). *Thought and language.* Cambridge, MA: The MIT Press.

— (1978). *Mind in society.* Cambridge, MA: Harvard University Press.

— (1981). The genesis of higher mental functions. In J. V. Wertsch (Ed.), *The concept of activity in Soviet psychology.* Armonk, NY: Sharpe.

— (1987). *Thinking and speech.* New York: Plenum. (Originally published 1934).

Wadsworth, B. J. (1984). *Piaget's theory of cognitive development: An introduction for students of psychology and education* (3d ed.). New York: Longman.

Waggoner, M., Chinn, C., Yi, H., and Anderson, R. C. (1993, April). *Reflective story discussions.* Paper presented at the Annual Meeting of the American Educational Research Association, Atlanta, GA.

Walker, L. J., DeVries, B., & Trevethan, S. D. (1987). Moral stages and moral orientations in real-life and hypothetical dilemmas. *Child Development, 58,* 842–858.

Walters, G. C., & Grusec, J. E. (1977). *Punishment.* San Francisco: Freeman.

Wang, M. C., Haertel, G. D., & Walberg, H. J. (1993). Toward a knowledge base of school learning. *Review of Educational Research, 63* (3), 249–294.

Wasik, B. A., & Karweit, N. L. (1994). Off to a good start: Effects of birth-to-three interventions on early school success. In R. E. Slavin, N. L. Karweit, & B. A. Wasik, *Preventing early school failure: Research on effective strategies.* Needham Heights, MA: Allyn & Bacon.

Watkins, D., & Astilla, E. (1984). The dimensionality, antecedents, and study method correlates of the causal attribution of Filipino children. *Journal of Social Psychology, 124* (2), 191–199.

Wechsler, D. (1958). *The measurement and appraisal of adult intelligence* (4th ed.). Baltimore, MD: Williams & Wilkins.

Weiner, B. (1980a). *Human motivation.* New York: Holt, Rinehart & Winston.

— (1980b). The role of affect in rational (attributional) approaches to human motivation. *Educational Researcher, 9,* 4–11.

— (1986). *An attributional theory of motivation and emotion.* New York: Springer-Verlag.

— (1992). *Human motivation: Metaphors, theories and research.* Newbury Park, CA: Sage Publications.

Weiner, H. (1969). Controlling human fixed-interval's performance. *Journal of Experimental Analysis of Behavior, 12,* 349–373.

Weinstein, C. S., & Mignano, A. (1993). *Elementary classroom management: Lessons from research and practice.* New York: McGraw-Hill.

Weinstein, C. S., Woolfolk, A. E., Dittmeier, L., & Shanker, U. (1994). Protector or prison guard? Using metaphors and media to explore student teachers' thinking about classroom management. *Action in Teacher Education, 16* (1), 41–54.

West, C. K., Farmer, J. A., & Wolff, P. M. (1991). *Instructional design: Implications from cognitive science.* Englewood Cliffs, NJ: Prentice Hall.

Wheeler, R. (1977 April). Predisposition toward cooperation and competition: Cooperative and competitive classroom effects. Paper presented at the Annual Meeting of the American Psychological Association, San Francisco.

White, B. Y. (1993). TinkerTools: Causal models, conceptual change, and science education. *Cognition and Instruction, 10,* 1–100.

Whitmore, J. R. (1986). Understanding a lack of motivation to excel. *Gifted Child Quarterly, 30,* 66–69.

Wiersma, W. (1995). *Research methods in education: An introduction* (6th ed.). Needham Heights, MA: Allyn & Bacon.

Wiggins, C. (1989). Teaching to the (authentic) test. *Educational Leadership, 46,* 1–47.

Wiggins, G. P. (1993). *Assessing student performance.* San Francisco: Jossey-Bass.

Williams J. D., & Snipper, G. C. (1990). *Literary and bilingualism.* White Plains, NY: Longman.

Willig, A. C. (1985). A meta-analysis of selection studies on the effectiveness of bilingual education. *Review of Educational Research, 55,* 269–317.

Wineburg, S. S. (1987). The self-fulfillment of the self-fulfilling prophecy: A critical appraisal. *Educational Researcher, 16,* 28–37.

Wittrock, M. C. (1974). Learning as a generative process. *Educational Psychologist, 11,* 87–95.

— (1990). Generative processes of comprehension. *Educational Psychologist, 24,* 345–376.

— (1991). Generative teaching and comprehension. *Elementary School Journal, 92,* 167–182.

Wittrock, M. C., Marks, C. B., & Doctorow, M. J. (1975). Reading as a generative process. *Journal of Educational Psychology, 67,* 484–489.

Woditsch, G. A. & Schmittroth, J. (1991). *The thoughtful teacher's guide to thinking skills.* Hillsdale, NJ: Erlbaum.

Wolf, D. P. (1989). Portfolio assessment: Sampling student work. *Educational Leadership, 46* (4), 36–38.

Wolf, M. M., Giles, D. K., & Hall, V. R. (1968). Experiments with token reinforcement in a remedial classroom. *Behavioral Research and Therapy, 6,* 51–64.

Wolf, R. M. (1979). Achievement in the United States. In H. J. Walberg (Ed.), *Educational environments and effects: Evaluation, policy, and productivity.* Berkeley, CA: McCutchan.

Wolfgang, C. H. (1995). *Solving discipline problems: Methods and models for today's teachers* (3d ed.). Needham Heights, MA: Allyn & Bacon.

Wolfgang, C. H., & Wolfgang, M. E. (1995). *Three Faces of Discipline for Early Childhood.* Needham Heights, MA: Allyn & Bacon.

Wollen, K. A., & Lowry, D. H. (1974). Conditions that determine effectiveness of picture-mediated paired-associated learning. *Journal of Experimental Psychology, 102,* 181–183.

Women's Educational Equity Program. (1983). *Fair play: Developing self-concept and decision-making skills in the middle school.* Newton, MA: Education Development Center.

Wong, K. K. (1994). Governance structure, resource allocation, and equity policy. *Review of Research in Education, 20,* 257–289.

Wood, B. S. (1981). *Children and communication: Verbal and nonverbal language development.* (2d ed.). Englewood Cliffs, NJ: Prentice Hall.

Wood, D., Bruner, J., & Ross, S. (1976). The role of tutoring in problem solving. *British Journal of Psychology, 66,* 181–191.

Woolfolk, A. E. (1995). *Educational psychology* (6th ed.). Needham Heights, MA: Allyn & Bacon.

Woolfolk, A. E., & Hoy, W. K. (1990). Prospective teachers' sense of efficacy and beliefs about control. *Journal of Educational Psychology, 82,* 81–91.

Woolfolk, A. E., & McCune-Nicolich, L. (1984). *Educational psychology for teachers* (2d ed.). Englewood Cliffs, NJ: Prentice Hall.

Worthen, B. R., & Spandel, V. (1991, February). Putting the standardized test debate in perspective. *Educational Leadership,* 65–69.

Wynn, E. A. (1987). Students and schools. In K. Ryan & G. McLean (Eds.), *Character development in schools and beyond.* New York: Praeger.

Wynn, R. L., & Fletcher, C. (1987). Sex role development and early educational experiences. In D. B. Carter (Ed.), *Current conceptions of sex roles and sex typing.* New York: Praeger.

Yao, E. L. (1985). Adjustment needs of Asian immigrant children. *Elementary School Guidance and Counseling, 19,* 222–227.

Yee, A. H. (1992). Asians as stereotypes and students: Misperceptions that persist. *Educational Psychology Review, 4,* 95–132.

Zerega, M. E., Haertel, G. D., Tsai, S., & Walberg, H. J. (1986). Late adolescent sex differences in science learning. *Science Education, 70* (4), 447–460.

Zessoules, R., Wolf, D., & Gardner, H. (1988). A better balance: Arts PROPEL as an alternative to discipline-based art education. In J. Burton, A. Lederman, and P. London (Eds.), *Beyond discipline-based art education.* North Dartmouth, MA: University Council on Art Education.

Zirpoli, T. J. (1989). Child abuse and children with handicaps. *Remedial and Special Education, 7* (2), 39–48.

GLOSSARY

absolute standard A grading system in which scores are compared to a set performance standard.

accommodation In Piaget's theory, a process of modifying existing cognitive structures or creating additional ones as a result of new experiences.

achievement motivation A person's desire or tendency to overcome obstacles and to accomplish some difficult task through the exercise of power.

acronym A word formed from the initial letters of a group of words (e.g., NASA).

acrostic A sentence used as a memory cue for information to be remembered.

action zones The areas in a classroom where a teacher directs most of his or her attention.

active learning Students engaging in meaningful tasks in which they have ownership of content.

additive bilingualism A form of bilingualism in which students have achieved complete literacy in two languages. Because of conceptual interdependence between languages, learning in one aids achievement in the other.

advance organizer Information presented prior to instruction that assists in understanding new information by relating it to existing knowledge.

affective domain Learning outcomes that relate to emotions, values, and attitudes, as classified by Krathwohl's taxonomy.

affordances Opportunities offered a person by his or her environment.

anticipatory set The first step in Hunter's approach to lesson delivery. This step establishes expectancies or a mind-set in students that anticipates the material to be covered.

applied behavior analysis The analysis of behavior problems and the prescription of remedies.

ARCS model A model teachers can use to identify and solve motivational problems in their classrooms. The ARCS model defines four categories of motivation that must exist for students to be motivated to learn: attention, relevance, confidence, and satisfaction.

arousal effects Consequences of modeling that change an observer's physical and psychological reactions caused by the model's expressed emotions and actions.

assertive discipline An approach to misbehavior based on principles of applied behavior analysis.

assessment The process of gathering, analyzing, and interpreting information about students and their progress in school.

assimilation In Piaget's theory, a process through which new experiences are incorporated into existing cognitive structures such as schemes.

assimilation A view of diversity in which a hierarchy of values is assumed so that members of ethnic groups are expected to adopt and live by the values of the dominant culture.

attention The process used to focus on one or more aspects of the environment to the exclusion of other aspects.

attitude According to Gagné, a learned capability that influences a person's choice of personal action.

attribution theory The explanations, reasons, or excuses students give for their own successes or failures in learning.

attribution training Attempting to change the student's style of explaining his or her own learning successes or failures.

authentic activities Instructional tasks that provide culturally and situationally relevant contexts for learning and development.

authentic assessment Assessment of higher-order skills such as problem solving and critical thinking in real-life contexts through the use of projects, exhibitions, demonstrations, portfolios, observations, science fairs, peer- and self-assessments.

authentic task An instructional task that is part of the world outside of school (e.g., comparison shopping) or part of the culture of a particular discipline (e.g., "exploiting extreme cases" in mathematics reasoning).

authoritative leadership Authority established through the flexible implementation of standards and characterized by discussion with and explanation to followers.

automatic attention The process of attention that occurs without effort.

automaticity The point at which a mental operation can be executed without conscious effort.

autonomy Independence. Autonomy versus shame and doubt marks Stage 2 of Erikson's theory of psychosocial development.

aversive Undesirable.

behavioral approach A school of thought in which learning is explained through observable aspects of the environment instead of mental or cognitive processes.

behavioral objectives Specific statements of goals, which include the behavior students should be able to perform as a result of instruction, the conditions of their performance, and the criteria used to judge attainment of the goals.

benchmarks Standards against which evaluative judgments are made.

bias The result of procedures or items used in assessment that unfairly discriminate among students.

bilingual education The teaching of English language skills to students with limited English proficiency. Two approaches are taken to bilingual education: Maintenance: Native Language (MNL) programs, in which students become fully literate in their home languages before studying English; and Transitional: English as a Second Language (TESL) programs, in which students begin studying English immediately.

bilingualism A term used to describe the ability to speak fluently in two different languages.

binary-choice items Any selected response item that offers two optional answers from which to select.

Bloom's taxonomy Bloom's classification of behavior in the cognitive domain. From simplest to complex, it consists of knowledge, comprehension, application, analysis, synthesis, and evaluation.

central tendency A score that is typical of a distribution of scores. Mode, median, and mean are three measures of central tendency.

chaining Successively linking together discrete, simpler behaviors already known to the learner in order to establish complex behaviors.

classical conditioning The process of bringing reflexes under control of the environment. Also known as Pavlovian and respondent conditioning.

classroom management Actions taken by a teacher to facilitate student learning.

cognitive development Changes in our capabilities as learners by which mental processes grow more complex and sophisticated.

cognitive domain Learning outcomes that relate to memory, understanding, and reasoning.

cognitive modeling An approach to instruction that combines demonstration of skill with verbalization of cognitive activity that accompanies the skill.

cognitive strategies A learned capability that enables learners to organize and regulate their own internal processes.

communication disorder Speech (voice) and language (symbols) disorders.

compensatory education Educational programs designed to combat the presumed effects of poverty on school performance.

competitive goal structure A class management structure in which students must compete for rewards so that they view attainment of goals as possible only if other students do not attain them.

componential intelligence Part of Sternberg's theory of intelligence, referring to a person's ability to reason abstractly, process information, and determine the kind and sequence of operations required for a task or problem.

computer-assisted instruction (CAI) Instruction delivered by a computer including tutorial, simulation, drill, and practice.

concrete concepts Abstractions based on objects, events, people, and relations that can be observed.

concrete operations Piaget's first stage of operational thought during which children develop skills of logical reasoning, but only about problems that are concrete.

conditioned reinforcer A neutral object or event that acquires the power to reinforce behavior as a result of being paired with one or more primary reinforcers, for example, money.

confidence bands An interval around a particular score in which the true score probably lies.

construct An idea devised by a theorist to explain observations and relationships between variables.

constructivist view of learning A cognitive view of learning whereby learners are assumed to construct knowledge in the context of the activity of the culture and knowing cannot be separated from doing.

content integration The degree to which teachers use content and examples in all subject areas that reflect both genders, diverse cultures, and different social classes.

contextual intelligence Part of Sternberg's theory of intelligence, relating to one's ability to adapt, select, or shape one's environment to optimize one's opportunities.

contingencies of reinforcement According to Skinner, learning principles based on the law of effect, the relationship between antecedent, response, and consequence.

continuous reinforcement A schedule of reinforcement in which reinforcement is delivered after every correct response.

contract grading Using an agreement that states what performances are required for a particular grade.

control theory The view that students need to be empowered to control to meet their own needs and thus experience success in school.

conventional morality Rules of conduct of older children (9 years–young adulthood) based on the conventions of society. This is Level 2 of Kohlberg's theory of moral reasoning.

cooperative goal structure A class management structure in which rewards for performance are given to a group, not to individuals within the group. As a consequence, students view attainment of goals as possible only through cooperation with members of their group.

cooperative integrated reading and composition (CIRC) Pairs of students from one homogeneous reading group join another pair from a different reading group to work cooperatively on comprehension and writing skills.

cooperative learning An instructional strategy whereby students work in cooperative groups to achieve a common goal. Conditions that promote effective cooperative learning include positive interdependence among group members, face-to-face interaction, clearly perceived individual accountability to achieve the group's goals, frequent use of interpersonal skills, and regular group processing to improve the group's functioning.

criterion-referenced judgments Assessment scores are compared to a set performance standard.

critical periods each one of Erikson's eight stages of psychosocial development; each stage identifies the emergence of a part of an individual's personality.

critical thinking Higher-level thinking used to analyze, synthesize, and evaluate.

cultural forces Four teaching strategies used to help students acquire thinking skills: (1) providing models of the culture, (2) explaining important cultural knowledge, (3) providing interaction among students and other members of the cultural community, and (4) providing feedback on students' use of thinking skills.

cultural pluralism A view of diversity that embraces cultural differences.

culture A way of life in which people share a common language and similar values, religion, ideals, habits of thinking, artistic expressions, and patterns of social and interpersonal relations.

curiosity An eager desire to know caused by stimuli that are novel, complex, or strange or that involve fantasy and ambiguity.

deficiency needs According to Maslow's hierarchy of needs, the basic needs that humans require for physical and psychological well-being.

deficit model The assumption that students who are members of ethnic minority groups are deficient in knowledge and skills required to contribute to the national culture.

defined concepts Abstractions that cannot be observed in the environment but must be defined (e.g., liberty).

developmental crisis According to Erikson, there is a conflict faced at each stage of psychological development. The way the crisis is resolved has a lasting effect on the person's self-concept and view of society in general.

developmentally appropriate instruction Instruction that is child-centered and provides activities appropriate to the developmental level of the student.

dialect A distinctive version or variation of a language in pronunciation, grammar, vocabulary, and usage.

difference model The assumption that students from different cultural groups will have unique learning styles and therefore different learning needs.

dimensions of good thinking Six aspects that characterize skill in thinking critically, which include a language of thinking, thinking dispositions, mental management, a strategic spirit, higher-order knowledge, and transfer.

direct instruction A form of teacher-centered instruction in which goals are clear and the teacher controls the material and the pace.

direct reinforcement Using direct consequences from the external environment to strengthen a desired behavior.

disability A diminished capacity to perform in a specific way.

discipline The extent to which students are engaged in learning or other classroom-appropriate activities.

discovery learning Bruner's approach to teaching, in which students are presented with specific examples and use these examples to form general principles. Discovery learning is inductive.

discrimination Distinguishing between and responding differently to two or more stimuli.

discriminative stimulus A stimulus that is present consistently when a response is reinforced and comes to act as a cue or signal for the response.

disinhibitory effects Consequences of modeling that increase a behavior already known but infrequently performed by the observer, by removing the inhibitions associated with that behavior.

dispersion An indication of how similar or different the scores in a distribution are from one another.

dominant bilingualism A form of bilingualism in which students are fully competent in their first language and nearly so in their second.

dual-code theory The assumption of two systems of memory representation, one for verbal information and one for nonverbal, or imaginal, information.

educational psychology The scientific study of the teaching–learning process.

elaborative rehearsal A type of encoding that relates new information to information already in LTS.

emotional/behavioral disorders A disorder in which people have difficulty controlling their feelings and behavior.

enactive learning Changes in thought or behavior that are a function of environmental consequences experienced by the learner.

encoding The process of converting a message from the environment to a cognitive code so that the information can be stored and later remembered.

enterprise schema An overall learning context that integrates multiple instructional goals and communicates the purpose for learning these goals.

environmental enhancement effects Consequences of modeling that direct an observer's attention to certain aspects or objects in the model's environment.

episodic memories Memories associated with specific personal experiences, including the time and place they occurred.

equilibration The self-regulating process in Piaget's theory through which people balance new experiences with present understanding.

essay items Test items that require students to construct written responses of varying lengths.

ethnic group The people who derive a sense of identity from their common national origin, religion, and, sometimes, physical characteristics.

ethnicity A term used to describe the cultural characteristics of people who identify themselves with a particular ethnic group.

ethnocentrism The assumption that one's own cultural ways are the right ways and universally appropriate to others.

evaluation The process by which teachers make specific judgments by answering the questions "How good?" or "How well?" (e.g., How well have students understood this concept? How good is this instruction?).

exceptional learners Learners who have special learning needs and who require special instruction.

experiential intelligence Part of Sternberg's theory of intelligence, describing a person's capacity to deal with novel tasks or new ideas and to combine unrelated facts.

explanation A clarification that provides a context or framework for a concept, event, or relationship.

extinction Removing reinforcement that is maintaining a behavior in order to weaken that behavior.

extrinsic motivation When learners work on tasks for external reasons, such as to please a parent or to avoid getting into trouble with the teacher.

fading The gradual withdrawal of a discriminative stimulus while the behavior continues to be reinforced.

foreclosure According to Marcia, adolescents who simply accept the decisions made for them by others. These decisions are often made by their parents.

forethought Anticipation of the future.

formal operations According to Piaget, the stage of development in which the abilities to reason abstractly and to coordinate a number of variables are acquired.

formative assessment An assessment used to diagnose learning difficulties and to provide feedback to students to improve their learning.

full inclusion The inclusion of all students in the regular classroom.

Gagné's events of instruction According to Gagné, the external conditions required to support and facilitate the cognitive processes that occur during learning.

gender role stereotypes Commonly held expectations about the roles of each sex.

generativity A sense of concern for future generations, expressed through childbearing or concern about creating a better world. Generativity versus stagnation marks Stage 7 of Erikson's theory of psychosocial development.

gifted and talented Students who are able to meet academic challenges better than the majority of their peers in any number of areas.

global education An aim of multicultural programs that helps students to understand that all peoples living on earth have interconnected fates.

goal structure A means by which teachers manage learning and evaluate and reward student performance.

grade equivalent score A standardized test score that uses grade-level performances to place individuals.

growth needs According to Maslow, the higher-level needs, the satisfaction of which enables human beings to grow psychologically.

growth spurt A dramatic increase in height and weight that signals the onset of puberty.

guided practice The sixth step in Hunter's approach to lesson delivery. This step begins the process of transfer.

handicap A disadvantage imposed on an individual.

hidden curriculum The tacit lessons and messages taught to students by the way teachers and schools operate.

hierarchy of needs A theory proposed by Abraham Maslow in which human needs are arranged in a hierarchy from basic needs to self-actualization, or self-fulfillment.

higher-order rules Rules formed by combining two or more rules, thus allowing students to solve problems.

I-message A clear statement by a teacher that tells how he or she feels about misbehavior but that does not lay blame on a student.

identity A sense of well-being, a feeling of knowing where one is going, and an inner assuredness of anticipated recognition from those who count. Identity versus role diffusion characterizes Stage 5 of Erikson's theory of psychosocial development.

identity achievement According to Marcia, adolescents who have made life-style decisions, although not in all areas.

identity diffusion To Marcia, adolescents who avoid thinking about life-style decisions and are unable to develop a clear sense of self.

identity statuses Different types of identity, as identified by Marcia.

independent practice Tasks that students complete independently either in the classroom or at home.

individual survival The first level of Gilligan's theory of moral reasoning, in which selfishness is identified as the primary concern.

individualistic goal structure A class management structure in which rewards are given on the basis of an individual's performance, unaffected by the performance of other students.

industry An eagerness to produce. Industry versus inferiority typifies Stage 4 of Erikson's theory of psychosocial development.

information-processing models Models of learning that rely on an analogy between the human mind and the computer to explain processing, storage, and retrieval of knowledge.

inhibitory effects Consequences of modeling that reinforce previously learned inhibitions.

initiative The quality of undertaking, planning, and attacking a new task. Initiative versus guilt characterizes Stage 3 of Erikson's theory of psychosocial development.

instruction According to Driscoll, the deliberate arrangement of learning conditions to promote the attainment of some intended goal.

instructional goals General statements of what students should be able to do as a consequence of instruction.

integration A view of diversity in which individual ethnic groups merge together to form a single, shared culture.

integrative model A view of moral development that combines cognition, affect, and behavior; method of lesson presentation that combines inductive skills, deductive skills, and content in one model.

integrity A sense of understanding how one fits into one's culture and the acceptance that one's place is unique and unalterable. Integrity versus despair marks Stage 8 of Erikson's theory of psychosocial development.

intellectual skills According to Gagné, learned capabilities that enable learners to make discriminations, identify and classify concepts, and apply and generate rules; procedural knowledge.

intelligence A personal capacity to learn, often measured by one's ability to deal with abstractions and to solve problems.

intermittent reinforcement A schedule of reinforcement in which reinforcement is delivered on some, but not all, occasions.

intersubjectivity In Vygotsky's theory, the process in which learning partners negotiate a mutual understanding of the task and how to proceed with its solution.

interview sheet A means of recording a teacher's observations during a conference with the student, which generally consists of a list of questions to be asked of each student together with space for recording the student's responses.

intimacy The state of having a close psychological relationship with another person. Intimacy versus isolation is Stage 6 of Erikson's theory of psychosocial development.

intrinsic motivation When learners work on tasks for internal reasons, such as pleasure or enjoyment in the activity.

isolation Failure to establish a close psychological relationship with another person leads to this feeling of being alone. The negative outcome of Stage 6 of Erikson's theory of psychosocial development.

item analysis A procedure used to evaluate test items for the purpose of determining whether the item functions in the way the teacher intends it to.

knowledge base of teaching The source from which a theory of teaching can be reflectively constructed; that which is known from educational psychology and classroom practice.

knowledge construction process A process by which knowledge is socially and culturally constructed.

language immersion A form of bilingual education in which students study the English language intensively for extended periods of time.

law of effect Thorndike's law of learning, which states that any action producing a satisfying consequence will be repeated in a similar situation. An action followed by an unfavorable consequence is unlikely to be repeated.

learned helplessness A depressed state when a person feels that no matter what he or she does, it will have no influence on important life events.

learning Change in thought or behavior that modifies a person's capabilities.

learning disability A generic term for disorders in cognitive processing that interfere with learning.

learning goal An aim of students who place primary emphasis on increasing competence.

learning outcomes According to Gagné, capabilities acquired by students resulting from the interaction of internal and external conditions of learning.

learning-oriented classrooms Classrooms in which the teacher values learning and facilitates, rather than directs, student activity.

lecturing A discourse given in class for the purpose of instruction.

limited English proficiency A phrase used to describe students whose first language is not English and who depend on their first language for communication and understanding.

logico-mathematical knowledge In Piaget's theory, knowledge that goes beyond physical experience and depends upon inventing or reorganizing patterns of ideas.

macroculture A larger shared culture representing core or dominant values of a society.

maintenance rehearsal Rote memorization, which does not guarantee understanding.

mastery teaching Refers to Madeline Hunter's seven-step lesson model.

matching items Any test item consisting of two columns of words or phrases to be matched.

mean The arithmetic average of a set of scores; one of the three measures of central tendency.

measurement The process of describing a student's particular characteristics. Measurement answers the question, "How much?"

median: The central score of a set of scores; the score that divides the set of scores into two equal halves; one of the three measures of central tendency.

medium-level questions Questions that guide a learner to new discoveries or to conceptual conflicts and inadequacies in his or her ways of thinking.

mental images Cognitive representations of, for example, pictures, sounds, and smells.

mental model A schema-based representation of experience, including perceptions of task demands and task performances.

mental retardation Significantly subaverage intellectual functioning, usually present at birth, resulting in or associated with impairments in adaptive behavior and manifested during the developmental period.

metacognition Knowledge about thinking, and the capability to monitor one's own cognitive processing, such as thinking, learning, and remembering.

metacognition Knowledge about thinking and the capability to monitor one's own cognitive processes, such as thinking, learning, and remembering.

metalinguistic awareness The ability to reflect on one's own knowledge of language.

metaphor A way to represent and talk about experiences in terms of other, more familiar, or more commonly shared events that seem comparable.

microcultures Groups within cultures that share particular values, knowledge, skills, symbols, and perspectives.

misbehavior According to Doyle, any behavior, by one or more students, that competes with or threatens learning activities.

mnemonic device A technique for remembering that connects new information with prior knowledge.

mode The most frequently occurring score in a set of scores; one of the three measures of central tendency.

model A person whose behavior acts as a stimulus to learning, according to Bandura.

modeling Learning by observing the behavior of others.

moral judgments Judgments about right or wrong.

morality of constraint According to Piaget, a type of moral thinking made by children under ten years of age; rules come from some external authority and strictly define what is right and wrong.

morality of cooperation According to Piaget, a type of moral thinking made by older children; rules provide general guidelines but should not be followed blindly without considering the context.

morality of nonviolence The third level of Gilligan's theory of moral reasoning, in which there is a realization that it is wrong to serve oneself at the expense of others.

moratorium According to Marcia, adolescents who have given thought to identity issues but have not reached any decisions.

motivation to learn A disposition of learners that is characterized by their willingness to initiate learning activities, their continued involvement in a learning task, and their long-term commitment to learning.

motivation The desire to produce modeled behavior.

motor skills According to Gagné, learned capabilities relating to movement or to muscles that induce movement, such as the ability to ride a bicycle or to operate a computer.

multiculturalism A recognition that ethnic groups make up and contribute to a national culture while they maintain an individual identity.

multiple acculturation The reciprocal idea that the general culture of the United States changes with the entry of each new ethnic and cultural group, which is itself changed by the national culture.

multiple-choice items Test items consisting of questions or incomplete sentences that are accompanied by three or more alternative responses, one of which is to be selected as the correct or best answer.

need for autonomy The need to initiate and regulate our own actions; self-determination.

negative reinforcement An aversive stimulus is removed or terminated following a desirable response in order to strengthen that response.

norm-referenced judgments The performance of one student is compared against the performances of others.

normal curve A mathematically defined function that approximates many educational phenomena.

objective tests Paper-and-pencil tests made up of items, such as true/false and multiple-choice, that can be objectively scored (i.e., scored in exactly the same way no matter who or what is doing the scoring).

observational learning effects Consequences of modeling that lead to the acquisition of cognitive and behavioral patterns that had no chance of occurring prior to modeling.

observer The learner is an observer, according to Bandura.

on-task behavior Any time a student is engaged with an academic task.

operant behavior According to Skinner, behavior that is not a simple reflex to a stimulus but an action that operates on the environment.

operant conditioning According to Skinner, learning through responses and their consequences.

outcomes-based education (OBE) A movement in school reform associated with the development of national and statewide standards in education that become the focus of local school improvement.

overlapping A teacher's ability to deal with more than one issue at the same time.

pair shares Short discussions between student dyads. Such discussions are usually interspersed with periods of lecture.

peer models Models who are from the same social environment.

peg mnemonics A strategy for memorization in which items of a list to be learned are associated with cue words and images.

perceived competence An observer's evaluation of how expert a model is.

perceived similarity An observer's perception of similarity between himself or herself and the model.

percentile rank A standardized score that gives the test taker the percentage of people in the norm group above whom he or she has scored.

performance Exhibiting a capability.

performance assessment A demonstration of learning, or an exhibition of curriculum mastery that typically involves tasks focusing on students' use of knowledge and skills in a variety of realistic situations and contexts.

performance goal An aim of students who place primary emphasis on gaining positive recognition from others and avoiding negative judgments.

phonology The study of the sound system of a language and the structure of those sounds.

physical disability Disorders of the skeleton, joints, and muscles, or health conditions that interfere with students' educational performances.

physical knowledge In Piaget's theory, any knowledge about objects in the world that can be gained through experiencing their perceptual properties.

placement A goal of assessment that determines what level of difficulty a student is capable of handling in instruction.

portfolio A collection of evidence pertaining to students' developing knowledge and expertise, serving a particular assessment purpose.

positive reinforcement The presentation of a satisfying stimulus, contingent on a response that results in strengthening the response.

postconventional morality Rules of conduct of adults who recognize the societal need for mutual agreement and the application of consistent principles in making judgments. This is Level 3 of Kohlberg's theory of moral reasoning.

pragmatics An area of language that refers to the effects of contexts on meaning and the ways to use language to create different contexts.

preconventional morality Rules of conduct of children (birth–9 years) who do not yet understand the conventions of society. This is Level 1 of Kohlberg's theory of moral reasoning.

Premack principle A special case of positive reinforcement in which a high-probability behavior is used to reinforce a low-probability behavior.

preoperational According to Piaget, the stage at which children learn to mentally represent things.

primary reinforcer Something that satisfies a basic biological need, such as food, water, or shelter.

prior knowledge Knowledge that has already been acquired and stored in long-term memory.

problem solving The activity of applying rules, knowledge, and cognitive strategies to move from the current situation, or initial state, to a desired outcome, or goal.

procedural knowledge Prior knowledge that involves knowing how to do something.

procedures Standards of behavior that are specific to a particular classroom task or set of related tasks.

production The act of producing modeled behavior.

psychomotor domain Learning outcomes that relate to skilled physical movements, as classified by Harrow's taxonomy.

psychosocial development According to Erikson, the process whereby relationships with others influence one's search for his or her own identity.

puberty The time of physical change during which individuals become sexually mature.

punishment The presentation of an aversive stimulus immediately following a response in order to weaken the incidence of the response.

Pygmalion effect The influence that a teacher's expectations may have on the behavior of students. Also called the teacher expectancy effect and the self-fulfilling prophecy.

qualitative information Information communicated through words.

quantitative information Information communicated through numbers.

questioning The act of asking questions as a tactic of instruction.

range The difference between the highest and lowest scores in a set of scores.

rating scale A measurement instrument used in observation-based assessment to make judgments about some continuing behavior or performance.

readiness A goal of assessment that shows whether students have the necessary prerequisite skills and knowledge to begin a unit of instruction.

reception learning Ausubel's approach to teaching, in which students are presented with material in a complete, organized form and are shown how to move from broad ideas to more specific instances. Reception learning is deductive.

reciprocal determinism In cognitive social theory, the three-way relationship that exists among personal factors, environment, and behavior.

reciprocal questioning A technique that uses question stems that students complete. The technique encourages critical thinking.

reciprocal teaching A technique that begins with the teacher's questions designed to enhance metacognitive skills and that progresses to a gradual transfer of the control of questioning to the students, who work cooperatively.

reflective construction Thinking critically about the principles and concepts of educational psychology and classroom practice in order to develop a theory of teaching.

reframing Rethinking an event or problem in terms of metaphors in order to gain a new perspective.

reinforcement The process by which the consequences of behavior establish and maintain it.

relative standard A grading system in which the performance of one student is compared against the performances of others.

reliability A property of assessment that concerns the degree to which assessments are free of measurement errors.

response cost A fine is exacted from an individual as punishment for misbehavior.

response facilitation effects Consequences of modeling that promote previously learned behavior by introducing inducements to perform that behavior.

retention The capacity to remember modeled behavior.

retrieval The process that transfers information from LTS to STS in order to be used.

rhymes Words that are identical to others in their terminal sound.

role diffusion The negative outcome of Stage 5 of Erikson's theory of psychosocial development, whereby an adolescent is unable to develop a clear sense of self.

rubric A scaled set of criteria clearly defining for the student and teacher the range of acceptable and unacceptable performance on a performance assessment.

rules General standards of behavior that are meant to apply across all classroom situations.

scaffolding The process in Vygotsky's theory whereby a more advanced partner changes the degree and quality of support provided to the less skilled partner as he or she becomes more proficient.

schema A mental structure for organizing information and representing knowledge. Any set of objects, experiences, or actions that is consistently classified forms a schema.

schemata Theoretical knowledge structures that contain information, facts, principles, and the relationships among them.

schemes In Piaget's theory, generalized ways of acting on the world that provide the basis for mental operations.

selection-type items A test item format in which students select an answer from possible alternatives.

selective attention The process of attention whereby the learner chooses to focus on a particular source of information from the environment.

selective perception The process of selectively attending to important aspects or details in stimulus information in order to process them further.

self-actualization Fulfilling one's personal potential.

self-concept One's description of self in terms of roles and characteristics.

self-efficacy A human being's judgment about his or her ability to deal effectively with tasks that need to be faced.

self-esteem One's judgments about self and the feelings associated with those judgments.

self-reflection The act of thinking about one's own experiences and reflecting on one's own thought processes.

self-regulation The act of applying an internal set of standards and criteria to regulate one's own behavior.

self-reinforcement Using consequences that come from within to strengthen a desired behavior.

self-sacrifice and social conformity The second level of Gilligan's theory of moral reasoning, in which there is a realization that caring for others rather than just caring for oneself is good.

semantic memories Memories of facts and general knowledge but not including the time and place they were learned.

semantics The study of the meanings of words and sentences.

sensorimotor stage The earliest stage in Piaget's theory of cognitive development, during which infants learn about their environment through their senses and motor actions.

sensory disorders Disorders such as hearing and visual impairments.

shaping The process of reinforcing responses that are successively closer to the ultimate desired behavior.

short answer items Supply-type items that include incomplete statements, such as fill-in-the-blanks or direct questions requiring a brief response.

short-term memory The phase of processing at which a limited amount of information is stored for a limited time.

situated learning Students engaging in problem solving of realistic or simulated problems that require the use of disciplinary knowledge and skills.

small group discussion Exchange of information and opinion among a small number of students.

social cognitive theory A learning theory, originated by Bandura, that draws on both cognitive and behavioral perspectives.According to the theory, people learn by observing the behavior of others in their social environment.

social learning Changes in thought or behavior brought about through observation of or interaction with one's social environment.

social-arbitrary knowledge In Piaget's theory, knowledge gained solely by one's interactions with other people within one's cultural group.

socioeconomic status Relative standing in society as measured by variables such as income, occupation, education, access to health coverage and community resources, and political power and prestige.

special education Specially designed instruction and services to meet the needs of exceptional learners.

standard deviation A statistic that expresses the variability in a distribution of scores.

standardized tests Tests that are prepared to provide accurate and meaningful data on students' performances compared to others at their age or grade levels.

stanine A standardized score from 1 to 9, each of which represents a range or band of raw scores.

story technique A memorization technique that helps in recalling ordered information by combining the elements to be remembered in the correct order in a brief story.

student teams–achievement divisions (STAD) A cooperative learning method that uses heterogeneous groups of four to five students. Rewards are given to teams whose members show the greatest improvement over their own past performance.

student-centered instruction Instruction in which the student is the focus of learning activity.

students at risk Students whose life circumstances make them more likely to fail in school

subtractive bilingualism A form of bilingualism in which students, although conversationally competent in both languages, are not fully literate in either one; this has an adverse effect on achievement.

summative assessment An assessment administered at the end of an instructional unit for the purpose of assigning a grade.

supply-type items A test item format in which items ask students to generate an answer.

symbolize To form mental representations of modeled events.

syntax The grammatical arrangement of words in sentences.

systemic validity A property of assessment in which assessment serves as an impetus for curriculum change.

T score A standardized score that converts raw scores to a distribution with a mean of 50 and a standard deviation of 10.

table of specifications Used for planning a test, a two-way chart or matrix that shows the content areas or objectives to be assessed along with the desired level of skill for each outcome.

teacher power The authority that teachers have available to them to manage student behavior; inversely, the extent to which students control their own behavior.

teacher-centered instruction Instruction in which the teacher is the focus of learning activity.

teaching Action taken with the intent to facilitate learning

teaching efficacy A teacher's belief that teaching, in general, will have an influence on students' learning.

teaching–learning process The process of taking action to produce change in thought or behavior and subsequent modification of capabilities.

team-assisted individualization(TAI) A teaching tactic in which students work on programmed materials as members of a heterogeneous group. Rewards for completing the work accurately and quickly are given to the team as a whole.

teams-games-tournaments (TGT) A cooperative learning method that uses heterogeneous groups of four to five students. Team members leave their teams to compete as individuals in homogeneous weekly tournaments. An individual's performance in the weekly tournament contributes to his or her team's score.

test bias An unfair disadvantage (less frequently an unfair advantage) that affects members of some subgroups because of some aspects of the test, the way the test is administered, or the way the result is interpreted.

test A formal procedure or an instrument used for measuring a sample of student performance.

theory of multiple intelligences Howard Gardner's theory of seven distinct intelligences or talents.

theory of teaching Description, explanations, and prediction of action staken with the intent to facilitate learning.

thinking dispositions Mental habits, inclinations, or tendencies in thinking behavior exhibited over time and across diverse thinking situations.

time-out The practice of separating a disruptive student from the rest of his or her classmates in order to decrease the probability of the response that precedes it.

token economy A behavioral program that allows students to earn objects for good behavior. The objects can be redeemed for desirable goods or privileges.

transfer of learning The application of knowledge acquired in one situation to other situations.

undermining effect Consequence that an extrinsic reward can have on behavior that is intrinsically motivated.

validity A property of assessment concerning the extent to which interpretations of assessment results will be appropriate, meaningful, and useful.

verbal information A learning outcome that enables learners to communicate about objects, events, or relations; declarative knowledge.

vicarious learning Changes in thought or behavior through observing the behavior of others and the consequences of those behaviors.

vicarious reinforcement Using consequences derived from viewing a model engaged in a desired behavior to strengthen that behavior.

wait-time I The length of time between the teacher's question and the student's response.

wait-time II The length of time between the student's response and the teacher's reaction to that response.

withitness According to Kounin, the teacher's ability to observe all situations in the classroom and to deal effectively with misbehavior.

work-oriented classrooms Classrooms in which the teacher values production and is directive of student activity.

working memory In some models, another term for STS because this is the stage at which a learner works on information from the environment.

Z score A score given in standard deviation units. The mean of any normal distribution is assigned a Z score of 0. Scores above the mean are plus scores; scores below the mean are minus scores.

zone of proximal development (ZPD) In Vygotsky's theory, the gap between actual and potential development—that is, between what a child can do unaided by an adult and what he or she can do under the guidance of an adult or in collaboration with more capable peers.

NAME INDEX

SUBJECT INDEX